# United States Law
# and the Armed Forces

edited by
**Willis E. Schug**

# United States Law and the Armed Forces

## Cases and Materials on Constitutional Law, Courts-Martial, and the Rights of Servicemen

**Praeger Publishers**   New York   Washington   London

PRAEGER PUBLISHERS
111 Fourth Avenue, New York, N.Y. 10003, U.S.A.
5, Cromwell Place, London S.W.7, England

Published in the United States of America in 1972
by Praeger Publishers, Inc.

© 1972 by Praeger Publishers, Inc.

Library of Congress Catalog Card Number: 75-167623

Printed in the United States of America

TO

MOTHER AND DAD

This book is provided as a basis for a course in military law. It is not limited to a survey of the courts-martial system of the armed services although those aspects of the system dissimilar to the federal law are adequately treated. What is also included are materials related in the constitutional sense to the sources of military law: the powers of Congress "to raise and support armies," "to make rules for the government" of the armed services, and "to declare war" and the power of the President as "Commander-in-Chief." In addition, materials are provided concerning the current organization of the armed services and the status of those persons who serve. The law regarding the constitutionality of conscription is included, but the administrative law regarding the implementation of Selective Service regulations is not. Finally, there are brief materials and notes related to the general powers of commanding officers, the processing of claims by and against the armed services, and the civil rights of servicemen.

It is hoped that a study of these materials and references, supplemented by the practical knowledge of the instructor, will cause the student to be better informed concerning some of the crucial problems of the times, such as the current complexities arising from the My Lai massacre.

I must mention my indebtedness to David Balcer of the Class of 1970 and Arthur Kaufman of the Class of 1971 of Columbia Law School for their assistance in assembling these materials. Obviously, I take full responsibility for the content and presentation. Finally, this book would never have been finished were it not for the secretarial assistance of Mrs. Jo Ferrante, her staff, and Miss Susan Johnson, and the patience and understanding of my wife.

# CONTENTS

x

# 1

## POWERS
## OF CONGRESS
## AND THE PRESIDENT
## CONCERNING THE ARMED FORCES

A careful reading of the Constitution of the United States will reveal a delicate balancing of the powers of Government concerning the armed forces between Congress and the President. One of the first cases decided by the Supreme Court interpreting this balance of power was Ex parte Milligan. A portion of the opinion follows.

## Ex parte MILLIGAN

Supreme Court of the United States, 1866.
71 U.S. (4 Wall.) 2, 18 L.Ed. 281.

MR. JUSTICE DAVIS delivered the opinion of the court.

On the 10th day of May, 1865, Lambdin P. Milligan presented a petition to the Circuit Court of the United States for the District of Indiana, to be discharged from an alleged unlawful imprisonment. The case made by the petition is this: Milligan is a citizen of the United States; has lived for twenty years in Indiana; and, at the time of the grievances complained of, was not, and never had been in the military or naval service of the United States. On the 5th day of October, 1864, while at home, he was arrested by order of General Alvin P. Hovey, commanding the military district of Indiana; and has ever since been kept in close confinement.

On the 21st day of October, 1864, he was brought before a military commission, convened at Indianapolis, by order of General Hovey, tried on certain charges and specifications; found guilty, and sentenced to be hanged; and the sentence ordered to be executed on Friday, the 19th day of May, 1865.

On the 2d day of January, 1865, after the proceedings of the military commission were at an end, the Circuit Court of the United States for Indiana met at Indianapolis and empanelled a grand jury, who were charged to inquire whether the laws of the United States had been violated; and, if so, to make presentments. The court adjourned

3

on the 27th day of January, having, prior thereto, discharged from further service the grand jury, who did not find any bill of indictment or make any presentment against Milligan for any offence whatever; and, in fact, since his imprisonment, no bill of indictment has been found or presentment made against him by any grand jury of the United States.

Milligan insists that said military commission had no jurisdiction to try him upon the charges preferred, or upon any charges whatever; because he was a citizen of the United States and the State of Indiana, and had not been, since the commencement of the late Rebellion, a resident of any of the States whose citizens were arrayed against the government, and that the right of trial by jury was guaranteed to him by the Constitution of the United States.

The prayer of the petition was, that under the act of Congress, approved March 3d, 1863, entitled, "An act relating to habeas corpus and regulating judicial proceedings in certain cases," he may be brought before the court, and either turned over to the proper civil tribunal to be proceeded against according to the law of the land or discharged from custody altogether.

With the petition were filed the order for the commission, the charges and specifications, the findings of the court, with the order of the War Department reciting that the sentence was approved by the President of the United States, and directing that it be carried into execution without delay. The petition was presented and filed in open court by the counsel for Milligan; at the same time the District Attorney of the United States for Indiana appeared, and, by the agreement of counsel, the application was submitted to the court. The opinions of the judges of the Circuit Court were opposed on three questions, which are certified to the Supreme Court:

1st. "On the facts stated in said petition and exhibits, ought a writ of habeas corpus to be issued?"

2d. "On the facts stated in said petition and exhibits, ought the said Lambdin P. Milligan to be discharged from custody as in said petition prayed?"

3d. "Whether, upon the facts stated in said petition and exhibits, the military commission mentioned therein had jurisdiction legally to try and sentence said Milligan in manner and form as in said petition and exhibits is stated?"

The importance of the main question presented by this record cannot be overstated; for it involves the very framework of the government and the fundamental principles of American liberty.

During the late wicked Rebellion, the temper of the times did not allow that calmness in deliberation and discussion so necessary to a correct conclusion of a purely judicial question. Then, considerations of safety were mingled with the exercise of power; and feelings and interests prevailed which are happily terminated. Now that the public safety is assured, this question, as well as all others, can be discussed and decided without passion or the admixture of any element not required to form a legal judgment. We approach the investigation of this case, fully sensible of the magnitude of the inquiry and the necessity of full and cautious deliberation.

. . .

The controlling question in the case is this: Upon the facts stated in Milligan's petition, and the exhibits filed, had the military commission mentioned in it jurisdiction, legally, to try and sentence him? Milligan, not a resident of one of the rebellious states, or a prisoner of war, but a citizen of Indiana for twenty years past, and never in the military or naval service, is, while at his home, arrested by the military power of the United States, imprisoned, and, on certain criminal charges preferred against him, tried, convicted, and sentenced to be hanged by a military commission, organized under the direction of the military commander of the military district of Indiana. Had this tribunal the legal power and authority to try and punish this man?

. . .

To the third question, then, on which the judges below were opposed in opinion, an answer in the negative must be returned.

It is proper to say, although Milligan's trial and conviction by a military commission was illegal, yet, if guilty of the crimes imputed to him, and his guilt had been ascertained by an established court and impartial jury, he deserved severe punishment. Open resistance to the measures deemed necessary to subdue a great rebellion, by those who enjoy the protection of government, and have not the excuse even of prejudice of section to plead in their favor, is wicked; but that resistance becomes an enormous crime when it assumes the form of a secret political organization, armed to oppose the laws, and seeks by stealthy means to introduce the enemies of the country into peaceful communities, there to light the torch of civil war, and thus overthrow the power of the United States. Conspiracies like these, at such a juncture, are extremely perilous; and those concerned in them are dangerous enemies to their country, and should receive the heaviest penalties of the law, as an example to deter others from similar criminal conduct. It is said the severity of the laws caused them; but Congress was obliged to enact severe laws to meet the crisis; and as our highest civil duty is to serve our country when in danger, the late war has proved that rigorous laws, when necessary, will be cheerfully obeyed by a patriotic people, struggling to preserve the rich blessings of a free government.

The two remaining questions in this case must be answered in the affirmative. The suspension of the privilege of the writ of habeas corpus does not suspend the writ itself. The writ issues as a matter of course; and on the return made to it the court decides whether the party applying is denied the right of proceeding any further with it.

5

If the military trial of Milligan was contrary to law, then he was entitled, on the facts stated in his petition, to be discharged from custody by the terms of the act of Congress of March 3d, 1863. . . .

The CHIEF JUSTICE delivered the following opinion.

Four members of the court, concurring with their brethren in the order heretofore made in this cause, but unable to concur in some important particulars with the opinion which has just been read, think it their duty to make a separate statement of their views of the whole case.

We do not doubt that the Circuit Court for the District of Indiana had jurisdiction of the petition of Milligan for the writ of <u>habeas corpus</u>.

. . .

We agree, therefore, that the first two questions certified must receive affirmative answers, and the last a negative. We do not doubt that the positive provisions of the act of Congress require such answers. We do not think it necessary to look beyond these provisions. In them we find sufficient and controlling reasons for our conclusions.

But the opinion which has just been read goes further; and as we understand it, asserts not only that the military commission held in Indiana was not authorized by Congress, but that it was not in the power of Congress to authorize it; from which it may be thought to follow, that Congress has no power to indemnify the officers who composed the commission against liability in civil courts for acting as members of it.

We cannot agree to this.

We agree in the proposition that no department of the government of the United States--neither President, nor Congress, nor the Courts--possesses any power not given by the Constitution.

We assent, fully, to all that is said, in the opinion, of the inestimable value of the trial by jury, and of the other constitutional safeguards of civil liberty. And we concur, also, in what is said of the writ of <u>habeas corpus</u>, and of its suspension, with two reservations: (1.) That, in our judgment, when the writ is suspended, the Executive is authorized to arrest as well as to detain; and (2.) that there are cases in which, the privilege of the writ being suspended, trial and punishment by military commission, in states where civil courts are open, may be authorized by Congress, as well as arrest and detention.

We think that Congress had power, though not exercised, to authorize the military commission which was held in Indiana.

We do not think it necessary to discuss at large the grounds of our conclusions. We will briefly indicate some of them.

The Constitution itself provides for military government as well as for civil government. And we do not understand it to be

6

claimed that the civil safeguards of the Constitution have application in cases within the proper sphere of the former.

What, then, is that proper sphere? Congress has power to raise and support armies; to provide and maintain a navy; to make rules for the government and regulation of the land and naval forces; and to provide for governing such part of the militia as may be in the service of the United States.

It is not denied that the power to make rules for the government of the army and navy is a power to provide for trial and punishment by military courts without a jury. It has been so understood and exercised from the adoption of the Constitution to the present time.

Nor, in our judgment, does the fifth, or any other amendment, abridge that power. "Cases arising in the land and naval forces, or in the militia in actual service in time of war or public danger," are expressly excepted from the fifth amendment, "that no person shall be held to answer for a capital or otherwise infamous crime, unless on a presentment or indictment of a grand jury," and it is admitted that the exception applies to the other amendments as well as to the fifth.

Now, we understand this exception to have the same import and effect as if the powers of Congress in relation to the government of the army and navy and the militia had been recited in the amendment, and cases within those powers had been expressly excepted from its operation. The states, most jealous of encroachments upon the liberties of the citizen, when proposing additional safeguards in the form of amendments, excluded specifically from their effect cases arising in the government of the land and naval forces. Thus Massachusetts proposed that "no person shall be tried for any crime by which he would incur an infamous punishment or loss of life until he be first indicted by a grand jury, except in such cases as may arise in the government and regulation of the land forces." The exception in similar amendments, proposed by New York, Maryland, and Virginia, was in the same or equivalent terms. The amendments proposed by the states were considered by the first Congress, and such as were approved in substance were put in form, and proposed by that body to the states. Among those thus proposed, and subsequently ratified, was that which now stands as the fifth amendment of the Constitution. We cannot doubt that this amendment was intended to have the same force and effect as the amendment proposed by the states. We cannot agree to a construction which will impose on the exception in the fifth amendment a sense other than that obviously indicated by action of the state conventions.

We think, therefore, that the power of Congress, in the government of the land and naval forces and of the militia, is not at all affected by the fifth or any other amendment. It is not necessary to attempt any precise definition of the boundaries of this power. But

7

may it not be said that government includes protection and defence as well as the regulation of internal administration? And is it impossible to imagine cases in which citizens conspiring or attempting the destruction or great injury of the national forces may be subjected by Congress to military trial and punishment in the just exercise of this undoubted constitutional power? Congress is but the agent of the nation, and does not the security of individuals against the abuse of this, as of every other power, depend on the intelligence and virtue of the people, on their zeal for public and private liberty, upon official responsibility secured by law, and upon the frequency of elections, rather than upon doubtful constructions of legislative powers?

But we do not put our opinion, that Congress might authorize such a military commission as was held in Indiana, upon the power to provide for the government of the national forces.

Congress has the power not only to raise and support and govern armies but to declare war. It has, therefore, the power to provide by law for carrying on war. This power necessarily extends to all legislation essential to the prosecution of war with vigor and success, except such as interferes with the command of the forces and the conduct of campaigns. That power and duty belong to the President as commander-in-chief. Both these powers are derived from the Constitution, but neither is defined by that instrument. Their extent must be determined by their nature, and by the principles of our institutions.

The power to make the necessary laws is in Congress; the power to execute in the President. Both powers imply many subordinate and auxiliary powers. Each includes all authorities essential to its due exercise. But neither can the President, in war more than in peace, intrude upon the proper authority of Congress, nor Congress upon the proper authority of the President. Both are servants of the people, whose will is expressed in the fundamental law. Congress cannot direct the conduct of campaigns, nor can the President, or any commander under him, without the sanction of Congress, institute tribunals for the trial and punishment of offences, either of soldiers or civilians, unless in cases of a controlling necessity, which justifies what it compels, or at least insures acts of indemnity from the justice of the legislature.

We by no means assert that Congress can establish and apply the laws of war where no war has been declared or exists.

Where peace exists the laws of peace must prevail. What we do maintain is, that when the nation is involved in war, and some portions of the country are invaded, and all are exposed to invasion, it is within the power of Congress to determine in what states or districts such great and imminent public danger exists as justifies the authorization of military tribunals for the trial of crimes and offences against the discipline or security of the army or against the public safety.

In Indiana, for example, at the time of the arrest of Milligan and his co-conspirators, it is established by the papers in the record, that the state was a military district, was the theatre of military operations, had been actually invaded, and was constantly threatened with invasion. It appears, also, that a powerful secret association, composed of citizens and others, existed within the state, under military organization, conspiring against the draft, and plotting insurrection, the liberation of the prisoners of war at various depots, the seizure of the state and national arsenals, armed cooperation with the enemy, and war against the national government.

We cannot doubt that, in such a time of public danger, Congress had power, under the Constitution, to provide for the organization of a military commission, and for trial by that commission of persons engaged in this conspiracy. The fact that the Federal courts were open was regarded by Congress as a sufficient reason for not exercising the power; but that fact could not deprive Congress of the right to exercise it. Those courts might be open and undisturbed in the execution of their functions, and yet wholly incompetent to avert threatened danger, or to punish, with adequate promptitude and certainty, the guilty conspirators.

In Indiana, the judges and officers of the courts were loyal to the government. But it might have been otherwise. In times of rebellion and civil war it may often happen, indeed, that judges and marshals will be in active sympathy with the rebels, and courts their most efficient allies.

We have confined ourselves to the question of power. It was for Congress to determine the question of expediency. And Congress did determine it. That body did not see fit to authorize trials by military commission in Indiana, but by the strongest implication prohibited them. With that prohibition we are satisfied, and should have remained silent if the answers to the questions certified had been put on that ground, without denial of the existence of a power which we believe to be constitutional and important to the public safety,--a denial which, as we have already suggested, seems to draw in question the power of Congress to protect from prosecution the members of military commissions who acted in obedience to their superior officers, and whose action, whether warranted by law or not, was approved by that up-right and patriotic President under whose administration the Republic was rescued from threatened destruction.

We have thus far said little of martial law, nor do we propose to say much. What we have already said sufficiently indicates our opinion that there is no law for the government of the citizens, the armies or the navy of the United States, within American jurisdiction, which is not contained in or derived from the Constitution. And wherever our army or navy may go beyond our territorial limits, neither can go beyond the authority of the President or the legislation of Congress.

There are under the Constitution three kinds of military juris-diction: one to be exercised both in peace and war; another to be ex-ercised in time of foreign war without the boundaries of the United States, or in time of rebellion and civil war within states or districts occupied by rebels treated as belligerents; and a third to be exer-cised in time of invasion or insurrection within the limits of the United States, or during rebellion within the limits of states maintain-ing adhesion to the National Government, when the public danger re-quires its exercise. The first of these may be called jurisdiction under MILITARY LAW, and is found in acts of Congress prescribing rules and articles of war, or otherwise providing for the government of the national forces; the second may be distinguished as MILITARY GOVERNMENT, superseding, as far as may be deemed expedient, the local law, and exercised by the military commander under the direction of the President, with the express or implied sanction of Congress; while the third may be denominated MARTIAL LAW PROPER, and is called into action by Congress, or temporarily, when the action of Congress cannot be invited, and in the case of justifying or excusing peril, by the President, in times of insurrection or in-vasion, or of civil or foreign war, within districts or localities where ordinary law no longer adequately secures public safety and private rights.

We think that the power of Congress, in such times and in such localities, to authorize trials for crimes against the security and safety of the national forces, may be derived from its constitutional authority to raise and support armies and to declare war, if not from its constitutional authority to provide for governing the national forces.

We have no apprehension that this power, under our American system of government, in which all official authority is derived from the people, and exercised under direct responsibility to the people, is more likely to be abused than the power to regulate commerce, or the power to borrow money. And we are unwilling to give our assent by silence to expressions of opinion which seem to us calculated, though not intended, to cripple the constitutional powers of the gov-ernment, and to augment the public dangers in times of invasion and rebellion.

MR. JUSTICE WAYNE, MR. JUSTICE SWAYNE, and MR. JUSTICE MILLER concur with me in these views.

10

## CONSTITUTIONALITY OF CONSCRIPTION

### SELECTIVE DRAFT LAW CASES*

Supreme Court of the United States, 1918.
245 U.S. 366, 38 S.Ct. 159, 62 L.Ed. 349.

*[ Footnotes have been omitted.  Ed.]

MR. CHIEF JUSTICE WHITE delivered the opinion of the court.
We are here concerned with some of the provisions of the Act
of May 18, 1917, c. 15, 40 Stat. 76, entitled, "An Act to authorize the
President to increase temporarily the Military Establishment of the
United States." The law, as its opening sentence declares, was intended to supply temporarily the increased military force which was
required by the existing emergency, the war then and now flagrant.
The clauses we must pass upon and those which will throw light on
their significance are briefly summarized:

The act proposed to raise a national army, first, by increasing
the regular force to its maximum strength and there maintaining it;
second, by incorporating into such army the members of the National
Guard and National Guard Reserve already in the service of the
United States (Act of Congress of June 3, 1916, c. 134, 39 Stat. 211)
and maintaining their organizations to their full strength; third, by
giving the President power in his discretion to organize by volunteer
enlistment four divisions of infantry; fourth, by subjecting all male
citizens between the ages of twenty-one and thirty to duty in the national army for the period of the existing emergency after the proclamation of the President announcing the necessity for their service;
and fifth, by providing for selecting from the body so called, on the
further proclamation of the President, 500,000 enlisted men, and a

second body of the same number should the President in his discretion deem it necessary. To carry out its purposes the act made it the duty of those liable to the call to present themselves for registration on the proclamation of the President so as to subject themselves to the terms of the act and provided full federal means for carrying out the selective draft. It gave the President in his discretion power to create local boards to consider claims for exemption for physical disability or otherwise made by those called. The act exempted from subjection to the draft designated United States and state officials as well as those already in the military or naval service of the United States, regular or duly ordained ministers of religion and theological students under the conditions provided for, and, while relieving from military service in the strict sense the members of religious sects as enumerated whose tenets excluded the moral right to engage in war, nevertheless subjected such persons to the performance of service of a non-combatant character to be defined by the President.

The proclamation of the President calling the persons designated within the ages described in the statute was made, and the plaintiffs in error, who were in the class and under the statute were obliged to present themselves for registration and subject themselves to the law, failed to do so and were prosecuted under the statute for the penalties for which it provided. They all defended by denying that there had been conferred by the Constitution upon Congress the power to compel military service by a selective draft, and asserted that even if such power had been given by the Constitution to Congress, the terms of the particular act for various reasons caused it to be beyond the power and repugnant to the Constitution. The cases are here for review because of the constitutional questions thus raised, convictions having resulted from instructions of the courts that the legal defences were without merit and that the statute was constitutional.

The possession of authority to enact the statute must be found in the clauses of the Constitution giving Congress power "to declare war; . . . to raise and support armies, but no appropriation of money to that use shall be for a longer term than two years; . . . to make rules for the government and regulation of the land and naval forces." Article I, §8. And of course the powers conferred by these provisions like all other powers given carry with them as provided by the Constitution the authority "to make all laws which shall be necessary and proper for carrying into execution the foregoing powers." Article I, §8.

As the mind cannot conceive an army without the men to compose it, on the face of the Constitution the objection that it does not give power to provide for such men would seem to be too frivolous for further notice. It is said, however, that since under the Constitution as originally framed state citizenship was primary and United States citizenship but derivative and dependent thereon, therefore the power conferred upon Congress to raise armies was only coterminous with United States citizenship and could not be exerted so as to cause that

citizenship to lose its dependent character and dominate state citizenship. But the proposition simply denies to Congress the power to
raise armies which the Constitution gives. That power by the very
terms of the Constitution, being delegated, is supreme. Article VI.
In truth the contention simply assails the wisdom of the framers of
the Constitution in conferring authority on Congress and in not retaining it as it was under the Confederation in the several States. Further
it is said, the right to provide is not denied by calling for volunteer
enlistments, but it does not and cannot include the power to exact enforced military duty by the citizen. This however but challenges the
existence of all power, for a governmental power which has no sanction to it and which therefore can only be exercised provided the citizen consents to its exertion is in no substantial sense a power. It is
argued, however, that although this is abstractly true, it is not con-
cretely so because as compelled military service is repugnant to a
free government and in conflict with all the great guarantees of the
Constitution as to individual liberty, it must be assumed that the authority to raise armies was intended to be limited to the right to call
an army into existence counting alone upon the willingness of the citizen to do his duty in time of public need, that is, in time of war. But
the premise of this proposition is so devoid of foundation that it leaves
not even a shadow of ground upon which to base the conclusion. Let us
see if this is not at once demonstrable. It may not be doubted that the
very conception of a just government and its duty to the citizen includes the reciprocal obligation of the citizen to render military service in case of need and the right to compel it. Vattel, Law of Nations,
Book III, c. 1 & 2. To do more than state the proposition is absolutely
unnecessary in view of the practical illustration afforded by the almost
universal legislation to that effect now in force. In England it is certain that before the Norman Conquest the duty of the great militant
body of the citizens was recognized and enforcible. Blackstone, Book
I, c. 13. It is unnecessary to follow the long controversy between
Crown and Parliament as to the branch of the government in which
the power resided, since there never was any doubt that it somewhere
resided. So also it is wholly unnecessary to explore the situation for
the purpose of fixing the sources whence in England it came to be
understood that the citizen or the force organized from the militia as
such could not without their consent be compelled to render service
in a foreign country, since there is no room to contend that such
principle ever rested upon any challenge of the right of Parliament
to impose compulsory duty upon the citizen to perform military duty
wherever the public exigency exacted, whether at home or abroad.
This is exemplified by the present English Service Act.

    In the Colonies before the separation from England there cannot
be the slightest doubt that the right to enforce military service was
unquestioned and that practical effect was given to the power in many
cases. Indeed the brief of the Government contains a list of Colonial

acts manifesting the power and its enforcement in more than two hundred cases. And this exact situation existed also after the separation. Under the Articles of Confederation it is true Congress had no such power, as its authority was absolutely limited to making calls upon the States for the military forces needed to create and maintain the army, each State being bound for its quota as called. But it is indisputable that the States in response to the calls made upon them met the situation when they deemed it necessary by directing enforced military service on the part of the citizens. In fact the duty of the citizen to render military service and the power to compel him against his consent to do so was expressly sanctioned by the constitutions of at least nine of the States, an illustration being afforded by the following provision of the Pennsylvania constitution of 1776. "That every member of society hath a right to be protected in the enjoyment of life, liberty and property, and therefore is bound to contribute his proportion towards the expense of that protection, and yield his personal service when necessary, or an equivalent thereto." Art. 8 (Thorpe, American Charters, Constitutions and Organic Laws, vol. 5, pp. 3081, 3083.) While it is true that the States were sometimes slow in exerting the power in order to fill their quotas--a condition shown by resolutions of Congress calling upon them to comply by exerting their compulsory power to draft and by earnest requests by Washington to Congress that a demand be made upon the States to resort to drafts to fill their quotas--that fact serves to demonstrate instead of to challenge the existence of the authority. A default in exercising a duty may not be resorted to as a reason for denying its existence.

When the Constitution came to be formed it may not be disputed that one of the recognized necessities for its adoption was the want of power in Congress to raise an army and the dependence upon the States for their quotas. In supplying the power it was manifestly intended to give it all and leave none to the States, since besides the delegation to Congress of authority to raise armies the Constitution prohibited the States, without the consent of Congress, from keeping troops in time of peace or engaging in war. Article I, §10.

To argue that as the state authority over the militia prior to the Constitution embraced every citizen, the right of Congress to raise an army should not be considered as granting authority to compel the citizen's service in the army, is but to express in a different form the denial of the right to call any citizen to the army. Nor is this met by saying that it does not exclude the right of Congress to organize an army by voluntary enlistments, that is, by the consent of the citizens, for if the proposition be true, the right of the citizen to give consent would be controlled by the same prohibition which would deprive Congress of the right to compel unless it can be said that although Congress had not the right to call because of state authority, the citizen had a right to obey the call and set aside state authority if he pleased to do so. And a like conclusion demonstrates the want of foundation for the contention that, although it be within the power to call the citizen into the army without his consent, the army into which he enters after the call is to be limited in some respects to services for which the militia it is assumed may only be used, since this admits the appropriateness of the call to military service in the army and the power to make it and yet destroys the purpose for which the call is authorized --the raising of armies to be under the control of the United States.

The fallacy of the argument results from confounding the constitutional provisions concerning the militia with that conferring upon Congress the power to raise armies. It treats them as one while they are different. This is the militia clause:

"The Congress shall have power . . . To provide for calling forth the militia to execute the laws of the Union, suppress insurrections and repel invasions; To provide for organizing, arming, and disciplining the militia, and for governing such part of them as may be employed in the service of the United States, reserving to the States, respectively, the appointment of the officers, and the authority of training the militia according to the discipline prescribed by Congress." Article I, §8.

The line which separates it from the army power is not only inherently plainly marked by the text of the two clauses, but will stand out in bolder relief by considering the condition before the Constitution was adopted and the remedy which it provided for the military situation with which it dealt. The right on the one hand of Congress under the Confederation to call on the States for forces and the duty on the other of the States to furnish when called, embraced the complete power of government over the subject. When the two were combined and were delegated to Congress all governmental power on that subject was conferred, a result manifested not only by the grant made but by the limitation expressly put upon the States on the subject. The army sphere therefore embraces such complete authority. But the duty of exerting the power thus conferred in all its plenitude was not made at once obligatory but was wisely left to depend upon the discretion of Congress as to the arising of the exigencies which would call it in part or in whole into play. There was left therefore under the sway of the States undelegated the control of the militia to the extent that such control was not taken away by the exercise by Congress of its power to raise armies. This did not diminish the military power or curb the full potentiality of the right to exert it but left an area of authority requiring to be provided for (the militia area) unless and until by the exertion of the military power of Congress that area had been circumscribed or totally disappeared. This, therefore, is what was dealt with by the militia provision. It diminished the occasion for the exertion by Congress of its military power beyond the strict necessities for its exercise by giving the power to Congress to direct the organization and training of the militia (evidently to prepare such militia in the event of the exercise of the army power) although leaving the carrying out of such command to the States. It further conduced to the same result by delegating to Congress the right to call on occasions which were specified for the militia force, thus again obviating the necessity for exercising the army power to the extent of being ready for every conceivable contingency. This purpose is made manifest by the provision preserving the organization of the militia so far as formed when called for such special purposes although subjecting the militia when so called to the paramount authority of the United States. Tarble's Case, 13 Wallace, 397, 408. But because under the express regulations the power was given to call for specified purposes without exerting the army power, it cannot follow that the latter power when exerted was not complete to the extent of its exertion and dominant. Because the power of Congress to raise armies was not required to be exerted to its full limit but only as in the discretion of Congress it was deemed the public interest required, furnishes no ground for supposing that the complete power was lost by its partial exertion. Because, moreover, the power granted to Congress to raise armies in its potentiality was susceptible of narrowing the area over which the militia clause operated, affords no ground for confounding the two areas which were distinct and separate to the end of confusing both the powers and thus weakening or destroying both.

And upon this understanding of the two powers the legislative and executive authority has been exerted from the beginning. From the act of the first session of Congress carrying over the army of the Government under the Confederation to the United States under the Constitution (Act of September 29, 1789, c. 25, 1 Stat. 95) down to 1812 the authority to raise armies was regularly exerted as a distinct and substantive power, the force being raised and recruited by enlistment. Except for one act formulating a plan by which the entire body of citizens (the militia) subject to military duty was to be organized in every State (Act of May 8, 1792, c. 33, 1 Stat. 271) which was never carried into effect, Congress confined itself to providing for the organization of a specified number distributed among the States according to their quota to be trained as directed by Congress and to be called by the President as need might require. When the War of 1812 came the result of these two forces composed the army to be relied upon by Congress to carry on the war. Either because it proved to be weak in numbers or because of insubordination developed among the forces called and manifested by their refusal to cross the border, the Government determined that the exercise of the power to organize an army by compulsory draft was necessary and Mr. Monroe, the Secretary of War, (Mr. Madison being President) in a letter to Congress recommended several plans of legislation on that subject. It suffices to say that by each of them it was proposed that the United States deal directly with the body of citizens subject to military duty and call a designated number out of the population between the ages of 18 and 45 for service in the army. The power which it was

recommended be exerted was clearly an unmixed federal power dealing with the subject from the sphere of the authority given to Congress
to raise armies and not from the sphere of the right to deal with the
militia as such, whether organized or unorganized. A bill was introduced giving effect to the plan. Opposition developed, but we need not
stop to consider it because it substantially rested upon the incompati-
bility of compulsory military service with free government, a subject
which from what we have said has been disposed of. Peace came before the bill was enacted.

Down to the Mexican War the legislation exactly portrayed the
same condition of mind which we have previously stated. In that war,
however, no draft was suggested, because the army created by the
United States immediately resulting from the exercise by Congress
of its power to raise armies, that organized under its direction from
the militia and the volunteer commands which were furnished, proved
adequate to carry the war to a successful conclusion.

So the course of legislation from that date to 1861 affords no
ground for any other than the same conception of legislative power
which we have already stated. In that year when the mutterings of the
dread conflict which was to come began to be heard and the Proclamation of the President calling a force into existence was issued it was
addressed to the body organized out of the militia and trained by the
States in accordance with the previous acts of Congress. (Proclamation of April 15, 1861, 12 Stat. 1258.) That force being inadequate to
meet the situation, an act was passed authorizing the acceptance of
500,000 volunteers by the President to be by him organized into a national army. (Act of July 22, 1861, c. 9, 12 Stat. 268.) This was soon
followed by another act increasing the force of the militia to be organized by the States for the purpose of being drawn upon when trained
under the direction of Congress (Act of July 29, 1861, c. 25, 12 Stat.
281), the two acts when considered together presenting in the clearest
possible form the distinction between the power of Congress to raise
armies and its authority under the militia clause. But it soon became
manifest that more men were required. As a result the Act of March
3, 1863, c. 75, 12 Stat. 731, was adopted entitled "An Act for enrolling
and calling out the National Forces and for other purposes." By that
act which was clearly intended to directly exert upon all the citizens
of the United States the national power which it had been proposed to
exert in 1814 on the recommendation of the then Secretary of War,
Mr. Monroe, every male citizen of the United States between the ages
of twenty and forty-five was made subject by the direct action of Congress to be called by compulsory draft to service in a national army
at such time and in such numbers as the President in his discretion
might find necessary. In that act, as in the one of 1814, and in this
one, the means by which the act was to be enforced were directly federal and the force to be raised as a result of the draft was therefore
typically national as distinct from the call into active service of the

militia as such. And under the power thus exerted four separate calls for draft were made by the President and enforced, that of July, 1863, of February and March, 1864, of July and December, 1864, producing a force of about a quarter of a million men. It is undoubted that the men thus raised by draft were treated as subject to direct national authority and were used either in filling the gaps occasioned by the vicissitudes of war in the ranks of the existing national forces or for the purpose of organizing such new units as were deemed to be required. It would be childish to deny the value of the added strength which was thus afforded. Indeed in the official report of the Provost Marshal General, just previously referred to in the margin, reviewing the whole subject it was stated that it was the efficient aid resulting from the forces created by the draft at a very critical moment of the civil strife which obviated a disaster which seemed impending and carried that struggle to a complete and successful conclusion.

Brevity prevents doing more than to call attention to the fact that the organized body of militia within the States as trained by the States under the direction of Congress became known as the National Guard (Act of January 21, 1903, c. 196, 32 Stat. 775; National Defense Act of June 3, 1916, c. 134, 39 Stat. 211). And to make further preparation from among the great body of the citizens, an additional number to be determined by the President was directed to be organized and trained by the States as the National Guard Reserve. (National Defense Act, supra.)

Thus sanctioned as is the act before us by the text of the Constitution, and by its significance as read in the light of the fundamental principles with which the subject is concerned, by the power recognized and carried into effect in many civilized countries, by the authority and practice of the colonies before the Revolution, of the States under the Confederation and of the Government since the formation of the Constitution, the want of merit in the contentions that the act in the particulars which we have been previously called upon to consider was beyond the constitutional power of Congress, is manifest. Cogency, however, if possible, is added to the demonstration by pointing out that in the only case to which we have been referred where the constitutionality of the Act of 1863 was contemporaneously challenged on grounds akin to, if not absolutely identical with, those here urged, the validity of the act was maintained for reasons not different from those which control our judgment. (Kneedler v. Lane, 45 Pa. St. 238.) And as further evidence that the conclusion we reach is but the inevitable consequence of the provisions of the Constitution as effect follows cause, we briefly recur to events in another environment. The seceding States wrote into the constitution which was adopted to regulate the government which they sought to establish, in identical words the provisions of the Constitution of the United States which we here have under consideration. And when the right to enforce under that instrument a selective draft law which was enacted, not differing in principle from the one here in question, was challenged, its validity was upheld, evidently after great consideration, by the courts of Virginia, of Georgia, of Texas, of Alabama, of Mississippi and of North Carolina, the opinions in some of the cases copiously and critically reviewing the whole grounds which we have stated. [Citation of cases omitted. Ed.]

In reviewing the subject, we have hitherto considered it as it has been argued, from the point of view of the Constitution as it stood prior to the adoption of the Fourteenth Amendment. But to avoid all misapprehension we briefly direct attention to that Amendment for the purpose of pointing out, as has been frequently done in the past, how completely it broadened the national scope of the Government under the Constitution by causing citizenship of the United States to be paramount and dominant instead of being subordinate and derivative, and therefore, operating as it does upon all the powers conferred by the Constitution, leaves no possible support for the contentions made, if their want of merit was otherwise not so clearly made manifest.

It remains only to consider contentions which, while not disputing power, challenge the act because of the repugnancy to the Constitution supposed to result from some of its provisions. First, we are of opinion that the contention that the act is void as a delegation of federal power to state officials because of some of its administrative features, is too wanting in merit to require further notice. Second, we think that the contention that the statute is void because vesting administrative officers with legislative discretion has been so completely adversely settled as to require reference only to some of the decided cases. Field v. Clark; 143 U.S. 649; Buttfield v. Stranahan, 192 U.S. 470; Intermountain Rate Cases, 234 U.S. 476; First National Bank v. Union Trust Co., 244 U.S. 416. A like conclusion also adversely disposes of a similar claim concerning the conferring of judicial power. Buttfield v. Stranahan, 192 U.S. 470, 497; West v. Hitchcock, 205 U.S. 80; Oceanic Steam Navigation Co. v. Stranahan, 214 U.S. 320, 338-340; Zakonaite v. Wolf, 226 U.S. 272, 275. And we pass without anything but statement the proposition that an establishment of a religion or an interference with the free exercise thereof repugnant to the First Amendment resulted from the exemption clauses of the act to which we at the outset referred, because we think its unsoundness is too apparent to require us to do more.

Finally, as we are unable to conceive upon what theory the exaction by government from the citizen of the performance of his supreme and noble duty of contributing to the defense of the rights and honor of the nation, as the result of a war declared by the great representative body of the people, can be said to be the imposition of involuntary servitude in violation of the prohibitions of the Thirteenth Amendment, we are constrained to the conclusion that the contention to that effect is refuted by its mere statement.

Affirmed.

This is the sole Supreme Court decision concerning the constitutionality of conscription.  In the "amazing case of Kneedler v.
Lane," 45 Pa 238 (1863), discussed in 53 A.B.A.J. 708 and 1132 (1967),
the Supreme Court of Pennsylvania initially decided that the draft act
of March, 1863, was unconstitutional.  Before the case was finally decided, however, a general election took place, and the litigation was
involved in a political fight.  The ruling of unconstitutionality was
subsequently reversed.  A similar draft act based on the Constitution
of the Confederate States, a document copied from the Constitution of
the United States, was held to be constitutional in Jeffers v. Fair, 33
Ga. 347 (1862).
        Tarble's Case, 80 U.S. (13 Wall.) 397, 20 L.Ed. 597 (1872), held
that a state judge had no jurisdiction to issue a writ of habeas corpus
for the discharge of a person held under the authority, or claim and
color of the authority, of the United States by an officer of that government.  MR. JUSTICE FIELD'S opinion in that case contains the
following:

Now, among the powers assigned to the National government,
is the power "to raise and support armies," and the power "to provide for the government and regulation of the land and naval forces."
The execution of these powers falls within the line of its duties; and
its control over the subject is plenary and exclusive.  It can determine, without question from any State authority, how the armies shall
be raised, whether by voluntary enlistment or forced draft, the age at
which the soldier shall be received, and the period for which he shall
be taken, the compensation he shall be allowed, and the service to
which he shall be assigned.  And it can provide the rules for the government and regulation of the forces after they are raised, define
what shall constitute military offences, and prescribe their punishment.  No interference with the execution of this power of the National
government in the formation, organization, and government of its
armies by any State officials could be permitted without greatly im-
pairing the efficiency, if it did not utterly destroy, this branch of the
public service.  Probably in every county and city in the several
States there are one or more officers authorized by law to issue
writs of habeas corpus on behalf of persons alleged to be illegally
restrained of their liberty; and if soldiers could be taken from the
army of the United States, and the validity of their enlistment inquired into by any one of these officers, such proceeding could be

taken by all of them, and no movement could be made by the National troops without their commanders being subjected to constant annoyance and embarrassment from this source. The experience of the late rebellion has shown us that, in times of great popular excitement, there may be found in every State large numbers ready and anxious to embarrass the operations of the government, and easily persuaded to believe every step taken for the enforcement of its authority illegal and void. Power to issue writs of habeas corpus for the discharge of soldiers in the military service, in the hands of parties thus disposed, might be used, and often would be used, to the great detriment of the public service. In many exigencies the measures of the National government might in this way be entirely bereft of their efficacy and value. An appeal in such cases to this court, to correct the erroneous action of these officers, would afford no adequate remedy. Proceedings on habeas corpus are summary, and the delay incident to bringing the decision of a State officer, through the highest tribunal of the State, to this court for review, would necessarily occupy years, and in the meantime, where the soldier was discharged, the mischief would be accomplished. It is manifest that the powers of the National government could not be exercised with energy and efficiency at all times, if its acts could be interfered with and controlled for any period by officers or tribunals of another sovereignty.

. . . 80 U.S. (13 Wall.) at 408-409, 20 L.Ed. at 600-601.

Prior to the Supreme Court's decision in the Selective Draft Law Cases, supra, the constitutionality of the Act of May 18, 1917, was also upheld in a case involving an indictment for conspiracy to induce others to refuse to register for the draft. United States v. Sugar 243 F. 423 (E.D. Mich. 1917), affirmed, 252 F. 74 (6th Cir. 1918), certiorari denied, 248 U.S. 578, 39 S.Ct. 19, 63 L.Ed. 429 (1918). Both the District Court and the Court of Appeals in that case held that the Act was not an improper delegation of legislative powers and did not violate the thirteenth amendment. On the thirteenth amendment issue of involuntary servitude, see also Story v. Perkins, 243 F. 997 (S.D. Ga. 1917), affirmed sub nom., Jones v. Perkins, 245 U.S. 390, 38 S.Ct. 116, 62 L.Ed. 358 (1918). For cases holding that compulsory civilian labor, as an alternative to military service, for conscientious objectors does not constitute involuntary servitude, see O'Conner v. United States, 415 F.2d 1110 (9th Cir. 1969), certiorari denied, 397 U.S. 968, 90 S.Ct. 1002, 25 L.Ed.2d 263 (1970); Boroski v. United States, 412 F.2d 668 (6th Cir. 1969), certiorari denied, 396 U.S. 1013, 90 S.Ct. 555, 24 L.Ed.2d 505 (1970); and Howze v. United States, 272 F.2d 146 (9th Cir. 1959).

UNITED STATES v. HENDERSON

United States Court of Appeals, Seventh Circuit, 1950.
180 F.2d 711.

SWAIM, Circuit Judge.

Each of the above named defendants was charged, either by indictment or information, with having unlawfully, knowingly, and wilfully failed and refused to present himself for, and submit to registration before a duly authorized registration official or local selective service board, all as required of him by the Selective Service Act of 1948, 50 U.S.C.A. Appendix, §§451-470, a Proclamation of the President of the United States, issued and promulgated thereunder July 20, 1948, No. 2799, 50 U.S.C.A. Appendix, §453 note, and Selective Service Regulations duly issued pursuant to said Act and then in full force and effect, all as the defendant then and there well knew. Three of the defendants were tried by a jury and one by the Court. All were found guilty as charged, sentenced to imprisonment for ninety days and fined $100.00. . . .

The defendants contend that the 1948 Selective Service Act is unconstitutional. They impliedly admit, as they must, that it is within the power of Congress to enact a selective service or draft law in time of war, Selective Draft Law Cases (Arver v. United States), 245 U.S. 366, 38 S.Ct. 159, 62 L.Ed. 349, L.R.A.1918C, 361, Ann.Cas. 1918B, 856, but contend that Congress may not exercise such power in time of peace. Both reason and the decided cases are against this contention of the defendants.

Congress was expressly given the power, "To raise and support Armies . . . ." U.S.Const., Art. I, Sec. 8, Cl. 12. This is an unqualified power given to Congress in order that it may protect the very existence of government. There is neither express nor implied limitation in the Constitution to this power. If, as contended by defendants, Congress could only exercise this power to conscript and train men when the country is at war, such action might then be unavailing, because it would come too late. To successfully fight modern war an army must be equipped with modern implements of war and be thoroughly trained in their use. This cannot be accomplished in a short time. One of the stated purposes of our Constitution was to "provide for the common Defense". It is fundamental that a nation must have the power to defend itself against enemies, both actual and threatened. Peace-time selective service acts have been held constitutional in United States v. Lambert, 3 Cir., 123 F.2d 395; United States v. Lamothe, 2 Cir., 152 F.2d 340; United States v. Rappeport, D.C., 36 F.Supp. 915, affirmed in United States v. Herling, 2 Cir., 120 F.2d 236.

The principal contention of the defendants is that the Act is unconstitutional as applied to them in that their religious belief, being contrary to war and even contrary to registering under a selective service act, which is, or may be, in aid of war, is protected by the First Amendment to the Constitution to the extent that they were not required by the Selective Service Act of 1948 to present themselves for, and submit to registration. Consequently, they contend that their right to exercise religious freedom cannot be abrogated by requiring their obedience to the Act. It is our opinion that the defendants have neither reason, nor authority, to sustain this contention.

. . .

It is true that each of the draft laws, including the Selective Service Act of 1948, has taken notice of the fact that we have citizens with the religious belief that war, and participation in war, is wrong, and each of these draft laws has made provision that those having such religious beliefs might be assigned to non-combatant service. The 1948 Selective Service Act goes even further and excuses them from non-combatant service if the local board finds that even that service would be against their religious scruples.

It seems that this recognition by Congress of the religious beliefs of some of our citizens has been interpreted by them as an admission that the religious freedom guaranteed by the First Amendment excuses them from participation, of any kind, in war or the preparation for war. With this interpretation we cannot agree. If this Nation were successfully attacked and conquered by enemies from without, or within, none of us would have the rights guaranteed to us by the First Amendment. It is this Constitution which gave us these rights, and it is the Government set up by this Constitution which has jealously protected these rights for us since the birth of this Nation.

To guarantee the survival of this Government for the protection of these rights the Constitution gave Congress the right to raise armies. To raise armies they must necessarily call on the manpower of this Nation. The power to call on only those who were willing to fight could not have been the intention of the framers of the Constitution. A nation engaged in war is fighting for its existence. The framers of the Constitution intended that Congress should have the power, if necessary, to call on every citizen to come to its aid. In these days of total war, war means just what that name implies, a war of all, as a unit, for the preservation of our Nation, our ideals and our freedoms. As said by the Supreme Court in the Selective Draft Law Cases, supra, 38 S.Ct. at page 161: ". . . a governmental power which has no sanction to it and which therefore can only be exercised provided the citizen consents to its exertion is in no substantial sense a power."

It is equally evident that the need for raising an army must be a question to be left to the final decision of Congress. It would be hard to conceive of our being engaged in any war to which there would

not be some objectors, conscientious or otherwise; where some of
our citizens would think the war not justified, who would think the
declaration of war and the waging of war unnecessary. If the question
of the necessity of war or the preparation for war were to be left to
the answer of the courts on the petition of individuals, instead of to
Congress, the war might well be over and our guaranteed freedom
something only to be remembered before Congress could act and raise
an army. Selective Draft Law Cases, 245 U.S. 366, 38 S.Ct. 159, 62
L.Ed. 349, L.R.A. 1918C, 361, Ann.Cas. 1918B, 856 . . . .

Certiorari was denied by the Supreme Court, 339 U.S. 963, 70
S.Ct. 997, 94 L.Ed. 1372 (1950).

For other cases holding that congressional power to raise and
support armies does not depend upon the existence of a declared war,
see United States v. Cornell, 36 F.Supp. 81 (D. Ida. 1940); United
States v. Garst, 39 F.Supp. 367 (E.D. Pa. 1941); Etcheverry v. United
States, 320 F.2d 873 (9th Cir.), certiorari denied, 375 U.S. 930, 84
S.Ct. 331, 11 L.Ed. 2d 963 (1963); and Baltimore Contractors, Inc. v.
Renegotiation Board, 383 F.2d 690 (4th Cir. 1967). Etcheverry v.
United States, supra, also holds that the draft law does not constitute
a deprivation of liberty in violation of the fifth amendment. For a
case holding that induction into the armed forces resulting in total
disability is not a taking of property in violation of the fifth amendment, see Commers v. United States, 66 F.Supp. 943 (D. Mont. 1946),
affirmed, 159 F.2d 248 (9th Cir.), certiorari denied, 331 U.S. 807, 67
S.Ct. 1189, 91 L.Ed. 1828 (1947).
For Supreme Court cases stating that exemption from service
in the armed forces for conscientious objectors is a matter of Congressional grace and not constitutional right, see United States v.
MacIntosh, 283 U.S. 605, 51 S.Ct. 570, 75 L.Ed. 1302 (1931) (naturalization case); and In re Summers, 325 U.S. 561, 65 S.Ct. 1307, 89 L.Ed.
1795 (1945) (denial of admission to state bar). In recent cases that
have expanded the scope of the definition of conscientious objection to
include those who do not adhere to organized religions and do not believe in a Supreme Being, the Supreme Court has avoided the consideration of constitutional issues. United States v. Seeger, 380 U.S.
163, 85 S.Ct. 850, 13 L.Ed.2d 733 (1965); Welsh v. United States, 398
U.S. 333, 90 S.Ct. 1792, 26 L.Ed.2d 308 (1970). Justice Harlan, however, in his concurring opinion in Welsh v. United States, states that:
"Congress of course, could, entirely consistently with the requirements of the Constitution, eliminate all exemptions for conscientious
objectors . . . However, having chosen to exempt, it cannot draw the

line between theistic or non-theistic religious beliefs on the one hand
and secular beliefs on the other.  Any such distinctions are not, in my
view, compatible with the Establishment Clause of the First Amendment."  398 U.S. at 356, 90 S.Ct. at 1805, 26 L.Ed.2d at 328.  See also
United States v. Sisson, 297 F.Supp. 902 (D. Mass. 1969), appeal dismissed, 399 U.S. 267, 90 S.Ct. 2117, 26 L.Ed.2d 608 (1970).

It is generally held that selective conscientious objectors, those
who do not oppose all wars, are not entitled to exemption from military service.  See, e.g., Gillette v. United States, 420 F.2d 298 (2d
Cir. 1970), certiorari granted, 399 U.S. 925, 90 S.Ct. 2236, 26 L.Ed.2d
791 (1970); United States v. Kurki, 255 F.Supp. 161 (E.D. Wis. 1966),
affirmed, 384 F.2d 905 (7th Cir. 1967), certiorari denied, 390 U.S. 926,
88 S.Ct. 861, 19 L.Ed.2d 987 (1968); and United States v. Kauten, 133
F.2d 703 (2d Cir. 1943).  But see United States v. McFadden, 309
F.Supp. 502 (N.D. Cal. 1970), which holds that section 6 (j) of the Selective Service Act, 50 U.S.C. App. §456 (j), discriminates against
Catholic selective objectors and is a violation of the free exercise
and establishment clauses of the first amendment and the equal protection and due process clauses of the fifth amendment.

The Selective Service Act of 1967, 50 U.S.C. App. §462 (a), provides that "any . . . person . . . who knowingly counsels, aids, or abets
another to refuse or evade registration or service in the armed forces
or any of the requirements of this title . . . shall, upon conviction . . .
be punished. . . ."  The constitutionality of this section was upheld in
Gara v. United States, 178 F.2d 38 (6th Cir. 1949), affirmed by an
equally divided court, 340 U.S. 857, 71 S.Ct. 87, 95 L.Ed. 628 (1950).
A conviction in a prosecution for conspiracy to counsel, aid, and abet
registrants to resist the draft law was set aside because of lack of
evidence and procedural irregularities in United States v. Spock, 416
F.2d 165 (1st Cir. 1969).  For an example of statements that would
not violate §462 (a), see Bond v. Floyd, 385 U.S. 116, 87 S.Ct. 339, 17
L.Ed.2d 235 (1966).  In that case, the Supreme Court held that Bond's
exclusion from the Georgia House of Representatives because of his
statements criticizing the war in Vietnam and the operation of the
Selective Service System violated his right of free expression guaranteed by the first amendment.  The Court indicated that Bond could
not have been convicted under §462 (a) consistently with the first
amendment for his statements.  For a case holding that draft-card
burning is not protected by the first amendment, see United States v.
O'Brien, 391 U.S. 367, 88 S.Ct. 1673, 20 L.Ed.2d 672 (1968), reversing
376 F.2d 538 (1st Cir. 1967).  See also Dorsen and Rudovsky, "Some
Thoughts on Dissent, Personal Liberty, and War," 54 A.B.A.J. 742
(1968).

In Gilbert v. Minnesota, 254 U.S. 325, 41 S.Ct. 125, 65 L.Ed.
287 (1943), the Supreme Court upheld the conviction of a man who was
charged with the violation of a state statute that made it unlawful "to
advocate or teach . . . that men should not enlist in the military or

naval forces of the United States or the State of Minnesota." The
plaintiff-in-error argued that under the Constitution, Congress has
exclusive power to legislate on the subject matter of the Minnesota
statute. The Court held that the statute did not encroach upon congressional power and that the statute could be supported as an exertion of the police power of the state. The Court also held that the
statute was not contrary to the first amendment guarantee of free
speech. Compare Taylor v. Mississippi, 319 U.S. 583, 63 S.Ct. 1200,
87 L.Ed. 1600 (1943), where the Supreme Court reversed convictions
based upon a Mississippi statute that made it unlawful for a person to
encourage disloyalty to the United States or Mississippi or to encourage others to refuse to salute, honor, and respect the flag of the
United States or Mississippi. The Court held that, as applied to the
defendants, the statute violated the fourteenth amendment.

## THE MILITIA

The militia clause of the Constitution is discussed in the Selective Draft Law Cases, supra, page 11. The view there taken is criticized by Professor Leon Friedman as inaccurate in that he believes
the framers of the Constitution intended to give the federal government wide discretion in the use of the army but not in gathering it,
while the militia's functions were specified but its manpower source
was unlimited (67 Mich. L. Rev. 1493 [1969]).

Whatever view may be correct historically there is no doubt of
the change in the concept of the "militia" from a state-based defence
force to an integral part of the United States armed forces.

In Hamilton v. Regents, 293 U.S. 245, 260, 55 S.Ct. 197, 79
L.Ed. 343 (1934), the Supreme Court stated that a "state has the authority to train its able-bodied male citizens of suitable age appropriately to develop fitness, should any such duty be laid upon them,
to serve in the United States army or in state militia," and "so long
as its action is within retained powers and not inconsistent with any
exertion of the authority of the national government, and transgresses
no right safeguarded to the citizen by the Federal Constitution, the
State is the sole judge of the means to be employed and the amount of
training to be exacted for the effective accomplishment of these ends."
Compare with Dunne v. People, 94 Ill. 120, 34 Am.Rep. 213 (1879).

In Presser v. Illinois, 116 U.S. 252, 6 S.Ct. 580, 29 L.Ed. 615
(1886), it was held that the Military Code of Illinois (Laws 1879, 192)

for the enrollment, organization, and government of the state militia was a valid exercise of the police power and was not unconstitutional as en-croaching upon the power of Congress under clause 16 of art. I, §8, or within the prohibition of art. I, §10; the provisions of article XI, sections 5 and 6 of The Military Code forbade unauthorized bodies of men to as-sociate themselves together as a military company or organization or to drill or parade with arms in any city or town. See also People v. Hill, 13 N.Y.S. 186 (1891), affirmed, 126 N.Y. 497, 27 N.E. 789 (1891).

The "federalization" of the militia became a very controversial subject in the early 1900's with the passage of the Dick Act (acts of Jan. 21, 1903, and May 27, 1908 [32 U.S.C.A. §§81a, 81b (1928 ed.)]) and the subsequent National Defense Act or Hay Bill (Act of June 3, 1916, as amended [32 U.S.C.A. §81 (1928 ed.)]). These acts are dis-cussed in Sweetson v. Emerson, 236 F. 161, Ann. Cas. 1917B, 244 (1916); see also notes in 30 Harv. L. Rev. 176 and 30 Harv. L. Rev. 712 (1916-17).

Additional comments on this subject: MacChesney, "National Defense--Constitutionality of Pending Legislation," 64 U. Pa. L. Rev. 449 (1916); Ansell, "Legal and Historical Aspects of the Militia," 26 Yale L.J. 471 (1917); Wiener, "The Militia Clause of the Constitu-tion," 54 Harv. L. Rev. 181 (1940); Colby and Glass, "The Legal Status of the National Guard," 29 Va. L. Rev. 839 (1943).

Other current statutes concerning the National Guard are set forth below:

_____/

## CALL OF ARMY NATIONAL GUARD TO FEDERAL SERVICE

Act of Jan. 21, 1903, c. 196. §4, as revised.
10 U.S.C.A. §3500

Whenever--

(1) the United States, or any of the Territories, Commonwealths, or possessions, is invaded or is in danger of invasion by a foreign nation;
(2) there is a rebellion or danger of a rebellion against the authority of the Government of the United States; or
(3) the President is unable with the regular forces to execute the laws of the United States;

the President may call into Federal service members and units of the Army National Guard of any State or Territory, Puerto Rico, the Canal Zone, or the District of Columbia in such numbers as he considers necessary to repel the invasion, suppress the rebellion, or execute those laws. Orders for these purposes shall be issued through the governors of the States, the Territories, Puerto Rico, and the Canal Zone, and, in the District of Columbia, through the commanding general of the National Guard of the District of Columbia. Aug. 10, 1956, c. 1041, 70A Stat. 199.

### ORDER INTO FEDERAL SERVICE

Act of July 9, 1952, c. 608, §201b, as revised.
10 U.S.C.A. §263

Whenever Congress determines that more units and organizations are needed for the national security than are in the regular components of the ground and air forces, the Army National Guard of the United States and the Air National Guard of the United States, or such parts of them as are needed, together with units of other reserve components necessary for a balanced force, shall be ordered to active duty and retained as long as so needed. Aug. 10, 1956, c. 1041, 70A Stat. 11.

### STATUS OF ARMY NATIONAL GUARD OF THE UNITED STATES

Act of July 9, 1952, c. 608, §709.
10 U.S.C.A. §3495

Members of the Army National Guard of the United States are not in active Federal service except when ordered thereto under law. Aug. 10, 1956, c. 1041, 70A Stat. 198.

Unless a National Guard unit has been ordered into active federal service, the members thereof are not employees of the United States within the meaning of the Federal Tort Claims Act. Satcher v. United States, 101 F.Supp. 919 (W.D.S. Car. 1952).

The phrase "when in actual service in time of war or public danger" in the Fifth Amendment applies only to "militia" (Johnson v. Sayre, 158 U.S. 109 [1894]).

The following extract summarizes the current composition of the United States Army and illustrates the practical demise of the state militia.

## COMPOSITION OF THE ARMY*

Extracted from Department of the Army Pamphlet 27-187,
Military Affairs, 1966.

*[ Footnotes have been omitted.  Ed.]

6.1  Purpose and Scope.  The purpose of this chapter is to explain the composition of the Army.  It deals with the various components and branches of the Army.

6.2  Components of the Army.  The Army consists of--
   (1)  The Regular Army, the Army National Guard of the
        United States, the Army National Guard while in the
        service of the United States, and the Army Reserve;
        and
   (2)  All persons appointed or enlisted in, or conscripted
        into, the Army without component.

The Army National Guard of the United States and the Army Reserve are the Reserve components of the Army.

6.3  The Regular Army.  By statute it is provided that--

a.  The Regular Army is the component of the Army that consists of persons whose continuous service on active duty in both peace and war is contemplated by law, and of retired members of the Regular Army.

   b.  The Regular Army includes--
   (1)  the officers and enlisted members of the Regular
        Army;
   (2)  the professors, registrar, and cadets of the United
        States Military Academy; and
   (3)  the retired officers and enlisted members of the
        Regular Army.

6.4  The Army National Guard.  a.  In General.  The Army National Guard as such is ordinarily not a component of the Army.  However, because of its essential relationship to the Army National Guard of the United States and because it is a component of the Army while in Federal service, some knowledge of the Army National Guard is necessary to an understanding of the composition of the Army.

The Army National Guard is part of the organized militia of the several states and territories, Puerto Rico, the Canal Zone, and the District of Columbia.  The Constitution gives Congress the following authority over the militia:

> To provide for organizing, arming, and disciplining
> the Militia, and for governing such Part of them as may
> be employed in the Service of the United States, reserv-
> ing to the States respectively, the Appointment of the
> Officers, and the authority of training the Militia accord-
> ing to the discipline prescribed by Congress.

The President is "Commander in Chief . . . of the Militia of the several States, when called into the actual Service of the United States." However, when not in the service of the United States, the Army National Guard of each state is a state force under the command of the governor of the state as commander in chief.

b. The Army National Guard in Federal Service. The Constitution empowers Congress to provide for calling forth the militia to execute the laws of the union, suppress insurrections, and repel invasions. Pursuant to this provision, Congress has authorized the President to call members and units of the Army National Guard into Federal service for each of these three purposes. Although any part of the Army National Guard entering Federal service pursuant to the President's call becomes a component of the Army, neither units nor individual members are merged into the Army. They retain their Army National Guard status. Members of the Army National Guard in Federal service may not be permanently assigned to a unit other than one from the Army National Guard of their own state nor may they be employed for a purpose other than that specified in the call.

c. Organization. The organization of the militia, even when not in the service of the United States, is a responsibility of Congress. Congress has provided generally that the organization of the Army National Guard and the composition of its units shall be the same as those prescribed for the Army, subject in time of peace to such exceptions as the Secretary of the Army may authorize.

The President is authorized to designate the units of the National Guard, by branch of the Army, to be maintained by each state, but no change in branch, organization, or allotment of a unit located entirely within a state may be made without the approval of its governor. The states may fix the locations of units within their borders.

The President may assign the Army National Guard to divisions or other tactical units and may detail officers of the Army National Guard or the Regular Army to command such units. However, the commanding officer of a unit organized wholly within a state may not be displaced. The President may also detail a Regular Army officer to perform the duties of chief of staff for each fully organized division of the Army National Guard.

d. Discipline. Congress has the responsibility for providing for the discipline of the militia. A court-martial system similar to that of the Army, except as to punishments, has been established for the Army National Guard when not in Federal service. The provisions of the Uniform Code of Military Justice are applicable to members of the Army National Guard in Federal service.

6.5 The Reserve Components. a. In General. Prior to the enactment of the Armed Forces Reserve Act of 1952, persons were appointed or enlisted in one of the Reserve components. Under current law, persons are appointed or enlisted as Reserves and then assigned to an appropriate Reserve component.

b. Army National Guard of the United States.
  (1) In General. The Army National Guard of the United
      States [hereafter referred to as ARNGUS] is a Reserve
      component of the Army all of whose members are mem-
      bers of the Army National Guard. One of the purposes
      for the establishment of the ARNGUS as a Reserve com-
      ponent of the Army was to enable the Federal Govern-
      ment to order trained personnel into active Federal
      service for purposes other than the three for which the
      militia (Army National Guard) may be called into Fed-
      eral service.
  (2) Federal Recognition. Federal recognition is an ac-
      knowledgment by the Federal Government that all pre-
      scribed qualifications and standards for the Army
      National Guard are met. Federal recognition is appli-
      cable both to organizations and to individual members.
          An organization of the state militia is not part of
      the Army National Guard unless it is federally recog-
      nized. . . .
              . . .
  (3) Personnel. A person becomes federally recognized as
      an enlisted member simply by enlisting in a federally
      recognized organization of the Army National Guard.
      A civilian who enlists in the Army National Guard is
      concurrently enlisted as a Reserve for service in the
      ARNGUS. A member of the Army Reserve who is en-
      listed in the Army National Guard in his Reserve
      grade, and is a member of a federally recognized unit
      or organization thereof, becomes a member of the
      ARNGUS and ceases to be a member of the Army Re-
      serve.
          The Constitution provides that the appointment of
      officers in the militia is reserved to the States. Upon
      appointment as an officer of the Army National Guard
      of a state, and subscribing to the oath of office, an in-
      dividual has a state status under which he can function.
      He becomes a member of the ARNGUS when he is fed-
      erally recognized and duly appointed as a Reserve in
      the same grade for service as a member of the
      ARNGUS. An officer of the Army Reserve who is ap-
      pointed in the same grade in the Army National Guard,
      and who is federally recognized in that grade, becomes
      an officer of the ARNGUS and ceases to be an officer
      of the Army Reserve.
  c. Army Reserve. The Army Reserve includes all Reserves
of the Army who are not members of the ARNGUS.

    d. General Organization of the Reserve Components. Each Reserve member of the Army must be placed in one of the following three categories.

        (1) Ready Reserve. The Ready Reserve is composed of both units and individual Reserves.

        . . .

        (2) Standby Reserve. All members of the Reserve components who are not in the Ready Reserve or Retired Reserve are in the Standby Reserve.

        . . .

        (3) Retired Reserve. The Retired Reserve consists of Reserves who are retired on the basis of 20 years of military service on active duty, or who have been transferred to the Retired Reserve upon their request, retaining their status as Reserves and meeting certain other qualifications.

Merlo J. Pusey in his book, The Way We Go to War (1969), presents a cogent argument against the almost unlimited powers of the President to put this country at war. He suggests a War Powers Act defining the roles of Congress and the Executive. See also The Ultimate Decision, edited by Ernest R. May (1960).

The following cases demonstrate the reluctance of the judiciary to review the acts of the President as Commander-in-Chief.

## PRIZE CASES

Supreme Court of the United States, 1863.
67 U.S. (2 Black) 635, 17 L.Ed. 459.

MR. JUSTICE GRIER. There are certain propositions of law which must necessarily affect the ultimate decision of these cases, and many others, which it will be proper to discuss and decide before we notice the special facts peculiar to each.

They are, 1st. Had the President a right to institute a blockade of ports in possession of persons in armed rebellion against the Government, on the principles of international law, as known and acknowledged among civilized States?

. . .

By the Constitution, Congress alone has the power to declare a national or foreign war. It cannot declare war against a State, or any

33

number of States, by virtue of any clause in the Constitution. The Constitution confers on the President the whole Executive power. He is bound to take care that the laws be faithfully executed. He is Commander-in-chief of the Army and Navy of the United States, and of the militia of the several States when called into the actual service of the United States. He has no power to initiate or declare a war either against a foreign nation or a domestic State. But by the Acts of Congress of February 28th, 1795, and 3d of March, 1807, he is authorized to called out the militia and use the military and naval forces of the United States in case of invasion by foreign nations, and to suppress insurrection against the government of a State or of the United States.

If a war be made by invasion of a foreign nation, the President is not only authorized but bound to resist force by force. He does not initiate the war, but is bound to accept the challenge without waiting for any special legislative authority. And whether the hostile party be a foreign invader, or States organized in rebellion, it is none the less a war, although the declaration of it be "unilateral." Lord Stowell (1 Dodson, 247) observes, "It is not the less a war on that account, for war may exist without a declaration on either side. It is so laid down by the best writers on the law of nations. A declaration of war by one country only, is not a mere challenge to be accepted or refused at pleasure by the other."

. . .

Whether the President in fulfilling his duties, as Commander-in-chief, in suppressing an insurrection, has met with such armed hostile resistance, and a civil war of such alarming proportions as will compel him to accord to them the character of belligerents, is a question to be decided by him, and this Court must be governed by the decisions and acts of the political department of the Government to which this power was entrusted. "He must determine what degree of force the crisis demands." The proclamation of blockade is itself official and conclusive evidence to the Court that a state of war existed which demanded and authorized a recourse to such a measure, under the circumstances peculiar to the case.

. . .

On this first question therefore we are of the opinion that the President had a right, jure belli, to institute a blockade of ports in possession of the States in rebellion, which neutrals are bound to regard.

### YOUNGSTOWN CO. v. SAWYER

Supreme Court of the United States, 1952.
343 U.S. 579, 72 S.Ct. 775, 96 L.Ed. 1344.

MR. JUSTICE BLACK delivered the opinion of the Court.
We are asked to decide whether the President was acting within his constitutional power when he issued an order directing the

Secretary of Commerce to take possession of and operate most of the
Nation's steel mills.  The mill owners argue that the President's
order amounts to lawmaking, a legislative function which the Constitution has expressly confided to the Congress and not to the President.
The Government's position is that the order was made on findings of
the President that his action was necessary to avert a national catas-
trophe which would inevitably result from a stoppage of steel production, and that in meeting this grave emergency the President was
acting within the aggregate of his constitutional powers as the Nation's Chief Executive and the Commander in Chief of the Armed
Forces of the United States. . . .

The order cannot properly be sustained as an exercise of the
President's military power as Commander in Chief of the Armed
Forces.  The Government attempts to do so by citing a number of
cases upholding broad powers in military commanders engaged in
day-to-day fighting in a theater of war.  Such cases need not concern
us here.  Even though "theater of war" be an expanding concept, we
cannot with faithfulness to our constitutional system hold that the
Commander in Chief of the Armed Forces has the ultimate power as
such to take possession of private property in order to keep labor
disputes from stopping production.  This is a job for the Nation's
lawmakers, not for its military authorities.

. . .

The judgment of the District Court is

Affirmed.

MR. JUSTICE FRANKFURTER.

Although the considerations relevant to the legal enforcement
of the principle of separation of powers seem to me more complicated
and flexible than may appear from what MR. JUSTICE BLACK has
written, I join his opinion because I thoroughly agree with the application of the principle to the circumstances of this case.  Even though
such differences in attitude toward this principle may be merely differences in emphasis and nuance, they can hardly be reflected by a
single opinion for the Court.  Individual expression of views in reaching a common result is therefore important.

MR. JUSTICE JACKSON, concurring in the judgment and opinion
of the Court.

. . .

The clause on which the Government next relies is that "The
President shall be Commander in Chief of the Army and Navy of the
United States . . . ."  These cryptic words have given rise to some of
the most persistent controversies in our constitutional history.  Of
course, they imply something more than an empty title.  But just what
authority goes with the name has plagued presidential advisers who
would not waive or narrow it by nonassertion yet cannot say where it
begins or ends.  It undoubtedly puts the Nation's armed forces under

presidential command. Hence, this loose appellation is sometimes advanced as support for any presidential action, internal or external, involving use of force, the idea being that it vests power to do anything, anywhere, that can be done with an army or navy.

That seems to be the logic of an argument tendered at our bar-- that the President having, on his own responsibility, sent American troops abroad derives from that act "affirmative power" to seize the means of producing a supply of steel for them. To quote, "Perhaps the most forceful illustration of the scope of Presidential power in this connection is the fact that American troops in Korea, whose safety and effectiveness are so directly involved here, were sent to the field by an exercise of the President's constitutional powers." Thus, it is said, he has invested himself with "war powers."

I cannot foresee all that it might entail if the Court should indorse this argument. Nothing in our Constitution is plainer than that declaration of a war is entrusted only to Congress. Of course, a state of war may in fact exist without a formal declaration. But no doctrine that the Court could promulgate would seem to me more sinister and alarming than that a President whose conduct of foreign affairs is so largely uncontrolled, and often even is unknown, can vastly enlarge his mastery over the internal affairs of the country by his own commitment of the Nation's armed forces to some foreign venture.*

---

*How widely this doctrine espoused by the President's counsel departs from the early view of presidential power is shown by a comparison. President Jefferson, without authority from Congress, sent the American fleet into the Mediterranean, where it engaged in a naval battle with the Tripolitan fleet. He sent a message to Congress on December 8, 1801, in which he said:
"Tripoli, the least considerable of the Barbary States, had come forward with demands unfounded either in right or in compact, and had permitted itself to denounce war on our failure to comply before a given day. The syle of the demand admitted but one answer. I sent a small squadron of frigates into the Mediterranean . . . with orders to protect our commerce against the threatened attack. . . . Our commerce in the Mediterranean was blockaded and that of the Atlantic in peril. . . . One of the Tripolitan cruisers having fallen in with and engaged the small schooner Enterprise, . . . was captured, after a heavy slaughter of her men . . . . Unauthorized by the Constitution, without the sanction of Congress, to go beyond the line of defense, the vessel, being disabled from committing further hostilities, was liberated with its crew. The Legislature will doubtless consider whether, by authorizing measures of offense also, they will place our force on an equal footing with that of its adversaries. I communicate all material information on this subject, that in the exercise of this important function confided by the Constitution to the Legislature exclusively

I do not, however, find it necessary or appropriate to consider the legal status of the Korean enterprise to discountenance argument based on it.

Assuming that we are in a war de facto, whether it is or is not a war de jure, does that empower the Commander in Chief to seize industries he thinks necessary to supply our army? The Constitution expressly places in Congress power "to raise and support Armies" and "to provide and maintain a Navy." [Emphasis supplied.] This certainly lays upon Congress primary responsibility for supplying the armed forces. Congress alone controls the raising of revenues and their appropriation and may determine in what manner and by what means they shall be spent for military and naval procurement. I suppose no one would doubt that Congress can take over war supply as a Government enterprise. On the other hand, if Congress sees fit to rely on free private enterprise collectively bargaining with free labor for support and maintenance of our armed forces, can the Executive, because of lawful disagreements incidental to that process, seize the facility for operation upon Government-imposed terms?

There are indications that the Constitution did not contemplate that the title Commander in Chief of the Army and Navy will constitute him also Commander in Chief of the country, its industries and its inhabitants. He has no monopoly of "war powers," whatever they are. While Congress cannot deprive the President of the command of the army and navy, only Congress can provide him an army or navy to command. It is also empowered to make rules for the "Government and Regulation of land and naval Forces," by which it may to some unknown extent impinge upon even command functions.

That military powers of the Commander in Chief were not to supersede representative government of internal affairs seems obvious from the Constitution and from elementary American history. Time out of mind, and even now in many parts of the world, a military commander can seize private housing to shelter his troops. Not so, however, in the United States, for the Third Amendment says, "No Soldier shall, in time of peace be quartered in any house, without the consent of the Owner, nor in time of war, but in a manner to be prescribed by law." Thus, even in war time, his seizure of needed military housing must be authorized by Congress. It also was expressly left to Congress to "provide for calling forth the Militia to execute the Laws of the Union, suppress Insurrections and repel Invasions . . . (U.S. Const., Art. I, §8, cl. 15)." Such a limitation on the command power, written at a time when the militia rather than a standing army, was contemplated as the military weapon of the Republic,

---

their judgment may form itself on a knowledge and consideration of every circumstance of weight." I Richardson, Messages and Papers of the Presidents, 314.

underscores the Constitution's policy that Congress, not the Executive, should control utilization of the war power as an instrument of domestic policy. Congress, fulfilling that function, has authorized the President to use the army to enforce certain civil rights (14 Stat. 29, 16 Stat. 143, 8 U.S.C. §55). On the other hand, Congress has forbidden him to use the army for the purpose of executing general laws except when expressly authorized by the Constitution or by Act of Congress (20 Stat. 152, 10 U.S.C. §15).

While broad claims under this rubric often have been made, advice to the President in specific matters usually has carried overtones that powers, even under this head, are measured by the command functions usual to the topmost officer of the army and navy. Even then, heed has been taken of any efforts of Congress to negative his authority.*

We should not use this occasion to circumscribe, much less to contract, the lawful role of the President as Commander in Chief. I should indulge the widest latitude of interpretation to sustain his exclusive function to command the instruments of national force, at least when turned against the outside world for the security of our society. But, when it is turned inward, not because of rebellion but because of a lawful economic struggle between industry and labor, it should have no such indulgence. His command power is not such an absolute as might be implied from that office in a militaristic system but is subject to limitations consistent with a constitutional Republic whose law and policy-making branch is a representative Congress. The purpose of lodging dual titles in one man was to insure that the civilian would control the military, not to enable the military to subordinate the presidential office. No penance would ever expiate the sin against free government of holding that a President can escape control of executive powers by law through assuming his military role. What the power of command may include I do not try to envision,

---

*In 1940, President Roosevelt proposed to transfer to Great Britain certain overage destroyers and small patrol boats then under construction. He did not presume to rely upon any claim of constitutional power as Commander in Chief. On the contrary, he was advised that such destroyers--if certified not to be essential to the defense of the United States--could be "transferred, exchanged, sold, or otherwise disposed of," because Congress had so authorized him. Accordingly, the destroyers were exchanged for air bases. In the same opinion, he was advised that Congress had prohibited the release or transfer of the so-called "mosquito boats" then under construction, so those boats were not transferred. Acquisition of Naval and Air Bases in Exchange for Over-age Destroyers, 39 Op. Atty. Gen. 484. See also Training of British Flying Students in the United States, 40 Op. Atty. Gen. 58.

but I think it is not a military prerogative, without support of law, to
seize persons or property because they are important or even essential for the military and naval establishment.
   . . .

   MR. JUSTICE CLARK, concurring in the judgment of the Court.
   One of this Court's first pronouncements upon the powers of the
President under the Constitution was made by Mr. Chief Justice John
Marshall some one hundred and fifty years ago. In Little v. Barreme
(2 Cranch 170 [1804]), he used this characteristically clear language
in discussing the power of the President to instruct the seizure of the
Flying Fish, a vessel bound from a French port: "It is by no means
clear that the president of the United States whose high duty it is to
'take care that the laws be faithfully executed,' and who is commander
in chief of the armies and navies of the United States, might not, without any special authority for that purpose, in the then existing state of
things, have empowered the officers commanding the armed vessels
of the United States, to seize and send into port for adjudication,
American vessels which were forfeited by being engaged in this illicit
commerce. But when it is observed that [an act of Congress] gives a
special authority to seize on the high seas, and limits that authority
to the seizure of vessels bound or sailing to a French port, the legislature seem to have prescribed that the manner in which this law shall
be carried into execution, was to exclude a seizure of any vessel not
bound to a French port" (Id., at 2 Cranch 177-178 [emphasis changed]).
Accordingly, a unanimous Court held that the President's instructions
had been issued without authority and that they could not "legalize an
act which without these instructions would have been a plain trespass."
I know of no subsequent holding of this Court to the contrary.*

---

   *Decisions of this Court which have upheld the exercise of
presidential power include the following: Prize Cases, 2 Black 635
(1863) (subsequent ratification of President's acts by Congress); In re
Neagle, 135 U.S. 1 (1890) (protection of federal officials from personal
violence while performing official duties); In re Debs, 158 U.S. 564
(1895) (injunction to prevent forcible obstruction of interstate commerce and the mails); United States v. Midwest Oil Co., 236 U.S. 459
(1915) (acquiescence by Congress in more than 250 instances of exercise of same power by various Presidents over period of 80 years);
Myers v. United States, 272 U.S. 52 (1926) (control over subordinate
officials in executive department) [but see Humphrey's Executor v.
United States, 295 U.S. 602, 626-628 (1935)]; Hirabayashi v. United
States, 320 U.S. 81 (1943), and Korematsu v. United States, 323 U.S.
214 (1944) (express congressional authorization); cf. United States v.
Russell, 13 Wall. 623 (1871) (imperative military necessity in area
of combat during war; United States v. Curtiss-Wright Export Corp.,
299 U.S. 304 (1936) (power to negotiate with foreign governments);

The limits of presidential power are obscure. However, Article II, no less that Article I, is part of "a constitution intended to endure for ages to come, and, consequently, to be adapted to the various crises of human affairs" (Mr. Chief Justice Marshall, in McCulloch v. Maryland, 4 Wheat. 316, 415 [1819]). Some of our Presidents, such as Lincoln, "felt that measures otherwise unconstitutional might become lawful by becoming indispensable to the preservation of the Constitution through the preservation of the nation" (Letter of April 4, 1864, to A. G. Hodges, in 10 Complete Works of Abraham Lincoln [Nicolay and Hay ed. 1894], 66). Others, such as Theodore Roosevelt, thought the President to be capable, as a "steward" of the people, of exerting all power save that which is specifically prohibited by the Constitution or the Congress (Roosevelt, Autobiography (1914 ed.), 371-372). In my view--taught me not only by the decision of Mr. Chief Justice Marshall in Little v. Barreme, but also by a score of other pronouncements of distinguished members of this bench--the Constitution does grant to the President extensive authority in times of grave and imperative national emergency. In fact, to my thinking, such a grant may well be necessary to the very existence of the Constitution itself. As Lincoln aptly said, "[is] it possible to lose the nation and yet preserve the Constitution?" (Letter of April 4, 1864, to A. G. Hodges, in 10 Complete Works of Abraham Lincoln [Nicolay and Hay ed. 1894], 66). In describing this authority I care not whether one calls it "residual," "inherent," "moral," "implied," "aggregate," "emergency," or otherwise. I am of the conviction that those who have had the gratifying experience of being the President's lawyer have used one or more of these adjectives only with the utmost of sincerity and the highest of purpose.

I conclude that where Congress has laid down specific procedures to deal with the type of crisis confronting the President, he must follow those procedures in meeting the crisis; but that in the absence of such action by Congress, the President's independent power to act depends upon the gravity of the situation confronting the nation. I cannot sustain the seizure in question because here, as in Little v. Barreme, Congress had prescribed methods to be followed by the President in meeting the emergency at hand.

Dissenting Opinion in DUNCAN v. KAHANAMOKU

Supreme Court of the United States, 1946.
372 U.S. 304, 342, 66 S.Ct. 606, 624, 90 L.Ed. 688.

BURTON, J. . . . . The conduct of war under the Constitution is largely an executive function. Within the field of military action in

---

United States v. United Mine Workers, 330 U.S. 258 (1947) (seizure under specific statutory authorization).

time of war, the executive is allowed wide discretion. While, even in the conduct of war, there are many lines of jurisdiction to draw between the proper spheres of legislative executive and judicial action, it seems clear that at least on an active battle field, the executive discretion to determine policy is there intended by the Constitution to be supreme. The question then arises: What is a battle field and how long does it remain one after the first barrage?

It is well that the outer limits of the jurisdiction of our military authorities is subject to review by our courts even under such extreme circumstances as those of the battle field. This, however, requires the courts to put themselves as nearly as possible in the place of those who had the constitutional responsibility for immediate executive action. For a court to recreate a complete picture of the emergency is impossible. That impossibility demonstrates the need for a zone of executive discretion within which courts must guard themselves with special care against judging past military action too closely by the inapplicable standards of judicial, or even military, hindsight. The nature of judicial authority is largely negative as contrasted with the generally positive nature of executive authority, and it is essential that the opportunity for well directed positive action be preserved and vigorously used if the Government is to serve the best interests of the people.

For this Court to intrude its judgment into spheres of constitutional discretion that are reserved either to the Congress or to the Chief Executive, is to invite disregard of that judgment by the Congress or by executive agencies under a claim of constitutional right to do so. On the other hand, this Court can contribute much to the orderly conduct of government, if it will outline reasonable boundaries for the discretion of the respective departments of the Government, with full regard for the limitations and also for the responsibilities imposed upon them by the Constitution.

---

The majority of the justices held that the "martial law" imposed in Hawaii, by virtue of the Organic Act of the Territory, did not justify the trial of civilians by military commissions when the civil courts could have functioned normally.

## LUFTIG v. McNAMARA

United States District Court, D.C., 1966.
252 F.Supp. 819.

HOLTZOFF, District Judge.

This is an action by a member of the United States Army against the Secretary of Defense and the Secretary of the Army to enjoin them from ordering him to proceed to Vietnam or to its immediate area to engage in the war in Vietnam. Before the Court at this time is a motion for a preliminary injunction.

Basically the underlying question is whether the Courts have any power to enjoin the Commander in Chief of the Army and Navy of the United States against either carrying on a war or hostilities of other types or, specifically, against transferring or stationing a member of the Armed Forces in some particular area. The Court is of the opinion that this is obviously a political question that is outside of the judicial function.

There are a number of cases to which the Court might refer without endeavoring to exhaust all of them. In State of Mississippi v. Johnson, 4 Wall. 475, 18 L.Ed. 437, there was an action brought in behalf of the State of Mississippi against President Andrew Johnson to enjoin him from stationing certain troops in the State of Mississippi for the purpose of carrying out what have become known in history as the Reconstruction Acts. The Supreme Court held that the action could not be maintained.

. . .

A companion case dating back to the same era is State of Georgia v. Stanton, 6 Wall. 50, 18 L.Ed. 721, in which a somewhat similar injunction was sought against Secretary of War Stanton by the State of Georgia, with the same result. At page 71 the Court stated:

> "The distinction between judicial and political pow-
> er is so generally acknowledged in the jurisprudence
> both of England and of this country, that we need do no
> more than refer to some of the authorities on the sub-
> ject. They are all in one direction."

If we now pass on to our own times, the decision of the Court of Appeals for this Circuit in Pauling v. McNamara, 118 U.S.App.D.C. 50, 331 F.2d 796, is pertinent. That case involved an action brought by a citizen against the Secretary of Defense to restrain and enjoin him, as well as the members of the Atomic Energy Commission, from carrying on certain experiments with nuclear weapons. The Court of Appeals held that such an action was outside of the judicial power.

. . .

Thus the Court concludes that the question involved in this case is a political one and, therefore, not cognizable by the judiciary.

There are also other grounds which lead the Court to the same result. The Courts may not substitute themselves for the Commander in Chief of the Army and Navy and determine the disposition of members of the Armed Forces. In Johnson v. Eisentrager, 339 U.S. 763, at 789, 70 S.Ct. 936, at 949, 94 L.Ed. 1255, it was said by Mr. Justice Jackson in the majority opinion:

"Certainly it is not the function of the Judiciary to entertain private litigation--even by a citizen--which challenges the legality, the wisdom, or the propriety of the Commander-in-Chief in sending our Armed Forces abroad or to any particular region." . . .

Finally, the Court is of the opinion that this action is barred by the very basic and fundamental principle that although ostensibly and in name it is a suit against officers of the government, it is actually and in essence a suit against the United States. The government has not consented to be sued in this matter for an injunction and, therefore, for this reason also, the action may not be maintained.

In view of these considerations the motion for a preliminary injunction is denied.

. . .

## UNITED STATES v. MITCHELL

United States Court of Appeals, Second Circuit, 1966.
369 F.2d. 323.

MEDINA, Circuit Judge.

David Henry Mitchell, III appeals from a conviction, after a trial to Judge Clarie and a jury, of wilful failure to report for induction into the Armed Forces in violation of 50 U.S.C., Appx., Section 462.

After initially registering with Selective Service Local Board 17, appellant "disaffiliated" himself from the Selective Service and thereafter refused to cooperate with his Board in any respect. In August, 1964, appellant was classified 1A and did not appeal. Subsequently, he was ordered to report for induction on January 11, 1965. Appellant acknowledged receipt of this notice by letter but did not report as ordered.

Appellant was indicted for violation of 50 U.S.C., Appx., Section 462, tried and found guilty. This Court reversed the first conviction because the trial judge had failed to allow sufficient time for appellant to obtain counsel. United States v. Mitchell, 354 F.2d 767 (2 Cir. 1966). He was retried before Judge Clarie and a jury. The wilfulness of his failure to report for induction was all too apparent, and he was again convicted and sentenced to five years imprisonment. At trial appellant made no claim to be a conscientious objector but sought to produce evidence to show that the war in Vietnam was being conducted in violation of various treaties to which the United States is a signatory and that the Selective Service system was being operated as an adjunct of this military effort. Judge Clarie ruled out all such evidence as immaterial and this ruling is assigned as error.

The government, citing a line of cases beginning with Falbo v. United States, 320 U.S. 549, 64 S.Ct. 346, 88 L.Ed. 305 (1944), would preclude consideration of appellant's claims because of his failure to exhaust his administrative remedies. But, as appellant does not seek any relief which the Selective Service is empowered to grant, we will assume these cases are not in point. Rather, he seeks a declaration, in effect, that the Service must cease to function. It would be pointless in this case to require appellant to press his claims before a Board which he claims is illegal.

Similarly, as appellant asserts that the Selective Service, and not merely the conduct of the war in Vietnam, is illegal, his defenses would seem not to be premature.

Nevertheless, appellant's allegations are not a defense to a prosecution for failure to report for induction into the Armed Forces and his evidence was properly excluded. Regardless of the proof that appellant might present to demonstrate the correlation between the Selective Service and our nation's efforts in Vietnam, as a matter of law the congressional power "to raise and support armies" and "to provide and maintain a navy" is a matter quite distinct from the use which the Executive makes of those who have been found qualified and who have been inducted into the Armed Forces. Whatever action the President may order, or the Congress sanction, cannot impair this constitutional power of the Congress.

Thus we need not consider whether the substantive issues raised by appellant can ever be appropriate for judicial determination. See United States v. Hogans, 2 Cir., 369 F.2d 359, decided by this Court on November 28, 1966.

Affirmed.

## MITCHELL v. UNITED STATES

Supreme Court of the United States, 1967.
386 U.S. 972 87 S.Ct. 1162, 18 L.Ed.2d. 132.

[The petition for a writ of certiorari was denied.]

MR. JUSTICE DOUGLAS, dissenting.
Petitioner did not report for induction as ordered, was indicted, convicted, and sentenced to five years' imprisonment and his

conviction was affirmed.  369 F.2d 323.  His defense was that the
"war" in Vietnam was being conducted in violation of various treaties
to which we were a signatory, especially the Treaty of London of
August 8, 1945, 59 Stat. 1544, which in Article 6(a) declares that
"waging of a war of aggression" is a "crime against peace" imposing
"individual responsibility."  Article 8 provides:

> "The fact that the Defendant acted pursuant to order
> of his Government or of a superior shall not free him
> from responsibility, but may be considered in mitigation
> of punishment if the Tribunal determines that justice so
> requires."

Petitioner claimed that the "war" in Vietnam was a "war of
aggression" within the meaning of the Treaty of London and that
Article 8 makes him responsible for participating in it even though
he is ordered to do so.

Mr. Justice Jackson, the United States prosecutor at Nurem-
berg, stated: "If certain acts in violation of treaties are crimes, they
are crimes whether the United States does them or whether Germany
does them, and we are not prepared to lay down a rule of criminal
conduct against others which we would not be willing to have invoked
against us."  (International Conference on Military Trials, Dept. of
State Pub. No. 3080, p. 330.)

Article VI, cl. 2, of the Constitution states that "Treaties" are
a part of the "supreme Law of the Land; and the Judges in every
State shall be bound thereby."

There is a considerable body of opinion that our actions in
Vietnam constitute the waging of an aggressive "war."

This case presents the questions:

(1)  whether the Treaty of London is a treaty within the meaning of Art. VI, cl. 2;

(2)  whether the question as to the waging of an aggressive
"war" is in the context of this criminal prosecution a justiciable
question;

(3)  whether the Vietnam episode is a "war" in the sense of
the Treaty;

(4)  whether petitioner has standing to raise the question;

(5)  whether, if he has, the Treaty may be tendered as a defense
in this criminal case or in amelioration of the punishment.

These are extremely sensitive and delicate questions.  But they
should, I think, be answered.  Even those who think that the Nurem-
berg judgments were unconstitutional by our guarantee relating to ex
post facto laws would have to take a different view of the Treaty of
London that purports to lay down a standard of future conduct for all
the signatories.

I intimate no opinion on the merits. But I think the petition for certiorari should be granted. We have here a recurring question in present-day Selective Service cases.

## MORA v. McNAMARA*

Supreme Court of the United States, 1967.
389 U.S. 934, 88 S.Ct. 282, 19 L.Ed.2d 287.

*[ Footnotes have been omitted. Ed.]

[The petition for a writ of certiorari was denied.]

MR. JUSTICE STEWART, with whom MR. JUSTICE DOUGLAS joins, dissenting.

The petitioners were drafted into the United States Army in late 1965, and six months later were ordered to a West Coast replacement station for shipment to Vietnam. They brought this suit to prevent the Secretary of Defense and the Secretary of the Army from carrying out those orders, and requested a declaratory judgment that the present United States military activity in Vietnam is "illegal." The District Court dismissed the suit, and the Court of Appeals affirmed.

There exist in this case questions of great magnitude. Some are akin to those referred to by MR. JUSTICE DOUGLAS in Mitchell v. United States, 386 U.S. 972. But there are others:

 I. Is the present United States military activity in Vietnam a "war" within the meaning of Article I, Section 8, Clause 11, of the Constitution?

 II. If so, may the Executive constitutionally order the petitioners to participate in that military activity, when no war has been declared by the Congress?

 III. Of what relevance to Question II are the present treaty obligations of the United States?

 IV. Of what relevance to Question II is the Joint Congressional ("Tonkin Gulf") Resolution of August 10, 1964?

 (a) Do present United States military operations fall within the terms of the Joint Resolution?

 (b) If the Joint Resolution purports to give the Chief Executive authority to commit United States forces to armed conflict limited in scope only by his own absolute discretion, is the Resolution a constitutionally impermissible delegation of all or part of Congress' power to declare war?

These are large and deeply troubling questions. Whether the Court would ultimately reach them depends, of course, upon the

resolution of serious preliminary issues of justiciability.  We cannot
make these problems go away simply by refusing to hear the case of
three obscure Army privates.  I intimate not even tentative views
upon any of these matters, but I think the Court should squarely face
them by granting certiorari and setting this case for oral argument.

MR. JUSTICE DOUGLAS, with whom MR. JUSTICE STEWART
concurs, dissenting.

The questions posed by MR. JUSTICE STEWART cover the wide
range of problems which the Senate Committee on Foreign Relations
recently explored, in connection with the SEATO Treaty of February
19, 1955, and the Tonkin Gulf Resolution.

Mr. Katzenbach, representing the Administration, testified that
he did not regard the Tonkin Gulf Resolution to be "a declaration of
war" and that while the Resolution was not "constitutionally necessary" it was "politically, from an international viewpoint and from a
domestic viewpoint, extremely important."  He added:

> "The use of the phrase 'to declare war' as it was used in
> the Constitution of the United States had a particular
> meaning in terms of the events and the practices which
> existed at the time it was adopted . . . .
> "[I]t was recognized by the Founding Fathers that the
> President might have to take emergency action to pro-
> tect the security of the United States, but that if there
> was going to be another use of the armed forces of the
> United States, that was a decision which Congress should
> check the Executive on, which Congress should support.
> It was for that reason that the phrase was inserted in the
> Constitution.
>     "Now, over a long period of time, . . . there have
> been many uses of the military forces of the United
> States for a variety of purposes without a congressional
> declaration of war.  But it would be fair to say that most
> of these were relatively minor uses of force. . . .
>         . . .
>     "A declaration of war would not, I think, correctly
> reflect the very limited objectives of the United States
> with respect to Vietnam.  It would not correctly reflect
> our efforts there, what we are trying to do, the reasons
> why we are there, to use an outmoded phraseology, to
> declare war."

The view that Congress was intended to play a more active role
in the initiation and conduct of war than the above statements might
suggest has been espoused by Senator Fulbright (Cong. Rec., Oct. 11,
1967, pp. 14683-14690), quoting Thomas Jefferson who said:

> "We have already given in example one effectual
> check to the Dog of war by transferring the power of let-
> ting him loose from the Executive to the Legislative body,
> from those who are to spend to those who are to pay."

These opposed views are reflected in the Prize Cases, 2 Black
635, a five-to-four decision rendered in 1863. Mr. Justice Grier,
writing for the majority, emphasized the arguments for strong presidential powers. Mr. Justice Nelson, writing for the minority of four,
read the Constitution more strictly, emphasizing that what is war in
actuality may not constitute war in the constitutional sense. During
all subsequent periods in our history--through the Spanish-American
War, the Boxer Rebellion, two World Wars, Korea, and now Vietnam
--the two points of view urged in the Prize Cases have continued to
be voiced.

A host of problems is raised. Does the President's authority
to repel invasions and quiet insurrections, do his powers in foreign
relations and his duty to execute faithfully the laws of the United
States, including its treaties, justify what has been threatened of
petitioners? What is the relevancy of the Gulf of Tonkin Resolution
and the yearly appropriations in support of the Vietnam effort?

The London Treaty (59 Stat. 1546), the SEATO Treaty (6 U.S.T.
81, 1955), the Kellogg-Briand Pact (46 Stat. 2343), and Article 39 of
Chapter VII of the UN Charter deal with various aspects of wars of
"aggression."

Do any of them embrace hostilities in Vietnam, or give rights
to individuals affected to complain, or in other respects give rise to
justiciable controversies?

There are other treaties or declarations that could be cited.
Perhaps all of them are wide of the mark. There are sentences in
our opinions which, detached from their context, indicate that what is
happening is none of our business:

> "Certainly it is not the function of the Judiciary to
> entertain private litigation--even by a citizen--which
> challenges the legality, the wisdom, or the propriety of
> the Commander-in-Chief in sending our armed forces
> abroad or to any particular region." Johnson v. Eisen-
> trager, 339 U.S. 763, 789.

We do not, of course, sit as a committee of oversight or supervision. What resolutions the President asks and what the Congress
provides are not our concern. With respect to the Federal Government, we sit only to decide actual cases or controversies within judicial cognizance that arise as a result of what the Congress or the
President or a judge does or attempts to do to a person or his
property.

In Ex parte Milligan, 4 Wall. 2, the Court relieved a person of the death penalty imposed by a military tribunal, holding that only a civilian court had power to try him for the offense charged. Speaking of the purpose of the Founders in providing constitutional guarantees, the Court said:

> "They knew . . . the nation they were founding, be its existence short or long, would be involved in war; how often or how long continued, human foresight could not tell; and that unlimited power, wherever lodged at such a time, was especially hazardous to freemen. For this, and other equally weighty reasons, they secured the inheritance they had fought to maintain, by incorporating in a written constitution the safeguards which time had proved were essential to its preservation. Not one of these safeguards can the President, or Congress, or the Judiciary disturb except the one concerning the writ of habeas corpus." Id., 125.

The fact that the political branches are responsible for the threat to petitioners' liberty is not decisive. As Mr. Justice Holmes said in Nixon v. Herndon, 273 U.S. 536, 540:

> "The objection that the subject matter of the suit is political is little more than a play upon words. Of course the petition concerns political action but it alleges and seeks to recover for private damage. That private damage may be caused by such political action and may be recovered for in a suit at law hardly has been doubted for over two hundred years, since Ashby v. White, 2 Ld. Raym. 938, 3 id. 320, and has been recognized by this Court."

These petitioners should be told whether their case is beyond judicial cognizance. If it is not, we should then reach the merits of their claims, on which I intimate no views whatsoever.

In Ashton v. United States, 404 F.2d 95 (8th Cir. 1968), certiorari denied, 89 S.Ct. 1308 (1969), the court upheld the constitutionality of draft laws in the absence of an emergency or declaration of war and denied defendant's standing to raise the question of the legality of use of draftees in Vietnam and of the Vietnam war itself since he had not received an order to go to Vietnam.

## UNITED STATES v. JOHNSON

United States Court of Military Appeals, 1967.
17 U.S.C.M.A. 246, 38 C.M.R. 44.

PER CURIAM:
The accused were convicted of willful disobedience of an order, in violation of Uniform Code of Military Justice, Article 90, 10 USC §890. In one instance, the order directed the individual concerned to board a sedan which would take him to McGuire Air Force Base for further transportation to Vietnam. In the other two, the order directed the individual to board an aircraft at McGuire for transportation to Vietnam. In each instance, the disobedience was judicially admitted. Prior thereto, each had been routinely ordered to Vietnam for duty. The main contention at the trial, as well as here, is that each of the orders was unlawful, as American participation in the Vietnamese conflict is illegal.

Under domestic law, the presence of American troops in Vietnam is unassailable. United States v Smith, 13 USCMA 105, 32 CMR 105. The legality under international law of the American presence in Vietnam is not a justiciable issue. As long ago as Martin v Mott, 12 Wheat 19, 29 (U.S. 1827), the Supreme Court rejected the idea that the orders of the President as Commander-in-Chief may be so questioned, either by the individual concerned or the judiciary. Inter alia, it said:

> ". . . If it be a limited power, the question arises, by whom is the exigency to be judged of and decided? Is the President the sole and exclusive judge whether the exigency has arisen, or is it to be considered as an open question, upon which every officer to whom the orders of the President are addressed, may decide for himself, and equally open to be contested by every militia-man who shall refuse to obey the orders of the President? We are all of opinion that the authority to decide whether the exigency has arisen, belongs exclusively to the President, and that his decision is conclusive upon all other persons."

The same Court has since likewise refused to entertain litigation "which challenges the legality, the wisdom, or the propriety of the Commander-in-Chief in sending our armed forces abroad or to any particular region." Johnson v Eisentrager, 339 US 763, 789, 94

L ed 1255, 1271, 70 S Ct 936 (1950).  See also Luftig v. McNamara,
373 F 2d 664 (CA DC Cir) (1967).

. . .

In like manner, an accused may not excuse his disobedience of
an order to proceed to foreign duty on the ground that our presence
there does not conform to his notions of legality.  We have examined
the other assignments of error, and find they have no merit.

The petition for review in each of the foregoing cases is denied.

Some very recent cases have examined more closely the President's powers to commit American military forces in Vietnam and
have found implicit, if not explicit, Congressional approval of the
President's actions.  See Berk v. Laird, CA 2d, 3 Selective Service
Law Reporter 3142 (1970), and Orlando v. Laird, E.D.N.Y., 3 Selective Service Law Reporter 3144 (1970).

The Supreme Court in 1970 denied a motion by the Commonwealth of Massachusetts to file a bill of complaint on behalf of its
citizens to obtain a declaration of unconstitutionality of the Vietnam
war (Massachusetts v. Laird, 91 S.Ct. 128).

## Questions

What is the purpose of the Commander-in-Chief clause of the
Constitution?  Are there any limitations on the President's power?
Are declarations of war obsolete?  What effects do treaty obligations
have?  Executive agreements?  Monroe Doctrine?  Nixon Doctrine?
Power of the President to conduct foreign affairs?  Are limitations
by Congress on the expenditure of appropriations (e.g., the Cooper-
Church Amendment) valid?  Can they be enforced?  How?

## LIABILITY FOR MILITARY DUTY

It is a fundamental principle of national law, essential to national life, that every citizen, whether of age to make contracts generally or not, is under obligation to serve and defend the constituted authorities of the state and nation, and for that purpose to bear arms, when of sufficient age and capacity to do so, and when such service is lawfully required of him. The power to enforce that obligation, so far as the necessities of the state may require, is an incident of state sovereignty, and the subject of state constitutional and statutory regulation. (Lanahan v. Birge, 30 Conn. 438, 443 [1862]).

Congress has the power to impose compulsory military service on all under the jurisdiction of the sovereign and no one is exempt except by the grace of the government. The obligation to render military service is inherent in citizenship. (United States ex rel. Lipsitz v. Perez, 260 F.Supp. 435, 440 [D. S. Car. 1966], affirmed, 372 F.2d 468 [4th Cir. 1967]).

Notwithstanding the provisions of section 405(b) of this Act, any alien who applies or has applied for exemption or discharge from training or service in the Armed Forces or in the National Security Training Corps of the United States on the ground that he is an alien, and is or was relieved or discharged from such training or service on such ground, shall be permanently ineligible to become a citizen of the United States. (8 U.S.C. §1426 [a] [1964]).

This section reinforces the idea that the obligation to render military service is inherent in citizenship. The law is not

unconstitutional as cruel and unusual punishment in violation of the
eighth amendment or as imposing a penalty without procedural safeguards guaranteed by the fifth and sixth amendments. In re Dulo, 237
F.Supp. 46 (D. Conn. 1965). It allows an alien "to avoid his obligation
for military service if he is willing to bargain away his eligibility for
American citizenship in exchange for the exemption." Naturalization
of Krummenacher, 202 F.Supp. 781, 784 (N.D. Cal. 1962). See also
Ceballos v. Shaughnessy, 352 U.S. 599, 77 S.Ct. 545, 1 L.Ed.2d 583
(1957), where the Supreme Court held that an alien's act of executing
and filing an application for exemption permanently barred him from
American citizenship, even though his draft board never issued an
alien exemption to him and classified him IV-F after he failed to pass
a physical examination. Accord, In re Lapenieks, 249 F.Supp. 398
(S.D. Cal. 1965), affirmed, 389 F.2d 343 (9th Cir. 1968), certiorari
denied, 391 U.S. 951, 88 S.Ct. 1846, 20 L.Ed.2d 864 (1968). An alien
is not relieved of his ineligibility for citizenship under this section
by attempting to withdraw his application for exemption after his
classification has been changed, even though he subsequently receives
an occupational deferment. Julran v. United States, 255 F.2d 81 (5th
Cir. 1958). He is barred from citizenship even if he withdraws his
application one week after he submits it to his draft board. Velasquez
v. United States, 241 F.2d 126 (2d Cir. 1957).

"It must be conceded that the Government has the right to demand the services, in time of war, of any of its citizens, whether
physically fit or not. If a man not physically fit is called into the
service of the country the Government has the right to take any measures, short, at least, of those which involve danger to life, which may
be necessary to restore the man to a proper physical condition. This
office has uniformly upheld the right of the Government to require
any officer or enlisted man in the service to submit to a physical operation which the Medical Department would certify was without
danger to life. The present case should be no exception to this general rule. If the man is in the service and is physically disqualified
to render full duty, and if such disqualification can be removed by an
operation which does not involve, in the opinion of the medical officers concerned, danger to life, then I see no reason for holding that
he can not be required to submit to such operation or be punished for
refusal so to submit. The fact that the man might have been rejected
if there had been a more rigid examination upon admission to the
service can not be held to affect the rights of the Government in his
case." (1918 Op. JAG 152 [1918]).

(b)  The Congress declares that an adequate armed strength must be achieved and maintained to insure the security of this Nation.

(c)  The Congress further declares that in a free society the obligations and privileges of serving in the armed forces and the reserve components thereof should be shared generally, in accordance with a system of selection which is fair and just, and which is consistent with the maintenance of an effective national economy.  (50 U.S.C. App. §451 [1964]).

Except as otherwise provided in this title (sections 451, 453, 454, 455, 456 and 458-471 of this Appendix), every male citizen of the United States and every male alien admitted for permanent residence, who is between the ages of 18 years and 6 months and 26 years, at the time fixed for his registration, or who attains the age of 18 years and 6 months after having been required to register pursuant to section 3 of this title (section 453 of this Appendix), or who is otherwise liable as provided in section 6(h) of this title (section 456(h) of this Appendix), shall be liable for training and service in the Armed Forces of the United States . . .  (50 U.S.C. App. §454 [a] [1964]).

## ENLISTMENT--IN GENERAL

### In re GRIMLEY

Supreme Court of the United States, 1890.
137 U.S. 147, 11 S.Ct. 54, 34 L.Ed. 636.

MR. JUSTICE BREWER delivered the opinion of the court.

John Grimley, the appellee, was on the 28th day of May, 1888, found guilty by a court-martial of the crime of desertion, and sentenced to be imprisoned six months.  While serving out this sentence at Fort Warren, Massachusetts, he sued out a writ of habeas corpus from the District Court of the United States for the District of Massachusetts.  That court, on June 25, 1888, discharged him from custody. The United States appealed to the Circuit Court for said District, which, on the 27th day of February, 1889, affirmed the decree of the District Court.  38 F. 84.  From this decision the United States has brought this appeal.

The Circuit Court found that the petitioner was forty years of age at the time of his alleged enlistment, although he represented himself to be but twenty-eight; and, under section 1116 of the Revised Statutes, 10 U.S.C.A. §621, ruled that the enlistment was void, and that Grimley never became a soldier, and was not subject to the jurisdiction of the court-martial.  That section reads: "Recruits enlisting in the Army must be effective and able-bodied men, and between the ages of sixteen and thirty-five years, at the time of their enlistment." It cannot be doubted that the civil courts may in any case inquire into the jurisdiction of a court-martial, and if it appears that the party condemned was not amenable to its jurisdiction, may discharge him from the sentence. And, on the other hand, it is equally clear that by habeas corpus the civil courts exercise no supervisory or correcting power over the proceedings of a court-martial; and that no mere errors in their proceedings are open to consideration. The single inquiry, the test, is jurisdiction. That being established, the habeas corpus must be denied and the petitioner remanded. That wanting, it must be sustained and the petitioner discharged. If Grimley was an enlisted soldier he was amenable to the jurisdiction of the court-martial; and the principal question, the one ruled against the government, is whether Grimley's enlistment was void by reason of the fact that he was over thirty-five years of age. This case involves a matter of contractual relation between the parties; and the law of contracts, as applicable thereto, is worthy of notice. The government, as contracting party, offers contract and service. Grimley accepts such contract declaring that he possesses all the qualifications prescribed in the government's offer. The contract is duly signed. Grimley has made an untrue statement in regard to his qualifications. The government makes no objection because of the untruth. The qualification is one for the benefit of the government, one of the contracting parties. Who can take advantage of Grimley's lack of qualification? Obviously only the party for whose benefit it was inserted. Such is the ordinary law of contracts. Suppose "A," an individual, were to offer to enter into contract with persons of Anglo-Saxon descent, and "B," representing that he is of such descent, accepts the offer and enters into contract; can he, thereafter, "A" making no objection, repudiate the contract on the ground that he is not of Anglo-Saxon descent? "A" has prescribed the terms. He contracts with "B" upon the strength of his representations that he comes within those terms. Can "B," thereafter, plead his disability in avoidance of the contract? On the other hand, suppose for any reason it could be contended that the proviso as to age was for the benefit of the party enlisting, is Grimley in any better position? The matter of age is merely incidental, and not of the substance of the contract; and can a party by false representations as to such incidental matter obtain a contract, and thereafter disown and repudiate its obligations on the simple ground that the fact in reference to this incidental matter was contrary to his representations? May he utter a falsehood to acquire a contract, and plead the truth to avoid it, when the matter in respect to which the falsehood is stated is for his benefit? It must be noted here, that in the present contract is involved no matter of duress, imposition, ignorance or intoxication. Grimley was sober, and of his own volition went to the recruiting office and enlisted. There was no compulsion, no solicitation, no misrepresentation. A man of mature years, he entered freely into the contract.

But in this transaction something more is involved than the making of a contract, whose breach exposes to an action for damages.

Enlistment is a contract; but it is one of those contracts which changes the status; and, where that is changed, no breach of contract destroys the new status or relieves from the obligations which its existence imposes. Marriage is a contract; but it is one which creates a status. Its contract obligations are mutual faithfulness; but a breach of those obligations does not destroy the status or change the relation of the parties to each other. The parties remain husband and wife, no matter what their conduct to each other--no matter how great their disregard of marital obligations. It is true that courts have power, under the statutes of most States, to terminate those contract obligations, and put an end to the marital relations. But this is never done at the instance of the wrongdoer. The injured party, and the injured party alone, can obtain relief and a change of status by judicial action. So, also, a foreigner by naturalization enters into new obligations. More than that, he thereby changes his status; he ceases to be an alien, and becomes a citizen, and when that change is once accomplished, no disloyalty on his part, no breach of the obligations of citizenship, of itself, destroys his citizenship. In other words, it is a general rule accompanying a change of status, that when once accomplished it is not destroyed by the mere misconduct of one of the parties, and the guilty party cannot plead his own wrong as working a termination and destruction thereof. Especially is he debarred from pleading the existence of facts personal to himself, existing before the change of status, the entrance into new relations, which would have excused him from entering into those relations and making the change, or if disclosed to the other party, would have led it to decline admission into the relation, or consent to the change.

By enlistment the citizen becomes a soldier. His relations to the State and the public are changed. He acquires a new status, with correlative rights and duties; and although he may violate his contract obligations, his status as a soldier is unchanged. He cannot of his own volition throw off the garments he has once put on, nor can he, the State not objecting, renounce his relations and destroy his status on the plea that, if he had disclosed truthfully the facts, the other party, the State, would not have entered into the new relations with him, or permitted him to change his status. Of course, these considerations may not apply where there is insanity, idiocy, infancy, or any other disability which in its nature, disables a party from changing his status or entering into new relations. But where a party is sui juris, without any disability to enter into the new relations, the rule generally applies as stated. A naturalized citizen would not be permitted, as a defense to a charge of treason, to say that he had acquired his citizenship through perjury, that he had not been a resident of the United States for five years, or within the State or Territory where he was naturalized one year, or that he was not a man of good moral character, or that he was not attached to the Constitution. No more can an enlisted soldier avoid a charge of desertion, and escape the consequences of such act, by proof that he was over age at the time of enlistment, or that he was not able-bodied, or that he had been convicted of a felony, or that before his enlistment he had been a deserter from the military service of the United States. These are matters which do not inhere in the substance of the contract, do not prevent a change of status, do not render the new relations assumed absolutely void. And in the case of a soldier, these considerations become of vast public importance. While our regular army is small compared with those of European nations, yet its vigor and efficiency are equally important. An army is not a deliberate body. It is the executive arm. Its law is that of obedience. No question can be left open as to the right to command in the officer, or the duty of obedience in the soldier. Vigor and efficiency on the part of the officer and confidence among the soldiers in one another are impaired if any question be left open as to their attitude to each other. So, unless there be in the nature of things some inherent vice in the existence of the relation, or natural wrong in the manner in which it was established, public policy requires that it should not be disturbed. Now, there is no inherent vice in the military service of a man forty years of age. The age of thirty-five, as prescribed in the statute, is one of convenience merely. The government has the right to the military service of all its able-bodied citizens; and may, when emergency arises, justly exact that service from all. And if for its own convenience, and with a view to the selection of the best material, it has fixed the age at thirty-five, it is a matter which in any given case it may waive; and it does not lie in the mouth of any one above that age, on that account alone, to demand release from an obligation voluntarily assumed, and discharge from a service voluntarily entered into. The government, and the government alone, is the party to the transaction that can raise objections on that ground. We conclude, therefore, that the age of the petitioner was no ground for his discharge. . . .

The remainder of the case concerns the question of whether Grimley was in fact enlisted. The Court held that Grimley's taking of an oath of enlistment, which included an acknowledgement that he had enlisted, was the "pivotal fact which changes the status from that of civilian to that of soldier." 137 U.S. at 157, 11 S.Ct. at 56, 34 L.Ed. at 640. See also Coe v. United States, 44 Ct.Cl. 419 (1909), and Tyler v. Pomeroy, 90 Mass. 480 (1864). On the question of when an inductee assumes the status of soldier, see Billings v. Truesdell, 321 U.S. 542, 64 S.Ct. 737, 88 L.Ed. 917 (1944), and Mayborn v. Heflebower, 145 F.2d 864 (5th Cir. 1944), certiorari denied, 325 U.S. 854, 65 S.Ct. 1087, 89 L.Ed. 1975 (1945).

"But, as will be illustrated as we proceed, the contract of enlistment is peculiar in that it is a contract made with the State, under the specific authority of the Constitution, and thus governed by those principles or considerations of expediency and economy expressed in the term 'public policy.' Thus, while the necessities of military discipline require that the soldier should be strictly obliged by the compact, the State, on the other hand, is not bound by the conditions though imposed by itself. Thus it may put an end to the term of enlistment at any time before it has regularly expired and discharge the soldier against his consent. So, pending the engagement, it may reduce the pay, or curtail any allowance, which formed a part of the original consideration. The contract of enlistment is thus a transaction in which private right is subordinated to the public interest. In law, it is entered into with the understanding that it may be modified in any of its terms, or wholly rescinded, at the discretion of the State. But this discretion can be exercised only by the legislative body, or under an authority which that body has conferred." Winthrop, Military Law and Precedents, 538-539 (2d ed. 1920).

UNITED STATES ex rel. PARSLEY v. MOSES*

United States District Court, D. New Jersey, 1956,
138 F.Supp. 799.

*[ Footnotes have been omitted. Ed.]

FORMAN, Chief Judge.
Relator, Robert A. Parsley, enlisted in the United States Army on August 15, 1950 for a term of three years. On January 3, 1951 relator absented himself without leave from the Army and made his way from his station at Fort Knox, Kentucky to Reno, Nevada. Reno was his destination because he had conceived a scheme which he thought would enable him to accumulate a fortune at roulette.

Like many predecessor research workers in this field, he soon found himself stranded in Reno without money. At this juncture, apparently, Army life once again seemed inviting, and, on January 7, 1951, relator surrendered himself to the Reno police as a soldier absent without leave. The police provided him with accommodations and contacted the local office of the Federal Bureau of Investigation, which, in turn, contacted Fort Knox, Kentucky. The reply from Fort Knox was that relator was "not wanted" there and accordingly upon authority obtained from the Federal Bureau of Investigation the Reno police released him. He then made an unsuccessful attempt to get the local Red Cross to provide him with transportation back to Fort Knox.

Relator obtained a few menial jobs in the Reno vicinity and eventually reached Seattle, Washington, where he resumed his civilian occupation of ship's radio officer.

On September 16, 1955, while relator was serving aboard a ship docked in New York harbor Army personnel took him into custody and transported him to Fort Dix, New Jersey. On November 18, 1955 relator was tried by a general court-martial at Fort Dix on a charge that he deserted on January 3, 1951. He pleaded guilty to the lesser charge of being absent without leave from January 3, 1951 to January 7, 1951, the day he surrendered himself to the Reno police. After trial he was found guilty of being absent without leave from January 3, 1951 to September 16, 1955. Relator was sentenced to serve 30 days at hard labor and to forfeit $55. The sentence has been served.

During the period of his absence from the Army relator made no effort to conceal either his identity or his whereabouts.

Under 10 U.S.C.A. §629 the Army has authority to add to a soldier's term of enlistment so-called "bad time"--time during which the enlistee has unauthorizedly absented himself from duty. However, the total amount of service that can be required may not exceed in length the original term of enlistment. Thus, relator is presently being required to serve the time that remained in his enlistment term after he absented himself from the Army on January 3, 1951. Relator's "bad time" amounts to about two years and seven months, since his original term expired on August 15, 1953.

It is relator's position that the Army lacks legal authority to hold him until he finishes the remainder of his three-year enlistment term. Upon the submission of a petition containing substantially all of the above facts, which the Army concedes to be an accurate description of the course of events, a writ of habeas corpus was issued, testimony taken and oral argument heard.

I

The first issue that must be met is whether the Army had jurisdiction to reacquire custody of relator and thus to apply 10 U.S.C.A. §629 to him.

In United States ex rel. Toth v. Quarles, 1955, 350 U.S. 11, 76 S.Ct. 1, the Supreme Court held, in dealing with a discharged soldier, that Congress lacks constitutional power to provide for military trial of civilians for crimes committed while in their former status as servicemen. Once a soldier's status has changed from soldier to civilian there is no courts-martial jurisdiction for the trial of crimes committed prior to the status-changing separation from the Armed Services. Future prosecution of civilians for their crimes committed while in the military must be by civilian courts subject to all the provisions of the Bill of Rights. United States ex rel. Toth v. Quarles, supra.

The Toth case stands for the proposition that once a soldier's status changes from that of soldier to that of civilian, military jurisdiction is lost and cannot be regained. It is apparent that that case will apply to relator only if at the time of the reacquisition of custody over him by the Army his status had changed to that of civilian. The issue becomes: Did his status change to that of civilian upon the expiration of his original term of enlistment? This requires an examination of the relationship between an enlisted man and the Army.

"Enlistment is a contract, but it is one of those contracts which changes the status, and where that is changed, no breach of the contract destroys the new status or relieves from the obligations which its existence imposes." In re Grimley, 1890, 137 U.S. 147, 151, 11 S.Ct. 54, 55, 34 L.Ed. 636. Discharge, of course, changes the status and turns a soldier into a civilian. Can it be said that the simple passage of time beyond the expiration date of the original term of enlistment creates the same effect?

In 1876 Attorney General Taft, in an opinion addressed to the then Secretary of War, construed the military contract of enlistment (absent statutory directions to the contrary) to impose a duty to serve only during the specific years covered by the contract. There was thought to be no duty to serve beyond the terminal date of the contractual period even if the enlistee deserted during his term and remained a deserter when the terminal date of the enlistment period was reached. 15 Op. Atty. Gen. 152, 161-163. Accord: NCM 133, Taylor, 4 CMR 450, 452 (1952).

In 1922 Attorney General Daugherty disagreed with his predecessor. In an opinion addressed to the then Secretary of the Navy he examined the contract of enlistment and found that "The contract is to serve for a certain period, and the status established is that of a soldier or sailor in the military service of the United States. . . . It is a contradiction in terms to say that this contract of service can be performed by desertion; that this status can be dissolved at the will of the enlisted man. The obligation can only be ended by complete performance, and the status is only satisfied by the prescribed continuous relationship of service." 33 Op.Atty.Gen. 121, 127-128. He further held that "There must be, in my judgment, some further act, such as a discharge, to terminate the actual state of service in which the contract of enlistment places the soldier or sailor." 33 Op.Atty.Gen. at page 129.

It is the latter interpretation of the military contract of enlistment that has found favor with the majority of civilian and military courts that have passed upon the problem. Two Federal District Courts have agreed with it, Ex parte Clark, D.C.E.D.N.Y. 1921, 271 F. 533 and Ex parte Wilson, D.C.E.D.Va. 1929, 33 F.2d 214, as has the Court of Claims, Peiffer v. United States, 1942, 96 Ct.Cl. 344 and the United States Court of Military Appeals, United States v. Klunk, 11 CMR 92 (USCMA 1953); see also United States v. Downs, 11 CMR 90 (USCMA 1953); United States v. Barrett, 12 CMR 50 (USCMA 1953);

CGCM 9737, Wilbert J. Meyer, 1 CMR 562 (1951). Any other construction of the enlistment contract would imperil military discipline.
Furthermore, Attorney General Taft's interpretation of the enlistment
contract runs counter to the provisions of 10 U.S.C.A. §652a, which
provides that no enlisted person shall be discharged without a certificate of discharge and, if the discharge is to take place before the enlistment term expires, in that event it must be in conformity with the
rules prescribed by the Secretary of the Army or the sentence of a
general or special court-martial. This statute clearly contemplates
a necessity for official military action before the cessation of an enlisted man's obligation to serve. A member of the Armed Forces
cannot discharge himself. It must be concluded that the Army had
jurisdiction to regain custody of the relator and therefore to apply the
provisions of 10 U.S.C.A. §629 to him.

## II

Relator also argues that he was deprived of procedural due
process by use of the administrative procedure utilized by the Army
in computing the amount of his "bad time".

. . .

. . . Under applicable Army regulations the power created by
10 U.S.C.A. §629 may be used independently of a court-martial conviction for unauthorized absence. . . .

. . .

Thus, it appears that there are two facets to every unauthorized
absence from the Army. One concerns liability to court-martial for
punishment and is akin to the criminal liability to which a wrongdoer
is exposed in civilian courts. The other is a liability to make good
time lost through unauthorized absence and is analogous to civil liability for breach of contract. When Army authorities set about determining the latter liability of a soldier Army regulations do not bind
them by the results of a court-martial, or even require that one be
held before an enlistment may be extended under 10 U.S.C.A. §629.

. . .

Relator's particular contention is that the administrative authority computed the length of his unauthorized absence in ignorance
of the true facts concerning his willingness to return to the Army
during January 1951, and his consequent frustration in that purpose
by the erroneous report from Fort Knox that he was "not wanted".
Furthermore, he asserts that his good faith in believing that the Army
had released him should be taken into consideration by the administrative authority. Since neither of these facts was sufficient to prevent
his court-martial conviction for unauthorized absence it is difficult to
see how they can rationally be expected to move an officer into dimin-
ishing the length of his "bad time". But the short answer to relator's
argument is to point out that if these facts were not considered in
computing the length of his "bad time" it is a defect of his own making.
He never took steps to put them before the administrative authority

who calculated his "bad time". The proper mechanism for him to use to secure a recomputation of the time he must make up by an authority with these additional facts before him is Article 138. It is no violation of the fundamental fairness due process requires for relator to bear the burden of going forward once the Army's records make out a prima facie case of unauthorized absence.

### III

Relator's final argument is that he was relieved from his obligation to serve by the Army when it, acting through the Federal Bureau of Investigation and the Reno police, told him he was "not wanted". Two theories are relied on in support of this argument: (1) that his release by the Reno police was actually a release from military custody which is binding on the Army and (2) that it is now estopped from asserting a contrary position.

Under 10 U.S.C.A. §652a "No enlisted person, lawfully inducted into the military service of the United States, shall be discharged from said service without a certificate of discharge, and no enlisted person shall be discharged from said service before his term of service has expired, except in the manner prescribed by the Secretary of the Department of the Army, or by sentence of a general or special court-martial." Civilian police officers are authorized by 50 U.S.C.A. §562 to apprehend deserters from the Armed Forces of the United States and to deliver them into the custody of military officials. But this is as far as their authority goes. There is no authority in civilian police or the Federal Bureau of Investigation to act as an agency of the Army in the granting of discharges. Only a discharge could relieve relator of his obligations to the Army and it was beyond the power of the Army to authorize the Reno police to give him one.

Nor can the relator validly assert the theory that the Reno police had apparent authority to release him from his obligation to the Army, and that the Army will not now be heard to deny the existence of that authority. The facts in this case present nothing from which a reasonable inference can be drawn that the Army so authorized the Reno police. . . .

The writ is discharged and the relator remanded to custody.

An enlisted member of an armed force who--

    (1)  deserts;
    (2)  is absent from his organization, station, or duty for more than one day without proper authority, as determined by competent authority;
    (3)  is confined for more than one day while awaiting trial and disposition of his case, and whose conviction has become final;
    (4)  is confined for more than one day under a sentence that has become final; or

(5)  is unable for more than one day, as determined by competent authority, to perform his duties because of intemperate use of drugs or alcoholic liquor, or because of disease or injury resulting from his misconduct;

is liable, after his return to full duty, to serve for a period that, when added to the period that he served before his absence from duty, amounts to the term for which he was enlisted or inducted. 10 U.S.C. §972.

## CONSTRUCTIVE ENLISTMENT

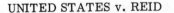

It has been stated that the taking of an oath is not essential to the validity of an enlistment contract and that such a contract may be implied from the conduct of a person such as the acceptance of pay and other benefits (see 1918 Op. JAG 488 (1918)).

## UNITED STATES v. REID

Board of Review, United States Air Force, 1954.
15 C.M.R. 899, A.C.M. 8288.

Upon trial the accused pleaded not guilty to but was found guilty of an assault thereby intentionally inflicting grievous bodily harm (Article 128).

The findings of guilty and the sentence are correct in law and fact if the accused was subject to the jurisdiction of the Court.

[On the basis of a plea of guilty to a robbery in the Superior Court of Los Angeles, the accused airman was committed to the California Youth Authority.  He was discharged from the service because of conviction by a civil court.  The discharge was later revoked as erroneously issued, and accused was returned to military control, prior to both the offense and date of trial.]

Accordingly it may readily be seen that when accused was certified to the Juvenile Court, found to be a fit subject and accepted as a ward of the Juvenile Court, the proceedings did not constitute a conviction for a criminal offense under California law. Since AFR 39-22 delegated discharge authority for civil conviction of a criminal offense only in cases where the person concerned had been so convicted, the discharge issued accused was null and void. The accused remained a member of the United States Air Force and subject to the jurisdiction of the court-martial.

In addition to the reasons stated above, we believe that there is another basis for holding that the accused on both the date of the offense and on date of trial herein was subject to the jurisdiction of the Uniform Code of Military Justice and a member of the United States Air Force. It is undisputed that the accused ate in the mess halls, slept in the barracks, performed duty as a driver in the motor pool, and received pay from the Air Force after his return from his stay with the civilian authorities. Such receipt is normally sufficient to constitute a "constructive enlistment".

A constructive enlistment is one which is implied in law. The decided cases in military law base a finding of constructive enlistment on two elements, the voluntary performance of military duties and the acceptance of benefits (Mayborn v. Heflebower, 145 F2d 864 (5th Cir 1944); U.S. v. Seldner ex rel. Mellis, 59 F Supp. 682 (DCMDNC 1945); Hibbs v. Catovolo, 145 F2d 866 (5th Cir 1944); Dig Op JAG 1912-40, AR 615-360 (220.815, July 26, 1919; 110.6, May 7, 1918) pp 999-1000). An examination of the facts related earlier in this opinion convinces us that both essential elements of a constructive enlistment are here present. However, accused's defense counsel argues that the rationale of ACM 2769, Holleman (BR) 3 CMR (AF) 450 applies thereby refuting the doctrine of constructive enlistment. In Holleman the accused was charged with desertion. The evidence showed that prior to the alleged desertion the accused had been restricted to a certain air base while his status was under investigation. During that period accused apparently received benefits in the nature of food and lodging and may have performed duty. However, he was not permitted to leave the base. It was determined by the Board of Review that the receipt of benefits and performance of duty was not voluntary by the accused in that case and therefore no constructive enlistment was discernible from those circumstances.

Thus we see that here, Reid, did not protest his return to the United States Air Force, in fact, he stated that he returned because his mother so desired. His receipt of pay and allowances and his performance of full duty was adequately established. It is uncontested that his receipt of benefits on the one hand and performance of duty on the other was voluntary rather than coerced within the meaning of the Holleman rule.  Reid's conduct, perforce, shows that he recognized himself to be a member of the United States Air Force in good standing.  Accordingly, he may not now complain of that status and assert to the contrary.

Article 66(c) having been complied with, the findings of guilty and the sentence are

Affirmed.

In United States ex rel. Norris v. Norman, 296 F.Supp. 1270 (N.D. Ill. 1969), the petitioner, Norris, was seeking release from the navy by writ of habeas corpus.  Prior to his entry into the service, he had taken an evaluation test that indicated that he was qualified as a Petty Officer second class.  In August, 1967, he presented himself for enlistment at a station in Maryland but refused to sign an enlistment contract because it indicated that he would be enlisted as a Petty Officer third class.  He made neither an oral nor a written oath.  He was sent to Washington, D.C., for two weeks for further processing, still refusing to take the oath of enlistment.  By this time, he had been issued a uniform.  He was told that an appropriate correction would be made to his enlistment contract, and he was directed to report for duty in California.

In October, the correction still had not been made.  At this time, he was directed to sign the contract and told that if he did not he would be prosecuted for fraudulent enlistment and unauthorized wearing of a uniform.  He then signed the contract, stating that he was signing involuntarily because of the threats of court-martial.  The oath was not subscribed before an officer.

In December, 1967, the petitioner left his base without permission.  He was subsequently apprehended and awaiting court-martial in Illinois when he petitioned the Court for his release.  From August until December, he had followed orders, performed his duties, accepted pay, and taken advantage of the navy's food and shelter.

After finding that his signature was coerced and that he had never voluntarily taken the required oath of enlistment, the Court considered the question of whether he had "ratified" the enlistment contract, or constructively enlisted, by his conduct.  The Court held that "under the circumstances, . . . the performances of duties and the acceptance of pay cannot be held to have constituted a voluntary constructive enlistment or ratification by Norris.  Rather his conduct represented a recognition that he had no real choice other than to succumb to the navy authorities until the matter was ultimately resolved and to keep up his efforts in the hope of that resolution." 296 F.Supp. at 1275.  The Court concluded that Norris was not a member of the navy and ordered that he be separated from the navy without prejudice, with provision for transportation back to Maryland and pay to date of separation, except for the period of his absence.

## UNITED STATES v. KING

United States Court of Military Appeals, 1959.
11 U.S.C.M.A. 19, 28 C.M.R. 243.

### Opinion of the Court

GEORGE W. LATIMER, Judge:

The facts in this case show a deceitful and fantastic scheme and, while the accused defrauded the United States Government, the issue before us is whether jurisdiction to try him for his offenses vested in a military court. We express no opinion as to the right of the Government to proceed in other forums, but we are constrained to hold that the accused was not triable by a court-martial.

Briefly stated, the facts disclose that on February 18, 1958, accused, then a Private E-1, was separated from the Army by means of an undesirable discharge, and he reverted to a civilian status. Some three days thereafter, with the asserted connivance of a member of Headquarters, United States Army Training Center, Infantry, and Fort Ord, California, orders were obtained by him purporting to authorize his shipment to Europe via Fort Dix, New Jersey, in the grade of master sergeant. Pursuant to these orders, the accused proceeded from Fort Ord, California, to Fort Dix, New Jersey. In the course of his travels between these two places, he applied for and received $194 in advance travel pay and $75 in partial pay. Upon his arrival at the latter station on March 22, 1958, he presented the false orders to the military authorities, and the United States Army Overseas Replacement Station, Fort Dix, New Jersey, relying on the documents, carried him as a member of the Army on a morning report for March 22, 1958. On March 25, 1958, travel orders were issued, and he was shipped to Germany. Upon arrival in that country, he was assigned to Headquarters Company, V Corps, and detailed with the Quartermaster Section in the food service field. He received pay and allowances from the United States Army from March 22, 1958, until he committed certain offenses on or about July 25, 1958, and we assume that at that time these payments ceased. Subsequent to the latter date he was charged with and tried for six separate offenses which, stated generally, were these: Fraudulent enlistment, absence without leave, failure to obey a lawful order, resisting apprehension, forgery, and possession of a false pass. At the time of arraignment, he moved to dismiss the specifications upon the grounds that he was a civilian and not a person subject to the Uniform Code of Military Justice. After the foregoing facts were brought to the attention of the law officer in an out-of-court hearing and counsel were afforded the opportunity of arguing their respective hypotheses, the law officer denied the motion. Thereupon, accused entered a plea of guilty, was convicted and sentenced by the court-martial to be dishonorably discharged from the service, to forfeit all pay and allowances and to be confined at hard labor for five years. The convening authority reduced the period of confinement to one year but otherwise approved the sentence, and while the board of review set aside the conviction for forgery, it affirmed the remaining findings and the sentence. We granted accused's petition for review on several grounds, but our holding that the accused was not subject to military law disposes effectively of all questions raised.

The theory relied on by the Government and the one used by lower reviewing authorities to support jurisdiction was that the accused constructively enlisted by voluntarily entering the Army and by receiving pay and allowances from that service. That is a firm principle, but we fail to conceive how it can be applied in this instance.

As a starting point, we refer to the well-recognized work of Colonel Winthrop. On page 733 of his Military Law and Precedents, 2d ed, 1920 Reprint, he states:

> "FRAUDULENT ENLISTMENT. By the recent enactment of July 27, 1892 ch. 272, sec. 3, it was provided-- 'That fraudulent enlistment, and the receipt of any pay or allowance thereunder, is hereby declared a military offence, and made punishable by court-martial under the 62d Article of War.'
>
> "Nature of The Offence. Prior to this legislation, fraudulent enlistment was not, in the opinion of the author, triable by court-martial, for the reason that the fraudulent representations, &c., in which the offence consisted must have been preliminary and made as an inducement to the enlistment, and so before it was consummated, and while therefore the individual was still a civilian and not constitutionally amenable to such trial. A statute assuming to make mere fraudulent enlistment so triable would not remove the objection, since a statute cannot do away with a constitutional incapacity or confer jurisdiction where the constitution denies it. But the receipt of 'pay' or an 'allowance' under an enlistment knowingly fraudulent is an offence, because the pay, &c., is not received till the enlistment has been completed and the party is actually in the military service. It is thus the

receipt of pay or of an allowance, (as an allowance of clothing or rations, for it is not considered that 'allowance' means necessarily pecuniary allowance,) which is the gist of the legal offence and which in fact constitutes it. A person who has procured himself to be enlisted by means of false representations as to his status is not, before having received pay or an allowance, or until he receives one or the other, amenable to military trial. And the Act would be more correctly worded thus--The receipt of any pay or allowance under a fraudulent enlistment is hereby declared, &c."

In the next paragraph he defines fraudulent enlistment as follows:

". . . And the offence is officially defined as follows--'A fraudulent enlistment is an enlistment procured by means of a wilful misrepresentation in regard to a qualification or disqualification for enlistment, or by an intentional concealment of a disqualification, which has had the effect of causing the enlistment of a man not qualified to be a soldier, and who, but for such false representation or concealment, would have been rejected.'"

Article 83(1) of the Uniform Code of Military Justice, 10 USC §883, which is controlling in the instant case, differs little from the quoted definition, as it provides for the punishment of:

"Any person who--
    (1) procures his own enlistment or appointment in the armed forces by knowingly false representation or deliberate concealment as to his qualifications for that enlistment or appointment and receives pay or allowances thereunder; . . ."

It is undisputed that the accused received pay and allowances, so the only question involved is whether his fraudulent representations or concealments procured his own enlistment in the Army. It is this ingredient of the crime which, as we view the facts, was not and cannot be established.

In developing our views, we must first look to the meaning of the word enlistment to ascertain if there was a voluntary entry into the Army. In Webster's New International Dictionary, Second Edition, enlist is defined as follows: "To enroll and bind oneself for military or naval service; as, to enlist in the army for the war." In Army Regulations 320-5, we find the following definition of enlistment:

"The voluntary enrollment for a specific term of
service in one of the Armed Forces, as contrasted with
induction under the Universal Military Training and
Service Act of 1948, as amended."

Certainly, when we measure the facts of this case by those definitions, the accused did not voluntarily enroll in the Army.  At best,
all he did was to put on the garb of a soldier and masquerade as a
member of the Army in good standing.  He did not solicit anyone in
authority to initiate steps which would result in his enrollment.  He
and the Government did not enter into any sort of a contract which
would change his status for he merely impersonated a member of the
Army, and that service was misled by the impersonation and not by
any mutual understanding with the accused.  By analogy, we suggest
that if a civilian reported into the Military District of Washington
under the guise of being an officer and he obtained monies by virtue
of his guile, he would not have procured an appointment as an officer.
Surely he would be guilty of some offense against the Government but
not one which required proof that he fraudulently induced a service
to appoint him a commissioned officer.

Admittedly, the question poses some difficulties, for it is obvious that when the accused used the forged orders he intended to procure some of the benefits which are secured to enlisted men.
However, as Colonel Winthrop pointed out in his treatise, supra,
fraudulent enlistment requires two separate and distinct acts and the
receipt of pay and allowances is usually subsequent to the execution
of a contract.  Moreover, monies and benefits can be obtained when
any civilian successfully poses as a serviceman and moves about
with a particular service.  In the case at bar, the accused fraudulently concealed that he had been separated from the Army by means
of an undesirable discharge and the orders he presented were ficti-
tious.  While the fraudulent concealments aided his scheme to be
shipped overseas, they did not procure an enlistment contract.  At
this point, it might be helpful to point out that there is a difference
between procuring an enlistment contract by false representation and
accepting its benefits after it has been executed.  Procure means to
induce or prevail upon another to perform a desired act, and the
record is barren of any evidence suggesting remotely that the Army
was prevailed upon to enter into any oral or written agreement by
which accused changed his status.  There was no offer by him and no
acceptance by the Army.  The most that can be said in that regard is
that the accused induced certain units to make entries in their morning reports showing him to be a member of the responsible commands.
Absent evidence to the contrary, these entries might be sufficient to
establish membership in the Army, but here the facts indubitably rebut that possibility.

Without going into all the preliminary details of an enlistment
contract, we point out that not one single step required by that form

of entry into a service was taken. Neither party intended to be bound by a contract. The accused did not solicit enlistment, he was not interviewed, he furnished no false information to a recruiting official, no papers were prepared, no term of service was contemplated, no conditions were agreed upon, no physical examination was given, no oath was given, and, unless the subsequent obtaining of benefits by the accused could change his status from civilian to soldier, there is nothing in this record to suggest any essentials of an enlistment contract.

That brings us to the question of a constructive contract of enlistment and, to support that theory, the Government cites a great many authorities. They are appropriate for the principle they announce, but they are inapposite to the present facts. In every cited case and others which we have considered, there was either a completed contract which could be vitiated by the service because of fraud on the part of the applicant or ratified by the service, regardless of the fraud; or, the preliminary arrangements had proceeded far enough that there was a meeting of the minds on the essentials of a contract, and both parties were bound by its express or implied terms. In most instances, the individual enlisted in fact and thereby sought to obtain the benefits flowing to a serviceman. In addition, the misrepresentations to the persons authorized to recruit enlistees caused the Government to agree to accept the applicants as members of the military community. The theory underlying those decisions is that there was a contract voidable by the service because a false representation had been made, but accused could not take advantage of his fraud to escape its terms. However, had the representations been true, the service involved would have been bound to accept the individual involved and he would have been obligated to serve for a specified period of time. One of the cardinal principles of contract law is that to change a status there must be a mutual understanding of the parties, and here there were no actual terms and conditions contemplated or agreed upon by them which remotely suggested a change in relationship. Accordingly, there is no framework from which to start the construction of a contract bringing about that result.

Obviously, there are instances where courts have held that the acts of the parties created a constructive enlistment. Usually that doctrine is applied where the parties have mutually agreed to change the applicant's status and subsequently he seeks to escape his obligations by asserting that the original agreement to change his status should be rejected because of his own fraud. It is in that sort of situation where constructive contracts find their roots for, in law, constructive means a condition assumed from other acts or conditions which are considered as amounting to or involving the act or condition assumed. Therefore, to find a constructive enlistment in this case, we would be required to assume that the accused became a soldier and that he was accepted by the Army as such merely because he posed as a serviceman and defrauded the Government.

Here, the thrust of the Government's argument is that the status was changed solely by accused's fraud in illegally obtaining money, food-stuffs, and other benefits; but such is not the law. Constructive contracts are imposed or created by law without regard to the party bound on the ground that they are dictated by reason and justice. They rest solely on a legal fiction and are not contract obligations at all in the true sense. They are predicated on the hypothesis that whatsoever it is certain that a man ought to do, the law supposes him to have promised to do. But the supposition cannot be expanded to the extent that criminal acts amount to enlistments and based on that premise a contract is constructed which is inimical to the interest of the in-nocent party. To construe the acts of the accused in such a manner that his status is changed and he becomes a member of the Army without its knowledge or intent that such a result obtains would sub-ject that service to the enrollment of undesirables merely because they were ingenious and their expertise at trickery resulted in obtain-ing pay and allowances. It is to be emphasized that this is not a case where the Army voluntarily accepted the accused and an enlistment contract--either with or without normal formalities--was executed. This record shows nothing more than a larceny or larcenies by trick in which the Army was undoubtedly duped but not in agreeing to en-roll the accused as a member of its community. It was just the victim of a crime committed by a civilian.

The Supreme Court in United States v Grimley, 137 US 147, 11 S Ct 54, 34 L ed 636 (1890), compared an enlistment contract to one of marriage and, in the course of the opinion, stated that:

> "But in this transaction something more is involved
> than the making of a contract, whose breach exposes to an
> action for damages. Enlistment is a contract, but it is one
> of those contracts which changes the status, and where
> that is changed, no breach of the contract destroys the new
> status or relieves from the obligations which its existence
> imposes."

The Court then went on to say:

> "By enlistment the citizen becomes a soldier. His
> relations to the state and the public are changed. He ac-
> quires a new status, with correlative rights and duties;
> and although he may violate his contract obligations, his
> status as a soldier is unchanged. He cannot of his own
> volition throw off the garments he has once put on nor
> can he, the state not objecting, renounce his relations
> and destroy his status on the plea that, if he had disclosed
> truthfully the facts, the other party, the state, would not

have entered into the new relations with him, or permitted him to change his status."

See also United States v Blanton, 7 USCMA 664, 23 CMR 128.

When that form of contract is being considered, it becomes apparent that both parties must intend to change the status before any
act or acts can result in the law saying it has been done. In the case
at bar, had there been any understanding between the Government and
the accused which contemplated a change in relationship, then his misconduct would preclude him from claiming a reversion to a civilian
status. Had there been an agreement to change his legal relationship
and he had become a member of the Army, neither his criminal conduct nor his false representation would have insulated him from
prosecution. However, we never reach that point, for there was no
act on his part which could be construed as offering to enlist in the
Army or misleading it into accepting him as a regular member of the
service. Before a person can become a serviceman by enlisting,
there must be some understanding that the steps taken by the service
in processing the applicant will result in a change of status. Here all
the Army did was to act in compliance with the purported authority of
accused's falsified documents, which served to indicate that his status
as a soldier had been accomplished at some prior time. As previously
mentioned, the fraudulent acts of this accused caused the Government
a loss, but they did not induce the Army to act on the assumption that
accused was enlisting, and the facts show that neither party could
properly assert that he initiated any process which would legally shed
his civilian garb. While the law could impose upon him the legal duty
to return his ill-gotten gains, that obligation would rest on the shoul-
ders of any similar wrongdoer, regardless of his status. Certainly,
it is most difficult for us to follow the reasoning that thievery changes
a civilian to a soldier. A mask of deceit may give rise to both civil
and criminal litigation in other courts but, in the military, prosecution can only be initiated legally when the accused is a member of the
military service. Membership cannot be established by criminal conduct alone, and a change in status cannot be constructed unless there
are legal remedies which should and can be enforced. Such is not the
case in this instance. To illustrate the point we ask, which of these
parties could be required to fulfill the terms of an enlistment contract? When a contract is constructed, one party, at least, should
have a legal civil remedy, and here we find none except the right of
the Army to proceed to recoup its losses. That remedy exists regardless of accused's status and, therefore, we are importuned to find a
temporary constructive enlistment solely for the purpose of permitting
the Army to prosecute the accused criminally. Changing a relationship for that purpose without some prior understanding by the parties
seems to us to be stretching a legal fiction beyond the limits of its

field. We have no doubt that under certain circumstances an accused
may be estopped from asserting that his misconduct released him
from his enlistment contract, but an estoppel cannot be used affirmatively to create a contract of entry into the service. Such a holding
would result in the unique principle that a civilian could steal his way
into the Army, a concept we unhesitantly reject.

Finally, the Government argues that if we cannot sustain jurisdiction under the theory of constructive enlistment, certain of the
findings must be supported upon the hypothesis that Article 2(11) of
the Code, 10 USC §802, permits the trial of civilians who accompany
the Army overseas. We need not develop that theory for the obvious
reason that under our holding the accused is a civilian and, generally
speaking, the crimes involved are not chargeable against one in that
status. Accused's conviction for forgery was set aside by the board
of review, and for the reasons we developed in the principal portion
of this opinion, the crime of fraudulent enlistment fails. The crimes
of absence without leave, failure to obey the order of a superior officer, and possession of a false pass are all predicated upon the theory
spelled out in the specification that the accused was a member of the
service which, of course, cannot be sustained. As to the offense of
resisting lawful arrest, it is apparent from the issues that all parties
assumed a legal apprehension for a military offense because the accused was believed subject to the Code. In light of the theory of the
case at the trial level, it is entirely probable that the accused was not
subject to arrest for purely military crimes and thus that finding cannot be affirmed.

For the foregoing reasons, the decision of the board of review
is reversed and, in view of our holding on jurisdiction, the case dismissed.

Judge FERGUSON concurs.

QUINN, Chief Judge (dissenting):
The record of trial shows more than a mere passing masquerade by the accused. It shows the procurement of an actual "entry into
service." See Manual for Courts-Martial, United States, 1951, paragraph 162. Among other things the accused presented an order showing purported enlistment for a period of six years with the estimated
time of separation as July 1963. Accordingly, he was placed on the
rolls of military organizations as a regular member and assigned
military duties. He performed those duties and received pay and
allowances therefor. In my opinion, these facts established beyond a
doubt that the accused intended to, and did, in fact, effect an entry
into the armed service for the ostensible period covered by his false
orders. He was, therefore, subject to trial and punishment by court-
martial.

As to the other assignments of error, the accused's plea of
guilty removed any basis for challenge of the specifications because

of ambiguity. See United States v Parker, 3 USCMA 541, 13 CMR 97; United States v Sell, 3 USCMA 202, 11 CMR 202; cf. United States v Fout, 3 USCMA 565, 13 CMR 121. I would affirm the decision of the board of review.

In United States v. Jenkins, 7 U.S.C.M.A. 261, 22 C.M.R. 51 (1956), the Court reversed the conviction of a person who was charged with fraudulent enlistment in violation of Article 83 of the Uniform Code of Military Justice, 10 U.S.C. §883 (1964). He had previously received an undesirable discharge from the army under the name of Webb. After his discharge, he was inducted into the army under the name of Jenkins. When he reported for induction, he failed to give notice of his prior service and undesirable discharge. The Court held that Article 83 does not apply to induction.

A court-martial has no jurisdiction to try an accused who did not participate in any induction ceremony and who continually protested all attempts to subject him to military life even though he accepted pay, executed an allotment for his wife, and wore the uniform (U.S. v. Hall, 17 USCMA 88, 37 CMR 352 [1967]). A person who fraudulently conceals facts that would bar his induction can be administratively discharged for that reason. JAGA 1959/6496 (Sept. 29, 1956).

ENLISTMENT OF MINORS

### In re MORRISSEY

Supreme Court of the United States, 1890.
137 U.S. 157, 11 S.Ct. 57, 34 L.Ed. 644.

MR. JUSTICE BREWER delivered the opinion of the court.

This case, appealed from the Circuit Court for the Eastern District of Missouri, presents, like that of Grimley, Petitioner, just decided, a question arising on habeas corpus as to the right of the petitioner, an enlisted soldier, to be discharged from military custody. An effort was made to bring this case here by writ of error; but that was abandoned, and an appeal rightfully substituted. In re Neagle, 135 U.S. 1, 42. The facts differ from those in that case, in this: The petitioner was seventeen years of age, and had a mother living who did not consent to his enlistment. Upon his enlistment he drew from the United States his uniform and equipments, and continued in actual service from the 23d day of August to the 13th day of September, 1883, when he deserted. He remained in concealment until February, 1889, at which time he had become of age, and then appeared at a recruiting office and demanded his discharge from the army on the ground that he was a minor when enlisted. In his oath of allegiance he swore that he was twenty-one years and five months old. It will be seen that the petitioner was within the ages prescribed by section 1116 of the Revised Statutes, to wit, sixteen and thirty-five years. Section 1117 provides that "no person under the age of twenty-one years shall be enlisted or mustered into the military service of the United States without the written consent of his parents or guardians: Provided, That such minor has such parents or guardians entitled to his custody and control." But this provision is for the benefit of the parent or guardian. It means simply that the government will not disturb the control of parent or guardian over his or her child without consent. It gives the right to such parent or guardian to invoke the aid of the court and secure the restoration of a minor to his or her control; but it gives no privilege to the minor.

The age at which an infant shall be competent to do any acts or perform any duties, military or civil, depends wholly upon the legislature. United States v. Bainbridge, 1 Mason, 71; Wassum v. Feeney, 121 Mass. 93, 95. Congress has declared that minors over the age of sixteen are capable of entering the military service, and undertaking and performing its duties.

An enlistment is not a contract only, but effects a change of status. Grimley's Case, ante, 147. It is not, therefore, like an ordinary contract, voidable by the infant. At common law an enlistment was not voidable either by the infant or by his parents or guardians. The King v. The Inhabitants of Rotherford Greys, 2 Dow. & Ryl. 628, 634; S. C. 1 B. & C. 345, 350; The King v. The Inhabitants of Lytchet Matravers, 1 Man. & Ryl. 25, 31; S. C. 7 B. & C. 226, 231; Commonwealth v. Gamble, 11 S. & R. 93; United States v. Blakeney, 3 Grattan, 405, 411-413.

In this case the parent never insisted upon her right of custody and control; and the fact that he had a mother living at the time is, therefore, immaterial. The contract of enlistment was good so far as the petitioner is concerned. He was not only de facto, but de jure, a soldier--amenable to military jurisdiction. His mother not interfering, he was bound to remain in the service. His desertion and concealment for five years did not relieve him from his obligations as a soldier, or his liability to military control. The order of the Circuit Court remanding him to the custody of the appellee was correct and must be

Affirmed.

## UNITED STATES v. BLANTON

United States Court of Military Appeals, 1957.
7 U.S.C.M.A. 664, 23 C.M.R. 128.

Opinion of the Court

ROBERT E. QUINN, Chief Judge:

Although the accused entered a plea of guilty to a charge of desertion, in violation of Article 85, Uniform Code of Military Justice,
10 USC §885, a board of review reversed his conviction and dismissed
the charge. Pursuant to Article 67(b)(2), The Judge Advocate General
of the Army asked this Court to review the correctness of the board
of review's decision. The issue raised is whether the enlistment of a
person under the statutory age is void so as to preclude trial by court-
martial for an offense committed by him while still under such age.

An agreement to enlist in an armed service is often referred to
as a contract. However, more than a contractual relationship is established. What is really created is a status. United States v Grimley,
137 US 147, 34 L ed 636, 11 S Ct 54 (1890); United States v Dickenson,
6 USCMA 438, 20 CMR 154. As a result, no useful purpose is served
by reviewing the common-law rules of contract and whether the contract of a minor is, under the common law, voidable at his election
and in his own time, with or without formal proceedings. The United
States Supreme Court has emphasized that the "age at which an infant
shall be competent to do any acts or perform any duties, military or
civil, depends wholly upon the Legislature." Morrissey v Perry, 137
US 157, 34 L ed 644, 11 S Ct 57 (1890). We must, therefore, look to
the statutes to determine whether Congress has established a minimum age at which a person is deemed incapable of changing his status
to that of a member of the military establishment.

Over the years Congress has passed several statutes on the subject of enlistment. Three statutes provide an appropriate beginning
point for the consideration of our problem. These are Revised Statutes, §§1116, 1117, and 1118. The first, as amended by Chapter 352,
§4, of the Act of March 2, 1899, 30 Stat 978, provided that recruits
enlisting in the Army shall be between the ages of 18 and 35; the
second directed that no person under 21 shall be enlisted without the
written consent of his parents or guardians; and the third provided
that "no minor under the age of 16" years shall be enlisted. The purpose and effect of these three acts were frequently before the Federal
courts. In In re Miller, 114 Fed 838 (1902), the Court of Appeals for
the Fifth Circuit held that the statutory scheme "peremptorily forbids
a minor under the age of 16 from being enlisted." Accord, In re
Lawler, 40 Fed 233 (ND Ga) (1889); In re Hearn, 32 Fed 141 (ND Ohio)
(1887); In re Davison, 21 Fed 618 (SD NY) (1884). In 1916 Congress
enacted the National Defense Act. 39 Stat 186. Section 27 of the Act

provided that no person under 18 shall be enlisted without the written
consent of his parents or guardian. Nothing in the Act referred to
the other provisions of the Revised Statutes. As a result, in Hoskins
v Pell, 239 Fed 279 (1917), the Fifth Circuit Court of Appeals reiterated its view that the enlistment of a minor under 16 years of age was
void. The Comptroller General of the United States reached the same
conclusion. Comptroller General Review No. 5550, October 25, 1923.

Despite the Hoskins case and the other Federal court decisions,
The Judge Advocate General of the Army took the position that under
the statutes the enlistment of all minors was merely voidable. That
same view, with a reservation, however, was expressed in the 1928
and 1949 Manuals for Courts-Martial. Manual for Courts-Martial,
U.S. Army, 1928, paragraph 157, page 198; Manual for Courts-Martial,
U.S. Army, 1949, paragraph 189, page 269. No reference to the matter
is made in the Manual for Courts-Martial, United States, 1951. Moreover, the Army regulations in effect before the commission of the
alleged offense which purported to give a commanding officer authority
to review the enlistment of a minor under 16 years of age, and, in his
discretion, to direct the retention of the minor in the service, or his
discharge, had been rescinded. AR 615-362, paragraph 15, July 14,
1947, rescinded by Change 4, August 23, 1948. Cf. AR 615-362, paragraphs 14(2), 19, April 7, 1952. Still, the Government contends that
the minimum age requirement is for the benefit of the Government,
not the minor, at least insofar as the minor is of the "age of discretion."

In our opinion, the Government's argument is wide of the mark.
As the Supreme Court pointed out in the Morrissey case, the question
is one of legal competency to effect a change of status. If there were
any doubts about the effect of the enlistment statutes in that regard,
we think that they were laid to rest by the Supreme Court in United
States v Williams, 302 US 46, 82 L ed 39, 58 S Ct 81. There, the
court reviewed the nature of the statute pertaining to enlistment in the
Navy of a minor over 14, which, except for the difference in age, was
substantially similar to the Army provision. It concluded that the
statute constitutes a "determination by Congress that minors over 14
have capacity to make contracts for service in the navy." The converse, namely that minors under 14 have no legal capacity to enlist,
is clearly implied. Significantly, the court cited In re Davison, supra,
in support of this holding. The Davison case construed the Army
statutes; it held that the "contract of enlistment of a minor under 16
years of age is void." Consequently, had no change been made in the
law, the weight of authority would compel the conclusion that minors
under 16 years of age had no capacity to enter into the military status
by enlistment. However, some statutory changes have been enacted.
Those in effect at the accused's enlistment are controlling.

In their informative brief, appellate defense counsel indicate
that Revised Statutes, §1118, which provided that no minors under the

age of 16 shall be enlisted, may not have been superseded by later statutes. The statement of law in §622, of Title 10 (repealed by Act of August 10, 1956, 70A Stat 641, and re-enacted as 10 USC §3253) seems to indicate a contrary view. We need not, however, pass upon that point. In our opinion, the subsequent statutes have carried on the Congressional purpose of limiting the capacity of certain minors to enlist in the Army. The governing statute is the Act of June 28, 1947, 61 Stat 191, 10 USC §628 (repealed by the Act of August 10, 1956, and re-enacted as 10 USC §3256). In material part it provides as follows:

> "Effective July 1, 1947, the Secretary of the Army is authorized, notwithstanding the provisions of section 634 of this title, to accept original enlistments in the Regular Army from among qualified male persons not less than seventeen years of age for periods of two, three, four, five, or six years: . . . Provided further, That no person under the age of eighteen years shall be enlisted without the written consent of his parents or guardian, and the Secretary of the Army shall, upon the application of the parents or guardian of any such person enlisted without their written consent, discharge such person from the military service with pay and with the form of discharge certificate to which the service of such person, after enlistment, shall entitle him. . . ."

It is axiomatic that in determining the meaning of a statute every provision must be given effect. The most striking fact which stands out in the provisions before us is the reference to two different ages. If, as the Government contends, every underage enlistment other than one below the "age of discretion," whatever age that may be, is merely voidable, why the difference? It would seem logical for Congress to have made the two age provisions the same. The difference manifestly indicates a difference in purpose. In the first provision Congress established a minimum age below which a youth is incompetent to acquire military status. Between the ages of 17 and 18 the minor is competent to serve, but his enlistment may be terminated by his parents or guardians, provided they had not consented to it.

Here, the stipulated facts show that the accused was born on June 9, 1936. Consequently, when he enlisted in the Army on March 9, 1951, he was not yet 15 years of age. He allegedly absented himself on June 8, 1952. At that time, he had not reached his 16th birthday. Thus, at no time was he on active duty at an age when he was legally competent to serve in the military. Cf. Ex parte Hubbard, 182 Fed 76 (D Mass) (1910). In sum, the court-martial had no jurisdiction over the accused. Article 85 of the Uniform Code, 10 USC §885, provides that only a "member of the armed forces" can commit an act of desertion. See United States v Ornelas, 2 USCMA 96, 6 CMR 96. The board of review, therefore was correct in holding that the accused was not subject to military law at the time of the alleged offense.

The certified question is answered in the affirmative, and the decision of the board of review is affirmed.

Judges LATIMER and FERGUSON concur.

The principal case states the current law with respect to the enlistment of minors under the age of seventeen. At one time there was a question of whether the enlistment of a minor under the minimum statutory age was void or only voidable at the election of the minor's parents. See, e.g., In re Cosenow, 37 F. 668 (E.D. Mich. 1889), and Hoskins v. Pell, 239 F. 279 (5th Cir. 1917). The current statutes relating to age qualifications of enlistees and to the discharge of minors are found at 10 U.S.C. §505 (Supp. V, 1970) and 10 U.S.C. §1170 (Supp. V, 1970), respectively.

As stated in Blanton v. United States, supra, a minor between the ages of seventeen and eighteen is competent to serve in the armed forces. The enlistment of a seventeen-year-old minor is voidable by his parents if he enlisted without their consent and if he is still under the age of eighteen. 10 U.S.C. §1170, supra. See also United States v. Bean, 13 U.S.C.M.A. 203, 32 C.M.R. 203 (1962). If a minor enlists before his seventeenth birthday and continues in the service until after he turns seventeen, his enlistment can "ripen into a valid enlistment." Barrett v. Looney, 158 F.Supp. 224 (D. Kan. 1957), affirmed, 252 F.2d 588 (10th Cir. 1958), certiorari denied, 347 U.S. 940, 78 S.Ct. 1390, 2 L.Ed. 1553 (1958). If a seventeen-year-old minor (whether he enlists before the age of seventeen and remains in service until reaching that age or enlists at the age of seventeen without his parent's consent) commits a military offense before his parents apply to have him discharged, the military authorities retain court-martial jurisdiction, and the parents are entitled to his release prior to the expiation of his offense, Barrett v. Looney, supra, United States v. Bean, supra, and cases cited therein. If the nonconsenting parents, however, make an attempt to obtain the discharge of a seventeen-year-old minor and subsequent to their attempt he commits a military offense, a court-martial does not have jurisdiction, and the minor must be released. United States v. Overton, 9 U.S.C.M.A. 684, 26 C.M.R. 464 (1968). Nonconsenting parents may waive their right to demand their child's discharge if they are aware of his enlistment and acquiesce in it. United States v. Scott, 11 U.S.C.M.A. 655, 29 C.M.R. 471 (1960).

The enlistment of persons ineligible for military duty presents a problem similar to that of the enlistment of minors. The enlistment of a person who is insane, intoxicated, a deserter, or who has been convicted of a felony is prohibited by law. The Secretary of the armed force concerned, however, may authorize the enlistment of deserters or felons in certain cases. 10 U.S.C. §504 (Supp. V, 1970). In addition, an original enlistment, in time of peace, is permitted only if the enlistee is a citizen of the United States or has been lawfully admitted to the United States for permanent residence. 10 U.S.C. §3253 (Supp. V, 1970) (Army), 10 U.S.C. §8253 (Supp. V, 1970) (Air Force).

It is unclear whether the enlistment of an insane person is void or voidable. The view that an enlistment is void if the enlistee was declared insane by a judicial determination prior to his entry into service is stated in 39 Comp. Gen. 742 (1960). Dicta in In re Grimley 137 U.S. 147, 11 S.Ct. 54, 34 L.Ed. 636 (1890), and In re Cosenow, 37 F. 668 (E.D. Mich. 1889), also support this position. But in In re Judge's Petition, 148 F.Supp. 80 (S.D. Cal. 1956), a District Court held that an enlistee had the burden of proving that he was insane at the time of his enlistment, even though he was adjudged insane by a California State Court one year before his enlistment and was not restored to capacity until he had served in the armed forces for more than fourteen months. If there has been no judicial determination of insanity prior to enlistment, the enlistment is presumably valid, and the person is a member of the armed forces until he is separated. The above rules would also apply to inductees. 39 Comp. Gen. 742, supra.

An intoxicated person would probably be in the same position as that of an insane person, and his enlistment would be void if he lacked capacity to enter into a contract at the time of his enlistment. See In re Cosenow, supra.

If a person at the time of his enlistment is a deserter from an armed force, has been convicted of a felony, or does not satisfy the citizenship requirements, his enlistment is only voidable, not void. Such a person has military status until his discharge and is subject to court-martial jurisdiction. See United States v. Robson, 24 C.M.R. 375, C.M. 396852 (B.R. [Army] 1957) (lack of citizenship), and In re McVey, 23 F. 878 (D. Cal. 1885) (deserter). Similarly, a person who should not have been enlisted because he failed to meet physical standards is not entitled to a discharge. Ex parte Blackington, 245 F. 801 (D. Mass. 1917). The induction of a person in violation of Selective Service statutes and regulations, however, is void (United States ex rel. Weidman v. Sweeney, 117 F.Supp. 739 [E.D. Pa. 1953]), so the induction of a person who is not physically qualified would be void.

The Federal Juvenile Delinquency Act is inapplicable to the military establishment and does not deprove a court-martial of jurisdiction over a minor offender for a violation of the U.C.M.J. (U.S. v. Baker, 14 U.S.C.M.A., 34 CMR 91 [1963]).

In Iroquois Iron Co. v. Industrial Commission, 294 Ill. 106, 128 N.E. 289, 12 A.L.R. 924 (1920), the Supreme Court of Illinois considered the question of whether a minor who enlists in the armed forces with the consent of his father is emancipated. The case arose when the Illinois Industrial Commission awarded $3,500 to the son of a man who was killed while working. The award was affirmed by the Circuit Court. The son, who was a member of the marines, was entitled to the award if his father was under a legal obligation to support him. The Supreme Court reversed the Circuit Court and held that by enlisting with parental consent, a minor "ceases to be a part of his father's family and puts himself under the control of the government and is consequently emancipated so long as this service continues." 294 Ill. at 109, 128 N.E. at 290, 12 A.L.R. at 927.

The question in Harwood v. Harwood, 182 Misc. 130, 49 N.Y.S.2d. 727 (Sup. Ct. 1944), was whether the induction of a minor into the armed forces operated as a "temporary emancipation" during the term of his service so as to suspend his father's obligation for support under a separation agreement. The Court held that the father's contractual obligation was not suspended by his son's induction. The support agreement that the mother was seeking to enforce had no provision concerning the induction of the son. The Court distinguished Iroquois Iron Co. v. Industrial Commission, supra, as a case concerning a question of legal dependency as opposed to an express covenant to pay for a minor's support and declined to follow that case to the extent that it was contrary to its own holding. A dissenting opinion advanced the view that the son's induction divested his mother of custody and control of her son and had the effect of bringing about a failure of consideration for the father's undertaking to support the son.

Other cases supporting the majority view in Harwood v. Harwood, supra, are Torras v. McDonald, 196 Ga. 347, 23 S.E.2d 598 (1943), and Carson v. Carson, 120 Ind. App. 1, 89 N.E.2d 555 (1950). Decisions in divorce decree modification proceedings in Missouri, however, follow the doctrine in Iroquois Iron v. Industrial Commission, supra: Swenson v. Swenson, 241 Mo. App. 21, 227 S.W.2d 103 (1950); Green v. Green, 234 S.W.2d 350 (Mo. Ct. App. 1950). Corbridge v. Corbridge, 230 Ind. 201, 102 N.E.2d 764 (1952), holds that an enlistment had emancipated a minor, distinguishing the case from Carson v. Carson, supra.

In United States v. Williams, 302 U.S. 46, 58 S.Ct. 81, 82 L.Ed. 39 (1937), a mother who had consented to the enlistment of her minor son on the condition that he take out war risk insurance sought to recover such insurance on the death of her son while serving. The son had ceased payment of premiums and requested termination of the insurance. The Supreme Court held the mother was not entitled to recover, the defendant not being bound by the condition on which the plaintiff consented to the enlistment.

# 4

The usual method of changing a person's status from a service-man to a civilian is by a formal discharge. Currently, there are five types of discharge: honorable, general, undesirable, bad conduct, and dishonorable. The first three are awarded administratively; the latter two may only be awarded judicially, by the sentence of a court-martial. A general discharge is normally awarded to a person who is unable to adjust to military service while an undesirable discharge is normally awarded to a person who is able but unwilling to adjust. As the follow-ing cases show, the characterization of service has effects far beyond military life.

## GRIFFIN v. UNITED STATES

United States District Court, W.D. Arkansas, 1953.
115 F.Supp. 509.

JOHN E. MILLER, District Judge.
On March 28, 1952, George Griffin, Sr., filed his complaint against the defendant and alleged that he was principal beneficiary of National Service Life Insurance Certificate Number V-1521-14-49, in the amount of $10,000, issued upon the life of his son, George Griffin, Jr.; that, while George Griffin, Jr., was in the military service, and while said insurance was in full force and effect, the said George Griffin, Jr., died on March 24, 1951; that he, George Griffin, Sr.,

applied to the Veterans' Administration of the United States of America for payment under the policy, but that his claim was finally and definitely denied on January 23, 1952, by R. J. Hinton, Director of Claims; and that as principal beneficiary he was entitled to recover judgment against the defendant for the principal sum of $10,000, interest, costs and attorneys' fee.

The defendant on May 21, 1952, filed its answer in which it admitted issuance of the policy and the death of the insured, George Griffin, Jr., but alleged that the said insurance had lapsed for non-payment of premiums, and further that the insured had forfeited all rights under the National Service Life Insurance Act because he had committed the offense of desertion.

. . .

### Findings of Fact

No. 1.  The original plaintiff, George Griffin, Sr., was, at the time of the filing of this suit, a citizen and resident of Johnson County, Arkansas.  A disagreement had arisen between the plaintiff and the defendant as to plaintiff's claim for $10,000 as beneficiary of National Service Life Insurance Certificate Number V-1521-14-49 issued upon the life of George Griffin, Jr., son of the said George Griffin, Sr.

No. 2.  On June 27, 1952, subsequent to the filing of this suit, the original plaintiff, George Griffin, Sr., died, and the present plaintiff, Rosa Griffin, is administratrix of the estate of George Griffin, Sr.  The said Rosa Griffin was the wife of George Griffin, Sr., and the mother of George Griffin, Jr.

No. 3.  "George Griffin, Jr., was inducted into and entered active duty in the Army of the United States on April 20, 1945, and was honorably discharged on January 23, 1946.  That on January 24, 1946, the said George Griffin, Jr., re-enlisted in the Army of the United States and continued in service until the 5th day of May, 1949, when he was discharged 'under honorable conditions', having served two years, eleven months and eight days overseas."  (Stipulation of fact No. 4.)

On May 6, 1949, the insured, George Griffin, Jr., enlisted in the Enlisted Reserve Corps, and on October 11, 1950, was called into extended active duty.  On October 13, 1950, he applied for and was granted National Service Life Insurance in the amount of $10,000, and Policy No. V1521-14-49 was issued to him.  Principal beneficiary of the policy was George Griffin, Sr., and contingent beneficiary was Rosa Griffin.  In the application the insured selected, as method of payment of premiums, an allotment to be taken from his active service pay.  (Class N allotment.)

On November 28, 1950, the insured left Camp Stoneman, California, and was absent without leave from that time until his death on March 24, 1951.  The insured died at the home of his mother and father, Mr. and Mrs. George Griffin, Sr., at Clarksville, Arkansas. The attending physician, Dr. R. E. King, certified that the insured's death was caused by a cerebral hemorrhage and bronchial pneumonia.

. . .

No. 4. Major Walter C. Hudson investigated the death of the insured and submitted a complete report of his findings, conclusions and opinions. This report was submitted April 10, 1951, and approved by the Adjutant General April 24, 1951, and sent to Secretary of the Army. On June 4, 1951, the Secretary of the Army, Frank Pace, Jr., after having an opportunity to read and consider this report, as well as the insured's military records and any other pertinent information, executed and caused to be delivered to George Griffin, Sr., the following Certificate of Honorable Service:

"Honorable Service
(The Great Seal
of the
United States.)
In the Armed Forces of the
United States of America
This Is To Certify That
Private George Griffin, Jr.
Died While in the Service of
Our Country
As a Member of the
Army of the United States
On the 24th Day of March 1951.  This
Certificate is
Awarded as a Testimonial of
Honest and Faithful Service
/s/ Frank Pace Jr.
Secretary of the Army"

. . .

No. 5. At the time the insured left Camp Stoneman, California, the United States was indebted to him in the sum of $64.31 as his regular service pay for the period from November 1 to November 28. This sum of money remained to insured's credit on the payroll until after his death. . . .

. . .

The monthly premium was $7.20 and the $64.31 held by the Army was more than sufficient to pay all premiums that accrued from the date of the policy to the date of the death of insured.

No. 6. None of the Army records of the insured indicate that he was ever considered or found by the Army to have been guilty of desertion. Nevertheless, on October 11, 1951, L. P. Payne, acting for C. A. Zoller, Jr., Director of Underwriting Service, executed a paper styled "Decision of Forfeiture" which purports to forfeit insured's policy as of November 28, 1950, on the ground that the insured was guilty of desertion. This instrument was never transmitted to George Griffin, Sr., or to Rosa Griffin.

No. 7. From the time insured left Camp Stoneman on November 28, 1950, until his death on March 24, 1951, his mental and physical condition was such as to cause him a great deal of difficulty. . . .

Throughout the time the insured was absent without leave, he actually intended to return to camp and would have done so had it not been for physical and mental difficulty he was experiencing.

. . .

### Discussion

Two questions are presented to the Court for determination: (1) Was the insured, George Griffin, Jr., guilty of desertion, thereby forfeiting his rights under the National Service Life Insurance Act? (2) Did the insured's policy lapse for non-payment of premiums?

In reference to the first question, 38 U.S.C.A. §812 provides:

"Any person guilty of mutiny, treason, spying, or desertion, or who, because of conscientious objections, refuses to perform service in the land or naval forces of the United States or refuses to wear the uniform of such force, shall forfeit all rights to insurance under this chapter. . . ."

The defendant contends that the insured was guilty of desertion, that the Director of Underwriting Service has so found, and that therefore he forfeited his rights under the Act. On the other hand, the plaintiff contends that the Certificate of Honorable Service conclusively establishes that the insured was not guilty of desertion, and, in any event, that he was not in fact guilty of desertion because he did not intend to remain away permanently.

As to the effect of the Certificate of Honorable Service, the Court feels that the same rules of law apply to said certificate as apply to an honorable discharge. An honorable discharge cannot be issued to a person after he is dead, and in lieu thereof a Certificate of Honorable Service, which is the equivalent thereto, is issued.

Under the law, an honorable discharge of a soldier is a formal final judgment passed by the government upon the entire military record of the soldier, and it is an authoritative declaration that he has left the service in a status of honor. United States v. Kelly, 15 Wall. 34, 82 U.S. 34, 21 L.Ed. 106; In re Fong Chew Chung, 9 Cir., 149 F.2d 904; Ex parte Drainer, D.C.Cal., 65 F.Supp. 410, affirmed in 158 F.2d 981; 6 C.J.S., Army and Navy, §32, page 415; 36 Am.Jur., page 208. See also, United States ex rel. Hirshberg v. Cooke, Commanding Officer, 336 U.S. 210, 69 S.Ct. 530, 93 L.Ed. 621.

In Ex parte Drainer, supra, Drainer had enlisted in the Marines and deserted after a month. He later was convicted of breaking and entering and served two years in a reformatory in Iowa. Thereafter he voluntarily enlisted in the Navy and after a year and a half of honorable service received an honorable medical discharge from the

United States Naval Service. Subsequently he was arrested, tried and found guilty of desertion from the United States Naval Service (Marines). He applied for writ of habeas corpus and the Court granted the petition, holding that the Marine Corps was a part of the Navy and that his honorable discharge from the United States Naval Service was a "formal final judgment upon the entire military record" of Drainer, thus foreclosing the attempted prosecution of Drainer for desertion.

Likewise, in the instant case the Court is of the opinion that the Certificate of Honorable Service conclusively establishes the fact that George Griffin, Jr., was not guilty of desertion. This is especially true in view of the fact that the Secretary of the Army, at the time he executed the Certificate, had previously received a complete report of the death of the insured and had before him all the pertinent facts and circumstances surrounding the death.

. . .

This leaves for disposition the question of whether the policy lapsed for non-payment of premiums. A determination of this question depends upon whether the defendant, while having in its possession accrued active service pay, may nevertheless discontinue a soldier's insurance allotment merely because he is absent without leave.

. . .

In the instant case, since the defendant had in its possession accrued active service pay owing to the insured, it had the duty to use this money to pay the premiums on his policy, and the fact that the premiums were not paid through error on the part of the Army officers does not defeat the right of the plaintiff herein to recover under the policy. . . .

. . .

Therefore, the policy was in full force and effect at the time of the death of George Griffin, Jr., and plaintiff is entitled to recover the proceeds of said policy under the provisions of 38 U.S. C.A. §802(t).

. . .

Prior to the decision in Harmon v. Brucker, infra, the judicial review of administrative discharges by the armed services was extremely limited. In Nordmann v. Woodring, 28 F.Supp. 573 (W.D. Okla. 1939), the Court found the Secretary of War's determination of discharge a discretionary act and not reviewable even though "a reasonable construction of the statute could have been made which would have permitted" retention. See also Gentila v. Pace, 193 F.2d 924 (D.C. Cir. 1951) and Michaelson v. Herren 242 F.2d 693 (C.A. 2d. 1957).

## HARMON v. BRUCKER

Supreme Court of the United States, 1958.
355 U.S. 579, 78 S.Ct. 433, 2 L.Ed.2d 503.

PER CURIAM.
The Secretary of the Army, relying upon 10 U.S.C. §652a (Act of June 4, 1920, §1, subch. II, 41 Stat. 809, as amended) and 38 U.S.C. §693h (Act of June 22, 1944, 58 Stat. 286, as amended), and upon Department of Defense and Army Regulations deemed to be authorized by those statutes, discharged petitioners from the Army and issued to each of them a discharge certificate in form other than "honorable." In so doing, he took into account preinduction activities of petitioners rather than basing his action exclusively upon the record of their military service. After having exhausted available administrative remedies, petitioners separately brought these proceedings in the District Court seeking judgments declaring those determinations and actions of the Secretary to be void as in excess of his powers under the circumstances, and directing him to issue "honorable" discharge certificates to them. Being of the view that it was without jurisdiction to consider the actions, the District Court dismissed them, 137 F. Supp. 475, and the Court of Appeals affirmed, with one judge dissenting, 100 U.S. App. D. C. 190, 256, 243 F. 2d 613, 834. We granted certiorari, 353 U.S. 956 and 354 U.S. 920.
The respective contentions made here may be summarized as follows:
(1) Petitioners contend (a) that the Secretary acted in excess of his powers, because the statutes referred to did not authorize, nor support Department of Defense and Army Regulations when taken to authorize consideration of petitioners' preinduction activities in determining the type of discharges to be issued to them upon separation from the Army, and (b) that the action of respondent in issuing to them less than "honorable" discharges, and the action of the District Court and of the Court of Appeals in refusing review for what they thought was lack of judicial power, deprived petitioners of due process under the Fifth Amendment, and of a judicial trial under the Sixth Amendment, of the Constitution;
(2) Respondent contends (a) that by 10 U.S.C. §652a, Congress required that, upon separation from the Army, a former soldier be given "a certificate of discharge, . . . in the manner prescribed by the Secretary of the Department of the Army . . ."; (b) that, inasmuch as all certificates of discharge are not required to be "honorable" ones, he was authorized to, and did, prescribe various types of discharge certificates running the gamut from the accolade of

"Honorable discharge" to the odious "Dishonorable discharge"; (c)
that by 38 U.S.C. §693h, Congress directed the establishment of an
Army Review Board with power to review, upon its own motion or that
of the former soldier, the type of discharge issued, and "to change,
correct, or modify any discharge or dismissal, and to issue a new
discharge in accord with the facts presented to the board," and prescribed that "the findings thereof [shall] be final subject only to review by the Secretary of the Army"; (d) that the findings of the Board,
made under those procedures so afforded to and availed of by petitioners, were _final_ subject only to review by the Secretary of the
Army; and (e) that, therefore, such administrative procedure is exclusive and the courts are without jurisdiction to review those
findings.

In keeping with our duty to avoid deciding constitutional questions presented unless essential to proper disposition of a case, we
look first to petitioners' non-constitutional claim that respondent
acted in excess of powers granted him by Congress. Generally, judicial relief is available to one who has been injured by an act of a government official which is in escess of his express or implied powers.
American School of Magnetic Healing v. McAnnulty, 187 U.S. 94, 108;
Philadelphia Co. v. Stimson, 223 U.S. 605, 621-622; Stark v. Wickard,
321 U.S. 288, 310. The District Court had not only jurisdiction to
determine its jurisdiction but also power to construe the statutes involved to determine whether the respondent did exceed his powers.
If he did so, his actions would not constitute exercises of his administrative discretion, and, in such circumstances as those before
us, judicial relief from this illegality would be available. Moreover,
the claims presented in these cases may be entertained by the District Court because petitioners have alleged judicially cognizable injuries. Cf. Joint Anti-Fascist Refugee Committee v. McGrath, 341
U.S. 123, 159, 160, and see Army Regulation 615-360, par. 7.

This brings us to the merits. The Solicitor General conceded
that if the District Court had jurisdiction to review respondent's determinations as to the discharges he issued these petitioners and if
petitioners had standing to bring these suits, the action of respondent
is not sustainable. On the basis of that concession and our consideration of the law and this record we conclude that the actions of the
Secretary of the Army cannot be sustained in law. By §652a, which
provides that no person be discharged from military service "without
a certificate of discharge," Congress granted to the Secretary of the
Army authority to issue discharges. By §693h it provided for review
by the Army Review Board of the exercise of such authority. Surely
these two provisions must be given an harmonious reading to the end
that the basis on which the Secretary's action is reviewed is coterminous with the basis on which he is allowed to act. Section 693h expressly requires that the findings of the Army Review Board "shall
be based upon all available records of the [Army] relating to the

person requesting such review. . . ." We think the word "records," as used in the statute, means records of military service, and that the statute, properly construed, means that the type of discharge to be issued is to be determined solely by the soldier's military record in the Army. An authoritative construction of the congressional grant of power is to be found in the regulations of the Department of the Army. Army Regulation 615-375, par. 2(b) states: "The purpose of a discharge certificate is to record the separation of an individual from the military service and to specify the character of service rendered during the period covered by the discharge." (Emphasis supplied.) Moreover, the Army's Regulation 615-360, par. 7 (which was in effect during the times here involved), further states: "Because the type of discharge may significantly influence the individual's civilian rights and eligibility for benefits provided by law, it is essential that all pertinent factors be considered so that the type of discharge will reflect accurately the nature of service rendered. . . ." (Emphasis supplied.)

The judgments of the Court of Appeals are reversed and the cases are remanded to the District Court for the relief to which petitioners are entitled in the light of this opinion.

Reversed.

MR. JUSTICE CLARK, dissenting.

I would affirm these cases on the basis of Judge Prettyman's opinion in the Court of Appeals. Harmon v. Brucker, 100 U.S. App. D. C. 190, 243 F.2d 613. Since this Court does not reach the constitutional claims considered and rejected by Judge Prettyman, however, it is appropriate to add a word about the Court's basis for asserting jurisdiction and reversing on the merits, namely, the finding that the action of the Secretary of the Army was in excess of his statutory authority.

At the outset it is well to state what Harmon and Abramowitz, petitioners in these cases, do not contend. They do not contest the decision that their retention in the Army was inconsistent with national security, nor do they claim that the procedures adopted violated their legally protected rights. They concede the Army "an absolute right to discharge," but object to issuance of discharge certificates that reflect the determinations underlying the fact of their discharges, insisting that the Secretary be required to issue them honorable discharges. The controversy thus is confined to the type of discharge certificate that may be issued to servicemen discharged because of preinduction activity deemed to render them undesirable security risks.

Throughout our history the function of granting discharge certificates has been entrusted by the Congress to the President and, through him, to the respective Secretaries of the Armed Forces. At no time until today have the courts interfered in the exercise of this military function. The lack of any judicial review is evidenced by the

fact that for over 70 years Congress itself reviewed military discharges and frequently enacted private bills directing the appropriate
Secretary to correct the type of discharge certificate given. By legislation in 1944 and 1946, Congress authorized creation of administrative boards to which it transferred the review of military discharges
in an effort to conserve its own time. That legislation makes no provision for judicial review; on the contrary, the 1944 Act expressly
states that the findings of the Army Discharge Review Board shall be
"final subject only to review by the Secretary of [the Army]," and the
1946 Act, as amended in 1951, expressly provides that the determination of the Board to Correct Military Records shall be "final and conclusive on all officers of the Government except when procured by
means of fraud." When this legislative expression of finality is
viewed in context with the uninterrupted history of congressional review, culminated by Congress' transfer of the review function to
administrative bodies, it cannot be said, in the absence of specific
legislative grant, that Congress intended to permit judicial review.
The Court avoids these considerations by positing jurisdiction to review simply on its determination that the Secretary's action exceeded
his statutory authority.

In reaching this exceptional position, the Court construes §693h
of the 1944 Act, supra, which provides that review of discharges shall
be based on "all available records" of the department involved, to include not "all available records" of the Army concerning petitioners,
but merely those "solely [concerned with] the soldier's military record in the Army." (Emphasis added.) This limitation of the clear
meaning of the words used by the Congress--so that "all" is deemed
to mean "some"--is lacking of any justification.

The construction adopted does enable the Court to by-pass the
constitutional questions raised by petitioners. It is true that we avoid
decision of constitutional questions "unless essential to proper disposition of a case." But as I see it, this rule should never compel a
transparently artificial construction of a statute. The Court's interpretation here of §693h must leave both the President and the Congress in a quandary as to the solution of an important problem
involving the security of our country.

It is to be regretted that the Justice Department and the Army
are at loggerheads over the proper disposition of these cases on the
merits. However, the frank confession thereof by the Solicitor General is hardly sufficient reason to abandon our long-established policy
of no review in such matters. If injustice has been done I have confidence in the Congress or the President to correct it. The proper recourse of petitioners is in that direction.

Judge Prettyman aptly stated: "Surely the President may apply
to military personnel the same program and policies as to security
and loyalty which he applies to civilian personnel. . . . [I]f [Harmon]
can be discharged as a security risk, the Army can determine whether

he is or is not a security risk. And in that determination surely no
data is more relevant and material than are his [preinduction] habits,
activities and associations." 100 U.S. App. D. C., at 197, 243 F. 2d,
at 620. The same type of data is commonly accepted among civilian
agencies as relevant to the security screening of its employees.
Those agencies also issue discharges in the form of severance papers
based upon, and frequently reciting, security grounds. Such papers
reflect the true condition upon which the discharge is made. It seems
incongruous to me that the military services should not be able to do
as much. I would not require the Secretary to issue a discharge certificate which on its face falsifies the real grounds for its issuance.

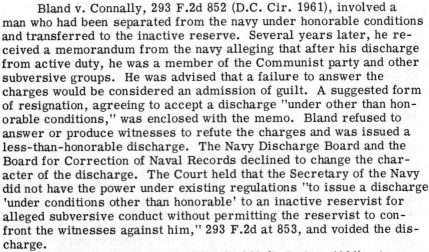

    Bland v. Connally, 293 F.2d 852 (D.C. Cir. 1961), involved a
man who had been separated from the navy under honorable conditions
and transferred to the inactive reserve. Several years later, he received a memorandum from the navy alleging that after his discharge
from active duty, he was a member of the Communist party and other
subversive groups. He was advised that a failure to answer the
charges would be considered an admission of guilt. A suggested form
of resignation, agreeing to accept a discharge "under other than honorable conditions," was enclosed with the memo. Bland refused to
answer or produce witnesses to refute the charges and was issued a
less-than-honorable discharge. The Navy Discharge Board and the
Board for Correction of Naval Records declined to change the character of the discharge. The Court held that the Secretary of the Navy
did not have the power under existing regulations "to issue a discharge
'under conditions other than honorable' to an inactive reservist for
alleged subversive conduct without permitting the reservist to confront the witnesses against him," 293 F.2d at 853, and voided the discharge.
    See also Davis v. Stahr, 293 F.2d 860 (D.C. Cir. 1961), where
the Court held that the Secretary of the Army does not have authority
to issue an undesirable discharge from the inactive reserve on the
ground that the former serviceman refused to discuss allegedly derogatory remarks about the army and the government while he was on
active duty, at least without permitting him to confront his accusers.

## REED v. FRANKE*

United States Court of Appeals, Fourth Circuit, 1961.
297 F.2d 17

*[ Footnotes have been omitted.  Ed.]

BOREMAN, Circuit Judge.

Plaintiff, Milton C. Reed, challenges the right of certain officers of the United States Navy to separate him from naval service with a general discharge under honorable conditions.  This appeal is from an order of the United States District Court for the Eastern District of Virginia setting aside prior restraining orders and denying plaintiff's request for a permanent injunction to prevent the defendants from so discharging him.  For the reasons hereinafter stated, we are of the opinion that the District Court should be affirmed in its denial of a permanent injunction.

. . . Reed, a Chief in the United States Navy with over eighteen years of service to his credit when this suit was brought, is under an enlistment which will not expire until March 21, 1962, at which time he will, unless sooner separated, have served sufficient time to permit his retirement with a pension.  On May 24, 1960, Reed was notified by the defendant, Commander Mayo, that he was being considered for an administrative discharge by reason of unsuitability.  Reed submitted a letter in support of his contention that he was not an alcoholic, and thus not unsuitable, although he freely conceded that he "occasionally overindulged" and that, in December 1959 and again in May 1960, he was properly convicted by court martial of operating an automobile when under the influence of intoxicants, such operations resulting in accidents occurring on Government property.

Prior to December 1959, on several occasions Reed had been observed under the influence of intoxicants and was warned by his Division Officer. . . .

. . .

On June 10, 1960, Commander Mayo, having reviewed the record of plaintiff, including an incident which occurred on November 2, 1956, recommended that the plaintiff be discharged from naval service by reason of unsuitability.  On July 6, 1960, the Chief of Naval Personnel directed that plaintiff be separated with a general discharge, under honorable conditions, by reason of unsuitability with the "reason not to be shown" on the discharge certificate.  On July 28, 1960, this injunction action was commenced, and the next day a temporary restraining order was entered which was thereafter continued pending final hearing.

. . .

The District Court held that it lacked jurisdiction on two grounds, namely, (1) plaintiff failed to exhaust his administrative remedies, and

(2) the facts of the case preclude the exercise of jurisdiction. Reed's principal contention is that an honorable discharge is a valuable property right and that, under the Constitution, he may not be deprived of this right except in accord with due process of law as required by the Fifth Amendment. He asserts that a hearing prior to discharge, under the facts of this case, is a requirement of due process. The principal constitutional claim, as we understand it, is not that plaintiff has a right to stay in the Navy until he has served sufficient time to retire with a pension. Such claim, if asserted, would be frivolous and would provide no basis for the court's jurisdiction to interfere with the normal operations of the military services.

. . .

The District Court below had jurisdiction to determine its jurisdiction and also to decide the merits of plaintiff's claim of violation of constitutional rights. If the claim were well founded, the Navy would have no authority to proceed with the discharge as contemplated, and judicial relief from this illegality would be available. The constitutionality of the discharge procedure is a justiciable issue but once the plaintiff's claim is found and declared to be without merit, the discharge procedure may continue as before. Here, as in Harmon v. Brucker, there is no direct judicial review of the administrative proceedings except insofar as necessary to determine the legality of prescribed administrative procedure. It is the basic procedure that is attacked and which may be reviewed.

. . .

We conclude that, where there is a substantial claim that prescribed military procedures violate one's constitutional rights, the District Courts have jurisdiction to resolve the constitutional questions. . . .

. . .

It is true that the regulations, pertinent here, make no provision for a hearing such as Reed contends he should be given prior to his general discharge from the Navy. But Congress has provided for a review of discharges and dismissals from military departments under 10 U.S.C. §1553. This statute contemplates a mandatory hearing, upon request after discharge, before a board of five members, at which hearing the person requesting review is permitted to appear in person or by counsel. Such review shall be based upon all available records of the military department concerned and such other evidence as may be presented. Witnesses shall be permitted to testify either in person or by affidavit. Certainly at such a hearing Reed would be entitled to present rebutting testimony and to have the decision based upon the record of the matters considered at the hearing. The board is granted the authority (except in case of a discharge or dismissal resulting from the sentence of a general court martial) to change, correct or modify any discharge or dismissal, and to issue a new discharge in accord with the facts presented to the board. Thus the reviewing board is empowered to nullify the action taken if determined to be erroneous and, in lieu thereof, to order an honorable discharge to which Reed claims to be entitled. The findings of the board are subject to review only by the Secretary of the military department affected.

Under 10 U.S.C. §1552, the Secretary of a military department is authorized to correct any military record when he considers it necessary to correct an error or remove an injustice. By this section there is no provision made for a formal hearing at which the serviceman or his counsel may be present and the procedure is not mandatory, yet a civilian board may be called to act in behalf of the Secretary in considering the matter.

If Reed were to be given a general discharge under honorable conditions as proposed, he could apply for relief under 10 U.S.C. §1552 and, if no relief were afforded thereby, he could proceed to obtain the mandatory hearing provided by 10 U.S.C. §1553.

There is no constitutional right to a particular form of remedy. Neblett v. Carpenter, 305 U.S. 297, 59 S.Ct. 170, 83 L.Ed. 182 (1938), rehearing denied, 305 U.S. 675, 59 S.Ct. 355, 83 L.Ed. 437 (1939). A fact-finding hearing prior to discharge is one way to protect plaintiff's alleged rights, but it is not the only means of protection and Congress has provided other ways of preventing injustices and correcting errors in connection with military discharges. By statute, Reed is provided an opportunity to avoid the injury he claims he will suffer when the discharge becomes effective.

Since we are of the opinion that 10 U.S.C. §1553 provides relief in the nature of a full hearing before a Board of Review, we will follow the accepted judicial practice of avoiding the resolution of constitutional issues where an alternative ground for disposing of the case is present. . . .

The fact that the hearing provided by statute does not precede, but follows, Reed's separation from the service does not make the hearing inadequate. The statutory review is a part of the protective procedure and due process requirements are satisfied if the individual is given a hearing at some point in the administrative proceedings. . . .

Those fundamental requirements of fairness which are of the essence of due process in the proceedings pursuant to the pertinent regulations are met by the provisions of the statutes above noted. Whether the absence from the regulations of the protections to which Reed is entitled would violate the demands of the Constitution is not an issue to be dealt with if the statute itself supplies these protections.

For the reasons herein stated, the decree of the District Court discharging prior restraining orders and denying plaintiff's request for a temporary and permanent injunction is affirmed without

prejudice to the plaintiff's resort to the adequate administrative
remedy provided by statute. The injunction pending appeal will be
vacated and discharged.

Affirmed.

It is unclear whether a serviceman can enjoin the armed forces
from discharging him pending review by the appropriate administrative agency. In Covington v. Schwartz, 230 F.Supp. 249 (N.D. Cal.
1964), modified and affirmed, 341 F.2d 537 (9th Cir. 1965), it was
held that an enlisted man could enjoin his undesirable discharge until
after review by the Discharge Board and the Army Board for Correction of Military Records if he was likely to prevail on the merits before the review boards, if he would otherwise suffer irreparable harm,
and if his retention in the army would not harm other interested persons or the public interest. See also Vitelli v. Warden, 247 F.Supp.
993 (S.D. Cal. 1965). In McCurdy v. Zuckert, 359 F.2d 491 (5th Cir.
1966), however, the Court of Appeals for the Fifth Circuit held that
the District Court lacked jurisdiction to entertain a motion for such
an injunction in a case involving a general discharge. The Court distinguished Covington v. Schwartz, supra, on the ground that a lesser
stigma attached to a general discharge than to an undesirable discharge and concluded that McCurdy would not suffer irreparable
harm. But see Tuggle v. Brown, 362 F.2d 801 (5th Cir. 1966), where
the same Court, relying on its decision in McCurdy v. Zuckert, supra,
refused to enjoin the issuance of an undesirable discharge to an airman.

## CLACKUM v. UNITED STATES

United States Court of Claims, 1960.
296 F.2d 226, 148 Ct. Cl. 404.

MADDEN, Judge.
        The plaintiff was separated from the United States Air Force
on January 22, 1952, with a discharge "under conditions other than
honorable." She asserts that the purported discharge was invalid,
and sues for her pay from the date of the purported discharge. The
following "Statement of Facts Alleged", contained in the following
four paragraphs, is copied from the Government's brief.

"On February 2, 1951, plaintiff was a reservist in the United States Air Force, (WAF--Women in the Air Force) and was ordered to active duty as an airman. She was stationed thereafter at Barksdale Air Force Base, Louisiana, in the grade of corporal, with duty in Headquarters and Headquarters Squadron, 301st Air Base Group.

"On April 18, 1951, plaintiff, among others, was called before her commanding officer and a representative of the O.S.I. (Office of Special Intelligence) and interrogated on matters of homosexuality concerning which plaintiff alleges she had no knowledge. Thereafter, until January 1952, plaintiff was repeatedly interviewed by an officer of the O.S.I. concerning homosexual activities and informed that she was under investigation. She was never informed of any charges against her by the Air Force, although in October 1951 she was informed that some action was contemplated against her. Also in October 1951 plaintiff was called before her commanding officer and was given an opportunity to resign under A.F.R. 35-66, (5b) (1). Upon being offered the opportunity to resign, plaintiff refused to resign and demanded in writing that she be tried by court-martial. The purpose of this demand was to require the Air Force to confront her with the basis of the accusations against her and to afford her an opportunity to present evidence in her own behalf.

"Although charges were preferred against plaintiff under the Uniform Code of Military Justice, the charges were not referred for investigation under the provisions of the Code, they were not brought to her attention, and she had no knowledge of them until after her discharge. After plaintiff was given an opportunity to resign and refused, she was given a psychiatric examination but was not informed of the report of the psychiatrist. No sworn evidence against plaintiff was taken or received by the O.S.I. or by the Air Force, and prior to her discharge plaintiff was not confronted with the nature of the evidence against her. Plaintiff was demoted to the grade of private on January 22, 1952 and on that same day was discharged from the service under conditions other than honorable under A.F.R. 35-66 dated January 12, 1951.

"Plaintiff brought suit in this Court on June 8, 1956. By agreement of the parties, the Court suspended proceedings in this Court to permit plaintiff to file an application before the Air Force Board for the Correction of Military Records on the ground that plaintiff had failed to

exhaust her administrative remedies. An application
was filed and was denied by the Air Force Board for the
Correction of Military Records. The suspension of proceedings in this Court was then removed."

Some of the effects upon a soldier of a discharge "under conditions other than honorable" are briefly stated in Air Force Regulations (A.F.R.) 35-66, dated January 12, 1951, 5(b) (1), which says
that the person so discharged may be deprived of many rights as a
veteran under both Federal and State legislation, and may expect to
encounter substantial prejudice in civilian life in situations where
the type of service rendered in any branch of the armed forces or the
character of discharge received therefrom may have a bearing.

One's reaction to the foregoing narrative is "What's going on
here?"

A woman soldier is interrogated about homosexual matters and
is orally told that some action is contemplated against her. She is
called before her commanding officer and is offered an opportunity to
resign. She indignantly denies the implied charges involved in the
situation and demands in writing that she be tried by a court-martial
so that she can learn what the charges are, face her accusers, and
present evidence in her own behalf. Although charges were preferred
against her, they were not referred for investigation as the statutes
governing courts-martial require, and neither the charges nor the
evidence upon which they were based were ever made known to the
soldier until after her discharge. She was summarily given a discharge "under conditions other than honorable", her reputation as a
decent woman was officially destroyed, her rights to her accrued pay
and accrued leave, and to the numerous and valuable benefits conferred by the nation and many of the states upon former soldiers were
forfeited.

Air Force Regulations 35-66 5(b) (1) related to the handling of
homosexual charges against enlisted personnel. They provided for a
resignation agreeing to accept an undesirable discharge with all its
damaging consequences. If the soldier refused to so resign, the regulations provided that a trial by general court-martial would be considered. If the evidence in the case indicated that conviction by a
general court-martial was unlikely, then the Secretary of the Air Force
was, by the regulations, authorized to "direct discharge and administratively determine whether an undesirable, general, or honorable type
of discharge will be furnished."

A dishonorable discharge is, for a soldier, one of the most
severe penalties which may be imposed by a court-martial. Elaborate
provisions for review of court-martial sentences within the military
hierarchy, and potentially by the Court of Military Appeals, are included in our military laws. Yet the Air Force regulations discussed
above provide that if the evidence at hand is so unsubstantial that a

conviction by a court-martial would be unlikely, the executive officers of the Air Force may themselves convict the soldier and impose the penalty. It is as if a prosecuting attorney were authorized, in a case where he concluded that he didn't have enough evidence to obtain a conviction in court, to himself impose the fine or imprisonment which he thought the accused person deserved.

The Government defends this remarkable arrangement, and its operation in the instant case, on the ground that it is necessary in the interest of an efficient military establishment for our national defense. We see nothing in this argument. The plaintiff being a member of the Air Force Reserve, on active duty, the Air Force had the undoubted right to discharge her whenever it pleased, for any reason or for no reason, and by so doing preserve the Air Force from even the slightest suspicion of harboring undesirable characters. But it is unthinkable that it should have the raw power, without respect for even the most elementary notions of due process of law, to load her down with penalties. It is late in the day to argue that everything that the executives of the armed forces do in connection with the discharge of soldiers is beyond the reach of judicial scrutiny. Harmon v. Brucker, 355 U.S. 579, 78 S.Ct. 433, 2 L.Ed.2d 503.

After her discharge, the plaintiff appealed to the Air Force Discharge Review Board. Such an appeal is provided for in the Air Force Regulations. Her appeal and that of another female non-commissioned officer were heard together. They were represented by counsel. They had access to a brief which had been written by an investigator, and which summarized conversations which he had had with various persons. The plaintiff and the other appellant testified at length, directing their testimony to the incidents mentioned in the conversations summarized in the investigator's brief. Their testimony was, of course, entirely favorable to themselves. Some members of the Board asked some questions of the appellants. None of the answers to these questions tended to show that the appellants were guilty. Testimonials of good character from Air Force superiors, civilian employers, clergymen and other acquaintances were placed in evidence.

No witnesses other than the two appellants testified. None of the persons mentioned in the investigator's brief as having made statements derogatory to the appellants were called to testify.

The appellants' counsel made an able argument on their behalf. Among other things, he pointed out the absurdity of the following oracular item in the investigator's brief:

> "Psychiatric evaluation of appl. (appellant) 21 Nov.
> 51 reflected a diagnosis of sexual deviate manifested by
> homosexuality latent.,"

in view of the plaintiff's uncontradicted testimony that the only psychiatric interview to which she was subjected lasted from 20 to 30 minutes.

The hearing was closed and the Discharge Review Board made the following

"Findings

After consideration of the evidence of record, including the 201 file in the case, the Board finds:

"a. That the discharge of the applicants under the provisions of AFR 35-66 (discharge of homosexuals) was in accord with the regulations in force at the time.

"b. That the character of the discharges was amply supported by the evidence of record.

"c. That no additional evidence of sufficient weight and credibility as to warrant reversal of the prior action in these cases has been adduced before the Air Force Discharge Review Board.

"Conclusions

"The Board recommends that no change be made in the type of discharge certificates presently in effect."

The "evidence of record" upon which the Board based its finding of guilt was obviously not the evidence received at the hearing. All of the evidence received at the hearing tended to prove the plaintiff's innocence. The "evidence of record" was a dossier of affidavits of persons, some of whom were not even mentioned in the investigator's brief which was made available to the plaintiff at the time of her hearing before the Discharge Review Board, although the statements made in their affidavits, if believed, were extremely damaging to the plaintiff. None of the affidavits was seen by the plaintiff or her counsel until July 24, 1959, long after the plaintiff's case was pending in this court.

The "evidence of record" also contained the confidential reports of the Office of Special Investigations which were forwarded to the Air Force Personnel Counsel and the Secretary of the Air Force, and which have never been made available to the plaintiff or her counsel.

The so-called "hearing" before the Air Force Discharge Board was not a hearing at all, in the usual sense of that word. It was a meaningless formality, to comply with the regulations. The "evidence" upon which the case was going to be decided, and obviously was decided, was not present at the hearing, unless the undisclosed dossier which contained it was in the drawer of the table at which the Board sat. The appellant and her counsel were futilely tilting at shadows. However vulnerable the secret evidence may have been, there was no possible way to attack it.

The plaintiff was, after the proceeding before the Discharge Review Board, as before, a soldier dishonorably discharged, officially

branded by her Government as an indecent woman, deprived of valuable rights and benefits which are given to other ex-soldiers. And all
this without any semblance of an opportunity to know what the evidence
against her was, or to face her accusers in a trial or hearing.

As we have said, the plaintiff is suing for her pay as a soldier,
on the theory that her purported discharge was illegal and invalid.
The Government says that even if the discharge actually issued was
invalid, the Air Force could have validly discharged her at the time
it invalidly did so, and therefore she is not entitled to be paid. There
are, of course, many situations in which, if a party had acted somewhat differently, he would not have violated the legal rights of the
other person and would not be liable for damages.

In the instant case, the dishonorable nature of the discharge was
its very essence, the most important thing about it. We feel no urge
to dissect the discharge and discard its essence, retaining only its
effect of getting the plaintiff out of the Air Force and off its payroll,
thus leaving her to suffer, without compensation, all the other penalties which the discharge imposed upon her.

Our conclusion is that the purported discharge of the plaintiff
was invalid, and did not effect the plaintiff's separation from the Air
Force.

Since the parties have filed a stipulation of facts which the court
has considered, the defendant's motion to dismiss the plaintiff's petition is, under our Rule 16(b), 28 U.S.C.A., treated as a motion for
summary judgment. The motion is denied.

It is so ordered.

JONES, Chief Judge, and LARAMORE and WHITAKER, Judges,
concur.

---

See also Glidden v. United States, 185 Ct.Cl. 515 (1968), where
the Court held that a former serviceman, who had been given an undesirable discharge for homosexuality, was denied procedural due
process before the Air Force Board by being denied the right to
crossexamine witnesses and by the introduction into evidence of sum-
maries of adverse testimony without an attempt being made to obtain
the presence of the witnesses whose testimony was summarized.

In Middleton v. United States, 170 Ct.Cl. 36 (1965), the Court
voided the undesirable discharge of a former serviceman who signed
a statement agreeing to accept the discharge "for the good of the
service and to escape trial by general court-martial!" 170 Ct.Cl. at
38-39. Prior to his acceptance of the discharge, he had been convicted in a police court but thereafter acquitted in a de novo trial in
another civilian court of a charge relating to homosexual acts. Navy
regulations did not permit a court-martial under the circumstances,

but naval investigators led him to believe that he would be court-martialed if he did not agree to an undesirable discharge. After the Board of Correction of Naval Records concluded that the discharge was improper and recommended that it be changed to an honorable discharge, the Secretary of the Navy changed it to a general discharge. The court held that the discharge was obtained as a result of wrongful pressure and that the serviceman "was denied due process and fair treatment by being faced with a harsh and disagreeable option which simply did not exist under Navy law." 120 Ct.Cl. at 41. Cf. Neal v. United States, 177 Ct.Cl. 937 (1966), where the Court voided the undesirable discharge that was issued on the basis of a confession obtained by naval investigators by threatening to court-martial the serviceman. The Navy Discharge Review Board and the Board of Correction of Naval Records refused to change the character of the discharge. The Court of Claims found that, unknown to the serviceman, he could not have been court-martialed without corroborative evidence and that the investigators had no such evidence. The Court held that the confession was improperly obtained and the discharge void.

In Ashe v. McNamara, 355 F.2d. 277 (C.A. 1st. 1965), the Court directed that a dishonorable discharge, awarded pursuant to a general court-martial sentence in 1948, be declared invalid because the accused was denied effective assistance of counsel guaranteed by the Sixth Amendment.

Guidelines for the separation of enlisted men, as well as commissioned and warrant officers, based upon claims of conscientious objection, are provided in A.R. 635-20 (1970). Under the regulation, the Army will consider requests for separation of those who object "to participation, in war in any form, when such objection develops subsequent to entry into the active military service." Id., para. 3 (a). Requests for discharge will not be favorably considered if it is based solely on an objection that existed, but was not claimed, prior to induction or enlistment or that was claimed and denied by the Selective Service System prior to induction. Id., para 3 (b) (1), (2). Consideration will be given to "claims based on conscientious objection growing out of experience prior to entering military service but which did not become fixed until entry into the service." Id., para. 3 (b). Pending a final determination on a request for discharge, the applicant is retained in his unit and assigned duties that conflict least with his asserted beliefs. Id., para. 6 (a). Enlisted men discharged under this regulation are entitled to an honorable or a general discharge certificate. Officers are furnished with a discharge certificate. Id., para. 10. Enlisted men with less than 180 days service, however, are referred to the Selective Service System with a request that they be inducted into the Conscientious Objectors' Work Program. Id., para. 7.

Extract from Department of the Army Pamphlet 27-187,
Military Affairs, 1967.*

*[ Footnotes have been omitted.  Ed.]

8.9  Retirement.  An enlisted member of the Regular Army with
30 years of active service must be retired on his request.  A Regular
Army enlisted member with at least 20, but less than 30, years of
active service may be retired on his request.  In the latter case, the
retiree becomes a member of the Army Reserve until his combined
active and retired service equals 30 years.  Nevertheless, all regular
enlisted men retired under either of the above provisions remain
members of the Regular Army and are subject to court-martial jurisdiction.

Regular enlisted members retire in the enlisted grade in which
serving on the date of retirement.  Provision is made for advancement
on the retired list to the highest temporary grade in which the member
served satisfactorily on active duty when his cumulative service,
active and retired, totals 30 years.

Only active service is creditable in determining the eligibility
of regular enlisted personnel for retirement and in computing their
retired pay.  All active service as an officer in the Army may be
credited as enlisted service for all purposes.  Retired pay is computed by multiplying the basic pay to which the member was entitled
on the day before retirement by 2-1/2 percent for each year of service credited, but not more than 75 percent.

There is no provision authorizing retirement of Reserve enlisted personnel specifically on the basis of active service.  However,
retired pay for non-Regular service, previously discussed, may be
paid on the basis of enlisted service as well as service as an officer.

## BLAKE v. UNITED STATES

Supreme Court of the United States, 1880.
103 U.S. 227, 26 L.Ed. 462.

MR. JUSTICE HARLAN delivered the opinion of the court.

The claim of Blake is placed upon the ground that before, at the date of, and after the letter addressed to the Secretary of War, which was treated as his resignation, he was insane in a sense that rendered him irresponsible for his acts, and consequently that his supposed resignation was inoperative and did not have the effect to vacate his office. Did the appointment of Gilmore, by and with the advice and consent of the Senate, to the post-chaplaincy held by Blake, operate, proprio vigore, to discharge the latter from the service, and invest the former with the rights and privileges belonging to that office? If this question be answered in the affirmative, it will not be necessary to inquire whether Blake was, at the date of the letter of Dec. 24, 1868, in such condition of mind as to enable him to perform, in a legal sense, the act of resigning his office; or, whether the acceptance of his resignation, followed by the appointment of his successor, by the President, by and with the advice and consent of the Senate, is not, in view of the relations of the several departments of the government to each other, conclusive, in this collateral proceeding, as to the fact of a valid effectual resignation.

From the organization of the government, under the present Constitution, to the commencement of the recent war for the suppression of the rebellion, the power of the President, in the absence of statutory regulations, to dismiss from the service an officer of the army or navy, was not questioned in any adjudged case, or by any department of the government.

107

Upon the general question of the right to remove from office, as incident to the power to appoint, Ex parte Hennen, 13 Pet. 225, is instructive. That case involved the authority of a district judge of the United States to remove a clerk and appoint some one in his place.

The court, among other things, said: "All offices, the tenure of which is not fixed by the Constitution or limited by law, must be held either during good behavior, or (which is the same thing in contemplation of law) during the life of the incumbent, or must be held at the will and discretion of some department of the government, and subject to removal at pleasure.

"It cannot for a moment be admitted that it was the intention of the Constitution that those offices which are denominated inferior offices should be held during life. And if removable at pleasure, by whom is such removal to be made? In the absence of all constitutional provision or statutory regulation, it would seem to be a sound and necessary rule to consider the power of removal as incident to the power of appointment. This power of removal from office was a subject much disputed, and upon which a great diversity of opinion was entertained in the early history of this government. This related, however, to the power of the President to remove officers appointed with the concurrence of the Senate; and the great question was whether the removal was to be by the President alone, or with the concurrence of the Senate, both constituting the appointing power. No one denied the power of the President and Senate jointly to remove, where the tenure of the office was not fixed by the Constitution; which was a full recognition of the principle that the power of removal was incident to the power of appointment. But it was very early adopted, as the practical construction of the Constitution, that this power was vested in the President alone. And such would appear to have been the legislative construction of the Constitution." 1 Kent, Com. 309; 2 Story, Const., 4th Ed., sects. 1537-1540, and notes; 2 Marshall, Life of Washington, 162; Sergeant, Const. Law, 372; Rawle, Const., c. 14.

During the administration of President Tyler, the question was propounded by the Secretary of the Navy to Attorney-General Legare, whether the President could strike an officer from the rolls, without a trial by a court-martial, after a decision in that officer's favor by a court of inquiry ordered for the investigation of his conduct. His response was: "Whatever I might have thought of the power of removal from office, if the subject were res integra, it is now too late to dispute the settled construction of 1789. It is according to that construction, from the very nature of executive power, absolute in the President, subject only to his responsibility to the country (his constituents) for a breach of such a vast and solemn trust. 3 Story, Com. Const. 397, sect. 1538. It is obvious that if necessity is a sufficient ground for such a concession in regard to officers in the civil service, the argument applies a mullo fortiori to the military and naval departments. . . . I have no doubt, therefore, that the President had the constitutional power to do what he did, and that the officer in question is not in the service of the United States." The same views were expressed by subsequent attorneys-general. 4 Op.Atty.Gen. 1; 6 id. 4; 8 id. 223; 12 id. 421; 15 id. 421.

In Du Barry's Case, 4 id. 603, 612, Attorney-General Clifford said that the attempt to limit the exercise of the power of removal to the executive officers in the civil service found no support in the language of the Constitution nor in any judicial decision; and that there was no foundation in the Constitution for any distinction in this regard between civil and military officers.

In Lansing's Case, 6 id. 4, the question arose as to the power of the President, in his discretion, to remove a military storekeeper. Attorney-General Cushing said: "Conceding, however, that military storekeepers are officers, or, at least, quasi officers, of the army, it does not follow that they are not subject to be deprived of their commission at the will of the President.

'I am not aware of any ground of distinction in this respect, so far as regards the strict question of law, between officers of the army and any other officers of the government. As a general rule, with the exception of judicial officers only, they all hold their commissions by the same tenure in this respect. Reasons of a special nature may be deemed to exist why the rule should not be applied to military in the same way as it is to civil officers, but the legal applicability to both classes of officers is, it is conceived, the settled construction of the Constitution. It is no answer to this doctrine to say that officers of the army are subject to be deprived of their commissions by the decision of a court-martial. So are civil officers by impeachment. The difference between the two cases is in the form and mode of trial, not in the principle, which leaves unimpaired in both cases alike the whole constitutional power of the President.

'It seems unnecessary in this case to recapitulate in detail the elements of constitutional construction and historical induction by which this doctrine has been established as the public law of the United States. I observe only that, so far as regards the question of abstract power, I know of nothing essential in the grounds of legal conclusion, which have been so thoroughly explored at different times in respect of civil officers, which does not apply to officers of the army."

The same officer, subsequently, when required to consider this question, said that "the power has been exercised in many cases with approbation, express or implied, of the Senate, and without challenge by any legislative act of Congress. And it is expressly reserved in every commission of the officers, both of the navy and army." 8 Opin. 223, 231.

Such was the established practice in the Executive Department, and such the recognized power of the President up to the passage of the act of July 17, 1862, c. 200, 12 Stat. 596, entitled "An Act to define the pay and emoluments of certain officers of the army, and for other purposes," the seventeenth section of which provides that "the President of the United States be, and hereby is, authorized and requested to dismiss and discharge from the military service, either in the army, navy, marine corps, or volunteer force, any officer for any cause which, in his judgment, either renders such officer unsuitable for, or whose dismission would promote, the public service."

In reference to that act Attorney-General Devens, 15 Opin. 421, said, with much reason, that so far as it "gives authority to the President, it is simply declaratory of the long-established law. It is probable that the force of the act is to be found in the word 'requested,' by which it was intended to re-enforce strongly this power in the hands of the President at a creat crisis of the State."

The act of March 3, 1865, c. 79, 13 Stat. 489, provides that, in case any officer of the military or naval service, thereafter dismissed by the authority of the President, shall make application in writing for a trial, setting forth, under oath, that he has been wrongfully and unjustly dismissed, "the President shall, as soon as the necessities of the service may permit, convene a court-martial to try such officer on the charges on which he was dismissed. And if such court-martial shall not award dismissal or death as the punishment of such officer, the order of dismissal shall be void. And if the court-martial aforesaid shall not be convened for the trial of such officer within six months from the presentation of his application for trial, the sentence of dismissal shall be void."

Thus, so far as legislative enactments are concerned, stood the law in reference to dismissals, of army or naval officers, by the President, until the passage of the army appropriation act of July 13, 1866, c. 176, 14 Stat. 92, the fifth section of which is as follows:--

"That section seventeen of an act, entitled 'An Act to define the pay and emoluments of certain officers of the army,' approved July seventeenth, eighteen hundred and sixty-two, and a resolution, entitled 'A Resolution to authorize the President to assign the command of troops in the same field, or department, to officers of the same grade, without regard to seniority,' approved April fourth, eighteen hundred and sixty-two, be, and the same are, hereby repealed. And no officer in the military or naval service shall, in time of peace, be dismissed from the service, except upon and in pursuance of the sentence of a court-martial to that effect, or in commutation thereof."

Two constructions may be placed upon the last clause of that section without doing violence to the words used. Giving them a literal interpretation, it may be construed to mean, that although the tenure of army and naval officers is not fixed by the Constitution, they shall not, in time of peace, be dismissed from the service, under any circumstances, or for any cause, or by any authority whatever, except in pursuance of the sentence of a court-martial to that effect, or in commutation thereof. Or, in view of the connection in which the clause

appears,--following, as it does, one in the same section repealing
provisions touching the dismissal of officers by the President, alone,
and to assignments, by him, of the command of troops, without regard
to seniority of officers,--it may be held to mean, that, whereas, under
the act of July 17, 1862, as well as before its passage, the President,
alone, was authorized to dismiss an army or naval officer from the
service for any cause which, in his judgment, either rendered such
officer unsuitable for, or whose dismissal would promote, the public
service, he alone shall not, thereafter, in time of peace, exercise such
power of dismissal, except in pursuance of a court-martial sentence
to that effect, or in commutation thereof. Although this question is
not free from difficulty, we are of opinion that the latter is the true
construction of the act. That section originated in the Senate as an
amendment of the army appropriation bill which had previously passed
the House of Representatives. Cong.Globe, 39th Congress, pp. 3254,
3405, 3575, and 3589. It is supposed to have been suggested by the
serious differences existing, or which were apprehended, between the
legislative and executive branches of the government in reference to
the enforcement, in the States lately in rebellion, of the reconstruction acts of Congress. Most, if not all, of the senior officers of the
army enjoyed, as we may know from the public history of that period,
the confidence of the political organization then controlling the legislative branch of the government. It was believed that, within the
limits of the authority conferred by statute, they would carry out the
policy of Congress, as indicated in the reconstruction acts, and suppress all attempts to treat them as unconstitutional and void, or to
overthrow them by force. Hence, by way of preparation for the conflict then apprehended between the executive and legislative departments as to the enforcement of those acts, Congress, by the fifth
section of the act of July 13, 1866, repealed not only the seventeenth
section of the act of July 17, 1862, but also the resolution of April 4,
1862, which authorized the President, whenever military operations
required the presence of two or more officers of the same grade, in
the same field or department, to assign the command without regard
to seniority of rank. In furtherance, as we suppose, of the objects of
that legislation, was the second section of the army appropriation act
of March 2, 1867, c. 170, 14 Stat. 486, establishing the headquarters
of the general of the army at Washington, requiring all orders and
instructions relating to military operations issued by the President or
Secretary of War to be issued through that officer, and, in case of his
inability, through the next in rank, and declaring that the general of
the army "shall not be removed, suspended, or relieved from command, or assigned to duty elsewhere than at said headquarters, except
at his own request, without the previous approval of the Senate, and
any orders or instructions relating to military operations issued
contrary to the requirements of this section shall be null and void;
and any officer who shall issue orders or instructions contrary to

the provisions of this section shall be deemed guilty of a misdemeanor in office," &c.

Our conclusion is that there was no purpose, by the fifth section of the act of July 13, 1866, to withdraw from the President the power, with the advice and consent of the Senate, to supersede an officer in the military or naval service by the appointment of some one in his place. If the power of the President and Senate, in this regard, could be constitutionally subjected to restrictions by statute (as to which we express no opinion), it is sufficient for the present case to say that Congress did not intend by that section to impose them. It is, in substance and effect, nothing more than a declaration, that the power theretofore exercised by the President, without the concurrence of the Senate, of summarily dismissing or discharging officers of the army or the navy, whenever in his judgment the interest of the service required it to be done, shall not exist, or be exercised, in time of peace, except in pursuance of the sentence of a court-martial, or in commutation thereof. There was, as we think, no intention to deny or restrict the power of the President, by and with the advice and consent of the Senate, to displace them by the appointment of others in their places.

It results that the appointment of Gilmore, with the advice and consent of the Senate, to the office held by Blake, operated in law to supersede the latter, who thereby, in virtue of the new appointment, ceased to be an officer in the army from and after, at least, the date at which that appointment took effect,--and this, without reference to Blake's mental capacity to understand what was a resignation. He was, consequently, not entitled to pay as post-chaplain after July 2, 1870, from which date his successor took rank. Having ceased to be an officer in the army, he could not again become a post-chaplain, except upon a new appointment, by and with the advice and consent of the Senate. Mimmack v. United States, 97 U.S. 426, 24 L.Ed. 1067.

As to that portion of the claim covering the period between April 28, 1869, and July 2, 1870, it is only necessary to say that, even were it conceded that the appellant did not cease to be an officer in the army by reason of the acceptance of his resignation, tendered when he was mentally incapable of understanding the nature and effect of such an act, he cannot recover in this action. His claim for salary during the above period accrued more than six years, and the disability of insanity ceased more than three years before the commencement of this action. The government pleads the Statute of Limitations, and it must be sustained. Congress alone can give him the relief which he seeks.

Judgment affirmed.

In Street v. United States, 24 Ct.Cl. 230 (1889), affirmed, 133 U.S. 299, 10 S.Ct. 309, 33 L.Ed. 631 (1890), the Court of Claims held that a commissioned officer was properly discharged pursuant to an Act of July 15, 1870, which provided for reduction of the army. The methods provided for reducing the army were (1) voluntary resignation, (2) placement on retired list, (3) sending officers "unfit for the proper discharge of their duties" before a military board, and (4) mustering out all officers who remained supernumerary as of January 1, 1871. The claimant was dismissed pursuant to the fourth alternative. The opinion of the Court contains the following:

> The power to dismiss an officer, as has been said, has been repeatedly exercised and has been recognized and sanctioned by Congress. But inasmuch as it carried with it a taint of dishonor, and was resorted to only in cases of shameful delinquency or gross incapacity, and was deemed by those most interested as one of the severest penalties known to military law, it was proper for Congress to regulate and restrict its application under the constitutional authority vested in them. Acts 17th July, 1862; 3d March, 1865; 17th July, 1866; 12 Stat.L., 596; 13 id., 489; 14 id., 92; Blake's Case, 103 U.S. 227, 26 L.Ed. 462.
>
> Still the limitation was itself limited. The purpose of the Act 17th July, 1866, was not to attach a life tenure or element of vested right to the office, but to save officers "in time of peace" from the ignominy of a hasty and dishonorable dismissal. The practical results of the statute, in connection with the other provisions of law bearing upon the subject, are these: that in time of war the President may dismiss an officer from the service at any moment and for any cause; that in time of peace he may dismiss him for cause with the co-operation of a court-martial, or remove him without cause with the consent of the Senate.
>
> The acts of 1866 and 1870 are therefore neither in conflict nor in pari materia. They spring from different provisions of the Constitution. The one is an exercise of the legislative power "to make rules for the government and regulation of the land and naval forces;" the other of the power "to raise and support armies." The former relates to the punishment or protection of the individual officer; the latter to the Army at large. It was the purpose of the one to secure to each officer a trial by court-martial in all cases "in time of peace;" it was the purpose of the other to reduce the Army of the United States from forty-five to twenty-five regiments. . . .

The question of the discharge of an officer in time of peace also arose in Crenshaw v. United States, 134 U.S. 99, 10 S.Ct. 431, 33 L.Ed. 825 (1890). The claimant in that case was an officer who had just completed a six-year course as a cadet at the Naval Academy. He was discharged pursuant to the Naval Appropriation Act of 1882, which provided, among other things, for the discharge of surplus graduates of the Academy. The Court considered the effect of the Act of 1866 and Blake v. United States, supra, on the power of Congress to provide for the removal of officers, holding that an officer does not have vested interest or contract right in his office that could not be taken away by Congress.

The question of whether a commissioned officer ceases to be a member of the Army when another is nominated by the President, and the nomination is confirmed by the Senate, was also considered in Wallace v. United States, 257 U.S. 541, 42 S.Ct. 221, 66 L.Ed. 360 (1922), affirming 55 Ct.Cl. 396 (1920). The appointment of the other officer filled the complement of officers in the rank. Relying on Blake v. United States, supra, and other cases, the Supreme Court held that the officer who originally held the position did cease to be a member under such circumstances. An underlying issue in the case concerned the President's power to dismiss officers in time of war. Although the Supreme Court did not discuss this issue in its opinion, the Court of Claims concluded that, under the 118th Article of War, the substance of which is now 10 U.S.C. §1161 (1964), the President could summarily dismiss officers in time of war.

Commissioned Officers: Limitations on Dismissal, 10 U.S.C. §1161 (1964).

(a) No commissioned officer may be dismissed from any armed force except--
(1) by sentence of a general court-martial;
(2) in commutation of a sentence of a general court-martial;
or
(3) in time of war, by order of the President.
(b) The President may drop from the rolls of any armed force any commissioned officer (1) who has been absent without authority for at least three months, or (2) who is sentenced to confinement in a Federal or State penitentiary or correctional institution after having been found guilty of an offense by a court other than a court-martial or other military court, and whose sentence has become final. Aug. 10, 1956, c. 1041, 70A Stat. 89.

In Myers v. United States, 272 U.S. 52, 47 S.Ct. 21, 71 L.Ed. 160 (1926), the Supreme Court passed upon a point that it had reserved in prior cases, namely, the power of Congress to prevent the

removal of executive officers by the President, officers who had been
appointed by him by and with the advice and consent of the Senate.
The Court held that the Tenure of Office Act of 1867, which attempted
to restrict the power of removal by the President, was in violation of
the Constitution and invalid. The intimation was that other enactments
of a similar nature of the Reconstruction period were likewise invalid,
e.g., the Act of July 13, 1866, which forbade dismissals of army and
navy officers in time of peace except by sentence of court-martial.

The doctrine of the Myers case was limited in Humphrey's
Executor v. United States, 295 U.S. 602, 55 S.Ct. 869, 79 L.Ed. 1611
(1935); in that case, a statutory restriction upon the President's power
of removal was upheld because the office in question was in its nature
quasi-legislative and quasi-judicial rather than executive. Then, however, it was decided in Morgan v. Tennessee Valley Authority, 115
F.2d 990 (6th Cir. 1940), certiorari denied, 312 U.S. 701, 61 S.Ct. 806,
85 L.Ed. 1135 (1941), that where an office was predominantly, if not
wholly, executive in nature, Congress could not constitutionally limit
the President's right of removal.

The possible effect of the Myers case on the right of the President to remove military officers without restriction was treated by
Colby, 15 Geo.L.J. 168-73 (1927), who pointed out that Congress has
long provided for removal from office in addition to court-martial
dismissal for cause. See note following Beard v. Stahr, infra. Actually, however, there has been no application of the Myers, Humphrey,
and Morgan cases to military personnel.

---

### BEARD v. STAHR

Supreme Court of the United States, 1962.
370 U.S. 41, 82 S.Ct. 1105, 8 L.Ed.2d 321.

PER CURIAM.
The judgment of the District Court is vacated and the cause is
remanded with directions to dismiss the complaint. The action is
premature. The appellant will not be removed from the active list of
the Regular Army unless the Secretary of the Army exercises the
discretionary authority to remove him conferred by 10 U.S.C. §3794.
The Secretary has not stated that he will so exercise his discretion
as to remove appellant. If the Secretary does not remove the appellant it will be unnecessary to pass on the constitutional objections
which have been urged. If appellant is removed, the Court is satisfied that adequate procedures for seeking redress will be open to him.
Compare Aircraft & Diesel Corp. v. Hirsch, 331 U.S. 752, 772-773.
Accordingly, the application for a stay is denied.

The CHIEF JUSTICE is of the opinion that further consideration of the question of jurisdiction should be postponed to the hearing of the case on the merits and would grant the application for a stay.

MR. JUSTICE FRANKFURTER took no part in the decision of this case.

MR. JUSTICE DOUGLAS, with whom MR. JUSTICE BLACK concurs, dissenting.

Appellant is a Major in the Regular Army and has the temporary rank of Lieutenant Colonel. He served in World War II and received the Bronze Star Medal. He at present has had over 19 years of active federal service and will be eligible for retirement in November 1962. But for the present charge against him his military record reflects exemplary conduct and high efficiency ratings.

These years of faithful service have now gone largely for naught under a decision of an Army Board of Review recommending that he be given a general discharge. Whatever the merits may be, I believe that the procedure used at his hearing violated our standards of fairness.

Under the statute here in question, 10 U.S.C. §3792 (c), an officer faced with a charge carries the burden of proof that "he should be retained on the active list."

The District Court held that there was no constitutional objection to placing this burden of proof on the officer. 200 F. Supp. 766, 775. It reasoned that since the President could dismiss an officer summarily,* Congress could place on the one removed "the onus of convincing his superiors that he should not be eliminated." Ibid. Dismissal is one thing; dismissal with stigma, as here, is quite another. Dismissal with stigma is a severe penalty. In comparable situations, the Government has been required to carry the burden of proof. Kwong Hai Chew v. Rogers, 103 U.S. App. D. C. 228, 257 F. 2d 606; Wood v. Hoy, 266 F. 2d 825, 830. Unless this burden is meticulously maintained, discharge for race, for religion, for political opinion, or for beliefs may masquerade under unproved charges. This right, like the right to be heard, is basic to our society. Cf. Joint Anti-Fascist Refugee Committee v. McGrath, 341 U.S. 123, 168 (concurring opinion); Beilan v. Board of Education, 357 U.S. 399, 421-423 (dissenting opinion); Wieman v. Updegraff, 344 U.S. 183, 191.

There is a second reason why we should remand this case for a new hearing. The one witness whose testimony was critical to the case was not called. Confrontation and cross-examination are, as I understand the law, vital when one's employment rights are involved (see Greene v. McElroy, 360 U.S. 474, 496)--the factor that distinguishes

---

*Which, of course, is a mistaken premise. See Wiener v. United States, 357 U.S. 349; Blake v. United States, 103 U.S. 227, 231.

Cafeteria Workers v. McElroy, 367 U.S. 886, where the only question was access to a military base. Perhaps the missing accuser--whose activities were described in uncomplimentary terms in Rittenour v. District of Columbia, 163 A. 2d 558--would have made such an unbecoming witness that the Board would have dismissed the charges. Faceless informers are often effective if they need not take the stand. A fair hearing requires the production of the accuser so that cross-examination can test his character and reliability. That question is very close to the one involved in No. 1123, Misc., Williams v. Zuckert, in which we granted certiorari only the other day. 369 U.S. 884. This case should be heard with that one.

I think the present case is ripe for review. Once the Secretary of the Army approves the decision now challenged, appellant will be severed from military service with less than an honorable discharge. If a wrong was committed, I assume that he could recover a judgment that restores any loss of salary or pension. More than dollars, however, are involved: at stake is a man's professional standing, his character, and his claim to an honorable discharge. Where the Army departs from the statutory standard which prescribes the basis on which discharges will be issued, the federal courts can intervene. See Harmon v. Brucker, 355 U.S. 579. Though the Court's opinion may be read as indicating that a collateral proceeding to set aside one discharge and to direct that an honorable one be granted may lie, we should nonetheless halt this irregular procedure in limine. For we are dealing here with the charge of "conduct unbecoming an officer," a charge that carries a heavy stigma. As Winthrop said: "Though it need not amount to a crime, it must offend so seriously against law, justice, morality or decorum as to expose to disgrace, socially or as a man, the offender, and at the same time must be of such a nature or committed under such circumstances as to bring dishonor or disrepute upon the military profession which he represents." Military Law and Precedents (2d ed. 1896) 1104.

If declaratory relief will be accorded, as it certainly could be (Bland v. Connally, 110 U.S. App. D. C. 375, 293 F. 2d 852), this action for an injunction is timely to prevent an injustice. As recently stated: "We think it must be conceded that any discharge characterized as less than honorable will result in serious injury. It not only means the loss of numerous benefits in both the federal and state systems, but it also results in an unmistakable social stigma which greatly limits the opportunities for both public and private civilian employment." 110 U.S. App. D. C. 375, 381, 293 F. 2d 852, 858.

I would reverse the judgment below and direct that appellant be accorded a hearing that comports with the requirements of due process.

In addition to dismissal and dropping from the rolls, considered above, an officer can be separated from the Army by discharge, resignation, or operation of law.

1. Discharge: Officers can be discharged pursuant to elimination proceedings for substandard performance of duties, 10 U.S.C. §§3781-3787 (1964), and for moral or professional dereliction or in the interests of national security, 10 U.S.C. §§3791-3797 (1964). General guidelines for discharges under these sections are found at A.R. 635-195, para. 2 (1968). The rights of an officer in this type of proceeding, considered in Beard v. Stahr, supra, are contained in 10 U.S.C. §3785 (1964), and in 10 U.S.C. §3795 (1964). In addition, an officer may be discharged if he fails to be selected for promotion twice and is not eligible for retirement, 10 U.S.C. §3303 (d) (3) (1964); or if he has less than three years of service, 10 U.S.C. §3814 (1964). Officers who are discharged are furnished with one of the following discharge certificates (A.R. 635-100, para. 1-4 [1970]):

| Type of discharge | Characterization of discharge |
| --- | --- |
| Honorable | Honorable |
| General | Under honorable conditions |
| Discharge | Under other than honorable conditions |

2. Resignation: The most important types of resignation are unqualified resignation, A.R. 635-120, para. 3 (1968), resignation in lieu of elimination, id., para 4, and resignation for the good of the service, id., para. 5.

Under A.R. 635-120, para. 4-1, an officer may tender a resignation in lieu of elimination if he has been recommended for elimination by the convening authority of a court-martial or if he has been selected for elimination pursuant to 10 U.S.C. §3781 or §3791 (1964). Elimination action is suspended pending a final determination by the Department of Army Headquarters on the tender of resignation. A.R. 635-120, para. 4-1 (c).

"An officer may submit a resignation for the good of the service when--(1) General court-martial charges are pending against him (2) He is under a suspended sentence of dismissal or (3) He elects to tender his resignation . . . prior to general court-martial charges being preferred against him [for homosexuality]." A.R. 635-120, para. 5-1 (a) (1970). The tender of resignation under these circumstances does not necessarily preclude or suspend disciplinary proceedings. Id., para. 5-1 (b).

3. Operation of Law: In addition to termination by appointment by the President of a successor with advice and consent of the Senate, an officer's appointment is terminated by operation of law under the following circumstances, among others: acceptance of any civil office, 10 U.S.C. §973 (Supp.V, 1970); acceptance of citizenship in a foreign country, with the resulting loss of United States citizenship, 10 U.S.C. §3285 (1) (1964); conviction for receiving a bribe, 18 U.S.C. §201 (1964); concealment, removal, or mutilation of public records, 18 U.S.C. §2071 (1964); treason, 18 U.S.C. §2381 (1964); advocation of the overthrow of the government, 18 U.S.C. §2385 (1964); encouragement of insubordination, disloyalty, or mutiny, 18 U.S.C. §2387 (1964).

Regarding retirement, there are two broad categories: voluntary and mandatory. A regular commissioned officer with at least twenty years of service may retire pursuant to 10 U.S.C. §3911 (1964) if at least ten years of his service has been as a commissioned officer. With at least thirty years of service, an officer may be retired at the discretion of the President. 10 U.S.C. §3918 (1964). After forty years of service, an officer shall be retired upon his request. 10 U.S.C. §3924 (1964). See also 10 U.S.C. §§3919, 3920 (1964).

Regular commissioned officers are subject to mandatory retirement for age, 10 U.S.C. §§3883-3886 (Supp.V, 1970), and for length of service, 10 U.S.C. §§3916, 3921, 3922, 3923 (1964), as amended, (Supp. V, 1970). If an officer is not recommended for promotion under 10 U.S.C. §3303 (c) (1964), he will be retired pursuant to 10 U.S.C. §3913 (a) (1964), as amended, (Supp.V, 1970) if he has at least twenty years of service. If he is within two years of becoming eligible for retirement, he must be retained on the active list until he completes twenty years of service. 10 U.S.C. §3913 (b) (1964). If he is not recommended for promotion under 10 U.S.C. 3303, supra, and is not eligible for retirement or within two years of eligibility, he is given an honorable discharge, with severance pay. 10 U.S.C. §3303 (d) (3) (1964).

In addition, an officer can be granted a request for retirement by the Secretary of the Army under 10 U.S.C. §§3786 (b) or 3796 (b) (1964) in lieu of elimination proceedings, if he is otherwise qualified for retirement.

PART

III

MILITARY

JUSTICE

Throughout Anglo-American history there have been separate systems of criminal justice for civilians and members of the armed forces. The reason for different systems is that they are designed to solve wholly different problems. Civilian criminal justice is designed in the main to deter individuals from abnormal or unconventional behavior in communities where there are few, if any, restrictions on, for example, their freedom to travel, or their selection of employment, residence, or mode of dress. Military justice, on the other hand, is designed to control individuals in very peculiar circumstances, such as combat, and to require from them the performance of oftentimes disagreeable and undesirable tasks. The soldier may not go where and when he pleases; he may not choose his job or quit if he doesn't like what he is ordered to do; he lives under abnormal conditions; and he is told what to wear. In short, the military justice system is designed to implement discipline as well as to punish obvious criminal conduct.

The following chapters provide an analysis of the current system of military justice in the United States. The sources and scope of military law are examined prior to a detailed consideration of courts-martial. Chapter 11 concerns the reviewability of decisions of courts-martial by civilian Courts.

Ex parte BRIGHT

Supreme Court of the Territory of Utah, 1874.
1 Utah 145.

On the 14th day of February, 1874, a verified petition, of which the following is a copy, was presented to the Chief Justice, to wit:

To the Honorable James B. McKean, Chief Justice of the Territory of Utah:

Your petitioner, Henry A. Morrow, for cause of complaint to your honor, states: That Frederick Bright is an enlisted private soldier in the Thirteenth Regiment (Company C), in the army of the United States, and belongs to the command of your petitioner, who is the officer in command of the forces of the United States stationed at Camp Douglas, in the Territory of Utah; that on the 12th day of February, 1874, said Bright was arrested by the police authorities of the corporation of Salt Lake City, and is now confined under a warrant of commitment, (a copy of which is hereto attached,) by one John D. T. McAllister, City Marshal; and that the alleged cause of his confinement is, that said Bright was guilty of violating an ordinance of said corporation forbidding drunkenness and disorderly conduct; that the sentence under which he is confined, as appears from said warrant, is that he pay a fine of five dollars, and, in default of payment, that he be imprisoned at labor on the public works of said city, at one dollar per day and board, until said fine is paid. All of which is illegal, as your petitioner is informed and believes, in this:--

That said Bright is not subject to the jurisdiction of said corporate authority for the offense charged.

That said sentence and judgment, having been rendered by one Jeter Clinton, a Justice of the Peace, for a violation of said ordinance, is void for want of jurisdiction.

. . .

Upon this petition a writ of <u>habeas corpus</u> was issued, and
Bright was brought before the Chief Justice. The return to the writ
corroborated the facts, alleged in the petition, and, after argument of
counsel, the soldier was discharged from custody. The city brought
an appeal to this court.

McKEAN, C. J., delivered the Opinion of the Court.
In our country the army derives its existence from the civil
government; and it can be controlled, increased, diminished, or
abolished by that government, either in time of war or of peace.
While it exists it is as amenable to the government as is any other
creature or authority emanating therefrom. "The Congress shall have
power, . . . to constitute tribunals inferior to the Supreme Court, . . .
to raise and support armies, . . . to provide and maintain a navy, . . .
to make rules for the government and regulation of the land and naval
forces." (Constitution, Art. 1, sec. 8.) Martial law and military law
are by no means the same thing. When a military chieftain, in time
of war, or in some great emergency, proclaims martial law, he may
limit its operation to a very narrow range, or he may make himself
a dictator whose word is law, save in so far as international law and
civilization require him to respect and enforce other laws. What
martial law is or may be depends so much upon the discretion of the
commander who proclaims it, that a description of its exercise in one
instance, would rarely describe it in any other.
Military law, however, is as clearly defined a system of laws
as are the statute and common laws, or the statute and civil laws,
prevailing in any State of the Union. Military law consists of the
Articles of War enacted by Congress; the Regulations and Instructions
sanctioned by the President; the orders of commanding officers; and
certain usages or customs constituting the unwritten or common law
of the army. These, taken together, are the law military of the land.
This law applies only to the army. Martial law has a wider scope,
and applies as well to the inhabitants of the country or district over
which it is proclaimed. Martial law now exists nowhere in the United
States, while military law must exist so long as we have an army.
. . .
We have therefore reached the following conclusions:
1st. That a soldier of the National army can be demanded by
and surrendered to the civil authorities, to be tried and punished by
them, only when he is charged with an offence, in time of peace, "such
as is punishable by the known laws of the land," that is, by the laws of
the United States, or of a State or Territory.
2d. That a city by-law or ordinance is not in this sense a law
of the land; but that a soldier who, when off duty, violates the ordinance of Salt Lake City forbidding drunkenness and disorderly conduct, may, in the absence of a Provost guard, be arrested in the act

and restrained by the civil authorities, but may not be tried and punished by them.

3d. That in case of such arrest and restraint, it is the duty of the civil authorities to deliver over such soldier to the military authorities, on the demand of the latter; and the duty of the military authorities to enforce against him the law military forbidding such offence.

4th. That if the civil authorities, after arresting such offender, refuse to deliver him over on such demand, or proceed to try and punish him, the military authorities may take him by force.

5th. That if, instead of resorting to force, the military authorities present a petition to a Federal Court or Judge of the Territory, the prisoner must be discharged from the custody of the civil authorities by the writ of habeas corpus.

The judgment appealed from must be affirmed.

. . .

The Articles of War, Chapter II of the National Defense Act of June 4, 1920, 41 Stat. 787, as amended (10 U.S.C. old §§1471 ff.) served as the basis of the code of military law for the army until the Uniform Code of Military Justice (UCMJ) went into effect, May 31, 1951. The act of June 25, 1948, 62 Stat. 1014, extended the Articles of War to the newly created United States Air Force.

The Articles for the Government of the Navy were set forth in R.S. §1624, 34 U.S.C. old §1200, primarily deriving from the act of July 17, 1862, itself tracing back to the act of July 1, 1797. These articles, with but minor changes and additions, were valid until the UCMJ went into effect. The AGN applied to members of the Coast Guard in time of war, act of Aug. 29, 1916, 39 Stat. 600, 14 U.S.C. §4f; in time of peace the Coast Guard was governed by the Disciplinary Laws of the Coast Guard, act of Aug. 4, 1949, 63 Stat. 538, 14 U.S.C. §§561 ff.

The act of May 5, 1950, 64 Stat. 108, 50 U.S.C. 551 ff. superseded the Articles of War and the Articles for the Government of the Navy and established the Uniform Code of Military Justice (UCMJ) applicable to all the Armed Services. The UCMJ was thereafter revised, codified, and enacted into law as part of Title 10, United States Code by the act of August 10, 1956 (70 A Stat. 1) and was subsequently further amended (see 10 U.S.C. 801-940). The act of October 24, 1968 (82 Stat. 1335) was the most recent amendment of the UCMJ.

## UNITED STATES v. LUCAS

United States Court of Military Appeals, 1951.
1 U.S.C.M.A. 19, 1 C.M.R. 19.

GEORGE W. LATIMER, Judge:
This cause comes to this court by certificate of the Judge Advocate General of the Navy pursuant to Article 67(b) (2) of the Uniform Code of Military Justice (Act of May 5, 1950, 64 Stat 108; 50 U.S.C. §§551-736). The particular point certified is whether or not the board of review erred in setting aside the conviction of the accused because a special court-martial failed to proceed in the manner required by Articles 51(a), 51(c), and 52 of the Uniform Code of Military Justice, and paragraph 73, Manual for Courts-Martial, 1951. The government seeks to have the decision of the board of review reversed and the accused contends the decision should be affirmed. In this decision we will refer to the Uniform Code of Military Justice as the "Code" and the Manual for Courts-Martial, 1951, as the "Manual."
. . .
In order to dispose of the certified question, it becomes necessary to construe subsections (a) and (c) of Article 51 and subsection (a) (2) of Article 52 of the Code, and their relationship to paragragh 73(b) of the Manual.
Subsection (a) of Article 51 of the Code provides as follows:

> "Voting by members of a general or special court-martial upon questions of challenge, on the findings, and on the sentence shall be by secret written ballot. The junior members of the court shall in each case count the votes, which count shall be checked by the president who shall forthwith announce the result of the ballot to the members of the court." (Italics ours)

Subsection (c) of the same article reads:

> "Before a vote is taken on the findings, the law officer of a general court-martial and the president of a special court-martial shall, in the presence of the accused and counsel, instruct the court as to the elements of the offense and charge the court--
> "(1) that the accused must be presumed to be innocent until his guilt is established by legal and competent evidence beyond reasonable doubt;
> "(2) that in the case being considered, if there is a reasonable doubt as to the guilt of the accused, the doubt shall be resolved in favor of the accused and he shall be acquitted;

"(3)  that if there is a reasonable doubt as to the degree of guilt, the finding must be in a lower degree as to which there is no reasonable doubt; and

"(4)  that the burden of proof to establish the guilt of the accused beyond reasonable doubt is upon the Government."

In compiling the Manual, the wording of Article 51(c) was changed and the law officer was required to charge the court in all cases.  Paragraph 73(b) of the Manual provides that after instructing the court as to the elements of each offense charged the law officer (president in special courts-martial) shall in all cases, including those in which a plea of guilty has been entered, charge the court on the four elements set forth in Article 51(c) of the Code, supra.  It will thus be observed that, while the Code does not require that the charge be given in those cases where a plea of guilty has been entered, the Manual does.

For the purposes of this case we can and do hold that the act of Congress (the Code) and the act of the Executive (the Manual) are on the same level and that the ordinary rules of statutory construction apply.  In that event the general rule is that statutes dealing with the same subject should, if possible, be so construed that effect is given to every provision of each.  Moreover, in dealing with each, its provisions should be construed so that no part will be inoperative, superfluous, void or ineffective.

The provisions of paragraph 73 of the Manual are clear and unambiguous and we can construe that section's provisions to be applicable without doing violation to the language of the Code.  The addition of the words "including those in which a plea of guilty has been entered" may place an additional burden upon the law officer and the president of courts-martial not expressly imposed by the Code, but the requirement encompassed within the phrase is not prohibited by the Code.  There is nothing in it which states that the law officer or president of a court-martial need not instruct the members of the court.  Silence on the part of Congress does not necessarily require like silence on the part of the Executive when, as here, the President has been expressly authorized to prescribe rules of procedure for courts-martial (Uniform Code of Military Justice, Article 36).  While we may be unable to ascertain any virtue in the additional requirement, we cannot ignore the plain meaning of the language used.

To be consistent with the foregoing principles, we hold that the provisions of Section 73 of the Manual are mandatory and should be complied with by the law officer and the president of courts-martial and that failure to follow out the mandate as required by that section when a plea of guilty is entered is error as a matter of law.

.  .  .

Paragraph 73b, MCM has been revised so as to require the charge to the Court "in all cases in which a not guilty plea has been entered and, when appropriate, in cases in which a plea of guilty to all charges and specifications has been entered. . . ."

## UNITED STATES v. JENKINS

United States Court of Military Appeals, 1956.
7 U.S.C.M.A. 261, 22 C.M.R. 51.

HOMER FERGUSON, Judge:
The accused was convicted by general court-martial of fraudulent enlistment, a purported violation of Article 83, Uniform Code of Military Justice, 50 USC §677, and larceny of a wrist-watch, a violation of Article 121, Uniform Code of Military Justice, 50 USC §715. He was sentenced to a dishonorable discharge, total forfeitures, and confinement for eighteen months. The convening authority and a board of review in the Army Judge Advocate General's office approved the findings and sentence. We granted review on the question as to whether an entry into the service by induction is included within the provisions of Article 83 of the Code.
. . .
Article 83 of the Code reads in part that any person who "procures his own enlistment or appointment in the armed forces by means of knowingly false representations or deliberate concealment" and receives pay and allowances thereunder shall be punished as a court-martial may direct. Paragraph 162, Manual for Courts-Martial United States, 1951, in discussing Article 83, contains the statement that "The term enlistment includes induction or any other means of entry into service in an armed force." If possible, provisions of the Code and the Manual will be reconciled; however, if the Manual in an authorized area conflicts with the Code, the latter must prevail. United States v Lucas, 1 USCMA 19, 1 CMR 19, and United States v LaGrange, 1 USCMA 342, 3 CMR 76. The power to prescribe rules provided for in the Manual is derived from Article 36 of the Code, 50 USC §611, which declares that the President may prescribe procedure, including modes of proof, provided that in this limited field nothing promulgated by the Manual shall be contrary or inconsistent with the Code. Modes of proof, as referred to by Article 36, according to the legislative history of the Act, mean only rules of evidence. See

Hearings before the House Committee on Armed Services, 81st Congress, 1st Session, on HR 2498, page 1016 et seq. It follows, therefore, that if Congress did not include inductees within the provisions of Article 83, the Manual interpretation cannot enlarge the scope of the Article and bring people within its provisions never contemplated by Congress. Such an enlargement could hardly be considered a procedural matter or a mode of proof, but would be more in the nature of a substantive rule of law. Maurizi v Western Coal and Mining Company, 321 Mo 378, 11 SW2d 268; King v Shumacher, 32 Cal App2d 172, 89 P2d 466, cert den 1939, 308 US 593, 60 S Ct 123, 84 L ed 496.

. . .

It would have been a simple matter--had the drafters of Article 83 been so minded--to have worded that Article to include inducted persons. Congress expressly failed to utilize such language and we cannot, in view of the clear wording of the statute, effect a different meaning from the Article. We therefore hold that Article 83 does not include inductees. The board of review decision with respect to the fraudulent enlistment charge is reversed and the charge dismissed. The record is returned to The Judge Advocate General of the Army for referral to a board of review for reconsideration of the sentence.

Chief Judge QUINN and Judge LATIMER concur.

In United States v. Rinehart, 8 U.S.C.M.A. 402, 24 C.M.R. 212 (1957), Judge FERGUSON stated in part for the Court of Military Appeals (COMA):

One further matter merits discussion. In the recent case of United States v Boswell, 8 USCMA 145, 23 CMR 369, we voiced our disapproval of the practice of permitting court members to consult "outside sources" for information on the law. We there said that "the Manual is no different from other legal authorities. It, too, has no place in the closed session deliberations of the court-martial." It was pointed out that court members may not understand the Manual's passages thereby creating an atmosphere of confusion and doubt during the closed deliberations. What was prophesied in Boswell, supra, has now come to pass. The prosecution in closing argument had directed the court's attention to paragraphs 76a(5) and 33h of the Manual. The court-martial in closed session, and on its own initiative, "discovered" paragraphs 76a(3) and 76a(4) of the Manual, neither paragraph being material in arriving at an appropriate sentence.  Thus a virtual race to the Manual had begun in spite of the fact that the law officer had fully and adequately instructed the members on the applicable law pertaining to the sentence.

We cannot sanction a practice which permits court members to rummage through a treatise on military law, such as the Manual, indiscriminately rejecting and applying a myriad of principles--judicial and otherwise--contained therein.  The consequences that flow from such a situation are manifold.  In the first place, many of the passages contained therein have been either expressly or impliedly invalidated by decisions of this Court. . . .  Secondly, we have consistently emphasized the role of the law officer in the instructional area.  In United States v Chaput, 2 USCMA 127, 7 CMR 3, we said that, "It is fundamental that the only appropriate source of the law applicable to any case should come from the law officer."  See also United States v Ginn, 1 USCMA 453, 4 CMR 45; United States v Beasley, 3 USCMA 111, 11 CMR 111.  Recently in United States v Wilson, 7 USCMA 713, 23 CMR 177, Judge Latimer, speaking on behalf of the Court, said:

> "We have said on numerous occasions that it is the law officer who is in charge of the trial proceedings and responsible for its orderly conduct.  One of his most important functions is to give adequate, comprehensive instructions on the issues of the case.  The trial of a criminal case is not a game to be regulated by the whims of counsel.  If we are to build a real system of military justice, we must ensure that the law officer is shouldered with the responsibility of seeing to it that the court-martial members are given proper guideposts to reach a fair and just verdict, . . ."

Thirdly, the great majority of court members are untrained in the law.  A treatise on the law in the hands of a nonlawyer creates a situation which is fraught with potential harm, especially when one's life and liberty hang in the balance.  We have absolutely no way of knowing whether a court-martial applied the law instructed upon by the law officer or whether it rejected such instructions in favor of other material contained in the Manual.  In United States v Chaput, supra, we reversed a conviction where a law officer had referred the court members to several board of review decisions to permit them to determine for themselves the applicable legal principles involved.  In the course of our opinion, we said:

> ". . . Notwithstanding the fact that the law officer acted and was motivated by what he considered to be the best means to inform the court as to the issue under discussion, nevertheless, the members of the court are not

learned in the law and they should not be given the responsibility of reading cases to determine the elements
of an offense."

In United States v Lowry, 4 USCMA 448, 16 CMR 22, we condemned
the practice wherein the law officer, in his instructions, provided the
court members with a list of cases for outside reference. We said
that if the court-martial is permitted to use them "for the purpose of
determining for themselves what law should be applied to the case,
then prejudice is present."

In civilian practice it would constitute a gross irregularity to
permit jurors to consult outside legal references. A case closely in
point is United States v Gordon, -- F2d -- (CA7th Cir), decided July
16, 1957. There jurors were furnished a pamphlet entitled "Handbook for Jurors," which was prepared for the use of jurors in the
Federal courts by the Administrative Office of the United States
Courts, upon the direction and under the supervision of the Committee
on the Operation of the Jury System upon authorization of the Judicial
Conference of the United States. Five United States District Court
Judges, who served as members of the Committee which prepared the
handbook, were listed. Many of the statements contained therein were
erroneous and misleading. The Court of Appeals held that the use of
such handbook constituted prejudicial error. . . . We see no compelling reason why a similar rule should not be adopted in courts-
martial practice. All the law a court-martial need know in order to
properly perform its functions must come from the law officer and
nowhere else.

We are fully aware that the change in the system of military
law occasioned by this decision represents a substantial departure
from prior service practices. However, we cannot but feel that such
change was imperatively needed if the system of military law is to
assume and maintain the high and respected place that it deserves in
the jurisprudence of our free society. Prior to the Code courts-
martial were neither instructed on the elements of the offense charged
nor the principles of law applicable to the case. The deliberations of
the court were in camera and a genuine need then existed for the use
of the Manual by the court members in determining the law to be
applied. However, with the advent of the Uniform Code of Military
Justice many of the problems which previously existed under the old
system disappeared. Congress created the role of law officer and
fashioned him in the image of a civilian judge. He was charged with
the responsibility of instructing the court on the elements of the offense and the applicable principles of law in order that informed and
intelligent findings and sentence could be reached. In a word, he was
made a fountainhead of the law in the court-martial scheme of things.
The sum total of these and other remedial changes inaugurated by the
Code was to bring court-martial procedure, wherever possible, into

conformity with that prevailing in civilian criminal courts. We believe that military law under the Code has come of age and the time has come when the use of the Manual by the court-martial must end.

This case is discussed in 72 Harv. L. Rev. 388 (1958) and 19 La. L. Rev. 715 (1959). The case was followed in United States v. Dobbs, 11 U.S.C.M.A. 328, 29 C.M.R. 144 (1960), but distinguished in United States v. Lewandowski, 17 U.S.C.M.A. 51, 37 C.M.R. 315 (1967).

## UNITED STATES v. SMITH

United States Court of Military Appeals, 1962.
13 U.S.C.M.A. 105, 32 C.M.R. 105.

KILDAY, Judge:

A general court-martial convened at Tachikawa Air Base, Japan, tried accused upon a charge of committing a lewd and lascivious act upon the body of his adopted seven-year-old daughter, in violation of Article 134 of the Uniform Code of Military Justice, 10 USC §934. In the course of those proceedings and, prior to the receipt of other testimony, the law officer received into evidence the pretrial statement of the accused. It will suffice to point out that accused's confession contained statements fully adequate to establish his guilt of the offense charged.

. . .

In his post-trial review the staff judge advocate concluded that the evidence of record, aliunde the accused's confession, fell short of meeting the military rule which requires a showing that the offense charged was probably committed by someone. Therefore, he recommended that the conviction and punishment be disapproved and a rehearing ordered. The convening authority, however, rejected the recommendation of the staff judge advocate and approved the findings and sentence.

The board of review reached the same conclusion as the staff judge advocate. It held that the corroboration of accused's confession was insufficient and that the law officer erred in permitting the court-martial to consider the same. Accordingly, the board set aside the findings of guilty and the sentence and dismissed the charge.

The Acting The Judge Advocate General of the Air Force has certified, under Article 67(b) (2), Uniform Code of Military Justice,

10 USC §867, two issues for decision by this Court. The first question inquires:

> "WAS THE BOARD OF REVIEW CORRECT IN
> HOLDING THAT AS A MATTER OF LAW THE COURT-
> MARTIAL SHOULD NOT HAVE BEEN PERMITTED TO
> CONSIDER THE ACCUSED'S CONFESSION?

Government counsel contend, in the first instance, that the corroboration in this case is sufficient when tested by the rule prescribed in paragraph 140a of the Manual for Courts-Martial, United States, 1951. Second, they assert that the corroborative evidence is sufficient when tested under the rule adopted by the Supreme Court of the United States in the case of Opper v United States, 348 US 84, 99 L ed 101, 75 S Ct 158 (1954).

The first contention need not delay us, as we are in agreement with the holding of the board of review. As we view the record, the evidence in corroboration of the accused's confession is insufficient, under the standards required by paragraph 140a of the Manual, supra, as the same have been construed and applied by the decisions of this Court, to establish the probability that the offense charged was committed. [Citing cases.]

We next proceed to a discussion of whether this Court should, or, conforming to Article 36, Uniform Code of Military Justice, 10 USC §836, and paragraph 140a of the Manual, supra, may, adopt the rule enunciated by the Supreme Court in Opper v United States, supra.

Appellate Government counsel candidly acknowledge that this Court has previously had the rule announced in Opper urged upon it "as one which commends itself for adoption by the military justice system." Counsel for the Government also concede that this Court has consistently refused to adopt such rule. However, they point out that members of the Court have not reached a common ground for their decisions. In effect, it is pointed out that, with changes in the composition of the Court, different reasons have been expressed for their holdings by different Judges. It is quite true that different reasons have been expressed; however, a majority of the Court has always sustained the rule as delineated in paragraph 140a of the Manual for Courts-Martial.

. . .

While the presence or absence of a corpus delicti, or the necessity that there be evidence to corroborate a confession, seems clearly to be a matter of substantive law, text writers, legal encyclopedias, and other authorities seem generally to consider the proof thereof to be a rule of procedure or a rule of evidence. . . .

. . .

Having established that the Constitution vests in Congress the power to make rules for the government and regulation of the armed forces, we must next consider the validity of a delegation by Congress

to the President, or another agency of Government, of any portion of
that power.

. . .

Thus the rule is well established that Congress may delegate to
the President, and other administrative officers, and to various agencies of government, the power to make regulations to fill up details
and implement statutory provisions, or to determine the details of the
legislative scheme. And, further, when regulations are so adopted,
they "have the force of law."

. . .

We conclude that Article 36, Uniform Code of Military Justice,
supra, falls within the category considered above. Accordingly, we
hold it is a valid delegation to the President of the power, by regulations, to prescribe the modes of proof before courts-martial.

That brings us to the critical question in the case at bar:
Whether paragraph 140a, supra, is a valid exercise of the power thus
delegated and, as such, carrying the force of law. Some of the cases
in this Court, in referring to paragraph 140a, state the same "is binding on this Court." This is possibly unfortunate language insofar as
it may carry a connotation that this Court is in anywise bound by
Presidential directives or regulations any more than is any other
court. Manifestly, any such implication must be rejected. But, at the
same time, we fully agree that a valid regulation promulgated by the
President, in conformity with a power properly delegated to him by
the Congress, has the force of law and is entitled to consideration by
this Court, as by all others, in that light.

As pointed out previously, that portion of paragraph 140a stating
"An accused cannot legally be convicted upon his uncorroborated confession or admission," appears to be substantive in nature. However,
as has also been noted earlier, that is a well recognized, indeed, a
cardinal principle. As such, it is stating the obvious to note that it
does not suffer any diminution in validity because the President directed that it be included in the Manual. It must be remembered that
in many instances facilities for legal research are not readily available, so it is wholly understandable--perhaps even desirable--that the
Manual, as a handy compendium on military justice, include statements
concerning substantive principles of law. The fact that it does so,
however, neither adds nor detracts from the validity of the rule set
forth, as Congress did not delegate to the President the authority to
fix substantive rules. In any event, in this instance the principle set
forth is clearly correct, so the matter need be of no concern to us.

What, then, of the balance of the Manual provision hereinbefore
quoted? As we have previously noted, the mode and manner of proof
of the so called corpus delicti is a matter of the laws of evidence.
Being such, it falls quite squarely within the authority delegated to
the President by the Congress in Article 36 of the Uniform Code,
supra. Accordingly, that portion of paragraph 140a, not being

contrary to or inconsistent with the Code, and not conflicting with other Manual provisions or principles of military justice, is a valid exercise of the delegated power, and has the force of law.

. . .

Both certified questions are answered in the affirmative and the decision of the board of review is affirmed.

Judge FERGUSON concurs.

[Dissenting opinion of Mr. Chief Judge Quinn omitted.]

The controversy in the principal case has been resolved by the rewriting of paragraph 140a of the MCM to accord with the current Federal practice. Section 3061 of Title 10, United States Code reads in its entirety: "The President may prescribe regulations for the government of the Army."

## UNITED STATES ex rel. HIRSCHBERG v. COOKE*

Supreme Court of the United States, 1949.
336 U.S. 210, 69 S.Ct. 530, 93 L.Ed. 621.

*[Footnotes have been omitted.  Ed.]

MR. JUSTICE BLACK delivered the opinion of the Court.

This case raises important questions concerning the statutory jurisdiction of general courts-martial of the Navy.

. . .

Accepting as we do the long-standing Army and Navy interpretation of the Articles previously referred to, an interpretation which necessarily would deny jurisdiction to the court-martial here, there remains the contention that the Navy has by a recent congressionally authorized regulation acquired such jurisdiction for its courts-martial. 34 U. S. C. §591 authorizes the Secretary of the Navy, with the approval of the President, to adopt and alter regulations and orders for control of the Navy. The Government claims that a regulation adopted pursuant to this authority has been promulgated, and that it vested the necessary power in this court-martial to try petitioner. This authorized regulation, it is contended, had the force of law, Ex parte Reed, 100 U.S. 13, 22, and consequently supplants the prior statutes which, as interpreted, had denied the jurisdiction here asserted. There has been considerable argument as to whether the language of the Navy regulation was sufficiently precise to endow it with the force of law. Passing over this argument, however, we are not able to agree that the Navy could in this manner acquire the expanded court-martial jurisdiction it claimed. For we cannot construe 34 U. S. C. §591 as permitting the Navy to extend its court-martial jurisdiction beyond the limits Congress had fixed. United States v. Symonds, 120 U.S. 46, 49-50.

The regulation stands no better if it be considered merely as an evidence of a revised naval interpretation of the Article. This revised naval interpretation was given in 1932. Before that time, both Army and Navy had for more than half a century acted on the implicit assumption that discharged servicemen, whether re-enlisted or not, were no longer subject to court-martial power. The Attorney General of the United States had proceeded on the same assumption. And see United States v. Kelly, 15 Wall. 34, 36. Under these circumstances, little weight can be given to the 1932 separate effort of the Navy to change the long-accepted understanding of its statutory court-martial power. For should this belated naval interpretation be accepted as correct, there would be left outstanding an Army interpretation of its statutory court-martial powers directly opposed to that of the Navy. Since the Army and Navy court-martial powers depend on substantially the same statutory foundations, the opposing interpretations cannot both be right, unless it be assumed that Congress has left each free to determine its own court-martial boundaries. We cannot assume that Congress intended a delegation of such broad power in an area which so vitally affects the rights and liberties of those who are now, have been, or may be associated with the Nation's armed forces.

Reversed.

Additional sources of military law besides statues, regulations and orders (see U.S. v. Brown, infra) are materials that may be loosely termed "judicial opinions". Opinions of the Judge Advocate General of the Army, including therein opinions of the Office, Judge Advocate General's Department (or Corps), decisions of the Board of Review, or Judicial Council. Full opinions of the JAG of the army were published for the years 1917 to 1919. Digest of Opinions from 1862 to 1912 in Howland, Dig. Op. JAG; cf. Winthrop, Dig. Op. JAG; (to 1895). Further digests of opinions are: 1912-17 Dig. Op. JAG; annual digests 1917 to 1930; 1912-30 Dig. Op. JAG and cumulative supplements; 1912-40 Dig. Op. JAG and supplement; Bull. JAG, vols. I-X (1942-51). For a list of the published opinions of the JAG, see Morse, 1942, 35 L. Lib. J. 476. In addition, there exist: Board of Review Decisions (81 vols.); Board of Review Decisions, European

Theater of Operations (31 vols.); Decisions of the Judicial Council
and the Army Board of Review (4 vols.); Memorandum Opinions of the
JAG Army, Relief under AW 53 (1949-50). For the Judge Advocate
General of the Air Force there have been published Court-Martial
Reports (3 vols.).

A selection of the opinions of the Judge Advocate General of the
Navy prior to 1916 are collected in Naval Digest, 1916. For the period 1916-37, there is a two-volume compilation of digests of opinions
(with an added index volume), entitled Compilation of Court-Martial
Orders. To 1951 opinions are digested in Court-Martial Orders,
issued monthly. As a result of the unification of court-martial procedure under the UCMJ, the series of publications of the JAG have
been revised. Annual volumes of Digests of Opinions, the Judge Advocates General of the Armed Forces, 1951 to date. In addition, there
is a quarterly advance Digest of Opinions.

The decisions of the United States Court of Military Appeals are
officially published in bound volumes (two or more volumes to a term),
and as Advance Opinions in pamphlet form, approximately bi-weekly.
These decisions are also included, along with decisions of the Boards
of Review (now Courts of Military Review) of the various services of
the armed forces, in an unofficial publication, Court-Martial Reports.
Citators and Indices to the latter series are invaluable aids in following up JAG opinions and USCMA decisions, as well as affording references to the citation of orders, laws and regulations in military
judicial opinions. See also Feld, Manual of Courts-Martial Practice,
§2, and Appendix 2.

One other source of military law is the "usages and customs of
the military service," sometimes referred to as "unwritten" law.
See Ex parte Bright, supra; Kirkman v. M'Claughry, 160 F. 436 (CCA,
8th Cir., 1908); and cases in Chapter 12 below.

[See Articles 2, 3 and 5
of the
Uniform Code of Military Justice.]

## OF THE PERSON

Assuming a person is in the military service, when does the jurisdiction of the military end?

### BARRETT v. HOPKINS

Circuit Court of the United States, D. Kansas, 1881.
7 F. 312.

Petition for <u>Habeas Corpus</u>.

The petitioner was, on the sixth of September, 1878, an enlisted soldier in the army of the United States, on duty in Wyoming territory, and on that day unlawfully assaulted and shot another soldier. For this offence he was arrested and held in custody, under charges properly preferred, awaiting the appointment and convening of a court-martial until the following March, 1879, when he was brought before a court-martial, convicted, and sentenced to five years' imprisonment in the Kansas penitentiary, where he is now confined, in the custody of respondent, as warden, in pursuance of said sentence. Between the time of the commission of said crime and the prisoner's arrest and the commencement of his trial his term of enlistment expired. He petitions for release from imprisonment upon the ground that the court-martial had no jurisdiction to try and convict him after the expiration of his term of enlistment. He avers that at the time of his trial he was a citizen, and not a soldier, and therefore entitled to a trial by jury.

141

. . .

McCRARY, C. J. . . .

. . .

The proceedings against the prisoner having been instituted while he was clearly within the jurisdiction of the military authority, by the prefering of the charges, and by his arrest, as well as by the forwarding of the charges to headquarters, with an application for the appointment of a court-martial for his trial, the question for determination is, did that jurisdiction cease and expire at the end of the prisoner's term of enlistment, so that all proceedings after that date were void?

The general rule is that when the jurisdiction of a court attaches in a particular case by the commencement of proceedings and the arrest of the accused, it will continue for all the purposes of the trial, judgment, and execution. This rule has long been recognized by the war department as applicable to cases properly instituted before a legally-constituted military court-martial, and in which, before the conclusion of proceedings, the term of enlistment of the accused expires. Winthrope's Dig. Opin. of Judge Advocate General, 1880, p. 210. The general rule is grounded in sound reason. Many of the greatest military offences are not cognizable by the courts of common law. A soldier might be guilty, on the eve of the expiration of his term of enlistment, of the grossest insult to his officers, or of disobedience of orders, or of desertion in the face of an enemy, and if he could not be held for trial after the end of his term he would escape punishment altogether. To hold that in every such case the jurisdiction of a court-martial would cease with the expiration of the term of enlistment, would be to shield the guilty from punishment, to encourage crime, and to greatly demoralize the military service. The jurisdiction, therefore, in such cases is to be maintained upon the highest considerations of public policy.

But such considerations are not alone sufficient to support the jurisdiction of a court which has power to deal with life, liberty, and property. The jurisdiction of a criminal court must rest upon sound principles of law, and not merely upon considerations of public interest and convenience. It frequently happens that the guilty go acquit because there is no lawful mode of trial and punishment provided. The jurisdiction in the cases named, and in many others of like character, must therefore be upheld upon the ground first mentioned, to-wit: that the court-martial acquired it by the proper commencement of proceedings, and could not be divested of it by any subsequent change in the status of the accused; and this reason applies as well to a case where the crime is one known to the common or statute law, as to one in which the offence is purely military. In both the jurisdiction is maintained, after the end of the term of enlistment, upon the same ground. This conclusion is supported by judicial interpretation, in the only cases, so far as I know, in which the question has

arisen.  U.S. v. Travers, 2 Wheeler, 509; In re Dew, 25 L. R. 540;
In re Bird, 2 Sawy. 33; In re Walker, 3 Am. Jurist, 281.
     What I have said is conclusive of the case, and it is therefore
not necessary to consider the question whether the term of enlistment
of a soldier in the army is for five years, or five years and until discharged.  In either case the prisoner must be remanded to the custody
of the warden to abide the sentence of the court-martial.  So ordered.

UNITED STATES v. DOWNS

United States Court of Military Appeals, 1953.<br>
3 U.S.C.M.A. 90, 11 C.M.R. 90.

PAUL W. BROSMAN, Judge:
     The essential probative facts of this case come to this.  The
appellant, Downs, enlisted in the United States Navy on December 7,
1946, for a period of four years.  The enlistment was, on December 6,
1950, involuntarily extended for one year--so that his term of obligated service was scheduled to expire on December 6, 1951.  Sometime prior to October, 1951, accused met with an accident in line of
duty in which he sustained a broken leg, and, in October, 1951, he was
transferred to the United States Navy Hospital, Portsmouth, Virginia,
for hospitalization and medical treatment.  He was retained at the
hospital beyond the period of his enlistment--in fact, until June,
1952--when he was granted leave for thirty days to visit his home.
He did not return to the hospital at the expiration of this leave, but
instead, and after an unauthorized absence of some two and a half
months, was apprehended and delivered to the United States Naval Receiving Station, United States Naval Base, Charleston, South Carolina.

II

     On the basis of this evidence, Downs was charged with, and con-
victed by general court-martial of, desertion with intent to remain
absent permanently, as proscribed by the Uniform Code of Military
Justice, Article 85 (a) (1), 50 USC §679 (a) (1).  The conviction was
approved by the convening authority.  However, upon review by a
board of review in the office of The Judge Advocate General, United
States Navy, the findings of guilty were set aside on the ground that
the court-martial lacked jurisdiction.  More specifically, the position
of the board of review was that the Navy had lost jurisdiction over the
person of the accused following the arrival of the extended expiration
date of his enlistment, namely, December 6, 1951--save for the
limited purpose of retaining him within service control for hospitalization and medical care.  Thereupon, The Judge Advocate General,
United States Navy, certified to this Court the question set out below:

'Is it an offense for an enlisted man, who has been
retained in the service beyond the expiration date of his

enlistment in order that he may receive medical and
hospital care for an injury incurred in line of duty prior
to the expiration of his enlistment, to fail to return from
an authorized leave?"

## III

We prefer to restate the issue as involving the simple question
of whether, under the facts of this case, the accused remained subject
to court-martial jurisdiction beyond the expiration date of his enlist-
ment--no formalities of discharge having been accomplished.  In the
course of its ably developed opinion, the board of review has cited numerous authorities to the effect that the expiration of a period of
enlistment effectively--and of its own force--operates as a discharge
from the Naval service.  We believe, however, that these authorities
are inapplicable to the factual situation presented in this case.

It was quite possible for the accused, under applicable provisions of the Bureau of Naval Personnel Manual, to have been retained
in service lawfully, with his consent, after the expiration of his enlistment period for treatment and care of an injury incurred in line of
duty.  However, accepting the view of the board that no specific attempt at compliance with those provisions was made, it does not at all
follow that accused was thereby relieved of subjection to military
law. . . .

An enlistment is a contract--not an ordinary contract but one
which accomplishes a change in status.  United States v. Grimley, 137
US 147, 34 L ed 636, 11 S Ct 54; In re Morrissey, 137 US 157, 34 L
ed 644, 11 S Ct 57.  The contract relationship, voluntarily established
at the beginning of the enlistment, could be--and here was--extended
by the mutual consent of the parties thereto.  Whether the accused
could have been restrained involuntarily for the purpose of medical
treatment beyond the expiration date of his period of service, we need
not now decide.  In any event, upon the expiration thereof under the
facts of this case, it was not within his power to effect his own discharge by any means which might seem satisfactory to him under
other circumstances--doubtless in the ordinary case--upon refusal
by the Naval authorities to issue the discharge to which he was entitled, he might have instituted appropriate judicial proceedings to
compel his release.  However, the doctrine of self-help was not open
to him here.  Because of the compelling necessity for an orderly
separation procedure, he cannot be permitted to take the law into his
own hands.  Until discharged through one of the "recognized legal
modes of separation from the service", he remained a military person
subject to the sanctions of military law.  See Winthrop's Military Law
and Precedents (1920 Reprint) 89; Dig Op JAG (1912-1940) §467.
Accordingly, the accused here was, at the date of his failure to return
from leave, subject to military law, and his unauthorized absence was
unlawful and subject to punishment.  The court-martial before which
he was tried for desertion was not without jurisdiction.

IV

As restated by us, the question certified by The Judge Advocate General, United States Navy, is, therefore, answered in the affirmative. The record is returned to that officer for reference to the board of review for reconsideration and disposition not inconsistent with this opinion.

Chief Judge QUINN and Judge LATIMER concur.

Accord, United States v. Klunk, 3 U.S.C.M.A. 92, 11 C.M.R. 92 (1953).

## UNITED STATES ex rel. HIRSHBERG v. COOKE

Supreme Court of the United States, 1949.
336 U.S. 210, 69 S.Ct. 530, 93 L.Ed. 621.

MR. JUSTICE BLACK delivered the opinion of the Court.

This case raises important questions concerning the statutory jurisdiction of general courts-martial of the Navy.

In 1942 the petitioner was serving a second enlistment in the Navy. Upon the surrender of the United States forces on Corregidor petitioner became a war prisoner of Japan. After liberation in September, 1945, petitioner was brought back to the United States and hospitalized. He was restored to duty in January, 1946. March 26, 1946, he was granted an honorable discharge because of expiration of his prior enlistment. The next day he re-enlisted, obligating himself to serve four years "subject to such laws, regulations, and articles for the government of the Navy as are or shall be established by the Congress . . . or other competent authority . . . ."

About a year later, petitioner was served with charges directing his trial by a general court-martial of the Navy. The specifications included charges that during his prior enlistment the petitioner had maltreated two other naval enlisted men who were also Japanese prisoners of war and who were members of groups of prisoners working under petitioner's charge. Petitioner filed a plea in bar of the trial, one ground being that the court-martial was without jurisdiction to try him for alleged offenses committed during a prior enlistment at the end of which he had received an honorable discharge. His plea was overruled. He was acquitted on some specifications but was convicted on others that charged maltreatment. His sentence was ten months confinement, reduction from chief signalman to apprentice seaman, and dishonorable discharge from the Navy.

Petitioner then brought this habeas corpus proceeding in a federal district court charging that the court-martial judgment was void because of want of statutory power to convict him for an offense committed if at all during his prior enlistment.* That court sustained petitioner's contention and ordered his release from custody. 73 F. Supp. 990. The Court of Appeals reversed, one judge dissenting. 168 F. 2d 503. The importance of the statutory construction, which appeared to affect the court-martial powers of the Army as well as the Navy, caused us to grant certiorari. 335 U.S. 842.

Aside from naval regulations to which reference will later be made, court-martial authority to try and to punish petitioner for his prior enlistment conduct primarily depends on the language in Article 8 (Second) of the Articles for the Government of the Navy (34 U. S. C. §1200, Art. 8), which particularly provides that "such punishment as a court-martial may adjudge may be inflicted on any person in the Navy . . . guilty of . . . maltreatment of, any person subject to his orders. . . ." The Government contends that this language given its literal meaning authorized the court-martial to try and to punish petitioner for conduct during a prior enlistment. It is pointed out that petitioner was "in the Navy" when the offense was committed and when he was tried; this language it is argued brings his case under the Article. In aid of this interpretation the Government emphasizes that during the whole period of time involved, petitioner was continuously "in the Navy" except for an interval of a few hours between his honorable discharge and his re-enlistment. This latter circumstance we think cannot justify the statutory interpretation urged. For if that interpretation is correct, court-martial jurisdiction would be satisfied if a sailor was merely "in the Navy" when the offense was committed and when brought before the court-martial, regardless of the duration of any interim period out of the naval service, provided the prosecution was not barred by the two-year limitation period provided by 34 U.S.C. §1200, Art. 61.

---

*Court-martial jurisdiction to try petitioner depends on a part of Article 8 (Second), which reaches only conduct of an offender charged with "maltreatment of, any person subject to his orders." Before the court-martial and in the District Court petitioner contended that the court-martial was without jurisdiction in his case because the alleged maltreatment was of naval enlisted men who were not "subject to his orders" by virtue of his United States Navy obligations, but that whatever authority he then had over the other Navy men came from duties assigned him by the Japanese as a prisoner of war. Both the District Court and the Court of Appeals rejected this suggested interpretation of the Article, and the contention is not urged here.

The concessions made by the Government in urging such a literal construction of this Article expose the whimsical and uncertain nature of the distinctions that would mark the boundaries of court-martial powers. It is conceded that had petitioner not re-enlisted in the Navy after his 1946 discharge, no Navy court-martial could have tried him for offenses committed during his prior naval service. Thus, under the construction here urged, naval court-martial jurisdiction for a prior enlistment offense is made wholly to depend on whether the naval offender either voluntarily re-enters the Navy or is drafted into its service. And punishment of the gravest nature might be imposed on a naval volunteer or draftee which no court-martial could have imposed but for such a voluntary or forced entry into the Navy. For under this interpretation had the same naval offender re-entered his country's service by way of the Army rather than the Navy, either by choice or by accident of draft assignment, no court-martial, either Navy or Army, could have punished him. Jurisdiction to punish rarely, if ever, rests upon such illogical and fortuitous contingencies. We therefore must look beyond the literal language of the Article, ambiguous at best, in order to determine whether this court-martial acted within its power. See Runkle v. United States, 122 U.S. 543, 555, 556; Ex parte Reed, 100 U.S. 13, 23.

While not itself determinative of the question here, 34 U. S. C. §1200, Art. 14 (Eleventh), has greatly influenced the Army and Navy in determining their court-martial jurisdiction to try service personnel for offenses committed in prior enlistments. That Article provides that where any person previously discharged or dismissed from the Navy has "while in the naval service" been guilty of certain types of fraud against the Government, such person "shall continue to be liable to be arrested and held for trial and sentence by a court martial, in the same manner and to the same extent as if he had not received such discharge nor been dismissed."

Article 14 (Eleventh) stems from an Act of Congress passed in 1863, particularly designed to punish frauds against the military branches of the Government in connection with the procurement of supplies for war activities. 12 Stat. 696. That the attention of the 1863 Congress was directly focused upon the powers that could and should be vested in courts-martial is made clear by the debates and by the fact that Congress deleted from the bill as proposed specific provisions which would have made civilian government contractors subject to trial before military and naval courts-martial. Cong. Globe, 37th Cong., 3d Sess. 952-958 (1863), and Appendix to Cong. Globe, 37th Cong., 3d Sess. 199 (1863). See Ex parte Henderson, 11 Fed. Cas. 1067, No. 6,349 (C. C. D. Ky. 1878). And see United States ex rel. Marcus v. Hess, 317 U.S. 537, 539-545. But after elimination of certain provisions which would further have expanded court-martial jurisdiction, Congress left in the bill §3, now Naval Article 14 (Eleventh), which makes naval personnel guilty of service frauds subject to court-martial after discharge or dismissal. The same 1863 provision has also been made applicable to Army personnel by Article of War 94, 10 U.S.C. §1566.

Congress in this 1863 Act plainly recognized that there was a significant difference between court-martial power to try men in the service and to try former servicemen after their discharge. The Government correctly argues that the attention of the 1863 Congress was not focused on the precise question here, namely, the extent of a military court's statutory power to punish a man presently "in the service" for an offense committed in a prior enlistment period from which he has been discharged. But the fact remains that the 1863 Congress did act on the implicit assumption that without a grant of congressional authority military courts were without power to try discharged or dismissed soldiers for any offenses committed while in the service. Acting on this assumption, Congress granted such a power to courts-martial but only in the very limited category of offenses there defined--frauds against the Government.* Since the 1863 Act, Congress has not passed any measure that directly expanded court-martial powers over discharged servicemen, whether they re-enlisted or not.

Obviously Article 8 (Second), which subjects to court-martial jurisdiction persons "in the Navy," supports an argument that petitioner was subject to trial by this court-martial. It is equally obvious that the language of Article 8 (Second) particularly in view of Article 14 (Eleventh) supports an argument that this court-martial could not try petitioner for an offense committed prior to his honorable discharge. Under these circumstances the manner in which court-martial jurisdiction has long been exercised by the Army and Navy is entitled to great weight in interpreting the Articles.

The question of the jurisdiction of a naval court-martial over discharged personnel was submitted by the Secretary of the Navy to the Attorney General in 1919. The precise question of whether re-enlistment could revive jurisdiction of a military court was not considered, but as to the power of military courts over discharged personnel in general the Attorney General reached the conclusion

---

*The discussion of the 1863 Act showed that Congress rather grudgingly conceded this comparatively slight expansion of the court-martial power apparently prompted by reports of particularly abhorrent recent frauds by war contractors, such as the supply of shells to the Army "filled not with the proper explosive materials for use, but with saw-dust." Cong. Globe, 37th Cong., 3d Sess. 955 (1863). This action of the 1863 Congress does not support an argument that Congress has been quick in response to appeals for expansion of court-martial jurisdiction. See Duncan v. Kahanamoku, 327 U.S. 304; Ex parte Milligan, 4 Wall. 2.

that a person discharged from the Navy before proceedings were instituted against him "for violations of the Articles Governing the
Navy, excepting article 14" could not "thereafter be brought to
trial . . . for such violations, though committed while he was in the
service." 31 Op. Atty. Gen. 521, 529. This conclusion of the Attorney
General relied on statements of the Judge Advocate Generals of the
Army and Navy that their offices had "from the beginning and uniformly held that a person separated from the service ceases to be
amenable" to military and naval jurisdiction. Previous to the Attorney
General's 1919 opinion neither the Navy nor Army had ever claimed
court-martial power to try their personnel for offenses committed
prior to an honorable discharge where proceedings had not been instituted before discharge. See Winthrop, Military Law and Precedents
93 (2d ed. 1920). The Government concedes that the Army has always
so construed its court-martial jurisdiction whenever the question
arose. And the Government concedes that the Navy also followed this
view of its jurisdiction until 1932. Many holdings and opinions of
Army and Navy authorities are cited to support these concessions.
The Government's brief quotes the following language by the Navy
Department in one of the cases which considered the precise issue
raised here. The case appears in CMO 12-1921, p. 11.

> "Except in cases of offenses in violation of Article
> 14 of the Articles for the Government of the Navy, there
> is no authority of law giving jurisdiction to a court-mar-
> tial to try an enlisted man for an offense committed in a
> prior enlistment from which he has an honorable discharge,
> regardless of the fact that he has subsequently reenlisted
> in the naval service and was serving under such reenlist-
> ment at the time the jurisdiction of the court was asserted."

[The remainder of this opinion is reprinted at page 137 supra.]
Reversed.

UNITED STATES v. SOLINSKY

United States Court of Military Appeals, 1953.
2 U.S.C.M.A. 153, 7 C.M.R. 29.

GEORGE W. LATIMER, Judge:
The facts necessary to a proper understanding of the single
issue involved in this review are these: The accused enlisted in the
Army in August 1947. On September 5, 1949, which was prior to the
expiration of his term of enlistment, he was stationed in Germany.
On that date, pursuant to some prior arrangements, he was given an
honorable discharge for "the convenience of the Government," in
order that he might re-enlist for an indefinite period of time. His

discharge was dated September 5, 1949, and his re-enlistment was effective the following day. From April to June 1948, he was a postal clerk in an engineer company stationed at or near Wolfgang, Germany, and it was during this period that the offenses were committed. He was returned to the United States to stand trial and on April 13, 1951, was arraigned on six specifications, four alleging alterations or forgeries of United States postal money orders, and the other two alleging larcenies of similar instruments. On August 29, 1951, he was convicted on all charges and specifications and sentenced to a dishonorable discharge, total forfeitures of pay and allowances, and confinement at hard labor for ten years. The findings and sentence were approved by the convening authority and a board of review in the office of The Judge Advocate General, United States Army, affirmed. We granted accused's petition for review to determine the single issue of whether the court-martial had jurisdiction to try him for offenses committed during his prior enlistment.

. . .

Appellate defense counsel contends the decision of the Supreme Court of the United States in Unites States ex rel. Hirshberg v. Cooke (1949) 336 US 210, 93 L ed 621, 69 S Ct 530, disposes of the issues in this case and that we must follow the holding in that case. We would agree with the latter part of the contention if the former were correct but the difference in facts poses different issues and requires us to reach a different result. . . .

. . .

Realizing we are bound by the principles of the Hirshberg case, we apply them to the facts as found in this record. There can be no dispute that at the time the offense was committed the accused was a person who was expressly made subject to military law by the Articles of War. The crux of the problem is the effect of a discharge for the benefit of the Government as there are special situations contemplated by Congress which are not encompassed within the Hirshberg doctrine.

On page 10 of the Manual for Courts-Martial, U.S. Army, 1949, we find the following statement which suggests an exception to the general rule that a discharge prevents prosecution where an offense, except in fraud cases, is committed in a prior period of enlistment:

> "In certain cases, if the person's discharge or other separation does not interrupt his status as a person belonging to the general category of persons subject to military law, court-martial jurisdiction does not terminate. Thus, when an officer holding an emergency commission was discharged from that commission by reason of his acceptance of a commission in the Regular Army, there being no interval between services under the respective commissions, it was held that there was no termination of the officer's military status--merely the accomplishment of a change

in his status from that of a temporary to that of a permanent officer--and that court-martial jurisdiction to try
him for an offense (striking enlisted men) committed pri-
or to the discharge was not terminated by the discharge
. . ." [Emphasis supplied.]

This provision was not first enacted by the promulgation of the
1949 Manual. It has been the law for approximately twenty-five years
as the Manual for Courts-Martial, U.S. Army, 1928, has substantially
the same provision. Moreover, it is amplified and expanded in the
Manual for Courts-Martial, United States, 1951, and this enactment
expressly mentions the type of case with which we are now dealing.
This Manual, paragraph 11, page 14, provides:

"The general rule is that court-martial jurisdiction
over officers, cadets, midshipmen, warrant officers, enlisted persons, and other persons subject to the code ceases
on discharge from the service or other termination of such
status and that jurisdiction as to an offense committed
during a period of service or status thus terminated is not
revived by re-entry into the military service or return into such status.
"b. Exceptions.--To this general rule there are,
however, some exceptions which include the following:
. . .
"In those cases when the person's discharge or
other separation does not interrupt his status as a person belonging to the general category of persons subject
to the code, court-martial jurisdiction does not terminate.
Thus when an officer holding a commission in a Reserve
component of an armed force is discharged from that commission, while on active duty, by reason of his acceptance
of a commission in a Regular component of that armed
force, there being no interval between the periods of
service under the respective commissions, there is no
termination of the officer's military status--merely the
accomplishment of a change in his status from that of a
temporary to that of a permanent officer--and court-
martial jurisdiction to try him for an offense committed
prior to such discharge is not terminated by the discharge.
Similarly, when an enlisted person is discharged for the
convenience of the Government in order to re-enlist before the expiration of his prior period of service, military
jurisdiction continues provided there is no hiatus between
the two enlistments. A member of the armed forces who
receives a discharge therefrom while serving without the
continental limits of the United States and without the

Territories enumerated in Article 2(11), and who immediately becomes a person accompanying, serving, or employed by the armed forces in such an oversea area,
remains amenable to trial by court-martial for offenses
committed prior to his discharge because such discharge
does not interrupt his status as a person subject to the
code. . . . "

. . .

A research of available authorities shows uniformity in holding
that the Government does not waive its right to proceed under the circumstances of this case. . . .

. . .

If there are good reasons for the holdings in the foregoing authorities, there are equally good reasons for differentiating this case
from the Hirshberg case. In this connection if we can determine the
reasons for adopting the general rule, we may be able to determine
the reasons prompting the exceptions. In Winthrop's Military Law
and Precedents, 2d ed., 1920 Reprint, pages 89 and 93, paragraphs
118 and 124, respectively, state as follows:

". . . . the general rule is that military persons--
officers and enlisted men--are subject to the military
jurisdiction, so long only as they remain such; that when,
in any of the recognized legal modes of separation from
the service, they cease to be military and become civil
persons, such jurisdiction can, constitutionally, no more
be exercised over them than it could before they originally
entered the army, or than it can over any other members
of the civil community."

. . .

If the rationale announced by Colonel Winthrop is the basis for
the rule, it might be well to consider whether the accused reverted to
a civilian status. This requires a consideration of the appropriate
Army Regulations and the evidence touching on the continuity of accused's service. The regulation under which his discharge and re-
enlistment were effected was AR 615-365, dated June 21, 1948, and
it is designated "Enlisted Men Discharge Convenience of Government." The pertinent part of the Regulation is as follows:

"2. Delegation of authority to order discharge--
Authority to order discharge of individuals for the convenience of the Government is delegated to the commanders
specified in paragraph 7, AR 615-360--

. . .

"b.  To permit immediate reenlistment for 3 years
or more as authorized, of individuals who apply for and
are qualified for such reenlistment.

(1)  At any time during the last 90 days of a
current enlistment.

(2)  For the purpose of--
. . .

(b)  Volunteering for foreign service, when
the amount of service remaining in current enlistment is not sufficient to complete a prescribed
foreign service tour in the oversea command to
which an individual is to be assigned; discharge
and reenlistment to be effected when the oversea
assignment is evidence;

(c)  Filling own vacancy where at least 12
months remain to complete a normal tour of foreign
service, when returning to the United States from
an oversea command on emergency or morale leave
and having less than 18 months remaining in current enlistment.
. . .

'Individuals being discharged from their present enlisted
status as provided above will be reenlisted on the day
following discharge.  The discharge certificate will not
be delivered to the individual until after reenlistment is
effected."  [Emphasis supplied.]

At the trial evidence was presented regarding the procedure required by the above regulation.  Qualified witnesses, well-acquainted
with its provisions, testified that the purpose of providing that discharge on one day be followed by immediate re-enlistment on the next
day was to insure continuous service; that upon discharge the current
enlistment ceased and the re-enlistment became effective immediately; that there would be no lapse of time between the two enlistments;
that the new enlistment contract would not be legal until after the person
was sown in for his re-enlistment, at which time his discharge would
be given him; and that there would be no break in his pay during the
period.  Concededly, one witness testified that the discharge would be
effective at midnight one day and the re-enlistment would become effective at 12:01 a.m. the following day, thereby leaving a hiatus of one
minute.  However, in the light of other testimony in the record, as it
may be influenced by the regulation, we do not believe that such a statement compels a conclusion that accused reverted to a civilian status.

When accomplished in the manner prescribed by the regulation,
accused's discharge did not terminate his membership in the Army.
This, because his then current term did not expire until sometime
after September 5, 1949, and his discharge for convenience could not

have been effective on that date without immediate re-enlistment. Had he accepted the discharge and thereafter failed to comply with the provision of the regulation requiring his re-enlistment, his discharge would have been fraudulently procured. . . .

. . .

In the case at bar, accused's discharge was conditioned upon his compliance with the provisions of the regulation and would have been voidable without such compliance. Clearly, the only purpose for a discharge and re-enlistment prior to the expiration of the then existing term of enlistment is to facilitate the administration and effectuation of a continuous term of service. It is not intended to return a soldier to a civilian status and then have him once again become a soldier, rather it is intended that the military status be not interrupted. The whole complexion of the proceedings argue against an interrupted status. The discharge was not delivered until the re-enlistment had been accomplished; there was no break in service or pay; the accused could have been ordered to perform a special mission covering that period; he was entitled to every benefit incidental to membership in the armed forces; there was not a fraction of a second that he was not subject to military orders or military control; and every fact and all circumstances point to a situation where the discharge and re-enlistment were to be simultaneous events for the sole purpose of preventing a hiatus or break in the service. Under the regulations and under the procedure outlined, one term could not end until the other commenced. If, by analogy, we compare the arrangement with a commercial contract, it was an extension before the end of the term. The only change was an extension of the term.

In the final analysis we find the following similarity and dissimilarity between the instant case and the Hirshberg case. The point of similarity is that in both instances the accused were subject to military law at the time the offenses were committed and the burden rested on the Government to establish that it did not lose jurisdiction by discharge. The point of departure is that in the Hirshberg case it appeared clearly that Congress, except in a limited field, had not reserved the right to proceed directly or indirectly against personnel of the armed forces who had reverted to a civilian status, but in this instance it had authorized a procedure which would retain jurisdiction. This conclusion is arrived at by virtue of the fact that Congress authorized the President to promulgate rules and regulations to govern the administration of military law and, as early as 1928, he had prescribed that so long as a discharge did not terminate an accused's status as a person belonging to a general category of persons subject to military law, courts-martial jurisdiction would not be lost. In spite of the fact that this regulation has been in the Manual since 1928, and that the Army has interpreted the regulations to continue jurisdiction over the dischargee, Congress has not seen fit to pass contrary regulations. Again, in this instance, we do not have conflicting Army regulations as the administrative construction has always been that under this type of discharge, jurisdiction does not terminate. Accordingly, if Congress has, by not requiring a change in the practice, approved the Army construction, the doctrine of the Hirshberg case would require an affirmance of the decision of the board of review. Moreover, the other tests laid down in that case can be applied here and the decision affirmed as the facts meet the requirements.

. . .

If we were to make what appears to us to be an unreasonable assumption, that is, that accused's status changed, we would be faced with this factual situation. For an infinitesimal period of time the accused became a civilian without the territorial jurisdiction of the United States. During this period he was housed, maintained, paid, and otherwise serviced by the United States Army. He was transported overseas and he was returned to the United States by the Army. Between these two events he was always a soldier. Under these circumstances he would either be accompanying or serving with the Armies of the United States from the moment he left these shores until he returned. If, for a moment, he stepped from his uniform into civilian clothes and then back again, he never stepped into a category which was not subject to military law. Under the principles announced in all the authorities, and under the Articles of War, he was always subject to courts-martial jurisdiction. A momentary break in service does not necessarily break court-martial jurisdiction. It did in the Hirshberg case but as we view the particular circumstances of this case, we find it did not do so here.

The decision of the board of review is affirmed.

Judge BROSMAN concurs.

QUINN, Chief Judge (dissenting):

I dissent.

In my opinion, United States ex rel. Hirshberg v. Cooke, 336 US 210, 93 L ed 621, 69 S Ct 530, is controlling here. I read Hirshberg to say that once an enlisted man has been discharged from the armed forces, that discharge operates as a bar to subsequent trial for offenses occurring prior to discharge, except in those situations expressly saved by applicable statute. I find no statutory provision-- and the majority cites none--that is applicable here.

It is immaterial, I think, that there may be persuasive policy arguments in support of the result reached by the majority. We are here concerned with courts-martial, special tribunals whose jurisdiction must be found solely within the confines of the statutes creating them. If jurisdiction is not conferred by statute, then it matters not that it should be conferred.

I should add that I find in this record no intimation that the accused procured his discharge by fraud.

I would dismiss the charges for lack of jurisdiction in the court-martial which tried them.

Cf. A.C.M. 5625, Isidore, 7 C.M.R. 595 (1952); A.C.M. 10047, Lucas, 19 C.M.R. 613 (1955); United States v. Kish, 176 F. Supp. 820 (D.C. Pa., 1959).

## UNITED STATES ex rel. TOTH v. QUARLES

Supreme Court of the United States, 1955.
350 U.S. 11, 76 S.Ct. 1, 100 L.Ed. 8.

MR. JUSTICE BLACK delivered the opinion of the Court.

After serving with the United States Air Force in Korea, Robert W. Toth was honorably discharged. He returned to his home in Pittsburgh and went to work in a steel plant. Five months later he was arrested by military authorities on charges of murder and conspiracy to commit murder while an airman in Korea.* At the time of arrest he had no relationship of any kind with the military. He was taken to Korea to stand trial before a court-martial under authority of a 1950 Act of Congress.** The Court of Appeals sustained the Act, rejecting the contention that civilian ex-servicemen like Toth could not constitutionally be subjected to trial by court-martial. 94 U.S. App. D. C. 28, 215 F. 2d 22. We granted certiorari to pass upon this important constitutional question. 348 U.S. 809.***

---

*The charges were violations of Articles 118 and 81 of the Uniform Code of Military Justice, 64 Stat. 140, 134, 50 U. S. C. §§712 and 675.

**Art. 3(a), Uniform Code of Military Justice, 64 Stat. 109, 50 U. S. C. §553, provides: "Subject to the provisions of article 43, any person charged with having committed, while in a status in which he was subject to this code, an offense against this code, punishable by confinement of five years or more and for which the person cannot be tried in the courts of the United States or any State or Territory thereof or of the District of Columbia, shall not be relieved from amenability to trial by courts-martial by reason of the termination of said status."

***This habeas corpus proceeding was brought in the District Court for the District of Columbia by Toth's sister while he was held in Korea. Without passing on any constitutional question the District Court ordered Toth discharged on the ground that he should not have

The 1950 Act cannot be sustained on the constitutional power of Congress "To raise and support Armies," "To declare War," or to punish "Offences against the Law of Nations" (see Ex parte Quirin, 317 U.S. 1; In re Yamashita, 327 U.S. 1). And this assertion of military authority over civilians cannot rest on the President's power as commander-in-chief, or on any theory of martial law. See Ex parte Milligan, 4 Wall. 2, 124-127. The Government's contention is that the Act is a valid exercise of the power granted Congress in Article I of the Constitution "To make Rules for the Government and Regulation of the land and naval Forces," as supplemented by the Necessary and Proper Clause.*

This Court has held that the Article I clause just quoted authorizes Congress to subject persons actually in the armed service to trial by court-martial for military and naval offenses (Dynes v. Hoover, 20 How. 65). Later it was held that court-martial jurisdiction could be exerted over a dishonorably discharged soldier then a military prisoner serving a sentence imposed by a prior court-martial (Kahn v. Anderson, 255 U.S. 1). It has never been intimated by this Court, however, that Article I military jurisdiction could be extended to civilian ex-soldiers who had severed all relationship with the military and its institutions.**   To allow this extension of military authority

---

been carried to Korea for trial without a hearing. 113 F.Supp. 330, 114 F. Supp. 468.

*The Fifth Amendment provides that "No person shall be held to answer for a capital, or otherwise infamous crime, unless on a presentment or indictment of a Grand Jury, except in cases arising in the land or naval forces, or in the Militia, when in actual service in time of War or public danger. . . ." This provision does not grant court-martial power to Congress; it merely makes clear that there need be no indictment for such military offenses as Congress can authorize military tribunals to try under its Article I power to make rules to govern the armed forces.

**In 1863 Congress passed a statute authorizing trial of ex-soldiers for commission of fraud against the Government while in the service; this law also authorized court-martial trial of contractors not part of the military forces. 12 Stat. 696. The latter provision of the 1863 law appears never to have been sustained by any court. Lower courts have disagreed as to the constitutional validity of the provision authorizing ex-soldiers to be tried. See, e. g., In re Bogart, 3 Fed. Cas. 796. Compare Ex parte Henderson, 11 Fed. Cas. 1067; United States ex rel. Flannery v. Commanding General, 69 F. Supp. 661, reversed by stipulation in unreported order of the Second Circuit, No. 20235, April 18, 1946. See United States ex rel. Hirshberg v. Cooke, 336 U.S. 210. A statute authorizing court-martial trial of inmates of the Soldiers' Home has been ruled unconstitutional by the

would require an extremely broad construction of the language used
in the constitutional provision relied on.  For given its natural meaning, the power granted Congress "To make Rules" to regulate "the
land and naval Forces" would seem to restrict court-martial jurisdiction to persons who are actually members or part of the armed forces.
There is a compelling reason for construing the clause this way: any
expansion of court-martial jurisdiction like that in the 1950 Act necessarily encroaches on the jurisdiction of federal courts set up under
Article III of the Constitution where persons on trial are surrounded
with more constitutional safeguards than in military tribunals.

Article III provides for the establishment of a court system as
one of the separate but coordinate branches of the National Government.  It is the primary, indeed the sole business of these courts to
try cases and controversies between individuals and between individuals and the Government.  This includes trial of criminal cases.  These
courts are presided over by judges appointed for life, subject only to
removal by impeachment.  Their compensation cannot be diminished
during their continuance in office.  The provisions of Article III were
designed to give judges maximum freedom from possible coercion or
influence by the executive or legislative branches of the Government.
But the Constitution and the Amendments in the Bill of Rights show
that the Founders were not satisfied with leaving determination of
guilt or innocence to judges, even though wholly independent.  They
further provided that no person should be held to answer in those
courts for capital or other infamous crimes unless on the presentment or indictment of a grand jury drawn from the body of the people.
Other safeguards designed to protect defendants against oppressive
governmental practices were included.  One of these was considered
so important to liberty of the individual that it appears in two parts of
the Constitution.  Article III, §2, commands that the "Trial of all
Crimes, except in Cases of Impeachment, shall be by Jury; and such
Trial shall be held in the State where the said Crimes shall have been
committed; but when not committed within any State, the Trial shall
be at such Place or Places as the Congress may by Law have

---

Judge Advocate General of the Army.  Dig. Op. J. A. G. (1912), pp.
1010, 1012.  It was declared that "such inmates are not a part of the
Army of the United States, but are civilians."  Id., at 1012.  Col.
Winthrop, concededly a leading authority on military law, expressed
the view that "this class of statutes, which in terms or inferentially
subject persons formerly in the army, but become finally and legally
separated from it, to trial by court-martial, are all necessarily and
alike unconstitutional. . . ."  1 Winthrop, Military Law and Precedents (2d ed. 1896), 146.  The War Department reprinted this classic
volume for the guidance of the Army in 1920.  Winthrop, Military Law
and Precedents (2d ed., Reprint 1920).

directed." And the Sixth Amendment provides that "In all criminal prosecutions, the accused shall enjoy the right to a speedy and public trial, by an impartial jury of the state and district wherein the crime shall have been committed. . . ." This right of trial by jury ranks very high in our catalogue of constitutional safeguards.*

We find nothing in the history of constitutional treatment of military tribunals which entitles them to rank along with Article III courts as adjudicators of the guilt or innocence of people charged with offenses for which they can be deprived of their life, liberty or property. Unlike courts, it is the primary business of armies and navies to fight or be ready to fight wars should the occasion arise. But trial of soldiers to maintain discipline is merely incidental to an army's primary fighting function. To the extent that those responsible for performance of this primary function are diverted from it by the necessity of trying cases, the basic fighting purpose of armies is not served. And conceding to military personnel that high degree of honesty and sense of justice which nearly all of them undoubtedly have, it still remains true that military tribunals have not been and probably never can be constituted in such way that they can have the same kind of qualifications that the Constitution has deemed essential to fair trials of civilians in federal courts. For instance, the Constitution does not provide life tenure for those performing judicial functions in military trials. They are appointed by military commanders and may be removed at will. Nor does the Constitution protect their salaries as it does judicial salaries. Strides have been made toward making courts-martial less subject to the will of the executive department which appoints, supervises and ultimately controls them. But from the very nature of things, courts have more independence in passing on the life and liberty of people than do military tribunals.

Moreover, there is a great difference between trial by jury and trial by selected members of the military forces. It is true that military personnel because of their training and experience may be especially competent to try soldiers for infractions of military rules. Such training is no doubt particularly important where an offense charged against a soldier is purely military, such as disobedience of an order, leaving post, etc. But whether right or wrong, the premise underlying

---

*A declaration of rights adopted by nine colonies in 1765 contained this statement: "That trial by jury, is the inherent and invaluable right of every British subject in these colonies." Harvard Classics, Volume 43, p. 148. The Declaration of Independence stated as one of the grievances of the colonies that the King of Great Britain had deprived the colonists of the benefits of trial by jury in many cases and that he had "affected to render the Military independent of and superior to the Civil power." Another charge was that he had transported colonials "beyond Seas to be tried for pretended offences."

the constitutional method for determining guilt or innocence in federal courts is that laymen are better than specialists to perform this task. This idea is inherent in the institution of trial by jury.

Juries fairly chosen from different walks of life bring into the jury box a variety of different experiences, feelings, intuitions and habits.* Such juries may reach completely different conclusions than would be reached by specialists in any single field, including specialists in the military field.** On many occasions, fully known to the Founders of this country, jurors--plain people--have manfully stood up in defense of liberty against the importunities of judges and despite prevailing hysteria and prejudices.*** The acquittal of William Penn is an illustrious example.**** Unfortunately, instances could also be cited where jurors have themselves betrayed the cause of justice by verdicts based on prejudice or pressures. In such circumstances independent trial judges and independent appellate judges have a most important place under our constitutional plan since they have power to set aside convictions (see II Wilson's Works [Andrews ed. 1896] 222).

---

*Chief Justice Cooley said: "The trial of criminal cases is by a jury of the country, and not by the court. The jurors, and they alone, are to judge of the facts, and weigh the evidence. The law has established this tribunal because it is believed that, from its numbers, the mode of their selection, and the fact that the jurors come from all classes of society, they are better calculated to judge of motives, weigh probabilities, and take what may be called a common sense view of a set of circumstances, involving both act and intent, than any single man, however pure, wise and eminent he may be. This is the theory of the law; and as applied to criminal accusations, it is eminently wise, and favorable alike to liberty and to justice." People v. Garbutt, 17 Mich. 9, 27.

**"Juries undoubtedly may make mistakes: they may commit errors: they may commit gross ones. But changed as they constantly are, their errors and mistakes can never grow into a dangerous system. The native uprightness of their sentiments will not be bent under the weight of precedent and authority. The esprit du corps will not be introduced among them; nor will society experience from them those mischiefs, of which the esprit du corps, unchecked, is sometimes productive." II Wilson's Works (Andrews ed. 1896) 222.

***An outstanding instance is the Dean of St. Asaph's Case, 21 How. St. Tr. 847, discussed in Stryker, For the Defense, 119-136.

****Penn and Mead's Case, 6 How. St. Tr. 951. After trial the jurors were fined for acquitting Penn contrary to the court's instructions. One was imprisoned for not paying the fine, but the Court of Common Pleas released him in a habeas corpus proceeding, upholding the freedom of the jury to decide the case. Bushell's Case, 6 How. St. Tr. 999.

The 1950 Act here considered deprives of jury trial and sweeps under military jurisdiction over 3,000,000 persons who have become veterans since the Act became effective. That number is bound to grow from year to year; there are now more than 3,000,000 men and women in uniform (Bureau of the Census, Current Population Reports, Series P-25, No. 101 [U.S. Dept. Commerce 1954]). These figures point up what would be the enormous scope of a holding that Congress could subject every ex-serviceman and woman in the land to trial by court-martial for any alleged offense committed while he or she had been a member of the armed forces. Every veteran discharged since passage of the 1950 Act is subject to military trial for any offense punishable by as much as five years' imprisonment unless the offense is now punishable in a civilian court. And one need only glance at the Military Code to see what a vast number and variety of offenses are thus brought under military jurisdiction (Arts. 77-134, Uniform Code of Military Justice, 64 Stat. 133-143, 50 U. S. C. §§671-728). Included within these are crimes such as murder, conspiracy, absence without leave, contempt toward officials, disrespect toward superior officers, willful or neglectful loss, damage, or destruction of government property, making false official statements, dueling, breach of the peace, forgery, fraud, assault, and many others.* It is true that with reference to some of these offenses, very minor ones, veterans cannot now be tried because of a presidential order fixing the punishment for such offenses at less than five years (see Table of Maximum Punishments, 127c, MCM, 1951, 16 Fed. Reg. 1364-1368). But that amelioration of the Military Code may be temporary, since punishment can be raised or lowered at the will of the President. It is also true that under the present law courts-martial have jurisdiction only if no civilian court does. But that might also be changed by Congress. Thus there is no justification for treating the Act as a mere minor increase of congressional power to expand military jurisdiction. It is a great change, both actually and potentially.

---

*A particularly sweeping offense, punishable by death and not subject to any statute of limitations, is found in Article 94, which provides in part that anyone "(2) who with intent to cause the overthrow or destruction of lawful civil authority, creates, in concert with any other person or persons, revolt, violence, or other disturbance against such authority is guilty of sedition; (3) who fails to do his utmost to prevent and suppress an offense of mutiny or sedition being committed in his presence, or fails to take all reasonable means to inform his superior or commanding officer of an offense of mutiny or sedition which he knows or has reason to believe is taking place, is guilty of a failure to suppress or report a mutiny or sedition." (Emphasis supplied.)

Fear has been 'expressed that if this law is not sustained discharged soldiers may escape punishment altogether for crimes they
commit while in the service. But that fear is not warranted and was
not shared by the Judge Advocate General of the Army who made a
strong statement against passage of the law.* He asked Congress to
"confer jurisdiction upon Federal courts to try any person for an offense denounced by the [military] code if he is no longer subject
thereto. This would be consistent with the fifth amendment of the
Constitution." The Judge Advocate General went on to tell Congress
that "If you expressly confer jurisdiction on the Federal courts to try
such cases, you preserve the constitutional separation of military and
civil courts, you save the military from a lot of unmerited grief, and
you provide for a clean, constitutional method for disposing of such
cases." It is conceded that it was wholly within the constitutional
power of Congress to follow this suggestion and provide for federal
district court trials of discharged soldiers accused of offenses committed while in the armed services. This concession is justified.
U.S. Const., Art. III, §2; and see, e.g., Jones v. United States, 137
U.S. 202, 211-212; United States v. Bowman, 260 U.S. 94, 97-98;
Skiriotes v. Florida, 313 U.S. 69, 73-74. There can be no valid argument, therefore, that civilian ex-servicemen must be tried by court-
martial or not tried at all. If that is so it is only because Congress
has not seen fit to subject them to trial in federal district courts.

None of the other reasons suggested by the Government are
sufficient to justify a broad construction of the constitutional grant of
power to Congress to regulate the armed forces. That provision itself
does not empower Congress to deprive people of trials under Bill of
Rights safeguards, and we are not willing to hold that power to cir-
cumvent those safeguards should be inferred through the Necessary
and Proper Clause. It is impossible to think that the discipline of the
Army is going to be disrupted, its morale impaired, or its orderly
processes disturbed, by giving ex-servicemen the benefit of a civilian
court trial when they are actually civilians. And we are not impressed
by the fact that some other countries which do not have our Bill of
Rights indulge in the practice of subjecting civilians who were once
soldiers to trials by courts-martial instead of trials by civilian courts.**

---

*Hearings before Subcommittee of Senate Committe on Armed
Services on S. 857 and H. R. 4080, 81st Cong., 1st Sess. 256-257. The
Assistant General Counsel of the Office of Secretary of Defense, who
was chairman of a committee that helped draft the Uniform Code of
Military Justice, expressed doubts as to the constitutionality of Arti-
cle 3 (a). Hearings before Subcommittee of House Committee on
Armed Services on H. R. 2498, 81st Cong., 1st Sess. 881.

**The historical background of this country's preference for
civilian over military trials was impressively presented in the

There are dangers lurking in military trials which were sought to be avoided by the Bill of Rights and Article III of our Constitution. Free countries of the world have tried to restrict military tribunals to the narrowest jurisdiction deemed absolutely essential to maintaining discipline among troops in active service. Even as late as the Seventeenth Century standing armies and courts-martial were not established institutions in England (3 Macaulay, History of England from the Accession of James the Second [London, 1855], 45). Court-martial jurisdiction sprang from the belief that within the military ranks there is need for a prompt, ready-at-hand means of compelling obedience and order. But Army discipline will not be improved by court-martialing rather than trying by jury some civilian ex-soldier who has been wholly separated from the service for months, years or perhaps decades. Consequently considerations of discipline provide no excuse for new expansion of court-martial jurisdiction at the expense of the normal and constitutionally preferable system of trial by jury.*

Determining the scope of the constitutional power of Congress to authorize trial by court-martial presents another instance calling for limitation to "the least possible power adequate to the end proposed" (Anderson v. Dunn, 6 Wheat. 204, 230-231). We hold that Congress cannot subject civilians like Toth to trial by court-martial. They, like other civilians, are entitled to have the benefit of safeguards afforded those tried in the regular courts authorized by Article III of the Constitution.

Reversed.

[Justices Reed, Burton, and Minton dissented. Opinions omitted.]

---

arguments of counsel and opinion of this Court in Ex parte Milligan, 4 Wall. 2, 121. And see Duncan v. Kahanamoku, 327 U.S. 304.

*Mr. Justice Sutherland writing for the Court in Dimick v. Schiedt, 293 U.S. 474, 485-486, said, "The right of trial by jury is of ancient origin, characterized by Blackstone as 'the glory of the English law' and 'the most transcendent privilege which any subject can enjoy' (Bk. 3, p. 379); and, as Justice Story said (2 Story on the Constitution, §1779), '. . . the Constitution would have been justly obnoxious to the most conclusive objection if it had not recognized and confirmed it in the most solemn terms.' With, perhaps, some exceptions, trial by jury has always been, and still is, generally regarded as the normal and preferable mode of disposing of issues of fact in civil cases at law as well as in criminal cases. Maintenance of the jury as a fact-finding body is of such importance and occupies so firm a place in our history and jurisprudence that any seeming curtailment of the right to a jury trial should be scrutinized with the utmost care. Compare Patton v. United States, 281 U.S. 276, 312."

UNITED STATES v. GALLAGHER

United States Court of Military Appeals, 1957.
7 U.S.C.M.A. 506, 22 C.M.R. 296.

GEORGE W. LATIMER, Judge:
The accused was convicted by general court-martial of two offenses of unpremeditated murder, in violation of Article of War 92, 10 USC §1564 (1946 ed); three offences of mistreatment of fellow-prisoners of war, in violation of Article of War 96, 10 USC §1568 (1946 ed); one offense of collaboration with the enemy, in violation of the 96th Article of War, 10 USC §1568 (1946 ed) and Article 134 of the Uniform Code of Military Justice, 10 USC §934; and one offense of misconduct as a prisoner of war, in violation of Article 105 of the Uniform Code, 10 USC §905. He was sentenced to dishonorable discharge, total forfeitures, and life imprisonment, and the convening authority approved. The board of review ordered the charges dismissed because it concluded the court-martial did not have jurisdiction to try the accused for the offenses charged. The Judge Advocate General of the Army certified this issue for our consideration and it is the sole question presently before us.
On November 2, 1950, while serving in combat with the 8th Cavalry Regiment in Korea, the accused was captured by the Chinese Communists. It is alleged that the murders and other atrocities of which he was convicted occurred while he was a prisoner of war. On August 27, 1953, he returned to the hands of the American Forces as a result of Operation "Big Switch." After his exchange, the accused returned to the United States where he was granted leave. Upon return from leave in October 1953, he requested re-enlistment for a period of three years. Pursuant to his request, he was processed for discharge in accordance with special standards prescribed by the Department of the Army for soldiers who desired re-enlistment. His prior term of enlistment, as extended by Presidential Order, had expired October 12, 1951, although he continued to remain subject to military jurisdiction while in enemy hands and at least until he was discharged from his then current enlistment. Charges were preferred on October 22, 1955, and the crucial question in this case is whether court-martial jurisdiction as to the offenses committed during his prior enlistment was lost by reason of an honorable discharge dated October 27, 1953.
The general rule is that court-martial jurisdiction over military personnel subject to the Code is terminated by a discharge from the service which returns the serviceman to the civilian community, and that jurisdiction as to offenses committed during the period of service prior to discharge is not revived by re-entry into the military service. Hirshberg v Cooke, 336 US 210, 69 S Ct 530, 93 L ed 621 (1949); Manual for Courts-Martial, United States, 1951, paragraph

11a, page 14.  The theory here appears to be that military persons, and those who serve with, accompany, or are dependent upon them, are subject to military jurisdiction only so long as they remain such, and that when that status is legally terminated they are no more subject to that jurisdiction than is any other member of the civil community.  The board of review held that this case could not be distinguished from Hirshberg, supra; that Article 3(a) of the Uniform Code of Military Justice, 10 USC §803, the only other possible basis of jurisdiction, had been ruled unconstitutional by the Supreme Court; and that no military jurisdiction existed as to these offenses.

. . .

## II

Each counsel at this level contends with much vigor that the Supreme Court holding in Hirshberg, supra, supports his theory of the case.  Because we believe that jurisdiction may be found to exist upon other grounds, we need not burden this opinion with our interpretation of the law announced by the Supreme Court in that case with respect to jurisdiction under what is now Article 2 of the Code, 10 USC §802.  Instead, we will turn to the development of another basis for concluding that the board of review erred in its decision, and Hirshberg v Cooke, supra, will be discussed only insofar as it is pertinent in that aspect.

Certainly we are not as easily convinced as was the board of review that there is no basis on which to found court-martial jurisdiction over this accused, for we believe Congress enacted legislation which permits military courts to try offenders who never really left the service between the time of the commission of the offense and the date of trial, and that this legislation is constitutionally valid when limited to the kind of situation presently before us.  For the purposes of this part of our discussion, we will assume, arguendo, that there was a nine-hour hiatus in the service of the accused.

Article 3(a) of the Uniform Code, supra, provides:

"(a)  Subject to section 843 of this title (article 43), no person charged with having committed, while in a status in which he was subject to this chapter, an offense against this chapter, punishable by confinement for five years or more and for which the person cannot be tried in the courts of the United States or of a State, a Territory, or the District of Columbia, may be relieved from amenability to trial by court-martial by reason of the termination of that status."

We have not the slightest doubt but what Congress passed this statute for the principal purpose of covering the situation brought about by the decision in Hirshberg v Cooke, supra.  The legislative history demonstrates beyond question that the attention of the 81st

Congress was focused on this precise issue, namely, the extent of a
military court's statutory power to punish a man in the service for an
offense committed in a prior enlistment period from which he had been
discharged. . . .
. . .
Accordingly, it is abundantly clear that Congress intended to
preserve jurisdiction over men like Gallagher. The statute is so
framed as to leave no doubt that it is sufficient to effectuate that result. The only remaining question, therefore, is whether Congress
was constitutionally empowered to work the desired change in military
law.
We are well aware that in Toth v Quarles, 350 US 11, 76 S Ct 1,
100 L ed 8 (1955), the Supreme Court held that Article 3(a), in so far
as it attempted to authorize the trial by courts-martial of ex-servicemen who are civilians at the time of trial, was unconstitutional, but
that holding must be considered in the light of the issues involved.
There the accused had severed all of his connections with the military
service and had reverted to a civilian status prior to apprehension.
Judging by the record, he was out of the Air Force for all purposes.
Here we are presented with a situation where the accused was in the
service when he committed the offense and when he was convicted.
Gallagher elected to cast his lot with the military a second time, Toth
did not. From our interpretation of that opinion, we do not believe the
Supreme Court intended to say that Congress could not provide for
trial in a military court of a person who, for all practical purposes,
was continuously a member of an armed force. On the contrary, we
conclude that the Supreme Court was dealing with a person who had
returned to the civilian community and whose prosecution had no
reasonable relationship to discipline and morale of the armed service. . . .
. . .
There is a sound basis for concluding that even though Article
3(a) offended against constitutional guarantees in that instance it
should be regarded as constitutional when applied in a situation such
as this. By Article I, Section 8, Clause 14, of the Constitution, Congress was granted the power "To make Rules for the Government and
Regulation of the land and naval Forces," and to make all laws which
were necessary and proper to carry those rules into execution. The
Supreme Court has ever been mindful of the need for the Armed
Forces to maintain good order and discipline within the military community itself. The entire body of military law and the system of
courts-martial is based on that premise and its validity when properly
used has often been upheld by the Supreme Court. Dynes v Hoover,
20 How 65 (US 1858); Kahn v Anderson, 255 US 1, 41 S Ct 224, 65 L ed
469 (1921); Gusik v Schilder, 340 US 128, 71 S Ct 149, 95 L ed 146
(1950). In the present case, Gallagher is, after all, a member of the
military service at the present time, just as he was at the time when

the offenses were committed.  Assuming that a short hiatus occurred in his service, his day to day contact with other servicemen was continuous, and an inability to deal with his delinquencies, committed during a prior enlistment, would clearly have an adverse impact on the morale and discipline of his fellow soldiers who kept faith with themselves and with each other in the face of adversity, and on good order among those who presently serve.  The services are filled with enlisted men who make military life a career and they re-enlist upon expiration of their term of service, which normally in the Army is every three years.  Laying aside the statute of limitations, there is no good reason why prosecution should be barred so long as the person committing the offense never really severed his relationship with the service for any practical purpose, whether or not a short hiatus appears as a matter of record.  We are mindful of the teaching of Toth v Quarles, supra, that the scope of the constitutional power of Congress to authorize trial by court-martial must be limited to "'the least possible power adequate to the end proposed.'"  When the caveat is given a reasonable application in this instance, however, we are led to the conclusion that Article 3(a) is constitutional.  As limited by us, the Article does not authorize any jurisdiction over the person which is not necessary and proper for the success of the services in accomplishing their mission.

. . .

We therefore conclude that we are free to, and do, decide that Article 3(a) is constitutional when applied so as to preserve jurisdiction over discharged servicemen who have re-enlisted.

For the foregoing reasons, the issue certified by The Judge Advocate General of the Army is answered in the affirmative.

[Concurring opinions of Mr. Chief Judge Quinn and Mr. Judge Ferguson omitted.]

Case is commented upon in 35 Texas L. Rev. 715 (1957); 26 Fordham L. Rev. 359 (1957); and 46 Georgetown L.J. 193 (1957).

Once court-martial jurisdiction attaches, it continues until appellate processes are completed despite an accused's intervening honorable separation from active duty (U.S. v. Speller, 8 USCMA 363, 24 CMR 173 [1957]; U.S. v. Robertson, 8 USCMA 421, 24 CMR 231 [1957]).

Since the Gallagher decision, the Court of Military Appeals has decided many cases involving application of the principles enunciated in that case and in Hirschberg and Solinsky.  Unfortunately, the decisions have depended upon the particular theories held by the judges of the Court.  Chief Judge Quinn has consistently taken the position

that, unless there is evidence to indicate that the discharge was not
intended to take immediate effect, a hiatus in service exists, the
Hirschberg rule is applicable, and jurisdiction does not exist in the
absence of the applicability of Article 3(a), UCMJ (see U.S. v. Solinsky,
supra, U.S. v. Noble, 13 USCMA 413, 32 CMR 413 [1962], U.S. v.
Ginyard, 16 USCMA 512, 37 CMR 132 [1967]).  However, Chief Judge
Quinn does not limit the applicability of Article 3(a) to its specific
language but instead includes as under military jurisdiction all offenses
involving frauds against the government even if triable in a Federal
District Court (U.S. v. Martin, 10 USCMA 636, 28 CMR 202 [1959]).
Judge Latimer, while on the Court, consistently adhered to his views
expressed in Solinsky that there was no hiatus in situations where the
discharge was in some way conditioned upon reenlistment.  Judge
Ferguson has consistently opposed Chief Judge Quinn's extension of
Article 3(a) to include fraud cases and has concurred in Judge Kilday's
statement of the rule that once "an enlisted man has been discharged
from the armed forces, that discharge operates as a bar to subsequent trial for offenses occurring prior to discharge, except in those
situations expressly saved by Article 3(a) of the Code" (U.S. v.
Ginyard, supra; see U.S. v. Martin, supra).

It thus appears that whether the armed forces may assert jurisdiction over a person who committed an offense during a prior enlistment may depend upon a detailed consideration of the circumstances
of the discharge and whether the alleged offense is punishable by confinement for five years or more, is triable in a Federal District
Court, and is a fraud against the government.

Expiration of the regular period of enlistment does not alter a
serviceman's status as a person subject to the UCMJ (U.S. v. Dickenson, 6 USCMA 438, 20 CMR 154 [1955]; cf. Dickenson v. Davis, 245
F.2d 217 [CA 10, 1957]).  An officer on terminal leave is still subject
to court-martial (Hironimus v. Durant, 168 F.2d 288 [CA 4, 1948]).

There are many cases that uphold or deny court-martial jurisdiction depending upon the legality of induction; see, inter alia, U.S.
v. Ornelas, 2 USCMA 96, 6 CMR 96 (1952); U.S. v. Rodriguez, 2
USCMA 101, 6 CMR 101 (1952); U.S. v. Lopez, 10 USCMA 334, 27
CMR 408 (1959); U.S. v. Hall, 17 USCMA 88, 37 CMR 352 (1957).

Persons "in custody of the armed forces serving a sentence imposed by a court-martial" are subject to trial by court-martial for
offenses under the Code (10 U.S.C. §802).  This provision and a
similar provision in the previous Articles of War have been held constitutional: U.S. v. Nelson, 14 USCMA 93, 33 CMR 305 (1963); Kahn
v. Anderson, 255 U.S. 1, 41 S.Ct. 224, 65 L.Ed 469 (1921).  See also
Ragan v. Cox, 320 F.2d 815 (CA 10, 1963); U.S. v. Ragan, 140 SCMA
119, 33 CMR 331 (1963).

The case of Wheeler v. Reynolds, 164 F.Supp. 951 (N.D. Fla.
1958), involved an accused who was convicted by a court-martial for
a murder committed in Germany prior to his release from active duty;

at his request, he was recalled to active duty for trial. Military jurisdiction was upheld. See also U.S. v. Wheeler 10 U.S.C.M.A. 646, 28 CMR 212 [1959].

The Wheeler case and other cases involving armed forces jurisdiction over "military-civilian hybrids" are discussed by Professor Joseph W. Bishop, Jr. in an article in 112 University of Pennsylvania Law Review 317 (1964). Of particular interest are his comments concerning retired officers, the subject of controversy in the following case.

## UNITED STATES v. HOOPER*

United States Court of Military Appeals, 1958.
9 U.S.C.M.A. 637, 26 C.M.R. 417.

*[Footnotes have been omitted. Ed.]

ROBERT E. QUINN, Chief Judge:

The accused was convicted by general court-martial of violations of Articles 125, 133 and 134, Uniform Code of Military Justice, 10 USC §§925, 933, 934, and was sentenced to dismissal and total forfeitures. The case is before this Court for mandatory review in accordance with Article 67(b) (1), Uniform Code, supra, 10 USC §867.

At the outset of this review we are met, as were the tribunals below, with a defense claim that the court-martial had no jurisdiction over the accused. The factual basis for this position is undisputed.

On December 1, 1948, upon Presidential approval, the accused was transferred to the Regular Navy retired list with the rank of Rear Admiral but with retired pay based on the rank of Captain, in accordance with the provisions of Title 34 USC §§410b and 410n. While in this status, the offenses occurred, and the charges were preferred against him. He was informed of said charges April 15, 1957, by the Acting Commandant, 11th Naval District. After full investigation was held, as required by Article 32, Uniform Code, supra, 10 USC §832, the Commandant, 11th Naval District, referred the charges for trial to a general court-martial convened at his discretion. Thereafter, a copy of the charges was served upon the accused. No pretrial restraint was imposed. On May 6, 1957, the date set for trial, the accused, together with civilian counsel of his own selection, and appointed military counsel, appeared before the court-martial. Upon arraignment, counsel interposed his challenge to the jurisdiction of the forum, but his contentions were denied. Rather than enter his pleas, the accused, as was his right, stood mute, so a plea of not guilty was entered as to each charge and specification.

The trial court relied upon Article 2 of the Uniform Code, supra, 10 USC §802, as its source of jurisdiction. This provides, in pertinent part:

"The following persons are subject to this chapter:
. . .
(4) Retired members of a regular component of the armed forces who are entitled to pay; . . ."

Neither by its express terms nor by any related provision of the Code, or other Congressional enactment, are any limitations or conditions put upon the exercise of the jurisdiction thus conferred. Hence, if this section is not contrary to the Constitution, it authorizes the proceedings in this case.

The defense argues, however, that jurisdiction over retired naval officers, such as the accused, cannot attach in the absence of an order effecting their return to active duty; that if the order directing trial is considered an order to active duty, it conflicts with 10 USC §6481, for it was not issued by the Secretary of the Navy, in time of war or national emergency declared by the President, nor with the consent of the officer concerned.

We cannot, consistently with well-established rules of statutory construction, accept this view. Engrafting such a requirement upon Article 2(4) would nullify its provisions completely. Article 2(1) makes all persons on active duty subject to the Code in the following language:

"The following persons are subject to this chapter:
(1) Members of a regular component of the armed forces, including those awaiting discharge after expiration of their terms of enlistment; volunteers from the time of their muster or acceptance into the armed forces; inductees from the time of their actual induction into the armed forces; and other persons lawfully called or ordered into, or to duty in or for training in, the armed forces, from the dates they are required by the terms of the call or order to obey it."

An officer recalled to duty from the retired list of a regular component is subject to the Code by virtue of this provision alone. It necessarily follows from this that if Article 2(4) requires the individual be recalled as a condition precedent to its effectiveness, its provisions are entirely unnecessary and could never be operative.
. . .
The final phase of the defense argument raises the applicability of the Fifth Amendment to the Constitution. He contends that if Article 2(4) of the Code, supra, is considered without reference to other

provisions, "it would seem to permit a military commander to snatch
a retired regular off the streets and thrust him before a court-martial."
Of course, this accused was not "snatched off the streets" nor was he
"thrust before a court-martial." After due notice of the charges, he
voluntarily appeared before the court-martial. Thus, there is found in
this case none of the brutal and shocking circumstances suggested by
the defense. If such circumstances ever operate to deprive a tribunal
of its otherwise lawful authority, the accused here is in no position to
avail himself of such a rule.

The Fifth Amendment to the Constitution provides:

> "No person shall be held to answer for a capital,
> or otherwise infamous crime, unless on a presentment
> or indictment of a Grand Jury, except in cases arising
> in the land or naval forces, or in the militia, when in
> actual service in time of war or public danger; . . . ."
> [Emphasis supplied.]

The sole problem left for resolution is whether or not the accused, as a retired member of a regular component of the Armed
Forces entitled to receive pay, is a part of the "land or naval forces."

Courts which have heretofore expressed opinions on this question have concluded that retired personnel are a part of the land or
naval forces. In arriving at this conclusion, each, with the exception
of United States v. Fenno, supra, appear to have assumed that being
a part of such forces, court-martial jurisdiction necessarily attaches
to them.

The Court of Claims has held retired personnel a part of the
military force of this country. Tyler v United States, 16 Ct Cl 223;
Runkle v United States, 19 Ct Cl 396; Franklin v United States, 29 Ct
Cl 6. When the Tyler case, supra, was before the United States Supreme Court, that tribunal, speaking through Mr. Justice Miller,
declared:

> "It is impossible to hold that men who are by stat-
> ute declared to be a part of the army, who may wear its
> uniform, whose names shall be borne upon its register,
> who may be assigned by their superior officers to spe-
> cified duties by detail as other officers are, who are sub-
> ject to the rules and articles of war, and may be tried,
> not by a jury, as other citizens are, but by a military
> court-martial, for any breach of those rules, and who
> may finally be dismissed on such trial from the service
> in disgrace, are still not in the military service."
> [United States v Tyler, 105 US 244, 26 L ed 985. Empha-
> sis supplied.]

. . .

Officers on the retired list are not mere pensioners in any sense of the word. They form a vital segment of our national defense for their experience and mature judgment are relied upon heavily in times of emergency. The salaries they receive are not solely recompense for past services, but a means devised by Congress to assure their availability and preparedness in future contingencies. This preparedness depends as much upon their continued responsiveness to discipline as upon their continued state of physical health. Certainly, one who is authorized to wear the uniform of his country, to use the title of his grade, who is looked upon as a model of the military way of life, and who receives a salary to assure his availability, is a part of the land or naval forces.

Left for determination is the applicability of the Articles herein involved to one in a retired status. Certainly conduct unbecoming an officer and gentleman--the subject of Charge II--and conduct of a nature to bring discredit upon the armed forces--the subject of Charge III--are offenses which do not depend upon the individual's duty status. Sodomy, the subject of Charge I, is an offense involving moral turpitude, and without doubt necessarily applies to all subject to military law without regard to the individual's duty status.

For the foregoing reasons, we hold that the court-martial had jurisdiction over this accused.

. . .

Judges LATIMER and FERGUSON concur.

The principal case is discussed in 57 Michigan L. Rev. 762 (1959) and 50 Georgetown L.J. 79 (1961). Admiral Hooper also lost in the Court of Claims, which upheld the constitutionality of Article 2(4) (Hooper v. U.S., 326 F.2d 982 (1964), certiorari denied 377 U.S. U.S. 977, 84 S.Ct. 1882, 12 L.Ed. 2d 746 (1964). An accused on the Temporary Disability Retired List is subject to court-martial jurisdiction (U.S. v. Bowie, 14 USCMA 631, 34 CMR 411 (1964)).

Paragraphs (10), (11) and (12) of Article 2, UCMJ, purport to grant court-martial jurisdiction over persons not actually in the armed services. The following cases illustrate the reluctance of the judiciary to accept such an expansive view.

## REID v. COVERT*

Supreme Court of the United States, 1957.
354 U.S. 1, 77 S.Ct. 1222, 1 L.Ed.2d 1148.

*[ Footnotes have been omitted.  Ed.]

MR. JUSTICE BLACK announced the judgment of the Court and
delivered an opinion, in which THE CHIEF JUSTICE, MR. JUSTICE
DOUGLAS, and MR. JUSTICE BRENNAN join.

These cases raise basic constitutional issues of the utmost concern.  They call into question the role of the military under our system
of government.  They involve the power of Congress to expose civilians
to trial by military tribunals, under military regulations and procedures, for offenses against the United States thereby depriving them of
trial in civilian courts, under civilian laws and procedures and with
all the safeguards of the Bill of Rights.  These cases are particularly
significant because for the first time since the adoption of the Constitution wives of soldiers have been denied trial by jury in a court of
law and forced to trial before courts-martial.

In No. 701 Mrs. Clarice Covert killed her husband, a sergeant
in the United States Air Force, at an airbase in England.  Mrs. Covert,
who was not a member of the armed services, was residing on the
base with her husband at the time.  She was tried by a court-martial
for murder under Article 118 of the Uniform Code of Military Justice
(UCMJ).  The trial was on charges preferred by Air Force personnel
and the court-martial was composed of Air Force officers.  The
court-martial asserted jurisdiction over Mrs. Covert under Article
2(11) of the UCMJ, which provides:

"The following persons are subject to this code:

. . .

"(11)  Subject to the provisions of any treaty or
agreement to which the United States is or may be a
party or to any accepted rule of international law, all
persons serving with, employed by, or accompanying
the armed forces without the continental limits of the
United States . . . ."

Counsel for Mrs. Covert contended that she was insane at the
time she killed her husband, but the military tribunal found her guilty
of murder and sentenced her to life imprisonment.  The judgment
was affirmed by the Air Force Board of Review, 16 CMR 465, but was
reversed by the Court of Military Appeals, 6 USCMA 48, because of
prejudicial errors concerning the defense of insanity.  While Mrs.
Covert was being held in this country pending a proposed retrial by
court-martial in the District of Columbia, her counsel petitioned the

District Court for a writ of habeas corpus to set her free on the ground that the Constitution forbade her trial by military authorities. Construing this Court's decision in United States ex rel. Toth v. Quarles, 350 U.S. 11, as holding that "a civilian is entitled to a civilian trial" the District Court held that Mrs. Covert could not be tried by court-martial and ordered her released from custody. The Government appealed directly to this Court under 28 U. S. C. §1252. See 350 U.S. 985.

In No. 713 Mrs. Dorothy Smith killed her husband, an Army officer, at a post in Japan where she was living with him. She was tried for murder by a court-martial and despite considerable evidence that she was insane was found guilty and sentenced to life imprisonment. The judgment was approved by the Army Board of Review, 10 CMR 350, 13 CMR 307, and the Court of Military Appeals, 5 USCMA 314. Mrs. Smith was then confined in a federal penitentiary in West Virginia. Her father, respondent here, filed a petition for habeas corpus in a District Court for West Virginia. The petition charged that the court-martial was without jurisdiction because Article 2(11) of the UCMJ was unconstitutional insofar as it authorized the trial of civilian dependents accompanying servicemen overseas. The District Court refused to issue the writ, 137 F. Supp. 806, and while an appeal was pending in the Court of Appeals for the Fourth Circuit we granted certiorari at the request of the Government, 350 U.S. 986.

The two cases were consolidated and argued last Term and a majority of the Court, with three Justices dissenting and one reserving opinion, held that military trial of Mrs. Smith and Mrs. Covert for their alleged offenses was constitutional. 351 U.S. 470, 487. The majority held that the provisions of Article III and the Fifth and Sixth Amendments which require that crimes be tried by a jury after indictment by a grand jury did not protect an American citizen when he was tried by the American Government in foreign lands for offenses committed there and that Congress could provide for the trial of such offenses in any manner it saw fit so long as the procedures established were reasonable and consonant with due process. The opinion then went on to express the view that military trials, as now practiced, were not unreasonable or arbitrary when applied to dependents accompanying members of the armed forces overseas. In reaching their conclusion the majority found it unnecessary to consider the power of Congress "To make Rules for the Government and Regulation of the land and naval Forces" under Article I of the Constitution.

Subsequently, the Court granted a petition for rehearing, 352 U.S. 901. Now, after further argument and consideration, we conclude that the previous decisions cannot be permitted to stand. We hold that Mrs. Smith and Mrs. Covert could not constitutionally be tried by military authorities.

I

At the beginning we reject the idea that when the United States acts against citizens abroad it can do so free of the Bill of Rights.

The United States is entirely a creature of the Constitution. Its power and authority have no other source. It can only act in accordance with all the limitations imposed by the Constitution. When the Government reaches out to punish a citizen who is abroad, the shield which the Bill of Rights and other parts of the Constitution provide to protect his life and liberty should not be stripped away just because he happens to be in another land. . . .

. . .

Trial by jury in a court of law and in accordance with traditional modes of procedure after an indictment by grand jury has served and remains one of our most vital barriers to governmental arbitrariness. These elemental procedural safeguards were embedded in our Constitution to secure their inviolateness and sanctity against the passing demands of expediency or convenience.

The keystone of supporting authorities mustered by the Court's opinion last June to justify its holding that Art. III, §2, and the Fifth and Sixth Amendments did not apply abroad was In re Ross, 140 U.S. 453. The Ross case is one of those cases that cannot be understood except in its peculiar setting; even then, it seems highly unlikely that a similar result would be reached today. Ross was serving as a seaman on an American ship in Japanese waters. He killed a ship's officer, was seized and tried before a consular "court" in Japan. At that time, statutes authorized American consuls to try American citizens charged with committing crimes in Japan and certain other "non-Christian" countries. . . .

The consular power approved in the Ross case was about as extreme and absolute as that of the potentates of the "non-Christian" countries to which the statutes applied. Under these statutes consuls could and did make the criminal laws, initiate charges, arrest alleged offenders, try them, and after conviction take away their liberty or their life--sometimes at the American consulate. Such a blending of executive, legislative, and judicial powers in one person or even in one branch of the Government is ordinarily regarded as the very acme of absolutism. Nevertheless, the Court sustained Ross' conviction by the consul. It stated that constitutional protections applied "only to citizens and others within the United States, or who are brought there for trial for alleged offences committed elsewhere, and not to residents or temporary sojourners abroad." Despite the fact that it upheld Ross' conviction under United States laws passed pursuant to asserted constitutional authority, the Court went on to make a sweeping declaration that "[t]he Constitution can have no operation in another country."

The Ross approach that the Constitution has no applicability abroad has long since been directly repudiated by numerous cases. That approach is obviously erroneous if the United States Government, which has no power except that granted by the Constitution, can and does try citizens for crimes committed abroad. Thus the Ross case rested, at least in substantial part, on a fundamental misconception

and the most that can be said in support of the result reached there
is that the consular court jurisdiction had a long history antedating
the adoption of the Constitution.  The Congress has recently buried
the consular system of trying Americans.  We are not willing to
jeopardize the lives and liberties of Americans by disinterring it.  At
best, the Ross case should be left as a relic from a different era.

   . . .

## II

At the time of Mrs. Covert's alleged offense, an executive
agreement was in effect between the United States and Great Britain
which permitted United States' military courts to exercise exclusive
jurisdiction over offenses committed in Great Britain by American
servicemen or their dependents.  For its part, the United States
agreed that these military courts would be willing and able to try and
to punish all offenses against the laws of Great Britain by such persons.  In all material respects, the same situation existed in Japan
when Mrs. Smith killed her husband.  Even though a court-martial
does not give an accused trial by jury and other Bill of Rights protections, the Government contends that Art. 2(11) of the UCMJ, insofar
as it provides for the military trial of dependents accompanying the
armed forces in Great Britain and Japan, can be sustained as legislation which is necessary and proper to carry out the United States'
obligations under the international agreements made with those
countries.  The obvious and decisive answer to this, of course, is
that no agreement with a foreign nation can confer power on the Congress, or on any other branch of Government, which is free from the
restraints of the Constitution.

   . . .

In summary, we conclude that the Constitution in its entirety
applied to the trials of Mrs. Smith and Mrs. Covert.  Since their
court-martial did not meet the requirements of Art. III, §2 or the
Fifth and Sixth Amendments we are compelled to determine if there
is anything within the Constitution which authorizes the military trial
of dependents accompanying the armed forces overseas.

## III

Article I, §8, cl. 14 empowers Congress "To make Rules for
the Government and Regulation of the land and naval Forces."  It has
been held that this creates an exception to the normal method of trial
in civilian courts as provided by the Constitution and permits Congress to authorize military trial of members of the armed services
without all the safeguards given an accused by Article III and the Bill
of Rights.  But if the language of Clause 14 is given its natural meaning, the power granted does not extend to civilians--even though they
may be dependents living with servicemen on a military base.  The
term "land and naval Forces" refers to persons who are members
of the armed services and not to their civilian wives, children and
other dependents.  It seems inconceivable that Mrs. Covert or Mrs.

Smith could have been tried by military authorities as members of
the "land and naval Forces" had they been living on a military post
in this country. Yet this constitutional term surely has the same
meaning everywhere. The wives of servicemen are no more members of the "land and naval Forces" when living at a military post in
England or Japan than when living at a base in this country or in
Hawaii or Alaska.

    The Government argues that the Necessary and Proper Clause
when taken in conjunction with Clause 14 allows Congress to authorize
the trial of Mrs. Smith and Mrs. Covert by military tribunals and
under military law. The Government claims that the two clauses together constitute a broad grant of power "without limitation" authorizing Congress to subject all persons, civilians and soldiers alike, to
military trial if "necessary and proper" to govern and regulate the
land and naval forces. It was on a similar theory that Congress once
went to the extreme of subjecting persons who made contracts with
the military to court-martial jurisdiction with respect to frauds related to such contracts. In the only judicial test a Circuit Court held
that the legislation was patently unconstitutional. Ex parte Henderson,
11 Fed. Cas. 1067, No. 6,349.

    It is true that the Constitution expressly grants Congress power
to make all rules necessary and proper to govern and regulate those
persons who are serving in the "land and naval Forces." But the
Necessary and Proper Clause cannot operate to extend military jurisdiction to any group of persons beyond that class described in Clause
14--"the land and naval Forces." Under the grand design of the Constitution civilian courts are the normal repositories of power to try
persons charged with crimes against the United States. And to protect persons brought before these courts, Article III and the Fifth,
Sixth, and Eighth Amendments establish the right to trial by jury, to
indictment by a grand jury and a number of other specific safeguards.
By way of contrast the jurisdiction of military tribunals is a very
limited and extraordinary jurisdiction derived from the cryptic language in Art. I, §8, and, at most, was intended to be only a narrow
exception to the normal and preferred method of trial in courts of
law. Every extension of military jurisdiction is an encroachment on
the jurisdiction of the civil courts, and, more important, acts as a
deprivation of the right to jury trial and of other treasured constitutional protections. Having run up against the steadfast bulwark of
the Bill of Rights, the Necessary and Proper Clause cannot extend
the scope of Clause 14.
    . . .
    Even if it were possible, we need not attempt here to precisely
define the boundary between "civilians" and members of the "land
and naval Forces." We recognize that there might be circumstances
where a person could be "in" the armed services for purposes of
Clause 14 even though he had not formally been inducted into the

military or did not wear a uniform.  But the wives, children and other
dependents of servicemen cannot be placed in that category, even
though they may be accompanying a serviceman abroad at Government expense and receiving other benefits from the Government.  We
have no difficulty in saying that such persons do not lose their civilian
status and their right to a civilian trial because the Government helps
them live as members of a soldier's family.

. . .

In light of this history, it seems clear that the Founders had no
intention to permit the trial of civilians in military courts, where
they would be denied jury trials and other constitutional protections,
merely by giving Congress the power to make rules which were
"necessary and proper" for the regulation of the "land and naval
Forces."  Such a latitudinarian interpretation of these clauses would
be at war with the well-established purpose of the Founders to keep
the military strictly within its proper sphere, subordinate to civil
authority.  The Constitution does not say that Congress can regulate
"the land and naval Forces and all other persons whose regulation
might have some relationship to maintenance of the land and naval
Forces."  There is no indication that the Founders contemplated setting up a rival system of military courts to compete with civilian
courts for jurisdiction over civilians who might have some contact or
relationship with the armed forces.  Courts-martial were not to have
concurrent jurisdiction with courts of law over non-military America.

. . .

The Milligan, Duncan and Toth cases recognized and manifested
the deeply rooted and ancient opposition in this country to the extension of military control over civilians.  In each instance an effort to
expand the jurisdiction of military courts to civilians was repulsed.

There have been a number of decisions in the lower federal
courts which have upheld military trial of civilians performing services for the armed forces "in the field" during time of war.  To the
extent that these cases can be justified, insofar as they involved trial
of persons who were not "members" of the armed forces, they must
rest on the Government's "war powers."  In the face of an actively
hostile enemy, military commanders necessarily have broad power
over persons on the battlefront.  From a time prior to the adoption of
the Constitution the extraordinary circumstances present in an area
of actual fighting have been considered sufficient to permit punishment of some civilians in that area by military courts under military
rules.  But neither Japan nor Great Britain could properly be said to
be an area where active hostilities were under way at the time Mrs.
Smith and Mrs. Covert committed their offenses or at the time they
were tried.

The Government urges that the concept "in the field" should be
broadened to reach dependents accompanying the military forces
overseas under the conditions of world tension which exist at the

present time.  It points out how the "war powers" include authority to
prepare defenses and to establish our military forces in defensive
posture about the world.  While we recognize that the "war powers"
of the Congress and the Executive are broad, we reject the Government's argument that present threats to peace permit military trial
of civilians accompanying the armed forces overseas in an area where
no actual hostilities are under way.  The exigencies which have required military rule on the battlefront are not present in areas where
no conflict exists.  Military trial of civilians "in the field" is an
extraordinary jurisdiction and it should not be expanded at the expense of the Bill of Rights.  We agree with Colonel Winthrop, an expert
on military jurisdiction, who declared:  "a statute cannot be framed
by which a civilian can lawfully be made amenable to the military
jurisdiction in time of peace."  (Emphasis not supplied.)

As this Court stated in United States ex rel. Toth v. Quarles,
350 U.S. 11, the business of soldiers is to fight and prepare to fight
wars, not to try civilians for their alleged crimes.  Traditionally,
military justice has been a rough form of justice emphasizing summary procedures, speedy convictions and stern penalties with a view
to maintaining obedience and fighting fitness in the ranks.  Because
of its very nature and purpose the military must place great emphasis
on discipline and efficiency.  Correspondingly, there has always been
less emphasis in the military on protecting the rights of the individual
than in civilian society and in civilian courts.

Courts-martial are typically ad hoc bodies appointed by a military officer from among his subordinates.  They have always been
subject to varying degrees of "command influence."  In essence, these
tribunals are simply executive tribunals whose personnel are in the
executive chain of command.  Frequently, the members of the court-
martial must look to the appointing officer for promotions, advan-
tageous assignments and efficiency ratings--in short, for their future
progress in the service.  Conceding to military personnel that high
degree of honesty and sense of justice which nearly all of them undoubtedly have, the members of a court-martial, in the nature of things,
do not and cannot have the independence of jurors drawn from the general public or of civilian judges.

We recognize that a number of improvements have been made in
military justice recently by engrafting more and more of the methods
of civilian courts on courts-martial.  In large part these ameliorations
stem from the reaction of civilians, who were inducted during the two
World Wars, to their experience with military justice.  Notwithstanding the recent reforms, military trial does not give an accused the
same protection which exists in the civil courts.  Looming far above
all other deficiencies of the military trial, of course, is the absence
of trial by jury before an independent judge after an indictment by a
grand jury.  Moreover the reforms are merely statutory; Congress--
and perhaps the President--can reinstate former practices, subject

to any limitations imposed by the Constitution, whenever it desires.
As yet it has not been clearly settled to what extent the Bill of Rights
and other protective parts of the Constitution apply to military trials.

It must be emphasized that every person who comes within the
jurisdiction of courts-martial is subject to military law--law that is
substantially different from the law which governs civilian society.
Military law is, in many respects, harsh law which is frequently cast
in very sweeping and vague terms. It emphasizes the iron hand of
discipline more that it does the even scales of justice. Moreover, it
has not yet been definitely established to what extent the President,
as Commander-in-Chief of the armed forces, or his delegates, can
promulgate, supplement or change substantive military law as well
as the procedures of military courts in time of peace, or in time of
war. In any event, Congress has given the President broad discretion
to provide the rules governing military trials. For example, in these
very cases a technical manual issued under the President's name with
regard to the defense of insanity in military trials was of critical importance in the convictions of Mrs. Covert and Mrs. Smith. If the
President can provide rules of substantive law as well as procedure,
then he and his military subordinates exercise legislative, executive
and judicial powers with respect to those subject to military trials.
Such blending of functions in one branch of the Government is the objectionable thing which the draftsmen of the Constitution endeavored
to prevent by providing for the separation of governmental powers.

In summary, "it still remains true that military tribunals have
not been and probably never can be constituted in such way that they
can have the same kind of qualifications that the Constitution has
deemed essential to fair trials of civilians in federal courts." In part
this is attributable to the inherent differences in values and attitudes
that separate the military establishment from civilian society. In the
military, by necessity, emphasis must be placed on the security and
order of the group rather than on the value and integrity of the individual.

It is urged that the expansion of military jurisdiction over
civilians claimed here is only slight, and that the practical necessity
for it is very great. The attitude appears to be that a slight encroachment on the Bill of Rights and other safeguards in the Constitution need
cause little concern. But to hold that these wives could be tried by the
military would be a tempting precedent. Slight encroachments create
new boundaries from which legions of power can seek new territory to
capture. "It may be that it is the obnoxious thing in its mildest and
least repulsive form; but illegitimate and unconstitutional practices
get their first footing in that way, namely, by silent approaches and
slight deviations from legal modes of procedure. This can only be
obviated by adhering to the rule that constitutional provisions for the
security of person and property should be liberally construed. A
close and literal construction deprives them of half their efficacy,

and leads to gradual depreciation of the right, as if it consisted more in sound than in substance. It is the duty of courts to be watchful for the constitutional rights of the citizen, and against any stealthy encroachments thereon." Moreover we cannot consider this encroachment a slight one. Throughout history many transgressions by the military have been called "slight" and have been justified as "reasonable" in light of the "uniqueness" of the times. We cannot close our eyes to the fact that today the peoples of many nations are ruled by the military.

We should not break faith with this Nation's tradition of keeping military power subservient to civilian authority, a tradition which we believe is firmly embodied in the Constitution. The country has remained true to that faith for almost one hundred seventy years. Perhaps no group in the Nation has been truer than military men themselves. Unlike the soldiers of many other nations, they have been content to perform their military duties in defense of the Nation in every period of need and to perform those duties well without attempting to usurp power which is not theirs under our system of constitutional government.

Ours is a government of divided authority on the assumption that in division there is not only strength but freedom from tyranny. And under our Constitution courts of law alone are given power to try civilians for their offenses against the United States. The philosophy expressed by Lord Coke, speaking long ago from a wealth of experience, is still timely:

"God send me never to live under the Law of Conveniency or Discretion. Shall the Souldier and Justice Sit on one Bench, the Trumpet will not let the Cryer speak in Westminster-Hall."

In No. 701, Reid v. Covert, the judgment of the District Court directing that Mrs. Covert be released from custody is

Affirmed.

In No. 713, Kinsella v. Krueger, the judgment of the District Court is reversed and the case is remanded with instructions to order Mrs. Smith released from custody.

Reversed and remanded.

MR. JUSTICE WHITTAKER took no part in the consideration or decision of these cases.

MR. JUSTICE FRANKFURTER, concurring in the result.
. . .
The Government, apparently recognizing the constitutional basis for the decision in Ross, has, on rehearing, sought to show that civilians in general and civilian dependents in particular have been subject to military order and discipline ever since the colonial period. The

materials it has submitted seem too episodic, too meager, to form a solid basis in history, preceding and contemporaneous with the framing of the Constitution, for constitutional adjudication. What has been urged on us falls far too short of proving a well-established practice-- to be deemed to be infused into the Constitution--of court-martial jurisdiction, certainly not in capital cases, over such civilians in time of peace.

MR. JUSTICE HARLAN, concurring in the result.

I concur in the result, on the narrow ground that where the offense is capital, Article 2(11) cannot constitutionally be applied to the trial of civilian dependents of members of the armed forces overseas in times of peace.

. . .

MR. JUSTICE CLARK, with whom MR. JUSTICE BURTON joins, dissenting.

The Court today releases two women from prosecution though the evidence shows that they brutally killed their husbands, both American soldiers, while stationed with them in quarters furnished by our armed forces on its military installations in foreign lands. In turning these women free, it declares unconstitutional an important section of an Act of Congress governing our armed forces. . . .

. . .

Before discussing the power of the Congress under Art. I, §8, cl. 14, of the Constitution it is well to take our bearings. These cases do not involve the jurisdiction of a military court-martial sitting within the territorial limits of the United States. Nor are they concerned with the power of the Government to make treaties or the legal relationship between treaties and the Constitution. Nor are they concerned with the power of Congress to provide for the trial of Americans sojourning, touring, or temporarily residing in foreign nations. Essentially, we are to determine only whether the civilian dependents of American servicemen may constitutionally be tried by an American military court-martial in a foreign country for an offense committed in that country. Congress has provided in Article 2(11) of the Uniform Code of Military Justice, 64 Stat. 109, 50 U. S. C. §552(11), that they shall be so tried in those countries with which we have an implementing treaty. The question therefore is whether this enactment is reasonably related to the power of Congress "To make Rules for the Government and Regulation of the land and naval Forces." U.S.Const., Art. I, §8, cl. 14.

Historically, the military has always exercised jurisdiction by court-martial over civilians accompanying armies in time of war. Over 40 years ago this jurisdiction was declared by Congress to include "all persons accompanying or serving with the armies of the United States without the territorial jurisdiction of the United States."

Art. of War 2(d), 39 Stat. 651. Article 2(11) of the present Uniform
Code of Military Justice was taken without material change from this
provision of the Articles of War. At the time of enactment of the
earlier provision Congress was plainly concerned with the maintenance of discipline and morale of American expeditionary forces composed of both military and civilian personnel. As pointed out in the
Senate Report to the Sixty-fourth Congress at the time Article 2(d)
was adopted:

> "The existing articles are further defective in that they
> do not permit the disciplining of these three classes of
> camp followers in time of peace in places to which the
> civil jurisdiction of the United States does not extend and
> where it is contrary to international policy to subject such
> persons to the local jurisdiction, or where, for other
> reasons, the law of the local jurisdiction is not applicable,
> thus leaving these classes practically without liability to
> punishment for their unlawful acts under such circum-
> stances--as, for example, . . . where such forces so
> accompanied are engaged in the nonhostile occupation of
> foreign territory, as was the case during the intervention
> of 1906-7 in Cuba." S. Rep. No. 130, 64th Cong., 1st
> Sess. 37-38.

. . .

In considering whether Article 2(11) is reasonably necessary to
the power of Congress to provide for the government of the land and
naval forces we note, as relevant, certain other considerations. As
a nation we have found it necessary to the preservation of our security
in the present day to maintain American forces in 63 foreign countries
throughout the world. In recent years the services have recognized
that the presence of wives and families at many of these foreign bases
is essential to the maintenance of the morale of our forces. This
policy has received legislative approval and the tremendous expense
to the Government involved in the transportation and accommodation
of dependents overseas is considered money well spent. It is not for
us to question this joint executive and legislative determination. The
result, however, has been the creation of American communities of
mixed civilian and military population on military bases throughout
the world. These civilians are dependent on the military for food,
housing, medical facilities, transportation, and protection. Often they
live in daily association in closely knit groups nearly isolated from
their surroundings. It cannot be denied that disciplinary problems
have been multiplied and complicated by this influx of civilians onto
military bases, and Congress has provided that military personnel
and civilians alike shall be governed by the same law administered
by the same courts.

Concerning the effect of civilian activities under such circumstances on the discipline and morale of the armed services, we have found no better statement than that of Judge Latimer of the United States Court of Military Appeals where the constitutionality of Article 2(11) was upheld in the recent case of United States v. Burney, 6 U. S. C. M. A. 776, 21 C. M. R. 98 (1956). Referring to the combat readiness of an overseas command, Judge Latimer stated:

"[I]t is readily ascertainable that black market transactions, trafficking in habit-forming drugs, unlawful currency circulation, promotion of illicit sex relations, and a myriad of other crimes which may be perpetrated by persons closely connected with one of the services, could have a direct and forceful impact on the efficiency and discipline of the command. One need only view the volume of business transacted by military courts involving, for instance, the sale and use of narcotics in the Far East, to be shocked into a realization of the truth of the previous statement. If the Services have no power within their own system to punish that type of offender, then indeed overseas crime between civilians and military personnel will flourish and that amongst civilians will thrive unabated and untouched. A few civilians plying an unlawful trade in military communities can, without fail, impair the discipline and combat readiness of a unit. At best, the detection and prosecution of crime is a difficult and time-consuming business, and we have grave doubts that, in faraway lands, the foreign governments will help the cause of a military commander by investigating the seller or user of habit-forming drugs, or assist him in deterring American civilians from stealing from their compatriots, or their Government, or from misusing its property." 6 U. S. C. M. A., at 800, 21 C. M. R., at 122.

In addition, it is reasonable to provide that the military commander who bears full responsibility for the care and safety of those civilians attached to his command should also have authority to regulate their conduct. Moreover, all members of an overseas contingent should receive equal treatment before the law. In their actual day-to-day living they are a part of the same unique communities, and the same legal considerations should apply to all. There is no reason for according to one class a different treatment than is accorded to another. The effect of such a double standard on discipline, efficiency, and morale can easily be seen.

. . .

My brothers who are concurring in the result seem to find some comfort in that for the present they void an Act of Congress only as to

capital cases. I find no distinction in the Constitution between capital
and other cases. In fact, at argument all parties admitted there could
be no valid difference. My brothers are careful not to say that they
would uphold the Act as to offenses less than capital. They unfortunately leave that decision for another day. This is disastrous to
proper judicial administration as well as to law enforcement. The
Congress and the Executive Department are entitled to know whether
a court-martial may be constitutionally utilized to try an offense less
than capital. If so, then all that is necessary is to eliminate capital
punishment insofar as Article 2(11) offenses are concerned. I deeply
regret that the former minority does not, now that it has become the
majority, perform the high duty that circumstance requires. Both the
Congress and the Executive are left only to conjecture as to whether
they should "sack" Article 2(11) and require all dependents to return
and remain within this country or simply eliminate capital punishment
from all offenses under the Article. The morale of our troops may
prevent the former and certainly the abstention of this Court prohibits
the latter. All that remains is for the dependents of our soldiers to
be prosecuted in foreign courts, an unhappy prospect not only for them
but for all of us.

The holding of Reid v. Covert, supra, was extended to apply to
non-capital crimes in time of peace in Kinsella v. Singleton, 361 U.S.
234, 89 S.Ct. 297, 4 L.Ed.2d 268 (1960). In Grisham v. Hagan, 361
U.S. 278, 80 S.Ct. 310, 4 L.Ed.2d (1960), and McElroy v. Guagliaido,
361 U.S. 281, 80 S.Ct. 305, 4 L.Ed.2d 282 (1960), the Supreme Court
held that the exercise of court-martial jurisdiction over civilian employees in time of peace was unconstitutional as to both capital and
non-capital offenses.

The determination of when the United States is "at war" may
have important ramifications. For example, the statute of limitations
(Article 43) of the UCMJ sets forth different time periods by which a
person must be charged with an offense depending upon whether it is
"time of war." For this purpose, the Court of Military Appeals has
held that an accused could be tried for absence without leave committed within the continental United States on December 23, 1950, because the United States was "at war" in Korea (U.S. v. Ayers, 4
USCMA 220, 15 CMR 220 [1954]) and that the state of war terminated
on July 27, 1953 (U.S. v. Shell, 7 USCMA 646, 23 CMR 110 [1957]).
Similarly, the Court found that the United States was at war in Vietnam (see U.S. v. Anderson, 17 USCMA 588, 38 CMR 386 [1968]). On
the other hand, the Court held that the words "in time of war," for
the purposes of Article 2(10) mean "a war formally declared by Congress" and that a court-martial had no jurisdiction to try a civilian

employed at an army installation in Vietnam (U.S. v. Averette, 19 USCMA 363, 41 CMR 363 [1970]); accord, Zamora v. Woodson, 19 USCMA 403, 42 CMR 5 (1970); cf. Latney v. Ignatius, 416 F.2d 821 (1969).

For other cases interpreting "wartime," see Hamilton v. McClaughrey, 136 F. 445 (1905) (Boxer Rebellion), and Lee v. Madigan, 358 U.S. 228, 79 S.Ct. 276, 3 L.Ed.2d 260 (1959) (World War II).

## OF THE OFFENSE

Prior to the following case, O'Callahan v. Parker, the question of court-martial jurisdiction depended primarily, if not entirely, upon the status of the accused.  The O'Callahan case introduced the question of the nature of the offense and held that, despite the fact that an accused was in the military service, he could not be court-martialed unless the offense was "service-connected."

## O'CALLAHAN v. PARKER*

Supreme Court of the United States, 1969.
395 U.S. 258, 89 S.Ct. 1683, 23 L.Ed.2d 291.

*[Footnotes have been omitted.  Ed.]

MR. JUSTICE DOUGLAS delivered the opinion of the Court.
Petitioner, then a sergeant in the United States Army, was stationed in July 1956, at Fort Shafter, Oahu, in the Territory of Hawaii. On the night of July 20, while on an evening pass, petitioner and a friend left the post dressed in civilian clothes and went into Honolulu. After a few beers in the bar of a hotel, petitioner entered the residential part of the hotel where he broke into the room of a young girl and assaulted and attempted to rape her.  While fleeing from her room onto Waikiki Beach, he was apprehended by a hotel security officer who delivered him to the Honolulu city police for questioning. After determining that he was a member of the Armed Forces, the

city police delivered petitioner to the military police. After extensive interrogation, petitioner confessed and was placed in military confinement.

Petitioner was charged with attempted rape, house-breaking, and assault with intent to rape, in violation of Articles 80, 130, and 134 of the Uniform Code of Military Justice. He was tried by court-martial, convicted on all counts, and given a sentence of 10 years' imprisonment at hard labor, forfeiture of all pay and allowances, and dishonorable discharge. His conviction was affirmed by the Army Board of Review and, subsequently, by the United States Court of Military Appeals.

Under confinement at the United States Penitentiary at Lewisburg, Pennsylvania, petitioner filed a petition for writ of habeas corpus in the United States District Court for the Middle District of Pennsylvania, alleging, inter alia, that the court-martial was without jurisdiction to try him for nonmilitary offenses committed off-post while on an evening pass. The District Court denied relief without considering the issue on the merits, and the Court of Appeals for the Third Circuit affirmed. This Court granted certiorari limited to the question:

> "Does a court-martial, held under the Articles of War, Tit. 10, U. S. C. §801 et seq., have jurisdiction to try a member of the Armed Forces who is charged with commission of a crime cognizable in a civilian court and having no military significance, alleged to have been committed off-post and while on leave, thus depriving him of his constitutional rights to indictment by a grand jury and trial by a petit jury in a civilian court?" 393 U.S. 822.

The Constitution gives Congress power to "make Rules for the Government and Regulation of the land and naval Forces," Art. I, §8, cl. 14, and it recognizes that the exigencies of military discipline require the existence of a special system of military courts in which not all of the specific procedural protections deemed essential in Art. III trials need apply. The Fifth Amendment specifically exempts "cases arising in the land or naval forces, or in the Militia, when in actual service in time of War or public danger" from the requirement of prosecution by indictment and, inferentially, from the right to trial by jury. (Emphasis supplied.) See Ex parte Quirin, 317 U.S. 1, 40. The result has been the establishment and development of a system of military justice with fundamental differences from the practices in the civilian courts.

If the case does not arise "in the land or naval forces," then the accused gets first, the benefit of an indictment by a grand jury and second, a trial by jury before a civilian court as guaranteed by the Sixth Amendment and by Art. III, §2, of the Constitution which provides in part:

> "The Trial of all Crimes, except in Cases of Impeachment, shall be by Jury; and such Trial shall be held in the State where the said Crimes shall have been committed; but when not committed within any State, the Trial shall be at such Place or Places as the Congress may by Law have directed."

Those civil rights are the constitutional stakes in the present litigation. What we wrote in Toth v. Quarles, 350 U.S. 11, 17-18, is worth emphasis:

> "We find nothing in the history or constitutional treatment of military tribunals which entitles them to rank along with Article III courts as adjudicators of the guilt or innocence of people charged with offenses for which they can be deprived of their life, liberty or property. Unlike courts, it is the primary business of armies and navies to fight or be ready to fight wars should the occasion arise. But trial of soldiers to maintain discipline is merely incidental to an army's primary fighting function. To the extent that those responsible for performance of this primary function are diverted from it by the necessity of trying cases, the basic fighting purpose of armies is not served. And conceding to military personnel that high degree of honesty and sense of justice which nearly all of them undoubtedly have, it still remains true that military tribunals have not been and probably never can be constituted in such way that they can have the same kind of qualifications that the Constitution has deemed essential to fair trials of civilians in federal courts. For instance, the Constitution does not provide life tenure for those performing judicial functions in military trials. They are appointed by military commanders and may be removed at will. Nor does the Constitution protect their salaries as it does judicial salaries. Strides have been made toward making courts-martial less subject to the will of the executive department which appoints, supervises and ultimately controls them. But from the very nature of things, courts have more independence in passing on the life and liberty of people than do military tribunals.
> "Moreover, there is a great difference between trial by jury and trial by selected members of the military forces. It is true that military personnel because of their

training and experience may be especially competent to
try soldiers for infractions of military rules. Such training is no doubt particularly important where an offense
charged against a soldier is purely military, such as disobedience of an order, leaving post, etc. But whether
right or wrong, the premise underlying the constitutional
method for determining guilt or innocence in federal
courts is that laymen are better than specialists to perform this task. This idea is inherent in the institution
of trial by jury."

A court-martial is tried, not by a jury of the defendant's peers
which must decide unanimously, but by a panel of officers empowered
to act by a two-thirds vote. The presiding officer at a court-martial
is not a judge whose objectivity and independence are protected by
tenure and undiminishable salary and nurtured by the judicial tradition, but is a military law officer. Substantially different rules of
evidence and procedure apply in military trials. Apart from those
differences, the suggestion of the possibility of influence on the actions of the court-martial by the officer who convenes it, selects its
members and the counsel on both sides, and who usually has direct
command authority over its members is a pervasive one in military
law, despite strenuous efforts to eliminate the danger.
A court-martial is not yet an independent instrument of justice
but remains to a significant degree a specialized part of the overall
mechanism by which military discipline is preserved.
That a system of specialized military courts, proceeding by
practices different from those obtaining in the regular courts and in
general less favorable to defendants, is necessary to an effective
national defense establishment, few would deny. But the justification
for such a system rests on the special needs of the military, and
history teaches that expansion of military discipline beyond its proper
domain carries with it a threat to liberty. This Court, mindful of the
genuine need for special military courts, has recognized their propriety in their appropriate sphere, e. g., Burns v. Wilson, 346 U.S. 137,
but in examining the reach of their jurisdiction, it has recognized that

"There are dangers lurking in military trials which
were sought to be avoided by the Bill of Rights and Article III of our Constitution. Free countries of the world
have tried to restrict military tribunals to the narrowest
jurisdiction deemed absolutely essential to maintaining
discipline among troops in active service.
"Determining the scope of the constitutional power
of Congress to authorize trial by court-martial presents
another instance calling for limitation to 'the least possible power adequate to the end proposed.'" Toth v. Quarles,
350 U.S. 11, 22-23.

While the Court of Military Appeals takes cognizance of some constitutional rights of the accused who are court-martialed; courts-martial as an institution are singularly inept in dealing with the nice subtleties of constitutional law. Article 134, already quoted, punishes as a crime "all disorders and neglects to the prejudice of good order and discipline in the armed forces." Does this satisfy the standards of vagueness as developed by the civil courts? It is not enough to say that a court-martial may be reversed on appeal. One of the benefits of a civilian trial is that the trap of Article 134 may be avoided by a declaratory judgment proceeding or otherwise. See Dombrowski v. Pfister, 380 U.S. 479. A civilian trial, in other words, is held in an atmosphere conducive to the protection of individual rights, while a military trial is marked by the age-old manifest destiny of retributive justice.

As recently stated: "None of the travesties of justice perpetrated under the UCMJ is really very surprising, for military law has always been and continues to be primarily an instrument of discipline, not justice." Glasser, Justice and Captain Levy, 12 Columbia Forum 46, 49 (1969).

The mere fact that petitioner was at the time of his offense and of his court-martial on active duty in the Armed Forces does not automatically dispose of this case under our prior decisions.

We have held in a series of decisions that court-martial jurisdiction cannot be extended to reach any person not a member of the Armed Forces at the times of both the offense and the trial. Thus, discharged soldiers cannot be court-martialed for offenses committed while in service, Toth v. Quarles, 350 U.S. 11. Similarly, neither civilian employees of the Armed Forces overseas, McElroy v. Guagliardo, 361 U.S. 281; Grisham v. Hagan, 361 U.S. 278; nor civilian dependents of military personnel accompanying them overseas, Kinsella v. Singleton, 361 U.S. 234; Reid v. Covert, 354 U.S. 1, may be tried by court-martial.

These cases decide that courts-martial have no jurisdiction to try those who are not members of the Armed Forces, no matter how intimate the connection between their offense and the concerns of military discipline. From these cases, the Government invites us to draw the conclusion that once it is established that the accused is a member of the Armed Forces, lack of relationship between the offense and identifiable military interests is irrelevant to the jurisdiction of a court-martial.

The fact that courts-martial have no jurisdiction over nonsoldiers, whatever their offense, does not necessarily imply that they have unlimited jurisdiction over soldiers, regardless of the nature of the offenses charged. Nor do the cases of this Court suggest any such interpretation. The Government emphasizes that these decisions-- especially Kinsella v. Singleton--establish that liability to trial by court-martial is a question of "status"--"whether the accused in the

court-martial proceeding is a person who can be regarded as falling
within the term 'land and naval Forces.'" 361 U.S., at 241. But that
is merely the beginning of the inquiry, not its end. "Status" is necessary for jurisdiction; but it does not follow that ascertainment of
"status" completes the inquiry, regardless of the nature, time, and
place of the offense.

Both in England prior to the American Revolution and in our own
national history military trial of soldiers committing civilian offenses
has been viewed with suspicion. Abuses of the court-martial power
were an important grievance of the parliamentary forces in the English
constitutional crises of the 17th century. The resolution of that conflict came with the acceptance by William and Mary of the Bill of
Rights in 1689 which established that in the future, Parliament, not
the Crown, would have the power to define the jurisdiction of courts-
martial. 1 W. & M., Sess. 2, c. 2. The 17th century conflict over the
proper role of courts-martial in the enforcement of the domestic
criminal law was not, however, merely a dispute over what organ of
government had jurisdiction. It also involved substantive disapproval
of the general use of military courts for trial of ordinary crimes.

Parliament, possessed at last of final power in the matter, was
quick to authorize, subject to annual renewal, maintenance of a standing army and to give authority for trial by court-martial of certain
crimes closely related to military discipline. But Parliament's new
power over courts-martial was exercised only very sparingly to
ordain military jurisdiction over acts which were also offenses at
common law. The first of the annual mutiny acts, 1 W. & M., c. 5, set
the tone. It established the general rule that

> "noe Man may be forejudged of Life or Limbe, or subjected
> to any kinde of punishment by Martiall Law or in any other
> manner than by the Judgement of his Peeres and according
> to the knowne and Established Laws of this Realme."

And it proceeded to grant courts-martial jurisdiction only over mutiny, sedition, and desertion. In all other respects, military personnel
were to be subject to the "Ordinary Processe of Law."

The jurisdiction of British courts-martial over military offenses
which were also common-law felonies was from time to time extended,
but, with the exception of one year, there was never any general military jurisdiction to try soldiers for ordinary crimes committed in the
British Isles. It was, therefore, the rule in Britain at the time of the
American Revolution that a soldier could not be tried by court-martial
for a civilian offense committed in Britain; instead military officers
were required to use their energies and office to insure that the accused soldier would be tried before a civil court. Evasion and erosion
of the principle that crimes committed by soldiers should be tried
according to regular judicial procedure in civil, not military, courts,

if any were available, were among the grievances protested by the American Colonists.

Early American practice followed the British model. The Continental Congress, in enacting articles of war in 1776, emphasized the importance of military authority cooperating to insure that soldiers who committed crimes were brought to justice. But it is clear from the context of the provision it enacted that it expected the trials would be in civil courts. The "general article," which punished "[a]ll crimes not capital, and all disorders and neglects, which officers and soldiers may be guilty of, to the prejudice of good order and military discipline, though not mentioned in the foregoing articles of war," was interpreted to embrace only crimes the commission of which had some direct impact on military discipline. Winthrop *1123. While practice was not altogether consistent, during the 19th century court-martial convictions for ordinary civil crimes were from time to time set aside by the reviewing authority on the ground that the charges recited only a violation of the general criminal law and failed to state a military offense. Id., *1124, nn. 82, 88.

During the Civil War, Congress provided for military trial of certain civil offenses without regard to their effect on order and discipline, but the act applied only "in time of war, insurrection, or rebellion." Act of Mar. 3, 1863, c. 75, §30, 12 Stat. 736; Rev. Stat. §1342, Art. 58 (1874). In 1916, on the eve of World War I, the Articles of War were revised, 39 Stat. 650, to provide for military trial, even in peacetime, of certain specific civilian crimes committed by persons "subject to military law" and the general article, Art. 96, was modified to provide for military trial of "all crimes or offenses not capital." In 1950, the Uniform Code of Military Justice extended military jurisdiction to capital crimes as well.

We have concluded that the crime to be under military jurisdiction must be service connected, lest "cases arising in the land or naval forces, or in the Militia, when in actual service in time of War or public danger," as used in the Fifth Amendment, be expanded to deprive every member of the armed services of the benefits of an indictment by a grand jury and a trial by a jury of his peers. The power of Congress to make "Rules for the Government and Regulation of the land and naval Forces," Art. I, §8, cl. 14, need not be sparingly read in order to preserve those two important constitutional guarantees. For it is assumed that an express grant of general power to Congress is to be exercised in harmony with express guarantees of the Bill of Rights. We were advised on oral argument that Art. 134 is construed by the military to give it power to try a member of the armed services for income tax evasion. This article has been called "a catch-all" that "incorporates almost every Federal penal statute into the Uniform Code." R. Everett, Military Justice in the Armed Forces of the United States 68-69 (1956). The catalogue of cases put within reach of the military is indeed long; and we see no way of saving to servicemen and servicewomen in any case the benefits of indictment and of trial by jury, if we conclude that this petitioner was properly tried by court-martial.

In the present case petitioner was properly absent from his military base when he committed the crimes with which he is charged. There was no connection--not even the remotest one--between his military duties and the crimes in question. The crimes were not committed on a military post or enclave; nor was the person whom he attacked performing any duties relating to the military. Moreover, Hawaii, the situs of the crime, is not an armed camp under military control, as are some of our far-flung outposts.

Finally, we deal with peacetime offenses, not with authority stemming from the war power. Civil courts were open. The offenses were committed within our territorial limits, not in the occupied zone of a foreign country. The offenses did not involve any question of the flouting of military authority, the security of a military post, or the integrity of military property.

We have accordingly decided that since petitioner's crimes were not service connected, he could not be tried by court-martial but rather was entitled to trial by the civilian courts.

Reversed.

MR. JUSTICE HARLAN, whom MR. JUSTICE STEWART and MR. JUSTICE WHITE join, dissenting.

I consider that the terms of the Constitution and the precedents in this Court point clearly to sustaining court-martial jurisdiction in this instance. The Court's largely one-sided discussion of the competing individual and governmental interests at stake, and its reliance upon what are at best wholly inconclusive historical data, fall far short of supporting the contrary conclusion which the majority has reached. In sum, I think that the Court has grasped for itself the making of a determination which the Constitution has placed in the hands of the Congress, and that in so doing the Court has thrown the law in this realm into a demoralizing state of uncertainty. I must dissent.

I

My starting point is the language of Art. I, §8, cl. 14, of the Constitution, which empowers the Congress "[t]o make Rules for the Government and Regulation of the land and naval Forces," and the Fifth Amendment's correlative exception for "cases arising in the land or naval forces."

Writing for a plurality of the Court in Reid v. Covert, 354 U.S. 1 (1957), MR. JUSTICE BLACK explained that if the "language of Clause 14 is given its natural meaning . . . [t]he term 'land and naval Forces' refers to persons who are members of the armed services . . . ," id., at 19-20, and that accordingly the Fifth Amendment's exception encompasses persons "'in' the armed services."

Id., at 22-23.  In Kinsella v. Singleton, 361 U.S. 234 (1960), again look-ing to the constitutional language, the Court noted that "military juris-diction has always been based on the 'status' of the accused, rather than on the nature of the offense," id., at 243; that is, whether the accused "is a person who can be regarded as falling within the term 'land and naval Forces.'"  Id., at 241.

In these cases and many others, Ex parte Milligan, 4 Wall. 2, 123 (1866); Coleman v. Tennessee, 97 U.S. 509 (1879); Smith v. Whitney, 116 U.S. 167, 184-185 (1886); Johnson v. Sayre, 158 U.S. 109, 114 (1895); Grafton v. United States, 206 U.S. 333, 348 (1907), this Court has consistently asserted that military "status" is a neces-sary and sufficient condition for the exercise of court-martial juris-diction.  The Court has never previously questioned what the language of Clause 14 would seem to make plain--that, given the requisite mili-tary status, it is for Congress and not the Judiciary to determine the appropriate subject-matter jurisdiction of courts-martial.  See Cole-man v. Tennessee, supra, at 514.

## II

English constitutional history provides scant support for the Court's novel interpretation of Clause 14, and the pertinent American history proves, if anything, quite the contrary.

The English history on which the majority relies reveals a long-standing and multifaceted struggle for power between the military and the Crown, on the one hand, and Parliament on the other, which focused, inter alia, on the King's asserted independent prerogative to try sol-diers by court-martial in time of peace.  See generally J. Tanner, English Constitutional Conflicts of the Seventeenth Century (1961). The martial law of the time was, moreover, arbitrary, and alien to established legal principles.  See 1 W. Blackstone's Commentaries 413; M. Hale, History and Analysis of the Common Law in England 42 (6th ed. 1820).  Thus, when, with the Glorious Revolution of 1688, Parliament gained exclusive authority to create peacetime court-martial jurisdiction, it exercised that authority sparingly; the early Mutiny Acts permitted trial by court-martial only for the crimes of mutiny, sedition, and desertion.  E. g., Mutiny Act of 1689, 1 W. & M., Sess. 2, c. 4.

Parliament subsequently expanded the military's peacetime jurisdiction both abroad and at home.  See Mutiny Act of 1712, 12 Anne, c. 13; Mutiny Act of 1803, 43 Geo. 3, c. 20.  And, significantly, §46 of the Mutiny Act of 1720, 7 Geo. 1, c. 6, authorized trial by court-martial for offenses of a nonmilitary nature, if the injured civilian made no request that the accused be tried in the civil courts.  See F. Wiener, Civilians Under Military Justice 13-14, 245-246 (1967).

The burden of English history was not lost on the Framers of our Constitution, who doubtless feared the Executive's assertion of an independent military authority unchecked by the people acting through the Legislature.  Article 9, §4, of the Articles of Confederation--from

which Art. I, §8, cl. 14, of the Constitution was taken--was responsive
to this apprehension:

> "The United States in Congress assembled shall . . .
> have the sole and exclusive right and power of . . . making
> rules for the government and regulation of the . . . land
> and naval forces, and directing their operations." [Empha-
> sis added.]

But nothing in the debates over our Constitution indicates that the
Congress was forever to be limited to the precise scope of court-
martial jurisdiction existing in 17th century England. To the contrary,
Alexander Hamilton stated that Congress' power to prescribe rules for
the government of the armed forces "ought to exist without limitation:
Because it is impossible to foresee or define the extent and variety of
national exigencies, or the corresponding extent & variety of the means
which may be necessary to satisfy them." The Federalist, No. 23.
[Emphasis omitted.]
    American exercise of court-martial jurisdiction prior to, and
contemporaneous with, adoption of the Constitution lends no support
to the Court's position. Military records between the end of the War
of Independence and the beginning of the War of 1812 show frequent
instances of trials by court-martial, east of the frontier, for offenses
against civilians and the civil laws, such as theft, assault, and killing
livestock. Military authority to try soldiers for such offenses derived
initially from the "general article" of war, first enacted by the Continental Congress in 1775, and incorporated today in Art. 134, 10
U. S. C. §934. W. Winthrop's Military Law and Precedents (2d ed.
1896), the leading 19th century treatise on military law, recognized
that the general article encompassed crimes "committed upon or
against civilians . . . at or near a military camp or post," id., at 724
(1920 reprint) (second emphasis added), and noted that even this
limiting principle was not strictly observed. Id., at 725, 730-732.
And in Grafton v. United States, 206 U.S. 333, 348 (1907), the Court
held, with respect to the general article, that:

> "The crimes referred to in that article manifestly em-
> brace those not capital, committed by officers or soldiers
> of the Army in violation of public law as enforced by the
> civil power. No crimes committed by officers or soldiers
> of the Army are excepted by the . . . article from the
> jurisdiction thus conferred upon courts-martial, except
> those that are capital in their nature. . . . [T]he juris-
> diction of general courts-martial [is] . . . concurrent
> with that of the civil courts."

Even if the practice of early American courts-martial had been
otherwise, this would hardly lead to the conclusion that Congress

lacked power to authorize military trials under the present circumstances. It cannot be seriously argued as a general matter that the constitutional limits of congressional power are coterminous with the extent of its exercise in the late 18th and early 19th centuries. And however restrictively the power to define court-martial jurisdiction may be construed, it would be patently wrong so to limit that power. The disciplinary requirements of today's armed force of over 3,000,000 men are manifestly different from those of the 718-man army in existence in 1789. Cf. The Federalist, No. 23, quoted, supra, at 277. By the same token, given an otherwise valid exercise of the Article I power, I can perceive no basis for judicial curtailment of court-martial jurisdiction as Congress has enacted it.

### III

In the light of the language and history of Art. I, §8, cl. 14, of the Constitution, and this Court's hitherto consistent interpretation of this provision, I do not believe that the resolution of the controversy before us calls for any balancing of interests. But if one does engage in a balancing process, one cannot fairly hope to come up with a meaningful answer unless the interests on both sides are fully explored. The Court does not do this. Rather, it chooses to ignore strong and legitimate governmental interests which support the exercise of court-martial jurisdiction even over "nonmilitary" crimes.

The United States has a vital interest in creating and maintaining an armed force of honest, upright, and well-disciplined persons, and in preserving the reputation, morale, and integrity of the military services. Furthermore, because its personnel must, perforce, live and work in close proximity to one another, the military has an obligation to protect each of its members from the misconduct of fellow servicemen. The commission of offenses against the civil order manifests qualities of attitude and character equally destructive of military order and safety. The soldier who acts the part of Mr. Hyde while on leave is, at best, a precarious Dr. Jekyll when back on duty. Thus, as General George Washington recognized:

> "All improper treatment of an inhabitant by an officer or soldier being destructive of good order and discipline as well as subversive of the rights of society is as much a breach of military, as civil law and as punishable by the one as the other." 14 Writings of George Washington 140-141 (Bicent. ed.).

A soldier's misconduct directed against civilians, moreover, brings discredit upon the service of which he is a member:

> "Under every system of military law for the government of either land or naval forces, the jurisdiction of courts martial extends to the trial and punishment of

acts of military or naval officers which tend to bring disgrace and reproach upon the service of which they are
members, whether those acts are done in the performance
of military duties, or in a civil position. . . ." Smith v.
Whitney, 116 U.S. 167, 183-184 (1886).

The Government, thus, has a proper concern in keeping its own house
in order, by deterring members of the armed forces from engaging in
criminal misconduct on or off the base, and by rehabilitating offenders
to return them to useful military service.

The exercise of military jurisdiction is also responsive to other
practical needs of the armed forces. A soldier detained by the civil
authorities pending trial, or subsequently imprisoned, is to that extent rendered useless to the service. Even if he is released on bail
or recognizance, or ultimately placed on probation, the civil authorities may require him to remain within the jurisdiction, thus making
him unavailable for transfer with the rest of his unit or as the service
otherwise requires.

In contrast, a person awaiting trial by court-martial may simply
be restricted to limits, and may "participate in all military duties and
activities of his organization while under such restriction." Manual
for Courts-Martial, United States (1969), ¶20 b. The trial need not
be held in the jurisdiction where the offense was committed. Id., ¶8.
See e. g., United States v. Voorhees, 4 U. S. C. M. A. 509, 515, 16
C. M. R. 83, 89 (1954); cf. United States v. Gravitt, 5 U. S. C. M. A.
249, 256, 17 C. M. R. 249, 256 (1954). And punishments--such as forfeiture of pay, restriction to limits, and hard labor without confine-
ment--may be imposed that do not keep the convicted serviceman from
performing his military duties. See Manual for Courts-Martial, supra,
¶¶126 g, h, k.

## IV

The Court does not explain the scope of the "service-connected"
crimes as to which court-martial jurisdiction is appropriate, but it
appears that jurisdiction may extend to "nonmilitary" offenses in
appropriate circumstances. Thus, the Court intimates that it is relevant to the jurisdictional issue in this case that petitioner was wearing
civilian clothes rather than a uniform when he committed the crimes.
Ante, at 259. And it also implies that plundering, abusing, and stealing
from, civilians may sometimes constitute a punishable abuse of military position, ante, at 270, n. 14, and that officers may be court-
martialed for purely civilian crimes, because "[i]n the 18th century
. . . the 'honor' of an officer was thought to give a specific military
connection to a crime otherwise without military significance." Ibid.
But if these are illustrative cases, the Court suggests no general
standard for determining when the exercise of court-martial jurisdiction is permissible.

Whatever role an ad hoc judicial approach may have in some
areas of the law, the Congress and the military are at least entitled

to know with some certainty the allowable scope of court-martial jurisdiction. Otherwise, the infinite permutations of possibly relevant
factors are bound to create confusion and proliferate litigation over
the jurisdictional issue in each instance. Absolutely nothing in the language, history, or logic of the Constitution justifies this uneasy state
of affairs which the Court has today created.

I would affirm the judgment of the Court of Appeals.

The O'Callahan case has been the subject of many articles,
comments, and notes. Among the best-written are: "The Wayward
Servicemen: His Constitutional Rights and Military Jurisdiction," by
James W. Hodges, 7 San Diego L. Rev. 185 (1970); 43 Temple Law
Quarterly 213 (1970); 15 Villanova L. Rev. 712 (1970); 68 Michigan
L. Rev. 1016 (1970); 3 Loyola Univ. of Los Angeles L. Rev. 188 (1970);
48 North Carolina L. Rev. 380 (1970); 22 Baylor L. Rev. 64 (1970); 54
Minnesota L. Rev. 1 (1969); "O'Callahan v. Parker-Milestone or Mill-
stone in Military Justice?", by Robinson O. Everett, 1969 Duke Law
Journal 853.

Among the suggestions for ameliorating the effects of O'Callahan
is the establishment of an accused's right of removal to the civilian
courts for "service-connected" offenses which right could be waived
if he preferred trial by court-martial. Is this feasible? Desirable?

RELFORD v. COMMANDANT*

Supreme Court of the United States, 1971.
401 U.S. 355, 91 S.Ct. 649.

*[ Footnotes have been omitted. Ed.]

MR. JUSTICE BLACKMUN delivered the opinion of the Court.
In O'Callahan v. Parker, 395 U.S. 258, decided June 2, 1969, by
a five-to-three vote, the Court held that a court-martial may not try
a member of our armed forces charged with attempted rape of a
civilian, with housebreaking, and with assault with intent to rape,
when the alleged offenses were committed off-post on American territory, when the soldier was on leave, and when the charges could have
been prosecuted in a civilian court. What is necessary for a court-
martial, the Court said, is the crime be "service connected." 395
U.S., at 272.

O'Callahan's military trial, of course, was without those constitutional guarantees, including trial by jury, to which he would have
been entitled had he been prosecuted in a federal civilian court in the
then Territory of Hawaii where the alleged crimes were committed.

O'Callahan already has occasioned a substantial amount of
scholarly comment. Much of it characterizes the decision as a significant one because it is said to depart from long-established, or at least
long-accepted, concepts. Some of the literature is generally approving.
Some of it is generally critical. Some of it, as did the O'Callahan dissent, 395 U.S., at 284, forecasts a period of confusion for both the civil
and the military courts. Not surprisingly, much of the literature is
concerned with the issue of O'Callahan's retrospectivity. Some writers
assert that the holding must be applied retroactively. Others predict
that it will not be so applied. Naturally enough, O'Callahan has had its
references in the federal courts of appeals and in a significant number
of cases in the United States Court of Military Appeals.

In the present federal habeas case, instituted several years after
the applicant's conviction by court-martial, certiorari was granted
"limited to retroactivity and scope of O'Callahan v. Parker. . . ."
397 U.S. 934 (1970). We thus do not reconsider O'Callahan. Our task
here concerns only its application.

I

Isiah Relford, in 1961, was a corporal on active duty in the United
States Army. He was stationed at Fort Dix, New Jersey.

On September 4, 1961, the visiting 14-year-old sister of another
serviceman, who was on leave from his Army station at Fort Campbell,
Kentucky, and who came to Fort Dix when his wife delivered a child at
the base hospital, was abducted at the point of a knife from an automobile in the hospital's parking lot as she waited for her brother. The
girl was raped by her abductor.

A few weeks later, on October 21, the wife of an Air Force man
stationed at McGuire Air Force Base, adjacent to Fort Dix, was driving from her home on the base to the post exchange concession, also
on the base, where she worked as a waitress. As the woman slowed
her automobile for a stop sign, a man gained entry to the car from the
passenger side and, with a knife at her throat, commanded the woman
to drive on some distance to a dirt road in the fort's training area.
She was raped there.

The second victim, with her assailant still in the automobile,
was able to make her predicament known to military police. The
assailant was apprehended and turned out to be Relford. He immediately admitted consensual intercourse with the victim. The next
morning, after a brief interrogation, he confessed to kidnaping and
raping both women.

At the time of each incident Relford was in civilian clothes.

It is undisputed that these events all took place on the military
reservation consisting of Fort Dix and the contiguous McGuire Air
Force Base.

Relford, in due course, was charged with raping and kidnaping each of the women, in violation of Articles 120 and 134, respectively, of the Uniform Code of Military Justice, 10 U. S. C. §§920 and 934. He was tried by a general court-martial in December 1961 and was convicted on the four charges. Relford's sentence was the forfeiture of all pay and allowances, reduction to the lowest enlisted grade, and death. The customary reference to the staff judge advocate was made and the convening authority approved. U. C. M. J. Arts. 60-65, 10 U. S. C. §§860-865. Upon the review by the Army Board of Review, required under the Code's Article 66, 10 U. S. C. §866, the conviction was sustained; the sentence, however, was reduced to hard labor for 30 years, total forfeitures, and a dishonorable discharge. The Court of Military Appeals denied a petition for review on September 24, 1963. United States v. Relford, 14 USCMA 678.

Relford's case thus became final more than five and a half years prior to this Court's decision in O'Callahan v. Parker.

In 1967, Relford, being in custody in the United States Disciplinary Barracks at Leavenworth, Kansas, filed his application for a writ of habeas corpus with the United States District Court for the District of Kansas. He alleged inadequate representation by counsel in the military proceeding. Chief Judge Stanley found no merit in the claim and denied the application. On appeal, Relford repeated the inadequate representation claim and, for the first time, raised questions as to the admissibility of his confession, as to a lineup procedure, and as to the fairness of his military trial. The Tenth Circuit reviewed all these claims on the merits, but affirmed the District Court's denial of relief. Relford v. Commandant, 409 F. 2d 824 (CA10 1969).

The Tenth Circuit's opinion was filed on April 23, 1969, several weeks prior to this Court's decision in O'Callahan v. Parker. The issue as to the propriety of trial by court-martial, perhaps understandably, was not raised before Judge Stanley or on the appeal to the Tenth Circuit; the issue, however, had been presented in O'Callahan's chronologically earlier appeal in his habeas proceeding. See United States ex rel. O'Callahan v. Parker, 390 F. 2d 360, 363-364 (CA3 1968).

II

This case, as did O'Callahan, obviously falls within the area of stress between the constitutional guarantees contained in the Constitution's Article III, §2, Clause 3, in the Sixth Amendment, and possibly in the Fifth Amendment, on the one hand, and, on the other, the power vested in the Congress, by the Constitution's Article I, §8, Clause 14, "to make Rules for the Government and Regulation of the land and naval Forces," with its supportive Necessary and Proper provision in Clause 18, and the Fifth Amendment's correlative exception for "cases arising in the land or naval forces."

Relford argues that O'Callahan's requirement that the crime be "service connected" before a court-martial may sit demands that the crime itself be military in nature, that is, one involving a level of conduct required only of servicemen and, because of the special needs of the military, one demanding military disciplinary action. He further states that the charges against him--like those against O'Callahan--do not involve a level of conduct required only of servicemen. He maintains that occurrence of the crimes on a military reservation and the military-dependent identity of one of his victims do not substantially support the military's claim of a special need to try him.

In further detail, it is stated that the Court in O'Callahan recognized that a court-martial "remains to a significant degree a specialized part of the overall mechanism by which military discipline is preserved," 395 U.S., at 265; that military courts, of necessity, are not impartial weighers of justice, but have as their primary consideration the enforcement of the unique discipline required of a fighting force; and that, as a consequence, the court-martial must be limited to the "least possible power adequate to the end proposed." United States ex rel. Toth v. Quarles, 350 U.S. 11, 22-23 (1955), citing Anderson v. Dunn, 19 U.S. (6 Wheat.) 204, 230-231 (1821).

It is then said that the level of conduct Relford is alleged to have violated, that is, intercourse only with consent, is the very same level required in the civilian community and is not altered by considerations of military dependency; that his alleged crimes are no more military than were O'Callahan's; that the ability of the military to perform its mission remains the same whether the crimes with which he was charged were committed on base or off base; that any interest in the maintenance of order on the base is adequately served by apprehension of the offender and trial in a civilian court; that the on-post/off-post distinction has little meaning; that it is the nature of the crime that is important; that the crimes charged to Relford stand in contrast to purely military crimes such as desertion, absence without leave, missing movement, assaulting a superior commissioned officer, and being drunk on duty, Arts. 85, 86, 87, 90, and 112, 10 U. S. C. §§885, 886, 887, 890, and 912; and that only crimes of the latter type have "an immediate adverse impact upon the ability of the military to perform its mission," and are "proper subjects for the exercise of military jurisdiction."

### III

In evaluating the force of this argument, the facts of O'Callahan and the precise holding in that case possess particular significance. We repeat: O'Callahan was in military service at the time and was stationed at a base in American territory. His offenses, however, took place off base in a civilian hotel while he was on leave and not in uniform.

MR. JUSTICE DOUGLAS, in speaking for the Court, said:

"In the present case petitioner was properly absent from his military base when he committed the crimes with

which he is charged.  There was no connection--not even
the remotest one--between his military duties and the
crimes in question.  The crimes were not committed on
a military post or enclave; nor was the person whom he
attacked performing any duties relating to the military.
Moreover, Hawaii, the situs of the crime, is not an armed
camp under military control, as are some of our far-flung
outposts.

"Finally, we deal with peacetime offenses, not with
authority stemming from the war power.  Civil courts
were open.  The offenses were committed within our
territorial limits, not in the occupied zone of a foreign
country.  The offenses did not involve any question of the
flouting of military authority, the security of a military
post, or the integrity of military property."  395 U.S., at
273-274.

We stress seriatim what is thus emphasized in the holding:

1.  The serviceman's proper absence from the base.
2.  The crime's commission away from the base.
3.  Its commission at a place not under military control.
4.  Its commission within our territorial limits and not in an
occupied zone of a foreign country.
5.  Its commission in peacetime and its being unrelated to authority stemming from the war power.
6.  The absence of any connection between the defendant's
military duties and the crime.
7.  The victim's not being engaged in the performance of any
duty relating to the military.
8.  The presence and availability of a civilian court in which
the case can be prosecuted.
9.  The absence of any flouting of military authority.
10.  The absence of any threat to a military post.
11.  The absence of any violation of military property.

One might add still another factor implicit in the others:

12.  The offense's being among those traditionally prosecuted
in civilian courts.

IV

This listing of factors upon which the Court relied for its result
in O'Callahan reveals, of course, that it chose to take an ad hoc approach to cases where trial by court-martial is challenged.  We therefore turn to those factors in Relford's case that, as spelled out in
O'Callahan's, bear upon the court-martial issue.

It is at once apparent that elements 4, 6, 8, 11, and 12, and perhaps 5 and 9, operate in Relford's favor as they did in O'Callahan's:
The offenses were committed within the territorial limits of the
United States; there was no connection between Relford's military
duties and the crimes with which he was charged; courts in New Jersey
were open and available for the prosecution of Relford; despite the
Vietnam conflict we may assume for present purposes that the offenses
were committed in peacetime and that they were unrelated to any problem of authority stemming from the war power; military authority, directly at least, was not flouted; the integrity of military property was
not violated; and the crimes of rape and kidnaping are traditionally
cognizable in the civilian courts.

Just as clearly, however, the other elements, present and relied
upon in O'Callahan's case, are not at hand in Relford's case.  These
are elements 1, 2, 3, 7, and 10:  Relford was not absent from the base;
the crimes were committed on the military enclave; the second victim,
because of her duties at the post exchange and because of the fact that
her abduction and the attack upon her took place as she was returning
to the PX at the end of a short and approved break in her work, was
engaged in the performance of a duty relating to the military; and the
security of two women properly on the post was threatened and, indeed, their persons were violated.

There are still other significant aspects of the Relford offenses:
The first victim was the sister of a serviceman who was then properly
at the base.  The second victim was the wife of a serviceman stationed
at the base; she and her husband had quarters on the base and were
living there.  Tangible property properly on the base, that is, two
automobiles, were forcefully and unlawfully entered.

## V

With the foregoing contrasting comparison of the pertinent
factual elements of O'Callahan with those of Relford's case, we
readily conclude that the crimes with which Relford was charged were
triable by a military court.  We do not agree with petitioner when he
claims that the "apparent distinctions" between this case and
O'Callahan "evaporate when viewed within the context of the 'service-
connected' test."  We stress:  (a) The essential and obvious interest
of the military in the security of persons and of property on the
military enclave.  Relford concedes the existence of this vital interest.  (b) The responsibility of the military commander for maintenance of order in his command and his authority to maintain that order.
See Cafeteria & Restaurant Workers Union, Local 473, AFL-CIO v.
McElroy, 367 U.S. 886 (1961).  Relford also concedes this.  (c) The
impact and adverse effect that a crime committed against a person
or property on a military base, thus violating the base's very security,
has upon morale, discipline, reputation and integrity of the base itself, upon its personnel and upon the military operation and the military mission.  (d) The conviction that Article I, §8, Clause 14, vesting

in the Congress the power "To make Rules for the Government and
Regulation of the land and naval Forces," means, in appropriate areas
beyond the purely military offense, more than the mere power to arrest a serviceman-offender and turn him over to the civil authorities.
The term "Regulation" itself implies, for those appropriate cases,
the power to try and to punish. (e) The distinct possibility that civil
courts, particularly nonfederal courts, will have less than complete
interest, concern, and capacity for all the cases that vindicate the
military's disciplinary problems within its own community. See W.
Winthrop, Military Law and Precedents, 725 (2d ed. 1896, 1920 Reprint); Wilkinson, 9 Washburn Law J. 193, 208 (1970). (f) The very
positive implication in O'Callahan itself, arising from its emphasis
on the absence of service-connected elements there, that the presence
of factors such as geographical and military relationships have important contrary significance. (g) The recognition in O'Callahan that,
historically, a crime against the person of one associated with the
post was subject even to the General Article. The comment from
Winthrop, 723-724:

> "Thus such crimes as theft from or robbery of an officer,
> soldier, post trader, or camp-follower . . . inasmuch as
> they directly affect military relations and prejudice mili-
> tary discipline, may properly be--as they frequently have
> been--the subject of charges under the present Article.
> On the other hand, where such crimes are committed
> upon or against civilians, and not at or near a military
> camp or post, or in breach or violation of a military duty
> or order, they are not in general to be regarded as within
> the description of the Article, but are to be treated as
> civil rather than military offenses." (Footnotes omitted.)

cited both by the Court in O'Callahan, 395 U.S., at 274, n. 19, and by
the dissent at 278-279, certainly so indicates and even goes so far as
to include an offense against a civilian committed "near" a military
post. (h) The mis-reading and undue restriction of O'Callahan if it
were interpreted as confining the court-martial to the purely military
offenses that have no counterpart in nonmilitary criminal law. (i) Our
inability appropriately and meaningfully to draw any line between a
post's strictly military areas and its nonmilitary areas, or between a
serviceman-defendant's on-duty and off-duty activities and hours on
the post.

This leads us to hold, and we do so hold, that when a serviceman is charged with an offense committed within or at the geographical boundary of a military post and violative of the security of a
person or of property there, that offense may be tried by court-martial.
Expressing it another way: a serviceman's crime against the person
of an individual upon the base or against property on the base is

"service connected," within the meaning of that requirement as specified in O'Callahan, 395 U.S., at 272. This delineation, we feel, fully
comports with the standard of "the least possible power adequate to
the end proposed" referred to in O'Callahan, 395 U.S., at 265.

By this measure, Relford's alleged offenses were obviously
service-connected. There is, therefore, no constitutional or statutory
barrier and Relford was properly tried by a court-martial.

## VI

We recognize that any ad hoc approach leaves outer boundaries
undetermined. O'Callahan marks an area, perhaps not the limit, for
the concern of the civil courts and where the military may not enter.
The case today marks an area, perhaps not the limit, where the court-
martial is appropriate and permissible. What lies between is for
decision at another time.

## VII

Having reached this result on the court-martial issue, the additional issue, that the parties have argued, of O'Callahan's retrospectivity, need not be decided. See Alabama State Federation of Labor v.
McAdory, 325 U.S. 450, 461 (1945). We recognize that the retroactivity
question has important dimensions, both direct and collateral, and that
the Government strongly urges that the question be decided here and
now. We have concluded, however, that the issue is better resolved in
other litigation where, perhaps, it would be solely dispositive of the
case. We take some comfort in the hope that the present decision
should eliminate at least some of the confusion that the parties and
commentators say has emerged from O'Callahan.

Affirmed.

Between the Supreme Court decisions in O'Callahan and Relford,
supra, the Court of Military Appeals rendered several decisions interpreting O'Callahan. Despite Chief Judge Quinn's opinion that the Supreme Court was attempting to remove from military jurisdiction only
crimes that could be tried in a federal civilian court, the majority decided that the military had no jurisdiction over an accused who had
been charged with rape, robbery, and sodomy occurring when he was
off-duty or on leave, off-post in civilian homes with civilian victims,
and the sole connection with the military being a bumper sticker on
his automobile that led to his apprehension (U.S. v. Borys, 18
U.S.C.M.A. 547, 40 CMR 259 [ 1969]). In U.S. v. Beeker, 18 U.S.C.M.A.
563, 40 CMR 275 (1969), the Court unanimously found that the use or
possession of marihuana on or off base by military persons was a
matter of direct concern to the military and within military jurisdiction; at the same time, the unlawful importation and transportation of

marihuana were found not triable by court-martial. If carnal knowledge occurs on-post, the perpetrator is triable by court-martial but not if it occurs off-post even though the victim in each instance is a dependent of a serviceman (compare U.S. v. Henderson, 18 U.S.C.M.A. 601, 40 CMR 313 [1969] with U.S. v. Smith, 18 U.S.C.M.A. 609, 40 CMR 321 [1969]). An airman accused of housebreaking and larceny involving the residence of a fellow airman located near but not on Tinker Air Force Base, Oklahoma, was subject to trial by court-martial (U.S. v. Rego, 19 U.S.C.M.A. 9, 41 CMR 9 [1969]). Reliance by the victim upon an accused's military status may be a sufficient basis for court-martial jurisdiction (see U.S. v. Morisseau, 19 U.S.C.M.A. 17, 41 CMR 17 [1969] and U.S. v. Peak, 19 U.S.C.M.A. 19, 41 CMR 19 [1969]). Petty offenses for which an accused is not constitutionally entitled to indictment or trial by jury may be tried by court-martial (see U.S. v. Sharkey, 19 U.S.C.M.A. 26, 41 CMR 26 [1969]). Finally, the Court of Military Appeals has held that the constitutional limitation on court-martial jurisdiction laid down in O'Callahan does not apply overseas (U.S. v. Keaton, 19 U.S.C.M.A. 64, 41 CMR 64 [1969]); accord, Gallagher v. U.S., 423 F.2d 1371 [Ct. Clms. 1970] and should not be given retroactive effect (Mercer v. Dillon, 19 U.S.C.M.A. 264, 41 CMR 264 (1970).

# 8

The following synopsis summarizes briefly the provisions of the UCMJ concerning the actions available to commanders in disposing of alleged offenses by members of their commands. The underlined words are words of art having a particular meaning in military law. Note that the administrative system is based upon the chain of command in the particular armed service; this synopsis deals with the army, but a similar hierarchical system exists in the air force and navy.

## SYNOPSIS OF ADMINISTRATION OF MILITARY JUSTICE

I.  Alleged offense is brought to the attention of the accused's company commander who is responsible for an investigation of the alleged offense and who may decide:
    A.  To do nothing;
    B.  To punish by administrative action, e.g. withdraw privilege;
    C.  To offer the accused non-judicial punishment (Art. 15); or
    D.  To act as accuser (Art. 1[9]), prefer charges for court-martial, recommend the type of court-martial (Art. 30) forward to:

*II.  The battalion or brigade commander, who may decide:
    A.  To convene and refer the charges to a summary court-martial for trial;
    B.  To convene and refer the charges to a special court-martial for trial; or

---

*Any superior commander has the same powers as any inferior commander.

C.   To appoint an <u>Article 32 Investigation Officer</u> and upon completion of that investigation, recommend trial by general
court-martial and forward to:

*III.  The division or post commander, who may decide:

A.   After receiving the advice of his Staff Judge Advocate (Art.
34), to <u>convene</u> and <u>refer</u> the charges to a general court-
martial for trial.

## COMMAND INFLUENCE

### UNITED STATES v. LITTRICE

United States Court of Military Appeals, 1953.
3 U.S.C.M.A. 487, 13 C.M.R. 43.

GEORGE W. LATIMER, Judge:

The accused was tried by general court-martial in Germany for
violation of Article 121, Uniform Code of Military Justice, 50 USC
§715, the three specifications thereunder alleging that he stole three
cameras. He was found guilty of two specifications, sentenced to dishonorable discharge, forfeiture of all pay and allowances, and confinement at hard labor for two years. The convening authority
approved but reduced the period of confinement to one year, and a
board of review in the office of The Judge Advocate General of the
Army affirmed. The accused petitioned this Court for a review of
his conviction and we granted his request limiting the scope of the
review to the single issue of whether the pretrial conference of the
acting commanding officer with the members of the court-martial
denied the accused a fair trial.

At the commencement of the trial, and prior to plea, defense
counsel interposed a motion which, in effect, was a challenge to all
members of the court. In support of this motion, Lieutenant Colonel
Lutz was placed on the stand to testify as to the instructions he had
given the members of the court-martial prior to trial. He was the
executive officer of Headquarters 8th Triple A Group, Wiesbaden Air
Base, Wiesbaden, Germany, and was acting for, and in the absence of,
the group commander. All officers detailed to the court-martial were
members of battalions which were under command of that officer.
The meeting was held immediately prior to the time the trial commenced, and the special order convening the court and detailing the

---

*Any superior commander has the same powers as any inferior
commander.

officers made reference to this particular case. Lieutenant Colonel Lutz testified in part as follows: That he had called all members of the court together and directed their attention to Circular 27-2, Seventh Army, dated February 29, 1952; that he inquired as to how many of the members had served on courts-martial previously, and ascertained that four or five had some experience; that he stated it was his duty, as senior army commander in the area, to brief the court as required by the circular and, to carry out its directions, he read verbatim one of its paragraphs; that he informed the members of the court-martial panel that they should not usurp the prerogatives of the reviewing authority; that it had been his experience that court-martial records received a thorough review in the Seventh Army; that he read excerpts from a letter from Headquarters, U.S. Army, Europe, September 8, 1952, on the subject of retention of thieves in the Army; that he explained that his reason for reading from this letter was that its distribution list disclosed it had been sent to group units only; and, that time had not permitted its reproduction for distribution to battalions.

Before leaving the witness stand, Colonel Lutz stated that he did not want to leave the documents with the court-martial because they were the only copies he had. He, however, volunteered the suggestion that the court take judicial notice of the contents of both the circular and letter. Defense counsel seized on the suggestion and the law officer replied that it could not be done unless they were made available for use by members of the court. Trial counsel suggested that the witness leave the papers with the court, and that defense counsel obtain additional copies for the record upon completion of trial. This was done and the two documents were admitted in evidence and identified in the record as appellate exhibits A and B, respectively. While Government counsel assert there is no showing that the members of the court had actual knowledge of the provisions of the two exhibits, the record is such that, as a matter of law and fact, we must charge them with knowing the contents. There is no showing that they were not informed generally of the complete contents of both exhibits at the pretrial meeting--the documents were discussed in open court, the members were required to judicially know their contents, and they were available for reading and inspection.

Appellate defense counsel contend that the instructions of the acting commanding officer constituted an exercise of improper influence over the court-martial, and thus deprived the accused of a fair trial. Appellate Government counsel, on the other hand, argue that the instructions given to the court by the commanding officer were proper and expressly authorized by the Code and Manual provisions.

Over the years that military justice has been under criticism, and particularly during the period the new Uniform Code of Military Justice was being prepared by the Morgan Committee and studied by Congressional Committees, one of the most controversial issues with which all interested parties was concerned dealt with the extent

officers in the chain of command should be authorized to influence
court-martial activities.  Recommendations came not only from those
who were directly connected with the armed services, but also from
civilians interested in the administration of military justice.  A number of boards of outstanding civilians have, at various times, considered different aspects of the military judicial system and many
individuals have objectively studied the problem. . . .
       . . .
    Thus, confronted with the necessity of maintaining a delicate
balance between justice and discipline, Congress liberalized the military judicial system but also permitted commanding officers to retain
many of the powers held by them under prior laws.  While it struck a
compromise, Congress expressed an intent to free courts-martial
members from any improper and undue influence by commanders
which might affect an honest and conscientious consideration of the
guilt or innocence of an accused.  Both the Code and the Manual announce the same caveat.  Article 37 of the Code, 50 USC §612, states
it in the following language:

> "No authority convening a general, special, or sum-
> mary court-martial, nor any other commanding officer,
> shall censure, reprimand, or admonish such court or any
> member, law officer, or counsel thereof, with respect to
> the findings or sentence adjudged by the court, or with
> respect to any other exercise of its or his functions in
> the conduct of the proceeding.  No person subject to this
> code shall attempt to coerce or, by any unauthorized
> means, influence the action of a court-martial or any
> other military tribunal or any member thereof, in reach-
> ing the findings or sentence in any case, or the action of
> any convening, approving, or reviewing authority with
> respect to his judicial acts."

On the command side of the ledger, we find some provisions
which indicate that he is not to be too tightly fettered by the new Code.
Article 25(c) (2), 50 USC §589, directs that he shall appoint to the
court-martial those persons who are, in his opinion, best qualified
because of training, experience and judicial temperament.  In addition,
the Manual for Courts-Martial, United States, 1951, permits him to
give certain general instructions to them.  The first portion of paragraph 38 of the Manual, supra, is as follows:

> 'INSTRUCTING PERSONNEL OF COURT.--A con-
> vening authority may, through his staff judge advocate or
> legal officer or otherwise, give general instruction to the
> personnel of a court-martial which he has appointed,
> preferably before any cases have been referred to the

court for trial. When a staff judge advocate or legal officer is present with the command such instruction should
be given through that officer. Such instruction may relate to the rules of evidence, burden of proof, and presumption of innocence, and may include information as to
the state of discipline in the command, as to the prevalence of offences which have impaired efficiency and
discipline, and of command measures which have been
taken to prevent offenses. Except as provided in this
manual, the convening authority may not, however, directly or indirectly give instruction to, or otherwise unlawfully influence, a court as to its future action in a
particular case. In this connection, see 67f ."

The same delicate balance which beset Congress now confronts
us. Justice can be dispensed and discipline maintained if one is not
permitted to overwhelm the other. Both should be given recognition
and both must be governed and guided by the necessities peculiar to
the military service. The difficult test in this case is in determining
whether the instructions given to the members of the court-martial
unnecessarily impinged on the right of the accused to have his case
heard by a court-martial unprompted by authority. Posed in a
slightly different manner the question is: Did the instructions given
by the acting commanding officer fall within the fair limits permitted
by the Manual or were they of such a coercive nature that there was a
violation of the Code restriction against the exercise of improper influence upon the court-martial members? For purpose of presenting
our answer to the question, we shall discuss the questioned instructions in the following order: First, those instructional or collateral
matters contained in or implied from Circular 27-2, Seventh Army,
dated February 29, 1952, regarding general court-martial proceedings; second, those pertaining to the letter from Headquarters, U.S.
Army, Europe, dated September 8, 1952, concerning the retention of
thieves in the Army.

Circular Number 27-2, Headquarters, Seventh Army, dated
February 29, 1952, is entitled "Military Law General Court-Martial
Procedures." It was issued some five months prior to the trial of
this case and its contents were general instructions applicable to all
courts under command of that headquarters. Colonel Lutz testified
that during the conference held prior to trial he read paragraph 3b(6)
verbatim. However, the document contains no paragraph enumerated
as 3b(6) but does contain a paragraph 3c(6), and while it seems to contain instructions for commanders and not court members, it was apparently the one referred to. It is as follows:

"Instruction of eligible personnel of his command
in the duties of members of courts-martial. In this

connection, it is desired that the commander nominating
a court, assemble the court prior to the receipt of any
cases if practicable. He will satisfy himself that the
court is qualified for courts martial duty; the need for
the utmost impartiality and highest judgment; the necessity for arriving accurately at the guilt or innocence of
the accused regardless of sentiment; the traditionally
high Army standards of honesty, integrity or leadership,
and moral conduct; and the necessity for dealing fairly
but firmly with offenders will be stressed. Commanders
nominating courts are expected to assume full responsibility that members of the court understand these matters
thoroughly. At the same time the commander issues his
briefing, a Staff Judge Advocate officer of this headquarters will instruct the court on matters listed in paragraph 38, MCM 1951, with particular emphasis on those
contained in paragraph 1b, above, and Army policies as
contained in Circular 21-1 and Circular 27-1 with Change
1, this headquarters."

Article 37, Uniform Code of Military Justice, supra, condemns
two types of coercive conduct. The first prohibits a convening authority, or other commanding officer, from censuring, reprimanding
or admonishing a court or member thereof because of the findings or
sentence adjudged. The second prohibits coercing or influencing a
court-martial member by any unauthorized means. The first part of
the Article is not involved in this case and we do not believe the portion read could in any way improperly influence a court or trespass
on the area protected by the second part. Obviously, emphasis on the
need for impartiality, accuracy, and fairness cannot be considered
objectionable, and admonitions concerning these matters come within
the type of general instruction authorized by Manual provision. Furthermore, efforts to have commanders instill in court members high
standards of honesty and integrity are commendable and are to be
encouraged. We find nothing in this Circular which should be the subject of condemnation.

Had Colonel Lutz been content to rely on the instructions set
forth in the Seventh Army Circular he would have stayed well within
bounds. However, he went much further as he told the members that
they should not usurp the prerogatives of the convening authority. In
addition, he informed them that from his own experience as a member
of a general court he had found that cases were thoroughly reviewed
by the reviewing authority of the Seventh Army. Those statements
more closely approach interference. As an abstract proposition,
there is some value in explaining to prospective members of a court
that a record, after completion of trial, would receive a thorough review. Cast in a proper background such a statement might be of

assistance in helping court-martial members to understand trial and appellate procedures. On the other hand, if the explanation is given just before a trial, it is subject to an interpretation damaging to the accused. Of necessity, the ultimate effect depends in part on the manner in which the matter is presented by the commander but demeanor cannot be extracted from the record. Be that as it may, when Congress enacted the new Code, it intended that court-martial members be independent and not influenced by suggestions that post trial reviewers would shoulder the responsibility. When a commanding officer suggests to court members that other higher commanders carefully scrutinize every record and that the court should not usurp the prerogatives of the convening authority, they are either coerced or confused. What is his authority and what is theirs? Do they not overlap on both findings and sentence? Directions such as those cannot help but lessen the court-martial members' appreciation of their own responsibility for the findings and sentence. The prerogatives Colonel Lutz had in mind are not disclosed and those the court members would consider are well concealed. The most apparent interpretation of this statement is that the court-martial should give the maximum sentence to the accused, and thus give the convening authority plenty of latitude in exercising his powers of clemency. This is contrary to the sentence procedure outlined in paragraph 76a (4), Manual for Courts-Martial, supra, and when the statement is considered in connection with the instructions which stress the principle that thieves should not be retained in the service, it places the members in a situation where they are coerced into adjudging a punitive discharge.

Even were we to concede that the instructions we have so far mentioned might have little impact on the members of the court when we heap on the next admonitions, we pass beyond the doubtful stage. These are the important provisions from the letter, Headquarters, U.S. Army Europe, Subject: Retention of Thieves in the Army:

> "In certain recent General Courts Martial cases courts have properly found the accused guilty of larceny of substantial sums of money and property and then after establishing that the accused was a thief, have given sentences which improperly retain him in the Service. In view of this it appears absolutely necessary that your attention be invited to the following provisions of the Manual so that you may take the necessary action to prevent other such errors from occurring.
>
> "First, the greatest care should be exercised in the selection of officers who are to be appointed as members of all courts-martial. They must be the best qualified by reason of age, education, training, experience, length of service, and judicial temperament. Moreover, when the individual members have verified by their

performance that they have those qualities, it is proper that you recognize that fact by appropriate notation on their efficiency report or by other written communication.

. . .

'The imposition by courts-martial of inadequate sentences upon military persons convicted of crimes which are punishable by the civil courts tends to bring the armed forces into disrepute as lacking in respect for the criminal laws of the land.'

The Manual also states:

'Offenses such as larceny . . . and the like involve moral turpitude and are not to be treated as minor.'

and states:

'. . . the retention in the armed forces of thieves and persons guilty of moral turpitude injuriously reflects upon the good name of the military service and its self-respecting personnel.' "

Here again the language of certain of the sections is permissible under the Manual provision allowing a commanding officer to give general instructions to the personnel of the court-martial, and to include therein information as to the state of discipline in the command and the prevalence of offenses which have impaired efficiency and discipline. We have no doubt about the accuracy of the statement that the prevalence of thievery among members of the armed forces is detrimental to morale. Frequent thefts of the personal property of members cannot be condoned, and a general policy discouraging the imposition of inadequate sentences for such offenses is entirely reasonable. Such a general policy may be necessary and desirable and its communication to the personnel of a court is proper. However, it is preferable to give it to the command rather than to a designated court-martial as there may be occasions when a court-martial, in good faith, and in a given case could conclude a punitive discharge was not warranted. It is one thing to announce a general policy and yet another to use that principle to influence the finding and a sentence in a particular case.

Undoubtedly the most offensive instruction given to the court members was the one dealing with efficiency reports. Again we have a perfectly fine concept put to a very questionable use. We cannot tear the statement out of the environment in which it was given nor can we ignore its obvious implications. It appears to have been a precept to the commanders but it was used inappropriately on court-martial members. No one would dispute that when services are well performed, the merits of the performance should be recognized. But commendations for outstanding performance should apply equally to all military duty and there is no compelling necessity to single out and emphasize the duties performed while a member of a court-martial and then mention efficiency report entries to personnel just before commencing consideration of a case. Actually the primary subject of the document was to place retention of thieves in the military service in its proper perspective. If considered for that purpose, no harm would be done; but immediately preceding the reference to efficiency report entries is a criticism of the sentences imposed by prior courts-martial. We believe that when the statement concerning the entering of commendatory remarks on the efficiency reports is considered in the context of a letter, there is a veiled threat that those members of the court who vote to convict an alleged thief and join in sentencing him to be dishonorably discharged from the service will receive a reward in the way of a commendation while those who do not will go unmentioned. Courts-martial are manned by officers whose opportunities for advancement and promotion are controlled largely by their commanding officers and it is no reflection on their honesty and integrity to conclude that they desire to make a fine record. When an officer is lectured on the policy of his commander and then told that if he performs his duties as a member of a courts-martial outstandingly, his record will reflect a high standard of performance, he is apt to be influenced to take action which might be highly regarded by the commander. At least he has more mental reservation than has an officer who has not been subjected to the influence of suggestion.

We return now to the ultimate question of the balance between command function and military justice as we view it from this record. Under the peculiar facts of this case, we find command coercion which was prejudicial to the accused. The total of all the facts, circumstances and instruction given compel that conclusion. Here the record presents a factual situation in which a court-martial was ordered to try an alleged thief. At the time the court was assembled to be given instruction by the commander, the members knew the nature of the accusation and the identity of the particular person to be tried. Immediately before trial, the members were ordered to assemble and certainly the message conveyed must have been considered of grave importance by them because the commander made a special personal appearance and announced he was doing so because the letter had not been distributed to the officers of that particular battalion. Involved in the dissertation were statements to the effect that sentences which permit one convicted of larceny to remain in the service are improper; that imposition of inadequate sentences brings the armed forces into disrepute; that prerogatives of the convening authority should not be usurped; that the court-martial's findings and sentence are relatively unimportant in view of the thorough review given by division headquarters; that failure to recognize that the Army is no place for thieves is a serious deficiency; that great care must be used in selecting officers to serve on courts-martial; and, that when individuals selected for that duty have verified by their performance that they have certain qualifications, appropriate notations will be made on their efficiency reports. With those admonitions ringing in their ears, the members began to hear this case on its merits. It requires little imagination to arrive at the reason why a finding of guilty was returned and the maximum sentence imposed.

. . .

In order to permit military justice to operate properly, commanders must use discrimination in the manner in which they seek to maintain discipline by directions to members of courts-martial. This case is a concrete example of how a combination of events and statements can deny an accused the fair and just trial contemplated by the Uniform Code of Military Justice. The conviction and sentence in this instance are the product of a trial not founded on those fundamental rights and privileges granted to one tried in the military system. The accused was convicted and sentenced by a court-martial which was not free from external influences tending to disturb the exercise of a deliberate and unbiased judgment. The attempt to enlighten the court members may have been prompted by the highest ideals but the method of presentation was steeped in prejudice.

The decision of the board of review is reversed, the findings and sentence are set aside and a rehearing is ordered.

BROSMAN, Judge (concurring):

I concur in the principal opinion. At the same time I must confess to some degree of general unfriendliness toward the sort of pretrial conference contemplated by paragraph 38 of the 1951 Manual-- quite apart from our action in this case. On the whole, I incline to believe that seances of this nature are less necessary than dangerous --and, all in all, they appear to be to be inconsistent with the character of law administration elsewhere contemplated by the Uniform Code. However, I feel sure that the law is solidly behind the author of the principal opinion in his view that there is nothing wrong per se with this sort of pretrial conference.

The only means by which I can reach a contrary conclusion is to hold that the language of paragraph 38 of the 1951 Manual constitutes a violation of Articles 37 and 66 of the Code, and hence must fall. On numerous occasions the members of this Court have united in holding that the provisions of the Code and the Manual occupy an identical authoritative position, in the absence of conflict. Certainly, therefore, before I may disregard paragraph 38, I must find it to be inconsistent with a mandate of the Code. And I cannot at all find this.

. . .

Chief Judge QUINN concurs in the result.

The issue of command influence involves a delicate balancing of interests as stated in U.S. v. Littrice, supra, between proper command functions and military justice. In U.S. v. Isbell, 3 USCMA 782, 14 CMR 200 (1954), the Court found no improper command influence in the distribution of a Staff Judge Advocate bulletin citing errors observed in records of trial supported by citations in the Manual for Courts-Martial and in the dissemination to the command as a part of a general program of indoctrination and instruction the same letter regarding the "retention of thieves" as considered in Littrice above. U.S. v. Hawthorne, 7 USCMA 293, 22 CMR 83 (1956) concerned the publication of a "policy declaration in regard to the elimination of Regular Army offenders," which was susceptible of an interpretation that such offenders should be tried by general court-martial; the Court found improper command influence in that the accused had been deprived of impartial consideration by his immediate commander and of an impartial trial because the members of the court-martial were aware of the policy.

Most cases involve lectures or publications by a commander or his Staff Judge Advocate pointing up command problems such as "barracks larceny" and the "proper" handling of such thieves. The Court has found prejudicial command influence when the content of the lecture or publication was erroneous or improper (see U.S. v. Zagan, 5 USCMA 410, 18 CMR 34 [1955]; U.S. v. Wright, 17 USCMA 110, 37 CMR 374 [1967]) or when the lecture was given to the court members immediately prior to a trial (U.S. v. Wright, supra). On the other hand, the Court did not find prejudicial command influence in such lectures or publications in U.S. v. Navarre, 5 USCMA 32, 17 CMR 32 (1954); U.S. v. Danzine, 12 USCMA 340, 30 CMR 350 (1971); or U.S. v. Davis, 12 USCMA 576, 31 CMR 162 (1961). Where the publication has been introduced at the trial, whether by trial or defense counsel, the Court has consistently found prejudicial command influence. See U.S. v. Fowle, 7 USCMA 349, 22 CMR 139 (1956); U.S. v. Estrada, 7 USCMA 635, 23 CMR 99 (1957); U.S. v. Rinehart, 8 USCMA 402, 24 CMR 212 (1957); U.S. v. Davis, 8 USCMA 425, 24 CMR 235 (1957).

Another facet of the command influence problem is the difficulty in obtaining a clear determination of the facts giving rise to the allegation. Often the allegation is not made at trial but comes to the attention of appellate agencies on review. See U.S. v. Ferguson, 5 USCMA 68, 17 CMR 68 (1954) and U.S. v. DuBay, (see below).

Some cases have concerned the remarks of a commander vis-à-vis the preparation of efficiency reports (an officer's rating form) and the performance of the officer's duties as a member of a court-martial. See U.S. v. Deain, 5 USCMA 44, 17 CMR 44 (1954) (prejudicial influence found); U.S. v. Navarre, supra (not prejudicial).

Other cases where the Court found improper command influence
include the replacement by a convening authority of a president of a
special court-martial after the trial had started (U.S. v. Whitley, 5
USCMA 786, 19 CMR 82 [1955]) and circumstances indicating a commander's personal interest in implementation of the Army's "fat-boy"
program (U.S. v. Shepherd, 9 USCMA 90, 25 CMR 352 [1958]).

## UNITED STATES v. DUBAY*

United States Court of Military Appeals, 1967.
17 U.S.C.M.A. 147, 37 C.M.R. 411.

*[Footnotes have been omitted.  Ed.]

PER CURIAM:
These cases involve the same basic issue, i.e., whether the Commanding General, Fort Leonard Wood, Missouri, violated the provisions of Uniform Code of Military Justice, Article 37, 10 USC §837,
with respect to the findings and sentence, or sentence alone, as adjudged by the particular general courts-martial appointed by him to
hear the causes.  Both parties are agreed that, at the very least, a
serious issue is raised concerning whether there was such command
interference with these judicial bodies.
In the nature of things, command control is scarcely ever apparent on the face of the record, and, where the facts are in dispute,
appellate bodies in the past have had to resort to the unsatisfactory
alternative of settling the issue on the basis of ex parte affidavits,
amidst a barrage of claims and counterclaims.  Compare United States
v Ferguson, 5 USCMA 68, 17 CMR 68, with United States v Shepherd,
9 USCMA 90, 25 CMR 352.  The conflicts here make resort to affidavits unsatisfactory and we determine upon the following as the means
of settling the matter herein, as well as in future cases in which a
similar issue may be raised either here or before a board of review.
See United States v Schalck, 14 USCMA 371, 34 CMR 151.
In each such case, the record will be remanded to a convening
authority other than the one who appointed the court-martial concerned
and one who is at a higher echelon of command.  That convening authority will refer the record to a general court-martial for another
trial.  Upon convening the court, the law officer will order an out-of-
court hearing, in which he will hear the respective contentions of the
parties on the question, permit the presentation of witnesses and evidence in support thereof, and enter findings of fact and conclusions of
law based thereon.  If he determines the proceedings by which the

accused was originally tried were infected with command control, he will set aside the findings or sentence, or both, as the case may require, and proceed with the necessary rehearing. If he determines that command control did not in fact exist, he will return the record to the convening authority, who will review the findings and take action thereon, in accordance with Code, supra. Articles 61 and 64, 10 USC §§861, 864. The convening authority will forward the record, together with his action thereon, to the Judge Advocate General for review by a board of review, in accordance with Code, supra, Article 66, 10 USC §866. From the board's decision, the accused may appeal to this Court on petition, or the decision may be certified here by the Judge Advocate General, under the provisions of Code, supra, Article 67, 10 USC §867.

In each of the above-styled cases, such disposition is ordered, without prejudice to the new convening authority's right to take appropriate action under Code, supra, Article 67(f) or Code, supra, Article 66(e), if he deems a rehearing on the issue of command control impracticable.

Article 37 of the UCMJ was amended by the Military Justice Act of 1968 to allow "general instructional or informational courses in military justice" and to prohibit the consideration by a commander of performance of duty as a member or a counsel of a court-martial in the preparation of efficiency reports. Other amendments in the same Act are directed toward the command-influence issue, such as the designation of military judges by the Judge Advocate General rather than by commanders (see Article 26, UCMJ).

Some persons still argue for a complete separation of the administration of military justice from any authority of commanders; for example, see "A History of Command Influence on the Military Judicial System," by Luther C. West, 18 U.C.L.A. L. Rev. 1 (1970).

## ORGANIZATION AND COMPOSITION OF COURTS-MARTIAL

The following synopsis is a brief summary of the provisions of the UCMJ concerning the composition of the different types of courts-martial. Cases and other materials must be studied to obtain a complete understanding of these provisions.

## Synopsis of Composition of Courts-Martial

| Type of C/M | Members[1] | Mil. Judge | Counsel[2] | Maximum Permissable Sentence | Remarks |
|---|---|---|---|---|---|
| Summary | 1 | No | No | Confinement: 1 month<br>Hard Labor: 45 days<br>Restriction: 2 months<br>Forfeiture: 2/3 of one month's pay | May not try an officer or any accused over his objection |
| Special | 3 or more | Varies[3] | Yes[4] | Confinement: 6 months<br>Hard Labor: 3 months<br>Forfeiture: 2/3 pay per month for 6 months<br>Bad Conduct Discharge[5] | |
| General | 5 or more | Yes | Yes | Any punishment not forbidden by UCMJ | Death may not be adjudged if case is referred as non-capital |

[1]An accused may request to be tried by a special or general court-martial consisting of a military judge only (see Art. 16).

[2]Counsel refers to the requirement that a "qualified" (see Art. 27[b]) counsel be appointed to represent the accused.

[3]If a military judge is not detailed to the trial because of "physical conditions or military exigencies," the convening authority must state the reasons and append the statement to the record of trial. If a military judge is not detailed without reasons, no BCD may be adjudged (see Art. 19).

[4]Trial may proceed without a qualified counsel appointed for an accused if one cannot be obtained on account of "physical conditions or military exigencies" (see Art. 27[c]).

[5]A bad conduct discharge may not be adjudged if a verbatim record is not kept.

The "convening authority" is the commander who appoints the members of a court-martial and refers the case to trial by such court. See Articles 22, 23, and 24 as to who may convene courts-martial. A convening authority otherwise authorized by law to convene a court-martial may not do so if he is the "accuser" or has a personal as opposed to official interest in the result of the trial. See U.S. v. Gordon, 1 USCMA 255, 2 CMR 161 (1952); U.S. v. Marsh, 3 USCMA 48, 11 CMR 48 (1953); U.S. v. Keith, 3 USCMA 579, 13 CMR 135 (1953); and U.S. v. McClemy, 5 USCMA 507, 18 CMR 131 (1955).

Paragraph 68h, MCM, states that a general court-martial convening authority may grant an accused immunity from prosecution. Such power was upheld in U.S. v. Kirsch, 15 USCMA 84, 35 CMR 56 (1964).

The "members" of a court-martial compare to a jury in a civilian trial. They are the fact-finders and decide on guilt or innocence of an accused after being instructed in the law by the military judge (formerly law officer). In courts-martial, they also have the responsibility of adjudging a sentence.

UNITED STATES v. CRAWFORD*

United States Court of Military Appeals, 1964.
15 U.S.C.M.A. 31, 35 C.M.R. 3.

*[Footnotes have been omitted. Ed.]

QUINN, Chief Judge:
The question on this appeal, and in several similar cases, is whether the method by which enlisted court members were selected discriminated against the lower enlisted ranks in such way as to threaten the integrity of the courts-martial system and violate the Uniform Code of Military Justice.

. . .

Beyond waiver, the first issue for consideration is the standard of selection of courts-martial members. Appellate defense counsel maintain military due process requires that the methods of selection approximate those in the civilian courts to insure a panel drawn from a cross section of the entire military community. Oppositely, the Government contends civilian standards are "antagonistic" to the military requirements. . . .

Under the Fifth and Sixth Amendments to the United States Constitution, persons in the armed forces do not have the right to indictment by grand jury and trial by petit jury for a capital or infamous

crime. Ex parte Quirin, 317 US 1, 87 L ed 3, 63 S Ct 2 (1942). However, courts-martial are criminal prosecutions, and those constitutional protections and rights which the history and text of the
Constitution do not plainly deny to military accused are preserved to
them in the service. United States v Culp, supra. Constitutional due
process includes the right to be treated equally with all other accused
in the selection of impartial triers of the facts. Methods of selection
which are designed to produce a court membership which has, or necessarily results in, the appearance of a "packed" court are subject
to challenge. . . .

. . .

It is unnecessary for present purposes to review the reasons
for, and the long evolution of, the qualification of enlisted persons for
service on courts-martial. Suffice it to say that the right to enlisted
court members was deemed important. Its importance is emphasized
by the exceedingly narrow and specifically defined conditions under
which a trial can be had without enlisted membership. As Mr. Felix
Larkin, one of the principal draftsmen of the Code, informed the Subcommittee of the House Armed Services Committee, which held hearings on the Uniform Code, the denial of the right to enlisted members
would be justifiable only "in the most exceptional type of case," where
the conditions "made it impossible for . . . [the convening authority]
to obtain enlisted men." Hearings before House Armed Services Committee on H. R. 2498, 81st Congress, 1st Session, pages 1150, 1151.

Here, the accused asked for, and was granted, enlisted court
members. Of the four persons appointed to the court, three were
sergeants major (E-9), and one was a master sergeant (E-7). The
accused contends the method by which these members were selected
violated the Uniform Code in that, all enlisted persons in grades lower
than E-7, and all specialists regardless of grade, all of whom were
otherwise eligible for appointment, were arbitrarily and discrimina-
torily excluded from consideration. He also contends the selection
process was invalid because a Negro enlisted man was arbitrarily
included in the court membership. The Government does not question
the facts upon which the accused's allegation of error is predicated,
but it denies the validity of the accused's conclusions. The facts are
set out in affidavits by persons who participated in the selection
process.

From the affidavits, it appears that in the late afternoon of the
day before trial, the accused, through his counsel, informed trial
counsel he desired to exercise his right to have enlisted members on
the court. The request was transmitted to the staff judge advocate,
who told his deputy to obtain from the adjutant general's office a list
of "senior noncommissioned officers who were regarded as responsible and available for court-martial duty." The staff judge advocate
requested senior noncommissioned officers because he regarded
"seniority of rank . . . [as an] indication of civic responsibility and

intelligence." He also asked, because the accused is Negro and the alleged assaults were against white soldiers, that the list include at least one member of that race. The deputy telephoned the instructions to the deputy adjutant general, who in turn passed them on to the noncommissioned officer in charge, Sergeant Major R. M. Nelson. Understanding he was to select "mature, responsible, and experienced senior noncommissioned officers," Sergeant Nelson compiled a list of eight or ten names by "random" selection from the "personnel rosters" in the office. The names were submitted by telephone to the staff judge advocate's office. A written list with the names of Negro nominees marked with asterisks was prepared, and given to the chief of staff. He took the list to the convening authority. Three or four of the eight or ten names on the list were selected by the convening authority. No Negro on the list was chosen. Instead, the general asked by name for a Sergeant Jones who was believed to be a Negro. Jones, however, was not a member of that race. The adjutant general suggested two other enlisted men believed to be Negro; one turned out to be white; the other was rejected because two members of his command were already "tapped" for the court. After further inquiry, the staff judge advocate succeeded in obtaining a "responsible" Negro sergeant first class from an engineer unit. He was accepted by the convening authority, and on the day of trial was added to the court. According to the staff judge advocate, his sole purpose was to obtain "court members with integrity and common sense." He regarded his method of selection as better designed to achieve that purpose than the mere submission of a list of names obtained "willy-nilly out of the . . . duty rosters of the Adjutant General." And he believed the method was sanctioned by the practice in the Federal courts as delineated in United States v Hoffa, 205 F Supp 710 (SD Fla) (1962).

Undeniably, the selection of mature, responsible, and available persons for court-martial membership is in the best tradition of the judicial process. All civilian jurisdictions have similar qualifications for jurors. See 28 USC §1861; United States v Dennis, 183 F2d 201 (CA 2d Cir) (1950), affirmed 341 US 494, 95 L ed 1137, 71 S Ct 857 (1951). In fact, the Uniform Code explicitly gives the convening authority a large measure of discretion in selecting court members to the end that he obtain the "best qualified for the duty by reason of age, education, training, experience, length of service, and judicial temperament." Article 25(d)(2), Uniform Code of Military Justice, 10 USC §825. As large as the discretion appears to be, the Uniform Code does not contemplate blanket exclusion of persons below specified rank as being unlikely to possess the statutory qualities.

Nothing in the Uniform Code expressly limits membership on a court-martial to persons of a particular rank. On the contrary, notwithstanding the reference to the selection of those "best qualified," Article 25 implies all ranks and grades are eligible for appointment. Subsection (d)(1) carries forward the venerable tradition that, whenever it can be avoided, no court member shall be junior in rank or grade to the accused. Since the provision allows a court member junior to the accused to serve (see Mullan v United States, 140 US 240, 35 L ed 489, 11 S Ct 788 (1891)), Congress, apparently, believed the lower ranks would contain qualified persons who would be appointed to courts-martial as occasions warranted. The practice, both before and after the Uniform Code, reflects this belief, at least as far as officer members are concerned. The many records of trial that have come before this Court show that lieutenants and captains in the Army are frequently appointed to courts-martial, although they probably have substantially less experience and years of service than colonels and generals. Similarly, Navy courts-martial often include lieutenants as members, but rarely have admirals. Much less variation in rank has been observed in the enlisted membership, but, even here, almost all ranks have been appointed.

    Enlisted grades range from E-1, the lowest, to E-9, the highest. Statistics presented by appellate defense counsel show that in the Army, during the period between 1959 through 1963, no enlisted court member was lower in grade than an E-4. Considering that E-1s and E-2s are normally persons with short periods of service, and allowing further for the statutory preference for persons senior in rank to the accused, the appellant's statistics appear to reflect a realization that all enlisted ranks are eligible for selection as court members. . . .

. . .

    We may take judicial notice that many enlisted persons below the senior noncommissioned ranks are literate, mature in years, and sufficiently judicious in temperament to be eligible to serve on courts-martial. It is equally apparent, however, that the lower enlisted ranks will not yield potential court members of sufficient age and experience to meet the statutory qualifications for selection, without substantial preliminary screening. It is permissible to anticipate, therefore, as did the staff judge advocate in this case, that the senior ranks will more readily provide a large number of persons possessing the varied qualities enumerated in the Uniform Code. In fact, the discussions of Article 25 in the hearings on the Code, which we quoted partially earlier, show a general understanding that the relationship between the prescribed qualifications for court membership, especially "training, experience, and length of service," and seniority of rank is so close that the probabilities are that those in the more senior ranks would most often be called upon to serve. House Hearings, supra, at page 724; see also Hearings before Senate Armed Services Committee on S. 857 and H. R. 4080, 81st Congress, 1st Session, page 183. In the civilian community, a preference for certain voting districts as potentially more fruitful sources of eligible jurors is not exclusionary discrimination. United States v Dennis, supra. Reliance upon a standard of selection which is directly and reasonably calculated to obtain persons with the qualifications prescribed by law does not vitiate the selection system. All enlisted persons may be eligible for membership on courts-martial; but not all enlisted ranks must, or for that matter can, be represented on any one court-martial. The Uniform Code requires a choice based upon a variety of qualities, not, as the staff judge advocate pointed out, "willy-nilly" recourse to the routine duty roster.

Appellate defense counsel argue that senior noncommissioned officers are to be distinguished from all other enlisted persons in that they have a predilection to convict. No evidence is presented or offered to support that contention. And we reject summarily, as obnoxious to the Uniform Code and the traditions of American justice, the assumption that a senior noncommissioned officer would violate his oath to decide the cause impartially, because he is afraid of, or desires to curry favor with, the officer-members of the court. Our experience, and our convictions, are to the contrary.

Career enlisted persons are no more inclined or likely to prejudge an accused, or to treat him with greater severity, than are career officers. This is not to say that all persons, commissioned and noncommissioned, are always free from fixed ideas and attitudes which may predispose them unfavorably toward an accused. Some individuals may be biased, actually or apparently, and are, therefore, subject to challenge. United States v Drain, 4 USCMA 646, 16 CMR 220; see also United States v Hedges, 11 USCMA 642, 29 CMR 458. Disqualification of an individual, however, does not vitiate the process by which the court members were selected. Here, the only purpose in looking to the senior noncommissioned ranks was to obtain persons possessed of proper qualifications to judge and sentence the accused. There was no desire or intention to exclude any group or class on irrelevant, irrational, or prohibited grounds. In short, the evidence leaves no room to doubt that the selection process was designed only to find enlisted men qualified for court service. The senior noncommissioned ranks provided a convenient and logically probable source for eligibles. To refer first to those ranks for prospective members is not an impermissible choice. United States v Dennis, supra.

We turn to the intentional selection of a Negro to serve as a court member. Complaints about color or race in the selection of jurors normally deal with the exclusion of qualified persons solely on such irrelevant and prohibited bases. See Annotation, "Violation of constitutional rights of defendant in criminal case by unfair practices in selection of grand or petit jury," 82 L ed 1053. However, in Collins v Walker, 329 F2d 100 (1964), the Court of Appeals for the Fifth Circuit granted a writ of habeas corpus on the ground the accused, a Negro, was unlawfully discriminated against when the panel of twenty grand jurors which indicted him was so organized as deliberately to include six Negroes. The court reasoned that the intentional inclusion of Negroes constituted "discrimination against . . . [the accused] because of his race or color." Id., at page 105. With due

respect to the learning and experience of the Court of Appeals, we
think it misapprehended the fundamental difference between inclusion
of a member of a particular group for the purpose of obtaining a fair
representation of a substantial part of the community, and exclusion
of members of that group so as to reduce the representational character of the jury.  In Avery v Georgia, 345 US 559, 562, 97 L ed 1244,
73 S Ct 891 (1953), which was relied upon by the Court of Appeals, the
Supreme Court criticized the practice of using a white ticket to designate a prospective white juror, and a yellow ticket to indicate a Negro
juror.  However, the criticism was related to the established fact that
no Negroes had been selected for service over an extended period of
time, although they numbered five percent of the jury list.  The flag-
ging of the tickets, together with the long continued failure to select
a single Negro for service, was held to establish a prima facie case
of exclusion of Negroes from jury duty.  It was exclusion, not inclusion,
that vitiated the selection process.  In Dow v Carnegie-Illinois Steel
Corporation, 224 F2d 414 (CA 3d Cir) (1955), cert den 350 US 971,
100 L ed 842, 76 S Ct 442 (1956), the clerk deliberately tried to place
more than one Negro juror on each panel.  To achieve that purpose,
the cards of eligible jurors were marked to show those who were
Negro.  The court pointed out that, unlike Avery, which was a case of
exclusion, the inclusion of Negroes on the jury was designed "to insure a fair representation" of that class, and was, therefore, proper.
Dow v Carnegie-Illinois Steel Corporation, 224 F2d 414, supra, at
pages 425-426.  Accord:  United States v Dennis, 183 F2d 201, supra,
at page 223; United States v Forest, 118 F Supp 504 (ED Mo) (1954).
If deliberately to include qualified persons is discrimination, it is discrimination in favor of, not against, an accused.  Equal protection of
the laws is not denied, but assured.  We hold, therefore, there was no
error in the deliberate selection of a Negro to serve on the accused's
court-martial.
    The decision of the board of review is affirmed.

KILDAY, Judge (concurring in the result):
    I concur in the result reached by Chief Judge Quinn.  I do not
agree with all of the reasons given by him in reaching that result.
Because the routes we follow are so divergent, I feel it is requisite
that my views be separately stated.
    The Congress has power "to make Rules for the Government
and Regulation of the land and naval Forces," Constitution of the
United States, Article I, Section 8, Clause 14.  This power is entirely
separate from the Congressional judicial powers as outlined in Article
III of the Constitution.  This is made clear in the early case of Dynes
v Hoover, 20 Howard 65 (U.S. 1858), in the following language:

        "These provisions show that Congress has the pow-
    er to provide for the trial and punishment of military and

naval offenses in the manner then and now practiced by civilized nations; and that the power to do so is given without any connection between it and the 3d article of the Constitution defining the judicial power of the United States; indeed that the two powers are entirely independent of each other."

. . .

It is to be noted that the appellant does not contend the court-martial which tried him was biased or prosecution minded. He does not contend the members appointed were not qualified, nor is there any indication the appellant did not receive a fair trial. Rather, he alleges that "Senior noncommissioned officers, quite naturally, would view a disturbance in a barracks in a different light than would lower grade enlisted men, and it is strenuously submitted that such senior non-commissioned officers would be likely to consider the entire matter more as a breakdown in discipline than anything else." There is, however, no contention that those who served on this court-martial were so oriented. Therefore, the naked question presented concerns the consideration for appointment and the appointment, as members of the court-martial, of senior noncommissioned officers only.

. . .

### III

Turning now to the language of Article 25(d)(1) and 25(d)(2), it is observed that the same is neither doubtful, obscure nor ambiguous, and resort to rules of statutory construction is unnecessary. United States v Davis, supra. The first clear and positive direction to the convening authority in appointing a court-martial is that: "When it can be avoided, no person in the armed forces shall be tried by a court-martial any member of which is junior to him in rank or grade." This is an ancient provision of military law. Winthrop, supra. The plain and unambiguous meaning of this provision is that an accused before a court-martial is to be tried by his superiors, not by his peers or equals as is the case of a civilian defendant before a jury.

The direction of Article 25(d)(2) is that the convening authority shall appoint as members thereof such persons as, in his opinion, are best qualified for the duty by reason of age, education, training, ex-perience, length of service, and judicial temperament. It would be difficult to conceive of words with which more adequately to commit the selection to the sound discretion of the convening authority. If the person under consideration for appointment is not junior to the ac-cused, the selection is of those who "in his opinion" are best qualified. The guidelines established are those which, among other worthwhile qualifications, tend to the accumulation of rank or grade. We are not blind to, nor ignorant of, the fact that under statutory provisions and ancient military procedures, age, education, training, experience, and length of service, do produce an accumulation of military rank and grade. This determination is within the sound discretion of the convening authority. He may not abuse that discretion by the choice of individuals who are not fair and impartial. He can no more "stack" the court against the interests of the accused than he can pollute the court by command control or influence against him. United States v Hedges, 11 USCMA 642, 29 CMR 458; United States v Kitchens, 12 USCMA 589, 31 CMR 175. In the case before us there is no contention nor intimation that the convening authority abused his discretion in the selection of the individuals who composed the court, nor that any of them were other than fair and impartial.

. . .

In view of the fact that Article 25, Uniform Code of Military Justice, supra, places the selection of the officer and enlisted members of a court-martial within the sound discretion of the convening authority and there being no evidence or contention of abuse of that discretion in the choice of the individuals who served on the court-martial, no error is reflected by this assignment.

Proceeding to the consideration of the efforts made by the convening authority to secure a Negro enlisted man as a member of the court-martial, I concur with the Chief Judge in his conclusion and the reasoning by which he reached the same. Here, again, there is no contention the enlisted man selected and appointed by the convening authority was biased, prosecution minded nor in anywise other than a fair and impartial member of the court. One of the officer-members was also of appellant's race, a Negro, and no complaint is made as to his membership on the court. This record reveals no more than that, in the exercise of his discretion, the convening authority chose this court member as qualified for membership on the court. As the Chief Judge points out, this contention is without merit.

I agree, the decision of the board of review should be affirmed.

FERGUSON, Judge (dissenting):

I dissent.

. . .

The statute, therefore, sets up a class of enlisted members who, after accused has filed his request for their appointment in writing, are all eligible for consideration by the convening authority. Not a single condition is inserted with regard to their rank or position within the military community, except those very general and personal factors which are to be considered by the convening authority in the exercise of his discretion. . . .

. . .

. . . I would conclude, therefore, that this accused's court-martial consisted in part of improperly chosen enlisted members, was not duly constituted, and would order another trial.

IV

It does not appear that the Chief Judge disagrees with the legal conclusion which I reach, for he, too, finds nothing in the "Uniform

Code expressly limits membership on a court-martial to persons of
a particular rank" and that Code, supra, Article 25, "implies all ranks
and grades are eligible for appointment." He finds, nevertheless, that
the evidence does not establish the practice of discriminatory exclusion in this case. . . .

. . .

In the instant case, however, the affidavits make quite clear
that the convening authority was limited to the class or group of
senior noncommissioned officers, thereby excluding from consideration all those not possessing one of those ranks. The statistics cited
show that in the Army there is a "systematic and intentional exclusion" from such court lists of the other ranks. Gorin, supra, at page
644. Hence, rather than the use of the ordinary screening process,
we are confronted with the intentional narrowing of the class of eligibles under the Article in question which, in respect to a similar
process under Federal jury enactments, the Supreme Court so vigorously condemned in Thiel v Southern P. Co., supra. In short, we have
that very departure from the statute which its drafters feared and pre-
dicted would occur. Taken all in all, the Chief Judge's reasoning to
the contrary notwithstanding, if such can be done through the device
of screening potential members, then the wording of the Article making
"[a]ny enlisted member" eligible to participate in the military judicial
process is indeed meaningless.

For these reasons, I record my disagreement with his conclusion.

V

The final question before us deals simply with whether a convening authority may ever select a member of a court-martial of the
same race as the accused solely on the grounds of that race, i.e.,
legitimately appoint a Negro member of a court solely on the grounds
that the defendant is colored. In my opinion, he clearly cannot.

. . .

VI

In sum, then, I am of the opinion that this record conclusively
establishes the convening authority impermissibly limited himself to
senior noncommissioned officers in choosing enlisted court members,
in violation of Code, supra, Article 25. Further, the detailed and
arduous quest for a Negro member of the court, selected solely on the
basis of his race, establishes beyond cavil that the ugly fact of race
was considered, at least in this jurisdiction, to be the standard by
which military jurors should be selected in the case of Negro defendants. I would not hesitate to strike this practice down and remind
commanders everywhere that neither race, nor color, nor creed,
enter into the administration of any American judicial system. Considering as I do that these errors go to the competency of the court-
martial which heard accused's case, I would order another trial
before a properly selected court. Thiel v Southern P. Co., supra.

I, therefore, dissent from the contrary view of my brothers.

The conviction of an enlisted accused who elected trial by a military judge in order to avoid trial by a court composed of lieutenant colonels and colonels was reversed because of doubts as to the propriety of the manner in which the Court was selected. U.S. v. Greene, 20 USCMA 232, 43 CMR 72 (1970).

Article 25, UCMJ, states that a person may not sit as a member of a court-martial if he is the "accuser or a witness for the prosecution or has acted as investigating officer or as counsel in the same case." The term "investigating officer" is not limited to the individual appointed under the provisions of Article 32 but extends to any other person who has conducted a personal investigation of a general matter involving the particular offense (U.S. v. Bound, 1 USCMA 224, 2 CMR 130 [1952]; U.S. v. Burkhalter, 17 USCMA 266, 38 CMR 64 [1967]). A member of a court-martial who had verified an extract of the accused's service record listing previous convictions was disqualified since he was "a witness for the prosecution" (U.S. v. Moore, 4 USCMA 675, 16 CMR 249 [1954]), but this disqualification may be waived (see U.S. v. Beer, 6 USCMA 180, 19 CMR 306 [1955]).

Prior to The Military Justice Act of 1968, the lawyer acting in the position comparable to the judge of a civilian Court was called the law officer. Judge FERGUSON, in his dissent in U. S. v. Mortenson, 8 USCMA 233, 24 CMR 43 (1957), discusses the role of the law officer:

One of the primary goals sought to be achieved by the enactment of the Uniform Code of Military Justice was the creation of the position of law officer with duties and functions comparable to those of a civilian trial judge. In the House Hearings on the Uniform Code of Military Justice, Professor Morgan, whose efforts were instrumental in securing Congressional adoption of the Code, stated in response to a Committee inquiry into the role of the law officer:

> "Well, the fundamental notion was that the law officer ought to be as near like a civilian judge as it was possible under the circumstances." [Hearings before House Armed Services Committee on H.R. 2498, 81st Congress, 1st Session, page 607.]

Similar sentiments are frequently interspersed throughout the House and Senate Hearings and Reports on the Uniform Code of Military Justice. Hearings before House Armed Services Committee on H.R.

2498, 81st Congress, 1st Session, page 1153; Hearings before Senate Armed Services Committee on S. 857 and H. R. 4080, 81st Congress, 1st Session, pages 40, 57, 287; Senate Report No. 486, 81st Congress, 1st Session, page 6.

A long unbroken line of decisions of this Court eloquently attests to the efforts made to equate the position occupied by the law officer to that held by a trial judge in civilian practice. It was recognized early in the history of this Court that only by such equation could the broad and sweeping remedial changes in the system of military justice envisioned by the Congress in the Code become a reality. In the early case of United States v Berry, 1 USCMA 235, 2 CMR 141, we held it to constitute reversible error for the president of a court-martial to usurp the functions of the law officer. In the course of our opinion we said:

> ". . . The complete independence of the law member and his unshackled freedom from direction of any sort or nature are, we entertain no doubt, vital, integral, even crucial, elements of the legislative effort to minimize opportunity for the exercise of control over the court-martial process by any agency of command. It follows that any abdication by the law member of his statutory duties and an attendant usurpation of those functions by the president--much more directly a representative of the convening authority--must be viewed with stern suspicion."

We made it crystal clear in that case that "the law member's position with respect to a court-martial is closely analogous to that of the judge in the criminal law administration of the civilian community," and that while occupying such position he represents "the external and visible symbol of the law in a process which has long been characterized as juristic and must be genuinely regarded as such."

In United States v Jackson, 3 USCMA 646, 14 CMR 64, we voiced the sentiment that the law officer was "not a mere figurehead in the courtroom drama," and that he must "direct the trial along paths of recognized procedure in a manner reasonably calculated to bring an end to the hearing without prejudice to either party." In United States v Stringer, 5 USCMA 122, 17 CMR 122, we discussed the inherent power existing in a law officer--similar to that found in a civilian trial judge--to declare a mistrial where warranted by the circumstances. A law officer may now properly entertain a motion for a change of venue where the interests of justice so require. United States v Gravitt, 5 USCMA 249, 17 CMR 249. The Federal rule permitting a trial judge to comment on the evidence--without infringing upon the accused's right to an impartial trial by jury--was adopted in military practice and a law officer may now comment upon the evidence in court-martial trials. United States v Andis, 2 USCMA 364,

8 CMR 164. In United States v Knudson, 4 USCMA 587, 16 CMR 161, we declared that: "Federal practice applies to courts-martial procedures if not incompatible with military law," and, accordingly, we held that the law officer in the exercise of his discretion was the proper person to rule on an application for continuance and that interference by the convening authority would not be tolerated. The practice familiar in civilian courts of reserving decision on a motion raising a question of law, until after the verdict of the jury has been returned, was approved by this Court where there was "no compelling reason requiring a different practice in the military." United States v Strand, 6 USCMA 297, 20 CMR 13. In accordance with the Federal Rules of Criminal Procedure we adopted a practice which permits the law officer to challenge a court member on his own motion. United States v Jones, 7 USCMA 283, 22 CMR 73. In United States v DeAngelis, 3 USCMA 298, 12 CMR 54, we advised law officers that they "should not hesitate to employ" the contempt powers contained in Article 48 of the Code against counsel who by their obstructive and abusive actions flout the authority of the law officer.

In United States v Smith, 6 USCMA 521, 20 CMR 237, we reversed a conviction, where the law officer failed to declare a mistrial on his own motion, because of the court-martial president's improper and accusatory questioning of an accused. In another case we reversed a conviction on the doctrine of cumulative error because of repeated acts of misconduct by the law officer during the trial. United States v Walters, 4 USCMA 617, 16 CMR 191. In the leading case of United States v Keith, 1 USCMA 493, 4 CMR 85, we voiced stern disapproval of the practice which permitted the law officer to confer with members of the court outside the presence of the trial counsel, defense counsel, and the accused. In reversing a conviction we there said:

> ". . . No one who has read the legislative history of the Code can doubt the strength of the Congressional resolve to break away completely from the old procedure and insure, as far as legislatively possible, that the law officer perform in the image of a civilian judge. This policy is so clear and so fundamental to the proper functioning of the procedural reforms brought about by the Uniform Code of Military Justice that it must be strictly enforced." [Emphasis supplied.]

Recently in United States v Fry, 7 USCMA 682, 23 CMR 146, we held that it "was not good practice for the law officer to review the investigating officer's report and the testimony of the witnesses" prior to trial. Although such conduct was not considered to fall within the overall pattern of disqualification established by the Code, "it is too close to a violation of its spirit to merit approval." In United States v Crunk, 4 USCMA 290, 15 CMR 290, we applied the doctrine of separation of functions by holding that a person who had acted as a law officer in a case was thereafter disqualified from participating in the preparation of the staff judge advocate's review. We even adhered to this doctrine in a case where the post-trial review was prepared by an officer who had previously served as law officer at the trial of a co-accused. United States v Turner, 7 USCMA 38, 21 CMR 164. In United States v Wilson, 7 USCMA 713, 23 CMR 177, we had occasion to reaffirm the principle of our earlier cases, which held that it is the law officer who bears the primary burden of insuring that the court-martial is instructed on all lesser included offenses raised by the evidence. In the course of our opinion, we said that:

> ". . . If we are to build a real system of military justice, we must ensure that the law officer is shouldered with the responsibility of seeing to it that the court-martial members are given proper guideposts to reach a fair and just verdict, counsel for the parties notwithstanding. If he is to find his proper place in the scheme of military law, and bear his responsibility to the Government, the accused and the system, we do not believe he can be stripped of the right of final decision as to what instructional guidance will lead the court to a proper decision."

The sum total of all these cases seeks for its purpose the sound erection of a trial system with the law officer at its apex. It was to elevate the role of the law officer that we clothed him with substantially the same rights, duties, functions, and obligations of a civilian trial judge. It is not too much to expect that one occupying a judicial position conduct himself in a judicious manner. From this Court's very inception we moved in the direction of creating an independent judicial officer who would demean himself with the dignity and stature customarily found in civilian trial judges. . . .

. . .

The Military Justice Act of 1968 made extensive changes in the procedures of courts-martial. "Law officers" became "military judges" and were given the authority to try an accused without members (jury) upon the accused's request except in capital cases (see Art. 16, UCMJ). Military judges were to be designated by and to be responsible to their Judge Advocate General rather than the particular unit or area commander where the trial is taking place. They were given the authority to hold pretrial sessions and to rule finally on challenges to Court members, a prerogative formerly in the hands of the members themselves. In essence, military judges now have almost the same powers and prerogatives as judges of federal district Courts.

The Court of Military Appeals has held that it is a jurisdictional prerequisite that the request by an accused to be tried by a military judge alone be in writing (U.S. v. Dean, 20 USCMA 212, 43 CMR 52 [1970]).

In courts-martial, the lawyer representing the government is referred to as the "trial counsel" while the lawyer representing an accused is called the "defense counsel." For the qualifications of counsel, see Article 27, UCMJ.

In United States v. Culp, 14 USCMA 199, 33 CMR 411 (1963), the Court of Military Appeals considered the question of the applicability of the right to counsel provisions of the Sixth Amendment to an accused before a special court-martial. A board of review had held that an accused was entitled to a counsel "qualified in the law unless such right was competently and intelligently waived by him." Judge KILDAY, writing the principal opinion, said:

First. When read in the light of the common law, the purpose of the Sixth Amendment was not to enlarge the right to counsel before courts-martial, but to provide it in those instances in which it was denied in civilian courts at that time.

Second. The reenactment by the First Congress on two occasions of the previously existing Articles adopted by the Continental Congress, and the action of Congress in 1806 in reenacting the identical provision as to counsel, must be regarded as contemporary construction of the constitutional provisions. It is a construction which has been followed since the founding of our government. Such construction is entitled to the greatest respect.

Third. In the light of the long-continued and consistent interpretation of the Sixth Amendment it cannot be taken to have extended the right to counsel, which did not exist at common law before courts-martial.

Considered in light of the foregoing and in light of Article I, Section 8, Clause 14, I find nothing in Article 27, Uniform Code of Military Justice, supra, when supplemented by Article 38(b) thereof, which conflicts with the Sixth Amendment; rather such provisions are compatible therewith.

In addition, the Congress having the undisputed right to enact the Uniform Code of Military Justice and to establish courts-martial and fix the qualifications of members thereof, it certainly has the power to prescribe the qualifications of counsel who appear before such courts. Nor is there anything to prevent the Congress from providing one qualification for counsel before general courts and another qualification for counsel before special courts.

A large percentage of cases heard by special courts-martial are by no means petty violations. However, the maximum sentence permitted is greatly diminished from that permitted by general courts-martial. Just as a distinction may be made as to trial by jury between serious and petty offenses, so too a distinction as to qualifications of counsel before general and special courts-martial is permissible. District of Columbia v Colts, 282 US 63, 75 L ed 177, 51 S Ct 52 (1930); Schick v United States, supra; District of Columbia v Clawans, supra; Ex parte Quirin, supra.

I would, therefore, hold that the board of review was in error in holding that the accused, as a matter of right, under the Sixth Amendment, was entitled to counsel; I would also hold that the defense counsel appointed for him met with the requirements of Article 27 and 38(b), Uniform Code of Military Justice, supra.

---

Chief Judge Quinn, disagreed with the conclusion that the Sixth Amendment's guarantee of the right to counsel is not applicable to courts-martial but found that the provisions of the UCMJ satisfied the Amendment's requirements and accordingly concurred in the remand of the case to the board of review for further action. Judge Ferguson also found the Sixth Amendment applicable to courts-martial but dissented on the basis that an accused before a special court-martial that has the authority to issue a bad conduct discharge should have a legally-trained counsel and hence that the UCMJ did not satisfy the requirements of the Amendment.

For further discussion of this issue, see Kennedy v. Commandant, USDB, 377 F.2d 339 (CA Tenth, 1967) (concurrence in Chief Judge Quinn's views), motion for leave to file petition for writ of habeas corpus and other relief denied, 389 U.S. 807 (1967).

UNITED STATES v. TEMPIA*

United States Court of Military Appeals, 1967.
16 U.S.C.M.A. 629, 37 C.M.R. 249.

*[Footnotes have been omitted. Ed.]

FERGUSON, Judge:
    This case, certified by the Judge Advocate General, United
States Air Force, presents important questions concerning the administration of military justice. Basically, it inquires whether the
principles enunciated by the Supreme Court in Miranda v Arizona,
384 US 436, 16 L ed 2d 694, 86 S Ct 1602 (1966), apply to military interrogations of criminal suspects. We hold that they do. As to cases
tried on and after June 13, 1966, the doctrine set forth in our earlier
decision in United States v Wimberley, 16 USCMA 3, 36 CMR 159, has
largely been set at naught by the Miranda decision.

I

    The accused was tried by general court-martial at Dover Air
Force Base, Delaware, and convicted of taking indecent liberties with
females under the age of sixteen, in violation of Uniform Code of
Military Justice, Article 134, 10 USC §934. He was sentenced to bad-
conduct discharge, forfeiture of all pay and allowances, confinement
at hard labor for six months, and reduction. Intermediate appellate
authorities affirmed, and the case was, as indicated above, certified
to this Court on the question:

    "WAS THE BOARD OF REVIEW CORRECT IN ITS
    DETERMINATION THAT THE ACCUSED'S PRETRIAL
    STATEMENT WAS PROPERLY RECEIVED IN EVI-
    DENCE?"

    The accused's trial commenced on June 14, 1966, one day after
the effective date of applying the principles set forth in Miranda,
supra. See Johnson v New Jersey, 384 US 719, 16 L ed 2d 882, 86
S Ct 1772 (1966). The testimony of the witnesses therein disclosed
the following evidence.
    On May 1, 1966, accused accompanied an Airman Keitel to the
base library. Upon request, Keitel pointed out the location of the
latrine. Accused left Keitel in the reading room and returned in five
or six minutes.
    From other testimony, it appears he went to the ladies' rest
room, stood in its partially opened door, and made obscene proposals
to three young girls. The victims left the library, returned with one
of their parents and the Air Police, and pointed accused out in the
reading room. Accused was asked "to come back to the office" by
one of the policemen. He did so.

At the Air Police office, accused was advised by Agent Blessing that he was suspected of taking indecent liberties with children; of his rights under Code, supra, Article 31, 10 USC §831; and " ' "that you may consult with legal counsel if you desire." ' " Agent McQuary assisted Agent Blessing in the interview. It was immediately terminated, as Tempia stated " 'he wanted counsel.' " He was released from custody.

On May 3, 1966, Tempia was again called to the "OSI Office" where he was once more advised by Blessing, in the presence of Agent Feczer, of his rights and entitlement to consult with counsel. Accused " 'stated he had not yet received legal counsel.' " Blessing thereupon called Major Norman K. Hogue, Base Staff Judge Advocate, and made an appointment for Tempia.

Blessing's interview with Tempia terminated at 8:50 a.m., and the latter proceeded to Major Hogue's office. Hogue informed him he was the Staff Judge Advocate and "that I could not accept an attorney-client relationship with him because if I did, it would disqualify me from acting in my capacity as Staff Judge Advocate." He further stated to Tempia that he would nevertheless "advise him of his legal rights and explained to him that this was different than acting as his defense counsel in that I did not want to hear any of his story, but I would answer any legal questions he had after I explained some rights to him."

Major Hogue also told accused he could not make a military lawyer available to him "as his defense counsel during that OSI investigation," but that he had the right to employ civilian counsel; would be given a reasonable time to do so; and that civilian counsel would be entitled to appear with him at the investigation. In addition, Hogue advised him of his rights under Code, supra, Article 31, and explained those rights to him, but:

> ". . . As I say, I told him no military lawyer would be appointed to represent him during the OSI investigation or any investigation by the law enforcement agents on this base. I told him that if charges are preferred--in his case, referred to trial by special court-martial or general court-martial, where it's referred to an investigation under Article 32b, he would be furnished a military lawyer at that time, one certified under Article 27b of the Uniform Code of Military Justice."

In addition, accused filled out a written form in which it was indicated he had been advised:

> a. That he had the right to retain civilian counsel at his own expense;

b. That no military lawyer would be appointed to represent him while under investigation by law enforcement agents;

c. That he would be furnished military counsel if charges were preferred and referred to trial or a pretrial investigation convened;

d. Of his rights under Code, supra, Article 31;

e. Of the maximum punishment involved; and,

f. That he had not discussed his guilt or innocence or any of the facts involved with Major Hogue.

Following his session with Major Hogue, Tempia returned to the Office of Special Investigations, at 9:24 a.m. He "was then called in . . . readvised of his rights, readvised of the nature of the investigation and of his rights to seek legal counsel the second time." He stated he had consulted with Major Hogue, and did not desire further counsel as "they could not help him. . . . He said, 'They didn't do me no good.'" Thereafter, he was interrogated by Blessing and Feczer, to whom he began to dictate his confession.

At the trial, defense counsel sought exclusion of the statement on the basis of the Supreme Court decision in Miranda, supra, as he had found it reported in the press. The law officer overruled his timely objection and admitted Tempia's confession in evidence.

II

The Judge Advocate General, United States Navy, has filed a brief amicus curiac in which it is urged that military law is in nowise affected by constitutional limitations and, in consequence, that the principles enunciated in Miranda v Arizona, supra, do not apply to the situation herein presented. The Government, however, takes a different tack. Conceding the application of the Constitution, it urges the Supreme Court has no supervisory power over military tribunals. Construing Miranda v Arizona, supra, as announcing only procedural devices designed to enforce a Constitutional right in the exercise of the Supreme Court's supervisory power, it contends this Court is neither required to follow Miranda, supra, nor are its stringent formulae necessary or desirable in the administration of military justice. In this latter connection, it adverts to our decision in United States v Wimberley, supra, and points to the safeguards erected by Congress in Code, supra, Article 31.

Counsel for the accused and other amicus curiae (who represented Miranda before the Supreme Court) disagree; point out that the decision in Miranda, supra, was one of constitutional dimensions; and, therefore, urge it is binding on military interrogations.

The time is long since past--as, indeed, the United States recognizes--when this Court will lend an attentive ear to the argument that members of the armed services are, by reason of their status, ipso facto deprived of all protections of the Bill of Rights.

Military jurisprudence is and has always been separated from the ordinary Federal and State judicial systems in this country. Such is the meaning of Mr. Chief Justice Vinson's language in Burns v Wilson, 346 US 137, 97 L ed 1508, 73 S Ct 1045 (1953), at page 140:

"Military law, like state law, is a jurisprudence which exists separate and apart from the law which governs in our federal judicial establishment. This court has played no role in its development; we have exerted no supervisory power over the courts which enforce it; the rights of men in the armed forces must perforce be conditioned to meet certain overriding demands of discipline and duty, and the civil courts are not the agencies which must determine the precise balance to be struck in this adjustment. The Framers expressly entrusted that task to Congress."

That military law exists and has developed separately from other Federal law does not mean that persons subject thereto are denied their constitutional rights. . . .

. . .

The impact of Burns v Wilson, supra, then, is of an unequivocal holding by the Supreme Court that the protections of the Constitution are available to servicemen in military trials. The issue on which the Court divided was not the applicability of constitutional rights but the scope of collateral review by the Federal courts--"the manner in which the Court should proceed to exercise its power." Burns v Wilson, supra, at page 139.

. . .

Thus, it will be seen that both the Supreme Court and this Court itself are satisfied as to the applicability of constitutional safeguards to military trials, except insofar as they are made inapplicable either expressly or by necessary implication. The Government, therefore, is correct in conceding the point, and the Judge Advocate General, United States Navy, as amicus curiae, is incorrect in his contrary conclusion. Indeed, as to the latter, it would appear from the authorities on which he relies that the military courts applied what we now know as the constitutional protection against self-incrimination in trials prior to and contemporaneous with the adoption of the Constitution. Hence, we find Major Andre being extended the privilege at his court-martial in 1780. Wigmore, Evidence, 3d ed, §2251. The same reference was made in the trial of Commodore James Barron in 1808. Proceedings of the General Court Martial Convened for the Trial of Commodore James Barron (1822), page 98. And the Articles of War of 1776, as amended May 31, 1786, provided for objection by the judge advocate to any question put to the accused, the answer to which might tend to incriminate him. See Winthrop's Military Law and Precedents, 2d ed, 1920 Reprint, pages 196, 972.

The point need not, however, be belabored. Sufficient has been said to establish our firm and unshakable conviction that Tempia, as any other member of the armed services so situated, was entitled to the protection of the Bill of Rights, insofar as we are herein concerned with it. We pass, therefore, to the Government's contention that Miranda, supra, involves a decision in the area of the Supreme Court's supervisory authority rather than constitutional principles.

. . .

A cursory scrutiny of the opinion in Miranda makes crystal clear that the formulae there laid down by the Court are constitutional in nature, although the door was left open for the legislative process to innovate "other procedures which are at least as effective in apprising accused persons of their right of silence and in assuring a continuous opportunity to exercise it." (Emphasis supplied.) Miranda, supra, at page 467. Thus, the Court noted, at the outset, it had "granted certiorari in these cases . . . to explore some facets of the problems, thus exposed, of applying the privilege against self-incrimination to in-custody interrogation, and to give concrete constitutional guidelines for law enforcement agencies and courts to follow." Id., at page 441. (Emphasis supplied.) It spoke not of the exercise of its supervisory authority over the Federal judicial system, but of the "constitutional issue"; "adequate safeguards to protect precious Fifth Amendment rights"; "whether the privilege is fully applicable during a period of custodial interrogation"; "the protection which must be given to the privilege against self-incrimination when the individual is first subjected to police interrogation"; "the issues presented are of constitutional dimensions"; and of similar matters, all indicative of the fact, hardly to be gainsaid, that the Court was laying down constitutional rules for criminal interrogation which are part and parcel of the Fifth Amendment.

. . .

### IV

We turn, therefore, to the merits of the controversy before us. Miranda v Arizona, supra, explicitly and at length lays down concrete rules which are to govern all criminal interrogations by Federal or State authorities, military or civilian, if resulting statements are to be used in trials commencing on and after June 13, 1966. We commend a reading of that opinion to all involved in the administration of military criminal law as well as the undertaking of educative measures to see that its precepts are not violated in pretrial interrogations. . . .

. . .

### a. Custodial Interrogation

The Government urges upon us the proposition that the accused was not in custody, and, hence, the need for appropriate advice and assistance did not arise. We may at once dispose of this contention. The accused was apprehended on May 1, 1966; freed to seek counsel;

recalled for interrogation on May 3, 1966; an appointment was made for him with Major Hogue, following which, he immediately returned to the Office of Special Investigations, where his interrogation was successfully completed. The test to be applied is not whether the accused, technically, has been taken into custody, but, absent that, whether he has been "otherwise deprived of his freedom of action in any significant way." Miranda, supra, at page 444. Here, the accused was clearly summoned for interrogation. Had he not obeyed, he would have undoubtedly subjected himself to being penalized for a failure to repair. Code, supra, Article 86, 10 USC §886; Manual for Courts-Martial, United States, 1951, paragraph 127b. In the military, unlike civil life, a suspect may be required to report and submit to questioning quite without regard to warrants or other legal process. It ignores the realities of that situation to say that one ordered to appear for interrogation has not been significantly deprived of his freedom of action. See People v Kelley, 57 West's Cal Rptr 363, 424 P2d 947 (1967). Hence, we conclude there was "custodial interrogation" in this case.

   b. The Warning.
   The accused was fully advised of his rights under Code, supra, Article 31, and of his right to consult with counsel. On indicating a desire to speak with counsel, he was initially freed and, ultimately, on May 3, was referred to Major Hogue for further advice concerning his rights. But that officer went no further than to emphasize to the accused that he could not form an attorney-client relationship with him; to advise him again of his rights under Code, supra, Article 31; and to inform him he could retain civilian counsel at his own expense, who could appear at his interrogation. He specifically told accused no military lawyer would be appointed "to represent him during the OSI investigation or any investigation by the law enforcement agents on this base."
   Miranda, supra, squarely points out "the person must be warned that he has a right to remain silent, that any statement he does make may be used as evidence against him, and that he has a right to the presence of an attorney, either retained or appointed." (Emphasis supplied.) In addition, if the accused "indicates in any manner and at any stage of the process that he wishes to consult with an attorney before speaking there can be no questioning. Likewise, if the individual is alone and indicates in any manner that he does not wish to be interrogated, the police may not question him."
   Undoubtedly, the advice given Tempia under Code, supra, Article 31, sufficed to inform him both of his right to remain silent and the purpose for which any statement he might make could be used. The advice as to counsel, however, was deficient.
   First, accused was only warned by the agents that he was entitled to consult with counsel. When Major Hogue elaborated on this

proposition, he limited the availability of counsel to private attorneys
employed by the accused at his own expense. He specifically told
accused no attorney would be appointed to represent him in any law
enforcement investigation. This is exactly contrary to the information which, under Miranda, supra, must be preliminarily communicated
to the accused. . . .

As accused was informed no counsel would be appointed for him,
it follows that the statement thereafter taken from him was inadmissible in evidence.

c. Waiver.

The Government suggests that accused knowingly and intelligently waived his rights against self-incrimination by making his
statement after being repeatedly warned under Code, supra, Article
31, and subjecting himself to further interrogation following his conference with Major Hogue. In connection with the latter circumstance,
it invites our attention to testimony that, on returning from Hogue's
office, accused stated he did not desire further counsel, "that they
could not help him. . . . 'They didn't do me no good.'"

Aside from the fact that accused was improperly advised as to
his entitlement to appointed counsel, we point out that he, in fact,
received no legal advice, as Major Hogue specifically declined to act
as his attorney. The testimony, taken as a whole, indicates not that
accused did not desire a lawyer's services but that he had been frustrated in obtaining advice on whether to exercise his rights--hence,
his comment: " 'They didn't do me no good.'" There should be small
wonder at his feelings, when he had just been refused the opportunity
to discuss the case with Hogue, relate any of the facts to him, or to
obtain any information as to a desirable course of action. "If the interrogation continues without the presence of an attorney and a statement is taken, a heavy burden rests on the government to demonstrate
that the defendant knowingly and intelligently waived his privilege
against self-incrimination and his right to retained or appointed
counsel." Miranda, supra, at page 475.

Quite apart from the insufficiency of the warning as to accused's
right to counsel, here the Government did not carry its burden, and
no waiver is made out. To the contrary, it merely shows accused's
entitlement to consult with counsel was frustrated by the Staff Judge
Advocate's well-meant but legally improper statements.

Finally, the Government urges it cannot be required in law to
furnish appointed counsel for accused during law enforcement investigations. Referring to language in our earlier decision in United
States v Gunnels, 8 USCMA 130, 23 CMR 354, and interpreting it to
mean that one is not entitled to appointed counsel prior to the reference of charges for investigation, it points out that no money has ever
been appropriated for providing counsel at an earlier time. Monies,
it states, which have been appropriated by the Congress must be used

for the purpose intended. See 31 USC §628. Hence, it argues that counsel paid from such funds may not be used as such earlier than was originally intended, i.e., at the initial investigation of charges.

We must confess an inability to follow out the intricacies of this argument. Undoubtedly, Congress provides funds for the payment of defense counsel, but we know of no prohibition in appropriation acts, the Uniform Code of Military Justice, or the Manual for Courts-Martial, United States, 1951, against such being made available to the accused when he is initially interrogated by police officers. Indeed, the impact of Miranda, supra, upon the administration of military justice should be far less than that in comparable civilian jurisdictions. The armed services are already provided with a complete, functioning system of appointed counsel, one which, in Miranda, supra, merited the approbation of our highest court. In most cases, defense counsel will eventually have to be appointed for the trial. All that will now be required is that the date of appointment be moved back. And should the investigation result in no trial, we daresay that the consequent savings will more than repay any costs involved in the earlier intervention of an appointed counsel.

Be that as it may, we point out another matter overlooked in the Government's claim of lack of authority to furnish counsel on this earlier occasion. Miranda, supra, does not specifically require such procedures or their equivalent to be followed. It merely prohibits the receipt in evidence of any statement taken, unless there is compliance with these constitutional standards. If the Government cannot comply with them, it need only abandon its reliance in criminal cases on the accused's statements as evidence. That is the essence of the Miranda holding, and it is the choice of the Government whether to pay this price for withholding counsel at the critical moment of police interrogation.

. . .

[Concurring opinion of Judge Kilday omitted.]

QUINN, Chief Judge (dissenting):

A good case can be made to show that Miranda v Arizona, 384 US 436, 16 L ed 2d 694, 86 S Ct 1602 (1966), was not intended by the Supreme Court to apply to the military legal system. The Supreme Court especially pointed out that an "understanding of the nature and setting" of the kind of in-custody interrogation it was concerned with was "essential" to its decision. It illumined and analyzed interrogation techniques that were "psychologically . . . oriented" to deprive the individual of the free and unfettered choice to speak or to remain silent. Id., at pages 445, 448. In United States v Wimberley, 16 USCMA 3, 10, 36 CMR 159, however, this Court observed that its experience with the conditions and methods of military interrogations indicated they did not tend to override or interfere with the individual's exercise of the right to remain silent. Perhaps even more

significant than the factual underpinning of Miranda is the approbation
accorded the military interrogative procedure by the Supreme Court.

The central purpose of Miranda was to effectuate the Fifth
Amendment right of the individual to remain silent. To achieve that
purpose, the Supreme Court deemed it necessary to adopt certain
"protective devices" to nullify the "inherent compulsions of the inter-
rogation process as it is presently conducted." Id., at pages 458, 467.
The devices adopted by the Court were patterned on safeguards in
effect in other jurisdictions. Among these jurisdictions was the United
States military. The Supreme Court commented on the procedure to
safeguard the right to remain silent, which had been prescribed by
Congress in Article 31 of the Uniform Code of Military Justice, 10
USC §831, and further delineated by this Court in United States v
Gunnels, 8 USCMA 130, 23 CMR 354, and United States v Rose, 8
USCMA 441, 24 CMR 251. It reasoned that "at least as much protection" of the right to remain silent should be accorded to individuals
in the civilian community. Miranda, at page 489. It seems to me that
this esteem for the military practice was expressed in Miranda only
because the Supreme Court was satisfied it provided effective counter-
balance to the inherent pressures of in-custody interrogation, and
assured the individual complete freedom to decide whether to speak
or to remain silent.

Assuming, however, I read too much into the praise accorded
the military system in Miranda, I am convinced that the military procedures to safeguard the right to remain silent are, within the framework of Miranda, "fully effective means . . . to notify the person of
his right of silence and to assure that the exercise of the right will
be scrupulously honored." The Supreme Court expressly disclaimed
any intention that Miranda operate as "a constitutional straightjacket"
of preconditions to in-custody interrogation. It expressly acknowledged
that means other than those prescribed by it may be equally effective
to safeguard the right. And, it expressly reaffirmed that a confession
is admissible in evidence against the accused when demonstrated to
have been "given freely and voluntarily without any compelling influences." Id., at pages 479, 467, 478. I am satisfied that the means
provided by Congress in the Uniform Code to safeguard the accused's
right to remain silent satisfy all constitutional requirements; to demand more, as the majority do, is to legislate, not adjudicate.

Military law starts with a safeguard not mentioned in Miranda,
Article 31 of the Uniform Code, supra, requires that, before any questioning, the individual be informed of the "nature of the accusation"
which prompts the proposed questioning. Thus, the individual is immediately and directly oriented to the purpose of the interrogation,
and is better able to determine whether to speak or to remain silent.
United States v Johnson, 5 USCMA 795, 803, 19 CMR 91. Next, for
many years military law has required, as Miranda interpreted the
Fifth Amendment to require, that, before questioning, the individual

be specifically informed "he has the right to remain silent," and if
he chooses to speak, anything he says can be used against him in court.
Id., at page 479; United States v Williams, 2 USCMA 430, 9 CMR 60;
see also United States v Diterlizzi, 8 USCMA 334, 24 CMR 144. The
third safeguard devised by the Supreme Court deals with advice to the
individual as to the right to counsel in connection with the interrogation. My brothers maintain the military procedure does not match
Miranda in this area. I pass the point for the moment to note the correspondence between the military procedure, and the fourth and final
procedural safeguard promulgated by Miranda. Miranda postulated
that the opportunity to exercise the right to remain silent and the right
to consult counsel "must be afforded . . . throughout the interrogation." Id., at page 479. Military law imposes a continuous duty upon
law enforcement agents to accord that right to the individual being
questioned. United States v Dickson, 16 USCMA 392, 37 CMR 12;
United States v Evans, 13 USCMA 598, 33 CMR 130; cf. United States
v Rogers, 14 USCMA 570, 34 CMR 350.

I turn now to the alleged difference between the mandate of
Miranda and the requirements of military law. Miranda held that one
of the minimum safeguards to assure the individual in an in-custody
situation the unfettered choice between speech and silence is that he
be advised he "has the right to the presence of an attorney, and that
if he cannot afford an attorney one will be appointed for him prior to
any questioning if he so desires." Id., at page 479.

Anticipating Miranda, and its precursor, Escobedo v Illinois,
378 US 478, 12 L ed 2d 977, 84 S Ct 1758 (1964), this Court held that
an accused has the right to the presence of counsel throughout interrogation by law enforcement officials. United States v Gunnels, supra,
at page 134. It did not, as Miranda does, impose an obligation upon the
agents to advise the individual explicitly that he has a right to counsel.
United States v Wimberley, supra. However, at least since Escobedo,
it has been common practice in the Air Force to provide such preliminary information. In fact, the accused in this case was affirmatively and fully informed he had a right to counsel and his lawyer
could be with him during any interrogation. This part of the counsel
safeguard expounded in Miranda was thus honored in fact, although it
had not yet been posited by Miranda as a requirement to assure that
the individual knows the nature of his right to remain silent and that
he is free to exercise it as he chooses. That brings us to the second
part of the Miranda formula which is to advise the individual that if
he "cannot afford an attorney one will be appointed for him prior to
any questioning if he so desires." In my opinion, military law provides the individual an equivalent, if not a greater, safeguard; and that
safeguard was accorded the accused in this case.

Miranda postulated that the circumstances of in-custody interrogation "can operate very quickly to overbear the will of one merely
made aware of his privilege by his interrogators." It, therefore,

concluded that a "once-stated warning, delivered by those who will conduct the interrogation," was insufficient to assure the right to choose between silence and speech. Id., at page 469. As a counterweight to the coercive influences of the in-custody interrogation, the Supreme Court determined that the individual was entitled to the assistance of counsel at the station house. Military procedure deals with the problem differently. It cuts off, abruptly and completely, the entire station house atmosphere. In its place it substitutes the dignity, the prestige, and the independence of the staff legal officer. Instead of a lawyer appointed by his interrogators, which itself may engender suspicion and fear, the individual is accorded the opportunity to consult the senior military legal officer of his command, or his representative, at a place removed from the interrogation site. United States v Gunnels, supra, at page 134. Instead of a "once-stated warning" by the interrogator, the individual discusses his right to remain silent with an impartial legal authority. And the legal officer is duty bound to advise the individual fully as to his right to remain silent and the means available to him to exercise the right. Gunnels, at page 138. Taking into account the individual's education, intelligence, and ability to understand English, the staff legal officer must be certain the individual understands that the law gives him the absolute right to face his interrogators and tell them, bluntly and immediately, that he does not want to talk. See United States v Hernandez, 4 USCMA 465, 16 CMR 39.

I fully appreciate that, in advising the accused in an interrogative situation, the staff legal officer does not act as a lawyer for the accused in the sense of the conventional attorney-client relationship. I do not, however, regard the absence of the conventional relationship as a defect in the military procedure. As I view the interrogation situation, the only advice any lawyer can give the individual is that if he keeps silent he will give the police nothing they can use against him, but if he talks whatever he says can be used against him. That is precisely the counsel the staff legal officer gives him. And, it seems to me, the impact of his advice upon the individual is greater than the probable impact of similar advice by a lawyer appointed through the efforts of the individual's interrogators.

The staff legal officer is the legal authority of the command, and his advice as to the dictates of the law is rarely disregarded by military persons within his jurisdiction. Consequently, if we consider operative psychological influences, as Miranda indicates we may, the legal officer's advice on the right to remain silent is likely to make a deeper and more lasting impact upon the individual than the advice given him at the station house by a lawyer secured by his interrogators. I am, therefore, convinced that according the individual faced with in-custody interrogation the right to consult the staff legal officer, or a legal member of his office, is fully as effective a safeguard of the right to remain silent, as informing the individual that if he "cannot afford an attorney one will be appointed for him . . . if he so desires." That opportunity was extended to, and accepted by, the accused. . . .

. . .

On the evidence in this record, I cannot avoid the conclusion that when the accused returned to the Office of Special Investigations he knew and fully understood his right to remain silent. He returned to the office determined to speak. He had been caught practically "redhanded" and there was no way out; but he could perhaps gain a measure of leniency by immediate cooperation with the police. Miranda does not proscribe a confession in such circumstances. On the contrary, it explicitly acknowledges "[t]here is no requirement that police stop a person who enters a police station and states that he wishes to confess a crime." Id., at page 478.

I would answer the certified question in the affirmative, and I would sustain the decision of the board of review.

One of the most difficult issues for any Appellate Court to handle is an allegation of inadequacy of counsel. In military practice, an accused rarely has the same defense counsel at trial and before the Appellate Court. For cases discussing the question of adequacy of representation by counsel, see U.S. v. Parker, 6 USCMA 75, 19 CMR 201 (1955); U.S. v. McMahan, 6 USCMA 709, 21 CMR 31 (1956); and U.S. v. Winchester, 12 USCMA 74, 30 CMR 74 (1961). For an historical analysis of the right to counsel in courts-martial, see "Military Justice and the Right to Counsel," by S. Sidney Ulmer (1970).

The Court of Military Appeals has directed that an accused must be personally questioned at the trial as to his understanding of his rights to counsel as set forth in Article 38(b), UCMJ (U.S. v. Donohew, 18 USCMA 149, 39 CMR 149 [1969]).

APPREHENSION AND RESTRAINT

Paragraphs 18 through 23, MCM, set forth the definitions, procedures, and authority for apprehension and restraint. Any physical restraint of a person is confinement. Moral restraint may be effected by a proper order directing an individual to remain within certain specified limits; such restraint is termed either arrest or restriction, the latter being distinguished from the former only if the person may be required to perform normal military duties. No restraint may be imposed as punishment, and confinement before trial may only be ordered when necessary to ensure the presence of the accused at trial or because of the seriousness of the offense charged. In U.S. v. Bayhand, 6 USCMA 762, 21 CMR 84 (1956), the Court of Military Appeals reversed a conviction of an accused, who was in pretrial confinement, for disobedience of an order to perform work with sentenced prisoners. In the course of his opinion, Judge LATIMER stated:

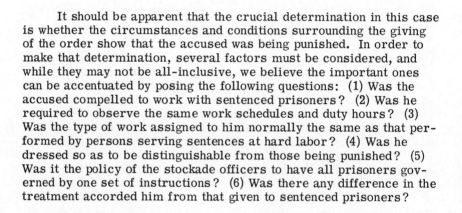

It should be apparent that the crucial determination in this case is whether the circumstances and conditions surrounding the giving of the order show that the accused was being punished. In order to make that determination, several factors must be considered, and while they may not be all-inclusive, we believe the important ones can be accentuated by posing the following questions: (1) Was the accused compelled to work with sentenced prisoners? (2) Was he required to observe the same work schedules and duty hours? (3) Was the type of work assigned to him normally the same as that performed by persons serving sentences at hard labor? (4) Was he dressed so as to be distinguishable from those being punished? (5) Was it the policy of the stockade officers to have all prisoners governed by one set of instructions? (6) Was there any difference in the treatment accorded him from that given to sentenced prisoners?

NONJUDICIAL PUNISHMENT

As noted above, a commander may choose to punish an accused for the commission of an offense under the Code by using his authority under the provisions of Article 15. With one minor exception, the accused may refuse such punishment and demand trial by court-martial. One advantage to an accused who accepts nonjudicial punishment is that he does not acquire a federal conviction as he would if found guilty by court-martial; in addition, the punishment that may be adjudged by a court-martial is usually more severe than may be awarded by a commander under Article 15. The specific punishments that may be awarded are listed in the Article itself.

Extract from
Manual for Courts-Martial, United States, 1969
(Revised edition).

128. AUTHORITY. a. <u>Who may impose nonjudicial punishment.</u> Unless otherwise provided by this chapter or regulations of the Secretary concerned, a commanding officer may, under Article 15, impose disciplinary punishments for minor offenses, without the intervention of a court-martial, upon commissioned officers, warrant officers, and other military personnel of his command. As used in this chapter, the term "commanding officer" or "commander" includes a warrant officer exercising command.

. . .

b. <u>Minor offenses</u>. The term "offenses," as used in connection with the authority to impose disciplinary punishment under Article 15 for minor offenses, includes only those acts or omissions constituting offenses under the punitive articles of the Uniform Code of Military Justice. The nature of an offense, and the circumstances surrounding its commission, are among the factors which must be considered in determining whether or not it is minor in nature. Generally, the term "minor" includes misconduct not involving any greater degree of criminality than is involved in the average offense tried by summary court-martial. This term ordinarily does not include misconduct of a kind which, if tried by general court-martial, could be punished by dishonorable discharge or confinement for more than one year. The imposition and enforcement of disciplinary punishment under this article for an act or omission is not a bar to trial by court-martial for a serious crime or offense which grew out of the same act or omission and which is not properly punishable under this article. See 68g and Article 15(f). However, the accused may show at the trial that he has been punished under Article 15 and, if he does, this fact must be considered in determining the measure of punishment to be adjudged if a finding of guilty results.

c. <u>Nonpunitive measures</u>. Article 15 and this chapter do not apply to, include, or limit the use of those nonpunitive measures that a commanding officer or an officer in charge is authorized and expected to use to further the efficiency of his command or unit, such as administrative admonitions, reprimands, exhortations, disapprovals, criticisms, censures, reproofs, and rebukes, written or oral, not imposed as punishment for a military offense. These nonpunitive measures may also include, subject to any applicable regulations, administrative withholding of privileges.

d. Double punishment and increase in punishment prohibited.
When punishment has been imposed upon a person under Article 15 for
an offense, punishment may not again be imposed upon him for the
same offense under Article 15 either by the commanding officer who
imposed the punishment or by any other commanding officer. But see
128b.

Once punishment has been imposed it may not be increased,
upon appeal or otherwise.

### UNITED STATES v. FRETWELL

United States Court of Military Appeals, 1960.
11 U.S.C.M.A. 377, 29 C.M.R. 193.

GEORGE W. LATIMER, Judge:

Upon his plea of guilty, a general court-martial convicted accused of violations of Articles 112 and 133, Uniform Code of Military
Justice, 10 USC §§912 and 933, respectively. The convening authority
approved, except that he reduced the adjudged punishment to forfeiture
of $100.00 per month for five months and a reprimand, and the record
was then referred to a board of review pursuant to Article 69 of the
Code, 10 USC §869. The board affirmed, and thereafter The Judge
Advocate General of the Navy certified the case to this Court under the
provisions of Article 67 (b) (2), Uniform Code of Military Justice, 10
USC §867, requesting our action on the following issue:

> "Was trial of the accused barred by punishment im-
> posed by his commanding officer under Article 15 ?"

The charges for which accused was tried grow out of events
that occurred January 16, 1959. On that date accused was assigned
as officer-of-the-deck for the midwatch aboard the aircraft carrier
U.S.S. HANCOCK. He judicially confessed and there is no dispute that
after having assumed and while on such duty he was found drunk in
uniform, lying unconscious in a passageway of the ship. However, before accused entered his plea admitting his guilt, the defense moved
to dismiss the charges on the ground of former punishment. It was
stipulated that on January 23, 1959, the commanding officer of the
U.S.S. HANCOCK imposed nonjudicial punishment upon accused under
Article 15, Uniform Code of Military Justice, 10 USC §815, for the
same acts of misconduct that were the basis of the charges being
tried, whereby he restricted accused to his stateroom for ten days
and recommended that the Commander, Fleet Air Alameda, issue accused a letter of reprimand. Accused served the imposed restriction,
but the Commander, Fleet Air Alameda, when the matter was referred
to him for the recommended letter of reprimand, stated his belief that
the nature of the alleged violations by accused more appropriately

warranted trial by court-martial, for he considered the actions did not constitute minor offenses. Subsequently, charges were preferred against accused and forwarded, together with the recommendations of the commanding officer, U.S.S. HANCOCK, and the Commander, Fleet Air Alameda, to the Commandant of the Twelfth Naval District, who acted as convening authority and referred them for trial to the instant general court-martial. After the Government and the defense had presented their respective arguments, the law officer denied the motion to dismiss.

At the outset, we deem it worthwhile to point out that we are not here concerned with a situation where true former jeopardy is asserted as the basis for relief. A plea in bar so predicated is available in the civilian and the military communities alike, for that fundamental protection to an accused is spelled out in the Fifth Amendment to the United States Constitution and Article 44, Uniform Code of Military Justice, 10 USC §844. It is to be borne in mind, however, that the right thereby extended to an accused concerns itself solely with prior judicial proceedings, as is clear from the terms of the last-mentioned Article. And there can be no doubt that the prior punishment visited upon accused in the case at bar is not of that nature. True it is that he was previously punished, but not judicially. To the contrary, the commanding officer of his ship undertook to discipline him under Article 15 of the Code, supra. Congress, in its wisdom recognizing the inherent necessity of administrative sanctions in the military, enacted that statute in order to permit summary disciplinary action by a commander for minor offenses committed by members of his command. The Congressional intent involved is obvious from even a casual perusal of the legislative history, the wording of the Article, and its entitlement: "Commanding officer's non-judicial punishment."

It is clear, then, that the prior punishment in the case at bar does not bring Article 44, Uniform Code of Military Justice, supra, into play. That is not to say, however, that our problem does not sound in jeopardy. Indeed, quite the contrary is true, as may be gleaned from our language in United States v Vaughan, 3 USCMA 121, 11 CMR 121. There, in discussing a somewhat similar situation involving disciplinary punishment, this Court alluded to the "double jeopardy provisions express and implied" in Article 15(e) of the Code, supra, and paragraphs 68g and 128b, Manual for Courts-Martial, United States, 1951. Perhaps it would be more technically correct to denote the basis for such a plea in bar as "former punishment"--to use the language of the Manual--instead of "double jeopardy." But regardless of the label we place upon it, there can be no question, and the parties are agreed, that the three last cited sections of the Code and the Manual govern the certified issue.

. . .

Our problem, then, narrows to whether the delicts charged against the accused were minor offenses, and paragraph 128b of the Manual, supra, affords us some assistance in that regard. . . .

Applying the above principles to the facts of the instant case, we are constrained to the conclusion that accused's acts of misconduct were not merely minor offenses. . . . Drunk and disorderly conduct, whether by an officer or by enlisted personnel, is a much more serious offense if committed aboard ship than otherwise and will permit imposition of six months' confinement and punitive separation from the service. And drunkenness on duty is one step further up the ladder of aggravated offenses, for it may be punished by punitive discharge and nine months' incarceration. . . . Without doubt accused's actions here constitute an even more flagrant breach of the law. Not only was he both drunk aboard ship and while on duty but, as the board of review pointed out, his duty was as officer-of-the-deck and, as such, he was the direct representative of the commanding officer of the ship, which position carries great responsibility. Thus, even apart from the punishment that could be permissibly adjudged, there can be no doubt that the accused's misconduct in so incapacitating himself and thus endangering the ship and its crew was attended with grave consequences and shows a "greater degree of criminality than is involved in the average offense tried by summary court-martial." It would be downgrading and belittling to the responsibility placed upon an officer-of-the-deck--whether on a ship at sea or, as here, in drydock--to conclude otherwise.

Accordingly, we hold that the law officer properly overruled the defense motion to dismiss, and the certified question is, therefore, answered in the negative. The decision of the board of review is affirmed.

Chief Judge QUINN concurs.

FERGUSON, Judge (dissenting):
I dissent.
. . .
. . . In short, a commanding officer has no authority to impose punishment under the Article for other than a minor offense. The difficulty lies in the fact that Congress nowhere included in the Code the characteristics which distinguish "serious" offenses and "minor" infractions.

It is in the resolution of this last problem that I differ fundamentally with my brothers. As evidenced by the principal opinion, they look to accused's delict and all the surrounding circumstances in determining whether a serious offense has been committed. I submit that this approach is demonstrably illogical, and I suggest that the proper method by which to classify a crime as "serious" or "minor" involves no more than an examination of the statute creating the offense and the punishment authorized for it by the President under the authority delegated to him by Congress in Code, supra, Article 56, 10 USC §856.

It is true, as Judge Latimer points out, that consideration of the particular circumstances surrounding an offense is supported by the discussion contained in paragraph 128b, Manual for Courts-Martial, United States, 1951. The Manual provision, however, does not purport to set forth a rule of procedure or evidence, published in accordance with the terms of Code, supra, Article 36, 10 USC §836. Hence, its relation of a "yardstick" for measuring the gravity of criminal misconduct is not binding on the Court, and I do not find its authoritative pronouncement persuasive.

. . .

In short, the rule set forth in the Manual, supra, and adopted in the principal opinion, allows a completely ad hoc determination to be made concerning whether, under the particular circumstances, an individual's crime is serious or petty. This is personal justice with a vengeance and effectively substitutes for the judgment of Congress and the President our individual reaction as Judges to the facts of each case. To such a proposition I cannot subscribe, and I prefer to measure the degree of accused's misconduct in light of whether Congress sought to make conduct felonious in enacting the statute involved or whether it attained that status from the punishment prescribed by the President.

. . .

The practical and legal conclusion which I believe should be drawn from the foregoing considerations is that we must hold that drunkenness on duty in time of peace is, as a matter of law, a "minor offense." While the statute is of little use to us in determining the degree of turpitude involved, the punishment prescribed for its violation establishes that it was to be treated as a misdemeanor. Neither a dishonorable discharge nor confinement in excess of one year is authorized for the delict. United States v Moore, supra. To the contrary, the only punitive separation involved is bad-conduct discharge which, as noted above, is imposed only for "bad conduct" and was not designed for the punishment of serious offenses. Manual, supra, paragraph 76a. In short, drunkenness on duty was considered by those charged with fixing punishments under Code, supra, Article 56, as a minor offense, and we should not now substitute our judgment for theirs.

I would answer the certified question in the affirmative, reverse the decision of the board of review, and order the charges dismissed.

---

The revision of the MCM in 1969 included a provision that permits a Secretary concerned to authorize consideration of personnel records of an accused during the sentencing part of a court-martial (para. 75d, MCM). Under this provision, records of the award of nonjudicial punishment may be admitted by the military judge subject to appropriate objections. The Court of Military Appeals has approved this provision on the grounds that it has an analogue under Rule 32 of the Federal Rules of Criminal Procedure and it does not empower a court-martial to adjudge additional punishments that are permitted in the case of prior <u>convictions</u> (U.S. v. Johnson, 19 USCMA 464, 42 CMR 66 [ 1970] ).

## ADDITIONAL PRE-TRIAL MATTERS

Appendix 6, MCM, contains forms to be used in the drafting of charges and specifications. A perusal of this appendix will give the reader an excellent view of the range of offenses proscribed by the UCMJ. Appendixes 5 and 7, MCM, are illustrations of a charge sheet and report of investigation conducted under the provisions of Article 32, UCMJ.

The Court of Military Appeals has established the following test to determine the sufficiency of a specification to allege an offense (U.S. v. Sell, 3 USCMA 202, 11 CMR 202 [1953 ]):

". . . The true test of the sufficiency of an indictment is not whether it could have been made more definite and certain, but whether it contains the elements of the offense intended to be charged, and sufficiently apprises the defendant of what he must be prepared to meet; and, in case any other proceedings are taken against him for a similar offense, whether the record shows with accuracy to what extent he may plead a former acquittal or conviction. Furthermore, when the pleadings have not been attacked prior to findings and sentence, it is enough to withstand a broadside charge that they do not state an offense, if the necessary facts appear in any form or by fair construction can be found within the terms of the specification." [Emphasis supplied.]

In addition to the foregoing test, a specification must be closely examined to ascertain whether it may be sufficient under the aider and abettor theory or under the theory of the military superior-subordinate relationship (see Article 77, UCMJ; U.S. v. Petree, 8 USCMA 9, 23 CMR 233 [1957]).

The MCM suggests that all charges against an accused should be consolidated and tried at a single trial (para. 30g, MCM). This provision is a precedural matter and is not reviewable in a habeas corpus proceeding in the civil Courts (Wigand v. Taylor, 285 F.2d 594 [CA, Tenth, 1960]).

## UNITED STATES v. GREEN

United States Court of Military Appeals, 1957.
7 U.S.C.M.A. 539, 23 C.M.R. 3.

GEORGE W. LATIMER, Judge:
The accused was convicted by general court-martial of two violations of a general regulation, in that he operated an unregistered motor vehicle and displayed invalid license plates thereon, both in violation of Article 92, Uniform Code of Military Justice, 10 USC §892. In addition, he was found guilty of receiving stolen property in violation of Article 134, Uniform Code of Military Justice, 10 USC §934. He was sentenced to a bad-conduct discharge, total forfeitures, and confinement at hard labor for nine months. The convening authority disapproved the offense relating to the receipt of stolen property but otherwise approved. The board of review affirmed, and we granted review to determine the admissibility of the accused's pre-trial statement.

During the time period encompassing these offenses, a general regulation published by Headquarters, United States Army, Europe, together with its annexes, provided that every owner of a motor vehicle must register his vehicle before operating it and that he must have affixed thereto valid license plates. On July 2, 1955, the accused registered an automobile with the United States Army Motor Vehicle Registration Office in Germany. After he produced a title certificate and insurance papers for the vehicle, license plates were issued to him. Four days later, these license plates and the registration certificate were cancelled, and the automobile was never thereafter re-registered with the official registrar.

Sometime during the period July 30, 1955, to August 13, 1955, a set of license plates bearing the number 5C-56962 were stolen from the automobile of Sergeant First Class Joseph Yemma. On November

12, 1955, the accused was transferred to a new unit and filled out an organizational form which was not transmitted to higher headquarters. In that document he listed his license number as being that of the plates which had been cancelled in July. However, he did not reveal the fact of cancellation.

On November 17, 1955, Mr. Richard Fuchs, a German national, was driving his automobile in the vicinity of Reichenbach, Germany, when he was forced to stop suddenly to avoid an on-coming truck. Suddenly, Mr. Fuchs' automobile was struck from behind by a car driven by the accused and bearing the license plates removed from the car of Sergeant Yemma. Two days thereafter, at about 7:00 p.m., Private Frederick Kellum, a military policeman who was off duty at the time, happened to see a vehicle bearing license plates numbered 5C-56962 as it was being parked by the accused near a cafe in Baumholder, Germany. He recalled a report to be on the lookout for these license plates and accordingly caused Lieutenant Edward R. Fye, the military police duty officer, to be notified. Lieutenant Fye picked up Private Kellum, proceeded to the cafe, entered, and questioned the accused to the extent shown in the out-of-court conference which will be subsequently discussed. Thereafter, Lieutenant Fye took the accused to the military police station and informed him of his rights under Article 31 of the Code, 10 USC §831. At that time, the accused admitted in substance that he was the owner of the vehicle upon which was displayed the stolen license plates but denied that he had known that they were stolen. His first assertion was to the effect that he had received the license plates from a sergeant friend but thereafter modified his story by stating that he had received the plates from a captain in the military police. At this time, the accused also handed over a certificate of title to the automobile.

In an out-of-court hearing, it was shown that the time when Lieutenant Fye approached the accused in the cafe, he merely asked the accused if he was the owner of the automobile in question and that an affirmative answer was given. The law officer ruled that this admission was inadmissible because the officer had not first advised the accused of his rights under Article 31 of the Code. Thereafter, defense counsel objected to the admission into evidence of the accused's later statement on the theory that the prior inadmissible admission had induced the subsequent statement. The objection was over-ruled by the law officer, and this is the ruling which accused contends was erroneous and prejudicial.

It is first of all worth repeating that the general regulation upon which this prosecution was bottomed required the registration of motor vehicles by those persons who owned such vehicles and that the accused's admission concerning ownership of the automobile regarded--within the meaning of Article 31(b)--the offenses alleged against the accused. United States v Taylor, 5 USCMA 178, 17 CMR 178. Furthermore, Lieutenant Fye occupied an official position in connection with law enforcement, the inquiry was made pursuant to an official investigation, and the facts were far enough developed so as to give Lieutenant Fye good cause to believe that the accused was the owner of the vehicle, for he had been seen operating it by Private Kellum. Accordingly, we have little hesitancy in concluding that the law officer had a reasonable basis for his ruling that the accused's initial admission of ownership, which was made before a warning was given, was inadmissible. Moreover, the ruling was beneficial to the accused and, for obvious reasons, he now relies upon the ruling as a supporting arch for his claim of error. Thus our present issue is whether, as a matter of law, the first admission rendered inadmissible the subsequent statement, which was made after warning, was in every other way voluntary and was used by the Government. United States v Dandaneau, 5 USCMA 462, 18 CMR 86.

We think the law officer had a solid ground for his ruling that the first admission of ownership did not induce the accused's later statement to the same effect. The accused was fully advised as to the meaning of Article 31 before his interrogation at the military police station, and stated that he understood its terms. It is a fair inference, then, that he was aware of his right to remain silent. He had been a master sergeant as late as July 1955, and it is unlikely that he was coerced or frightened by the rank of his interrogator, for surely he was not a newcomer to the Service. He had previously registered this vehicle with the appropriate authorities and certainly knew that they would have a record of his ownership, even though the registration had been cancelled. All that the investigating officer needed to do to ascertain the true ownership was to communicate with the appropriate registration official. Just one week prior to his questioning, the accused had listed his automobile with his unit, had admitted ownership at that time, and must have known that that record was available. When the last interrogation began, Lieutenant Fye asked him for the certificate of title to the vehicle. The accused replied that this document was at his home. When the Lieutenant observed that the best way to settle this matter would be to go to his home and obtain the title, the accused replied that such a trip would not be necessary, meanwhile removing the certificate of title from his pocket and handing it to the officer. All of this time, of course, the accused knew that he was in possession of the evidence of title and that a search would reveal it.

When these factors are marshaled, they lead to the conclusion, within the operation of a fair mind, that the accused admitted ownership of the automobile, not because he had orally disclosed the information to the Lieutenant earlier, but, because he knew he could not successfully deny it and silence would avail him nothing. Information as to his ownership was available from too many convenient sources to permit him to be coercively influenced by his earlier answer to one question. Any carry-over from the first admission to the final confession, if present, is not measurable. It necessarily follows that the law officer's ruling is supported by the evidence and cannot be overturned here. United States v Bennett, 7 USCMA 97, 21 CMR 223.

The decision of the board of review is affirmed.

Chief Judge QUINN concurs.

FERGUSON, Judge (concurring in part):

I concur.

I agree with the principal opinion that the law officer was correct in his ruling that the statement made by the accused after he had been advised of his rights under Article 31, Uniform Code of Military Justice, 10 USC §831, was not induced by an earlier inadmissible statement and was therefore admissible. Under the circumstances of this case I cannot say that the law officer erred as a matter of law in his holding that the subsequent statement was not involuntary.

However, in the result reached by a majority of the Court in United States v Dutcher, 7 USCMA 439, 22 CMR 229, it was noted that if a ruling by the law officer can properly be sustained on one ground, it is unnecessary to consider whether it satisfies other grounds. For that reason I believe it unnecessary to go into the question of whether the law officer was correct in ruling that the first statement was inadmissible because it was obtained in violation of Article 31(b). In particular, I wish to disassociate myself from the proposition set forth in United States v Gibson, 3 USCMA 746, 14 CMR 164, and United States v Dandaneau, 5 USCMA 462, 18 CMR 86, and endorsed above, that a prerequisite to the application of the provisions of Article 31, supra, is "officiality" of investigation or of the questioner. All persons subject to the Code must fulfill the prerequisites of Article 31 before they may interrogate or request any statement from an accused or person suspected of an offense. The fact that a person compelling another person to incriminate himself or answer a question, the answer to which might incriminate him, is not acting in an official capacity does not mean that Article 31(a) has not been violated. Any person subject to the Code is, in my opinion, required to fulfill the provisions of Article 31(b) before asking any questions, of a person accused or suspected of an offense, pertaining to the suspected offense.

However, in this case the challenged ruling was that a subsequent statement was not "tainted"; i.e., that the circumstances of the first statement did not render the questioned statement involuntary and hence inadmissible. We agree that it was not.

See U.S. v. Tempia, supra, at p. 340. See also, U.S. v. Johnson, 20 USCMA 320, 43 CMR 160 (1971), which concerns an alleged failure of an investigator to advise an accused fully of the particular offense of which he was suspected. Compare U.S. v. Reynolds, 16 USCMA 403, 37 CMR 23 (1966), and U.S. v. Davis, 8 USCMA 196, 24 CMR 6 (1957).

## UNITED STATES v. MICKEL

United States Court of Military Appeals, 1958.
9 U.S.C.M.A. 324, 26 C.M.R. 104.

ROBERT E. QUINN, Chief Judge:
The Judge Advocate General of the Air Force has certified the case to this Court for review of the following question:

"Was the Board of Review correct in holding that the failure to provide accused with counsel qualified within the meaning of Article 27(b) at the Article 32 investigation constituted reversible error in the absence of specific prejudice and timely objection?"

An accused is entitled to qualified counsel during the Article 32 investigation. United States v Tomaszewski, 8 USCMA 266, 24 CMR 76. The investigation here was held in May 1957. The report of the investigating officer shows that the accused had requested either of two officers as his counsel, but neither was reasonably available. Accordingly, First Lieutenant R. L. Ostertag was assigned as counsel. Lieutenant Ostertag was not then a member of the bar. The board of review noted he was not certified by The Air Force Judge Advocate General under the provisions of Article 27(b), Uniform Code of Military Justice, 10 USC §827, until August 16, 1957. It further noted that at the trial there was no objection to the lieutenant's qualification to represent the accused. The board of review also recognized that, under ordinary circumstances, the failure to make timely objection to a defect in the pretrial investigation is a waiver of the defect. See United States v McCormick, 3 USCMA 361, 12 CMR 117. However, it concluded that the accused did not waive Lieutenant Ostertag's disqualification because he "could not, at that time, have fully understood a right concerning which authorities on military jurisprudence disagreed."

We agree with the board of review that the pretrial investigation is an integral part of the general court-martial proceedings, and the right to counsel is a fundamental right therein. However, there is a substantial difference between a defect in the preliminary proceedings and a defect in the trial proceedings. A defect in the preliminary proceeding will not justify setting aside a conviction unless it clearly appears that the error prejudiced the accused in some material respect at the trial. In the Federal criminal practice a person under arrest is entitled to be brought before the nearest available commissioner, or other officer empowered to commit, who must inform him of his right to counsel, of his right to a preliminary examination, and that he is not required to make a statement. Rule 5, Federal Rules of Criminal Procedure. But deprivation of these preliminary rights does not, standing alone, constitute a denial of due process to the extent that the conviction must be set aside. Blood v Hunter, 150 F2d 640 (CA 10th Cir) (1945); Barber v United States, 142 F2d 805 (CA 4th Cir) (1944).

In the Federal criminal practice and in military law, an accused must object to defects in the preliminary proceedings before he goes to trial on the merits. If he fails to make timely objection, the defect is waived unless the court grants relief for good cause. Rule 12, Federal Rules of Criminal Procedure; Manual for Courts-Martial, United States, 1951, paragraph 67b; United States v McCormick, supra. Of course, if the accused does not know his rights, an appellate court will not "presume acquiescence" in their loss. Wood v United States, 128 F2d 265 (CA DC Cir) (1942). Nor will an appellate court apply the rule of waiver if it results in a miscarriage of justice. United States v Smith, 2 USCMA 121, 6 CMR 121. These are different ways of expressing the fundamental rule that an accused is entitled to a fair and impartial trial in accordance with the requirements of the law.

Among the fundamentals of a fair trial is the right of an accused to the assistance of counsel and the right to an adequate opportunity to prepare his defense. No question was raised by the accused before the board of review regarding the qualification or the competency of trial defense counsel; nor did the board of review find disqualification or incompetency. Neither did the accused question the adequacy of the defense counsel's preparation for trial, or the sufficiency of time accorded him for such preparation; nor did the board of review find inadequacy of preparation or the need for additional time. Had evidence obtained during the pretrial investigation been admitted against the accused at the trial, the error in the preliminary proceedings would be carried over to the trial, and consideration of its effect would be required. United States v Gunnels, 8 USCMA 130, 23 CMR 354; United States v Tomaszewski, supra; Wood v United States, supra; see also, Dainard v Johnston, 149 F2d 749 (CA 9th Cir) (1945). However, here there was no assertion, much less a showing, that the failure to provide qualified counsel at the pretrial investigation in any way affected the accused's rights at the trial. On the contrary, the

record of trial affirmatively shows that <u>the defense used evidence ob-</u>
<u>tained at the pretrial investigation to impeach an important Govern-</u>
<u>ment witness.</u>  In the absence of any possibility of harm, what reason
justifies reversal of the accused's conviction?
. . .

The law demands that an accused, who is aware of error in preliminary procedures, make timely objection to preserve his rights.
From one who is not aware of the error until after trial, we can expect no less than a showing that the pretrial error prejudiced him at
the trial.  Here, the board of review concluded that the accused
"could not" have fully understood his rights to qualified counsel at the
pretrial investigation, but it did not inquire whether the failure to provide such counsel prejudiced him at the trial.  In the absence of such
prejudice, the pretrial error did not contaminate the proceedings in
which the accused's guilt was actually determined.  The board of review was wrong in holding that the accused was denied due process.
Accordingly, we answer the certified question in the negative.

The decision of the board of review is reversed.  The record of
trial is returned to The Judge Advocate General of the Air Force for
submission to the board of review for further proceedings consistent
with this opinion.

Judge FERGUSON concurs.

LATIMER, Judge (concurring in the result):
I concur in the result.

In United States v Tomaszewski, 8 USCMA 266, 24 CMR 76, a
majority of the Court reached the conclusion that an accused was entitled as a matter of right to have a certified lawyer appointed to
represent him at an Article 32 investigation, and that is now the law.
In the case at bar, the officer appointed was a graduate of an ac-
credited law school and shortly after the hearing was admitted to a
State bar and certified by The Judge Advocate General of the Air
Force as competent to try cases before general courts-martial.  While
there was a lack of certification at the time of the pretrial hearing,
there is no claim of specific prejudice, and the record shows the absence of harm to the accused.  Therefore, I join in reversing the decision of the board of review.

The Article 32 investigation, above, is often compared to the
grand jury in civilian practice.  Actually, a reading of the article will
indicate that it might more aptly be called a discovery proceeding for
the defense.

## UNITED STATES v. FOTI

United States Court of Military Appeals, 1961.
12 U.S.C.M.A. 303, 30 C.M.R. 303.

GEORGE W. LATIMER, Judge:
The instant case was forwarded to this Court for review under the provisions of Article 67(b)(2), Uniform Code of Military Justice, 10 USC §867, and involves an inquiry by The Judge Advocate General of the Army as to whether the board of review was correct in reassessing accused's sentence. The latter was tried by a general court-martial for larceny of $75.00, in violation of Article 121, Uniform Code of Military Justice, 10 USC §921. He pleaded not guilty to the alleged offense but guilty of the lesser crime of wrongful appropriation. After a trial on the merits, he was found guilty as charged, and the convening authority approved the adjudged sentence of dishonorable discharge, total forfeitures, and confinement at hard labor for two years. A board of review in the office of The Judge Advocate General of the Army determined the accused was prejudiced by inadequate pretrial advice to the convening authority and, to remove any possible harm, reassessed sentence upon the basis of the entire record. In its opinion, the board of review not only mentioned curing any semblance of prejudice but went further and stated it was considering such extenuating and mitigating factors as the accused's youth, his belated realization of the seriousness of the offense, his repentance, his prior good record, and his earnest desire and potentiality for future military service.

From the foregoing statement, it is apparent that the opinion of this Court in United States v Higbie, 12 USCMA 298, 30 CMR 298, decided this day, is dispositive of the certified question and requires affirmance of the board of review's decision. However, a few observations touching on the insufficiency of the pretrial advice are considered appropriate.

The staff judge advocate to the convening authority submitted his opinion on a form which included the minimal requirements set out in paragraph 35c of the Manual for Courts-Martial, United States, 1951. The Government seeks to sustain it as adequate or, in the alternative, to invoke the doctrine of waiver. In view of our disposition, we need not discuss either issue but, like the board of review, we conclude the advice fell far short of serving the ends of justice. The Manual, supra, requires that a case be referred to the lowest court which can adjudge an appropriate sentence for the crime committed. See paragraph 33h at page 42. In order to aid the convening authority in that determination, facts which have a substantial effect

on his decision ought to be called to his attention and thus save him
the duty of going through a record with a fine tooth comb. Although
in most instances furnishing the minimal information might be sufficient, for the record may not contain additional guides and, while in
usual cases forms might be a convenient means to inform the convening authority, they may be snares when extraordinary circumstances
are present.

Here the staff judge advocate had before him cogent facts which
might have aided the convening authority immeasurably in arriving at
a proper decision. These included testimony showing the offense was
not aggravated; the company commander's recommendation for trial
by special court-martial, his belief that the accused would become a
useful soldier, and his desire to have the accused retained in his command; a psychiatrist's evaluation that the accused appeared generally
motivated for further military service; the Article 32 investigating
officer's recommendation that the offense be reduced to wrongful
appropriation and tried by a special court-martial; and accused's explanation of his intent which impressed the pretrial investigating
officer, his confession to taking the money and its immediate return,
and his desire to rehabilitate himself and serve out his obligation.
While obviously the convening authority is not bound by any or all of
these facts, as he is authorized to use his own independent judgment
as to which type of court should try the accused, it ought to be obvious
that the better he is informed the more fairly and justly will he exercise his discretion.

In this connection, we do not intend to postulate rigid rules to
control pretrial legal officers on their advice, but we do suggest that
criminal charges should receive individualized treatment and when,
as here, there are factors which would have a substantial influence on
the decision of the convening authority, they should be furnished to him.
We, therefore, agree with the observations of the board of review that
the pretrial advice in this case is subject to criticism for being too
scanty.

The decision of the board of review is affirmed.

Chief Judge QUINN concurs.

FERGUSON, Judge (concurring in the result):

I concur in the result.

. . .

# 9

## COURTS-MARTIAL:
## TRIAL
## CONSIDERATIONS

Appendix 8 of the Manual for Courts-Martial contains detailed trial procedure guides. An Article 39(a) session, during which the military judge alone rules upon various motions and inquiries into any plea of guilty by an accused, usually precedes the trial proper. This pre-trial session was first authorized by the Military Justice Act of 1968; before that amendment the court-martial members had to be assembled and then excused for out-of-court hearings.

## PLEAS AND MOTIONS

The right of an accused before a court-martial to a public trial is discussed fully in U.S. v. Brown, 7 USCMA 251, 22 CMR 41 (1956). In that case, the Court reversed the conviction of an accused for obscene and threatening phone calls because the convening authority had ordered that the courtroom be closed to the public except that the accused could have anyone present that he wished. The Court found the order too broad and intimated that had the order not excluded the press, it may have been upheld.

UNITED STATES v. SCHALCK*

United States Court of Military Appeals, 1964.
14 U.S.C.M.A. 371, 34 C.M.R. 151.

*[Footnotes have been omitted. Ed.]

KILDAY, Judge:

Upon a plea of guilty to two specifications of being absent without leave and one specification of willful disobedience of a lawful order of a superior officer, the accused was sentenced to a bad-conduct discharge, total forfeitures, and confinement at hard labor for two years. The findings and sentence were approved by the convening authority.

Before the board of review, Schalck, for the first time, asserted he was denied his right to military due process, by reason of the fact that he was confined for a period of ninety-six days during which time no charges were preferred against him, allegedly in violation of his rights under Articles 10 and 33, Uniform Code of Military Justice, 10 USC §§810 and 833, respectively.

The board of review, finding that the accused was confined for the period alleged without charges and that the record was devoid of any data detailing the reasons why the pertinent Articles of the Code were not complied with, set aside the findings of guilty of all charges and specifications and ordered them dismissed.

The Judge Advocate General of the Army certified the following questions to this Court:

(1) Was the board of review correct in holding that the delay in preferring charges against the accused was not waived by his failure to raise the issue at trial and by his plea of guilty?

(2) Was the board of review correct in summarily dismissing the charges against the accused on the factor alone of delay in preferring charges when the Government, because the issue was not raised at the trial, was never accorded a hearing upon the question?

The facts to which the accused pleaded guilty are not in dispute for they were entered into the record by way of stipulation between counsel for the Government and the defense with the express consent of the accused. Rather it is the lapse of time (ninety-six days) between his confinement on June 19, 1962, and his release on September 23, 1962, without charges being filed, that formed the basis for accused's allegation of denial of due process.

The Government does not dispute the confinement issue, but contends that the accused waived his right to such an assertion by his

failure to make a timely objection prior to or at time of trial and by
his plea of guilty. In the alternative, the Government argues that it
should be afforded an opportunity to explain the delay and to have the
issue decided at the trial level.

Appellate defense counsel assert that the doctrine of waiver
does not apply, despite a plea of guilty, where the defect involves, as
in this case, a denial of due process of law; and that the Government
has itself waived its opportunity to explain the delay by its failure to
do so during the post-trial review and before the board of review.

The record of trial reflects that the accused was in fact confined, as alleged, in the post stockade, Fort Jay, New York, from June
19, 1962, to September 23, 1962, and that charges were not preferred
against him until October 5, 1962. Defense counsel referred generally
to this situation in his argument on sentence and the law officer informed the court-martial members that in determining the sentence
to be adjudged, they could take into consideration, "the nature and
duration of the pretrial restraint." However, neither of these individuals detailed or discussed further this situation and the Government, at trial, was silent in regard thereto.

Review of the allied papers in this case reveals that subsequent
to the decision of the board of review, the office of The Judge Advocate
General of the Army obtained from trial counsel a chronology of events,
dated July 12, 1963, covering the pertinent period of accused's confinement. Although these data are revealing of the events occuring
during that period, the chronology was not utilized, except in a general
way, by the Government in its argument before this Court, and was
not, of course, considered by the board of review, having been prepared at a later date.

As asserted by the Government, the law of this Court and other
Federal courts clearly establishes that the right to a speedy trial is
personal and can be waived if not promptly asserted by a timely
demand. . . .

. . .

The issues of speedy trial and denial of due process are frequently inextricably bound together and the line of demarcation is not
always clear. Such, allegedly, is the situation in this case. According to accused, the Government's delay herein is coupled with a failure
to comply with Articles 10 and 33, Uniform Code of Military Justice,
10 USC §§810 and 833, respectively. Article 10 guarantees to an accused his constitutional right to a "speedy trial," while Article 33
establishes that charges are to be forwarded within eight days after
arrest or confinement, or a written explanation given for failure to do
so, if not practicable. These provisions are further strengthened by
Article 98 of the Uniform Code, 10 USC §898, which provides punishment for anyone responsible for an unnecessary delay. Failure to
comply with these provisions of the Code, accused urges, amounts to
more than mere failure to accord the accused a speedy trial but rather results in a denial of due process.

The Government's position is that the accused was immediately informed of the wrong for which he was confined at time of confinement and that this is borne out by the fact that accused signed a form, on the day of his apprehension, in which he acknowledged that sections (a) and (b) of Article 31, Uniform Code of Military Justice, 10 USC §831, had been read and explained to him, that he understood them and his rights thereunder and that he did not desire to make a statement. On the reverse side of this form is a certificate, signed by the accused, that Article 31 had been read and explained to him prior to "requesting my authority to be absent from my organization or to any questioning whatsoever.'" It is this certificate, plus a notation on the confinement order that accused stated he had been absent without leave since January 24, 1962, which forms the basis for the Government's position that accused was immediately informed of the reason for his confinement. Since he was immediately served with a copy of the formal charges, which were sworn to on October 5, 1962, the Government argues it has discharged its responsibility and that "accused was not deprived of the right granted by Congress to be informed of the wrong he committed or of the charges against him."

While the Government's position hardly seems tenable in view of the specific language of Articles 10 and 33, supra, and the sanctions imposed for violation thereof, we are not constrained to decide the issue at this level. There are numerous, unanswered factual questions here that should be resolved at a level where testimony can be taken, witnesses examined, and testimony offered in rebuttal. In this manner the rights and interests of the accused and the Government will be preserved. United States v Thomas, 13 USCMA 163, 32 CMR 163.

Accordingly, we hold, that in the posture of this record, the board of review was correct in holding that delay in preferring charges against the accused was not waived by his failure to raise the issue at trial and by his plea of guilty. We also hold that the board of review was not correct in summarily dismissing the charges against the accused on the factor alone of delay in preferring charges when the Government, because the issue was not raised at trial, was never accorded a hearing upon the question.

The first certified question is answered in the affirmative. The second certified question is answered in the negative. The decision of the board of review is reversed and the record is returned to The Judge Advocate General of the Army for further proceedings not inconsistent with this opinion.

Chief Judge QUINN and Judge FERGUSON concur.

In U.S. v. Williams, 16 USCMA 589, 37 CMR 209 (1967), the
Court of Military Appeals unanimously reversed the conviction and
dismissed the charges against an accused for the presentation of
false claims for pay because the accused was denied military due
process and his right to the speedy disposition of charges against
him. In that case, the accused was restricted to his company area
from April 14, 1963, to August 30, 1965, and charges were not preferred until November 9, 1965; the trial did not commence until
February 26, 1966. The government's explanation of the delay, based
upon alleged difficulties in completing the investigation, was deemed
unacceptable by the Court.

A motion to dismiss for lack of speedy trial does not deal with
the guilt or innocence of the accused; hence, a convening authority
may reverse the granting of such a motion by a military judge. See
Article 62(a), UCMJ; and U.S. v. Boehm, 17 USCMA 530, 38 CMR 328
(1968).

In U.S. v. Blackwell, 19 USCMA 196, 41 CMR 196 (1970), the
Court of Military Appeals considered the applicability of Articles 10
and 33 to an accused in confinement after his conviction had been
reversed and prior to a rehearing. Judge Ferguson found the Articles inapplicable to such a situation; Chief Judge Quinn disagreed and
Judge Darden did not state an opinion on this point. The case was reversed for reassessment of the sentence on the grounds that in any
event the accused should have been given credit for the time served,
i.e., that it was not pre-trial confinement.

## UNITED STATES v. CARE

United States Court of Military Appeals, 1969.
18 U.S.C.M.A. 535, 40 C.M.R. 247.

DARDEN, Judge:

The Court selected this case for a grant of review to consider
again the extent to which a law officer or a president of a special
court-martial must question an accused about the latter's actions and
his understanding of the law applicable to these actions before accepting a guilty plea.

Private Care pleaded guilty to desertion, in violation of Article
85, Uniform Code of Military Justice, 10 USC §885. Under the terms
of a pretrial agreement, the convening authority would approve no
sentence in excess of a bad-conduct discharge, total forfeitures, and
confinement at hard labor for two years, compared with the maximum sentence of a dishonorable discharge, total forfeitures, and

confinement at hard labor for three years. Because of the guilty plea no evidence was presented; an absence of almost fifteen months terminated by apprehension was alleged. After the findings of guilty and the sentence were approved by the board of review, this Court granted a petition for review on the issue of whether the plea of the accused was provident in view of the law officer's failure to delineate the essential elements of the offense and to determine the factual basis of the plea.

After our grant of review, the accused submitted an affidavit asserting that his counsel did not specifically explain the elements of the offense to him; that he had denied any intent to remain away permanently; that his counsel had told him a plea of not guilty would delay his trial for four months; that inevitably he would be convicted and receive the maximum sentence, but that a negotiated pretrial agreement could limit his confinement sentence to two years; that this advice resulted in his pleading guilty; and that if he were tried again he would plead not guilty.

In a reply affidavit, Care's trial defense counsel insists that although he does not recall the specific words used in the first of at least six conferences with the accused before trial, he is certain that he followed a written guide or checklist he had prepared earlier to assure that his clients were fully informed of their rights. The items on his checklist included the lawyer-client privilege; the elements of the offense; the proof needed to convict; the maximum punishment; the effect of pleas of guilty and not guilty; pretrial agreement; and related subjects. The counsel's affidavit also indicates that he informs each client of his absolute right to plead not guilty and that he should plead guilty only if he is, in fact, guilty and "did everything the Government is charging him with." The counsel denies that he told Care there was no possibility of an acquittal or that "a guilty plea would take four months longer than a not guilty." Near the end of the affidavit he affirms that Private Care informed him that Care was guilty of desertion and that he knew the elements of the offense before he signed the pretrial agreement.

. . .

In United States v Chancelor, 16 USCMA 297, 36 CMR 453, this Court exhaustively considered the legislative background of Article 45 relating to guilty pleas and pointed out the congressional intent that the acceptance of a guilty plea be accompanied by certain safeguards to insure the providence of the plea, including a delineation of the elements of the offense charged and an admission of factual guilt on the record. The Court strongly recommended that the armed forces require a form of inquiry that would satisfy this congressional intent.

. . .

Appendix A is a verbatim record of the examination of Care by the law officer. It will be seen that the law officer explained that he had to determine voluntariness and providency personally and asked the accused (1) if he knew his plea subjected him to a finding of guilty without further proof; (2) if he knew he could be sentenced to the maximum sentence; (3) if he understood the meaning and effect of his plea; (4) if he knew that the burden was on the Government to prove his guilt beyond a reasonable doubt; (5) if he knew he was entitled to plead not guilty; (6) if he knew the elements of the offense; (7) if he had adequate opportunity to consult with counsel on any matters he felt necessary; (8) if he was satisfied with his counsel; (9) whether counsel advised him of the maximum punishment; (10) if the decision to negotiate a plea originated with him; (11) if his plea was given voluntarily; (12) if anyone used force or coercion to get him to enter a guilty plea; (13) if he believed it was in his best interest to plead guilty; (14) if his plea was the product of free will and a desire to confess his guilt; and (15) if he knew he could withdraw his plea. In each instance, the answer was "yes."

The procedure that was followed here fell short of the one recommended in United States v Chancelor, supra, because the law officer did not personally inform the accused of the elements constituting the offense and he did not establish the factual components of the guilty plea. That the Chancelor recommendation was not an inflexible requirement is shown by this Court's having denied, after Chancelor and before Care, many petitions for review of cases involving guilty plea where delineation of the elements was lacking. Taken as a whole, the evidence in this record satisfies us the accused knew what he was pleading guilty to, what he must have done for his acts to constitute desertion, and that he did, in essence, know the elements of the offense just as his acknowledgment to the law officer indicates.

The specification itself, furthermore, sets forth in simple comprehensible terms all the elements of the relatively uncomplicated offense of desertion:

"In that Private David E. CARE, U.S. Marine Corps, Support Company, Headquarters Battalion, Headquarters Regiment, Marine Corps Base, Camp Pendleton, California did, on or about 18 May 1967, without proper authority and with intent to remain away therefrom permanently, absent himself from his unit, to wit: Headquarters & Service Company, 2d Battalion, 6th Marines, 2d Marine Division, Fleet Marine Force, Camp Lejeune, North Carolina, and did remain so absent in desertion until apprehended on or about 13 August 1968." [Emphasis supplied.]

This specification appears on the charge sheet, a copy of which was served on the accused. Moreover, a copy of the charge and specification was handed to the accused at the trial.

Beyond this, the elements of desertion are (1) unauthorized absence and (2) an intent to remain away permanently. Unauthorized absence is probably one of the simplest of all military offenses. It consists of being away from duty without permission. After arguing that members of the armed forces have common knowledge that they may not leave their duty without permission, the Government points out that Care "has a special claim to expertise, in that he is one of the Marine Corp's [sic] more experienced absentees. Two of Appellant's three prior convictions by courts-martial were for three separate unauthorized absences." With this history, we find it difficult to believe that Care did not know he needed permission to be away from his duty.

The second element of desertion is an intent to remain away permanently. Care was absent for about fourteen months. Extraordinary duration of absence, standing alone, will not establish the intent required for a finding of desertion. United States v Cothern, 8 USCMA 158, 23 CMR 382. But when an unauthorized absence of extended duration is combined with apprehension 3,000 miles from the last duty station, an inference of an intent to remain away permanently may be drawn. United States v Montoya, 15 USCMA 210, 35 CMR 182; United States v Bonds, 6 USCMA 231, 19 CMR 357.

The affidavit of the appellant concedes that his defense counsel asked him if he intended to remain away permanently. He states further that he did not intend to remain away permanently. But in the interrogation by the law officer he responded to a question that he knew the elements of the offense with which he was charged. At which point are we to believe him? United States v Boberg, 17 USCMA 401, 38 CMR 199. The affidavit of the trial counsel states his certainty that he explained the elements of the offense to the appellant. Hence, again this Court must determine controverted issues on the basis of the "blizzard of . . . affidavits" that the opinion in Chancelor decried.

We are satisfied that at the time of his guilty plea Private Care knew the acts and intent necessary to prove desertion and consequently that his plea was voluntary. We believe, however, that further action is required toward the objective of having court-martial records reflect fully an awareness by an accused pleading guilty of what he is admitting that he did and intended and of the law that applies to his acts and intentions.

The Court noted earlier in the opinion that its recommendation in Chancelor that the armed forces take remedial action to assure compliance with the requirement for inquiry into guilt-in-fact. This recommendation has received less than satisfactory implementation as is evidenced by review of many records of trial in which the law officer or the president fails to explain personally the elements of an offense and to establish factual guilt directly. Although the Manual for Courts-Martial, United States, 1969, which became effective January 1, 1969, adds the elements of the offense as one of the subjects that should be included in the explanation prescribed by paragraph 70b when a guilty plea is entered, we note also that the language applicable to the explanation by a law officer or a president of a court-martial of the meaning and effect of a guilty plea has been changed from "will explain" to "should explain." Perhaps this is only a stylistic change that is not intended to convert the explanation into a discretionary procedure. But we are concerned that the new Manual's Trial Procedure Guide (Appendix 8a), Manual for Courts-Martial, supra, still contains no suggestion for an explanation of the elements of offenses and no suggestions for questions eliciting the facts leading to a guilty plea.

In any event, the record of trial for those courts-martial convened more than thirty days after the date of this opinion must reflect not only that the elements of each offense charged have been explained to the accused but also that the military trial judge or the president has questioned the accused about what he did or did not do, and what he intended (where this is pertinent), to make clear the basis for a determination by the military trial judge or president whether the acts or the omissions of the accused constitute the offense or offenses to which he is pleading guilty. United States v Rinehart, 8 USCMA 402, 24 CMR 212; United States v Donohew, 18 USCMA 149, 39 CMR 149. This requirement will not be satisfied by questions such as whether the accused realizes that a guilty plea admits "every element charged and every act or omission alleged and authorizes conviction of the offense without further proof." A military trial judge or a president personally addressing the accused to explain the elements of the offense with which he is charged and to question him about his actions and omissions should feel no obligation to apologize or to disclaim any intent that his actions reflect on the competence of the accused's counsel. We believe the counsel, too, should explain the elements and determine that there is a factual basis for the plea but his having done so earlier will not relieve the military trial judge or the president of his responsibility to do so on the record.

Further, the record must also demonstrate the military trial judge or president personally addressed the accused, advised him that his plea waives his right against self-incrimination, his right to a trial of the facts by a court-martial, and his right to be confronted by the witnesses against him; and that he waives such rights by his plea. Boykin v Alabama, supra. Based upon the foregoing inquiries and such additional interrogation as he deems necessary, the military trial judge or president must make a finding that there is a knowing, intelligent, and conscious waiver in order to accept the plea.

The decision of the board of review is affirmed.

Chief Judge QUINN concurs.

FERGUSON, Judge (dissenting):
I dissent.
[Opinion omitted. Ed.]
. . .

## UNITED STATES v. RODGERS

United States Court of Military Appeals, 1957.
8 U.S.C.M.A. 226, 24 C.M.R. 36.

HOMER FERGUSON, Judge:
The single issue before us is whether the statute of limitations had run as to the specifications of Charge III. The accused was charged with, and pleaded guilty to, an unauthorized absence of five days' duration occurring in December 1952, a violation of Article 86, Uniform Code of Military Justice, 10 USC §886 (Charge I). He was also charged with, pleaded not guilty to, but convicted of, two specifications alleging desertion, in violation of Article 85, Uniform Code of Military Justice, 10 USC §885, from the periods of December 13, 1952, to January 23, 1953, and from January 26, 1953, to June 2, 1956, respectively (Charge II). Under Charge III, he was found guilty-- despite his plea to the contrary--of two specifications alleging the failure to obey a lawful order to report to his unit, in contravention of Article 92, Uniform Code of Military Justice, 10 USC §892. It is these two specifications upon which the issue granted was based. Specification 1 of Charge III alleged that the accused had failed to obey an order "on or about 13 December 1952" and specification 2 alleged another failure to obey "on or about 26 January 1953."

The charge sheet upon which the accused was tried was dated July 3, 1956, and prepared at Camp Pendleton, California, the place of trial. These charges were received by the officer exercising summary court-martial jurisdiction the same day, a date obviously more than two years after the commission of the offenses alleged in the specifications of Charge III. . . .

It is well established in military jurisprudence that whenever it appears the statute of limitations has run against an offense, the court "will bring the matter to the attention of the accused and advise him of his right to assert the statute unless it otherwise affirmatively appears that the accused is aware of his rights in the premises." Paragraph 68c, Manual for Courts-Martial, United States, 1951. This Manual provision is substantially repeated in paragraphs 53h and 74h, Manual for Courts-Martial, supra. Service boards of review have consistently applied this well-settled doctrine on numerous occasions and have held it to be reversible error for a law officer to fail to advise an apparently uninformed accused of his right to interpose the statute or to fail to determine if there has been a conscious waiver by him of his right to do so. United States v Snyder, 15 CMR 856; United States v Sparks, 15 CMR 584; United States v Rowland, 14 CMR 649; United States v Berry, 14 CMR 396. When we look to the record in the instant case, we find nothing which suggests that the accused was aware of his rights in the premises and his failure therefore cannot possibly operate as a waiver. Accordingly, we conclude that the law

officer erred in failing to advise this uninformed accused of his right
to plead the statute in bar of trial and punishment.

One further matter merits consideration. Found among the
allied papers in the record of trial--in addition to the charge sheet
dated July 3, 1956--is another charge sheet bearing the date of November 8, 1954, and prepared at Headquarters, U.S. Marine Corps, Washington, D.C. This earlier charge sheet lists substantially the same
offenses as those contained in the charge sheet of July 3, 1956, upon
which the accused was tried. The earlier charges were received by
an officer exercising summary court-martial jurisdiction on November 10, 1954, a date less than two years after the alleged commission
of the offenses found in specifications 1 and 2 of Charge III. We suppose that this earlier charge sheet was drafted and charges subsequently filed for the express purpose of tolling the statute of
limitations, as to the specifications of Charge III, against which only
a two-year statute of limitations applies.

The redrafted charges were then prepared for the purpose of
showing apprehension and termination of the absence alleged in specification 2 of Charge II. From these circumstances the Government
argues that the statute of limitations was tolled by the first charge
sheet, which became a part of the record and that it is "clearly inferable" that both charge sheets were exhibited to the accused by the
pretrial investigating officer. It is then contended that the accused,
by not questioning the validity of the first charge sheet, is precluded
from doing so now. This argument need not detain us for long, for
the obvious answer is that the record must affirmatively show that
the accused was made aware of his right to assert the statute or that
having been aware he consciously waived that right. Here the record
is silent as to any indication that the accused was aware of his rights.
The charge sheet of July 3, 1956, was the only one before the law officer and the court. Furthermore, we do not presume that the accused
waived a substantial right which the record fails to show he even
knew of.

. . .

It would have been perfectly proper to have brought the accused
to trial on the original charge sheet which was seasonably filed with
the officer exercising summary court-martial jurisdiction. All that
would have been necessary was an amendment to specification 2 of
Charge II fixing the termination date of the alleged desertion. The
practice of filing charges prior to the statute of limitations running
its course is commendable and is to be encouraged. Paragraph 33b,
Manual for Courts-Martial, supra. We inferentially approved this
practice in our early decision of United States v Nichols, 2 USCMA
27, 6 CMR 27. However, if such charges are later redrafted in a new
charge sheet--as distinguished from amended--the risk of running
the statute of limitations is present. Modern judicial theory looks
with favor upon statutes of limitations and they are liberally construed

on behalf of an accused in furtherance of their manifest objectives. We conclude, therefore, that the statute of limitations had run as to the specifications of Charge III and that the law officer erred in failing to advise the accused of his right to interpose that defense. In view of the fact that the Government has not been given the opportunity to show--if possible--whether the statute may have been tolled under the provisions of Article 43(d), Uniform Code of Military Justice, supra, we return the case to The Judge Advocate General of the Navy for reference to a board of review. In its discretion, the board may order a rehearing as to Charge III, or it may dismiss that charge and reassess the sentence on the basis of the remaining approved findings of guilt.

[Concurring opinion of Chief Judge Quinn omitted.]

LATIMER, Judge (dissenting):

I dissent.

The decision in this case is a classic example of elevating form over substance. The findings on two perfectly good specifications are set aside merely because the pleader, when faced with the necessity of amending another specification, elected to make the addition by preparing a new charge sheet instead of making interlineations on the first.

. . .

For cases concerning the effect of amendment of charges and the statute of limitations, see U.S. v. Busbin, 7 USCMA 661, 23 CMR 125 (1957); U.S. v. Shell, 7 USCMA 646, 23 CMR 110 (1957); and U.S. v. Arbic, 16 USCMA 292, 36 CMR 448 (1966).

Paragraph 56, MCM, purports to authorize a convening authority to "withdraw" specifications from consideration by a court-martial under certain circumstances; unless withdrawn prior to the actual commencement of trial, "good cause," such as urgent and unforeseen military necessity," must be shown. In some instances, withdrawal after trial has commenced may result in a complete trial in the sense of Article 44(c) and, hence, bar future prosecution. See U.S. v. Stringer, 5 USCMA 122, 17 CMR 122 (1954); Wade v. Hunter, 336 U.S. 684, 69 S.Ct. 834, 93 L.Ed. 974 (1949).

Withdrawal of charges because of the leniency of previous sentences adjudged by the court-martial in similar cases is prejudicial error (U.S. v. Williams, 11 USCMA 459, 29 CMR 275 [1960]). What constitutes "good cause" for the withdrawal of charges? See U.S. v. Fleming, 18 USCMA 254, 40 CMR 236 (1969).

## UNITED STATES v. WILLIAMS

United States Court of Military Appeals, 1959.
10 U.S.C.M.A. 615, 28 C.M.R. 181.

HOMER FERGUSON, Judge:
At his trial by special court-martial, the accused was found guilty of using disrespectful language to a noncommissioned officer, violation of a lawful general regulation by possessing alcoholic beverages, breach of restriction, being disorderly in station, and wrongfully and materially altering, with intent to defraud, a promotion roster, in violation, respectively, of Uniform Code of Military Justice, Articles 91, 92, and 134, 10 USC §§891, 892, and 934. Following disapproval of the charge of violating Article 92, Code, supra, and conduct of a rehearing on sentence, the convening authority approved a penalty of bad-conduct discharge (suspended), partial forfeiture of pay, and confinement at hard labor for six months. The board of review affirmed the findings and sentence, and we granted the accused's petition for review on the question whether the president of the court-martial erred in overruling a defense motion to dismiss Charge III and its specification, alleging that accused was disrespectful in language to a noncommissioned officer.
The specification of Charge III states that the accused:

". . . [A]t, Amarillo Air Base . . . on or about 17 October 1958, was disrespectful in language toward Staff Sergeant J. W. Connell, his superior Non-Commissioned Officer, who was then in the execution of his office, by saying to him, 'To hell with you Sergeant, I don't have to do anything', or words to that effect."

At the commencement of the trial, the defense counsel moved to dismiss Charge III and its specification on the ground that the accused had previously suffered punishment for this breach of discipline. In support of his motion, evidence was adduced which establishes that the accused, having been apprehended for other offenses, was delivered to the Amarillo Air Base guardhouse for incarceration pending disposition of charges. While being administratively processed by confinement personnel, he was disrespectful in the manner indicated to the noncommissioned officer in charge. On the following morning, pursuant to the provisions of Air Force Manual 125-2, September 2, 1956, entitled "Operation of Confinement Facilities," and the authorization of the commander who later convened the special court-martial, he was placed in "disciplinary segregation" on a reduced diet for an indefinite period not to exceed fourteen days. The imposition of this punitive measure was based solely on the incident forming the basis for the later charge of disrespect. The president of the court denied the defense motion.

The Government urges affirmance of the findings on the basis that accused's segregation was administrative rather than judicial in nature and that, in any event, his offense was a major violation of the Code, supra, thus rendering inapplicable the defense of former punishment. On the other hand, the accused argues that his offense was minor in nature and that, in effect, he suffered nonjudicial punishment for the breach of the Code involved. Hence, his later trial was barred. Manual for Courts-Martial, United States, 1951, paragraph 68g; Code, supra, Article 15(e), 10 USC §815. While neither argument is precisely dispositive of the granted issue, we conclude that, for the reasons hereinafter stated, the ultimate conclusion of appellate defense counsel has merit.

In enacting the Uniform Code of Military Justice, Congress recognized the necessity for maintaining discipline and order in military confinement facilities, and provided in Article 13, Code, supra, 10 USC §813, that an accused "while being held for trial or the result of trial, . . . may be subjected to minor punishment during that period for infractions of discipline." It is apparent that the provisions of Air Force Manual 125-2, supra, authorizing the imposition of disciplinary segregation on reduced rations, were promulgated on the basis of this statutory provision and to contend that their invocation did not constitute punishment is to disregard the obvious. Not only does the statute use that term, but the Air Force directive refers to the procedure as a "major disciplinary measure" to be imposed only as "a last resort" for the "control and correction" of the individual concerned. Finally, common sense dictates the conclusion that solitary segregation and deprivation of a normal diet are punitive measures. Thus, we reject any notion that these disciplinary measures, even though properly authorized and invoked, are not punitive in nature.

The argument that the accused's offense was not minor need not long detain us. The Table of Maximum Punishments, Manual, supra, paragraph 127c, authorizes the imposition for this misconduct of a penalty not to exceed confinement at hard labor for three months and forfeiture of two-thirds pay for a like period. In discussing the same concept with relation to the exercise of nonjudicial powers under Article 15, Code, supra, 10 USC §815, the Manual, supra, in paragraph 128b, points out that the term generally includes misconduct not involving moral turpitude or any greater degree of criminality than is involved in the average offense tried by summary court-martial. These considerations, as well as the attendant circumstances, persuade us that the accused's delict was not so serious as the Government contends and, thus, was properly punishable by disciplinary action under Article 13, Code, supra. Cf. United States v Vaughan, 3 USCMA 121, 11 CMR 121.

Thus, we are confronted with the basic question whether imposition of disciplinary punishment pursuant to Article 13, Code, supra, for a minor offense bars the accused's subsequent trial for the same misconduct.

In United States v Vaughan, supra, we faced a similar issue. There, however, the accused had been both previously punished and subsequently tried for escape from a United States Disciplinary Barracks. In rejecting the defense contention that the doctrine of former punishment was applicable, we acted on the basis that escape from a disciplinary barracks was a major offense. Nevertheless, we noted our reservations concerning the present problem:

> ". . . Some prisoner offenses are grave and 'merit' trial by court-martial despite prior disciplinary action. Others are venial--and as to them court action is barred by earlier administrative punishment. This answer is furnished alike by reason and regulations. While care should be exercised to appreciate fully the peculiar character of the prison commandant's task and responsibilities and the demanding nature of his problems, we would not hesitate in a proper case to hold trial by court-martial barred in a setting similar to the present one."

The Government seeks to distinguish Vaughan, supra, on the basis that it involved Army regulations authorizing the use of disciplinary measures and specifically providing that the punishment of the accused thereunder for a minor offense would bar his subsequent trial, whereas Air Force Manual 125-2, supra, contains no comparable limitation. See SR 210-185-1, May 31, 1951. Conceding the existence of that distinction, we do not believe it has the asserted effect. On the contrary, the Army regulations do no more than recognize the intent of Congress in enacting the authority for disciplinary punishment conferred in Article 13, Code, supra. Therein it sought to provide for the punishment of infractions "not warranting trial by court-martial." Hearings before House Armed Services Committee on H.R. 2498, 81st Congress, 1st Session, page 916. From that description of legislative purpose, we infer that Congress intended the exception stated in Article 13, Code, supra, to be utilized only when the infraction was not deemed worthy of reference to trial, and that the imposition of punishment thereunder would finally dispose of the matter. We conclude, therefore, that the silence of the Air Force Manual is immaterial, and we now hold unequivocally that disciplinary punishment in military confinement facilities for minor offenses bars any subsequent trial by court-martial of the accused for the same infraction, regardless of the terms of the regulations designed to implement Article 13, Code, supra. As the accused's misconduct was not a serious violation of the Code and as he suffered disciplinary punishment therefor, the president of the court-martial erred in overruling his motion to dismiss Charge III and its specification.

The decision of the board of review is reversed and the record of trial is returned for reassessment of the sentence. Charge III and its specification are ordered dismissed.

Chief Judge QUINN concurs.

LATIMER, Judge (concurring):

I concur.

Article 13 of the Uniform Code of Military Justice, 10 USC §813, authorizes commanding officers of military confinement installations to subject inmates to minor punishment for infractions of discipline. The legislative history of the Article suggests that it was enacted principally to prevent an accused, held pending trial for an offense, from being punished therefor while in pretrial confinement. However, members of Congress realized that incarcerated persons might, before being tried, become recalcitrant and insubordinate and as a means of deterring that sort of misbehavior it authorized confinement officials to take summary action to enforce and maintain the discipline required for proper operation of the facility. Merely because of that grant of authority it would be difficult to ascribe to Congress an intent to change a well-established principle of criminal law and authorize a person to be twice punished for the same offense. Particularly is that true in light of Article 44(a) of the Code, 10 USC §844, which provides that no person shall, without his consent, be tried a second time for the same offense.

In the case at bar, there can be no question that the reason disciplinary segregation was imposed was to punish the accused for an offense which had been completed prior to the time disciplinary action was taken. Obviously, at times, there may be a combination of punitive, preventive and security reasons prompting disciplinary sanctions and in that situation a different principle might apply, but I find only the first reason present in this case. In that connection, I have not overlooked the contention that the action taken was to maintain peace and order in the stockade but I do not find that assertion sustainable under the facts of this case.

This record bears out the conclusion that the commanding officer proceeded under Article 13 of the Code, supra, for he never employed the procedural steps required by Article 15, Uniform Code of Military Justice, 10 USC §815. But that is not to say he did not impose nonjudicial punishment, because Article 13 suggests a summary proceeding and it does not furnish any procedural or penalty guides. Absent any other Congressional restrictions on administrative or nonjudicial punishment, which are not covered by Article 44(a), supra, I believe Article 15 must be deemed to mark out the limitations Congress intended to impose to prevent double punishment for the same crime when the pretrial offense is minor and nonjudicial punishment for the misconduct is imposed. When the two Articles are construed together in that manner, Article 15 supplements Article 13 and a statutory privilege accorded an accused is thereby protected. Moreover, the officials in charge of military prisons or stockades are left with adequate means to cope with the problems of control and discipline.

I make these brief observations because I believe it advisable to point out that confinement officials have the right to take administrative disciplinary measures to keep order in penal institutions without regard to the powers granted by either Articles 13 or 15, supra. However, if they elect to impose punishment for infractions of a minor nature merely to chastise for that which is past and not for security or the prevention of agitation or trouble, then trial for the same offense is barred.

---

Nonjudicial punishment previously imposed for a "minor offense" may be interposed in bar of trial for the same offense (para. 68g, MCM). A promise by one commander not to prefer charges is not binding upon a subsequent commander and may not be urged in bar of trial (U.S. v. Werthman, 5 USCMA 440, 18 CMR 64 [ 1955]). If an officer exercising general court-martial jurisdiction unconditionally restores a deserter to duty without trial with knowledge of the alleged desertion, this action amounts to a constructive condonation of the desertion and may be interposed in bar of trial subsequently ordered (para. 68f, MCM).

The fact that an accused's conviction was reversed by appellate authority does not bar a retrial of the accused for the offense of which he was formerly convicted or of a lesser included offense. See Sanford v. Robbins, 115 F.2d 435 (1940), certiorari denied 312 U.S. 697 (1941); Wrublewski v. McInerney, 166 F.2d 243 (1948); Brewster v. Swope, 180 F.2d 984 (1950).

Acquittal by court-martial does not bar trial in a State court for the same act. See State v. Rankin, 4 Cold. Tenn. 145 (1867); Bartkus v. Ill., 359 U.S. 121 (1959); Abbate v. U.S., 359 U.S. 187 (1959).

Article 14, UCMJ, allows the delivery of a member of the armed forces to the civil authorities for trial. See Kennedy v. Sanford, 166 F.2d 568 (1948); Peek v. U.S., 321 F.2d 934 (1963).

For cases concerning a requested "change of venue," see Durant v. Hiatt, 81 F.Supp. 948 (1948); U.S. v. Gravitt, 5 USCMA 249 (1954); and U.S. v. Carter, 9 USCMA 108 (1958).

CHALLENGES

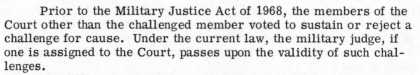

Prior to the Military Justice Act of 1968, the members of the Court other than the challenged member voted to sustain or reject a challenge for cause. Under the current law, the military judge, if one is assigned to the Court, passes upon the validity of such challenges.

The following extract from the MCM sets forth various grounds for challenges. If a member, upon disclosing the grounds for challenge against him, also discloses facts that might prejudice other members against the accused, the military judge should declare a mistrial. See U.S. v. Richard, 7 USCMA 46, 21 CMR 172 (1956).

Courts-martial members are permitted to ask questions of witnesses after examination by counsel. If they exercise this privilege, they must be careful not to depart from an impartial role. For cases where convictions were reversed because of members' excessive questioning, see U.S. v. Blankenship, 7 USCMA 328, 22 CMR 118 (1956); U.S. v. Marshall, 12 USCMA 117, 30 CMR 117 (1961); and U.S. v. Pratt, 15 USCMA 558, 36 CMR 56 (1965).

Extract from
Manual for Courts-Martial, United States, 1969
(Revised edition).

62. CHALLENGES. a. Statutory provisions. The military judge and members of a general or special court-martial may be challenged by the accused or the trial counsel for cause stated to the court. The military judge, or if none has been detailed, the court members shall determine the relevancy and validity of challenges for cause, but a challenge may not be received to more than one person at a time. Challenges by the trial counsel shall ordinarily be presented and decided before those by the accused are offered. Each accused and the trial counsel is entitled to one peremptory challenge, but the military judge may not be challenged except for cause (Art. 41).

b. Disclosing grounds for challenges. After the members of the court, the military judge, and counsel have been sworn, the trial counsel will announce to the court the general nature of the charges, the name of the accuser, the investigating officer, the officer or officers forwarding the charges to the convening authority, and the name of any court member or military judge who participated in any proceedings already had. He will then disclose in open session every ground for challenge believed by him to exist in the case and will request that the military judge and each member do likewise with respect to grounds of challenge, whether against the military judge or member himself or against any others who are subject to challenge for cause. . . .

. . .

c. Action upon disclosure. If it appears from any disclosure that the military judge or a member is subject to challenge on any ground stated in clauses (1) through (8) of 62f, and the fact is not disputed, the military judge or member will be excused forthwith. If the military judge is excused or the court is reduced below a quorum, the court will adjourn pending detail of a new military judge or additional members. Except as just stated, no action is required under this subparagraph (62c) with respect to any disclosure that may be made; but proceedings under this paragraph are without prejudice to any rights of challenge on either side.

. . .

e. Peremptory challenges. A peremptory challenge does not require any reason or ground therefor to exist or to be stated. It may be used before, during, or after challenges for cause, or against a member unsuccessfully challenged for cause, or against a new member if not previously utilized in the trial. It cannot be used against the military judge. A member challenged peremptorily will be excused forthwith.

In a joint or common trial each accused is entitled to one peremptory challenge.

f. Challenges for cause--grounds for. Among the grounds of challenges for cause against members of special and general courts-martial and, unless otherwise indicated by the context, the military judge are the following:

(1)  That the challenged military judge or member is not eligible to serve as military judge or member, respectively, on courts-martial.

(2)  That he is not a member or military judge of the court.

(3)  That he is the accuser as to any offense charged. See Article 1(9) for definition of accuser.

(4)  That he will be a witness for the prosecution. See 63 for definition of witness for the prosecution.

(5)  That he was the investigating officer as to any offense charged. See 64 for definition of investigating officer.

(6) That he has acted as counsel for the prosecution or the accused as to any offense charged.

(7) That upon a rehearing or a new or other trial of the case he was a member of the court which first heard the case.

(8) That he is an enlisted member who is a member of the same unit as the accused. See 4b and Article 25(c)(2) for definitions of the word "unit."

(9) That he has forwarded the charges in the case with his personal recommendation concerning trial by court-martial.

(10) That he has formed or expressed a positive and definite opinion as to the guilt or innocence of the accused as to any offense charged, except that this shall not necessarily apply to a military judge who has formed or expressed such an opinion solely in his role as military judge sitting alone in a previous trial of the same or a closely related case.

(11) That he has acted in the same case as the convening authority or as the legal officer or staff judge advocate to the convening authority.

(12) That he will act in the same case as the reviewing authority (84) or as the legal officer or staff judge advocate to the reviewing authority (85a).

(13) Any other facts indicating that he should not sit as a member or military judge in the interest of having the trial and subsequent proceedings free from substantial doubt as to legality, fairness, and impartiality. Examples of the facts which may constitute grounds for challenge are: That he will be a witness for the defense; that he testified or submitted a written statement in connection with the investigation of the charges, unless at the request of the accused; that he has officially expressed an opinion as to the mental condition of the accused; that, when it can be avoided, a member is junior in rank or grade to the accused; that he has a direct personal interest in the result of the trial; that he is in any way closely related to the accused; that he participated as a member or as counsel in the trial of a closely related case; that he is decidedly hostile or friendly to the accused; that, not having been present as a member when testimony on the merits was heard, or other important proceedings were held in the case, his sitting as a member will involve an appreciable risk of injury to the substantial rights of an accused, which risk will not be avoided by a reading of the record. In connection with this last example, see 41e and f, and 62h(1).

g. Limitations on inquiry as to eligibility of military judge. A challenge against a military judge based on the ground that he is not eligible to act as military judge (62f (1)) will not be sustained unless it is shown: (1) That he is not a commissioned officer; or (2) that he is not on active duty with an armed force; or (3) that he is not a member of the bar of a Federal court or of the highest court of a State of the United States; or (4) that he has not been certified to be qualified for duty as a military judge (Art. 26(b)); or (5) that in a general court-martial he is not designated and assigned in accordance with Article 26(c). The hearing on such a challenge will be limited to the issue of determining whether any one of the reasons enumerated above exists. In this connection, it may be inferred that a person detailed as the military judge of a court-martial is a commissioned officer on active duty with an armed force, and the recital of his qualifications in the convening order is evidence of the facts recited therein. An inquiry into the general educational, legal, or judicial experience of the military judge is improper.

## EVIDENCE

See Article 36, UCMF. Chapter 27, MCM, 1969 (rev. ed.), contains the rules of evidence as prescribed by the President. See United States v. Smith, supra, p. 134. The use of deposition testimony is probably more frequent in courts-martial than in civilian trials because of the migrant nature of members of the armed forces, but the Court of Military Appeals has by various opinions placed the practice under stringent restrictions. See U.S. v. Davis, 19 USCMA 217, 41 CMR 217 (1970).

### UNITED STATES v. LANGE

United States Court of Military Appeals, 1965.
15 U.S.C.M.A. 486, 35 C.M.R. 458.

KILDAY, Judge:
A general court-martial convened at Wurtsmith Air Force Base, Michigan, convicted accused for the separate thefts of three wallets, in violation of Article 121, Uniform Code of Military Justice, 10 USC

§921. Accused was sentenced to bad-conduct discharge, total for-feitures, confinement at hard labor for one year, and reduction to the grade of airman basic. The findings and sentence were approved by the officer exercising general court-martial jurisdiction. A board of review, however, ruled that the law officer erred in admitting the three wallets into evidence, as the same had been recovered through an illegal search. Accordingly, the board set aside the findings and sentence, and ordered a rehearing.

Pursuant to the provisions of Article 67(b)(2), Uniform Code of Military Justice, 10 USC §867, the Acting The Judge Advocate General of the Air Force certified the case to this Court for review, request-ing that we resolve the following issue:

"WAS THE BOARD OF REVIEW CORRECT IN ITS
DETERMINATION THAT PROSECUTION EXHIBITS 1,
2 AND 3 WERE SEIZED AS THE RESULT OF AN IL-
LEGAL SEARCH?"

The record reflects that on separate dates in February 1964, the wallets of two airmen were taken without permission. In June, the wallet of a third man was stolen. These are the wallets that were alleged to have been the res of the thefts with which accused was charged, and they were admitted into evidence as prosecution exhibits 1, 2, and 3.

On August 14, 1964, the commander of accused's squadron was conducting an inspection of the barracks. He was accompanied by the base commander and by the squadron administrative officer. During the course of that inspection the base commander suggested to the commanding officer of the squadron that he conduct periodic "stand-by" or "shake-down" type inspections more frequently than had been the practice, commenting " 'You would be surprised at what you might find.' " The latter, in turn, immediately told his administrative offi-cer to see that this was done " 'when you get an opportunity,' " indi-cating the inspections should be made about once a month.

The squadron administrative officer understood his superior's order to direct him to conduct such inspections, at his discretion, as a regular future routine. Generally, the purpose of such a "stand-by" or "shake-down" inspection would be "for the health, welfare and morals of the individual, and also to see that his belongings are clean, properly kept and maintained, uniforms are right, and if there's any property in his possession that does not belong there." It would en-tail checking the billets and lockers, and going through personal be-longings.

Subsequently, on the first of September, a theft of a watch and money was reported to the squadron administrative officer. He was also aware of other such reports over the past two months, and the most recent theft caused him to remember the order given him by the commanding officer of the squadron as to monthly inspections, for he had not yet taken any such action. Accordingly, he undertook to conduct such an inspection immediately. He tried to apprise the squadron commander of his intended action--for the sole purpose of keeping him informed, he testified--but was unsuccessful in contacting him.

Specifically, the administrative officer testified he undertook to make a thorough check for cleanliness, Government property, and recently stolen property, describing his action as "just an over-all typical shakedown inspection." In order that the squadron's operations be disrupted as little as possible during the inspection, the administrative officer determined to call the men back to the barracks in groups of ten. He further testified that he believed the property reported stolen that day, if it were to be recovered, would likely be found in close proximity to the victim's room. He therefore included in the first group of ten, the men sharing quarters with the victim and those living in adjoining billets. As accused was that victim's roommate, he was in the first group called to the barracks from their duty stations.*

In the course of checking accused's room and effects, the three wallets which he was convicted for stealing were found among his possessions. Subsequently, after proper warning of his rights under Article 31, Uniform Code of Military Justice, 10 USC §831, accused executed a sworn statement confessing the three thefts.

The board of review held that the record fails to establish that the search leading to the seizure of the wallets was legal. Accordingly, the board concluded the law officer erred in overruling defense counsel's objection to admitting the wallets into evidence.

In the course of its opinion, the board of review recognized the necessity to determine whether the actions of the squadron administrative officer constituted an inspection, or whether he in fact performed a search. With regard to the former, the board stated its satisfaction:

". . . that a commander has the inherent power (and continuing duty) to inspect his organization, in the strict sense of the word, formally or informally, at any time, to determine its ability to perform its mission. We are equally satisfied that he possesses broad discretion in the exercise of this responsibility. He may inspect in person or direct a subordinate to do so. Evidence of criminal activity discovered during the inspection would ordinarily be admissible in a court-martial. The discovery of the evidence during an inspection would not taint a statement,

_____

*Prior to arrival of this group, two men who happened to come to the orderly room were taken to their rooms and inspected.

made pursuant to a confrontation with the evidence, as
'the fruit of the poison tree', for the simple reason there
would be no poison tree."

The board distinguished such an inspection from both particularized
or generalized searches, in the following language:

"Comparing 'search' with 'inspection', we find that
a search is made with a view toward discovering contra-
band or other evidence to be used in the prosecution of a
criminal action. In other words, it is made in anticipation of prosecution.* On the other hand, an inspection is
an official examination to determine the fitness or readiness of the person, organization, or equipment, and,
though criminal proceedings may result from matters
uncovered thereby, it is not made with a view to any
criminal action. It may be a routine matter or special,
dictated by events, or any number of other things, including merely the passage of time. There is no requirement
for 'probable cause', as that term is used in the law, but
it may result from a desire of the commander to know
the status of his organization or any part of it, including
its arms, equipment, billets, etc.

In that connection, the board of review referred to Chief Judge Quinn's
opinion in United States v Gebhart, 10 USCMA 606, 28 CMR 172. His
language there, at page 610, on this subject is illuminating:

"While it is difficult to lay down a general rule applicable to every conceivable situation, it can be said
with assurance that the exercise of the authority to search
must be founded upon probable cause, whether the search
be general in that it includes all personnel of the command
or subdivision, or limited only to persons specifically
suspected of an offense. United States v Doyle, supra;
United States v Brown, 10 USCMA 482, 28 CMR 48. A
search founded upon mere suspicion is illegal and the
fruits thereof inadmissible. United States v Brown,
supra.** To hold otherwise would require us to deny to

---

*"The term 'prosecution', as here used, may include administra-
tive actions, but the distinction does not affect the reasoning here involved.

**Both the generalized and particularized types of searches are
not to be confused with inspections of military personnel entering or
leaving certain areas, or those, for example, conducted by a

military personnel the full protections of the United States
Constitution itself.  This, neither we, nor the Congress,
nor the Executive, nor any individual can do.

The Government does not quarrel with that portion of the board's
opinion.  Indeed, quite to the contrary, appellate Government counsel
endorse the board's analysis in that respect as "eminently correct."
But, the Government contends, a bona fide inspection of the sort above
described, does not lose its character as such and become an illegal
search merely because the officer conducting the inspection has been
apprised of larcenies from squadron members.
     Briefly, the thrust of the Government's position is that the
squadron commanding officer had undisputedly ordered his administrative officer to conduct what may be termed an inspection in the strict
sense.  He did so legitimately it is asserted; in good faith and wholly
without any suspicion of crime or specific wrongdoing by anyone.  The
administrative officer, in turn, they argue, was merely complying
with his commander's order--as he was obliged to do--and the fact
that he had been apprised of stealing in the squadron neither relieved
him of complying with the commanding officer's direction, nor changed
the basic nature of his action.
     We cannot accede to appellate Government counsel's importunity
to adopt this approach.  To do so would require that we ignore the uncontested evidence that, although the squadron commander, on August
14th, authorized his administrative officer to conduct an inspection,
seventeen days had passed without any action by the latter.  He had
neither complied with his superior's directive, nor had he scheduled
any inspection for a future time.  It was not until September 1st, when
a theft was brought to his attention, that the administrative officer
determined to check the billets, lockers, and effects of the squadron.
Significantly, he frankly conceded that he intended to look for recently
stolen property, among other things.  And manifestly this part of his
quest was dictated by the theft report he had just received, as he
determined to check first those persons and that area, where he believed the property recently stolen would most likely be found.
     In short, all the evidence points to what the board concluded
was a search, and we agree.  Over two weeks had passed without any
action whatever taken to conduct an inspection; the administrative
officer did not determine to conduct a "shake-down" until he learned
of a recent theft; he admittedly was seeking to recover the property
reported stolen; and he undertook to look first where he believed that
property was likely to be.

---

commander in furtherance of the security of his command.  These are
wholly administrative or preventive in nature and are within the commander's inherent powers.  United States v Brown, 10 USCMA 482,
28 CMR 48.

We are not here concerned with an inspection that had been held earlier, and the wallets thereby recovered; or with an inspection that had been already scheduled at the time the administrative officer received the report of the larceny, where the situation conceivably would be different. However, an "inspection" cannot be used as a pretext to cover up unlawful invasions of the personal rights of members of the armed services. True it is that the administrative officer steadfastly maintained he was acting in good faith to comply with the commanding officer's order, and was not guilty of such an abuse. Indeed, we do not in anywise intend to impugn or reflect on his honesty. His integrity and good faith, however, cannot change the character of what he actually did. It is clear from the evidence of record, as the board of review held, that what was conducted in the present case was in fact a search.

As such, as the board pointed out, it is clear on this record that it was not made pursuant to a warrant or incident to lawful apprehension. Nor can accused be said to have consented to the search of his effects. To the contrary, his action was manifestly mere peaceful acquiescence in the face of authority. See United States v Westmore, 14 USCMA 474, 34 CMR 254; United States v Justice, 13 USCMA 31, 32 CMR 31; and cases therein collated. Likewise, the board held, and we agree, that the record does not establish that immediate action was necessary to prevent removal or disposition of stolen property. See United States v Swanson, 3 USCMA 671, 14 CMR 89; United States v Davis, 4 USCMA 577, 16 CMR 151.

Left then, is the question whether the administrative officer was permitted to order a search by virtue of a commander's authority. Regardless of whether he had the requisite probable cause to order this generalized search (see United States v Drew, 15 USCMA 449, 35 CMR 421; United States v Schafer, 13 USCMA 83, 32 CMR 83)--a question with which we need not concern ourselves in the present case--there is no showing that the administrative officer was the senior officer present in the organization. Nor can it be contended, in the posture of this record, that his commander delegated to him the power to authorize searches. See United States v Drew, 15 USCMA 449, 35 CMR 421. To the contrary, his superior's earlier direction to him was, as the Government concedes, limited strictly to inspections, and he received no subsequent authorization.

Accordingly, the board of review correctly held the wallets inadmissible, as the record fails to establish they were seized in the course of a legal search. The certified question, therefore, is answered in the affirmative.

The decision of the board of review is affirmed.

Judge FERGUSON concurs.

QUINN, Chief Judge (dissenting):

The principal opinion presents a curious situation. On the one hand, my brothers have consistently held that, no matter how implausible and incredible it may be, the accused's testimony as to the nature of his act is sufficient to raise an issue requiring determination by the fact finder. See United States v Kuefler, 14 USCMA 136, 33 CMR 348; United States v Callaghan, 14 USCMA 231, 34 CMR 11. Here they profess not "to impugn or reflect on" the administrative officer's honesty and integrity, but they totally reject his testimony that the theft merely reminded him of his neglect of duty, and that the inspection he ordered was "just an over-all typical shakedown inspection."

At the very least, the administrative officer's testimony raises a question of fact as to the nature of the inspection. Surely, the majority do not mean that once he received the report of the theft he could not thereafter hold a shakedown inspection. Surely, they do not mean that the theft precluded him from carrying out his duties.

In the first instance, the question of whether he acted on a purely administrative basis, as he testified he did, or whether he was directly engaged in ferreting out the fruits of a crime, as the accused contended, was for the law officer's determination. His ruling must be sustained, unless new and contrary findings of fact are made. See United States v Brown, 10 USCMA 482, 28 CMR 48. As I read the opinion of the board of review, it did not, as the majority here do not, question the administrative officer's credibility. Rather, it held that the circumstances established as a matter of law that the inspection was legally a search for the fruits of a crime. I disagree with that conclusion because, in my opinion, there is evidence to support a finding that the inspection was merely administrative in purpose and execution. The latter finding is implicit in the law officer's ruling. Since the board of review made no findings of fact contrary to those made by the law officer, I would sustain the law officer's ruling. United States v Alaniz, 9 USCMA 533, 26 CMR 313. I would, therefore, answer the certified question in the negative, and return the record of trial to the board of review for further consideration.

---

The Lange case illustrates the major area in which the rules of evidence in courts-martial differ somewhat from the rules in federal district Courts. A thorough understanding of these rules may only be achieved by a study of the cited cases.

CONTEMPT

Article 48, UCMJ, provides for the punishment of any person for contempt in courts-martial. See U.S. v. De Angelis, 3 USCMA 298, 12 CMR 54 (1953), for an example of a case where the Court of Military Appeals implied that a counsel should have been so punished.

INSTRUCTIONS

## UNITED STATES v. CLAY

United States Court of Military Appeals, 1951.
1 U.S.C.M.A. 74, 1 C.M.R. 74.

GEORGE W. LATIMER, Judge:
A certificate from The Judge Advocate General of the Navy in accordance with the Uniform Code of Military Justice, Article 67(b)(2) (Act of May 5, 1950, 64 Stat. 108, 50 U. S. C. §§551-736) brings this case before us. Accused was tried by a special court-martial on two charges, one for violation of Article 8(1), and the other for violation of Article 22(a), of the Articles for the Government of the Navy. The charge under the first mentioned article was for an alleged disorder, while the one charged under the latter was for improperly wearing the uniform. The offenses were committed prior to the effective date of the Uniform Code of Military Justice, supra, but the arraignment was not held until after that date. Under the provisions of Executive Order No. 10214, dated February 8, 1951, it was permissible to prefer the charges under the Articles for the Government of the Navy, but because the accused was not arraigned before May 31, 1951, the trial procedure was governed by the new code. (See United States v. Merritt, 1 USCMA 56, 1 CMR 56, decided November 20, 1951).
Accused pleaded guilty to the charge involving the wearing of an improper uniform and not guilty to the charge of disorder. After the presentation of evidence, and after both parties had rested, the president closed the court to consider the findings. He, however, neglected to charge the court on the elements of the offense, the presumption of innocence, and the burden of proof, as required by the Uniform Code of Military Justice, Article 51(c), supra, and Paragraph

73(b), Manual for Courts-Martial, United States 1951. The court found the accused guilty on both charges. After the findings of guilty were announced, but prior to sentence, the defense counsel pointed out the failure of the president to instruct in accordance with the above cited article and paragraph. The court, after considering the point raised, conceded the possibility of errors in procedure but instead of correcting them overruled the objection, sentenced the accused, and attached a letter of explanation to the record for the information of the convening authority. The convening authority concluded that the error was not prejudicial to the substantial rights of the accused, and the board of review affirmed the conviction by a written decision which reached the same conclusion. The Judge Advocate General of the Navy then certified the case to this Court for a decision on that question.

We can eliminate from further consideration the charge dealing with improperly wearing the uniform, for the reason that in the case of United States v. Lucas, 1 USCMA 19, 1 CMR 19, decided November 8, 1951, we held that when an accused, after a full and fair explanation of the effect of a guilty plea, nevertheless insists on pleading guilty to a charge, his rights are not substantially prejudiced by the failure to instruct as required by the Code and Manual. This opinion will, therefore, deal only with the charge which alleges disorderly conduct in violation of Article 8(1), Articles for the Government of the Navy.

. . .

The board of review in its decision went to some length to avoid the effect of the error by attempting to show that there was no substantial right of the accused materially prejudiced because there was competent evidence to establish all elements of the offense, the evidence was of such quality and quantity that the presumption of innocence was overcome, and the evidence established beyond a reasonable doubt the guilt of the accused. We do not accept the reasoning used by the board. But, before we touch that question, we look to the acts of Congress to determine whether it has declared that there are fundamental rights inherent in the trial of military offenses which must be accorded to an accused before it can be said that he has been fairly convicted.

There are certain standards in the military accusatorial system which have been specifically set by Congress and which we must demand be observed in the trials of military offenses. Some of these are more important than others, but all are of sufficient importance to be a significant part of military law. We conceive these rights to mold into a pattern similar to that developed in federal civilian cases. For lack of a more descriptive phrase, we label the pattern as "military due process" and then point up the minimum standards which are the framework for this concept and which must be met before the accused can be legally convicted. The Uniform Code of Military Justice, supra, contemplates that he be given a fair trial and it commands us to see that the proceedings in the courts below reach that standard.

Generally speaking, due process means a course of legal proceedings according to those rules and principles which have been
established in our system of jurisprudence for the enforcement and
protection of private rights. For our purposes, and in keeping with
the principles of military justice developed over the years, we do not
bottom those rights and privileges on the Constitution. We base them
on the laws as enacted by Congress. But, this does not mean that we
can not give the same legal effect to the rights granted by Congress
to military personnel as do civilian courts to those granted to civilians by the Constitution or by other federal statutes.

As we have stated in previous opinions, we believe Congress
intended, in so far as reasonably possible, to place military justice
on the same plane as civilian justice, and to free those accused by
the military from certain vices which infested the old system. Believing this, we are required to announce principles consistent therewith.

A cursory inspection of the Uniform Code of Military Justice,
supra, discloses that Congress granted to an accused the following
rights which parallel those accorded to defendants in civilian courts:
To be informed of the charges against him; to be confronted by witnesses testifying against him; to cross-examine witnesses for the
government; to challenge members of the court for cause or peremptorily; to have a specified number of members compose general
and special courts-martial; to be represented by counsel; not to be
compelled to incriminate himself; to have involuntary confessions excluded from consideration; to have the court instructed on the elements of the offense, the presumption of innocence, and the burden of
proof; to be found guilty of an offense only when a designated number
of members concur in a finding to that effect; to be sentenced only
when a certain number of members vote in the affirmative; and to
have an appellate review.

By mentioning the foregoing rights and benefits, we have not
intended to make the list all-inclusive, nor to imply others might not
be substantial. We have merely enumerated those which are of such
importance as to be readily catalogued in that category. In addition,
we disclaim any intent to classify these as jurisdictional or non-
jurisdictional. Under our powers as an appellate court we can reverse for errors of law which materially prejudice the substantial
rights of the accused, and we need go no further than to hold that the
failure to afford to an accused any of the enumerated rights denied
him military due process and furnishes grounds for us to set aside
the conviction.

Previously adjudicated federal court cases are a source from
which we can test the prejudicial effect of denying an accused the
rights we have set out as our pattern of "military due process. . . ."
. . .

Aside from the constitutional due process concept threading its
way through federal cases, we find federal appellate courts passing

directly on the prejudicial error of failure of trial judges properly to instruct a jury. We have not found any reported cases in which a court refused to give any instructions, but there are numerous in which the instructions were so inadequate and incomplete that it could be said the same result was reached. . . .

. . .

We may have belabored the importance of the question herein involved. If so, it is to impress on courts-martial the undesirability of short-cutting the plain mandate of Congress. To follow strictly the required procedure may at times seem unimportant, but the only way by which Congress can make certain what it deems important is by saying so in its legislative pronouncement. In this instance, it proclaimed that the giving of instructions was a valuable right, the court-martial crashed through that mandate, and now we are asked to say that right was unsubstantial. It was for Congress to set the rules governing military trials. It legislated on the subject and not without adequate consideration. We are not concerned with the wisdom of the enactment, but we might suggest that there are many reasons which may have prompted Congress to demand that instructions be given to members of courts-martial. It is reasonable to require that members trying an accused should not be permitted to deliberate upon the guilt of an accused without having been told the nature of the crime and the essential elements of the offense. It is necessary and desirable that the law be explained to them, that the law officer or president point out the issues involved, and that someone with authority and knowledge of the law bring into focus the relationship of the evidence to those issues. Unless the court is in some way limited as to what are the essential elements, the members become unguided and unconfined. What evidence might be considered by them as relevant to establish the crime may be outside the limits of the charge and the material evidence influencing them might have no reasonable relationship to the elements of the offense. Moreover, assuming, as contended, that most members of a court-martial have a smattering knowledge of the law and do not need to be informed, Congress could reasonably demand that immediately before deliberating upon a finding those who know have their memory refreshed and those who do not be enlightened.

A conviction supported by a proceeding which is so lacking in correct procedure should fall of its own weight. However, we proceed one step further and point out why we believe the board of review erred in its appraisal of prejudice. We are not here concerned with the questions answered in the Lucas case, supra. There, the accused pleaded guilty and waived his right to demand the full protective safeguards accorded to him. Cast in the background of a plea of guilty with a full understanding of its consequences, the failure to instruct could not be prejudicial error. But, not so when the accused insists on his full measure of protection. An accused might waive some of the safeguards thrown around him but the court cannot waive them for him. The members of a court should not force a situation by taking

away substantial benefits and then seek to have us justify their act by
saying, in effect, "They are of little value, the evidence is such the
court would have found him guilty anyway."

   . . .

    What we have previously stated goes with like effect to the fail-
ure of the court to instruct on the presumption of innocence and the
burden of proof. We are not impressed with the argument made by
the board of review that it was clothed with authority to determine
the sufficiency of the evidence and that it found the failure to instruct
was not prejudicial because the evidence overcame the presumptions
of innocence; that the elements were established beyond a reasonable
doubt; and that it was satisfied the court or the board of review could
not have made a finding other than that of guilty. Assuming without
deciding that the evidence compels such a finding, we are, nevertheless, required to hold the error materially prejudiced the substantial
rights of the accused, for the reason that we cannot say one of the
historic cornerstones of our system of civil jurisprudence is merely
a formality of military procedure. If Congress specifically grants
what it considers to be a substantial right, we cannot deny the authoritative requirement by refusing to recognize it. There is importance
attached to a benefit given by Congress, and the importance should
not be diluted by an assumption that doubtful cases call for its protection but those appearing certain permit it to be discarded. By way
of analogy, the government could as well argue that when an accused
is denied the right of counsel, the error is not prejudicial because the
evidence points unmistakenly toward the guilt of the accused. We must
reject such contentions as their adoption would effectively eat away
what Congress has declared to be military justice.

    It is argued by counsel for the government that the members
sitting on the court were Navy officers and were familiar with the
rules of law that the accused is presumed innocent, that the burden
of proof is upon the government, and that the elements of the offense
must be established beyond a reasonable doubt; and, therefore, they
need not be instructed as they considered these principles while deliberating upon their verdict. This is an assumption made by counsel,
and it need be answered only to the extent of saying that members of
Congress were undoubtedly aware of the standards of the service and
may have known that members of courts-martial might have knowledge of these fundamental rights; but, nevertheless, and in spite of
this knowledge, they made it mandatory that instructions be given for
the benefit of the accused. Without question, Congress not only considered the qualifications of members of the court, but also considered the accused and in so doing directed that the court be instructed
in his presence and in the presence of his counsel so that, if desired,
objections could be made to the charge given or additional instructions could be requested. Moreover, we are not convinced all members of courts-martial are sufficiently versed in law to know all the

elements of all offenses; but, even were we to make this assumption, the accused is an interested party and entitled to know to what extent the court-martial is controlled by law in considering his guilt.

In applying the concepts we have discussed to this case we find the trial of the accused far short of what is deemed essential to military justice. In the final analysis, the record as a whole convinces us that the accused was denied those necessary elements of military due process by which Congress sought to protect him.

The decision of the board of review is reversed.

Chief Judge QUINN and Judge BROSMAN concur.

---

A court-martial must be instructed not only on the elements of the offense charged but also on the elements of every lesser offense included therein that is reasonably placed in issue by the evidence. The application of this principle to specific factual situations is not easy. In U.S. v. Thompson, 11 USCMA 5, 28 CMR 229 (1959), the Court of Military Appeals affirmed a board of review decision that the law officer did not err when he failed to instruct on the lesser included offense of assault and battery, to which the accused pleaded guilty, and the accused was found guilty of aggravated assault, upon which the law officer did instruct.

In U.S. v. Morgan, 8 USCMA 659, 25 CMR 163 (1958), the Court reversed the conviction of an accused for voluntary manslaughter because the law officer did not instruct on that offense even though he did instruct on the charged offense of unpremeditated murder, involuntary manslaughter, and assault and battery, and the defense counsel specifically asked that the Court not be instructed on voluntary manslaughter.

In U.S. v. Kuefler, 14 USCMA 136, 33 CMR 348 (1963), the Court remanded a case to the board of review with instructions that it could affirm findings of guilty to the lesser included offense of unlawful entry (because the Court said that he judicially confessed thereto) even though the law officer had not instructed on that offense but only on the major offense of housebreaking of which he had been found guilty by the law officer.

## UNITED STATES v. PATTERSON

United States Court of Military Appeals, 1964.
14 U.S.C.M.A. 441, 34 C.M.R. 221.

QUINN, Chief Judge:
    The question presented on this appeal is whether the board of
review prejudiced the accused in modifying the findings of guilty of
three of the several offenses of which he was convicted by a special
court-martial.
    Specification 1, Charge II, alleged the accused committed an
assault with a dangerous weapon--a knife--upon another airman. The
charge was laid under Article 128, Uniform Code of Military Justice,
10 USC §928, and the accused was convicted as charged. Exercising
its power to make new findings of fact, the board of review held the
evidence did not establish that the accused used the knife in a manner
likely to produce grievous bodily harm. It reduced the court-martial's
finding of guilty of assault with a dangerous weapon to the lesser offense of simple assault. At trial, the court-martial had not been
instructed that simple assault was in issue, and could be considered
as an alternative offense to that charged.
    Specification 2, Charge II, alleged the accused intentionally in-
flicted grievous bodily harm upon another airman in an assault with
a knife. No instruction was given on any lesser offense; and the
court-martial found the accused guilty, as charged. The board of
review concluded the accused's testimony about this encounter could
be "viewed" as the denial of any intention to inflict harm. It held
that the failure of the president to instruct on the lesser offense of
assault with a dangerous weapon was error. To "cure the prejudice
resulting from" the error, it affirmed findings of guilty of only the
lesser included offense of assault with a dangerous weapon.
    Charge III and its specification alleged the accused was drunk
and disorderly in station, in violation of Article 134 of the Uniform
Code, 10 USC §934. The evidence showed the accused was involved
in an automobile accident in Indianapolis, Indiana. Apparently against
his will, he was placed in an ambulance and taken to an Army hospital. While being administered treatment at the hospital, he was abusive and belligerent to hospital and other military personnel; and he
used foul and profane language. Before the board of review, the
accused's counsel contended that since the accused had been involuntarily brought to the hospital while in a state of intoxication he
could not properly be convicted of the offense charged. See United
States v Bailey, 10 USCMA 95, 27 CMR 169. The board of review
sustained the assignment of error so far as it related to drunkenness, and affirmed only that part of the court-martial's findings
which held the accused was disorderly in station.
    In substance, the accused challenges the correctness of the
disposition by the board of review of the errors affecting the findings

of guilty. He contends that instead of affirming lesser offenses, it should have directed a rehearing or dismissed the charges. There is, he maintains, "no more reason or authority for permitting reviewing authorities to convict accused on lesser included offenses not before the trial forum than there is for permitting the trial court to return findings without instructions." The argument makes no distinction between appellate modification of findings of guilty because the evidence of record does not support one or more of the elements of the offense found by the court-martial, and appellate modification of the findings of guilty to cure a deficiency in the instructions.

Affirmance of a lesser included offense by a reviewing authority is specifically sanctioned by the Uniform Code of Military Justice. . . . . . .

A different kind of problem is presented by the board of review's action on specification 2, Charge II. Here we are not concerned with the sufficiency of the evidence to support the findings of fact made by the court-martial, but with a definite error in trial procedure. A court-martial must be instructed not only on the elements of the offense charged, but also on the elements of every lesser offence included therein which is reasonably placed in issue by the evidence. Article 51(c), Uniform Code of Military Justice, 10 USC §851; United States v Clark, 1 USCMA 201, 2 CMR 107. The failure to instruct on a lesser offense reasonably in issue is error. United States v Kuefler, 14 USCMA 136, 33 CMR 348; United States v Strong, 1 USCMA 627, 5 CMR 55. The problem that faces the reviewing authority in this situation is to determine the effect of the error. Can all possibility of prejudice to the accused resulting from the error be eliminated, without invalidating all the court-martial's findings of guilty? In other words, can part of the findings of guilty manifestly not affected by the instructional error be affirmed? The accused contends that the only fair procedure is to reverse all the findings of guilty. So far as his argument advances the formula that error equals reversal, this Court has consistently rejected it.

Generally, an error at the trial level which presents no fair risk of prejudice to the accused does not justify reversal of his conviction. Article 59(a), Uniform Code of Military Justice, 10 USC §859; United States v Oliver, 14 USCMA 192, 33 CMR 404. The general rule is applicable to errors in regard to the instructions. See United States v Crawford, 6 USCMA 517, 20 CMR 233. It follows that reversal of every finding of the court-martial is not required if the trial error affects only one of the findings. Disapproval of the finding affected by the error eliminates all harm to the accused resulting from the error. If the evidence supports the remaining findings, and those findings amount to an offense included within that found by the court-martial, that offense can be affirmed. In United States v Cline, 2 USCMA 411, 413, 9 CMR 41, the accused was charged with desertion, in violation of Article 85 of the Uniform Code, 10 USC §885. We set aside the conviction on the ground the law officer failed to instruct adequately on the lesser included offense of absence without leave, in violation of Article 86 of the Code, 10 USC §886, which had been placed in issue by the evidence.  But, we held it was "unnecessary to order a rehearing since there . . . [was] indisputable and substantial evidence that the accused" was guilty of the included offense.  During our last term, we considered the Kuefler case, supra.  There, the evidence indicated that an instruction on a lesser included offense should have been given.  The accused's sworn testimony, however, amounted to a confession of the commission of a lesser offense included within that charged.  Referring to the effect of the accused's testimony on the instructional error, we said: "In light of the accused's judicial confession to the lesser included offense of unlawful entry, the board of review may affirm findings of guilty of that offense . . . [or] it may order a rehearing." Id., at page 139.  In United States v Miller, 13 USCMA 66, 32 CMR 66, the accused was charged with assault upon a superior noncommissioned officer.  The evidence reasonably placed in issue the lesser included offense of simple assault.  There was no instruction on the lesser offense.  We set aside the findings of guilty by the court-martial, but returned the record of trial to the board of review to consider, in its discretion, whether to affirm the lesser offense and reassess the sentence, or to direct a rehearing of the principal offense.  In United States v Baguex, 2 USCMA 306, 310, 8 CMR 106, Judge BROSMAN succinctly stated the general rule as follows:

> ". . . We do not doubt that the error presented by a failure to instruct as to lesser included offenses may be expunged by an appellate body's affirmance of the lowest of the lesser offenses fairly raised by the evidence, since the accused would thereby have the benefit of the most he could expect from proper instructions.  Whether we thus affirm in a particular case clearly rests within our sound discretion--for Article 59(b) of the Code, 50 USC §646, is phrased in permissive terms only.  At this point it would not be amiss for us to state parenthetically that--in view of our want of fact-finding power--we will doubtless exercise sparingly our power in this particular, reserving it for cases presenting a clear and clean-cut difference between the offense of which the accused was found guilty and another as to which it may be said as a matter of law that the evidence indicates guilt.  The present case is of this sort, because, on rehearing, accused could be convicted only of unpremeditated murder or voluntary manslaughter.
>
> "Accordingly, the decision of the board of review here is affirmed in so far as it extends to guilt of voluntary manslaughter. . . ."

On the basis of this unbroken chain of precedent, the board of review correctly purged the error affecting the findings of guilty of specification 2, Charge II, by affirming only the lesser included offense of assault with a dangerous weapon. Its action is not inconsistent with our opinion in United States v Morgan, 8 USCMA 659, 25 CMR 163. . . .

The decision of the board of review is affirmed.

Judges FERGUSON and KILDAY concur.

In U.S. v. Neal, 17 USCMA 363, 38 CMR 161 (1968), the Court of Military Appeals held that prior to arguments, the law officer (now military judge) should hold an out-of-court conference on instructions in order to act upon requests therefor, hear objections thereon, and, in addition, inform counsel of his action thereon.

## SENTENCE-PUNISHMENT

In addition to the jurisdictional limitations on each type of court-martial found in the UCMJ, paragraphs 125 and 126, MCM set forth specific types of punishment and other limitations. Paragraph 127 sets forth the maximum punishments that may be imposed for each specific offense under the UCMJ.

There are with regard to sentences two significant differences between military and civilian law: (1) an accused serves only one sentence at a time; there are no concurrent sentences in military law; (2) a court-martial adjudges one sentence for all the offenses of which an accused is found guilty.

In U.S. v. Bryant, 12 USCMA 133, 30 CMR 133 (1961), the defense urged that the UCMJ required that sentences be served concurrently. The Court of Military Appeals rejected this contention and summarized its opinion as follows:

First, cumulative or consecutive sentences have long been a part of military law. Second, there is no indication Congress intended to engraft concurrent sentences into military justice when it enacted the Code. Rather Article 57(b) seems to have been designed to insure that an accused received credit against a sentence to confinement for time served from the date the court-martial adjudged sentence instead of some later date when punishment was approved by reviewing authority. Third, service regulations such as Air Force Manual 125-2, supra, are merely designed to preserve the concept of consecutive sentences while implementing the codal requirement that a sentence to confinement begins to run from the date adjudged, and such directives are not inconsistent with Article 57(b). Last, the Secretaries of the respective services may properly promulgate such regulations. Clearly, then, we must rule adversely to accused on this arm of his assigned error.

Accord, McDonald v. Lee, 217 F.2d 619 (CA 5th Cir., 1954). The single gross sentence for more than one offense was approved by the Supreme Court of the United States in Jackson v. Taylor, 353 U.S. 569, 77 S.Ct. 1027, 1 L.Ed.2d 1054 (1957). See also Carter v. McClaughry, 183 U.S. 365, 393 (1902); McDonald v. Lee, supra. In the Jackson case, the accused had been found guilty of premeditated murder and attempted rape and had been given the mandatory sentence of life imprisonment required for a conviction of murder. The board of review disapproved the findings of guilty of murder, approved the findings of guilty of attempted rape, and reassessed the sentence to 20 years' confinement, the maximum imposable for that offense. The accused urged that the board of review had exceeded its powers and that the sentence should be reassessed by the former or by a new court-martial. The Supreme Court rejected the contention of the accused.

The question of "commutation" of a sentence by military appellate review authorities has been developed by the Court of Military Appeals since the enactment of the Uniform Code of Military Justice. It must be remembered that the sentence adjudged by the court-martial fixes the absolute maximum sentence that may be approved by reviewing authorities.

UNITED STATES v. JOHNSON

United States Court of Military Appeals, 1962.
12 U.S.C.M.A. 640, 31 C.M.R. 226.

FERGUSON, Judge:
The accused was tried by general court-martial and, upon his
plea, was found guilty of absence without leave, in violation of Uniform Code of Military Justice, Article 86, 10 USC §886. He was sentenced to be confined at hard labor for one year and to forfeit all pay
and allowances. Upon review, the staff judge advocate concluded that
the sentence was "correct in law and fact" but, because of accused's
"propensity for becoming absent without authority, the nature of the
civil offense committed by him while absent without leave [using an
automobile without the owner's permission], and his poor record of
conduct while in confinement," an opinion was expressed that he had
demonstrated his "lack of suitability for retention in the Army."
Accordingly, the staff judge advocate recommended "commutation"
of the sentence from confinement at hard labor to a punitive discharge.
A copy of the review was served on the accused on June 17, 1961, and
he expressed approval of the proposed change in sentence, requesting
that it be effected and that he be released from confinement.
On July 18, 1961, the convening authority acted upon the record
in accordance with his staff judge advocate's recommendation. Approving the sentence adjudged, he "commuted" it to a bad-conduct
discharge.
On September 19, 1961, the board of review concluded the convening authority's action on the sentence was illegal in that it increased the severity of the penalty. It set aside his action and
ordered the record of trial forwarded to another convening authority
for preparation of a new post-trial review and action.
Based upon the action of the board of review, The Judge Advocate General of the Army has certified the following question:

"WAS THE BOARD OF REVIEW CORRECT IN
HOLDING THAT, AS A MATTER OF LAW, THE ACTION
OF THE CONVENING AUTHORITY IN THIS CASE IN-
CREASED THE SEVERITY OF THE SENTENCE AD-
JUDGED?"

A few preliminary observations are in order before we proceed
to determine the ultimate answer to this issue. First, we apprehend
from the Government's brief and the position of both sides on oral
argument a belief that the resolution of the question before us does
not involve consideration of the factor whether the accused desired
or consented to the change in the sentence. Except insofar as it may
bear upon his counsel's performance of duty on appeal, we agree

with this conclusion. Whether the convening authority may change a
sentence of confinement and forfeitures to a punitive discharge is an
issue which must be resolved without regard to the accused's desires.
There is language to the contrary in the principal opinion in United
States v Christensen, 12 USCMA 393, 30 CMR 393, but we call attention to the fact that the relative position of the Judges in that case
requires that it be regarded as expressing only the view of the author
Judge.

In United States v Russo, 11 USCMA 352, 29 CMR 168, this
Court had before it the issue whether a death sentence might be
changed to dishonorable discharge, forfeiture of all pay and allowances, and confinement at hard labor for life or a lesser term. Reviewing the pertinent authorities, we found that only our opinions in
United States v Freeman, 4 USCMA 76, 15 CMR 76, and United States
v Goodwin, 5 USCMA 647, 18 CMR 271, squarely held that the nature
of a punishment could not be changed in reducing it to what was
deemed an appropriate penalty. Our re-examination of these decisions was in light of the Congressional purpose in providing that a
convening authority had the duty to approve only that sentence which
"he in his discretion determines should be approved," Code, supra,
Article 64, 10 USC §864, and that a board of review in like manner
could only approve such punishment as it "finds correct in law and
fact and determines, on the basis of the entire record, should be
approved," Code, supra, Article 66, 10 USC §866. It was concluded
that these appellate authorities had been granted the power to change
one classification of punishment to another of lesser degree in order
to affirm an appropriate sentence, and it is important to note that no
particular label was attached to this process, the Court being satisfied to determine, upon the basis of an overwhelming demonstration
of legislative intent, that:

> ". . . [W]hether it be termed commutation, miti-
> gation, or merely a reduction in punishment, . . . both
> the convening authority and a board of review have the
> authority to lessen the severity of a death penalty by
> converting it to dishonorable discharge and confinement
> at hard labor." [United States v Russo, supra, at page
> 358.]

The second case which came before us involving a change in the
nature of punishment in order to make it appropriate was United States
v Plummer, 12 USCMA 18, 30 CMR 18. There, an accused officer had
been sentenced to dismissal and forfeiture of all pay and allowances.
In his action, the convening authority approved the sentence but, in
view of the accused's prior good record and his apparently sincere
repentance, recommended that the dismissal be commuted to an administrative discharge under conditions other than honorable. We

found the action ambiguous. It was arguable either that the convening authority had found the dismissal appropriate and recommended a change in its characterization to a class with which he was not empowered to deal or that he had found a punitive separation inappropriate but was unaware of his authority to lessen its severity under United States v Russo, supra. Accordingly, we ordered the record of trial returned for a new review and action in light of the Russo case.

The last opinion in which we had occasion to concern ourselves with this problem is United States v Christensen, supra. There, an officer was sentenced to be reprimanded and suspended from rank for twelve months. In acting on the record, the convening authority affirmed the reprimand but changed the suspension from rank for twelve months to forfeiture of $25.00 per month for a like period. The board of review affirmed. Upon certification to this Court, Judge Latimer, in a lengthy opinion, set forth his views and ultimately concluded that the sentence approved by the convening authority was a permissible alternative to that adjudged by the court-martial. For a variety of reasons, which need not be accorded post hoc treatment here, the Chief Judge and I disassociated ourselves from our brother's rationale and concurred only in the disposition which his opinion ordered.

From the foregoing cases, a number of principles helpful to the resolution of the issue before us may be gleaned. First, and most importantly, we have consistently emphasized that we here deal with the power of the convening authority and the board of review to make a determination regarding the appropriateness of a particular sentence with due regard to the accused and the crimes of which he has been convicted. Congress did not think it wise to attach labels to this process, for attempts so to classify changes in sentences tend to bring into play technical niceties and narrowly based distinctions which are completely at odds with the legislative intent to have the sentence reassessed at various levels until it fits the particular offender. In short, Congress desired intermediate appellate authorities to look again at the penalty adjudged and reduce the severity of its impact until it was deemed appropriate. Code, supra, Articles 64, 66.

Secondly, in both Russo, supra, and in Plummer, supra, the sentence was one which, if deemed inappropriate, could not be reduced in kind. Accordingly, the appellate authorities were apparently faced with the choice of either approving the punishment which had been adjudged or indulging in the rarely seen process of disapproving the entire penalty. Cf. United States v Speller, 8 USCMA 363, 24 CMR 173, and United States v Atkins, 8 USCMA 77, 23 CMR 301. The decisions in the cited cases merely pointed out that Congress had afforded a broader choice of alternatives. Compare United States v Sippel, 4 USCMA 50, 15 CMR 50, and United States v Kelley, 5 USCMA 259, 17 CMR 259.

Thirdly, in each case, it had been determined below, or was at least left in doubt, that the sentence adjudged was inappropriate for the accused and his offenses.

Finally, in each case, it was clearly indicated that the convening authority and the board of review, in taking such action with respect to the sentence, must thereby lessen its severity. It is axiomatic that exercise of appellate authority on the sentence may not increase its impact and if the change in form of penalty is to be equally damaging, it would follow that there was no need to alter the sentence, for that adjudged would logically be as appropriate as that sought to be imposed on appeal. In short, neither the convening authority nor the board of review may change the nature of a penalty merely because that sought to be approved is administratively more convenient than that imposed by the court-martial. Thus, it may appear desirable to a convening authority to convert an adjudged sentence which did not extend to a punitive discharge into one which effects such a separation rather than either to retain an accused in confinement for a lengthy period or to invoke separate administrative discharge proceedings. That he may not so combine his judicial and administrative authority scarcely requires extended citation of authority. See United States v Simpson, 10 USCMA 229, 27 CMR 303, and United States v Armbruster, 11 USCMA 596, 29 CMR 412.

With these guidelines in mind we turn to the certified question. At the outset, it is apparent there are several reasons for agreeing with the conclusion of the board of review. Thus, we note that the convening authority found the adjudged punishment appropriate but nevertheless changed its nature because it seemed more convenient for the service to have accused punitively separated. We also call attention to the fact that the sentence to confinement and forfeitures, here found to be appropriate, might have been reduced in kind in order to lessen its severity. Putting these factors to one side, however, we prefer to approach the problem principally from the standpoint taken by the board.

The board of review reasoned that a convening authority might not commute a sentence from confinement and forfeitures to a bad-conduct discharge because so to act would permit circumvention of 10 USC §3811, which commands that:

> "(b)  No enlisted member of the Army may be discharged before his term of service expires, except--
>      (1)  as prescribed by the Secretary of the Army;
>      (2)  by sentence of a general or special court-martial; or
>      (3)  as otherwise provided by law."

We agree with the board's rationale. The statute in question expressly and unequivocally prohibits the discharge of individual members of the Army except by affirmative action of certain authorities. Provision is made for such action "by sentence of a general or special court-martial." This obviously and directly refers to the adjudication of punitive discharges, the only sort of separations which may form a part of military sentences. United States v Phipps, 12 USCMA 14, 30 CMR 14. The only meaning which we can draw from the explicit language of the statute is that, in order to be a valid penalty, the sentence itself must expressly include direction of the discharge. And, as we have many times noted,

> ". . . If the words used in the statute convey a clear and definite meaning, a court has no right to look for or to impose a different meaning. . . . 'a plain and unambiguous statute is to be applied, and not interpreted, since such a statute speaks for itself, and any attempt to make it clear is a vain labor and tends only to obscurity.'"
> [United States v Dickenson, 6 USCMA 438, 449, 20 CMR 154, 165.]

See also United States v Hicks, 6 USCMA 621, 20 CMR 337.

Nor does it appear that our decisions in United States v Russo, supra, and United States v Bigger, 2 USCMA 297, 8 CMR 97, are inconsistent with the application of the statute's prohibitory language to the situation before us. In both cases, the accused were sentenced to be put to death. While nothing was said about dishonorable or bad-conduct discharge, it is quite obvious that every legal and appropriate punishment is included within the supreme penalty. Thus, when the board of review acted in the Bigger case to affirm findings of guilty of unpremeditated murder and a sentence which included a dishonorable discharge, it did no more than to approve a lesser included penalty just as it might have, in an appropriate case, reduced an expressly adjudged dishonorable discharge to a bad-conduct discharge. Our interpretation of Code, supra, Article 66, expressly recognized and accorded effect to this principle by reference to the Bigger opinion and adoption of the position taken by the Chief Judge in United States v Goodwin, 5 USCMA 647, 18 CMR 271. We are convinced, therefore, that these holdings offer no impediment to our adoption of the position taken by the board of review in this case.

Unlike the death penalty, it should be equally clear that a sentence to confinement at hard labor and forfeitures does not, by implication, include a punitive discharge to which the penalty might be reduced. The truth of this proposition may be demonstrated by a comparison of the two latter punishments--a process which inevitably leads to the conclusion that the dishonorable or bad-conduct discharge may not be so classified.

Confinement at hard labor involves placing a military accused under physical restraint in a designated facility and there requiring him to perform such tasks as may be lawfully assigned. Code, supra,

Articles 9, 58, 10 USC §§809, 858; United States v Dunn, 9 USCMA
388, 26 CMR 168. When the accused's term of imprisonment is over,
he is entitled to be returned to duty with his armed service, unless,
of course, it has in the meantime ended his military status administratively. Indeed, it is the purpose of the Army's fine disciplinary
barracks system to use confinement in such a way that, where possible, the prisoner is restored to society as one willing and able to
abide by its mores. See, generally, Herrod, The United States Disciplinary Barracks System, Military Law Review, April 1960 (Department of the Army Pamphlet 27-100-8), pages 35, 36.

Further, it is certain that the damage visited upon an accused
by a sentence to confinement may not involve the serious consequences
of a punitive discharge. As we have on occasion noted, a bad-conduct
discharge affects entitlement to those benefits which a grateful nation
has made available to individuals who have served it honorably.
United States v Quesinberry, 12 USCMA 609, 31 CMR 195. And see
Lerner, Effect of Character of Discharge and Length of Service on
Eligibility to Veterans' Benefits, Military Law Review, July 1961
(Department of the Army Pamphlet 27-100-13), page 121. Moreover,
the ineradicable stigma of a punitive discharge is commonly recognized by our modern society, and the repugnance with which it is regarded is evidenced by the limitations which it places on employment
opportunities and other advantages which are enjoyed by one whose
discharge characterization indicates he has been a good and faithful
servant. Indeed, we have implicitly recognized that its burden may
exceed that of confinement to the extent that we have approved an
instruction which permitted a court-martial on rehearing to adjudge
this physical restraint in lieu of a former sentence to a bad-conduct
discharge. United States v. Smith, 12 USCMA 595, 31 CMR 181. And
it was noted by the late Judge BROSMAN, in United States v. Kelley,
supra, at page 264, that:

> ". . . Viewed realistically and practically, I doubt
> that scarcely any punishment is more severe than a puni-
> tive discharge."

We agree that a punitive discharge is a severe punishment, and
we are reinforced in our conclusion by the attitude of the Congress
through the postwar years. It has demonstrated uncommon concern
for punishments extending to dishonorable or bad-conduct discharges.
Thus, aside from judicial review under the Code, it has provided administrative machinery in the form of discharge review boards and
boards for the correction of military and naval records to insure
that these iniquitous penalties receive continuing and unremitting
attention. 10 USC §§1552, 1553. This, and the other considerations
outlined above, indicate the propriety of our belief that punitive discharges are not lesser included in confinement and forfeitures.

In sum, then, we hold that the board of review properly decided that the convening authority's action was illegal. We emphasize particularly the fact that he had before him a sentence which he, in fact, found appropriate, but which, if inappropriate in amount, could have been reduced in kind. Thus, it would clearly appear that his resort to a change in the nature of the sentence overreached the scope of Code, supra, Article 64. United States v Russo, supra; United States v Plummer, supra. More importantly, however, the sentence which he approved contravened 10 USC §3811, supra, and his action, therefore, went beyond his judicial authority.

The certified question is answered in the affirmative, and the decision of the board of review is affirmed.

Chief Judge QUINN and Judge KILDAY concur.

The Court of Military Review (formerly board of review) may "commute" a bad conduct discharge to confinement at hard labor for three months (U.S. v. Prow, 13 USCMA 63, 32 CMR 63 [1962]). On a rehearing, the military judge must instruct the members of a court-martial that they may substitute confinement at hard labor and forfeitures for a previously adjudged punitive discharge (U.S. v. Smith, 12 USCMA 595, 31 CMR 181 [1961]). On "commutation" by the convening authority, see U.S. v. Brown, 13 USCMA 333, 32 CMR 333 (1962); and U.S. v. Brousseau, 13 USCMA 624, 33 CMR 156 (1963).

Although an accused may be found guilty of two or more offenses arising out of the same act, if each offense requires proof of an additional fact that the other does not, the offenses may be held multiplicious for sentencing purposes and the accused may only be sentenced to the maximum punishment for the major offense. See U.S. v. McVey, 4 USCMA 167, 15 CMR 167 (1954); U.S. v. Brown, 8 USCMA 18, 23 CMR 242 (1957); and U.S. v. Gibbons, 11 USCMA 246, 29 CMR 62 (1960).

A law officer [military judge] must tailor his instruction on sentence to the law and the evidence just as in the case of prefindings advice; an instruction solely setting forth the maximum imposable sentence is prejudicial error (U.S. v. Wheeler, 17 USCMA 274, 38 CMR 72 [1967]).

Article 58(a), UCMJ, requires that an enlisted man be reduced to the lowest pay grade if his approved sentence by court-martial includes a punitive discharge, confinement, or hard labor without confinement. Military judges should instruct a court-martial before sentencing concerning the effect of this article; if a court-martial adjudges reduction to an intermediate pay grade and confinement, the confinement portion of the sentence must be disapproved (see U.S. v. Koleff, 16 USCMA 268, 36 CMR 424 [1966]).

Article 57(d), UCMJ, permits a general court-martial convening authority to defer service of a sentence to confinement; the deferment may be rescinded at any time by the officer who granted it or by the officer then exercising general court-martial jurisdiction over him. In Collier v. U.S., 19 USCMA 511, 42 CMR 113 (1970), the Court of Military Appeals held that the convening authority abused his discretion when he rescinded a deferment granted by another commander.

All courts-martial receive an automatic review; no request or other action by the accused is necessary. The following chart summarizes the provisions of the UCMJ and the MCM concerning review of different types of courts-martial.

## INITIAL REVIEW

Not all error constitutes reversible error; corrective action is necessary only when on the basis of the entire record the rights of the accused have been materially prejudiced. See U.S. v. Lee, 1 USCMA 212, 2 CMR 118 (1952).

# BRIEF SUMMARY OF REVIEW OF COURTS-MARTIAL

| | Summary | Special | Special (BCD Adjudged) | General |
|---|---|---|---|---|
| Action by Convening Authority | Complete discretion to approve only such findings of guilty and sentence as correct in law and fact (Art. 64). | | | Same, but must first obtain written opinion of Staff Judge Advocate (Art. 61; note para. 85c, MCM). |
| Review by Supervisory Authority (officer exercising GCM jurisdiction) | Final review by SJA (Art. 65). Complete discretion (Para. 94, MCM). | As outlined for GCMs above (Art. 65). | | (Not applicable) |
| Court of Military Review (Board of Review) | | | Reviews all cases in which sentence affects a general or flag officer or extends to death, dismissal, dishonorable discharge, bad conduct discharge, or confinement for one year or more. Limited discretionary review (Art. 66). | |
| The Judge Advocate General | Possible action on stated grounds in Article 69. | | Examines all other GCM cases, if legal error found or at his discretion, may refer to Court of Military Review (Art. 69). | |
| Court of Military Appeals | | | Reviews all cases in which sentence affects a general or flag officer or extends to death, cases reviewed by CMR and sent by TJAG, and cases upon petition of accused. Review only as to matters of law (Art. 67). | |

## UNITED STATES v. GRICE

United States Court of Military Appeals, 1957.
8 U.S.C.M.A. 166, 23 C.M.R. 390.

HOMER FERGUSON, Judge:
The accused, despite his plea of not guilty, was convicted by general court-martial of conspiracy to commit larceny and larceny, in violation of Articles 81 and 121, Uniform Code of Military Justice, 10 USC §§881 and 921, respectively. He was sentenced to be dishonorably discharged from the service, to forfeit all pay and allowances, and to be confined at hard labor for one year. The convening authority approved the findings and the sentence, but suspended the execution of the dishonorable discharge until the accused's release from confinement or until completion of appellate review, whichever occurs later. The convening authority ordered the unsuspended portion of the sentence executed. The board of review set aside that portion of the convening authority's action that ordered immediate execution of the sentence as violative of the provisions of Article 71 (c), Uniform Code of Military Justice, 10 USC §871, but otherwise approved the findings of guilty and the sentence as correct in law and fact.

The sole issue presented on this appeal is whether the advice of the staff judge advocate to the convening authority in the post-trial review--wherein an allegedly incorrect standard for measuring the sufficiency of the evidence was applied--deprived the accused of his right to a legally correct review of his case at the level of the convening authority.

It is not essential to the determination of this issue that a full recital of the facts be set forth. It will suffice to say that the sole issue at trial concerned whether the accused was involved in the alleged larceny and conspiracy. Testifying in his own behalf, he denied complicity in the crimes despite the assertions of two Korean conspirators who sought to implicate him. The court-martial, however, chose to disbelieve the accused and found him guilty as charged. The staff judge advocate, in his post-trial review, after summarizing the testimony adduced in behalf of both the prosecution and the defense, advised the convening authority under the separate section heading "Sufficiency of the evidence" as follows:

"The fact that the alleged larceny occurred was not contested; the sole issue in the case was whether or not the accused was involved. This issue could be resolved only by a comparison of the credibility of the witnesses, Kang and Mike, with the credibility of the accused. Since that issue was resolved against the accused by the court who observed the demeanor of all witnesses and heard all the evidence first-hand, the under-signed may not disagree with that decision.  There is sufficient evidence in the record of trial to sustain the findings of guilty." [Emphasis supplied.]

It is the italicized portion of this advice which gives rise to the issue presently before us.  Appellate defense counsel contend that this advice of the staff judge advocate erroneously informed the con-vening authority that he was bound by the findings of the court-martial. The Government, on the other hand, argues that the advice cannot be construed as having informed the convening authority that he was pre-cluded from making an independent determination of the sufficiency of the evidence.

. . .

In pursuing the advisory function set forth in Article 61, supra, it is incumbent upon the staff judge advocate to apply the same legal standards that would be employed by the convening authority in deter-mining a given legal problem.  A staff judge advocate has no command authority and no test is to be applied by him except in his capacity as legal adviser to the commander.  His advice, therefore, must utilize the standards that the commander himself would use.

. . .

The advice given in this case is unambiguous.  The staff judge advocate stated that he was bound by the findings of the court-martial on questions of fact.  The convening authority, however, is not so limited and since the staff judge advocate has no authority or function but to advise his commander, we believe the advice was tantamount to informing the commander that he also was bound by the findings of the court-martial.  While it is true that the convening authority should generally recognize that "the trial court saw and heard the witness" it is equally true that he is empowered and required to judge the credibility of witnesses, determine controverted questions of fact, and otherwise apply the trial level test of sufficiency rather than the more restrictive test reserved to appellate tribunals.  He must be satisfied in his action that the accused is guilty beyond a reasonable doubt.

. . . We disagree with the board of review's conclusion in this case that the staff judge advocate was merely saying that he per-sonally saw no reason to disagree with the court-martial's findings. He not only has failed to fulfill his function as imposed by the Code and detailed by the Manual, but he has couched his "opinion" in terms of mandatory compliance with the court-martial's findings of facts. The staff judge advocate does not say that he doesn't disagree with the court-martial.  He says specifically and unambiguously that he "may not disagree."  This was error.

We are not unmindful of the fact that a convening authority may completely disregard the advice of his staff judge advocate.  Paragraph

85c, Manual for Courts-Martial, supra, however, provides that the convening authority should "ordinarily" accept the opinion of a staff judge advocate on questions respecting the inadequacy of the evidence. In the case at bar the convening authority did not disregard the advice of his staff judge advocate. Our problem then resolves to this: Did there exist a fair risk that the convening authority's action was prompted by reliance upon the erroneous advice of his legal adviser? We believe such a fair risk existed. United States v Doherty, 5 USCMA 287, 17 CMR 287.

Since the staff judge advocate considered himself bound by the court-martial's findings, we conclude that the convening authority also considered himself bound. To hold otherwise would, in the language of the Greenwalt case, supra, "ignore the practicalities of the situation." In United States v Schuller, 5 USCMA 101, 17 CMR 101, we had occasion to discuss the duties of a staff judge advocate with respect to the pretrial advice and in the course of our opinion we said:

> "We recognize that, under Article 34, the convening authority, not the Staff Judge Advocate, actually makes the final decisions as to whether the expected evidence is sufficient to support the charges, and whether they should be referred to trial. . . . Our interest is in the fact that the convening authority was given an advice which purported to show a legal evaluation of the sufficiency of the evidence. If we presume regularity, we cannot doubt that his decision to refer the charges to trial was substantially influenced by the advice of his Staff Judge Advocate. Yet, that advice was not based upon any examination of the evidence. Essentially, therefore, the convening authority himself did not make a proper determination of the sufficiency of the evidence."

This reasoning applicable to the pretrial advice is equally valid with regard to the post-trial review.

In view of what we have said, we conclude that as a result of the staff judge advocate's erroneous advice, the accused has not received that legally correct review of his case at the convening authority level that he is guaranteed by the Uniform Code of Military Justice and the Manual for Courts-Martial, supra. The decision of the board of review is reversed. In United States v Papciak, 7 USCMA 412, 22 CMR 202, we said that the officer to whom the record must be returned for corrective action in situations of this nature "should necessarily be determined by the particular facts of the case." Here, we feel it is perfectly proper to return the case to the same convening authority, who will refer the record to his staff judge advocate for further review in accordance with the principles expressed in this opinion.

Chief Judge QUINN concurs.

LATIMER, Judge (dissenting):
I dissent.

I dissent from the result reached by my associates in the opinion of the Court and, if they are branching out into the fields of staff concepts, I disassociate myself from the view that, because a legal officer does not have command responsibility, he must measure a record of trial by the standards of his commander. Such a concept overlooks entirely the relationship between the commander and his legal consultant. While the superior can set generally the manner in which he desires his counselor to perform, the former does not expect the latter to cut all the cloth by his measurements for, if he did, he would find little use for his adviser on the law. Commanders vary in their method of operation, and one convening authority may want his expert on the Code to limit his advice to legalistic concepts, leaving to the commander the responsibility of making all final decisions required by law, regulation, and customs of the service. If the commander operates in that manner, the staff judge advocate must confine his reviews within the minimum requirements of the Code and the Manual. On the other hand, a commander may operate in such a way that he may allow his legal subordinates much greater latitude and solicit help and advice on matters which go far beyond strictly legal limits. In that event, the legal expert may expand his views and offer helpful recommendations in many areas. However, regardless of the manner of operation used by the convening authority, it has always been my belief that, to be of any value as an adviser, a legal officer's recommendations must be based on his own judgment and not on any yardstick carved out by his immediate superior. And I believe that was the concept envisioned by Congress and the President when they enacted the Code and promulgated the Manual.
. . .

In the case at bar, the reporting staff officer chose one method of setting out his recommendations and the reasons underlying them, and the Court finds fault with his manner of approach. I take the opposite view, for I find nothing wrong with a staff judge advocate writing like a lawyer, using legal standards to measure the record, and freely expressing his opinion as to why he--not the convening authority--would affirm or reverse a conviction or lessen the punishment. Part of the difficulty I encounter in finding prejudice in post-trial reviews is that the words and phrases found in a staff judge advocate's review are merely advisory and they are considered by the commander as such. They seldom, if ever, reflect the thought and consideration given to the case by the officer who has the authority to act. Therefore, I see no good reason to interpret the language used with such rigidity that all common sense is forced out. Nor do I find any justification for treating the review as a verbatim transcript of all that transpires between the commander and his staff consultant. There are such things as personal conferences, and I am reasonably certain that most commanders converse frequently with their legal advisers on general court-martial convictions and that many matters not appearing in the reviews or not fully developed therein are discussed informally. Sometimes there is unanimity of opinion between the two on both the law and the facts, while in other instances there may be disagreement on either or both; but if a legal counselor must obtain the guideposts for his review from his superior, there is little chance for an objective opinion. Perhaps I can rephrase the old adage by saying that two heads are no better than one if they are compelled to read the record with the same pair of spectacles.

. . .

## UNITED STATES v. DEAN

United States Court of Military Appeals, 1957.
7 U.S.C.M.A. 721, 23 C.M.R. 185.

ROBERT E. QUINN, Chief Judge:
This appeal brings up for review an important question of post-trial procedure. The accused was convicted of rape, in violation of Article 120, Uniform Code of Military Justice, 10 USC §920, and sentenced to a dishonorable discharge, total forfeitures, and confinement at hard labor for twenty years. However, the convening authority approved only findings of guilty of assault with intent to commit rape, in violation of Article 134, Uniform Code, 10 USC §934, and reduced the period of confinement to two years. At the same time he suspended the execution of the discharge. A board of review set aside his action because he had referred to matter outside the record of trial. The board of review noted that the extra-hearing matter induced the convening authority to disapprove the findings of guilty of the offense charged, but "reinforce[d] the . . . evidence that accused was guilty" of the lesser offense. It directed that the convening authority withdraw his action and forward the case to a different court-martial authority for a new review.

On the second review, the Staff Judge Advocate reasoned that the new reviewing authority "should not approve findings or sentence more severe than those approved" by the original convening authority. His reasoning was rejected by the reviewing authority. Without stating his reasons in a separate letter, as required by paragraph 85, Manual for Courts-Martial, United States, 1951, he affirmed the court-martial's finding of rape. He also approved a sentence which did not provide for suspension of the discharge, and which included confinement at hard labor for five years. A board of review affirmed his action, but, in the exercise of its appellate power, reduced the confinement to two years. We granted review to consider whether the second action taken by the reviewing authority was legally correct.

Article 64 of the Uniform Code, 10 USC §864, defines the power of the convening authority in reviewing a conviction. He can "approve only such findings of guilty, and the sentence . . . as he finds correct in law and fact and as he in his discretion determines should be approved." (Emphasis supplied.) In analyzing the limits of this grant of power, we must distinguish between action approving a conviction and that which disapproves the results of the court-martial. As far as the former is concerned, the reviewing authority is not unrestrained. He cannot, for example, approve a conviction on the basis of evidence outside the record of trial, United States v Duffy, 3 USCMA 20, 11 CMR 20; nor can he approve the sentence on the basis of a predetermined and fixed policy. United States v Wise, 6 USCMA 472, 20 CMR 188. However, in disapproving a finding or a sentence, the convening authority is not confined to the record of trial. Instead, he can properly consider matter outside the record of proceedings in regard to the findings, United States v Massey, 5 USCMA 514, 18 CMR 138, and in connection with the sentence, United States v Lanford, 6 USCMA 371, 20 CMR 87. Whether in disapproving findings of guilty or a sentence, in whole or in part, he exercises his discretion wisely or ineptly cannot be questioned by a subsequent reviewing authority. As we said in United States v McDaniel, 7 USCMA 56, 58 21 CMR 182, subsequent reviewing authorities are "limited by the convening authority's action on the findings and the sentence." Earlier, in United States v Massey, supra, page 520, we had occasion to consider the Congressional hearings on the subject, and we pointed out that the draftsmen of the Uniform Code intended to confer upon the convening authority the right to disapprove the accused's conviction "for no reason at all."

Although the principle is different in several states, in the Federal criminal procedure, if an accused appeals his conviction and obtains an order or reversal and rehearing from the appellate tribunal, at the rehearing he is subject to trial and punishment upon the same basis as though the first trial had not been had. The reason for the rule is explained in Trono v United States, 199 US 521, 533-534, 50 L ed 292, 26 S Ct 121, as follows:

"In our opinion the better doctrine is that which does not limit the court or jury, upon a new trial, to a consideration of the question of guilt of the lower offense of which the accused was convicted on the first trial, but that the reversal of the judgment of conviction opens up the whole controversy, and acts upon the original judgment as if it had never been. The accused, by his own action, has obtained a reversal of the whole judgment, and we see no reason why he should not, upon a new trial, be proceeded against as if no trial had previously taken place.

> ". . . When, at his own request, he has obtained a
> new trial, he must take the burden with the benefit, and
> go back for a new trial of the whole case." [See also
> Green v United States, 236 F 2d 708 (CA DC Cir) (1956);
> cert granted 352 US 915, 1 L ed2d 122, 77 S Ct 217
> (1956).]

In the absence of any jurisdictional issue (see United States v Ban-
croft, 3 USCMA 3, 11 CMR 3; United States v Padilla, 1 USCMA 603,
5 CMR 31) the Trono rule does not apply in the military. Under the
Uniform Code a court-martial is expressly bound by the findings and
the sentence of the first trial. Article 63(b), Uniform Code of Military Justice, 10 USC §863. In United States v King, 5 USCMA 3, 8,
17 CMR 3, a majority of this Court held that the same restriction
applies in regard to the convening authority's action. As we have
already noted, the convening authority has absolute discretion in
approving or disapproving findings of guilty by the court-martial and
in modifying the adjudged sentence. His action, therefore, fixes the
limits of both the findings of guilty and the sentence in all subsequent
proceedings in the case. This holding is consonant with two general
principles applicable to military criminal law.

First, Congress intended that the review of the convening authority's action by appellate bodies be for the benefit of the accused. . . .

The second principle is that a well-settled administrative interpretation of an existing statute can be read into a re-enactment of that
statute. See United States v Butts, 7 USCMA 472, 22 CMR 262. Article 63(b) of the Uniform Code, which limits the court-martial's authority on a rehearing, is phrased almost in identical language with
Article of War 50-1/2 and Article of War 52, its predecessors. These
latter statutes were interpreted by service boards of review for almost
fifteen years before the enactment of the Uniform Code. . . .

. . .

The decision of the board of review is reversed. The findings
of guilty and the sentence are set aside. In accordance with our general practice of referring a case back to the level of proceedings at
which the error occurred (United States v Clisson, 5 USCMA 277, 17
CMR 277), we return the record of trial to The Judge Advocate General for reference to another competent court-martial authority for
proceedings consistent with this opinion.

Judge FERGUSON concurs.

[Dissenting opinion of Judge Latimer omitted.]

UNITED STATES v. GRIFFIN

United States Court of Military Appeals, 1957.
8 U.S.C.M.A. 206, 24 C.M.R. 16.

ROBERT E. QUINN, Chief Judge:

The accused was convicted of two specifications of unauthorized absence, one of which was almost two months in duration, and of a failure to obey a lawful order. Considering two previous convictions, including one for desertion, the court-martial adjudged a sentence of dishonorable discharge, total forfeitures, and confinement at hard labor for 2-1/2 years. In reviewing the case the convening authority's Staff Legal Officer referred to "other facts concerning the accused's absence" which he found in the record of trial of another Marine. These purported "facts" were contained in testimony of the accused in the other case and were of a derogatory nature. The staff legal officer concluded that he could find nothing "on which to base a recommendation for clemency." Accordingly, he recommended approval of the sentence, and the recommendation was accepted by the convening authority.

When the case came before the board of review, appellate defense counsel contended that the accused was prejudiced by the failure of the convening authority to accord him an opportunity to rebut the extra-record derogatory matter, and that the sentence was excessive and inordinately severe. "Proceeding on the basis" that error had been committed by the convening authority, the board of review re-evaluated the sentence upon the record and without regard to "that portion of the statement of the legal officer complained of here." It concluded that the period of confinement was too severe and that a dishonorable discharge was "not in keeping with the nature of the offenses of which the accused" was convicted. The board of review, therefore, mitigated the dishonorable discharge to a bad-conduct discharge and reduced the period of confinement by nine months. The accused now contends that the board of review could not itself cure the error, but was required to order a new post-trial review.

Unquestionably, it was error for the convening authority to consider, in his deliberations on the sentence, adverse matter from outside the record without affording the accused an opportunity to rebut or explain that matter. United States v Lanford, 6 USCMA 371, 20 CMR 87. How to cure this error in the sentence is another problem. The answer depends upon the facts in the particular case. Sometimes error can best be cured by returning the case to the level of proceedings at which the error occurred; in other instances, the reviewing authority, by the exercise of its own powers, can effectively eliminate the harmful consequences of the error in earlier proceedings. See Feld, A Manual of Courts-Martial Practice and Appeal,

§§95, 113, 147 (1957). For example, an erroneous instruction on the
limits of the sentence can sometimes be cured by the board of review
by reassessing the sentence in the light of the error; other times
what is required is a rehearing by the court-martial. Cf. United
States v Reiner, 8 USCMA 101, 23 CMR 325; United States v Oakley,
7 USCMA 733, 23 CMR 197. A similar balance of factors exists when
the reviewing authority sets aside one or more of a number of findings of guilty. The critical inquiry is whether justice to the accused
requires redetermination of the sentence by the "primary" authority.
United States v Kowert, 7 USCMA 678, 23 CMR 142.

   At all times the paramount consideration is to do justice to the
accused. As we pointed out in United States v Papciak, 7 USCMA 412,
416, 22 CMR 202, in another, but related, connection, the reviewing
authority must consider whether "a new start as it were--is important
to an equitable and fair administration of justice." But that principle
cannot be applied with slide rule exactitude. There is, and necessarily must be, an area of discretion in a matter of this kind. United
States v Stene, 7 USCMA 277, 22 CMR 67.

   After careful review of the nature of the extra-record evidence
and considering all the other evidence relating to the sentence, we
conclude that the board of review properly corrected the error here,
making it unnecessary to return the case to the convening authority.
Cf. United States v Atkins, 8 USCMA 77, 23 CMR 301. United States
v Papciak, supra. Accordingly, we affirm the decision of the board
of review.

   [Concurring opinion of Judge Ferguson omitted; Judge Latimer
concurred in the result without opinion.]

   A convening authority may suspend the execution of any sentence except a death sentence (Article 71[d], UCMJ). If a convening
authority suspends a special court-martial sentence that includes a
bad conduct discharge or any general court-martial sentence, such
action automatically creates a status of probation that may not be
altered except as provided in Article 72, UCMJ; i.e., by a hearing
held by the special court-martial convening authority having jurisdiction over the accused. U.S. v. May, 10 USCMA 358; 27 CMR 432
(1959).

## COURTS OF MILITARY REVIEW

A Court of Military Review, composed of one or more panels, has been established by each Judge Advocate General pursuant to the amended Article 66, UCMJ. These courts have assumed the powers formerly exercised by "boards of review" and any references concerning those powers would appear to be applicable to the Courts of Military Review.

UNITED STATES v. LANFORD

United States Court of Military Appeals, 1955.
6 U.S.C.M.A. 371, 20 C.M.R. 87.

ROBERT E. QUINN, Chief Judge:

This case raises novel and important questions relating to appellate review of the sentence adjudged by a court-martial.

On December 1, 1954, the accused was arraigned before a special court-martial on a charge alleging an unauthorized absence of approximately eleven hours. He pleaded guilty and was convicted. During the sentence procedure, trial counsel read the service data from the charge sheet and introduced evidence of two previous convictions. Both convictions were by a summary court-martial. The first was for a two day absence without leave in 1952, and the second for a nineteen hour absence without leave in May 1954.

In mitigation, the accused made a brief sworn statement in which he explained that he was in a "little fight" the evening before his present absence. The civilian police locked him up for the night. On his release the next morning, he returned to his station as speedily as possible. Additionally, defense counsel asserted that the accused had been restricted for eight days before the trial, and that he was serving his second enlistment.

The accused was sentenced to a bad-conduct discharge and to confinement at hard labor for one month. Two days later the convening authority approved the sentence. However, he also provided for suspension of the execution of the discharge and for automatic remission at the end of the period of confinement and five months thereafter. Included in his formal action is a statement that in "approving the sentence . . . the convening authority has also considered the entire service record of the accused." The statement is followed by a recital of certain entries from various sections of the accused's service record. These show that the accused served on the USS Iowa when it was commended for high morale and devotion to duty during bombardments of enemy coastal transportation and supply lines in Korea, and that the accused was eligible for the United Nations Service Medal and Korean Service Medal with one Bronze Star. Also set out is a list of nine nonjudicial punishments imposed upon the accused during the period from February 1951 to July 1954, a period within the accused's current enlistment.

All the matter in the convening authority's action was apparently noted in compliance with a directive from the Chief of Naval Personnel. BUPERS Instruction 1626.13, October 7, 1954. . . .

After the convening authority completed his action, the case was forwarded under Article 66(b), Uniform Code of Military Justice, 50 USC §653, to the officer exercising general court-martial jurisdiction. It appears that while the latter had the case, the accused submitted an affidavit for consideration with the record. In it the accused asserts that his trial testimony about a "little fight" was misleading since "no blows actually were struck." The accused again emphasized that he was released by the civilian authorities without trial or bond. The affidavit appears at the end of the trial exhibits. See Manual for Courts-Martial, United States, 1951, Appendix 10b, page 535. On December 19, 1954, the general court-martial authority approved the sentence and forwarded the case for review in accordance with the provisions of Article 66, supra.

In due course, the case was referred to a board of review in the office of The Judge Advocate General of the Navy. There, appellate defense counsel moved to strike from the record the references to nonjudicial punishment which were set out in the convening authority's action. The motion was denied. However, the board of review held that it could not, and would not, consider the additional information in its deliberation on the sentence. It concluded that, on the basis of the offense charged and the character of the two previous convictions admitted into evidence, a punitive discharge was inappropriate. Accordingly, the board of review affirmed only so much of the sentence as provided for confinement. One member of the board concurred in the result. In a separate opinion, he said that the board of review not only could, but should, consider the supplemental matter in the convening authority's action, which he described as being of "invaluable assistance." He also said that a board of review can reduce a sentence as an "act of grace," that is, as an act of clemency. . . .

The accused's argument is based upon the contention that the supplemental matter relating to the sentence which is considered by the convening authority cannot properly be reviewed by the board of review. And if the allegedly improper matter should come before the board of review, it would necessarily prejudice the board against the accused. See: United States v Steber, 6-54-S-1273, February 15, 1955.

These contentions bring us to the other certified questions. In combination, they concern the authority of the board of review to consider the convening authority's synopsis of the information taken from the accused's service record. The questions are as follows:

"(1) Was the action of the Board of Review correct in denying the defense motion to strike from the convening authority's action all references to non-judicial punishments previously imposed upon the accused?

"(2) If (1) above is answered in the affirmative, should the Board of Review have considered all of the matter contained in the said synopsis in its determination of the appropriateness of the sentence?

"(3) Is a Board of Review authorized to exercise clemency, and if so, to what extent?

"(4) If (3) above is answered in the affirmative, should the Board of Review consider all of the matter contained in the said synopsis in the determination of whether or not to exercise clemency?"

For purposes of military law a board of review is a judicial body, United States v Whitman, 3 USCMA 179, 11 CMR 179. It is however, the creation of Congress. It can, therefore, act only within the direct or reasonably implied scope of the powers given to it by the Uniform Code. United States v Reeves, 1 USCMA 388, 3 CMR 122; United States v Brasher, 2 USCMA 50, 6 CMR 50. The grant of authority to the board of review is found in Article 66, supra. Important here is that part of the Article which provides that the board of review shall:

". . . affirm . . . the sentence or such part or amount of the sentence, as it finds correct in law and fact and determines, on the basis of the entire record, should be approved."

Since the effective date of the Uniform Code, we have decided more than a score of cases which considered some aspect of the board of review's power over the sentence. In most instances, it was sufficient to note that the board of review has the power "to affirm so much of the sentence as it deems appropriate on the basis of the entire record." United States v Fleming, 3 USCMA 461, 465, 13 CMR 17. Generally, when we set aside a finding of guilty or affirm only a lesser included offense to that charged, we remand the case to The Judge

Advocate General for reference to a board of review for determination of an "appropriate sentence." United States v Crawford, 4 USCMA 701, 16 CMR 275; United States v Keith, 1 USCMA 442, 4 CMR 34. . . .

. . .

One of the principal matters Congress considered at the time of the enactment of the Uniform Code was the establishment of a procedure for review of the sentence which would insure a fair and just punishment for every accused. To achieve that purpose, Congress gave the convening authority the power to approve a sentence in his discretion. But it made his decision subject to review by a board of review. United States v Brasher, 2 USCMA 50, 6 CMR 50; United States v Cavallaro, 3 USCMA 653, 14 CMR 71. The name by which the board's power is denominated is really unimportant. What is important is that, within the limitations of its own authority, the board of review can, in the interests of justice, substantially lessen the rigor of a legal sentence. The board of review, therefore, can be compassionate; it can be lenient; it can be forbearing. If one prefers to call the influence of those human qualities in the mitigation of a sentence the exercise of the judicial function of determining legal appropriateness, the description is proper. Tah Do Quah v State, 62 Okla Cr 139, 70 P2d 818. On the other hand, if one wishes to call it clemency, that description also is proper. The title applied to the power matters little, so long as it is clearly understood that the law invests boards of review with the power to treat "an accused with less rigor than their authority permits." United States v Cavallaro, supra, page 655.

. . .

The accused argues that the "entire record" means merely the evidence adduced at the trial. In support of his contention, he relies upon United States v Duffy, 3 USCMA 20, 11 CMR 20. In that case, this Court held that the accused's conviction could not be sustained by the reviewing authority on the basis of evidence contained in the allied papers, but not presented at the trial. See also: United States v Whitman, 3 USCMA 179, 11 CMR 179. Undeniably, evidence not presented at the trial cannot be used to support or reverse a conviction. Both the accused and the Government are entitled to challenge the admissibility of the evidence according to accepted rules of law; and each has a right to test the trustworthiness and the probative value of proffered evidence by cross-examination, and by other evidence. Different considerations apply to the sentence.

In the first instance the sentence is fixed by the court-martial. The court, of course, will normally act on the evidence presented to it. The sentence imposed by the court is not final. It cannot be increased, but it may be mitigated by the reviewing authorities. The question then arises as to whether the interests of justice require these reviewing authorities to look no further than the trial

proceedings for facts which would justify a reduction in the sentence.
It seems to us that an accused would be the last person to urge that
rule. In any event, we think that the law is less harsh. In our opinion,
justice is fostered by giving the reviewing authorities power to go outside the record of trial for information as to the sentence. See Rule
32 (c), Federal Rules of Criminal Procedure. Its purpose is to benefit, not to harm, the accused. But what of a case like this one in which
some of the extra-trial facts militate against a reduction in the sentence? Would not consideration of these facts harm the accused by
persuading the reviewing authorities to affirm the sentence imposed
by the court-martial? The answer is necessarily "yes." But, it must
be remembered that appeal from the court-imposed sentence is a
matter of legislative grant not of inherent right. Congress might have
provided that a legal sentence adjudged by a court-martial cannot be
altered in any way by a reviewing authority. Instead, it chose to provide a procedure under which the court's sentence can be materially
reduced. This procedure insures justice; it does not defeat it. We
conclude, therefore, that, contrary to the accused's contention, the
words "entire record" mean more than the evidence presented at the
trial. In fact, previous decisions of the Court clearly indicate that a
board of review may look beyond the trial record for mitigating evidence.
. . .

In view of the language of Article 66 and the purpose and the
scope of the power given to the board of review to reassess the sentence, we believe that there should be a free interchange of facts
affecting the sentence. Certainly, Congress did not intend the sentence review to be a guessing game. Rather, it desired that the
judgment of each reviewing authority be an informed judgment; that
is, a judgment based on facts not fancy. We believe, therefore, Congress intended that, as far as possible, the board of review would have
available to it the same facts relating to the sentence which were considered by the convening authority in his action. If the accused submits nothing to the court-martial or to the convening authority, and
the staff judge advocate's review or the convening authority's action
does not contain a statement of the factors considered in evaluating
the sentence, the board of review will have little information upon
which to base its determination of the fairness of the sentence. Necessarily, it is limited to a consideration of the trial proceedings and
the provisions of paragraph 76a of the Manual for Courts-Martial.
United States v Cavallaro, supra, page 657. It seems to us to be
vastly more desirable to have a "free exchange of information between boards of review and other military authorities charged with
the responsibility of considering the appropriateness of any sentence."
United States v Cavallaro, supra. And, in our opinion, Congress intended that result. Consequently, we hold that, under Article 66, a
board of review is authorized to review as part of the "entire record"

a statement of the matters considered by the convening authority in his action on the sentence. This statement may be included in the post-trial review of the convening authority's legal officer, or in his own action, or even in a separate statement included with the allied papers. Of course, justice to the accused requires that he be given a fair and reasonable opportunity to rebut or to explain any matter which may be detrimental to him. In that connection what we said in United States v Long, 5 USCMA 572, 574, 18 CMR 196, is appropriate here:

> ". . . If an appellate agency is going to use any post-trial information as a basis for its decision, on jurisdictional matters or in any other permissible areas, each party should be afforded an opportunity to present his, or its, side of the dispute."

The certified questions are answered as indicated. Since the majority of the board of review apparently was influenced in its review of the sentence by a mistaken idea of the legal scope of its power, we remand the case to The Judge Advocate General of the Navy for submission to the board of review for reconsideration of the sentence, or for such other action as The Judge Advocate General may deem appropriate and which is consistent with this opinion. United States v Cavallaro, 3 USCMA 653, 14 CMR 71.

LATIMER, Judge (concurring):

I concur.

In considering the principles controlling this issue, I believe it well to accentuate a point made in the Chief Judge's opinion to the effect that we are resolving the rights and privileges of an accused after a finding and sentence. Some of the strict formality demanded before conviction is relaxed after an accused is convicted and his punishment imposed, and adherence to the rules of evidence is not compelled. In military law, a reviewing authority cannot add to the punishment imposed by a court-martial and so, if any change is made in the sentence, it must be scaled downward. Because of that restriction, an accused cannot be harmed legally by the convening authority, but he can, and often is, helped. His only privilege is to have the sentence re-evaluated in the light of the record and his service behavior pattern. But any favorable action taken by a reviewing officer is largely a matter of grace as, unless the sentence is legally excessive, the reviewing authority has the discretion to affirm the sentence as imposed.

. . .

BROSMAN, Judge (concurring):

I concur in the views set out in the principal opinion.

. . .

Appellate authorities are not bound by the mandatory sentence provisions of Articles of the Code; for example, a board of review may reappraise the appropriateness of a sentence to life imprisonment even though it affirms findings of guilty of premeditated murder under Article 118, which requires the court-martial to adjudge either death or life imprisonment. See U.S. v. Jefferson, 7 USCMA 193, 21 CMR 319 (1956).

Unlike a convening authority, who may disapprove findings of guilt for any reason, a board of review may only disapprove such findings as it finds incorrect in law and fact; a setting aside of a conviction solely on the basis of "substantial justice" is outside the authority of a board of review. See U.S. v. Waymire, 9 USCMA 252, 26 CMR 32 (1958).

A board of review did not abuse its discretion when it affirmed a sentence of dismissal even though at the same time it set aside the conviction for one of three specifications (U.S. v. Stene, 7 USCMA 277, 22 CMR 67 [1956]; compare U.S. v. Voorhees, 4 USCMA 509, 16 CMR 83 [1954]).

## UNITED STATES v. JUDD

United States Court of Military Appeals, 1960.
11 U.S.C.M.A. 164, 28 C.M.R. 388.

ROBERT E. QUINN, Chief Judge:
A general court-martial convicted the accused of the murder of his wife in their trailer home near Anchorage, Alaska, and imposed a sentence which included a dishonorable discharge and confinement at hard labor for twenty-five years. On review, a board of review reduced the findings of guilty to involuntary manslaughter and reassessed the sentence by reducing the period of confinement to three years. The Judge Advocate General of the Air Force certified the case to this Court to review the correctness of the board of review's action, reducing the findings of guilty. From the opinion of the board of review, we were unable to determine whether it based its decision upon new findings of fact, or upon an erroneous conception of the applicable principles of law. Accordingly, we returned the record of trial to the board of review for clarification of its action. United States v Judd, 10 USCMA 113, 27 CMR 187.

On further review, the board of review emphasized that its earlier action had been predicated upon its interpretation of the rules

of law. It affirmed the court-martial's finding of guilty of murder, and approved a sentence which includes confinement at hard labor for twenty years. The accused then petitioned this Court for review alleging eight grounds of error.
. . .

The remaining allegations of error relate to the further action of the board of review after the remand. The first allegation is to the effect that the action of the board of review on remand was "inconsistent and anomalous" with the action it took on the first review. It is contended that since the board of review said on the second review that it was basing its finding on "facts supplied by the accused," there was not "any scintilla of evidence to warrant an instruction on [Article] 118(2)." Therefore, the argument continues, the board of review was wrong when it held initially that the evidence was sufficient to support an instruction on both subsections 2 and 3 of Article 118. The argument overlooks the fact that the amount of evidence required to raise an issue for instruction purposes is less than the amount of evidence required to support a finding of guilty. There may be enough evidence to require an instruction, yet not enough to justify affirmance of a conviction of guilt beyond a reasonable doubt. The board of review held that the evidence was not sufficient to support a finding of guilty of subsection 2. As a result, errors that may have been committed by the admission of evidence tending to support a conviction of that offense, which seems to be the accused's real complaint, were eliminated as a basis for further review, and the board of review acted properly in choosing to pass over a discussion of them. See United States v McCluskey, 6 USCMA 545, 20 CMR 261; United States v Reese, 5 USCMA 560, 18 CMR 184.

Next, the accused contends the board of review erred by failing to obey the mandate of this Court. We returned the record of trial to the board of review indicating we were not sure of the grounds upon which it based its holding reducing the findings of guilty from murder to involuntary manslaughter. United States v Judd, supra, page 119. We noted that if the findings were predicated upon the erroneous principles of law announced in the opinion, the board of review was wrong in its conclusion; but if the finding was based upon a factual determination, the board of review was "legally and properly within . . . [its] province." The accused maintains that on remand, the board of review did not define the basis for its initial action but merely proceeded to hold what this Court had already determined, namely, that as a matter of law it was sufficient to support a finding of guilty of murder under subsection (3) of Article 118. We do not so read the board of review's decision upon further review. The board of review expressly refers to our mandate, and then proceeds to enumerate the findings of fact it made in its previous review. These "former finding[s] of fact," the decision observes, establish, under the principles announced in our opinion on remand, that the accused was guilty of a violation of Article 118(3). All that the board of review did, was to reaffirm, as it was bound to do, the findings of fact it had previously made. These, the board pointed out, establish the accused's guilt beyond a reasonable doubt. We conclude, therefore, that the board of review adhered literally to the terms of our mandate.

Finally, the accused contends the board of review erred in regard to the sentence. The first part of the claim is addressed to a statement by the board of review in which it said it had considered the "sentences finally approved in over a hundred other military cases . . . of unpremeditated murder." It is asserted that this statement shows the board of review considered matters outside the record to sustain the sentence. Whether a board of review, as a permanent appellate tribunal, may consider sentences adjudged in other cases as a circumstance bearing upon appropriateness of a sentence in a particular case need not detain us. Cf. United States v Mamaluy, 10 USCMA 102, 27 CMR 176. The statement here was made in an effort to assess the harmful effects of certain inadmissible evidence. It is arguable that the purpose and the result did not prejudice the accused. Be that as it may, it is clear the board of review reassessed the sentence on the facts of this particular case, and affirmed a sentence which it believed was just and appropriate.

The second part of the sentence assignment of error is that the board of review could not reassess a sentence which extends to confinement at hard labor for more than three years. We considered a similar contention in regard to the convening authority in United States v Jones, 10 USCMA 532, 533, 28 CMR 98. We pointed out in that case that a sentence approved on initial review is binding in all subsequent proceedings in the case, unless the sentence action was "expressly and solely predicated on an erroneous conclusion of law." Since the reduction effected by the board of review on the first review was based solely upon an erroneous view of the applicable law, the board of review was not precluded from reassessing the sentence on the basis of the correct findings of guilty.

The decision of the board of review is affirmed.

Judge LATIMER concurs.

FERGUSON, Judge (concurring in the result):

I concur in the result.

While I agree generally with the discussion of the assigned errors and the disposition ordered, I am disturbed by the implication of the principal opinion that a board of review may average out the "sentences finally approved in over a hundred other military cases . . . of unpremeditated murder" in determining the quantum of the penalty which should be approved in this case.

. . .

The accused in this case filed a petition for a writ of habeas corpus in the United States District Court for the District of Kansas, challenging the Board's action in reassessing the sentence. The United States Court of Appeals, Tenth Circuit, affirmed the District Court's discharge of the writ (296 F.2d 737 [1961]). Certiorari was denied by the Supreme Court (369 U.S. 889, 82 S.Ct. 1163, 8 L.Ed.2d 289 [1962]).

Although a board of review may not suspend a sentence in the first instance, it may reduce the period of suspension (U.S. v. Estill, 9 USCMA 458, 26 CMR 238 [1958]).

A convening authority and a board of review have the authority to commute a death sentence to dishonorable discharge and confinement at hard labor (U.S. v. Russo, 11 USCMA 352, 29 CMR 168 [1960]). See also U.S. v. Johnson at page 303, supra.

## COURT OF MILITARY APPEALS

### UNITED STATES v. BUNTING

United States Court of Military Appeals, 1955.
6 U.S.C.M.A. 170, 19 C.M.R. 296

GEORGE W. LATIMER, Judge:

I

Despite his plea to the contrary, the accused was found guilty by a general court-martial of unpremeditated murder, in violation of Article 118, Uniform Code of Military Justice, 50 USC §712; robbery, in violation of Article 122, Uniform Code of Military Justice, 50 USC §716; and three offenses of aggravated assault, in violation of Article 128, Uniform Code of Military Justice, 50 USC §722. He was sentenced to dishonorable discharge, total forfeitures, and confinement at hard labor for life. The convening authority approved but the board of review set aside the proceedings, holding that the court was appointed by an officer having no legal authority to convene a general court-martial. The Judge Advocate General of the Navy certified that question to this Court, and we reversed the board of review. United States v. Bunting, 4 USCMA 84, 15 CMR 84. In our disposition of that certificate, we returned the record to the board of review and directed that appellate tribunal to consider the appeal on its merits. Pursuant to this mandate, a majority of the board concluded that as a matter of fact, and after consideration of all the evidence in the record, they had a reasonable doubt as to the sanity of the accused at the time of the commission of the offenses. Accordingly, the board set aside the findings and sentence, and dismissed

the charges. The Judge Advocate General of the Navy then certified
to this Court the following questions:

> "(a)  Did the Board of Review err, as a matter of
> law, in its analysis of the testimony and thereby abuse its
> discretion in reversing the findings of the court-martial?

. . .

### III

We have previously considered the power granted to us by the
Uniform Code of Military Justice to interfere with a decision of a
board of review, and we have suggested certain limits beyond which
our authority does not run.  In United States v. Zimmerman, 2 USCMA
12, 6 CMR 12, we recognized our power to review questions of law
resolved by a board of review by saying:

> ". . . Article 67(d), supra, [of the Code] explicitly
> gives to the Court power to act with respect to findings
> and sentence which have been 'set aside as incorrect in
> law' by a board of review.  A board of review decision
> clearly based on matter of law, therefore, does not pos-
> sess such finality that it may be assimilated to court-
> martial findings of not guilty."

It is implicit in the grant of authority found in Article 67 of the
Code that a board of review may not permissibly defeat review in this
Court by labeling a matter of law, or a mixed holding of law and fact,
as a question of fact.  To avoid that impasse, we look to the substance
of the holding, and its rationale, not to the characterization by the
board of review.  United States v. Benson, 3 USCMA 351, 12 CMR 107.
Furthermore, we have consistently held that where a board of review
makes a truly factual determination based upon the evidence of record,
we may not overturn it.  United States v. Thompson, 2 USCMA 460,
462, 9 CMR 90.  When faced with such a determination, we are free
only to insist that the holding, if it affirms a finding, be based upon
substantial evidence, United States v. Hernandez, 4 USCMA 465, 16
CMR 39, and that the board of review express clearly the exercise
of its fact-finding powers.  United States v. Sell, 3 USCMA 202, 11
CMR 202; United States v. Moreno, 5 USCMA 500, 18 CMR 124.

As an offshoot to the foregoing principle is the precise concept
which is presented by this certificate.  Here the board of review found
that the evidence in the record was insufficient to establish the sanity
of the accused beyond a reasonable doubt.  The nature of this finding
does not permit us to say accurately that the evidence is sufficient to
support the finding, for to do so would suggest that we are placing a
burden on the accused to establish his insanity.  The test we view as
more appropriate in this instance may be found in this reasoning:

On the one hand, if all reasonable men would conclude that the Government had established sanity beyond a reasonable doubt, then as a matter of law the board of review erred. On the other hand, if all reasonable men would conclude that the accused was insane, a holding to that effect by a board of review would be untouchable. Between the two extremes there exists an area where reasonable minds would differ as to whether the Government had established its burden beyond a reasonable doubt. If the facts place the issue in that area, then the board of review may resolve the conflict either way--in the exercise of its fact-finding powers--without abusing its discretion. Obviously, intertwined within the board's power to resolve disputed questions of fact is its authority to believe or disbelieve witnesses.

As we read the board of review decision which is before us, we find nothing more than a factual determination of an evidential dispute. The issue of the sanity of this accused was one of fact, not law, and as noted by a majority of the board, the medical testimony concerning his mental responsibility was conflicting. . . .

We have been faced with some cases in which we were doubtful of the power a board of review was seeking to exercise when it reversed a court-martial on a finding of guilt, but we are morally certain in this instance that the board was attempting to do the very thing Congress authorized it to do. The evidence for both the Government and the defense was paired off, compared and evaluated. The experience and training of the experts were considered and their qualifications measured. A conscious effort was made to balance the evidence in the pans of scales weighted by reasonable doubt. When the scales showed the evidence was wanting in that quality and quantity which would require all reasonable men to conclude the accused was sane, a majority of the board refused to find the accused sane. . . .

. . .

It is our conclusion, then, that the board of review did not err, as a matter of law, in concluding that the evidence did not establish mental responsibility at the time of this occurrence beyond a reasonable doubt, and in not requiring a further mental examination.

. . .

The Court of Military Appeals will not decide a hypothetical question (see U.S. v. Harris, 10 USCMA 69, 27 CMR 143 [1958]).

UNITED STATES v. FRISCHHOLZ*

United States Court of Military Appeals, 1966.
16 U.S.C.M.A. 150, 36 C.M.R. 306.

*[ Footnotes have been omitted. Ed.]

QUINN, Chief Judge:
    In 1960, this Court denied the accused's petition to review his
conviction, by a general court-martial in Japan, of three specifications of wrongdoing, in violation of Article 134, Uniform Code of
Military Justice, 10 USC §934, and his sentence to dismissal and forfeiture of all pay and allowances. United States v Frischholz, 12
USCMA 727, 30 CMR 417. Thereafter, the sentence was executed and
the accused was dismissed from the United States Air Force. Five
years later, he applied to the United States District Court for the
District of Columbia for relief from his conviction. District Judge
Hart denied the application, indicating that the merits should be considered first by this Court. Thereupon, the accused filed the present
Petition for Writ in the Nature of Error Coram Nobis.
    Reversing its position in the United States District Court, the
Government contends that this Court has no power "to entertain and
consider" the accused's application because it is outside the scope of
jurisdiction conferred upon this Court by Article 67, Code, supra,
10 USC §867, and prohibited by Article 76, Code, supra, 10 USC §876.
The latter Article provides that "all dismissals . . . carried into
execution under sentences by courts-martial" are final and conclusive
upon all courts, subject only to a petition for a new trial, action by the
Secretary concerned, and the authority of the President. This provision does not insulate a conviction from subsequent attack in an appropriate forum. At best it provides finality only as to interpretations
of military law by this Court. United States v Armbruster, 11 USCMA
596, 29 CMR 412. It has never been held to bar review of a court-
martial, when fundamental questions of jurisdiction are involved. See
Burns v Wilson, 346 US 137, 97 L ed 1508, 73 S Ct 1045 (1953);
Shapiro v United States, 69 F Supp. 205 (Ct Cl) (1947); Application of
Stapley, 246 F Supp 316 (DC Utah) (1965). As the Supreme Court of
the United States observed in a related case, a finality clause of the
kind in question describes the normal "terminal point for proceedings
within the court-martial system." Gusik v Schilder, 340 US 128, 132,
95 L ed 146, 71 S Ct 149 (1950).
    Whether this Court has jurisdiction to grant relief encompassed
within the writ of coram nobis has been before us on other occasions.
See United States v Buck, 9 USCMA 290, 26 CMR 70; United States v
Tavares, 10 USCMA 282, 27 CMR 356. In those cases, we found it
unnecessary to explore or define the limits of our jurisdiction, but we
have pointed out that we possess powers incidental to, and protective

of, those defined in Article 67. In re Taylor, 12 USCMA 427, 430, 31 CMR 13. On that premise, appellate defense counsel maintain this Court comes within the purview of the All Writs Act which confers upon "all courts established by Act of Congress" authority to issue "writs necessary or appropriate in aid of their respective jurisdictions." 28 USC §1651(a). Despite the broad language of the All Writs Act, the Government would exclude this Court from its provisions on the ground the Act applies only to courts established by Congress under Article III of the Constitution of the United States. This Court, it contends, was not established under Article III.

We have no desire, and there is no need, to assess the precise Constitutional nature of the jurisdiction conferred upon this Court. Contrary to the Government's interpretation, Title 28 does not apply exclusively to courts created by Congress in exercise of its Article III power and to the judges thereof. Many provisions in the Title relate to courts, and the judges thereof, which were established by Congress in exercise of powers other than those possessed under Article III. See, for example, sections 373, 414, 457, 1732, 1738, 1739, and 2071. Section 1732, which deals with the admissibility of evidence of business records, is especially illuminating. In material part it provides as follows: "In any of the United States and in any court established by Act of Congress, any writing or record . . . made as a . . . record of any act . . . shall be admissible as evidence of such act. . . ." If "any court established by Act of Congress" means the same thing as "any court of the United States," then Congress was absurdly redundant. Common sense and a respect for the seriousness of the legislative task compel the conclusion that the two terms have different meanings. The difference is made crystal clear in section 451. There, Congress defined the term " 'court of the United States'" as a court created by act of Congress, the judges of which are entitled to hold office during good behavior. Manifestly, as used in Title 28, the term "court of the United States" is not synonymous with the term "court established by Act of Congress." The latter is more comprehensive, and includes courts other than those established by Congress under Article III. It is further apparent that when Congress wanted to limit applicability of a particular provision in Title 28 to specific courts, it did so explicitly. In most of the chapters of the Title, Congress used the term "court of the United States" which it specially defined; but when it was convenient to use an undefined and broader term such as "any court," Congress ended the chapter with a provision enumerating the courts covered by the chapter. See Chapter 41, section 610; Chapter 57, section 963. No such delineation was made with respect to the All Writs Act.

As originally approved by the House of Representatives, the bill providing for the establishment of this Court included tenure for the judges corresponding to that of the judges of Article III courts. However, the concept of direct review of courts-martial by a civilian tribunal was a "revolutionary" aspect of the Uniform Code of Military Justice, and the Court iself was regarded as "experimental." House Report No. 491, 81st Congress, 1st Session, page 6; Hearings before Senate Armed Services Committee on S 457 and HR 4080, 81st Congress, 1st Session, page 43. In its wisdom, the Senate determined to substitute for the House approved provision tenure for a term of years. In the conference to resolve various differences between the House approved bill and the Senate bill, the House conferees acceded to the Senate reservations. The change in tenure, however, did not change the fundamental nature of this tribunal. As summarized by counsel to the House Subcommittee that recommended the bill, the intention was to constitute this Court "a specialized Federal court." Hearings before House Armed Services Committee on HR 2498, 81st Congress, 1st Session, page 1280.

The All Writs Act merely makes "explicit" the right to exercise powers implied from the creation of such courts." Reviser's Note, Historical and Revision Notes, 28 USC §1651. See United States v Morgan, 346 US 502, 506, 98 L ed 248, 74 S Ct 247, footnote 6 (1954). The fact that a court is empowered by Congress to act only in a specially defined area of law does not make it any the less a court established by Congress. Glidden Co. v Zdanok, 370 US 530, 561, 8 L ed 2d 671, 82 S Ct 1459 (1962). Part of our responsibility includes the protection and preservation of the Constitutional rights of persons in the armed forces. Burns v Wilson, supra; see also Chief Justice Warren, "The Bill of Rights and the Military," 37 New York University Law Review 182 (1962). We entertain no doubt, therefore, that this Court is a court established by act of Congress within the meaning of the All Writs Act. Consequently, the Government's motion to dismiss the accused's petition because this Court lacks jurisdiction to grant relief is denied.

So far as the pleading filed by the accused is concerned, our conclusion as to our jurisdiction under the All Writs Act does not help him. Coram nobis is not a substitute for an appeal. It is extraordinary relief predicated upon "exceptional circumstances" not apparent to the court in its original consideration of the case. United States v Tavares, supra, page 284. It may not be used to seek a reevaluation of the evidence or a reconsideration of alleged errors. Lipscomb v United States, 273 F2d 860, 865 (CA 8th Cir) (1960), certiorari denied, 364 US 836, 5 L ed 2d 61, 81 S Ct 72 (1960). Yet, in the brief on the merits of the application, the accused acknowledges that the issues which he now seeks to raise were merely not "fully presented" in his original appeal. Each assignment of error could have been raised on the appeal from the conviction, and most, in fact, were included in the petition for grant of review in 1960. Thus, the accused has not established any acceptable basis for extraordinary relief. Accordingly, as an application for coram nobis relief, the petition is denied.

In substance, the accused is really asking for reconsideration of our 1960 decision denying his petition under Article 67(b)(3) of the

Uniform Code of Military Justice.  Under Rule 49 of the rules of this Court, an application for reconsideration must be filed within five days of receipt of notice of entry of the original order or decision.  Rule 49, Rules of Practice and Procedure, United States Court of Military Appeals.  For good cause, this Court can grant relief from the time limit imposed by the Rule, but no reasons have been advanced by the accused to excuse his delay.  Nevertheless, to insure that the accused's conviction was not a miscarriage of justice, we have examined the record of trial in detail and we are satisfied that the accused was fairly charged, convicted, and tried, without any error prejudicial to a substantial right.  We, therefore, deny this application for relief.

Judges FERGUSON and KILDAY concur.

## JONES v. IGNATIUS

United States Court of Military Appeals, 1968.
18 U.S.C.M.A. 7, 39 C.M.R. 7.

FERGUSON, Judge:

Accused was convicted on June 25, 1968, by a special court-martial convened at Camp Pendleton, California, of one specification of absence without leave, in violation of Uniform Code of Military Justice, Article 86, 10 USC §886, and sentenced to a bad-conduct discharge, confinement at hard labor for six months, and forfeiture of $68.00 per month for a similar period.  On July 15, 1968, the convening authority, in part, took the following action:

> "In the foregoing case of Private James E. JONES, 2344062, U.S. Marine Corps, tried by special court-martial on 25 June 1968, the bad conduct discharge is commuted to confinement at hard labor for five months and forfeiture of $68.00 per month for five months.
> "Only so much of the sentence as commuted which provides for confinement at hard labor for eleven months and forfeiture of $68.00 per month for eleven months is approved and will be duly executed."

The supervisory authority at Camp Pendleton approved the sentence "as commuted, approved and ordered executed by the convening authority."  The order reflecting this approval also contained the following statement:

> "This record has been reviewed in accordance with Article 65(c), Uniform Code of Military Justice, and is thus final and conclusive in the sense of Article 76, Uniform Code of Military Justice."

The accused, through counsel, has petitioned this Court for a Writ of Habeas Corpus or, in the alternative, such other further or different and appropriate relief as may be required, on the ground that the convening authority erred in his attempted commutation of this sentence. Specifically, it is asserted that since the maximum period of confinement imposable by a special court-martial is six months, and the maximum imposable forfeiture is two-thirds pay per month for six months, Code, supra, Article 19, 10 USC §819, the approval of confinement and forfeitures of eleven months is illegal, being in direct contravention of the Code.

The Government contends in the alternative that: (1) This Court has no jurisdiction to act in this case, under either the Habeas Corpus or All Writs Act of the U.S. Code, 28 USC §§2241 (a), 1651 (a); and (2) a special court-martial convening authority has the power to commute a sentence to one that is less severe, even though not within the jurisdictional limits of a special court-martial.

The Government concedes that the sentence, as approved, was one that a special court-martial could not adjudge; however, it asserts that that portion of the approved sentence to confinement and forfeitures in excess of the statutory limitation "was not adjudged by the court-martial," rather "[i]t came about as the result of the exercise by the convening authority of his powers of commutation."

The power of reviewing authorities to commute a sentence to one of less severity than that adjudged by a court-martial is no longer in dispute. . . .

The landmark case in the area of commutation is United States v Russo, supra. Subsequently, in United States v Plummer, 12 USCMA 18, 30 CMR 18, we held that "a convening authority may not approve a penalty which is not included within the sentencing power of a court-martial." There the convening authority approved the court's sentence to dismissal but recommended that it be commuted by higher authorities to an administrative form of discharge under other than honorable conditions. We reversed because the convening authority's action was ambiguous. While actual reduction in severity of sentence was not the precise issue in Plummer, we therein expressed what had been implied in Russo; namely, that the power of commutation encompassed only those penalties that are within the power of the court to adjudge. See also United States v Christensen, 12 USCMA 393, 30 CMR 393.

Turning now to the matter before us, it is at once apparent that, as the Government concedes, the convening authority approved a sentence to confinement and forfeitures which is in excess of that which could have been imposed by the court. It matters not that he first approved the adjudged sentence and thereafter commuted a portion thereof. His authority to commute any portion thereof is not unrestricted but limited as we have noted. If a special court-martial is restricted by law from imposing a sentence of confinement and partial

forfeitures for a period of eleven months, it can hardly be argued
that the convening authority can achieve such a result by his powers
of commutation.  The logic of an argument to the contrary escapes
us.  Having attempted to do so in the case at bar, we hold his action
illegal. . . .

Conversion of a discharge into another form of punishment is
not the same as total disapproval; and at least to the extent that it is
used to increase the remaining punishment beyond that allowed by
law, the discharge must be considered as still inherent in the sentence.  In our opinion, therefore, the convening authority's action did
not bar further review under the provisions of Code, supra, Articles
66(b) and 67(b)(3).  Proceedings in this Court to preserve the right of
review are, therefore, appropriate.  Gale v United States, 17 USCMA
40, 37 CMR 304; United States v Frischholz, 16 USCMA 150, 36 CMR
306.

Accordingly, the accused's petition for appropriate relief is
granted and the action of the convening authority is set aside.  The
record of trial is returned to the Judge Advocate General of the Navy.
A new action by the convening authority should be ordered.

Chief Judge QUINN concurs.

## UNITED STATES v. BEVILACQUA*

United States Court of Military Appeals, 1968.
18 U.S.C.M.A. 10, 39 C.M.R. 10.

*[ Footnotes have been omitted.  Ed.]

QUINN, Chief Judge:
In 1967, a special court-martial in Turkey convicted the petitioners of wrongful possession and use of marihuana, in violation of
Article 134, Uniform Code of Military Justice, 10 USC §934, and sentenced them to reduction in grade and partial forfeiture of pay.  The
conviction was approved and ordered executed by the convening authority.  An application for further review was made to the general
court-martial authority and denied.  Cf. Article 65(b), (c), Code,
supra, 10 USC §865.  Thereafter, two applications for relief from
the conviction were filed with the Air Force Board for Correction of
Military Records and both were denied.  The petitioners then filed
this application for Writ of Error Coram Nobis.  Petitioner Bevilacqua
is no longer in the service, but Braun is, and he asserts that the conviction "is an unwarranted burden upon his career and his life."

Air Force appellate Government counsel, and the United States
Army and the United States Coast Guard appearing as amici curiae,
contend that this Court lacks power to grant relief of any kind to
petitioners.  They point to the fact that the sentence adjudged by the
court-martial and approved by the convening authority did not include

a punitive discharge or confinement at hard labor for one year or more, as provided in Articles 66 and 67 of the Uniform Code, 10 USC §§866 and 867, respectively. They maintain that the Court is powerless to act in any case not expressly defined in Article 67 and, since the sentence adjudged by the court and approved by the convening authority is not within those cases set out in the Article, the Court lacks jurisdiction to consider the petition.

So far as direct appeal for the purpose of reviewing alleged irregularities of procedure or other defects is concerned, we have indeed determined that our power to review is "expressly conditioned" by the provisions of Article 67. United States v Bondy, 13 USCMA 448, 450, 32 CMR 448. For that reason, we have not entertained a petition to review by direct appeal the validity of a conviction not within the scope of Article 67. See United States v Hardy, 17 USCMA 100, 37 CMR 364. However, Article 67 does not describe the full panoply of power possessed by this Court. In United States v Frischholz, 16 USCMA 150, 151-152, 36 CMR 306, we noted that we "possess powers incidental to, and protective of, those defined in Article 67," and that part of our responsibility under the Uniform Code "includes the protection and preservation of the Constitutional rights of persons in the armed forces." In Gale v United States, 17 USCMA 40, 42, 37 CMR 304, we commented on the "intent of Congress to confer upon this Court a general supervisory power over the administration of military justice" and determined that we possessed authority to grant relief, in appropriate circumstances, before completion of pending court-martial proceedings. In part, we said: "We cannot believe Congress, in revolutionizing military justice and creating for the first time in the armed services a supreme civilian court in the image of the normal Federal judicial system, intended it not to exercise power to grant relief on an extraordinary basis, when the circumstances so require." Id., at page 43. These comments and decisions certainly tend to indicate that this Court is not powerless to accord relief to an accused who has palpably been denied constitutional rights in any court-martial; and that an accused who has been deprived of his rights need not go outside the military justice system to find relief in the civilian courts of the Federal judiciary. See Application of Stapley, 246 F Supp 316 (D Utah) (1965); Ashe v McNamara, 355 F2d 277 (CA 1st Cir) (1965). We need not, however, demarcate the boundaries of our power. . . .

The record of the special court-martial which convicted the accused is not before us. However, the petition for relief sets out three assignments of error. None of them demonstrates the accused was denied a constitutional right. In the first assignment, the accused, in effect, seeks review of the sufficiency of the evidence to show compliance with the requirements for issuance of a search warrant; the petition itself indicates that at least one witness testified that the officer who authorized the search was properly informed of the articles for which the search was to be made and of circumstances indicating probable cause for the search. The two remaining assignments of error are couched in terms of a denial of the right to prepare for trial but, in substance, they raise only a question as to whether the petitioners were prejudiced by the refusal of the prosecution to disclose the name of an informant. The petitioners admit they suspected the informant of framing them. Manifestly, therefore, the putative informant was known to the petitioners, and they could have subpoenaed him as a witness to determine his exact role, if any, in the case. In Frischholz, supra, we pointed out that collateral proceedings to overturn a conviction which has become final by law cannot be used merely to seek reevaluation of the evidence or the potential prejudice of alleged trial irregularities. The present application discloses no deprivation of any constitutional right or the denial of any fundamental right accorded by the Uniform Code of Military Justice. The petition, therefore, is denied.

Judge FERGUSON concurs.

## UNITED STATES v. SNYDER

United States Court of Military Appeals, 1969.
18 U.S.C.M.A. 480, 40 C.M.R. 192.

### Memorandum Opinion of the Court

Tried by special court-martial convened at Travis Air Force Base, California, the accused was found guilty of adultery, in violation of Article 134, Uniform Code of Military Justice, 10 USC §934, and sentenced to detention of $50.00 per month for two months and reduction to the grade of sergeant. On March 14, 1969, the convening authority approved only so much of the sentence as provided for reduction to the grade of sergeant and ordered the punishment, as thus modified, executed.

Thereafter, accused submitted an appeal to the Judge Advocate General, United States Air Force, under the provisions of Article 69, Code, supra, 10 USC §869, which as amended by the Act of October 24, 1968, 82 Stat 1335, 1342, permit that officer to grant relief, on the ground of newly discovered evidence, fraud on the court, lack of jurisdiction over the accused or the offense, or error prejudicial to the substantial rights of the accused, in any case "which has been finally reviewed, but has not been reviewed by a Court of Military Review [under the provisions of Code, supra, Article 66, 10 USC §866]." On May 13, 1969, the Judge Advocate General denied accused's claim for relief.

Subsequently, accused filed a "Petition for Review and Writ of Coram Nobis" with this Court. Among other errors, it alleges accused's court-martial lacked jurisdiction to try him for the offense of adultery under the principles laid down in O'Callahan v Parker, 395 US 258, 23 L Ed 2d 291, 89 S Ct 1683 (1969). In response thereto, the Government urges jurisdiction may be premised upon the fact that the victim was another serviceman's wife and that the meretricious relationship grew out of their association as employees at the Travis Air Force Base Hospital.

We do not reach the merits of the question thus presented, for, at the outset, we are met with a more serious question, i.e., that of our own jurisdiction to entertain an "appeal" from a decision of the Judge Advocate General, taken pursuant to the provisions of Code, supra, Article 69.

Article 67, Code, supra, 10 USC §867, empowers this Court to review the record of a court-martial in three categories of cases:

> ". . . (1)  all cases in which the sentence, as affirmed by a Court of Military Review, affects a general or flag officer or extends to death;
>
> "(2)  all cases reviewed by a Court of Military Review which the Judge Advocate General orders sent to the Court of Military Appeals for review; and
>
> "(3)  all cases reviewed by a Court of Military Review in which, upon petition of the accused and on good cause shown, the Court of Military Appeals has granted a review."

From the foregoing, it is apparent that appeals to this Court in the ordinary course are from decisions of the Courts of Military Review--formerly designated boards of review. Those bodies' jurisdiction, in turn, depends upon the sentence adjudged and approved in particular cases, i.e., whether such affects a general or flag officer or extends to death, dismissal of a commissioned officer, cadet, or midshipman, dishonorable or bad-conduct discharge, or confinement for one year or more. Code, supra, Article 66, 10 USC §866. In addition, where the sentence in a general court-martial, as approved below, does not extend to those set out above, and the case, therefore, is reviewed only at the convening authority level and "examined in the office of the Judge Advocate General," it may be reviewed by a Court of Military Review "[i]f any part of the findings or sentence is found unsupported in law, or if the Judge Advocate General so directs." Code, supra, Article 69. In such event, however, "there may be no further review by the Court of Military Appeals except under section 867(b)(2)," providing for certification of the case here.

Other courts-martial, which do not fall into the mentioned categories, are finally reviewed at the supervisory authority level. The Judge Advocate General, however, is empowered--notwithstanding the finality of such convictions under Code, supra, Article 76, 10 USC §876--to hear an appeal therefrom and to vacate or modify the findings of guilty or sentence, or both, on "the ground of newly discovered evidence, fraud on the court, lack of jurisdiction over the accused or the offense, or error prejudicial to the substantial rights of the accused." Code, supra, Article 69.

It is into this last classification that accused's case falls. As his approved sentence extended only to reduction to the grade of sergeant and as he was tried only by special court-martial, the record was neither reviewable as a matter of right by a Court of Military Review under Code, supra, Article 66, nor was he entitled to have it "examined" in the office of the Judge Advocate General under the provisions of Code, supra, Article 69. However, accused was entitled to appeal the conviction and sentence to the Judge Advocate General and to seek invocation of the latter's powers under Code, supra, Article 69, for the reasons set forth in that Article.* This is the course which he has followed, the unsuccessful termination of which he desires reviewed here.

Accused does not contend, nor, indeed, could he do so, that his case is one reviewable by this Court in the ordinary course of appellate review. His record is not one reviewable by a Court of Military Review, nor, as we have noted, one which could be referred to that body by the Judge Advocate General, or, indeed, certified here under Code, supra, Article 67. Instead, accused refers to our decision in United States v Bevilacqua, 18 USCMA 10, 39 CMR 10, and asserts such stands for the proposition that this Court may review a special court-martial even if the approved sentence therein does not require the case to be reviewed by a Court of Military Review. Specifically, he invokes our jurisdiction on the basis of the Court's comment, at page 11, that it:

> ". . . is not powerless to accord relief to an accused who has palpably been denied constitutional rights in any court-martial; and that an accused who has been deprived of his rights need not go outside the military justice system to find relief in the civilian courts of the Federal judiciary."

Accused's reading of the foregoing language in Bevilacqua, supra, is over-broad. We specifically noted in that case that we "need not . . . demarcate the boundaries of our power," for, in any event, the accused was entitled to no relief on the merits of his claim, and that

---

*In fairness to the Judge Advocate General, it should be noted that his action herein was taken several weeks prior to the decision of the Supreme Court in O'Callahan v Parker, 395 US 258, 23 L Ed 2d 291, 89 S Ct 1683 (1969), and it does not, therefore, appear that he considered the merits of the case in light of that opinion's guidelines.

an attempt to invoke this Court's extraordinary powers could not be made a substitute for the ordinary appellate process. Cf. United States v Frischholz, 16 USCMA 150, 36 CMR 306. Moreover, in setting forth the concept on which accused relies, we referred to our prior decisions in United States v Frischholz, supra, and Gale v United States, 17 USCMA 40, 37 CMR 304, as well as that in Jones v Ignatius, 18 USCMA 7, 39 CMR 7, all of which dealt, not with the creation of a new jurisdiction, but with the exercise of this Court's powers ancillary to the jurisdiction which it possesses under Code, supra, Article 67. Indeed, we specifically referred to the fact that "we 'possess powers incidental to, and protective of, those defined in Article 67.'" United States v Bevilacqua, supra, at page 11.

There can be no doubt of the fact that this Court does possess the authority to resort to extraordinary writs under the All Writs Act, 28 USC §1651. Noyd v Bond, 395 US 683, 23 L Ed 2d 631, 89 S Ct-- (1969), specifically recognizes our authority in this area. And see United States v Frischholz, supra; Jones v Ignatius, supra. But such resort is had, under the very terms of the statute, in aid of the exercise of our jurisdiction over cases properly before us or which may come here eventually. Our jurisdiction to hear appeals, no matter how well-founded, is set out by Congress in Code, supra, Article 67. We cannot by judicial fiat enlarge the scope of our appellate review to embrace those cases which Congress thought justified no remedy beyond the powers it so recently confided to the Judge Advocate General under Code, supra, Article 69.

In sum, then, we believe the accused misreads our language in United States v Bevilacqua, supra. What we there stated concerning our duty and responsibility to correct deprivations of constitutional rights within the military system must be taken to refer to cases in which we have jurisdiction to hear appeals or to those to which our jurisdiction may extend when a sentence is finally adjudged and approved. Resort to extraordinary remedies such as those available under the All Writs Act, supra, cannot serve to enlarge our power to review cases but only to aid us in the exercise of the authority we already have. As such, therefore, we find no basis which permits us to review a special court-martial in which the adjudged and approved sentence extends only to reduction.

The petition is dismissed.

The U.S. Army Court of Military Review has held that it has the authority declared in the All Writs Act and this may grant relief through extraordinary writs (see U.S. v. Draughton, CM 419184, 20 March 1970). Question: does a military judge have such authority?

The following case illustrates the application of a Status of Forces Agreement (SOFA) with a foreign country where American armed forces are serving. Similar agreements are in effect with many countries throughout the world. The particular agreement with a foreign country must be consulted in connection with actions contemplated by commanders of armed forces stationed in such country.

## AUTRY v. HYDE

United States Court of Military Appeals, 1970.
19 U.S.C.M.A. 433, 42 C.M.R. 35.

### Memorandum Opinion of the Court

Petitioner is confined in the Correctional Center, Headquarters First Naval District, Boston, Massachusetts, awaiting trial by general court-martial upon a charge of desertion, and other charges alleging offenses arising out of incidents occurring subsequent to the commencement of such confinement. He has filed a Petition for Writ of Habeas Corpus in this Court alleging his confinement is illegal, for reasons hereinafter set forth. Upon preliminary consideration of the petition, an order was issued to respondents requiring that they show cause, in writing, why the relief sought should not be granted. Thereafter, it appearing that the pending charges had been referred to a general court-martial and that the prosecution was ready to proceed to trial, this Court ordered the proceedings of said general court-martial stayed pending further order.

. . .

The following facts are disclosed by the pleadings.

On June 23, 1968, shortly after registering for the draft, petitioner enlisted in the Naval Reserve. Called to active duty on November 20, 1968, he was assigned to the U.S.S. McCAFFREY, as a fireman apprentice. While on a North Atlantic cruise, the vessel docked at Halifax, Nova Scotia, Canada. Petitioner left his ship July 20, 1969, allegedly without authority, and missed its movement on July 22, 1969. The petition avers that petitioner renounced his United States citizenship and applied for Land Immigrant Status in Canada through the Canadian Immigration Office in Halifax. We note that there is some dispute between the parties as to the manner in which the latter step was taken, but this is not material to the merits of any issue now before us, and need not be resolved.

On September 23, 1969, the United States Defense Attache at Ottawa, Canada, requested the Canadian authorities to apprehend and return petitioner to United States military control (Exhibit 27) pursuant to the provisions of section 10, Visiting Forces Act. The Canadian Minister of National Defense directed the requested apprehension and delivery on October 1, 1969. Thereafter, and in compliance with the Defense Minister's order, two Canadian military policemen, accompanied by a Halifax City Police official, apprehended petitioner in Halifax, October 16, 1969. Upon learning they were Canadian officials, petitioner denied their jurisdiction over him and requested permission to make a telephone call. The request was denied. While at the Provost Station awaiting delivery to United States custody, petitioner unsuccessfully requested a lawyer. Later, on the same day, Lieutenant Commander Hildebrand, United States Navy, accepted custody of petitioner at the Halifax International Airport, where they enplaned for Boston, Massachusetts. Lieutenant Commander Hildebrand did not advise him of his rights under Article 31, Uniform Code of Military Justice, 10 USC §831, nor of his constitutional rights in accordance with Miranda v Arizona, 384 US 436, 16 L Ed 2d 694, 86 S Ct 1602 (1966). Indeed, that officer's affidavit indicates he did not question the accused in any way. Although the pair conversed during the flight, the subject of their conversation is not material to the present issue. It is sufficient to observe that Hildebrand's affidavit makes no mention of a request by petitioner for counsel while in Canada.

Petitioner alleges that his arrest and subsequent return to the United States "were accomplished by means of an unlawful conspiracy between and among members of the American military establishment and the American Department of State, on the one hand, and members of the Canadian Department of Manpower and Immigration and the Canadian Department of Defense, on the other hand." In support of this assertion, he relies on a message from the United States Embassy to the Secretary of State that Canadian authorities intended instituting deportation proceedings against petitioner unless a request for his arrest under section 10, Canadian Visiting Forces Act, was made. The Canadian preference for action under the Visiting Forces Act, as well as the reasons for such preference, were also reported.

.  .  .

Lieutenant Commander Hildebrand and other armed forces personnel of the United States are authorized to apprehend service personnel "upon reasonable belief that an offense has been committed and that the person apprehended committed it." (Article 7(b), Code, supra, 10 USC §807.) The exercise of this power in Canada, however, is limited by the "Agreement Between The Parties To The North Atlantic Treaty Regarding The Status of Their Forces," June 19, 1951, 4 UST 1792, and by the Visiting Forces Act, Statutes of Canada, 1967-68, chapter 23. Paragraph 5(a), Article VII, of the Agreement provides:

"The authorities of the receiving and sending States shall assist each other in the arrest of members of a force

or civilian component or their dependents in the territory
of the receiving State and in handing them over to the authority which is to exercise jurisdiction in accordance
with the above provisions."

Desertion by a member of the armed forces of the United States
is an offense under the Uniform Code, as noted, but it is not a violation
of Canadian law. Therefore, under paragraph 2(a), Article VII of the
Agreement, only United States authorities have jurisdiction of the
offense.

To complete the jurisdiction contemplated by paragraph 2(a),
Article VII, supra, over one who has left his organization and has
entered the Canadian civilian community, section 10 of the Visiting
Forces Act provides:

> "For the purpose of enabling the service authorities
> and service courts of a visiting force to exercise more
> effectively the powers conferred upon them by this Act,
> the Minister of National Defence, if so requested by the
> officer in command of the visiting force or by the desig-
> nated state, may from time to time by general or special
> orders to the Canadian forces, or any part thereof, direct
> the officers and men thereof to arrest members of the
> visiting force or dependents alleged to have been guilty of
> offences against the law of the designated state and to hand
> over any person so arrested to the appropriate authorities
> of the visiting force."

Unquestionably the United States Navy is a "visiting force"
within the meaning of the foregoing provision, and members thereof
are, and at all pertinent times have been, stationed at Argentia, New-
foundland.

The record before us makes it abundantly clear that when the
petitioner's absence was noted, and his presence within the civilian
community was ascertained, the Naval authorities, rather than
abandon him--and thereby subject him to the deportation proceedings
which would, or could, result in his involuntary return to the United
States--elected to proceed under the Status of Forces Agreement and
the Visiting Forces Act, and so advised the Department of State.
That Department, of course, has the primary responsibility for invoking such international agreements.

Each step taken by the United States and the Canadian officials
completely conformed to the provisions of the Agreement and of the
implementing Visiting Forces Act. The claim that reliance on international agreements of the type here involved is evidence of a "conspiracy," is patently a fiction. In no way does this record support
petitioner's claim.

It is next urged that denial of an opportunity to consult with counsel, who would then present a petition to the Canadian courts to test the legality of his arrest, denied petitioner his right to counsel as guaranteed by the Fifth and Sixth Amendments to the Constitution of the United States, and his right to a hearing as guaranteed by the Sixth Amendment. The short answer to this complaint is that the provisions of the Constitution of the United States are not binding upon Canadian officials in the performance of their respective functions as defined by the laws of Canada.

Article VI, Constitution of the United States, provides, in pertinent part:

> "This Constitution, and the Laws of the United States which shall be made in Pursuance thereof; and all Treaties made, or which shall be made, under the Authority of the United States, shall be the supreme Law of the Land. . . ."

Since every step pursued by the United States to effect the apprehension and return of the petitioner to military control conformed to the provisions of the Agreement, supra--the "supreme Law of the Land"--there is no basis for a finding that petitioner's present confinement is illegal. On this subject, MR. CHIEF JUSTICE MARSHALL, declared in Foster v. Neilson, 2 Peters 253, 314 (U. S. 1829):

> ". . . Our Constitution declares a treaty to be the law of the land. It is, consequently, to be regarded in courts of justice as equivalent to an Act of the Legislature, whenever it operates of itself without the aid of any legislative provision."

In summary, petitioner became subject to military law upon reporting for active duty pursuant to his orders, and nothing had occurred in the interim to terminate that status.

The Petition for Writ of Habeas Corpus is denied, and the Order staying proceedings of the general court-martial is vacated.

# 11

---

The review of courts-martial by civilian courts is a very controversial legal question. For two particularly enlightening discussions of the subject, see 83 <u>Harvard L. Rev.</u> 1208 (1970) and 69 <u>Columbia L. Rev.</u> 1259 (1969).

---

Ex parte DICKEY

District Court, Maine, 1913.
204 F. 322.

Petition by William W. Dickey for a writ of habeas corpus to review the validity of his imprisonment under a judgment of a naval court-martial on a charge of scandalous conduct tending to the destruction of good morals. Writ denied.

HALE, District Judge. . . .
. . .
The decisions of the Supreme Court in reference to the power of military tribunals is founded upon the doctrine that the third article of the Constitution has conferred upon Congress the power to create certain federal courts; that another power is conferred upon Congress in the first article of the Constitution, namely, to make rules for the government and regulation of the land and naval forces. These powers are independent of each other. They are derived from different

349

articles of the Constitution. When courts organized under these respective powers are proceeding within the limits of their jurisdiction,
it is clear that they must be held free from any interference.

It has been repeatedly held, where the charge against a person,
tried in a military court, is within the jurisdiction of the court, and
is authorized by army or navy regulations, that the matter of setting
out the offense is a matter of pleading rather than of jurisdiction;
that it is for the court having such jurisdiction to decide upon the
validity of the pleadings necessary to bring that charge before the
court; that the only question before the civil court is whether or not
the military court had the right to try and determine the cause; that
the jurisdiction of the trial court cannot depend upon his decision on
the merits of the cause, but upon the court's right to hear and decide
it; that where a military or naval tribunal has the right to try the
cause, even though a civil court had the concurrent right, the civil
court cannot enter upon the consideration of the evidence adduced before the court-martial, or of the question whether the accused was
guilty of the offense over which the military court has jurisdiction;
that if the military court had jurisdiction to impose sentence authorized by the regulations of the army or navy, the civil court cannot
pass upon the severity of such sentence; that errors in law, however
numerous, committed by the trial court in a cause within its jurisdiction, can be reviewed only by appeal or writ of error in the court
exercising supervisory jurisdiction; that it is only where the trial
court is without the jurisdiction of the person or the cause, and the
party is subjected to illegal imprisonment, that a writ of habeas corpus may be invoked, and the party discharged from imprisonment.
Civil courts are not courts of error to review the proceedings and
sentence of a court-martial, where such court-martial has jurisdiction of the offense and of the person of the accused, has complied with
the statutory requirements governing the proceedings of the court,
and acts within the scope of its lawful powers. Mullan v. United States,
212 U.S. 516, 29 Sup. Ct. 330, 53 L. Ed. 632; Swaim v. United States,
165 U.S. 553, 566, 17 Sup. Ct. 448, 41 L. Ed. 823; Carter v. McClaughry,
183 U.S. 365, 22 Sup. Ct. 181, 46 L. Ed. 236; United States v. Maney
(C. C.) 61 Fed. 140; Ex parte Watkins, 7 Pet. 572, 8 L. Ed. 786; Ex
parte Ulrich (C. C.) 43 Fed. 661.

. . .

I am of the opinion that I have no power to review the proceedings of the court-martial, or to set aside its conclusions, or annul the
sentence imposed by it. If the petitioner was harshly dealt with, and
a sentence of undue severity was imposed, such sentence seems to
have been within the powers of the court-martial; and it is held by the
Supreme Court of the United States that the remedy must be found
elsewhere than in courts of law.

The petition for writ of habeas corpus is dismissed.

The opinion of Judge Hale in Ex parte Dickey, supra, concisely
states the scope of review of courts-martial by civilian courts for
many years.  In Hiatt v. Brown, 339 U.S. 103, 70 S.Ct. 495, 94 L.Ed.
691 (1950), Justice Clark stated in part: "It is well settled that 'by
habeas corpus the civil courts exercise no supervisory or correcting
power over the proceedings of a court-martial. . . . The single inquiry, the test is jurisdiction' [citing In re Grimley, supra] ."  See
Fratcher, 10 Ohio St. L.J. 271 (1949).

## GUSIK v. SCHILDER*

Supreme Court of the United States, 1950.
340 U.S. 128, 71 S.Ct. 149, 95 L.Ed. 146.

*[ Footnotes have been omitted.  Ed.]

MR. JUSTICE DOUGLAS delivered the opinion of the Court.
This is a petition for a writ of habeas corpus filed in the District Court on behalf of petitioner challenging the legality of his detention by respondent.  Respondent holds Gusik pursuant to a court-
martial judgment convicting him of murder while he was stationed in
Italy as a member of the United States Army.  After conviction by the
court-martial petitioner exhausted all his remedies for reversal or
modification of the judgment of conviction which then existed under
the Articles of War.  When he secured no relief from the military
authorities he filed this petition in which he challenges the jurisdiction of the court-martial both under the Articles of War and the
Constitution.  The District Court, after a hearing, sustained the writ
and released Gusik on bond.  It found that the court-martial did not
have jurisdiction, because no thorough and impartial pretrial investigation was conducted in compliance with Article 70 of the Articles
of War, because the Trial Judge Advocate failed to call material
witnesses, and because Gusik was denied the effective assistance of
counsel.  The Court of Appeals reversed, 180 F. 2d 662.  It did not
reach the merits of the case; it held that there was an administrative
remedy which petitioner had not exhausted and that the petition must
be dismissed without prejudice to the filing of a new petition after
resort to the additional administrative remedy had been made.
The new remedy is Article 53 of the Articles of War, 62 Stat.
639, 10 U. S. C. (Supp. III) §1525.  It gives the Judge Advocate General

discretion, <u>inter alia</u>, to grant a new trial in any court-martial
case. . . .

     . . .

An argument is woven around the finality clause of Article 53
as a foundation to a claim of unconstitutionality. The provision is that
all action by the Judge Advocate General under Article 53 shall be
"final and conclusive" and shall be "binding upon all departments,
courts, agencies, and officers of the United States." It is argued that
this clause deprives the courts of jurisdiction to review these military judgments and therefore amounts to a suspension of the writ. We
do not so read Article 53. Congress was legislating as respects tribunals over which the civil courts have traditionally exercised no
power of supervision or review. See <u>In re Grimley</u>, 137 U.S. 147,
150. These tribunals have operated in a self-sufficient system, save
only as habeas corpus was available to test their jurisdiction in specific cases. We read the finality clause of Article 53 as doing no
more than describing the terminal point for proceedings within the
court-martial system. If Congress had intended to deprive the civil
courts of their habeas corpus jurisdiction, which has been exercised
from the beginning, the break with history would have been so
marked that we believe the purpose would have been made plain and
unmistakable. The finality language so adequately serves the more
restricted purpose that we would have to give a strained construction
in order to stir the constitutional issue that is tendered.

Petitioner says that resort to Article 53 will be futile. If it
proves to be, no rights have been sacrificed. Habeas corpus will then
be available to test any questions of jurisdiction which petitioner may
offer.

Trial of the case in the District Court had ended before the
effective date of Article 53 and the question of the exhaustion of the
new remedy which the Article affords was not raised until the case
was in the Court of Appeals. We conclude that in the interests of
justice the Court of Appeals, instead of reversing the District Court
and ordering the petition to be dismissed, should have done what the
Court of Appeals in <u>Whelchel v. McDonald</u>, <u>ante</u>, p. 122, did under
like circumstances and held the case pending resort to the new
remedy under Article 53. If relief is obtained from the Judge Advocate General, the case will then be remanded for dismissal. If the
relief is not obtained under Article 53, petitioner will not be put to
the time and expense of trying anew the case which he tried when he
had no relief other than habeas corpus.

We agree with the Court of Appeals on the main issue tendered
under Article 53. But since we think a different disposition of the
case should be made pending resort to the new remedy which Article
53 affords, we reverse the judgment below and remand the cause to
the Court of Appeals for further proceedings in conformity with this
opinion.

So ordered.

Following the decision in Gusik v. Schilder, the JAG, deciding that good cause for granting a new trial did not appear, denied the petition. The Court of Appeals thereafter dismissed the petition for writ of habeas corpus, Gusik v. Schilder, 195 F.2d 657 (CA 6th, 1952), certiorari denied, 344 U.S. 844, 73 S.Ct. 60, 97 L.Ed. 657 (1952).

## NOYD v. BOND

Supreme Court of the United States, 1969.
395 U.S. 683, 89 S.Ct. 1876, 23 L.Ed.2d 631.

MR. JUSTICE HARLAN delivered the opinion of the Court.

Petitioner is a career officer in the Air Force who has come to believe that this country's participation in the Vietnamese conflict is unjust and immoral. Having decided that he would do nothing to further the Nation's military effort in Southeast Asia, Captain Noyd refused to obey an order, issued December 5, 1967, requiring him to teach one of the junior officers at the Cannon Air Force Base, New Mexico, to fly a military airplane.*

---

*Before this incident took place, Captain Noyd sought to invoke the jurisdiction of the civilian federal courts in an effort to require the Air Force either to assign him to duties consistent with his beliefs or to dismiss him. The United States District Court for the District of Colorado denied relief because petitioner had not yet been court-martialed for refusing to obey orders and so had not fully exhausted his remedies within the military system. Noyd v. McNamara, 267 F. Supp. 701 (1967). The Court of Appeals for the Tenth Circuit affirmed, 378 F. 2d 538, and this Court denied certiorari, 389 U.S. 1022 (1967). The Courts of Appeals for the Second and Fifth Circuits have, however, subsequently decided that the exhaustion doctrine did not necessarily require a serviceman to await the military's decision to convene a court-martial before seeking relief in the civilian courts. Hammond v. Lenfest, 398 F. 2d 705 (C. A. 2d Cir. 1968); In re Kelly, 401 F. 2d 211 (C. A. 5th Cir. 1968). Cf. Brown v. McNamara, 387 F. 2d 150 (C. A. 3d Cir. 1967). We have not found it necessary to resolve this conflict among the circuits in order to decide the narrow issue in this case.

In response, Major General Charles Bond, Jr., the Commander of the Twelfth Air Force, convened a general court-martial at the Cannon Base. On March 8, 1968, the court-martial found Noyd guilty of wilfully disobeying a lawful order; on the following day petitioner was sentenced to one year's confinement at hard labor, forfeiture of all pay and allowances, and dismissal from the Air Force. As soon as the court-martial announced its sentence, Captain Noyd was ordered confined to his quarters. The court-martial's judgment was then forwarded to General Bond for the review required by 10 U. S. C. §864, and on May 10, 1968, the General approved the sentence, ordering that: "Pending completion of appellate review, the accused will be confined in the United States Disciplinary Barracks, Fort Leavenworth, Kansas."

At this point, petitioner's attorneys undertook two courses of action. On the one hand, they appealed the merits of petitioner's conviction to the Air Force Board of Review, which is the appellate military tribunal Congress has established to oversee the administration of criminal justice in petitioner's branch of the Armed Forces. On the other hand, they sought habeas corpus relief from the civilian courts, arguing that the Uniform Code of Military Justice required that petitioner be released from confinement pending the outcome of his military appeal.

At the present time, petitioner's appeal from his conviction is still pending in the higher reaches of the military court system. While the Air Force Board of Review has now affirmed the judgment of the court-martial, the Court of Military Appeals, the highest military tribunal, has agreed to review Captain Noyd's case. Petitioner does not suggest that we may properly interfere with the orderly process of military review by considering the merits of his conviction at this juncture. Rather, we are now only asked to vindicate his asserted right to remain free from confinement while the validity of his conviction is still being litigated in the appellate military courts.

I

Captain Noyd's effort to invoke the assistance of the civilian courts was precipitated by General Bond's order transferring petitioner to the disciplinary barracks at Fort Leavenworth. Shortly after the order was issued, and before it was carried out, petitioner sought a writ of habeas corpus from the United States District Court for the District of New Mexico, arguing that both his confinement at the Cannon Air Force Base and his proposed transfer to Fort Leavenworth were in violation of two provisions of the Uniform Code of Military Justice. . . .

The Government, in addition to opposing Captain Noyd's claims on the merits, argued that petitioner should be required to exhaust his military remedies before seeking habeas corpus relief from the civilian courts. The District Court, however, refused to apply the exhaustion principle in the present case, finding that the military

court system did not provide petitioner with an adequate remedy by
which he could test the validity of his confinement, pending appeal,
in an expedited manner. Turning to the merits, the District Judge
granted petitioner part of the relief he requested. While the court
refused to review the legality of Noyd's confinement at the Cannon Air
Force Base, the court did find that petitioner's incarceration at Fort
Leavenworth would constitute an "execution" of his sentence in violation of Article 71 (c), and so declared General Bond's order invalid.*

Both sides appealed to the Court of Appeals for the Tenth Circuit, which reversed the District Court's grant of partial relief.
Relying on this Court's decision in Gusik v. Schilder, 340 U.S. 128
(1950), a unanimous panel held that the District Court could not properly grant petitioner any form of relief until he had first challenged
the validity of his confinement before the appellate tribunals within
the military system. The court emphasized that "the Court of Military Appeals has recently held that it possesses the power to issue
a habeas corpus writ" if a serviceman could demonstrate that he was
illegally restrained pending appeal, and it could perceive no justification for petitioner's failure to seek the military court's assistance.
402 F. 2d 441, 442-443. We granted certiorari to consider the propriety of the application of the rule of Gusik v. Schilder in the circumstances of this case. 393 U.S. 1048 (1969).

## II

Shortly after the Court of Appeals announced its decision, petitioner recognized that since his sentence was scheduled to expire on
December 26, 1968,** he might well be released from custody before
this Court would have an opportunity to pass upon his claims for re-
lief pending his appeal to the military courts. In order to avoid the
possibility of mootness, petitioner promptly requested the Court of
Appeals to stay its mandate and order his release pending this
Court's decision on his petition for certiorari. On December 6, the
Court of Appeals agreed to stay its mandate, thereby keeping the
District Court's order in effect, but refused to require the military

---

*After the District Court held that petitioner could not be law-
fully transferred to Fort Leavenworth, the military significantly increased the degree of restraint that was imposed upon Captain Noyd
at the Cannon Air Force Base. Petitioner was permitted to see his
family only twice each week and was forbidden to leave his quarters
except for narrowly limited purposes. See Letter Regarding Arrest
in Quarters, from Col. George R. Doerr, Appendix 32-34.

**While petitioner's one-year sentence began to run on March
9, 1968, when it was announced by the court-martial, the Air Force
awarded him sentence credits for good behavior, thereby permitting
him to obtain his release from custody after a period of some nine
and one-half months.

to release Captain Noyd from custody at the Cannon Air Force Base.

Petitioner then applied to MR. JUSTICE WHITE, Circuit Justice for the Tenth Circuit, for temporary release from all confinement pending this Court's action on his certiorari petition. When the Circuit Justice denied this application on December 18, 1968, a second motion of the same tenor was made to MR. JUSTICE DOUGLAS on the following day. Noting that the Court was then in recess and would not meet again until January 10, 1969, MR. JUSTICE DOUGLAS ordered that "petitioner . . . be placed in a non-incarcerated status" until the full Court could have an opportunity to pass on the issues raised in a considered manner. Pursuant to MR. JUSTICE DOUGLAS' order, petitioner was released from confinement on Christmas Eve, two days before his sentence was scheduled to expire.*

Despite MR. JUSTICE DOUGLAS' order of release, the Government now suggests that this case has become moot. . . .

. . .

We hold that the principles of the Manual for Courts-Martial operated to interrupt the running of Captain Noyd's sentence at the time of his release on December 24, 1968, and hence that the case before us is not moot.

### III

We now turn to consider whether petitioner could properly seek his release in civilian courts without making any effort to invoke the assistance of the courts within the military system. Gusik v. Schilder, 340 U.S. 128 (1950), established the general rule that habeas corpus petitions from military prisoners should not be entertained by federal civilian courts until all available remedies within the military court system have been invoked in vain. . . . It is true, of course, that the principles of federalism which enlighten the law of federal habeas corpus for state prisoners are not relevant to the problem before us. Nevertheless other considerations require a substantial degree of civilian deference to military tribunals. In reviewing military decisions, we must accommodate the demands of individual rights and the social order in a context which is far removed from those which we encounter in the ordinary run of civilian litigation, whether state or federal. In doing so, we must interpret a legal tradition which is radically different from that which is common in civil courts.

It is for these reasons that Congress, in the exercise of its power to "make Rules for the Government and Regulation of the land

---

*When this Court granted certiorari on January 20, 1969, we also ordered that the "[s]tay heretofore granted by MR. JUSTICE DOUGLAS shall remain in effect pending issuance of judgment of this Court or until further order of this Court." 393 U.S. 1048.

and naval Forces" (Constitution of the United States, Art. I, §8, cl.
14), has never given this Court appellate jurisdiction to supervise
the administration of criminal justice in the military. When after the
Second World War, Congress became convinced of the need to assure
direct civilian review over military justice, it deliberately chose to
confide this power to a specialized Court of Military Appeals, so that
disinterested civilian judges could gain over time a fully developed
understanding of the distinctive problems and legal traditions of the
Armed Forces.

Almost one year before petitioner sought habeas corpus relief
from the Federal District Court sitting in New Mexico, the Court of
Military Appeals had held that it would, in appropriate cases, grant
the relief petitioner now demands from us. Levy v. Resor, 17 U. S.
C. M. A. 135, 37 C. M. R. 399 (1967).* Petitioner, however, has made
no effort to invoke the jurisdiction of the Court of Military Appeals.
Nevertheless, he would have civilian courts intervene precipitately
into military life without the guidance of the court to which Congress
has confided primary responsibility for the supervision of military
justice in this country and abroad.

Petitioner emphasizes that in the present case we are not called
upon to review prematurely the merits of the court-martial proceeding itself. Instead, we are merely asked to determine the legality of
petitioner's confinement while he is exercising his right of appeal to

---

*The Government does not renew the arguments it has on occa-
sion advanced before the Court of Military Appeals, see Brief in
Support of Motion to Strike and Dismiss Petition, United States v.
Frischholz, Docket No. 14,270 (1965), to the effect that the Court of
Military Appeals lacks the power to grant emergency writs. In its
decision in the Frischholz case, 16 U. S. C. M. A. 150, 36 C. M. R.
306 (1966), the Court of Military Appeals properly rejected the
Government's argument, holding that the All Writs Act, 28 U. S. C.
§1651 (a), permitted it to issue all "writs necessary or appropriate
in aid of [its] . . . jurisdiction." Since the All Writs Act applies
by its terms to any "courts established by Act of Congress," and
since the Revisers of 1948 expressly noted that "[t]he revised section extends the power to issue writs in aid of jurisdiction, to all
courts established by Act of Congress, thus making explicit the right
to exercise powers implied from the creation of such courts," we do
not believe that there can be any doubt as to the power of the Court
of Military Appeals to issue an emergency writ of habeas corpus in
cases, like the present one, which may ultimately be reviewed by
that court. A different question would, of course, arise in a case
which the Court of Military Appeals is not authorized to review under
the governing statutes. Cf. United States v. Bevilacqua, 18 U. S. C.
M. A. 10, 39 C. M. R. 10 (1968).

the higher military courts. It is said that there is less justification
for deference to military tribunals in ancillary matters of this sort.
We cannot agree. All of the reasons supporting this Court's decision
in Gusik v. Schilder, supra, are applicable here. If the military
courts do vindicate petitioner's claim, there will be no need for
civilian judicial intervention. Needless friction will result if civilian
courts throughout the land are obliged to review comparable decisions of military commanders in the first instance. Moreover, if we
were to reach the merits of petitioner's claim for relief pending his
military appeal, we would be obliged to interpret extremely technical
provisions of the Uniform Code which have no analogs in civilian
jurisprudence, and which have not even been fully explored by the
Court of Military Appeals itself. There seems little reason to blaze
a trail on unfamiliar ground when the highest military court stands
ready to consider petitioner's arguments.*

Accordingly, the judgment of the Court of Appeals is affirmed.
In light of the substantial questions raised by petitioner, however, we
think it plain that petitioner in no sense acted in bad faith when he
failed to exhaust his military remedies before invoking the jurisdiction of the District Court. Consequently, we consider it appropriate
for us to continue MR. JUSTICE DOUGLAS' order in effect until our
mandate issues, in order to give petitioner an opportunity to present
his arguments to the Court of Military Appeals. See 28 U. S. C.
§1651 (a); cf. Phillips v. United States, 312 U.S. 246, 254 (Mr. Justice
Frankfurter). While it is true that Captain Noyd has only two days
yet to serve on his sentence, he should not be required to surrender
his freedom for even this short time unless it is found that the law
so requires.

It is so ordered.

MR. JUSTICE BLACK concurs in the result.

---

*Petitioner contends that our decisions in Toth v. Quarles, 350
U.S. 11 (1955); Reid v. Covert, 354 U.S. 1 (1957); and McElroy v.
Guagliardo, 361 U.S. 281 (1960), justify his position that exhaustion
of military remedies is not required in this case. The cited cases
held that the Constitution barred the assertion of court-martial jurisdiction over various classes of civilians connected with the military,
and it is true that this Court there vindicated complainants' claims
without requiring exhaustion of military remedies. We did so, however, because we did not believe that the expertise of military courts
extended to the consideration of constitutional claims of the type
presented. Moreover, it appeared especially unfair to require exhaustion of military remedies when the complainants raised substantial arguments denying the right of the military to try them at all.
Neither of these factors is present in the case before us.

MR. JUSTICE WHITE, dissenting.

The petition for certiorari in this case sought a determination that petitioner was being subjected to illegal restraints pending the appeal of his court-martial conviction to the appropriate tribunals. Since his sentence had begun to run at the time it was imposed, it would have expired on December 26, 1968, unless suspended or otherwise interrupted. Hence when the petition was filed here, the most petitioner had to gain from this litigation, which does not reach the merits of his conviction, was that for the duration of his sentence-- two days at the time MR. JUSTICE DOUGLAS ordered his release from confinement--he was not to be subject to the restraints then being imposed on him. Surely this is a picayune issue which does not warrant decision here in any event, either alone or in conjunction with the exhaustion question. Petitioner should not have brought the custody question to the federal courts in the first place; and by the same token, if to preserve the issue he desired suspension of his sentence or its equivalent, that matter also should have been presented first to the military tribunals rather than to the District Court. I would dismiss the writ as improvidently granted.

---

The Court of Military Appeals affirmed the conviction in United States v. Noyd, 18 U.S.C.M.A. 483, 40 C.M.R. 195 (1969).

---

## BURNS v. WILSON*

Supreme Court of the United States, 1953.
346 U.S. 137, 73 S.Ct. 1045, 97 L.Ed. 1508.

*[Footnotes have been omitted. Ed.]

MR. CHIEF JUSTICE VINSON announced the judgment of the Court in an opinion in which MR. JUSTICE REED, MR. JUSTICE BURTON and MR. JUSTICE CLARK join.

Tried separately by Air Force courts-martial on the Island of Guam, petitioners were found guilty of murder and rape and sentenced to death. The sentences were confirmed by the President, and petitioners exhaused all remedies available to them under the Articles of War for review of their convictions by the military tribunals. They then filed petitions for writs of habeas corpus in the United States District Court for the District of Columbia.

In these applications petitioners alleged that they had been denied due process of law in the proceedings which led to their conviction by the courts-martial. They charged that they had been subjected to illegal detention; that coerced confessions had been extorted from them; that they had been denied counsel of their choice and denied effective representation; that the military authorities on Guam had suppressed evidence favorable to them, procured perjured testimony against them and otherwise interfered with the preparation of their defenses. Finally, petitioners charged that their trials were conducted in an atmosphere of terror and vengeance, conducive to mob violence instead of fair play.

The District Court dismissed the applications without hearing evidence, and without further review, after satisfying itself that the courts-martial which tried petitioners had jurisdiction over their persons at the time of the trial and jurisdiction over the crimes with which they were charged as well as jurisdiction to impose the sentences which petitioners received. 104 F. Supp. 310, 312. The Court of Appeals affirmed the District Court's judgment, after expanding the scope of review by giving petitioners' allegations full consideration on their merits, reviewing in detail the mass of evidence to be found in the transcripts of the trial and other proceedings before the military court. 91 U.S. App. D. C. 208, 202 F. 2d 335.

We granted certiorari, 344 U.S. 903. Petitioners' allegations are serious, and, as reflected by the divergent bases for decision in the two courts below, the case poses important problems concerning the proper administration of the power of a civil court to review the judgment of a court-martial in a habeas corpus proceeding.

In this case, we are dealing with habeas corpus applicants who assert--rightly or wrongly--that they have been imprisoned and sentenced to death as a result of proceedings which denied them basic rights guaranteed by the Constitution. The federal civil courts have jurisdiction over such applications. By statute, Congress has charged them with the exercise of that power. Accordingly, our initial concern is not whether the District Court has any power at all to consider petitioners' applications; rather our concern is with the manner in which the Court should proceed to exercise its power.

The statute which vests federal courts with jurisdiction over applications for habeas corpus from persons confined by the military courts is the same statute which vests them with jurisdiction over the applications of persons confined by the civil courts. But in military habeas corpus the inquiry, the scope of matters open for review, has always been more narrow than in civil cases. Hiatt v. Brown, 339 U.S. 103 (1950). Thus the law which governs a civil court in the exercise of its jurisdiction over military habeas corpus applications cannot simply be assimilated to the law which governs the exercise of that power in other instances. It is sui generis; it must be so, because of the peculiar relationship between the civil and military law.

Military law, like state law, is a jurisprudence which exists separate and apart from the law which governs in our federal judicial establishment. This Court has played no role in its development; we have exerted no supervisory power over the courts which enforce it; the rights of men in the armed forces must perforce be conditioned to meet certain overriding demands of discipline and duty, and the civil courts are not the agencies which must determine the precise balance to be struck in this adjustment. The Framers expressly entrusted that task to Congress.

Indeed, Congress has taken great care both to define the rights of those subject to military law, and provide a complete system of review within the military system to secure those rights. Only recently the Articles of War were completely revised, and thereafter, in conformity with its purpose to integrate the armed services, Congress established a Uniform Code of Military Justice applicable to all members of the military establishment. These enactments were prompted by a desire to meet objections and criticisms lodged against court-martial procedures in the aftermath of World War II. Nor was this a patchwork effort to plug loopholes in the old system of military justice. The revised Articles and the new Code are the result of painstaking study; they reflect an effort to reform and modernize the system--from top to bottom.

Rigorous provisions guarantee a trial as free as possible from command influence, the right to prompt arraignment, the right to counsel of the accused's own choosing, and the right to secure witnesses and prepare an adequate defense. The revised Articles, and their successor--the new Code--also establish a hierarchy within the military establishment to review the convictions of courts-martial, to ferret out irregularities in the trial, and to enforce the procedural safeguards which Congress determined to guarantee to those in the Nation's armed services. And finally Congress has provided a special post-conviction remedy within the military establishment, apart from ordinary appellate review, whereby one convicted by a court-martial may attack collaterally the judgment under which he stands convicted.

The military courts, like the state courts, have the same responsibilities as do the federal courts to protect a person from a violation of his constitutional rights. In military habeas corpus cases, even more than in state habeas corpus cases, it would be in disregard of the statutory scheme if the federal civil courts failed to take account of the prior proceedings--of the fair determinations of the military tribunals after all military remedies have been exhausted. Congress has provided that these determinations are "final" and "binding" upon all courts. We have held before that this does not displace the civil courts' jurisdiction over an application for habeas corpus from the military prisoner. Gusik v. Schilder, 340 U.S. 128 (1950). But these provisions do mean that when a military decision has dealt fully and fairly with an allegation raised in that application, it is not open to a federal civil court to grant the writ simply to re-evaluate the evidence. Whelchel v. McDonald, 340 U.S. 122 (1950).

We turn, then, to this case.

Petitioners' applications, as has been noted, set forth serious charges--allegations which, in their cumulative effect, were sufficient to depict fundamental unfairness in the process whereby their guilt was determined and their death sentences rendered. Had the military courts manifestly refused to consider those claims, the District Court was empowered to review them de novo. For the constitutional guarantee of due process is meaningful enough, and sufficiently adaptable, to protect soldiers--as well as civilians--from the crude injustices of a trial so conducted that it becomes bent on fixing guilt by dispensing with rudimentary fairness rather than finding truth through adherence to those basic guarantees which have long been recognized and honored by the military courts as well as the civil courts.

. . .

These records make it plain that the military courts have heard petitioners out on every significant allegation which they now urge. Accordingly, it is not the duty of the civil courts simply to repeat that process--to re-examine and reweigh each item of evidence of the occurrence of events which tend to prove or disprove one of the allegations in the applications for habeas corpus. It is the limited function of the civil courts to determine whether the military have given fair consideration to each of these claims. Whelchel v. McDonald, supra. We think they have.

. . .

Petitioners have failed to show that this military review was legally inadequate to resolve the claims which they have urged upon the civil courts. They simply demand an opportunity to make a new record, to prove de novo in the District Court precisely the case which they failed to prove in the military courts. We think, under the circumstances, that due regard for the limitations on a civil court's power to grant such relief precludes such action. We think that although the Court of Appeals may have erred in reweighing each item of relevant evidence in the trial record, it certainly did not err in holding that there was no need for a further hearing in the District Court. Accordingly its judgment must be

Affirmed.

MR. JUSTICE JACKSON concurs in the result.


MR. JUSTICE MINTON, concurring in the affirmance of the judgment.

I do not agree that the federal civil courts sit to protect the constitutional rights of military defendants, except to the limited extent indicated below. Their rights are committed by the Constitution and by Congress acting in pursuance thereof to the protection of the military courts, with review in some instances by the President. Nor do we sit to review errors of law committed by military courts.

This grant to set up military courts is as distinct as the grant to set up civil courts. Congress has acted to implement both grants. Each hierarchy of courts is distinct from the other. We have no supervisory power over the administration of military justice, such as we have over civil justice in the federal courts. Due process of law for military personnel is what Congress has provided for them in the military hierarchy in courts established according to law. If the court is thus established, its action is not reviewable here. Such military court's jurisdiction is exclusive but for the exceptions contained in the statute, and the civil courts are not mentioned in the exceptions. 64 Stat. 115, 50 U. S. C. (Supp. V) §581.

If error is made by the military courts, to which Congress has committed the protection of the rights of military personnel, that error must be corrected in the military hierarchy of courts provided by Congress. We have but one function, namely, to see that the military court has jurisdiction, not whether it has committed error in the exercise of that jurisdiction.

. . .

MR. JUSTICE FRANKFURTER.

This case raises questions of great delicacy and difficulty. On the one hand is proper regard for habeas corpus, "the great writ of liberty"; on the other hand the duty of civil courts to abstain from intervening in matters constitutionally committed to military justice. The case comes to us on a division of opinion in the Court of Appeals. In the interest of enabling indigent litigants to have the case reviewed in this Court without incurring the enormous cost of printing, we have required to be brought here only one copy of a record consisting of a mass of materials in their original form. Consideration of the case has fallen at the close of the Term. Obviously it has not been possible for every member of the Court to examine such a record. In any event there has not been time for its consideration by me. An examination of it, however, is imperative in view of what seem to me to be the essential issues to be canvassed. I can now only outline the legal issues that are implicit in the case.

. . .

In the light of these considerations I cannot assume the responsibility, where life is at stake, of concurring in the judgment of the Court. Equally, however, I would not feel justified in reversing the judgment. My duty, as I see it, is to resolve the dilemma by doing neither. It is my view that this is not just a case involving individuals. Issues of far-reaching import are at stake which call for further consideration. They were not explored in all their significance in the submissions made to the Court. While this case arose prior to the new Code of Military Justice, 64 Stat. 107, it necessarily will have a strong bearing upon the relations of the civil courts to the new Court of Military Appeals. The short of it is that I believe this case should be set down for reargument.

MR. JUSTICE DOUGLAS, with whom MR. JUSTICE BLACK concurs, dissenting.

The charges which are made concerning the confessions exacted from these accused are quite lurid. But the basic, undisputed facts, though not dramatic, leave the clear impression that one of the petitioners was held incommunicado and repeatedly examined over a 5-day period until he confessed.

. . .

I think petitioners are entitled to a judicial hearing on the circumstances surrounding their confessions.

Congress has power by Art. I, §8, cl. 14 of the Constitution "To make Rules for the Government and Regulation of the land and naval Forces." The rules which Congress has made relative to trials for offenses by military personnel are contained in the Uniform Code of Military Justice. 64 Stat. 108, 50 U. S. C. §551 et seq. Those rules do not provide for judicial review. But it is clear from our decisions that habeas corpus may be used to review some aspects of a military trial.

The question whether the military tribunal has exceeded the powers granted it by Congress may be tested by habeas corpus. See Hiatt v. Brown, 339 U.S. 103; Whelchel v. McDonald, 340 U.S. 122; Gusik v. Schilder, 340 U.S. 128. But it is also clear that that review is not limited to questions of "jurisdiction" in the historic sense.

Of course the military tribunals are not governed by the procedure for trials prescribed in the Fifth and Sixth Amendments. That is the meaning of Ex parte Quirin, 317 U.S. 1, holding that indictment by grand jury and trial by jury are not constitutional requirements for trials before military commissions. Nor do the courts sit in review of the weight of the evidence before the military tribunal. Whelchel v. McDonald, supra, p. 124. But never have we held that all the rights covered by the Fifth and the Sixth Amendments were abrogated by Art. I, §8, cl. 14 of the Constitution, empowering Congress to make rules for the armed forces. . . .

. . .

The opinion of the Court is not necessarily opposed to this view. But the Court gives binding effect to the ruling of the military tribunal on the constitutional question, provided it has given fair consideration to it.

If the military agency has fairly and conscientiously applied the standards of due process formulated by this Court, I would agree that a rehash of the same facts by a federal court would not advance the cause of justice. But where the military reviewing agency has not done that, a court should entertain the petition for habeas corpus. In the first place, the military tribunals in question are federal agencies subject to no other judicial supervision except what is afforded by the federal courts. In the second place, the rules of due process which they apply are constitutional rules which we, not they, formulate.

. . .

Whether Burns v. Wilson, supra, expanded the jurisdiction of the civil courts to review courts-martial was the issue in many cases. In Easley v. Hunter, 209 F.2d 483 (CA, Tenth Cir., 1953), Judge Pickett stated that the Burns decision "does no more than hold that a military Court must consider questions relating to the guarantees afforded an accused by the Constitution and when this is done, the civil Courts will not review its action." Accord, Suttles v. Davis, 215 F.2d 760 (CA 10th, 1954); Dickenson v. Davis, 245 F.2d 317 (CA 10th, 1957); Thomas v. Davis, 249 F.2d 232 (CA 10th, 1957); Jacobi v. United States, 257 F.2d 184 (CA 10th, 1958). Judge Wisdom, in Rushing v. Wilkinson, 272 F.2d 633 (CA 5th Cir., 1959), questioned the Burns holding but acquiesced in the law as stated above. Judge Cameron, in Williams v. Heritage, 323 F.2d 731 (CA 5th Cir., 1963), characterized the Burns decision as a "prior short-lived more liberal view."

The Court of Appeals for the District of Columbia has no jurisdiction to review decisions of the Court of Military Appeals as if those decisions were the same as an administrative agency (Shaw v. United States, 209 F.2d 811 (1954)).

KAUFFMAN v. SECRETARY OF THE AIR FORCE

United States Court of Appeals, D.C. Circuit, 1969.
415 F.2d 991.

EDGERTON, Senior Circuit Judge:
Appellant brought suit in the District Court to have his court-martial conviction and sentence declared void on the ground that they rested upon violations of his constitutional rights. He also asked for restoration to active duty with full rank, and the seniority and allowances to which he would have been entitled had he not been discharged, resting his claim on the record made in the court-martial proceeding. The case was decided upon cross-motions for summary judgment and the government's alternative motion to dismiss for want of jurisdiction in the District Court. The District Court held that it had jurisdiction to entertain an action for declaratory relief attacking a court-martial conviction, but granted summary judgment for the government on the ground that the issues raised by appellant were fully and fairly considered in the military proceedings.

Three questions are presented: (1) whether the District Court has jurisdiction to entertain a collateral attack on a military judgment not presented in the form of a petition for writ of habeas corpus; (2) the proper standard for review of military judgments by civilian courts; and (3) the validity of appellant's conviction and sentence. We agree that the District Court had jurisdiction but find that it applied an unduly limited standard for review of alleged constitutional errors. We think the scope of review of military judgments should be the same as that in habeas corpus review of state or federal convictions, and constitutional requirements should be qualified by the special conditions of the military only where these are shown to require a different rule. Imposing this standard of review, we nonetheless agree that appellant's conviction and sentence were valid. Accordingly, we affirm the judgment of the District Court in favor of the government.

. . .

## II
## JURISDICTION

Article 76 of the Uniform Code of Military Justice, 10 U.S.C. §876, provides that military review of court-martial convictions shall be "final and conclusive" and "binding upon all . . . courts . . . of the United States." The legislative history of the finality clause demonstrates that Congress intended to preserve the collateral remedy of habeas corpus in civilian courts, S. Rep. No. 486, 81st Cong., 1st Sess. 32 (1949); H. Rep. No. 491, 81st Cong., 1st Sess. 35 (1949); and the Supreme Court has held that review by this route in civilian courts remains available. Gusik v. Schilder, 340 U.S. 128, 132-133, 71 S.Ct. 149, 95 L.Ed. 146 (1950); Burns v. Wilson, 346 U.S. 137, 142, 73 S.Ct. 1045, 97 L.Ed. 1508 (1953). The question presented in this case is whether habeas corpus to secure release from confinement is the exclusive collateral remedy, so that any jurisdictional attack on a court-martial judgment in civilian courts is barred if the plaintiff is no longer in custody.

We think that confinement is not a jurisdictional requirement for collateral review of military judgments in civilian courts. For many years, the Court of Claims has entertained suits for back pay by servicemen not in custody who based their claims on allegations that their courts-martial convictions were invalid. See, e.g., Runkle v. United States, 122 U.S. 543, 7 S.Ct. 1141, 30 L.Ed. 1167 (1887); Shaw v. United States, 357 F.2d 949, 174 Ct.Cl 899 (1966). Other courts have held that the remedy of mandamus to require administrative correction of military records pursuant to 10 U.S.C. §1552* is available

---

*Section 1552(a) of 10 U.S.C. provides in part:

The Secretary of a military department, under procedures established by him and approved by the Secretary of Defense, and acting through boards of civilians of the executive part of that military department, may correct

to a serviceman seeking to void a punitive sentence imposed by a court martial in violation of his constitutional rights. Ashe v. McNamara, 355 F.2d 277 (1st Cir. 1965); Smith v. McNamara, 395 F.2d 896 (10th Cir. 1968). And in Gallagher v. Quinn, 124 U.S. App. D.C. 172, 363 F.2d 301, cert. denied, 385 U.S. 881, 87 S.Ct. 167, 17 L.Ed.2d 108 (1966), this court held that the District Court had jurisdiction of a serviceman's suit for a mandatory injunction and other relief attacking his court martial, where he claimed that the statute denying him a right of review by the Court of Military Appeals was unconstitutional, even though the petitioner was not in custody.*

We reserved decision on the jurisdictional issue in this case pending the decision of the Supreme Court in United States v. Augenblick, 393 U.S. 348. 89 S.Ct. 528, 21 L.Ed.2d 537 (1969). . . .
. . .

The errors alleged in this case do rise to a constitutional level, and we follow Gallagher in holding that the District Court had jurisdiction to review appellant's conviction. The Gallagher court reasoned that the serviceman need not be in prison, for the continuing disabilities attending a dishonorable discharge provided a case or controversy, and "the right to due process would be lost if one deprived of it could not obtain redress because not in confinement." 124 U.S. App.D.C. at 175, 363 F.2d at 304. Both elements of this reasoning are sound. First, the deprivation of liberty under an invalid conviction is a grievous injury, but a military discharge under other than honorable conditions imposes a life-long disability of greater consequence for persons unlawfully convicted by courts martial. "In terms of its effects on reputation, the stigma experienced by the recipient of a discharge under other than honorable conditions is very akin to the concept of infamy. . . ." Everett, Military Administrative Discharges--The Pendulum Swings, 1966 Duke L. J. 41, 50.

Second, the enactment of the Uniform Code of Military Justice and the establishment of the Court of Military Appeals made up of civilian judges to enforce its procedural guarantees are proof of Congress' concern that the system of military justice afford the maximum protection to the rights of servicemen. The writ of habeas corpus has played a unique role in the system by affording the basis

---

any military record of that department when he considers it necessary to correct an error or remove an injustice.

*Other opinions of this court have suggested that the decisions of courts martial are open to collateral attack other than by a habeas corpus proceeding. See Shaw v. United States, 93 U.S.App.D.C. 300, 302, 209 F.2d 811, 813 (1954); and Levy v. Corcoran, 128 U.S.App. D.C. 388, 389 F.2d 929, cert. denied, 389 U.S. 960, 88 S.Ct. 337, 19 L.Ed.2d 369 (1967).

for ultimate Supreme Court review of constitutional errors.  But for reasons related to the efficiency of the services, the military may prefer to discharge an offender without imposing a term of imprisonment, thus removing the traditional predicate for habeas corpus review. Everett, op. cit., 1966 Duke L.J. at 96; and see United States v. Augenblick, supra, 393 U.S. at 350, 89 S.Ct. 528.  To hold that collateral review is contingent on confinement in every case would arbitrarily condition the serviceman's access to civilian review of constitutional errors upon a factor unrelated to the gravity of the offense, the punishment, and the violations of the serviceman's rights.

Finally, the result of requiring confinement as a condition of servicemen's access to collateral remedies would be especially arbitrary in a case such as this.  Appellant lost his opportunity to obtain civilian review by writ of habeas corpus because he had completed his two-year term of confinement at hard labor before he had exhausted his military remedies.  In Carafas v. La Vallee, 391 U.S. 234, 88 S.Ct. 1556, 20 L.Ed.2d 554 (1968), the Supreme Court held that a civilian petitioner was entitled to review of his criminal conviction by writ of habeas corpus even though he was free by the time his petition came up for review.  It stated that the disabilities of a criminal conviction kept the case from being moot and that collateral relief should not be denied because of exhaustion requirements and delays in court processes.  If the custody requirement may be relaxed in habeas corpus review of state convictions, subject to direct review of violations of federal rights, 28 U.S.C. §1257, it may surely be dispensed with in review of military judgments not otherwise reviewable by a constitutional court.

### III
### SCOPE OF REVIEW

The government contends that even if civilian courts have jurisdiction to entertain collateral attacks on military judgments not presented upon petition for habeas corpus, the scope of review is narrower than the scope of collateral review of state and federal convictions.  First, it contends that in collateral review of military judgments courts may inquire into only the traditional elements of jurisdiction--whether the court martial was properly constituted, and had jurisdiction of the person and the offense and the power to impose the sentence--and not the constitutional errors held to oust courts of jurisdiction since Johnson v. Zerbst, 304 U.S. 458, 58 S.Ct. 1019, 82 L.Ed. 1461 (1938).  Second, the government asserts that even if collateral review extends to constitutional errors, the duty of the civilian court is done if it finds that the military court has considered the serviceman's constitutional claims, even if its conclusions are erroneous by prevailing Supreme Court standards.  We find no support for the first proposition, and no persuasive authority for the second.

In Burns v. Wilson, 346 U.S. 137, 73 S.Ct. 1045, 97 L.Ed. 1508, rehearing denied, 346 U.S. 844, 74 S.Ct. 3, 98 L.Ed. 363 (1953), the leading case on the scope of review, only one Justice was willing to affirm dismissal of a serviceman's petition for habeas corpus upon the narrow jurisdictional test. Upon the denial of rehearing in Burns, Justice Frankfurter wrote an opinion asking that the decision be clarified, and expressing doubt "that a conviction by a constitutional court which lacked due process is open to attack by habeas corpus while an identically defective conviction when rendered by an ad hoc military tribunal is invulnerable." 346 U.S. at 851, 74 S.Ct. at 7. We see no argument for such a distinction. Deference to the peculiar needs of the military does not require denying servicemen the contemporary reach of the writ.

The argument that military judgments are subject to less exacting scrutiny on collateral review than state or federal judgments relies upon the statement of a plurality of the Court in Burns v. Wilson, supra, that "when a military decision has dealt fully and fairly with an allegation raised in that application [for a writ of habeas corpus], it is not open to a federal civil court to grant the writ simply to re-evaluate the evidence." 346 U.S. at 142, 73 S.Ct. at 1049. (Emphasis supplied.) The Supreme Court has never clarified the standard of full and fair consideration, and it has meant many things to many courts. One commentator has observed that in following Burns, "a court may simply and summarily dismiss a petition upon the ground that the military did not refuse to consider its allegations or it may, with equal ease or upon the same authority, stress the requirement that military consideration shall have been full and fair." Bishop, Civilian Judges and Military Justice, 61 Col.L.Rev. 40, 47 (1961).

We think it is the better view that the principal opinion in Burns did not apply a standard of review different from that currently imposed in habeas corpus review of state convictions. The Court's denial of relief on the merits of the serviceman's claims can be explained as a decision based upon deference to military findings of fact, similar to the general non-reviewability of state factual findings prevailing at the time. But cf. Townsend v. Sain, 372 U.S. 293, 311, 83 S.Ct. 745, 9 L.Ed.2d 770 (1962). Note, Servicemen in Civilian Courts, 76 Yale L.J. 380, 392-395 (1966). Courts taking this view have interpreted Burns to require review of military rulings on constitutional issues for fairness. See, e.g., Application of Stapley, 246 F.Supp. 316 (D.Utah 1965); Gibbs v. Blackwell, 354 F.2d 469 (5th Cir. 1965).

The District Court below concluded that since the Court of Military Appeals gave thorough consideration to appellant's constitutional claims, its consideration was full and fair. It did not review the constitutional rulings of the Court of Military Appeals and find them correct by prevailing Supreme Court standards. This was error. We hold that the test of fairness requires that military rulings on constitutional issues conform to Supreme Court standards, unless it is shown that conditions peculiar to military life require a different rule.* The military establishment is not a foreign jurisdiction; it is a specialized one. The wholesale exclusion of constitutional errors from civilian review and the perfunctory review of servicemen's remaining claims urged by the government are limitations with no rational relation to the military circumstances which may qualify constitutional requirements. The benefits of collateral review of military judgments are lost if civilian courts apply a vague and watered-down standard of full and fair consideration that fails, on the one hand, to protect the rights of servicemen, and, on the other, to articulate and defend the needs of the services as they affect those rights.

. . .

We conclude that the Court of Military Appeals fully and fairly considered appellant's claims of constitutional error and disposed of them in accordance with Supreme Court standards. The judgment of the District Court is

Affirmed.

The principal case is discussed in 19 American U. L. Rev. 84 (1969).

The Gallagher v. Quinn case, cited in the above opinion, upheld the constitutionality of the UCMJ, which denied the accused a right of review of his conviction by the Court of Military Appeals even though such a review is accorded a general or flag officer. Review of the principal case was denied by the Supreme Court, 391 U.S. 1013 (1970).

---

*For example, it has been pointed out that what might be an illegal search by a police officer may be a routine inspection in the services, and that here the balancing of interests will be affected by the military context. Note, Servicemen in Civilian Courts, 76 Yale L.J. at 399. Similarly, the government has suggested elsewhere that military rank has its penalties as well as its privileges, and that conduct which is excusable for an enlisted man may be punishable for an officer. Brief for the Government at 38, United States v. Augenblick, 393 U.S. 348, 89 S.Ct. 528, 21 L.Ed.2d 537 (1969).

## UNITED STATES v. AUGENBLICK*

Supreme Court of the United States, 1969.
393 U.S. 348, 89 S.Ct. 528, 21 L.Ed.2d 537.

*[ Footnotes have been omitted.  Ed.]

MR. JUSTICE DOUGLAS delivered the opinion of the Court.

Respondents, who had been convicted by courts-martial, brought these suits for back pay.  Augenblick, though charged with sodomy, was convicted of a lesser offense, an indecent act, and Juhl was convicted of selling overseas merchandise of an Air Force Exchange. Augenblick was sentenced to dismissal from the service; Juhl was sentenced to reduction in rank, partial forfeiture of pay, and confinement for six months.  Each exhausted the remedies available to him and, not having obtained relief, brought suit in the Court of Claims to recover back pay, on the ground that the court-martial infringed on his constitutional rights.  The Court of Claims undertook to review the judgments of the courts-martial for constitutional defects and rendered judgments for respondents.  180 Ct. Cl. 131, 377 F. 2d 586; 181 Ct. Cl. 210, 383 F. 2d 1009.  The case is here on petition for writs of certiorari which we granted because of the importance of the question concerning the jurisdiction of the Court of Claims to review judgments of courts-martial.  390 U.S. 1038.

Article 76 of the Uniform Code of Military Justice, 10 U. S. C. §876, provides that military review of court-martial convictions shall be "final and conclusive" and "binding upon all . . . courts . . . of the United States."  The legislative history of the provision makes clear that relief by way of habeas corpus was an implied exception to that finality clause (S. Rep. No. 486, 81st Cong., 1st Sess., 32; H. R. Rep. No. 491, 81st Cong., 1st Sess., 35)--an exception not available to respondent Augenblick because he was discharged from the service, not imprisoned, and a remedy apparently not invoked by respondent Juhl during his short period of detention.

An additional remedy, apparently now available but not clearly known at the time of these court-martial convictions, is review by the Court of Military Appeals.  In United States v. Bevilacqua, 18 U. S. C. M. A. 10, 11-12, 39 C. M. R. 10, 11-12, decided November 8, 1968, that court held that it has jurisdiction "to accord relief to an accused who has palpably been denied constitutional rights in any court-martial; and that an accused who has been deprived of his rights need not go outside the military justice system to find relief in the civilian courts of the Federal judiciary."

Prior to the enactment of Article 76, the Court of Claims had entertained suits for back pay brought by servicemen who had been convicted by courts-martial.  See, e.g., Keyes v. United States, 109 U.S. 336; Runkle v. United States, 122 U.S. 543; Swaim v. United

States, 165 U.S. 553; United States v. Brown, 206 U.S. 240. These decisions, it is argued, were based on the theory that the Court of Claims had jurisdiction over back-pay suits where the courts-martial lacked "jurisdiction" in the traditional sense, viz., where "there is no law authorizing the court-martial, or where the statutory conditions as to the constitution or jurisdiction of the court are not observed." Keyes v. United States, supra, at 340. From this premise it is urged that when, in review of state convictions by way of federal habeas corpus, the concept of "jurisdiction" was broadened to include deprivation by the trial tribunal of the constitutional rights of a defendant (Moore v. Dempsey, 261 U.S. 86; Johnson v. Zerbst, 304 U.S. 458), the scope of collateral review of court-martial convictions was also broadened. That is the position of the Court of Claims which rejected the view that the adoption of Article 76 introduced a new regime and that 10 U. S. C. §1552 which provides a remedy to correct a military record in order to "remove an injustice," see Ashe v. McNamara, 355 F. 2d 277, is, apart from habeas corpus, the exclusive remedy.

On that issue there have been a variety of views expressed in this Court. See Burns v. Wilson, 346 U.S. 137, 149, 152-153. There is likewise unresolved the question whether, if the view of the Court of Claims is correct, the District Courts might have a like jurisdiction over suits not exceeding $10,000 under the Tucker Act, 28 U. S. C. §1346 (a) (2). After hearing argument and studying the record of these cases we do not reach those questions. For we conclude that, even if we assume arguendo, that a collateral attack on a court-martial judgment may be made in the Court of Claims through a back-pay suit alleging a "constitutional" defect in the military decision, these present cases on their facts do not rise to that level.

The Court of Claims gave relief to Juhl because of the provision in paragraph 153(a) of the Manual for Courts-Martial which states that the court-martial "cannot" base a conviction "upon the uncorroborated testimony of a purported accomplice in any case, if such testimony is self-contradictory, uncertain, or improbable."

We do not stop to review the evidence which bears on this issue and which the Court of Claims sets forth in detail. See 181 Ct. Cl., at 215-225, 383 F. 2d, at 1012-1017.

The Manual was prescribed by the President pursuant to Article 36 of the Uniform Code, 10 U. S. C. §836. It is a guidebook that summarizes the rules of evidence applied by court-martial review boards. See Levy v. Resor, 17 U. S. C. M. A. 135, 37 C. M. R. 399. The paragraph regarding accomplice testimony is a statutory rule of evidence. Such rules do not customarily involve constitutional questions. See Humphrey v. Smith, 336 U.S. 695; Whelchel v. McDonald, 340 U.S. 122. The Whelchel case involved various paragraphs of the Manual dealing with the defense of insanity. We did not sanction review of those paragraphs in a collateral remedy but held that only a denial of the opportunity for the military to consider the defense of insanity "goes to the question of jurisdiction"; and we added that, "[a]ny error that may be committed in evaluating the evidence tendered is beyond the reach of review by the civil courts." 340 U.S., at 124.

Rules of evidence are designed in the interest of fair trials. But unfairness in result is no sure measure of unconstitutionality. When we look at the requirements of procedural due process, the use of accomplice testimony is not catalogued with constitutional restrictions. Of course, if knowing use of its perjured character were linked with any testimony (Mooney v. Holohan, 294 U.S. 103; Brady v. Maryland, 373 U.S. 83), we would have a problem of different dimensions. But nothing of the kind is involved here.

Augenblick's claim of constitutional defect in his court-martial concerns a phase in the discovery of evidence. He and a young airman, Hodges, were apprehended late at night in a parked car. The civilian police who arrested them turned them over to the Armed Forces Police who questioned them separately at a naval station in Washington, D.C. Hodges was then taken to an Air Force base in Maryland where he swore to a five-page written statement.

Augenblick was questioned at the naval station after Hodges. During this questioning of both men, Agent James made a tape recording of the conversations. Agent Mendelson either took some notes or wrote up some notes later.

Hodges apparently started out by denying that anything happened in the parked car and later maintained that sodomy had taken place, though, as we have said, Augenblick's conviction was for an indecent act, not for sodomy. Hodges later received an honorable discharge; and it was the theory of the defense that he may have been induced to change his testimony on a promise that one would be given. It is indeed heavily impressed on us that Hodges was kept available for some months and left in good standing, in spite of his reprehensible conduct, and given an honorable discharge only after Augenblick was convicted.

The defense moved for the production of the notes which Mendelson had taken--or later typed up--and of the tape which James had made. As to the notes, the law officer, without examining them in camera or otherwise, denied the request. As to the tapes, the law officer ordered that they be produced or that the Government produce witnesses at an out-of-court hearing who could explain their non-existence. The tapes were not produced; but each agent who had had contact with the recording was called, except Mendelson who was in Norfolk. James testified that there was a tape but no one knew where it was or what had happened to it. The defense urged that Mendelson, to whom the tapes had apparently once been delivered, be called; but the law officer after reading the record of Mendelson's testimony on the tape recording at a pretrial investigation, refused.

The question of the production of Mendelson's "notes" as well as the question of the production of the tapes bring into focus the Jencks Act, 18 U. S. C. §3500. This Act, enacted after our decision in Jencks v. United States, 353 U.S. 657, provides that when a witness testifies for the United States the Government may be required to produce "any statement" of the witness which relates to his testimony. §3500 (b). The term "statement" is defined in subsection (e) as:

"(1)   a written statement made by said witness and signed or otherwise adopted or approved by him; or

"(2)   a stenographic, mechanical, electrical, or other recording, or a transcription thereof, which is a substantially verbatim recital of an oral statement made by said witness to an agent of the Government and recorded contemporaneously with the making of such oral statement."

There is considerable doubt if Mendelson's "notes" fall within the definition of subsection (e). He testified at the court of inquiry that he made "rough pencil notes"; and he said at the pretrial investigation, "I did jot down a couple of rough notes." Both the law officer and the Board of Review concluded that these "notes" were not a "substantially verbatim" statement producible under the Jencks Act.

It is difficult to tell from this record the precise nature of Mendelson's "notes," whether they recorded part of Hodges' interview or whether they were merely a memorandum giving names, places, and hours. Certainly they were not a statement covering the entire interview; and if they were a truncated version, they would pose the question reserved in Palermo v. United States, 360 U.S. 343. Since on examination of the record we are left in doubt as to the precise nature of the "notes," we cannot say that the command of the Jencks Act was disobeyed when they were not ordered to be produced.

Moreover, we said in Palermo v. United States, supra, at 353, that the administration of the Jencks Act must be entrusted to the "good sense and experience" of the trial judges subject to "appropriately limited review of appellate courts." We cannot conclude that when it came to the "rough notes" of Mendelson, the law officer and Board of Review abused their discretion in holding that they need not be produced under the Jencks Act.

The same is true of the rulings concerning production of the tapes. There is no doubt but that the tapes were covered by the Jencks Act; and an earnest effort was made to locate them. Their nature and existence were the subject of detailed interrogation at the pretrial hearing convened at the request of the defense. Four government agents testified concerning the interrogation of Hodges, the recording facilities used, the Navy's routine in handling and using such recordings, and the fate of the tape containing Hodges' testimony. The ground was covered once again at the court-martial. The tapes were not produced; the record indeed shows that they were not found; and their ultimate fate remains a mystery. The law officer properly ruled that the Government bore the burden of producing them or explaining why it could not do so.

The record is devoid of credible evidence that they were suppressed. Whether Mendelson should have been recalled is a matter of debate and perhaps doubt. But questions of that character do not rise to a constitutional level. Indeed our Jencks decision and the Jencks Act were not cast in constitutional terms. Palermo v. United States, supra, at 345, 362. They state rules of evidence governing trials before federal tribunals; and we have never extended their principles to state criminal trials. It may be that in some situations, denial of production of a Jencks Act type of a statement might be a denial of a Sixth Amendment right. There is, for example, the command of the Sixth Amendment that criminal defendants have compulsory process to obtain witnesses for their defense. Palermo v. United States, supra, at 362 (BRENNAN, J., concurring in result). But certain it is that this case is not a worthy candidate for consideration at the constitutional level.

The Court of Claims, in a conscientious effort to undo an injustice, elevated to a constitutional level what it deemed to be an infraction of the Jencks Act and made a denial of discovery which "seriously impeded his right to a fair trial" a violation "of the Due Process Clause of the Constitution." 180 Ct. Cl., at 166, 377 F. 2d, at 606-607. But apart from trials conducted in violation of express constitutional mandates, a constitutionally unfair trial takes place only where the barriers and safeguards are so relaxed or forgotten, as in Moore v. Dempsey, supra, that the proceeding is more a spectacle (Rideau v. Louisiana, 373 U.S. 723, 726) or trial by ordeal (Brown v. Mississippi, 297 U.S. 278, 285) than a disciplined contest.

Reversed.

See Gallagher v. United States, 423 F.2d 1371 (Ct. Clms. 1970).

## SMALLWOOD v. CLIFFORD*

United States District Court, D.C., 1968.
286 F. Supp. 97.

*[ Footnotes have been omitted.  Ed.]

CURRAN, Chief Judge.

On May 3, 1968, petitioner, a Specialist Fourth Class in the United States Army stationed in the Republic of Korea, was permitted to file in this court in forma pauperis a pro se petition for a writ of habeas corpus. Petitioner alleges that he is being illegally detained by officials of the United States Army in the Republic of Korea. He was initially placed in pretrial confinement on February 29, 1968, after having been implicated in the murder of a female Korean national which occurred off post in the early morning hours of February 28, 1968. . . .

On March 11, 1968, pursuant to the provisions of the present Status of Forces Agreement between the Republic of Korea and the United States, the Korean Minister of Justice notified the Commander, United States Forces, Korea, that the Korean Government intended to exercise its primary right of jurisdiction over Specialist Smallwood on charges of murder and arson. On March 21, 1968, petitioner was also formally charged by the United States military authorities with violating Article 118(2) (unpremeditated murder) and Article 92 (failure to obey lawful general regulation) of the Uniform Code of Military Justice. Thereafter, on April 25, 1968, petitioner was indicted by the Seoul District Prosecutor, Republic of Korea. While awaiting trial by the Korean authorities, petitioner has been incarcerated at the United States Army Stockade at ASCOM City, Korea. Proceedings in the Korean courts began on June 4, 1968. Pursuant to the terms of the existing Status of Forces Agreement, petitioner will remain in the custody of the American military authorities pending final disposition of the criminal charges in the Korean court.

. . .

Petitioner asserts that respondents do not have legitimate authority to release him to the Republic of Korea for trial by a Korean court. His argument to this end may be summarized as encompassing two major points:

1. The United States-Republic of Korea Status of Forces Agreement of 1966 was not approved by the United States Government in a constitutionally acceptable manner;

2. The fair trial guarantees in the United States-Republic of Korea Status of Forces Agreement are insufficient in law and practice to protect the petitioner against violations of his Fourteenth Amendment due process rights.

. . .

It should be stated at the outset that under the applicable principles of international law, Korea should have exclusive jurisdiction to punish offenses committed within its territory, unless it expressly or impliedly consents to surrender its jurisdiction. Thus, the Status of Forces Agreement embodied the consent of the Korean government to a diminished role in the enforcing of its territorial laws. The United States did not waive any jurisdiction over crimes committed

within its territory. The Agreement constituted a unilateral waiver
by Korea of criminal jurisdiction in certain limited cases. Where a
crime falls outside the area covered by this limited waiver, primary
jurisdiction is maintained by the nation within which the crime
occurred. Ratification of this principle by the United States Senate
is clearly unnecessary, since Senate approval could have no effect
on a grant of jurisdiction by the Republic of Korea, which the United
States could not rightfully claim.

. . .

Petitioner states that both the Constitution and the Uniform
Code of Military Justice provide the method of trying servicemen
abroad and that this method cannot be altered by an Executive Agreement. This contention has merit only in instances in which there has
been no violation of the criminal code of a foreign state. However,
when the offense is against the laws of another nation, primary jurisdiction lies with that nation, and only when it expressly or impliedly
waives its jurisdiction will the provisions of the Uniform Code of
Military Justice apply. The Girard case holds that the primary right
of jurisdiction belongs to the nation in whose territory the serviceman commits the crime.

. . .

Petitioner's final contention is that the fair trial guarantees of
the Agreement of 1966 are insufficient to protect his due process
rights under the Fourteenth Amendment. He alleges that the nature
of the Korean system of criminal justice is inherently violative of
the Fourteenth Amendment requirements of due process. To this
end, petitioner asserts several unsubstantiated shortcomings
allegedly inherent in Korean courts. The numerous provisions of
the Status of Forces Agreement pertaining to the protection of the
rights of the accused are ignored by petitioner. Furthermore, the
petitioner fails to point out to the satisfaction of this court by what
authority the United States may dictate to a sovereign nation the
procedure to be followed by that nation in the exercise of its primary
jurisdiction over alleged violators of its criminal laws. . . .

The rule to show cause is discharged and the petition for a
writ of habeas corpus is dismissed.

Articles 77 through 134 of the UCMJ, referred to as the punitive articles, set forth all the offenses that are cognizable by a court-martial. Paragraphs 155 through 213 of the MCM contain discussions of each of the punitive articles and include an enumeration of the essential elements of proof applicable to each offense. Appendix 6c of the MCM contains suggested forms for specification under each punitive article; in this connection, it is noteworthy that some 63 separate forms are listed under Article 134.

The following cases and materials do not concern even a majority of these offenses, many of which compare to civilian offenses; the primary emphasis is placed upon offenses peculiar to military law.

## DESERTION

See Articles 85 and 86, UCMJ.

### UNITED STATES v. BONDAR

United States Court of Military Appeals, 1953.
2 U.S.C.M.A. 357, 8 C.M.R. 157.

ROBERT E. QUINN, Chief Judge:
The accused in this case, Private Louis E. Bondar, United States Army, was tried by general court-martial on a charge of

desertion in violation of the Uniform Code of Military Justice, Article 85, 50 USC §679. He was convicted, instead, of the offense of unauthorized absence in violation of Article 86 of the Code, 50 USC §680. The findings and sentence were set aside and the charges were ordered dismissed by the board of review. The case is before us on certificate of The Judge Advocate General, United States Army, pursuant to the provisions of the Uniform Code of Military Justice, Article 67(b)(2), 50 USC §654, raising the following issues:

> "1. Is the offense absence without leave included in a specification alleging that an accused 'did, . . . with intent to shirk important service, . . . quit his organization . . . and did remain so absent in desertion until he was apprehended . . .'?
> "2. If the answer to (1) is in the affirmative, does a finding that the accused 'did . . . quit his organization . . . and did remain so absent until he was apprehended . . .' allege the offense of absence without leave, or was it necessary for the court to make substitutions finding that accused did quit his organization 'without proper authority'?"

. . .

It will be noted that the element of absence without authority, required for desertion with intent to remain absent permanently, is not specifically mentioned in the definition of desertion with intent to avoid hazardous duty or to shirk important service. Instead, the drafters of the Code used the word "quits." Determination of the meaning of this word is essential to resolution of this controversy. If "quits" equals absence alone, then a specification alleging desertion with intent to shirk important service contains no allegation of unauthorized absence and, a fortiori, does not necessarily include as a lesser offense the crime of absence without authority. See Manual for Courts-Martial, United States, 1951, paragraph 158. On the other hand, if "quits" is synonymous with "absence without authority" then the lesser offense of absence without leave is necessarily included within a specification alleging desertion with intent to shirk important service in the words of Article 85, supra.

It is important to note at the outset that absence without leave has always been considered to be a lesser included offense of desertion with intent to remain absent permanently, to avoid hazardous duty, and to shirk important service. . . .

Appellate defense counsel makes much of the fact that the present wording of Article 85, supra, represents a change from preceding statutes. It is contended that, while prior law required proof of absence without leave to support a finding of desertion with intent to avoid hazardous duty or to shirk important service, this requirement is conspicuously absent in Article 85 of the Code. We do not agree with this rationale. . . .

It would be a distinct novelty to military law if absence without authority were not lesser included within the three major types of desertion and we are not disposed to adopt such a view without some positive indication of a desire for change by Congress.

We may note also that it is extremely difficult, from a logical standpoint, to give to the word "quits" as used in Article 85 of the Code any interpretation other than an absence without authority. Otherwise, an authorized absence from a unit, organization or place of duty could form the basis for an offense under the article. If "quits" does not import leaving without authorization, then the Article just does not make sense.

It is our conclusion that the word "quits" is used in Article 85 as a word of art legally synonymous with "goes absent without authority." Under this view, both of the questions certified must be answered in the affirmative.

The decision of the board of review is reversed and the case is remanded to The Judge Advocate General of the Army for action not inconsistent with this opinion.

Judges LATIMER and BROSMAN concur.

## UNITED STATES v. APPLE*

United States Court of Military Appeals, 1953.
2 U.S.C.M.A. 592, 10 C.M.R. 90.

*[Footnotes have been omitted. Ed.]

PAUL W. BROSMAN, Judge:
The accused, Apple, was convicted in Korea by an Army general court-martial of desertion with intent to avoid hazardous duty. Following approval by the convening authority and affirmance by a board of review, this Court granted his petition for further review, limited, however, to the question of sufficiency of instructions.

II

The evidence adduced at the trial served to paint this factual backdrop. Accused absented himself without authority from his unit, which was then on the main line of resistance in Korea, and was absent therefrom for several days. It is clear beyond cavil that his organization was in fact engaged in "hazardous duty" during that period. However, as a witness in his own behalf, the accused related that in leaving his place of duty and going to the rear, he had no intention whatever of doing so for the purpose of avoiding hazardous duty--but rather that he proposed only to see what had occasioned the evident confusion in his records with respect to rotation points. This explanation is strongly supported by the fact that he had then been in Korea for some twenty months, of which approximately thirteen had been spent on the front lines.

Desertion with intent to avoid hazardous duty--by its very terms--connotes an absence without leave the prompting for which is a specific intent entertained by the offender to avoid the hazardous duty present or in prospect. As a matter of law, the offense is not committed by reason of a naked unauthorized absence, without more, from a unit engaged in hazardous duty. However, the fact of the absence and the presence of hazardous duty may in themselves be considered sufficient evidence--under some circumstances--that the latter was the moving force behind the former. United States v. Squirrell (No. 657), 7 CMR 22, decided January 26, 1953. Let us seek to put the matter in a somewhat different way. In terms of legal distinction it is manifest that desertion with intent to avoid hazardous duty is not identical with absence without leave from a unit engaged in hazardous duty. Instead, the entertainment of a particular purpose lies at the very heart of the desertion offense. Where the assignment of an entirely different purpose is made by the accused, it is clear beyond doubt that an instruction that evidence of this other objective should be disregarded as irrelevant would constitute error. It would seem to follow, therefore, that where the existence of another aim is fairly placed in issue, it is incumbent on the law officer to instruct as to a lesser included offense, if any, of which the legally demanded purpose--that is, one to avoid hazardous duty--is not an element, and that it is error to fail to do so. . . .

. . .

Examining the instructions of the law officer as given, we observe that, although he adverted to absence without leave at one point--in the form of a comment on the evidence--at no juncture did he state that this offense was, on the facts of the case, lesser included within that charged, much less did he instruct the court on the elements thereof. Neither the fact that no request for such instructions was made by defense counsel, nor the possibility that the members of the court, qua officers of the service, may have known that it was open to them to return a finding of guilty of absence without leave, can serve to excuse the failure of the law officer. His failure constituted prejudicial error. United States v. Lowery, supra.

A concluding caveat should be entered. Our holding here in no sense involves a failure to recognize fully the distinction between "intent" and "motive"--traditional in the common law of crimes. This is not the problem at all. Our single task here has been to determine the intent of Congress in setting the elements of the offense of desertion with intent to avoid hazardous duty.

III

Accordingly, the decision of the board of review is reversed. The record is returned to The Judge Advocate General, United States Army, for rehearing, for reference to the board of review for

consideration of affirmance of the lesser included offense, or for
other action not inconsistent with this opinion.
    Chief Judge QUINN concurs.
    [Concurring opinion of Judge Latimer omitted.]

## UNITED STATES v. McKENZIE

United States Court of Military Appeals, 1964.
14 U.S.C.M.A. 361, 34 C.M.R. 141.

FERGUSON, Judge:
    Tried by general court-martial, the accused was found guilty
of desertion with intent to avoid important service, in violation of
Uniform Code of Military Justice, Article 85, 10 USC §885. He was
sentenced to bad-conduct discharge, forfeiture of all pay and allowances, and confinement at hard labor for one year. The convening
authority approved the sentence. The board of review affirmed findings of guilty of absence without leave for the period involved and
only so much of the sentence as provided for bad-conduct discharge,
total forfeitures, and confinement at hard labor for ten months. Its
decision has been certified to this Court by The Judge Advocate General of the Army upon the following question:

> "WAS THE BOARD OF REVIEW CORRECT IN
> HOLDING THAT EVIDENCE OF THE ACCUSED'S
> ORDERS ASSIGNING HIM TO THE EIGHTH UNITED
> STATES ARMY PERSONNEL CENTER WAS AS A
> MATTER OF LAW INSUFFICIENT TO SUPPORT A
> FINDING THAT THIS SERVICE WAS 'IMPORTANT
> SERVICE' WITHIN THE MEANING OF ARTICLE
> 85(a) (2) OF THE UNIFORM CODE OF MILITARY
> JUSTICE?"

    . . .
    According to the evidence, the accused, while stationed at Fort
Bragg, North Carolina, was issued orders directing him to report to
the United States Army Overseas Replacement Station, Oakland Army
Terminal, California, on March 19, 1962, for transfer to the Eighth
United States Army Personnel Center, APO 20, San Francisco,
California. Apparently, he departed from Fort Bragg, North Carolina, in compliance with such orders on February 6, 1962. He did
not, however, report to the Oakland Army Terminal, nor did he report to the Eighth United States Army Personnel Center. On January
5, 1963, accused surrendered himself to civilian authorities and was
returned to military control on the same date.
    The Eighth United States Army Personnel Center is located in
Korea, and accused's orders indicated his military occupational

specialty to be that of infantryman. In a voluntary statement executed on January 7, 1963, accused declared that this absence was motivated by an intent to avoid shipment to Korea. He further stated that, if given the opportunity to remain in service, he "would go AWOL again" and "I don't like it, I hate it."

The board of review reduced the findings of guilty to absence without leave, as it found nothing in the record upon which a finding might be predicated that the service which the accused intended to avoid was "important," in the sense of Code, supra, Article 85. Before us, the Government contends the board erred and compares present day overseas service in Korea to " 'foreign service during time of war or under emergency conditions and in or near a combat area.' " United States v Taylor, 2 USCMA 389, 9 CMR 19, at page 391; United States v Shull, 1 USCMA 177, 2 CMR 83. The analogy, we believe, is inapt.

. . .

If Korea, then, is not to be specially differentiated from the other overseas outposts at which our troops are on guard against potentially aggressive forces, there was, as the board of review said, nothing presented to the court-martial upon which its members might base a finding that accused's intended service possessed any of those peculiar hallmarks which branded it as "important" within the meaning of Code, supra, Article 85. In a very general sense, of course, any military service is important both to the Nation as a whole and to the particular unit and individuals involved. But that is not the sort of duty Congress had in mind when it enacted the applicable punitive sanction. As we have heretofore held, the usual course of duty overseas is excluded from the ambit of Article 85. Thus, in United States v Boone, 1 USCMA 381, 3 CMR 115, we declared, at page 384:

> "Undoubtedly, service beyond the continental limits of the United States may, under certain circumstances, be considered 'important service,' but we believe that phrase as used in the Article of War and as explained in the Manual denotes something more than the ordinary everyday service of every member of the armed forces stationed overseas. If it does not, then absence without leave and desertion outside the continental limits of the United States would be synonymous." [Emphasis supplied.]

To the same effect, see United States v Hemp, 1 USCMA 280, 3 CMR 14; United States v Deller, 3 USCMA 409, 12 CMR 165; United States v Stabler, 4 USCMA 125, 15 CMR 125; and United States v Hyatt, 8 USCMA 67, 23 CMR 291. Indeed, in this very Term, we pointed out:

> ". . . Assignment to overseas duty or to sea duty may, under some conditions, be important service; under

others it may not be. Thus, assignment to an overseas unit 'during time of war or under emergency conditions and in or near a combat area' is substantially different from assignment today to a unit stationed in Okinawa or Spain. . . . As we noted in the Hyatt case, at page 68, whether 'the "something more" (that distinguishes important service from ordinary every day service of the same kind) is present depends entirely upon the circumstances of the particular case.' " [Merrow, supra, at page 267.]

It is this "something more" which is conspicuously absent from this record. The accused is shown to have been ordered in the ordinary course of duty to a personnel replacement center in Korea. His specialty was that of the usual infantryman. Thus, what is made out is nothing more than intent to avoid "the ordinary everyday service of every member of the armed forces stationed overseas." United States v Boone, supra, at page 384. As this is not enough to characterize the accused's service as "important," the board of review correctly decided the evidence was insufficient in law to support the findings of guilty. The certified issue, therefore, must be answered in the affirmative.

. . .

Chief Judge QUINN and Judge KILDAY concur.

See also U.S. v. Hyatt, 8 USCMA 67, 23 CMR 291 (1957). In U.S. v. Smith, 18 USCMA 46, 39 CMR 46 (1968), the Court of Military Appeals found that proof of the accused's assignment to Saigon and of the fact that hostile pay was afforded personnel on duty in that area was insufficient as a matter of law to sustain a finding of guilty of desertion with intent to avoid hazardous duty.

## UNITED STATES v. COTHERN

United States Court of Military Appeals, 1957.
8 U.S.C.M.A. 158, 23 C.M.R. 382.

HOMER FERGUSON, Judge:

Despite his plea to the contrary, Ralph Estell Cothern, a seaman apprentice in the United States Navy, was tried and convicted of desertion and failure to obey a lawful order, in violation of Articles 85 and 92, Uniform Code of Military Justice, 10 USC §§885 and 892, respectively. He was sentenced to be discharged from the service with a bad-conduct discharge, to forfeit all pay and allowances, to be confined at hard labor for one year and six months, and to be reduced to the grade of seaman recruit. The convening authority, after providing that forfeitures should apply to pay and allowances becoming due on and after the date of his action, approved the findings and the sentence. A board of review affirmed the findings and sentence as approved below. This Court granted petition for review on the single following issue:

> "Whether the law officer erred by permitting the court-martial to base a finding of guilty of desertion upon the theory that seventeen days was a much prolonged absence."

At trial, evidence was introduced by the prosecution which showed that the accused had been the subject of a series of absences most of which had been terminated by apprehension. The last such absence and apprehension are the subject of the present desertion charge. The accused presented evidence of family difficulties and the physical condition of a brother who had been seriously injured. He denied an intention to desert the Naval Service and explained that his absences were made necessary by the exigencies of his family situation. In particular he claimed he wanted to be near his injured brother and to accomplish the rehabilitation of his father. A detailed examination of the evidence is unnecessary for the disposition of this case. It is also unnecessary to discuss the facts relating to the charge of disobedience of a lawful order.

Among his instructions to the court-martial, the law officer included the following remarks:

> "If the condition of absence without proper authority is much prolonged and there is no satisfactory explanation of it, the court will be justified in inferring from that fact alone an intent to remain absent permanently.
>
> "If the court finds that an absence of approximately 17 days has been proved, it is for the court to determine if such period of absence is a much prolonged one under all the facts and circumstances in this case, and it is for the court to determine from the evidence whether the absence has been satisfactorily explained.
>
> "To warrant a conviction, evidence of a much prolonged absence or of other circumstances must be introduced from which the intent to desert can be inferred."
> [Emphasis supplied.]
>
> . . .

. . .

The first paragraph of the instructions set forth above states that if the absence alleged is characterized as much prolonged, and is not explained to the court-martial's satisfaction, they might infer from that "fact" alone that the accused intended to desert. Thus, on the basis of this first paragraph, the court-martial could believe that if they found that the absence was much prolonged they would not have to consider the intent of the accused. This, of course, is contrary to the doctrine set forth in the case of Morissette v United States, 342 US 246, 72 S Ct 240, 96 L ed 288, and is error. See also United States v Miller, 8 USCMA 33, 23 CMR 257. The court-martial must consider the specific intent of the accused and not some substituted "established fact" of a justifiable inference. Seventeen days is merely one fact from which, when considered with all the other evidence in the case, an intent to desert may be inferred.

It is clear that justifiable inferences are a proper subject in the instruction of the court-martial. United States v Ball, 8 USCMA 25, 23 CMR 249; United States v Miller, supra. In those cases we stated that the important question is not what nomenclature is used in describing justifiable inferences, but what effect these inferences are to be allowed in the court-martial's determinations. Happily, in the instant case we are free of the problem of nomenclature as the law officer here used only the direct terminology. He spoke in terms of justifiable inferences but not in the ambiguous terminology of presumptions. Unhappily, we are, however, still faced with the problem of the effect that this justifiable inference had on the court-martial.

. . .

One necessary ingredient of the offense of desertion as charged in the instant case is that the accused intended to remain away permanently from his place of service. Article 85(a)(1), Uniform Code of Military Justice, 10 USC §885. The court-martial must consider the necessary ingredient of intent and if the instructions as given would have allowed them to convict the accused of desertion without their considering his specific intent, such instructions were in error and he was prejudiced. This is exactly what occurred in this case. The "established fact" in this justifiable inference is a period of absence. The fact that a court-martial is admonished to consider all the facts and circumstances in arriving at an adjectival characterization of a period of absence is of no consequence. Neither the law officer nor the Manual for Courts-Martial, supra, may substitute a period of absence for the necessary ingredient of intent--regardless of the character of such a period. An absence of seventeen days, or seventeen months, or seventeen years, is only an absence--though its probative value may be great--and it is not a substitute for intent. The court-martial must consider the intent of the accused. See, for a general discussion on other aspects of this problem, H. H. Brandenburg, Proof of Intent to Desert 17 The Federal Bar Journal, April-June, 1957.

The third paragraph of the above-quoted instructions, rather than helping to explain the effect of this inference, explains in the disjunctive that evidence of a much prolonged absence is sufficient alone to permit an inference of intent. This compounds the error.

The accused pleaded not guilty to desertion and the central issue in this case was the intent of the accused. Though the question of a "much prolonged absence" was not an issue, the court-martial could have considered it and thereby have eliminated from their consideration the accused's intent. The decision of the board of review is therefore reversed. The findings of guilty of Charge I are set aside, and the record is returned to The Judge Advocate General of the Navy for reference to a board of review. The board in its discretion may approve the lesser offense of absence without leave and reassess the entire sentence, or it may order a rehearing on the desertion charge.

Chief Judge QUINN concurs.

[Concurring opinion of Judge Latimer omitted.]

## UNITED STATES v. SOCCIO

United States Court of Military Appeals, 1957.
8 U.S.C.M.A. 477, 24 C.M.R. 287.

HOMER FERGUSON, Judge:

We granted review in this case to consider the correctness of the law officer's instructions. The accused was convicted of desertion, in violation of Article 85, Uniform Code of Military Justice, 10 USC §885, for an absence of some four and one-half years' duration, terminated by apprehension. He had entered a plea of guilty to the lesser offense of absence without leave, in violation of Article 86 of the Code, supra, 10 USC §886, but not guilty to the greater offense of desertion. The only issue before the court-martial concerned the question of the accused's intent.

Testifying in his own behalf, he related in detail the reasons underlying his unauthorized absence during the period alleged. After having spent several weeks at home on leave he found that he lacked sufficient funds to return to his organization. He obtained civilian employment in order to earn funds to return. It became necessary, however, to give the money earned to his father who was unemployed at the time. While at home he met a young lady whom he married after a brief engagement. He informed her of his status as an absentee from the Army and of his intent to return to the service. She became pregnant shortly after their marriage and because of her weak physical condition, he decided to remain at home in order to take care of her. Her pregnancy ended in a miscarriage. He made preparations to return to the service only to be told by his wife that she was again pregnant. This second pregnancy also unfortunately ended in a miscarriage. After this the accused "wanted to come back real bad" but lacked the means of adequately caring for his wife. She subsequently became pregnant a third time and a child was born shortly before he was apprehended. He further testified that he again decided to return but delayed his departure because the child was too young and his wife too ill at the time. He then decided to wait until a few bills were paid before he returned. During his absence he had lived in the same city where he had resided prior to his entry into the service. He steadfastly maintained that he intended to return throughout his absence. The accused's wife corroborated his testimony that during their marriage he had frequently expressed an intent to return to the service and that on several occasions he had started to turn himself in only to be dissuaded by her pleas begging him to remain.

After opposing counsel had presented closing argument, the law officer outlined to the court the elements of the offense. He then instructed as follows:

> "You are advised that the statement 'and a purpose to return provided a particular but uncertain event happens in the future may be considered an intent to remain away permanently' contained in paragraph 164a(1), to be found at page 311 of the Manual, is an incorrect statement of the law. With regard to a contingent intent to return, you are advised that a purpose to return provided a particular but uncertain event happens in the future may not, standing alone, be considered proof of an intent to remain away permanently. Such evidence should be considered by you along with other relevant evidence, if any, of intent in the record in determining whether or not an intent to remain away permanently exists."

Several instructional errors are assigned as grounds for reversal. The first contention made is that the law officer erred in advising the court that concerning the issue of intent, it could consider--"along with other relevant evidence"--that a purpose to return provided a particular but uncertain event happens in the future is proof of an intent to remain away permanently. In discussing the offense of desertion, paragraph 164a(1), Manual for Courts-Martial, United States, 1951, contains the statement that:

> ". . . a purpose to return, provided a particular but uncertain event happens in the future, may be considered an intent to remain away permanently."

We have had occasion in the past to fully consider the correctness of this Manual provision. In United States v Rushlow, 2 USCMA 641, 10 CMR 139, the accused--as in the instant case--was found

guilty of desertion terminated by apprehension. At trial he had testified that upon arriving home he found his mother in need of an operation and because of his parents' financial difficulties, he decided to
obtain employment in order to help defray expenses. He further contended that he did not intend to desert the service but instead intended to return when his brother was discharged from the service.
The law officer in instructing the court, read the Manual passage set
forth above. We held the instruction erroneous and, in the course of
our opinion, said:

> ". . . The instruction thus told the court members
> that if they believed the accused had a purpose to return,
> but that this purpose was conditioned upon his brother's
> relief from active duty, and contributions to the support
> of the family, it might find the accused intended to remain
> away permanently. The instruction did not require that
> that factor be considered with other relevant evidence of
> intent in the record as it stated that his intent not to return
> could be gathered from that fact alone. To inform a court
> it could so find seems to be converting a probable intent
> to return to the service into an intent not to do so. The
> practical effect of such an instruction was to render the
> accused's explanation no more than a judicial confession
> and its legal effect was to announce a new rule of law, that
> is, specific intent to remain away may be established by
> proving an intent to return if the latter is based on a con-
> tingency. Accused's only defense was predicated upon a
> qualified intent to return to the service but the members
> of the court-martial were instructed that this mental con-
> dition could be considered as equivalent to one which
> purposed an intent to remain away forever. While an in-
> tent to return based on a contingency might be rejected
> as a defense to a crime otherwise established, it is diffi-
> cult to support a statement to the effect that it establishes
> an essential element to remain away permanently when
> it has a tendency to prove the opposite." [Emphasis
> supplied.]

The law officer in the instant case was obviously familiar with
our Rushlow holding for he had earlier informed the court that the
passage "contained in paragraph 164a(1), to be found at page 311 of
the Manual, is an incorrect statement of law." He was in error, however, when he advised the court that although it could not consider a
contingent intent to return "standing alone" as proof of an intent to
remain away permanently, it could consider such evidence "along
with other relevant evidence." Evidence of an intent to return provided a particular but uncertain event happens in the future is not

in any manner indicative of an intent to remain away permanently, but, on the contrary, is evidence of a probable intent to return. It is within the exclusive province of the court-martial to believe or reject such evidence in reaching its findings unfettered by any instruction which seeks to convert a probable intent to return into an intent to desert. The entire thrust of the accused's defense other than his own statements that he never intended to desert the service, was based on a contingent intent to return when his wife was able to care for herself and their baby. In such a setting, the erroneous instruction was prejudicial to the accused.

. . .

One further matter merits attention. Twice the law officer in the brief instruction here under consideration informed the court that an intent to remain away permanently might be inferred from the length of absence "in the absence of satisfactory explanation." We believe this had the effect of compounding the other errors found in the instructions. As the length of absence was undisputed, the accused was thus required to convince the court of his innocence by a "satisfactory" explanation of his absence. Such an instruction has the effect of shifting the burden of proof to an accused in order to establish his innocence rather than placing the burden on the Government throughout the trial to prove the accused's guilt beyond a reasonable doubt. Article 51(c) of the Uniform Code of Military Justice.

. . .

The burden is always on the prosecution to establish the guilt of an accused beyond a reasonable doubt. Price v United States, 200 F2d 652 (CA 5th Cir) (1953). To misplace that burden, as was done in the instant case by instructing the court that the accused must satisfactorily explain his absence, requires an accused to acquit himself rather than requiring the Government to convict him. Lambert v United States, 101 F2d 960 (CA 5th Cir) (1939). We believe a sound rule is the one stated in Dillon v United States, 218 F2d 97 (CA 8th Cir) (1955), where the court said:

> "Great care should be observed in the exercise of judicial discretion to the end that no shifting of the burden placed upon the prosecution to prove guilt result in requiring to any degree or extent that a defendant prove his innocence. The burden of proof must remain on the prosecution to establish guilt. The administration of justice is not a game of chess or of hide-and-seek. It is a search for truth and the application of the law to the true facts in order that substantial justice be done under the law."

In view of the several errors contained in the law officer's instructions, the accused's conviction of desertion cannot stand. The decision of the board of review is reversed. The record of trial is returned to The Judge Advocate General of the Army for reference to a board of review. The board, in its discretion, may approve the lesser offense of absence without leave and reassess the sentence or it may order a rehearing on the principal charge.

Chief Judge QUINN concurs.

[Concurring opinion of Judge Latimer omitted.]

The question of the sufficiency of the evidence to require instruction on the lesser included offense of absence without leave in a trial for desertion has been considered by COMA on many occasions. In U.S. v. Swain, 8 USCMA 387, 24 CMR 197 (1957), the Court held the law officer had erred in not instructing even though the accused was absent for 12 years! Compare U.S. v. Williams, 9 USCMA 3, 25 CMR 265 (1958), where the Court upheld the law officer's refusal to instruct even though there was evidence that the accused "turned himself in."

## OFFENSES CONCERNED WITH THE
## SUPERIOR-SUBORDINATE RELATIONSHIP

See Articles 89-92, UCMJ.

### UNITED STATES v. BROWN

United States Court of Military Appeals, 1957.
8 U.S.C.M.A. 516, 25 C.M.R. 20.

ROBERT E. QUINN, Chief Judge:

The accused stands convicted of disobeying a lawful general order, in violation of Article 92, Uniform Code of Military Justice, 10 USC §892, and committing an assault in which grievous bodily harm was intentionally inflicted, in violation of Article 128, Uniform Code of Military Justice, 10 USC §928. We granted review to consider two questions regarding the first offense.

The order which the accused is charged with violating is described as a general order of Company A, 855th Engineer Battalion. The organization was commanded by a first lieutenant in the Corps of Engineers, and he issued the order as part of a "Standard

Operating Procedure" for the whole company. The first question is whether a first lieutenant commanding a company has power to issue a general order.

In pertinent part, Article 92 provides that a person subject to the Uniform Code who fails to obey "any lawful general order or regulation," or "any other lawful order issued by a member of the armed forces" shall be punished as a court-martial may direct. In the Table of Maximum Punishments, the President established a maximum punishment for the offense. See Article 56, Uniform Code of Military Justice, 10 USC §856; Manual for Courts-Martial, United States, 1951, paragraph 127c, Section A. The Table differentiates between a "general order or regulation" and "any other lawful order." The former carries the relatively severe penalty of a dishonorable discharge, total forfeitures, and confinement at hard labor for two years; the punishment for the latter is limited to a bad-conduct discharge, total forfeitures, and confinement at hard labor for not more than six months. Therefore, the determination of the nature of a particular order has serious punitive consequences for an accused.

A definition of a general order is set out in paragraph 171a of the Manual. It says that a "general order . . . is one which is promulgated by the authority of a Secretary of a Department and which applies generally to an armed force, or one promulgated by a commander which applies generally to his command." As a matter of substantive law, the definition is not binding upon us in construing the meaning of the Code provision. For two reasons, however, it is a proper starting point for consideration of this case. First, it is a practical administrative interpretation, and, as such, is entitled to weight. See United States v Garcia, 5 USCMA 88, 17 CMR 88. Second, the President is authorized to prescribe the maximum punishment for an offense in violation of Article 92, Uniform Code of Military Justice, 10 USC §892. He has set out a separate punishment for a general order. Necessarily his definition of such an order is important.

Under the Manual definition, an order qualifies as a general order only if it is promulgated by either of two classes of persons, namely, the Secretary of an armed force or a commander. The Manual does not define a commander. Consequently, the Government argues that we should look to the service regulations for the definition. Army Regulations describe the officer in charge of a company or larger administrative or tactical unit as a "commander"; the person in charge of a unit smaller than a company is called a "leader." SR 320-5-1, paragraph 2, November 24, 1953. See also Dictionary of United States Military Terms for Joint Usage, Fourth Revision, February 1957, page 48. It would follow from this argument that, since the lieutenant in this case was in charge of a company, he was authorized to promulgate a general order. The argument, however, overlooks other important considerations.

The Manual lists only two classes empowered to promulgate a general order. One is at the top of the hierarchy of command in an armed force. If the Government's definition of a commander is accepted, the other class could be the lowest in the hierarchy and include enlisted personnel, if so defined by service regulation. In our opinion, the President did not intend to create such a situation. It seems to us that his specific joinder of the Secretary of a service with the term commander contemplates that the latter occupy a substantial position in effectuating the mission of the service. Consequently, the Manual definition argues against, not for, the view that the commander of minor and administrative tactical units have power to issue general orders, which would subject a violator to a dishonorable discharge, total forfeitures of pay and allowances, and confinement at hard labor for two years.

Another circumstance which militates against the possession of power to issue a general order by commanders of minor commands is found in the background of the Uniform Code. Article 92 was intended to apply to all the services. The Army and the Navy already had a history of use of the term "general order" before enactment of the Code. The Navy differentiated between a general order and a local order. The general order was one promulgated only by the Secretary of the Navy. Article 8(20), Articles for the Government of the Navy. An order issued by a local commander was not a general order, and a violation of such an order was punishable under Article 22, which provided generally for the punishment of other offenses not expressly listed in the Articles for the Government of the Navy. The frequency of the latter offense prompted Navy authorities to propose its delineation as a separate offense. See Proposed Articles for the Government of the Navy, Revised, June 30, 1945, Articles 4a(70) (71), Appendix B, page 39.

In the Army, the Articles of War did not, as did the Articles for the Government of the Navy, expressly distinguished between a general order by the Secretary of the Department and the order of subordinate commanders, but the practice was substantially the same as in the Navy. The Secretary of War promulgated as "general orders" directives intended for servicewide applicability. Lesser commanders sometimes designated their commandwide precepts as "standing orders" (See United States v Snyder, 1 USCMA 423, 4 CMR 15), but it was usual for Army commanders of major areas and installations to use the term "general orders" for directives applying to all members of their command. Army regulations in effect at the time of enactment of the Uniform Code classified orders into two main groups, routine orders and combat orders. AR 310-110, May 26, 1949, as supplemented by SR 310-110-1, May 26, 1949. The former classification was further subdivided as follows: General orders, special orders, letter orders, orders (detachment, company, or similar unit), general court-martial orders, special court-martial orders, bulletins, circulars, and memorandums. Of these, the general order was plainly authorized for use under normal conditions only by major commanders. . . .

. . . In the light of the then existing practice, we doubt that Congress intended to grant to all inferior commanders the same authority to promulgate general orders which had previously been reserved to the Secretary of a Department and to commanders of major commands. We hold, therefore, that the order in this case is not a "general order" but merely "another lawful order" within the meaning of Article 92 of the Uniform Code.

. . .

The decision of the board of review as to the sentence is set aside. The record of trial is returned to The Judge Advocate General of the Army for submission to a board of review for reconsideration of the sentence on the basis of a violation of a "lawful order" contrary to Article 92 and the findings of guilty on the assault charge.

Judges LATIMER and FERGUSON concur.

---

An order to perform close-order drill indefinitely given for legitimate training and not as punitive action was upheld as legal (U.S. v Trani, 3 CMR 27 [1952]). An order given an accused not to talk to anyone in a unit concerned with an investigation, however, was held to be too broad and illegal (U.S. v Wysong, 9 USCMA 249, 26 CMR 29 [1958]).

---

## UNITED STATES v. MILLDEBRANDT

United States Court of Military Appeals, 1958.
8 U.S.C.M.A. 635, 25 C.M.R. 139.

GEORGE W. LATIMER, Judge:

This case reaches us by certificate of The Judge Advocate General of the Navy and only the facts and circumstances necessary to a disposition of the questions certified by him will be related. A special court-martial inter alia found the accused guilty of willfully disobeying a lawful command of his superior officer, in violation of Article 90, Uniform Code of Military Justice, 10 USC §890. The convening authority in his action affirmed only the lesser included offense of failing to obey a lawful order, contrary to Article 92, Uniform Code of Military Justice, 10 USC §892.

A board of review in the office of The Judge Advocate General of the Navy reversed the findings and sentence but the reasons assigned for reaching that result were not unanimous. A majority of the board concluded that the order imposed upon the accused a duty which was inconsistent with his leave status and therefore was not a legal order. The third member of the board concluded that illegality of the order arose out of the nature and extent of the duty saddled on the accused. The Judge Advocate General of the Navy thereupon certified the case to us requesting that we answer the following questions:

"1. Was the order as stated in the specification of Charge I a lawful one?
"2. If so, was the accused required to comply therewith during a period of authorized leave?"

The operative facts necessary to place the questions in their proper perspective are as follows: During the latter part of 1956, the accused was heavily burdened with personal financial problems. In order to augment his income, he requested a thirty-day leave of absence during which time he anticipated civilian employment. The leave was granted but it was conditioned upon the accused making certain weekly reports. The officer authorizing the leave testified that he was required to submit a weekly written report to the executive officer on the accused's financial condition and to do that it was necessary that he receive progress reports from the accused. He therefore ordered the accused to report his financial transactions at certain specified times. The direction for the first period was not complied with and shortly thereafter a telegram was dispatched ordering him to report back to his command. There appears to be some question as to whether this telegram was ever received by the accused, but four days thereafter a second message was dispatched to him and, pursuant to the direction contained therein, he reported back to his station.

In order to answer the first question, it is necessary that we consider the facts alleged in the specification. The charge and specification here involved are as follows:

"Charge I: Violation of the Uniform Code of Military Justice, Article 90
"Specification: In that James R. Milldebrandt, Disbursing Clerk Second Class, U.S. Navy, Naval Administrative Command, U.S. Naval Training Center, San Diego, California, having received a lawful order from Lieutenant W. B. McDonald, Naval Administrative Command, U.S. Naval Training Center, San Diego, California, his superior officer, to report to him, Lieutenant McDonald, during the week beginning Monday, 5 November

1956 and ending Friday, 9 November 1956 concerning his,
the said Milldebrant's indebtedness, did, at San Diego,
California, on or about 9 November 1956, willfully disobey the same."

The first certified question is not stated aptly, for the specification does not give us sufficient information to ascertain the full extent and scope of the report to be submitted by the accused.
Pretermitting the duty to report while on leave, the parties agree
that an order to report about the status of indebtedness may be lawfully issued by a commanding officer.  For the purpose of this case,
we need not express an opinion on the concession, but that is not to
say that every order directing an accused to make a full disclosure
about his personal business may be valid.  A command to file a complete and comprehensive report may compel an accused to disclose
transactions which have a tendency to incriminate him, or which
might subject him to the imposition of sanctions, or which would
breach confidential communications.  Furthermore, such a directive
might require him to publicize financial involvements which are of
no concern to the military community.  Certainly the legality or
illegality of the order must be determined by its terms, and here the
allegations of the specification leave everything to the imagination
of the pleader.  Unless orders concerning personal dealings by their
terms are limited to the furnishing of information which essentially
does not narrow or destroy the rights and privileges granted to an
accused by the Code or other principles of law, they should not be
considered as legal.  From the foregoing and in view of the general
nature of the pleading, it becomes necessary to look to the facts to
determine the sweep of the order given.
    In this instance, the evidence found in the record is of no
assistance in determining the legality or illegality of the order.  The
officer merely directed the accused to report to him on his financial
affairs during stated periods.  The nature of the information ordered
to be furnished is not shown and for aught that appears, the accused
might have been required to give a detailed statement of every financial transaction engaged in by him while off duty.  It should be
apparent that if the order was as broad as that, the accused might be
prosecuted for failure to disclose information of a confidential or
incriminating nature.  While we do not pass on the legality of all
orders dealing with personal business, we do not believe the authority
of a commanding officer extends to the point that an accused can be
ordered to make all facets of his personal dealings public.  By way
of illustration to support our theory, we mention one fact set out in
accused's pretrial statement.  He concedes obtaining some money
but says he lost it gambling.  Had he been interrogated about that
transaction, he would have been entitled to a prior warning, but under
the order given he was required to disclose an incriminating fact

without the benefit of the privileges accorded to him by Article 31 of the Code. Accordingly, under the facts of this case, we believe the order given to be so all-inclusive that it is unenforceable. Certainly we believe that, unless an order of this type is so worded as to make it specific, definite, and certain as to the information to be supplied so that it can be measured for legality, the only penalty which can be enforced is revocation of the leave.

The second question is one of first impression in this Court, and counsel argue the issue as though there were two conflicting concepts. The first is that a member of the Armed Forces on leave is not required to perform military duty. The second is that certain military orders given to a member of the Services prior to or while on leave must be obeyed. If the two are not reconcilable, a doctrine we do not necessarily support, we believe that the nature of this order brings it under the former rule. . . .

It seems reasonable to conclude that when an enlisted man is granted leave, he ought not to be subject to orders requiring him to perform strictly military duties unless their performance is compelled by the presence of some grave danger or unusual circumstance. It seems a bit inconsistent to authorize a period of absence from duty and at the same time require the person on leave status to return intermittently to a duty status. A serviceman should be either on a leave status or a duty status, and when on the former he should not be saddled with duties which can await his return. Undoubtedly there may be instances when complete freedom from military duties cannot be the rule, for a serviceman on leave must hold himself amenable to orders of revocation and a commander should be authorized to direct him to furnish changes of address or to report where he may be reached for recall to duty if an emergency arises. However, we need not concern ourselves with the exceptions to the general rule, for in this instance we see no immediate military necessity for a commander to issue this particular type of order. It is to be remembered that the order was not to contact the creditor and thus improve the civilian-service relationship; it was to file a report. That order was not necessary to the successful pursuit of any military mission, and it was not required to maintain the morale, discipline, or good order of the unit or to keep the military free from disrepute. Assuming arguendo that the financial irresponsibility of service people has a tendency to bring discredit on the military, a report could have been furnished upon return. No doubt the officer who issued the order was prompted to do so by his desire to have the accused use the leave for the purposes intended, and obviously the latter breached the faith of those who were working to help him, but they were not left without effective measures of relief if the accused failed to comply. The leave orders were subject to revocation when accused failed to comply with the conditions imposed, and this method of returning the accused to his unit was employed by the Naval authorities when the reports were not forthcoming. It, therefore, appears to us that failure to obey this type of order might be made the basis for revoking authorized leave, but it should not be considered a crime when the accused has been freed from performance of all but extraordinary military duties. The basis of a criminal prosecution for failing to obey an order rests on a duty to comply. If there is any duty on a serviceman to furnish personal financial data, it cannot be made mandatory while he is not on a duty status. We will leave for future determination how far military commanders may go in carrying out a financial responsibility program, if at all, but for the purpose of this case, we hold that the duty imposed was illegal in the light of accused's status at the time it was disobeyed.

The decision of the board of review is affirmed.

Judge FERGUSON concurs in the result.

QUINN, Chief Judge (concurring in the result):

I have serious doubts about the validity of a number of the implications of the present opinion. Among them are the following: (1) That we approve Colonel Winthrop's dictum that military personnel on leave are "not subject to the military jurisdiction"; (2) that when an order can be construed as legal or illegal, the latter is preferable to the former. Cf. United States v Trani, 1 USCMA 293, 3 CMR 27; and (3) that it is a rule of law rather than a statement of policy that persons on leave cannot be required to perform "strictly military duties," unless "compelled by . . . some grave danger or unusual circumstance." However, I agree with the result.

Persons in the military service are neither puppets nor robots. They are not subject to the willy-nilly push or pull of a capricious superior, at least as far as trial and punishment by court-martial is concerned. In that area they are human beings endowed with legal and personal rights which are not subject to military order. Congress left no room for doubt about that. It did not say that the violation of any order was punishable by court-martial, but only that the violation of a lawful order was. Article 92, Uniform Code of Military Justice, 10 USC §892.

The legality of an order is not determined solely by its source. Consideration must also be given to its content. If an order imposes a limitation on a personal right, it must appear that it is "reasonably necessary to safeguard and protect the morale, discipline and usefulness of the members of a command and . . . directly connected with the maintenance of good order in the services." United States v Martin, 1 USCMA 674, 676, 5 CMR 102. I suppose that no one would doubt the invalidity of an order which directs military personnel who purchase an automobile to buy only from a particular manufacturer or the illegality of an order which requires military personnel who telephone family or friends by long distance to call on a person to person basis, instead of station to station. In cases of this kind, we must look closely to the connection between the personal act required by the order, and the needs of the military service. United States v Martin, supra; see also United States v Voorhees, 4 USCMA 509, 16 CMR 83; cf. United States v Noriega, 7 USCMA 196, 21 CMR 322. As the principal opinion points out, the order here is completely unrelated to any requirement of the military service. On that basis it is not a "lawful order" within the meaning of Article 92 of the Code. I would, therefore, answer the first certified question in the negative and affirm the decision of the board of review.

### UNITED STATES v. BUCKMILLER*

United States Court of Military Appeals, 1952.
4 C.M.R. 96.

*[Footnotes have been omitted. Ed.]

ROBERT E. QUINN, Chief Judge:
The accused in this case was tried and convicted by special court-martial at Fort George G. Meade, Maryland, on November 20, 1951, on charges alleging failure to obey the lawful order of a noncommissioned officer, and absence without leave. The court sentenced the accused to a bad-conduct discharge, forfeiture of pay of $25.00 per month for six months and confinement at hard labor for six months. The convening authority approved but the Army board of review, in a decision to be hereinafter discussed, reduced the confinement at hard labor to three months and the forfeiture of pay to $25.00 per month for a like period.

It appears from the record that on September 20, 1951, Sergeant First Class Jarrett, Acting First Sergeant of the Rear Detachment of the 70th Gun Battalion, ordered accused to report to the Battalion Ration Breakdown Section for duty. Accused replied that he did not have to work, or could not work, because of a boil under his arm. Although accused was advised that he would be given light work which would not interfere with his boil, accused again stated that he did not have to work, turned, and walked away. Accused did not report for ration breakdown detail at any time on the day in question.

The case was certified to us by The Judge Advocate General of the Army, and upon motion was consolidated for hearing with the case of United States v. James F. McNeely (No. 494), -- USCMA --, 4 CMR 102, decided this date, upon the following issue:

> "Does the sentence adjudged by the court-martial exceed the maximum punishment prescribed in Manual for Courts-Martial, United States, 1951, for the offenses of which the court-martial convicted the accused?"

The accused was charged with failing to obey a lawful order under Article 92 of the Uniform Code of Military Justice, 50 USC §686. The maximum punishment for this offense is a bad-conduct discharge, total forfeiture of pay and confinement at hard labor for six months. Paragraph 127c, Manual for Courts-Martial, United States, 1951, page 221. Such punishment is further limited, however, by Footnote 5, on that same page, which states that "The punishment for this offense does not apply in those cases wherein the accused is found guilty of an offense which, although involving a failure to obey a lawful order, is specifically listed elsewhere in this table." Article 86(1) of the Code, 50 USC §680, provides that any member of the armed forces who, without proper authority, fails to go to his appointed place of duty at the time prescribed shall be punished as a court-martial may direct. Paragraph 127c, supra, page 220, provides that the maximum punishment for "Failing to go to, or going from, the appointed place of duty" is confinement at hard labor for one month and forfeiture of two-thirds pay for a like period. The board of review took the position that the offense here charged as a failure to obey an order under Article 92, supra, constituted a violation of Article 86(1), supra, the maximum punishment for which is "specifically listed elsewhere in" the Table of Maximum Punishment, and that accordingly the maximum punishment is limited by Footnote 5 to confinement at hard labor for one month and forfeiture of two-thirds pay for a like period.

The problem before us is whether the restrictions of Footnote 5 apply to this case. If they do, then the board of review's action was correct. . . . The language of the footnote, even as amplified in the discussion of the drafters of the Manual, is exceedingly ambiguous. A technical and entirely literal interpretation of the footnote leads to a conclusion that in no case can an accused be convicted of knowingly failing to obey a lawful order under Article 92, supra, if the circumstances of the offense also involve, in any way, "failing to go to . . . the appointed place of duty" under Article 86. This, we think, cannot have been the result intended. The footnote becomes much more sensible if interpreted to require a comparison of the gravamen of the offense set out in the specification with the charge it is laid under and other articles under which it might have been laid.

Here, the specification alleged that the accused, having been specifically ordered to perform a certain duty, did fail to obey the order. The board of review held that this constituted a violation of Article 86(1), supra--the Code counterpart of the old "failure to repair." We have no doubt that the facts alleged in the specification would support a charge under Article 86(1). That, however, is not the test. The gravamen of the offense as spelled out in the specification is the disrespect for authority as evidenced by the disobedience of the direct order of a superior. This is obviously an offense of a more serious character than that condemned by Article 86(1). The latter article contemplates, generally, a failure to report for routine duties as prescribed by routine orders. An example may be found in United States v. Wiley, SpCM 3746, decided October 2, 1951, where the footnote under consideration was, we think, properly applied. There, the accused had been informed that his sentence by summary court-martial, including hard labor for 20 days, had been approved, and he was ordered by a Captain to report for fulfillment of the hard labor to the First Sergeant, "who would direct him to the time and place every day to report and the extra duty." The First Sergeant instructed the accused to report to the Charge of Quarters in the orderly room at 1:00 p.m. on Saturday and Sunday and at 6:00 p.m. on week days to perform two hours extra duty. The accused complied with this order until June 30, 1951, on which day he failed to report to the Charge of Quarters for extra duty. Accused was then charged with failing to obey a lawful order of Captain McCarty. The board of review applied Footnote 5 and reduced the sentence to that authorized for a violation of Article 86(1), supra.

. . .

Where a member of the Armed Forces is given a direct, personal order by a superior to report to a particular place, and this order is disobeyed, Article 92, supra, is violated. This offense is a serious one, and properly allows a more severe sentence than the avoidance of routine duty proscribed by Article 86(1), supra. The gravamen of the offense disclosed by the acts alleged in the specification here was a knowing failure to obey the direct, personal order of a superior. As such, the accused could legally have been sentenced for a violation of Article 92, supra, despite the fact that the acts alleged may also be interpreted to constitute a violation of Article 86(1), supra.

The question certified is answered in the negative. The case is remanded to The Judge Advocate General of the Army for further action consistent with this opinion.

Judge BROSMAN concurs.

GEORGE W. LATIMER, Judge (concurring in results):

I concur in the results.

. . .

The language of footnote 5 to paragraph 127c, MCM, has been revised to read as follows:

This punishment does not apply in the following cases:
(1) If in the absence of the order or regulation which was violated or not obeyed the accused would on the

same facts be subject to conviction for another specific offense for which a lesser punishment is prescribed in this table.

(2) If the violation of failure to obey is a breach of restraint imposed as a result of an order.

In these instances, the maximum punishment is that specifically prescribed elsewhere in this table for the
offense.

---

## UNITED STATES v. PINKSTON

United States Court of Military Appeals, 1956.
6 U.S.C.M.A. 700, 21 C.M.R. 22.

ROBERT E. QUINN, Chief Judge:

The accused was tried and convicted by a special court-martial
convened in Hawaii, of a failure to obey the lawful order of a superior
officer, in violation of Article 92, Uniform Code of Military Justice,
50 USC §686. The sentence, as approved by the convening and supervisory authorities, is a bad-conduct discharge, confinement at hard
labor for a period of four months, and reduction to the grade of private.
A board of review in the office of The Judge Advocate General, United
States Navy, affirmed the findings and sentence without opinion. We
granted the accused's petition for review on two issues: (1) the adequacy of the president's instructions to the court, and (2) the legal
sufficiency of the evidence to support the findings of guilty.

During an "operational readiness inspection," conducted on
October 19, 1954, by the treasurer of the commissioned officer's
club at which the accused was serving, the latter's effects were
found not to include two required tropical uniforms. He was ordered
by the treasurer, a Captain Turner, to procure this apparel by
October 22, 1954, and also to have available at that time the quartermaster's slip indicating the date on which, and the person by whom,
the purchases were made. The accused acknowledged the order, and
spoke no further of the matter to Captain Turner. However, he did
not possess the demanded clothing on the date specified.

Testifying in his own behalf at the trial, Pinkston admitted that
he had received the order in question; that he had understood its
meaning; and that he had failed to comply with it. However, in support of his plea of not guilty, he asserted that it had simply been impossible for him to remedy the uniform deficiency within the prescribed
period because of his poor financial situation. In this connection, he
testified that, since he was without funds at the time of the order, he

had sought immediately to obtain a "checkage" on his pay account. Under this procedure he might have been allowed to draw compensation in advance of pay day--the amount advanced to be diminished by deductions from forthcoming pay periods.

Following the usual chain of command, he presented an oral request to his sergeant-major for an appropriate "checkage." However, it appears that the commanding officer of the accused's unit had previously directed that all such applications be denied, in the absence of emergency need. The stipulated testimony of the sergeant-major fully corroborated the accused's assertion that his application-- tendered promptly on the date of the order--had been denied by the former on the theory that the accused's need was not one of a critical character. Thereafter, Pinkston informed his immediate noncommissioned superior of this development, but was informed that, under the circumstances, he had no choice but to await the following pay day, and thereafter to purchase the necessary uniforms.

According to the accused, the disallowance of his request for a "checkage" effectively exhausted all possibility of obtaining the requisite funds in timely fashion. He had attempted several times to borrow from members of his command for the present purpose, but he had been unable to do so, because it seems to have been recognized universally that he was a "bad loan risk." This unfortunate reputation existed, he said, for the reason that it was known that he was obliged to support not only his wife and infant child, but the offspring of a previous marriage as well.

Prior to its retirement to deliberate on findings, the court was fully and properly instructed for the record by the president on the elements of the offense charged, the presumption of innocence, reasonable doubt, and the burden of proof. No reference was made to the accused's defense of impossibility, and no further instructions were requested either by the prosecution or the defense.

Appellant's initial assignment of error raises the question of whether financial inability may, in an appropriate case, be regarded as a valid defense against a charge of failure to obey. We have previously determined that at least one variety of impossibility of performance constitutes a good defense to a charge of willful disobedience under Article 91. United States v Heims, 3 USCMA 418, 12 CMR 174; United States v King, 5 USCMA 3, 17 CMR 3. Each of the cited cases concerned an impossibility created by physical incapacity. Although the Court recognized that provision for such a defense had not been made explicitly in the Manual for Courts-Martial, United States, 1951, it nevertheless determined that the accused's claim of inability, if accepted by the court-martial, amounted to an answer to the Government's charge since he could not be deemed to have evinced that "intentional defiance of authority" on which criminality is based in these premises.

As in the case of the willful disobedience situation, the current Manual contains no mention of impossibility as a possible defense to a charge of failure to obey. It is arguable that less reason exists for a determination in favor of its utility in a "failure" situation, since in this offense there is involved no content of "intentional defiance," the absence of which was regarded as pivotal in Heims, supra. Appellate defense counsel urged, however, that the rationale of the mentioned cases is applicable--and the Government's lawyers seem to accept this point of view. We are inclined to agree.

It appears to us that, in general, failures to obey may be divided, in terms of source, into two categories. The first of these springs from conduct falling short--perhaps just short--of willful disobedience, and the second is generated by forgetfulness or other cause having its origin in simple negligence. We are concerned here only with the first, and possibly the larger, group--and it seems clear that an offense of this variety possesses at least one basic similarity to an instance of willful disobedience. By this we mean that a failure to obey brought about by such a cause as indifference to recognized authority, general rebelliousness, vague refractoriness, or the like--all wanting in that willfulness requisite for the Article 91 offense--contains some measure of conscious deliberation and choice. Indeed, such a personal decision against compliance is identical in kind, if not in degree or manifestation, to that involved in the more serious offense. By necessity, we believe, such a choice presupposes some degree of voluntariness or purposefulness. And in a situation such as that which now confronts us, it is within this area that the quality of offense--of criminality--lies. In sum, this type of a failure to obey can be considered to involve a sort of mens rea--albeit a different and more dilute one than that found in the crime of willful disobedience. On the other hand such a failure arising out of some aspect of neglect is quite without this factor of election, and is thereby rendered distinct from the situation in which compliance is available and recognized, but is simply not chosen.

Since it appears that the accused was prepared to obey the order, ostensibly at least, but was prevented from doing so by the existence or intervention of an extrinsic fact over which, for the time, he could exercise no control, that necessary element of voluntariness is absent.

Certainly, every conceivable "incapacity" cannot exonerate from criminal accountability. As we said in this regard in United States v Heims, supra:

> ". . . Incapacity, of course, may be--to some extent, at least--a matter of degree. . . . Inability . . . must, we think, be weighed in the balances of reasonableness. . . . In view of this essential element of reasonableness, it seems impossible to formulate a general rule for application to all cases. Perforce each must rest largely on the conclusions of the triers of fact, reached after a consideration of all of the evidence presented, together with

the realities of the situation as evaluated by rational military persons, and against a background of the transaction's
total setting."

Therefore--while making no attempt to devise a universal solvent for
application in this area--we deem it sufficient to hold here that impossibility of compliance with an order to purchase goods within an
assigned time, which inability is brought about by financial incapacity,
raises an affirmative defense to a charge of misconduct laid under
Article 92 of the Code.

We are not unaware of the Service conception that Article 92
provides for an "insurer" type of crime--that is, one with respect
to which the existence of any sort of affirmative defense is precluded
by the very nature of the charge. We appreciate that the present ruling will have some effect on the conduct and possible result of future
prosecutions based on failures to obey. Whereas the result was once
dependent solely on satisfactory proof of the basic elements of the
offense, these latter, standing alone, are insufficient, where the accused adduces believable evidence establishing a defense such as that
with which we are presently concerned. To this extent, therefore,
Article 92 is not an "insurer" offense. However, this result, we
believe, is demanded by considerations of essential fairness. To view
the problem otherwise would serve to perpetuate a result based solely
on the strict and empty letter of the Manual's language--one entirely
devoid of regard for the manifest and overriding spirit of moderation
implicit in every segment of the Code and the Manual. We refuse to
hold, under the facts of this case, that the accused must be deemed
guilty of a criminal offense, no matter how sincerely he may have
sought to comply with Captain Turner's direction. Any other result
is downright shocking.

It has been observed earlier that there was no request to this
special court-martial for further instructions. Was it nevertheless
necessary for the senior member to instruct respecting the claimed
incapacity? We have previously held that the law officer of a general
court-martial is required to instruct sua sponte where the evidence
operates fairly to raise an affirmative defense. . . . But shall a
similar requirement be applied to the president of a special court-
martial?
     . . .

In short--and as a general rule--the law established for the
guidance of the military judicial system by this Court must attach
with equal force to every tribunal over which we exercise appellate
jurisdiction. Our instructional decisions dictated clearly the conclusions we reached in the Heims and King cases, supra. Faced now
with a similar problem found in this lower court, consistency, and
especially sound practice, demands that we come to an identical
result.

Of course, neither the president of a special court, nor the law officer of a general, will be required to supply such an instruction unless the issue has been raised reasonably by evidence brought before the judicial agency. United States v Stout, 1 USCMA 639, 5 CMR 67, and cases cited. However, in the present case, there can be no doubt that the claimed inability of the appellant to comply with the order in suit was squarely placed before the court's members. The accused's testimony concerning his efforts to secure a "checkage" was completely corroborated--as was that having to do with the refusal of his request. Nor was his story regarding his failure to secure the necessary funds elsewhere either incredible, inherently improbable, or otherwise unworthy of belief. In other words, the appellant's account was sufficient, in our view, fairly to raise the issue of incapacity for the court's consideration. United States v Simmons, 1 USCMA 691, 5 CMR 119. That he may not have done all that he possibly could in the premises is plainly beside the point--so far as raising the issue is concerned. Any omission of his to plumb every conceivable source of funds is relevant only as it may serve to throw light on the "jury" question of whether impossibility exists in fact.

Moreover, and apart from his unfortunate credit rating, a loan from Sergeant Pinkston's service associates would probably have been difficult to obtain--this for the reason that existing Naval regulations place severe restrictions on certain aspects of this practice. Articles 1259, 1260, United States Naval Regulations, 1948. It is also to be observed that the Government's lawyer at the trial conceded in his opening argument that the accused had genuinely attempted to obtain the necessary funds. Of course, he thereafter argued, in effect, that these efforts would not serve to avail the latter here--because the charge is one of failure to obey, and not of willful disobedience, with the result that conviction is inescapable, once the fact of a failure is established beyond reasonable doubt. Following this presentation-- and supplied with no more than the bare elements of the offense alleged--the members of the court plainly had no choice but to convict. In such a setting, the president's omission was manifestly prejudicial to the accused, and demands reversal.

Since the conclusion we have reached on the initial assignment of error is dispositive of this appeal, we need not consider the second in detail. Suffice it to say, however, that, had all issues been submitted to the court here under proper instructions, we would have no disposition to question the legal sufficiency of the evidence to support findings of guilty.

Accordingly, the decision of the board of review must be, and hereby is, reversed. A rehearing is ordered.

LATIMER, Judge (concurring in the result):

I concur in the result.

The accused's testimony raised reasonably the issue that it was impossible for him to comply with the order, and the instructions

given by the president of the court neither directed the court's attention to that ingredient nor required that it be considered in arriving
at a finding. Under those circumstances, the court-martial could
find the accused guilty, even though the members believed it was impossible for him to comply with the order. That is not the law, and
so a reversal is required.

Neither motivation nor respectful demeanor determine whether
the disobedience of an order is willful. See U.S. v. Ferenczi, 10
USCMA 3, 27 CMR 77 (1958).

## OFFENSES INVOLVING COMBAT CONDITIONS

See Articles 99-106, UCMJ.

### UNITED STATES v. CAREY

United States Court of Military Appeals, 1954.
4 U.S.C.M.A. 112, 15 C.M.R. 112.

ROBERT E. QUINN, Chief Judge:
Upon common trial by general court-martial in Korea, Corporal
Herman M. Carey, and Private First Class Herman W. Clark, were
convicted of misbehavior before the enemy, in violation of Article 99,
Uniform Code of Military Justice, 50 USC §693. The accused, Corporal Carey, was sentenced to bad conduct discharge, total forfeitures,
and confinement at hard labor for three years. Private Clark was
sentenced to bad conduct discharge, total forfeitures, and confinement
at hard labor for one year. The convening authority approved the
findings and sentences, but suspended the execution of the sentence
imposed upon Clark for six months with a provision for remission
at the expiration of that period. The board of review affirmed these
actions, and the accused, Carey, petitioned this Court for review on
the ground of insufficiency of the evidence to support the findings.
We granted the petition to determine the issue thus raised.
    The material facts are as follows: On December 3, 1952, the
9th Infantry Regiment was in position on the main line of resistance
in Korea. Twenty-two tanks were arrayed immediately in front of
the regiment with the mission of maintaining a defensive position and

providing fire support for friendly patrols in their respective sectors. The accused, Carey, was commander of a tank supporting Company B. As such he was responsible for its operation and mechanical condition, and was in charge of the crew. Normally, the crew consisted of five men, including the commander. However, on the day in question, there were only four in the crew. When not on duty, the members were permitted to sleep in a bunker near the tank, but they could not leave the immediate vicinity. While in the area, the crew was on constant alert and each man was required to assume his assigned station when a call to supply fire support to a patrol was received. This tank was located 2500 yards from the Communist lines, and was within artillery, mortar, and sniper range.

During the day, Versteeg, a crew member went to the rear to obtain gasoline for the tank. While there, he purchased five bottles of whiskey with funds supplied by the accused and at his direction. By rule of the Tank Company, whiskey was prohibited in the front lines. That night Clark reported enemy activity to the Tank Company command post. His suspicions aroused by Clark's manner, the accused's platoon leader investigated the report and learned it was unfounded. The officer then went to the tank position where he discovered that both Clark and Carey were intoxicated. When the Tank Commander arrived at the site to relieve the accused, the latter was in such a stupor that he could not be aroused for a half-hour.

As a result of this conduct, Carey and Clark were charged with misbehavior before the enemy. The specification of the charge against Carey alleged that he:

> ". . . did, at APO 248, on or about 3 December 1952, before the enemy, endanger the safety of his unit, Tank Company, 9th Infantry Regiment, which it was his duty to defend, by intentional misconduct in that he became drunk while on duty as Tank Commander."

At the trial the evidence established that during that period patrols from Company B were operating in front of their lines, but did not require any support from the accused's tank. It was also indicated that no necessity for repelling hostile advances arose during the night.

In his single assignment of error, the accused contends that intoxication alone does not constitute the offense of misbehavior. He argues that Article 99 of the Code, supra, requires proof either that the condition of intoxication was induced for the purpose of evading combat, or that the accused intended thereby to endanger his unit. In support of this position the defense relies upon excerpts from Samuel's History of the British Army, London, 1816, pages 597-598, and Winthrop's Military Law and Precedents, 2d ed, 1920 Reprint, page 623. In the absence of a showing of either state of mind,

the argument concludes, the evidence is legally insufficient to support
the finding of the court-martial.

As originally enacted the American Articles of War of 1776,
provided:

> "Section XIII
> "Art. 13. Whatsoever officer or soldier shall mis-
> behave himself before the enemy, and run away, or shame-
> fully abandon any fort, post or guard, which he or they
> shall be commanded to defend, or speak words inducing
> others to do the like; or who, after victory, shall quit his
> commanding officer, or post, to plunder and pillage . . .
> shall suffer death, or such other punishment, as, by a
> general court-martial, shall be inflicted on him.
> "Art. 14. Any person, belonging to the forces of
> the United States, who shall cast away his arms and am-
> munition, shall suffer death, or such other punishment
> as shall be ordered by the sentence of a general court-
> martial."

The general provisions of these Articles were combined in
Article 52 of the 1786 Articles of War which authorized the imposition of the death penalty "or such other punishment as shall be
ordered by the sentence of a general court-martial." These provisions remained virtually unchanged until the Articles of War were
revised by Chapter II, Act of June 4, 1920, 41 Stat 787. Although this
enactment did not further define the term "misbehave himself," it
did add a new provision relating to the endangering of a command "by
any misconduct, disobedience, or neglect." Under the 1921 revision,
Article of War 75, provided:

> "ARTICLE 75. Misbehavior Before the Enemy.--
> Any officer or soldier who, before the enemy, misbehaves
> himself, runs away, or shamefully abandons or delivers
> up or by any misconduct, disobedience, or neglect en-
> dangers the safety of any fort, post, camp, guard, or other
> command which it is his duty to defend, or speaks words
> inducing others to do the like, or casts away his arms or
> ammunition, or quits his post or colors to plunder or
> pillage, or by any means whatsoever occasions false
> alarms in camp, garrison, or quarters, shall suffer death
> or such other punishment as a court-martial may direct."

Decisions of military tribunals, throughout the existence of the
"misbehavior" article, consistently construed the term as encompassing any conduct not conformable to the standard of behavior before the enemy required by the custom of our arms. Manual for

Courts-Martial, U.S. Army, 1921, paragraph 425; Manual for Courts-Martial, U.S. Army, 1928, paragraph 141; Manual for Courts-Martial, U.S. Army, 1949, paragraph 163. Numerous instances of acts constituting this offense are listed by Colonel Winthrop at pages 622 and 623 of his Precedents, supra. In discussing misbehavior he states:

> "The act or acts, in the doing, not doing, or allowing of which consists the offence, must be conscious and voluntary on the part of the offender. The mere circumstance that he is found in a condition of intoxication, when called upon to march or operate against the enemy, will not constitute the offence, unless such condition should have been induced for the express purpose of evading such service."

Samuel, in his History of the British Army, pages 597-598, similarly concludes that mere intoxication in the presence of the enemy, without more, does not constitute the offense. In his view, the offense is committed only when there is an abandonment of some positive or demonstrative duty.

It is evident that the guides thus fixed for determining guilt or innocence could be known only to one thoroughly acquainted with the decisions of military tribunals defining from time to time the standard of behavior before the enemy. Recognizing that this was an unsatisfactory method of determining the elements of a capital offense, Congress eliminated from the Uniform Code of Military Justice the general term "misbehaves himself." Moreover, it took this action only after a clear demonstration of the historical background of the term had been presented to it in a vigorous attempt by The Judge Advocate General of the Army to preserve it as a part of the Uniform Code. Hearings before Senate Committee on Armed Services, 81st Congress, 1st Session, on S 857 and HR 4080, page 275. In Article 99 of the Code, supra, the acts constituting misbehavior before the enemy are set out in eight categories. By combining the provisions of Article of War 75 and Article 4 (paragraphs 12-20) of the Articles for the Government of the Navy, 31 USC §1200, this Article seeks to particularize the conduct proscribed and to provide clear standards by which violations may be determined.

Insofar as it is pertinent to this case, Article 99, supra, provides:

> "Any member of the armed forces who before or in the presence of the enemy--
>
>     . . .
>
>     (3) through disobedience, neglect, or intentional misconduct endangers the safety of any such command, unit, place, or military property;
>
>     . . .

shall be punished by death or such other punishment as
a court-martial may direct."

As used in this Article, misconduct implies a wrongful intention,
not a mere error of judgment. Manual for Courts-Martial, United
States, 1951, paragraph 178d. The term contemplates "a transgression
of some established and definite rule of action, where no discretion is
left, except what necessity may demand; . . . a violation of a definite
law." Manual for Courts-Martial, U.S. Army, 1921, paragraph 425
IV. Under the provisions of this Article, any disobedience, neglect,
or intentional misconduct of a member of the armed forces, before
or in the presence of the enemy, the natural and probable consequence
of which is the endangering of the safety of any command, unit, place,
or military property, which it is his duty to defend, constitutes misbehavior before the enemy. Thus the essential elements of this offense are correctly summarized by paragraph 178c, Manual for
Courts-Martial, United States, 1951, as follows:

"(a)  That it was the duty of the accused to defend
a certain command, unit, ship, or place, or certain military property; (b) that he committed certain disobedience,
neglect, or intentional misconduct, as alleged; (c) that
thereby he endangered the safety of the command, unit,
place, ship, or military property; and (d) that this act
occurred while the accused was before or in the presence
of the enemy."

In the instant case, the tank to which the accused was assigned
as commander occupied a vital link in a defensive chain. The loss of
that link endangered not only the infantry company to which it was
attached, but also the safety of other regimental units because of the
havoc resulting from the rupture of a defensive line. The accused's
duty to defend his unit, therefore, was clearly established by the
general conditions shown to exist, as well as by the evidence of his
assignment and of the mission of his tank. Similarly established was
the element of "presence of the enemy." The unit was located in advance of an infantry company occupying positions on the main line of
resistance; there were no friendly troops located between it and the
enemy positions 2500 yards away; and it was required to furnish fire
support for friendly patrols while well within range of hostile fire.
United States v. Sperland, 1 USCMA 661, 5 CMR 89; United States v.
Smith, 2 USCMA 197, 7 CMR 73. At a time when full responsibility
for the operational efficiency of this vital defensive and offensive
instrumentality was upon him, the accused voluntarily consumed
sufficient liquor to intoxicate him. That such intoxication constitutes
intentional misconduct there is no doubt, for drunkenness is a violation of Article 134 of the Code, supra, 50 USC §728, and, when it

occurs while on duty, it is a violation of Article 112 of the Code, 50 USC §706. In that condition the accused was incapable of directing the operation of the tank, the delivery of fire support, or of defending his position against an enemy advance, should occasion arise. With Clark in the same condition, only two men were available to carry out the mission which ordinarily required the services of a crew of five. Under these circumstances, the safety of the unit was jeopardized, because the tank was out of action for all practical purposes, and the defensive chain was broken. This was the natural and probable consequence of the accused's intentional misconduct. Manual for Courts-Martial, United States, 1951, paragraph 138a.

Every essential element of the offense charged was established beyond a reasonable doubt. The evidence is legally sufficient to sustain the findings.

The decision of the board of review is affirmed.

Judges LATIMER and BROSMAN concur.

Article 99 covers the entire range of offenses that are assimilable to misbehavior before the enemy; Article 134 is not applicable in this area (U.S. v. Hallett, 4 USCMA 378, 15 CMR 378 [1954]). This is an application of the so-called "preemptive doctrine" discussed in U.S. v. Norris, infra, p. 450.

## UNITED STATES v. WILLIAMS

United States Court of Military Appeals, 1968.
17 U.S.C.M.A. 358, 38 C.M.R. 156.

QUINN, Chief Judge:

Appellant stands convicted of cowardice before the enemy in Vietnam and disobedience of the order of a superior noncommissioned officer "to move forward and join" his squad, in violation of Articles 99 and 91, Uniform Code of Military Justice, 10 USC §§899 and 891, respectively. His sentence extends to a dishonorable discharge and confinement at hard labor for three years. On this appeal, he contends the evidence is insufficient to support the findings of guilty of cowardice, and that he was prejudiced by certain remarks of trial counsel and the law officer.

As to the first issue, the specific question is whether the accused misbehaved himself as the result of cowardice. On the date
alleged, his squad was engaged in a heliborne operation against the
Vietcong forces. The helicopter missed the designated landing zone,
and came down in a rice paddy. As the squad members left the helicopter, they were subjected to "moderate" to "heavy" machine gun
and small arms fire from Vietcong forces in a village to the left of
the rice paddy. The squad was divided into two teams, Team A and
Team B. Team A consisted of four men; Team B had five men, including the accused. Following standard procedure, Team A moved
forward to set up a base of fire, while Team B maneuvered forward.
In turn, Team B provided a base of fire, and Team A maneuvered.
The squad reached a large dike, which was the "prior designated
position." From that position, it acted as a security force to protect
the landing of other elements of the operation. Sergeant Wolfe, the
Team B leader, reported to Platoon Sergeant Billy L. Bowlin, the
squad leader, that the accused had not moved forward with his Team.
The accused remained "out in the middle of the rice paddy where he
got off the chopper," about seventy to one hundred meters to the rear.
He was behind a small dike.

Intermittently, during the next thirty-five to forty minutes,
Sergeant Bowlin "hollered" to the accused to move up; and at least
once he told accused he was giving him a "lawful order" to "get . . .
over here." The accused made different responses to Bowlin's calls.
During the "first 15 or 20 minutes" he maintained he was "hit" and
"could not stand up." Then, he said he "had a pungi stick in his leg."
On a number of occasions, he replied "that his weapon was jammed."
Finally, Sergeant Carlos Torres "checked . . . out" the accused,
and the accused said: " 'I'm moving, I'm moving.' "* In a "low
crawl," the accused crossed the rice paddy and came up to Sergeant
Bowlin. He told the Sergeant his weapon, an M-16, was jammed.
The weapon appeared to be "still intact." According to Sergeant
Bowlin, once an M-16 jams, it "will never fire again" because "the
bolt will bust." Bowlin told the accused to test fire the rifle into a
pond. The accused "fired his weapon one time and then it jammed."
(Emphasis supplied.) Thereupon, Sergeant Torres gave the accused
a rifle that had belonged to a man who was wounded.

About ten to fifteen minutes after the accused rejoined the squad,
it moved down the dike, as the last element in the advance toward the
village. Although, because of the "turmoil," Sergeant Bowlin did not
specifically examine Williams for injury, to the "best" of his knowledge, Williams "had not been shot; had no pungi stick" wound "or
nothing." He put Williams "up in front" of him "to prod . . . [him]

---

*Before trial, Sergeant Torres was wounded and had been re-
turned to the United States.

along" as they moved into the village. After the village had been secured, Specialist Four Charles L. Lostanau, another member of the squad, met the accused. He had earlier heard the accused call to Sergeant Bowlin from the rice paddy that he had been hit and could not stand up, but he observed that the accused "wasn't limping or anything."

Two items of evidence form the linchpins of the defense argument as to the insufficiency of the evidence. The first is that the accused's state of mind during the period in issue is best indicated by his own statements that he was "hit" and "could not stand up"; that he had a pungi stick in his leg; and that his weapon was "jammed." All these statements, say appellate defense counsel, demonstrate the accused did not act through fear, but because of "injury or inoperative equipment." The second is that the accused joined the squad "of his own volition," and this evidence "weighs heavily against any inference of fear."

All the evidence is opposed to the defense contention that the accused moved forward of his "own volition" to join the squad. For more than half an hour he repeatedly told Sergeant Bowlin he was " 'moving,' " but he did not move. It is apparent that he did not move until Sergeant Torres "checked him out." Bowlin was not allowed to testify as to what Sergeant Torres told him about the results of his examination of the accused, but from the evidence the court members could reasonably infer, as we shall point out below, that the accused was neither shot nor wounded by a pungi stick. Consequently, after Sergeant Torres' examination the accused was in an untenable position and could no longer remain in the rice paddy. His movement forward, therefore, was not an act of his own choosing.

There is an abundance of evidence to justify the conclusion by the court members that the accused's successive and different replies to Sergeant Bowlin were false. While Bowlin admitted he did not personally examine the accused for signs of a wound, the circumstantial evidence establishes that he saw no evidence of any injury. The accused was in Bowlin's immediate presence. Bowlin observed him test fire his rifle, and he also had him under his direct observation during the move into the village. His testimony clearly implies he closely watched all accused's movements. In addition, Bowlin testified he knew that the first squad, which included the accused, "took no casualties"; and that the first casualty in the entire platoon occurred "the following day--that's when Kantz was hit." The court members, therefore, had a substantial factual basis upon which to credit Bowlin's testimony that, to the "best" of his knowledge, the accused "had not been shot; had no pungi stick" wound "or nothing" wrong with him while he was in the rice paddy.

Sergeant Bowlin's testimony is corroborated by that of another member of the squad. It will be recalled that Specialist Lostanau encountered the accused in the village. He had heard the accused call from the rice paddy that he had been hit and could not stand, but he testified that when he met the accused, he "wasn't limping or anything."

Besides disputing the accused's representations of injury, Sergeant Bowlin's testimony also conflicts with the accused's statement that his weapon was jammed. Bowlin testified he knew that a jammed M-16 will not fire again without exploding the bolt; consequently, when the accused finally came up to the dike he had him fire his weapon into a pond. The rifle fired once then jammed on the second shot. Bowlin's testimony also indicates that, during the time the accused remained in the rice paddy, other elements of the company debarked from helicopters and deployed along the dike, so that eventually "friendly troops" extended "all the way down" the dike. It is reasonably inferable that the accused witnessed the movement of these elements before he moved forward.

It is arguable that some of the evidence in the record of trial can be viewed as indicating that the accused was not motivated by cowardice in remaining in the rice paddy. For example, his position in the rice paddy was at least as exposed to enemy fire as the position of the other members of the platoon at the dike. Even this evidence, however, is not wholly opposed to the prosecution's case. As Government counsel point out, it is not unreasonable to infer that the accused believed himself safer "away from the main body" which was "drawing fire" from the enemy.

Much of the evidence against the accused is circumstantial, but circumstantial evidence can as effectively prove the existence of a fact as direct evidence. United States v Mason, 8 USCMA 329, 24 CMR 139. Considering all the evidence, and the permissible inferences therefrom, the court members could, in our opinion, conclude beyond a reasonable doubt that by remaining in the rice paddy, instead of moving forward against the enemy with the others in his squad, the accused was motivated by fear. United States v Smith, 2 USCMA 197, 7 CMR 73.

[The Court found no merit in the other assignments of error and affirmed the decision of the board of review.]

A specification under Article 99 may be drafted to allege more than one type of misbehavior--for example, running away and cowardly conduct--and the court-martial may find either offense. See U.S. v. Parker, 3 USCMA 541, 13 CMR 97 (1953); U.S. v. Gross, 17 USCMA 610, 38 CMR 408 (1968).

## UNITED STATES v. DICKENSON

United States Court of Military Appeals, 1955.
6 U.S.C.M.A. 438, 20 C.M.R. 154.

ROBERT E. QUINN, Chief Judge:
This case concerns the conduct of an American soldier in a
Chinese prisoner of war camp in Korea. We take judicial notice of
the fact that many prisoners were subjected to severe brutality or to
tremendous psychological pressures which made them do and say
things which they would otherwise have avoided. The British have
reported that the Chinese used the same methods on British prisoners
of war. "Treatment of British Prisoners of War in Korea," Ministry
of Defence (1955). However, of the fourteen assignments of error
set out in the accused's petition for grant of review not one alleges
that the offenses of which he stands convicted were the result of
force or coercion on the part of his captors.
. . .
In sum, none of the dramatic and momentous prisoner of war
problems, which have occupied the attention of the Government and
the American people since the Armistice Agreement in Korea, are
present on this appeal. The issues before us are entirely routine.
In November 1950, the accused was captured by Chinese Communist forces. Two months later, he was interned in Camp No. 5,
Pyoktong, Korea. After the armistice, he refused to return to the
United Nations forces during "Operation Big Switch," which provided
for the exchange of prisoners of war who wanted to be repatriated.
However, on the evening of October 20, 1953, he approached an Indian
guard at the Repatriation Center in the neutral zone. He complained
of a toothache. When taken to headquarters, he notified an Indian
officer that he wanted to return to the United States. The next morning, his request for repatriation was approved by the United Nations
Repatriation Commission and he was returned to United States military control.
All repatriates were examined by counter-intelligence agents
regarding their conduct and their treatment during captivity. The
accused was flown from Korea to Tokyo, Japan, for his examination.
He was quartered at the Tokyo Army Hospital, but his questioning took
place at the Dai Iti Hotel, in a room occupied by one of two agents conducting the inquiry. At the outset of the examination, Article 31, 50
USC §603, was read and explained to the accused. He indicated that
he was familiar with its provisions because "the Communists had
coached him on them" and G-2 (Intelligence) in Korea had also explained them to him. At intervals during the inquiry, the agents told
the accused that he did not have to answer any questions unless he
wanted to.
The examination extended over a period of weeks. It proceeded
according to a standard form of questions. Throughout the period of

examination, the accused was "at ease." He had lunch and coffee breaks with the agents. On seven or eight occasions the accused went on pass. In the course of the questioning, the accused submitted several handwritten statements. Finally, on November 6, 1953, a nine-page typewritten statement was drafted by the agents. This statement was a "collection" of the oral and written information obtained from the accused. After it was prepared, the statement was given to the accused. For two and one-half hours he read it. He made certain changes in the text; he initialed each change, every erasure, and every page. The accused then swore to and signed the statement.

On termination of the counter-intelligence examination, the accused was returned to the United States. He was granted leave. When he returned, he was served with charges alleging that while a prisoner of war he communicated with the enemy in violation of Article 104 (Charge I), 50 USC §698, and that in order to secure favorable treatment for himself he informed on other prisoners in violation of Article 105 (Charge II, specifications 1 and 2), 50 USC §699. The charges were referred to trial before a general court-martial.

At the close of the prosecution's case, the law officer, without objection by any member of the court, granted a motion for a finding of not guilty of specification 2, Charge II. In addition, the court-martial returned findings of not guilty on some of the allegations of the specification of Charge I. However, the accused was convicted of the remaining allegations of the specification under Charge I and of Charge II, specification 1. He was sentenced to a dishonorable discharge, total forfeitures, and confinement at hard labor for ten years. The convening authority approved the findings of guilty and the sentence without modification, but a board of review set aside one of the findings under the specification of Charge I. The board of review affirmed all other findings of guilty and the sentence. We granted the accused's petition for review to consider a number of assignments of error.

Our first problem relates to the legality of Charge I which alleges unauthorized communication, correspondence, and holding intercourse with the enemy in violation of Article 104. The accused's attack on this charge is two-fold. First, he contends that Article 104 is unconstitutional. Second, he argues that, if constitutional, Article 104 does not apply to prisoners of war in the hands of the enemy.

. . .

By its terms the Article applies to all persons, whether or not subject to the Uniform Code at the time of the commission of the offense. However, the accused contends that to apply the Article to persons not subject to the Uniform Code violates Section 2 of Article III of the United States Constitution, which describes the offense of treason, and also Section 3 of Article III which prescribes essential procedures in the prosecution of crimes against the United States. Conversely, the Government argues that global warfare has made the whole world a theater of military operations and justifies the exercise of military jurisdiction over all civilians. See United States

v Ayers, 4 USCMA 220, 15 CMR 220; United States v McDonald, 265
Fed 754 (ED NY) (1920).

Although not specifically set out, the accused's analogy of
Article 104 to the offense of treason implies that the Article represents only a particularization of different overt acts of treason. But,
if we were to conclude that offenses under Article 104 are different
and separate from that of treason and constitute violations of the laws
of war, there would be no repugnancy between the constitutional provisions cited by the accused and the Uniform Code of Military Justice.
See Ex parte Quirin, 317 US 1, 63 S Ct 2, 87 L ed 3. However, we
need not reach those broad problems. We may assume that civilians
not otherwise validly subject to the Uniform Code cannot be tried by
a military tribunal if the offense charged is not a violation of the laws
of war, or if martial law has not been constitutionally established.
Ex parte Quirin, supra; Ex parte Milligan, 4 Wall 2, 18 L ed 281.

Ordinarily, one cannot seek "vindication of the constitutional
rights of some third party." Barrows v Jackson, 346 US 249, 255, 73
S Ct 1031, 97 L ed 1586; see also George v United States, 196 F 2d
445 (CA 9th Cir) (1952), cert den 344 US 843, 73 S Ct 58, 97 L ed 656.
In United States v Thompson, 2 USCMA 460, 462, 9 CMR 90, this
Court indicated that we were inclined "to decide issues of law only
in so far as such issues are raised in individual cases coming before
the Court." Does the accused then have standing to urge the unconstitutionality of Article 104? In other words, does he fall within the
class of persons described as being constitutionally free from trial
by a military tribunal?

The accused's status as a person subject to trial by court-
martial was not disputed at the trial. The omission, of course, does
not deprive him of the right to contest jurisdiction over his person at
any stage of the proceedings, including his appeal to this Court.
United States v Robertson, 5 USCMA 806, 19 CMR 102. But, the accused does not deny that, at all times important to this case, he was
subject to the Uniform Code. The strongest assertion that he makes
is that there is "grave doubt" on that point. We do not share that view.

The evidence shows unmistakably that the accused was a member of the United States Army in 1950. There was no evidence that
he was ever discharged. Mere expiration of the regular period of
enlistment does not alter a serviceman's status as a person subject
to the Uniform Code. Article 2(1), 50 USC §552, Uniform Code of
Military Justice. United States v Johnson, 6 USCMA 320, 20 CMR
36. Consequently, the accused was and still is subject to the Uniform
Code. As a person subject to the Code, he is not within the class of
civilians who might have a possible objection to trial by a military
tribunal for a violation of Article 104. See Ex parte Quirin, supra.
As a person subject to the Code, unquestionably he can be constitutionally tried by a court-martial for a violation of its provisions.
United States v Marker, 1 USCMA 393, 3 CMR 127.

To avoid the effect of his status, the accused contends that the words "all persons" are indivisible, that is, that the Article cannot be interpreted as applicable to persons subject to the Code and inapplicable to persons not subject to the Code. See: United States v Reese, 92 US 214, 23 L ed 563. The difficulty with this argument is that it disregards the clear intention of Congress that all persons enumerated in Article 2 are subject to the Articles of the Uniform Code. The particular designation in each Article is intended principally to restrict or to enlarge the general applicability of the Code as in the case of Article 104. Thus, there is no question of divisibility or segmentation.

As an alternative attack on the specification laid under Article 104, the accused contends that the Article has no application to prisoners of war in actual custody of the enemy. The contention is predicated on two theories. First, the accused maintains that offenses committed in captivity are chargeable only under Article 105, which is titled, "Misconduct as a Prisoner." The argument is untenable.

. . .

Nothing in the language of that Article even remotely implies that every act of misconduct by a prisoner of war must be charged as a violation of its provisions. Its plain purpose is to prohibit one prisoner from gaining favor with his captors at the expense of another prisoner. Many crimes may be committed by a prisoner of war which have no bearing whatever on his standing with his captors. So, for example, an ordinary prisoner, having no authority over any other person, may steal cigarettes belonging to another prisoner and secretly smoke them. It can hardly be argued that the wrongdoer acted for the purpose of enhancing his stature in the eyes of his captors. Or, suppose the owner of the cigarettes detects the thief in the act, and to avoid apprehension, the thief strangles him. Is the murder to go unpunished because it was committed by the culprit while he was a prisoner of war? Yet, the offense cannot properly be charged as a violation of Article 105 because the Article requires that the act be done with the specific purpose of securing favorable treatment, not to escape apprehension and punishment for a crime.

Neither the language nor the purpose of Article 105 supports the conclusion that it embraces every offense perpetrated by a prisoner of war. In our opinion Article 105 is not a general catchall statute. It proscribes specific conduct by a prisoner of war which is in addition to, not exclusive of, other provisions of the Uniform Code. We conclude, therefore, that there is no merit in the accused's argument that Article 104 does not apply to prisoners of war because the totality of their conduct is governed exclusively by Article 105.

The second phase of the accused's argument, relating to the scope of Article 104, is based upon a strained construction of its provisions. He interprets the Article to prohibit only such

communication or correspondence with the enemy as goes "across
the lines, from territory under United States control to the enemy."
On the basis of this construction, he maintains that the specification
does not state an offense for two reasons: (1) In substance, it alleges
only that the accused corresponded or communicated with the enemy,
but is devoid of any allegation that he gave "intelligence" to the enemy
in any way, and (2) it alleges that the offenses were committed while
the accused was a prisoner of war in the hands of the enemy. It follows therefrom that the accused's communications with his captors
did not go "across the lines" between the United States and the enemy.
Both of the accused's reasons lack merit.

. . .

Not every communication is prohibited by Article 104. The
entire subsection in issue is qualified by the phrase "without proper
authority." Consequently, a communication with the enemy which is
authorized is not a violation of the Article. Service custom, which
merely recognizes the applicable laws of war, authorizes a prisoner
of war to disclose his name, rank, and service number. The laws of
humanity authorize communications in connection with the necessities
of life. Long past are the days of "no quarter" when a prisoner of war
was summarily put to death on capture. A prisoner of war has a recognized claim to life. In furtherance of this claim, he may demand sus-
tenance from his captors. He may ask for, and is entitled to receive,
"food, clothing if necessary, and proper lodging and medical attendance." Winthrop's Military Law and Precedents, 2d ed, 1920 Reprint,
page 789. Moreover, the laws of war authorize communications between prisoners of war and their captors in regard to matters other
than the bare necessaries of life. So, for example, a prisoner of war
is required to conform to the laws, regulations, and orders of the
place in which he is confined. Winthrop, supra, page 792. See also:
Geneva Convention Relative to the Treatment of Prisoners of War of
August 12, 1949, which the United Nations Command declared that it
would apply in the treatment of its war prisoners. If he is required
to communicate with the enemy in the course of compliance with these
regulations and orders, the communication is authorized, and, therefore, not a violation of Article 104. It is thus apparent that the practicalities of the prisoner of war status are not such as to justify an
interpretation of Article 104 different from that indicated by the plain
language of its provisions.

Also lacking in merit is the accused's claim that the specification laid under Article 104 does not state an offense because the communication did not pass "across the lines" between the United States
and the enemy. The impassable "line" between belligerents is not
geographic. The geographic line merely marks off the territory subject to the separate control of each belligerent and provides a convenient basis for establishing defensive and offensive measures. The
true line between enemies is philosophical. That line is not measured

by the inches, yards, or miles separating the opposing military forces. It is established and measured by the existence of a state of war. The Prize Cases, 2 Black 635, 688, 17 L ed 459; Hiatt v Brown, 15 Wall 177, 21 L ed 128; United States v Grossmayer, 9 Wall 72, 19 L ed 627.

Whatever the place, whether within or without an area controlled by the United States, there can be no unauthorized intercourse between a citizen of the United States and an enemy. In Hiatt v Brown, supra, the Supreme Court held that even the courts of each belligerent are closed to the citizens of the other. We hold, therefore, that a prisoner of war in the hands of the enemy is bound by the provisions of Article 104. He is not exempt from the provisions of that Article because he is outside an area subject to the control of the United States.

Before turning to the accused's attack on some of the findings of guilty, it is appropriate to consider his claim of error regarding the admission in evidence of his statement to the counter-intelligence agents. . . .

[The Court found no error in the admissibility of his statement and found the evidence sufficient to support the findings.]

United States v. Batchelor, 7 USCMA 354, 22 CMR 144 (1956), also concerns an accused who was a prisoner of war in Korea and who was charged with violations of Articles 104 and 105, in addition to other charges. The Court of Military Appeals held that Article 104 requires proof only of a general criminal intent as opposed to a specific intent. In the course of the opinion, Judge Latimer quoted from Judge Magruder's opinion in the case of Chandler v. United States, 171 F.2d 921 (CA 1st Cir. 1948), as follows:

". . . Suppose Chandler had obtained advance information of the Anglo-American plans for the invasion of North Africa and had passed the information on to the enemy. Would a treason prosecution fail if he could convince the jury that, in his fanatical and perhaps misguided way, he sincerely believed his country's ultimate good would be served by an early withdrawal from the war; that he sincerely believed that the best, perhaps the only, way to accomplish this good end was to bring it about that the first major military operation of the United States should be a resounding fiasco, thereby stimulating such a revulsion among the American people that the perfidious administration would be forced to negotiate a peace? It is hardly necessary to state the answer to that question.

"When war breaks out, a citizen's obligation of allegiance puts definite limits upon his freedom to act on his private judgment. If he trafficks with enemy agents, knowing them to be such, and being aware of their hostile mission intentionally gives them aid in steps essential to the execution of that mission, he has adhered to the enemies of his country, giving them aid and comfort, within our definition of treason. He is guilty of treason, whatever his motive."

The term "military commission" appears in Articles 21, 36, 104, and 106 of the Code. The case of Ex parte Quirin, 317 U.S. 1, 63 S.Ct. 2, 87 L.Ed. 3 (1942), concerns the trial by military commission of eight saboteurs who were landed on the coast of the United States by German submarines. The petitioners contended that they were entitled to be tried in the civil courts with the safeguards guaranteed by the Fifth and Sixth Amendments. The Supreme Court denied this contention and held the trial to be valid and the provisions of the Amendments inapplicable to such military commissions. See also Colepaugh v. Looney, 235 F.2d 429 (CA, Tenth Cir., 1956), certiorari denied 352 U.S. 1014, 77 S.Ct. 568, 1 L.Ed.2d 560 (1957).

## THE GENERAL ARTICLES

See Articles 133 and 134.

### FLETCHER v. UNITED STATES

Court of Claims of the United States, 1891.
26 Ct. Cl. 541.

NOTT, J., . . . :
. . .
It must be confessed that, in the affairs of civil life and under the rules and principles of municipal law, what we ordinarily know as fraud relates to the obtaining of a man's money, and not to refusing to pay it back. It is hard for the trained lawyer to conceive of an indictment or declaration which should allege that the defendant defrauded A or B by refusing to return to him the money which he had borrowed from him. Our legal training, the legal habit of mind, as it is termed, inclines as to dissociate punishment from acts which the law does not define as offenses. As one of our greatest writers of fiction puts it, with metaphysical fitness and accurate sarcasm, as she describes one of her legal characters, "His moral horizon was limited by the civil code of Tennessee." That it is a fraud to obtain

a man's money by dishonest representations, but not a fraud to keep it afterwards by any amount of lying and deceit, is a distinction of statutory tracing. The gambler who throws away other people's money and the spendthrift who uses it in luxurious living instead of paying it back, cheat and defraud their creditors as effectually as the knaves and sharpers who drift within the meshes of the criminal law. We learnt as law students in Blackstone that there are things which are malum in se and, in addition to them, things which are merely malum prohibitum; but unhappily in the affairs of real life we find that there are many things which are malum in se without likewise being malum prohibitum. In military life there is a higher code termed honor, which holds its society to stricter accountability; and it is not desirable that the standards of the Army shall come down to the requirements of a criminal code. Moreover, the specifications aver in one instance that the claimant used his honorable military position to borrow money upon, and assured his creditors of payment from the pay which the Government allows to officers on the retired list. It may or it may not be dishonorable for a man not to pay his debts; but that may depend upon how he incurred them and whether it is within his human possibilities to pay them. Certainly the Government does not give officers the respectability of rank and the support of retired pay to enable them to prey upon their fellow citizens. Remembering the honorable military record of the claimant, the court is averse to commenting upon the details of the specifications, especially as it is not at liberty to review the evidence, but at the same time can not hold that refusing to pay a debt may not be conduct unbecoming an officer and a gentleman.

. . .

Reversed on other grounds, United States v. Fletcher, 148 U.S. 84, 13 S.Ct. 552, 37 L.Ed. 378 (1893).

### UNITED STATES v. KIRKSEY*

United States Court of Military Appeals, 1955.
6 U.S.C.M.A. 556, 20 C.M.R. 272.

*[Footnotes have been omitted. Ed.]

PAUL W. BROSMAN, Judge:

We are once more called on to determine whether certain ostensible offenses reflected in the findings of a general court-martial constitute crimes known to military law. Charged with dishonorably failing to pay a debt and--in twelve specifications--with dishonorably failing to maintain sufficient funds in a banking account, the accused officer was convicted of no more than "discreditably" failing to deal with both sorts of financial obligation. After receiving a sentence to dismissal from the service, which was affirmed--together with all findings--Captain Kirksey now comes before us on petition, contending that the offenses of which he was found guilty by the court-martial are not lesser crimes included within those alleged in the several specifications. Briefs and arguments concerning this issue, and three related ones, were submitted to us for consideration--and, after a careful study of the positions taken by both the appellant and the Government, we are convinced that the conviction cannot stand.

. . .

### III

A contemporary opinion of this Court furnishes a complete answer to the question of whether a negligent failure to maintain bank funds to meet outstanding checks constitutes "conduct of a nature to bring discredit upon the armed forces," in violation of the Uniform Code of Military Justice. In United States v Downard, 6 USCMA 538, 20 CMR 254, we held--and clearly--that no such offense is cognizable under Article 134. . . .

The rationale of the Downard decision is applicable with equal vigor to the case before us now. The present appellant stands convicted under twelve counts of "discreditably" failing to maintain funds--findings identical with these returned against Downard. Furthermore, by explicitly excepting the term "dishonorably" from the findings, the members of the court-martial necessarily eliminated the gravamen of the offense contemplated by the draftsman of the specifications--this for the reason that the word itself has been construed by this Court to connote bad faith or gross indifference, a state of mind in the absence of which no crime of this nature may be recognized. United States v Downard, supra. Therefore, we hold unhesitatingly that the findings of the present court-martial under the worthless check specifications reduce to nullities and, as such, are wholly ineffective to form a basis for punitive action.

### IV

We reach now the question posed by the court's determination that the accused "discreditably" failed to discharge a debt. It is difficult, of course, for one unfamiliar with the principles of military criminal law to accept the notion that any sort of nonpayment of a pecuniary obligation may subject a member of the Armed Services to penal sanctions. Traditionally, the American concept of justice has excluded the abhorrent practice of imprisonment for debt--with the result that the constitutions of the several states almost invariably contain clauses specifically forbidding action of this character. Sound reasons familiar to us all, and too numerous to mention here, lend full support to the constitutional protection which enables even the most imprudent debtor to retain his liberty--and we have no slightest wish to derogate from the importance of such a safeguard. Indeed, we heartily agree that, within the civilian community, the direct use of criminal sanctions to enforce the collection of debts must be condemned.

When we consider the problem created by a failure to meet financial obligations as it is found in the military scene, however, additional and perhaps overriding factors must be taken into account. Since the military establishment is composed in large part of transient --often unselected--personnel removed from the customary restraints of civilian society, it is readily apparent that resolute measures are required to insure the prompt liquidation of fiscal obligations. Civil suits are always difficult in such a setting, and are seldom effective against service personnel, who may be found within the jurisdiction of local courts at one time and far removed therefrom at another shortly thereafter. Indeed, if normal civil processes constituted the sole remedies available to creditors of military people, it is conceivable, at least, that an unscrupulous soldier, sailor or airman calculatedly might amass substantial liabilities in advance of impending transfer, and--on completion of the movement--find himself immune from civil action for all practical purposes. Moreover, members of the military community--easily identified through the wearing of the uniform--are inevitably grouped in the public mind as a class--with the result that a failure by one to discharge monetary responsibilities tends to brand all not only as criminal persons, but as poor credit risks as well, in the eyes of the civilian population. Too, the ancient ethical traditions of the profession of arms cannot safely be left out of account in this connection. Historically, of course, these moral customs have possessed a particularly binding force in the case of commissioned officers--but they have not at all been rejected in that of enlisted personnel. And they have always dictated a high standard of promissory responsibility.

For these reasons, the Armed Services have sought for years to impose on their members a standard of financial accountability somewhat higher than that demanded of the civilian. It is therefore well established in military law that a failure to discharge obligations when characterized by a certain culpable type of motivation may result in court-martial charges against the debtor. If the offender be an officer, he has been dealt with traditionally under that clause of the military code of the period which proscribed conduct unbecoming an officer and a gentleman. Where an enlisted man is involved, the offense customarily has been laid under the "General article"--that is, that section of the legislation which, in broad language, provides that all misconduct of a nature to bring disrepute on the Armed Services shall be cognizable by court-martial. However, it is our view that a mere negligent omission--in either case--is not of itself a wrongdoing of sufficient moment to justify punitive action based on the nonpayment of a debt.

. . .

We are, of course, perfectly willing to concede that the failure of a member of the Armed Forces to pay his just debts will, in every instance, reflect some measure of discredit on the service concerned.

Indeed, this phenomenon has not gone unnoticed by the services themselves. See United States v Young [ACM 7391], 12 CMR 939; United
States v Walden, supra. But we cannot hold--in the absence of clear
Code authorization or long established custom--that a negligent omission in this respect rises to the type of dishonorable conduct, which
is the gravamen of the offense in question. The term "dishonorable"
itself connotes bad faith or gross indifference--a state of mind not
fairly attributable to one who is no more than careless. See United
States v Downard, supra. Therefore, since boards of review have
consistently required proof of some variety of fraudulent or deceitful
purpose to support a conviction of failure to pay debts, we are sure
that the Manual language cited by the Government is entirely consistent with our holding that only a dishonorable neglect constitutes that
measure of misconduct which reflects discredit on the military establishment for present purposes.

As was observed in the opening paragraph of this section of the
opinion, the imposition of punishment for debt is alien to the civilian's
concept of criminal law--and justly so. In addition, we have suggested
that only because of the necessarily unique composition of the military community are we willing to recognize the service custom by
which penal sanctions are invoked against uniformed debtors--and then
only provided that the failure to pay is accompanied by a course of
conduct best described by the Armed Forces themselves as "dishonorable." Beyond that we will not, and, in good conscience, cannot go.
Accordingly, we must hold that the instant findings of guilty of neglect to pay debts--based as they are on a determination that the accused did not more than fail to exercise reasonable care--does not
state an offense cognizable under military law.

V

It follows from what has been said that the case against the
accused must fall. This disposition of the case obviates discussion
of the remaining assignments of error. The decision of the board of
review is reversed and the charges are dismissed.

Chief Judge QUINN and Judge LATIMER concur.

## UNITED STATES v. GIORDANO*

United States Court of Military Appeals, 1964.
15 U.S.C.M.A. 163, 35 C.M.R. 135.

*[Footnotes have been omitted. Ed.]

KILDAY, Judge:
Tried jointly by a general court-martial convened at Fort Hood,
Texas, the two accused officers entered pleas of not guilty. Both
were, however, convicted as charged of conspiracy to violate a lawful order, five specifications of violating the same order, and two

counts of conduct unbecoming officers and gentlemen, contrary to Articles 81, 92, and 133, Uniform Code of Military Justice, 10 USC §§881, 892, and 933, respectively. The court-martial sentenced accused Sims to dismissal and total forfeitures. It fixed accused Giordano's punishment at dismissal. The convening authority approved, and a board of review in the office of The Judge Advocate General of the Army affirmed the findings and sentence as to each accused.

Thereafter, both officers sought review by this Court under the provisions of Article 67(b)(3), Uniform Code of Military Justice, 10 USC §867. We granted their petitions for review in order to consider arguments on the following issues:

1.   Whether the order involved was legal.
2.   Whether the law officer erred in instructing that the accused could be convicted of an offense under specification 2 of Charge III even if they did not know about the order.
3.   Whether specification 1 of Charge III is sufficient to allege the offense of conspiracy as conduct unbecoming under Article 133, in the absence of an allegation of an overt act.
4.   Whether the law officer was correct in instructing the maximum punishment was dismissal and total forfeitures.
5.   Whether the law officer erred in not instructing on multiplicity.

The case at bar has its roots in what may fairly be described as loan shark activity. Generally, the evidence presented by the prosecution showed that three lieutenants--including both the accused officers--of the company commanded by accused Sims, joined in backing a loan operation. It was agreed that one Private First Class Harver, an enlisted member of the same unit, would act as a "front man" for the operation in lending money to other various enlisted personnel. Five men from the same company testified Harver lent them money during April 1963. The loans were for a period of one month, and interest was charged at the rate of fifty percent. Private Harver admitted making loans for a "syndicate." The borrowers did not know where the money came from, but Harver testified it was from a pool, and that his dealings with the commissioned participants in the enterprise were through accused Giordano. A regulation issued by the Commanding General, Fort Hood, Texas, governed loans among military personnel. It specifically prohibited, as usurious and unconscionable, interest rates in excess of three percent per month on loans for a one month period and of the amounts with which we are concerned in the instant case.

Such additional facts as are pertinent to determination of the respective issues will be set forth in the discussion of each.

I

The first issue draws into question the lawfulness of the Fort Hood circular regulating interest rates on loans among military personnel. Appellate defense counsel contend the same is illegal because it invades the accused's private rights without showing of its necessity to protect discipline or its connection with maintenance of good order in the service. Moreover, they assert the order is so broad and uncertain as to be objectionable for that reason. It is claimed "that this is a less than ingenious attempt to sidestep the restrictions placed by this Court in United States v Day, 11 USCMA 549, 29 CMR 365."

Day was an Army case in which this Court dismissed specifications alleging usury under the General Article, 10 USC §934, on the ground there was no such offense in military law in the absence of any statute or regulation fixing a maximum legal rate of interest. We noted in Day, however, that the Navy had such a regulation, and suggested that one might be provided by the Army. In the present instance that void is filled by the Fort Hood order.

. . .

Interest rates are commonly regulated in the various civilian jurisdictions, and no extended argument is necessary to demonstrate the obvious impact on morale, discipline, and good order, of loans among military personnel at unconscionable rates of interest in excess of those fixed as proper. Here, we agree with the board of review, which pointed out that:

". . . the order does not prohibit the loaning or borrowing of money but regulates the rate of interest so that, in the interest of morale and discipline, a borrower may maintain his self-respect as a soldier and not become the tool of a harassing money-lender."

The regulation is neither arbitrary nor unreasonable, and we conclude it falls within the scope of the class of orders that may properly be promulgated. By its terms, the regulation clearly applies to the individuals and transactions with which we are concerned and we reject the assertion that it is in anywise vague or uncertain.

We agree with the board of review that the regulation in question is a lawful order, and therefore must rule adversely to the accused on the first issue.

II

Under the second specification of Charge III, the accused were convicted of conduct unbecoming officers and gentlemen by loaning money to enlisted personnel at fifty percent interest per month in violation of the Fort Hood order. The second issue upon which we granted review questions the law officer's instruction that the court-martial might convict the accused of this offense regardless of whether they had knowledge of the order.

In support of their position on this issue, appellate defense counsel again advert to this Court's opinion in United States v Day, supra. Briefly, they argue that "the illegality of usury derives merely from statutory prohibition"; that usury is malum prohibitum as opposed to malum in se. Because usury's wrongfulness springs from specific prohibition rather than the nature of the act being wrong in itself, the defense argues that the misconduct stems from knowing violation of the order regulating loans. Without proof of knowing violation of a valid order, it is asserted, the accused's conduct "is not the type which breaches the minimal standards of a gentleman and officer and subjects an officer to criminal conviction and disgrace."

. . .

Conduct unbecoming an officer has long been recognized as a military offense, and it is to be noted that the quoted language from the present Manual is substantially identical to the treatment given the same offense by the services under the law prior to the enactment of the Uniform Code. . . . Indeed, the understanding of the nature of conduct contemplated as being unbecoming an officer and gentleman goes back even further. Thus, Colonel Winthrop, in his treatise Military Law and Precedents, 2d ed, 1920 reprint, noted at pages 711-712:

> ". . . To constitute therefore the conduct here denounced, the act which forms the basis of the charge must have a double significance and effect. Though it need not amount to a crime, it must offend so seriously against law, justice, morality or decorum as to expose to disgrace, socially or as a man, the offender, and at the same time must be of such a nature or committed under such circumstances as to bring dishonor or disrepute upon the military profession which he represents."

From the foregoing, it is evident that the essence of an Article 133 offense is not whether an accused officer's conduct otherwise amounts to an offense--although, of course, it may--but simply whether the acts meet the standard of conduct unbecoming an officer as spelled out. Manifestly this is so for, in the face of a well-defined and long standing interpretation extant under the precursor statutes--particularly Article of War 95--Congress substantially reenacted the prior law as Article 133 of the Uniform Code, with the single exception of the punishment prescribed. . . .

. . .

Against the foregoing backdrop, we turn our attention to the conduct charged against the accused officers, and the law officer's advice that they might be found guilty of the second specification laid under Article 133 regardless of whether they had knowledge of the Fort Hood order. It may be legitimately contended that the instructions of the law officer in this regard were not in error.

The question is whether taking fifty percent monthly interest, on loans by the accused officers to enlisted members of their own unit, under their command and supervision, constitutes conduct unbecoming an officer and gentleman. It is not unfair to describe conduct of this sort as wholly incompatible with the necessary attributes of character, honesty, integrity, and fair dealing to be expected of an officer in his relationship with enlisted personnel under his command. Milking personal financial gain of this magnitude from one's own men in such a fashion is bound to have a demoralizing impact, and supplant the respect that is an officer's due with the legitimate resentment of his subordinates. Exorbitant and unconscionable gain by an officer at the expense of an enlisted man is patently unfair, and wholly inconsistent with the officer's duty as to the welfare and interests of those he commands. Selling liquor to enlisted men at excessive prices has been recognized as conduct unbecoming an officer, and the misconduct with which we are concerned in this issue is analogous.

In this connection, we point out that our opinion in United States v Day, supra, adverted to the possibility that exacting unconscionable interest from an enlisted man might constitute conduct unbecoming an officer even in the absence of a provision setting legitimate rates of interest. United States v Day, supra, 11 USCMA at page 550. And in the case at bar, it must be remembered that, apart from whether the accused knew of the Fort Hood order, the Commanding General's directive did prohibit the excessive interest exacted. See United States v Marker, 1 USCMA 393, 398 and 399, 3 CMR 127.

Additionally, we invite attention to Winthrop's discussion of the offense, to which we referred earlier. He observed it has been recognized since the early 1800's, that conduct unbecoming an officer may consist of abuse of authority over soldiers by exacting from them excessive interest. Winthrop's Military Law and Precedents, supra, at page 716. Indeed, by interesting coincidence, the examples cited by Colonel Winthrop involved exacting interest of twenty-five percent and one hundred percent per month, exactly braketing the rate charged by the accused officers presently before us.

To paraphrase the language of the present Manual, the accused's conduct, as the court-martial was permitted to find under the questioned instruction, may be said to fall below the limit of tolerance required of commissioned officers. See United States v Sadinsky, supra. And the board of review concluded, in the case at bar, that knowledge of the order was not an essential element of this Article 133 offense.

Beyond spelling out the general principles involved, however, there is no need for us to determine firmly their applicability in the present instance. For another reason, under the facts peculiar to this case, it is clear we must find against the accused on this issue.

It is settled law that incorrect or incomplete instructions do not require reversal where there is no possibility of prejudice to the accused from the omission. United States v Leach, 5 USCMA 466, 18 CMR 90. Cf. United States v Clay, 1 USCMA 74, 1 CMR 74. This Court has held that even where the instructions given to the court-martial on one aspect of an offense are deficient, such error is not prejudicial where, on another offense the findings of the court as to the same matter are returned under correct advice. See United States v Demetris, 9 USCMA 412, 26 CMR 192; United States v Higgins, 4 USCMA 143, 15 CMR 143; United States v Kubel, 1 USCMA 645, 5 CMR 73.

In the case at bar, the accused were both separately convicted on five counts of violating Article 92 of the Code, supra. These specifications involved the same five loans to enlisted men which were involved in the second specification charging conduct unbecoming an officer. With regard to the Article 92 violations, the law officer instructed the court-martial that it could not convict the accused unless convinced beyond a reasonable doubt they had actual knowledge of the Fort Hood order. The court members obviously found such knowledge, for they returned findings of guilty on these five counts. Manifestly, therefore, since the same transactions--same men, money, and dates--and the same order, were involved in those five specifications as in specification 2 of the Article 133 offense, the court-martial could not but have found the knowledge that appellate defense counsel assert is essential to the conduct unbecoming offense. Accordingly, even assuming, for the purpose of argument only, that the law officer's instruction was erroneous, there is absolutely no risk that his advice resulted in prejudice to the accused.

Accordingly, we find no merit in the defense position on the second issue.

### III

Next, we turn our attention to the first specification of Charge III. It purports to allege another Article 133 violation in the following language:

> "In that First Lieutenant Jackie Hartwell Sims
> . . . and Second Lieutenant Robert Rocco Giordano
> . . . in conjunction with Second Lieutenant James Nelson Embree . . . did, at Fort Hood, Texas, from on or about 1 April 1963 to on or about 21 May 1963, conduct themselves in a manner unbecoming officers and gentlemen by conspiring with Private First Class (E-3) William Harver . . . and among themselves, to commit an offense under Article 92 of the Uniform Code of Military Justice, to wit: failure to obey a lawful order issued by the

Commanding General Fort Hood, Texas, to wit: paragraph 2, Regulation 22-11, Headquarters, Fort Hood, Fort Hood, Texas, dated 1 February 1963."

It is to be noted that no overt act in pursuance of the conspiracy is alleged therein and, in the absence thereof, the third issue before us questions the sufficiency of the above averments to allege the offense of conspiracy as conduct unbecoming.

. . .

Absent any additional averments of circumstances reflecting wherein the accused wrongfully and dishonorably compromised their standing as officers and gentlemen, we conclude that the instant specification--lacking as it does any allegation of an overt act--fails to state an offense in violation of Article 133, Uniform Code of Military Justice, 10 USC §933. Accordingly, the findings of guilty under the first specification of Charge III must be overturned.

IV

The fourth point upon which we elected to hear arguments concerns the law officer's instruction to the members of the court-martial on sentence. He advised that maximum punishment, for the offenses of which the accused were convicted, was dismissal from the service and forfeiture of all pay and allowances.

The law officer's advice was apparently bottomed on the theory that, insofar as imprisonment was concerned, all of the offenses would be punishable as usury, which carries no confinement. See footnotes four and five, Table of Maximum Punishments, paragraph 127c, Manual for Courts-Martial, United States, 1951, at pages 219 and 221.

Appellate defense counsel necessarily follow the approach of the law officer in applying footnote five to all offenses here involved. In doing so, they point out that the punishment listed for usury in the Table includes imposition of forfeitures only; not only is confinement omitted, but punitive separation is not thereby permitted. Thus, in the case of an enlisted accused, the defense contends the instant offenses would not permit punitive discharge.

. . .

The resolution of this issue is not difficult. The short answer is that the punitive Articles under which the accused were convicted all provide punishment "as a court-martial may direct." And Article 56, Uniform Code of Military Justice, 10 USC §856, authorizes the President to fix maximum limits on the sentence a court may adjudge. Thus, it is evident that Presidential implementations in conformity with such authority have the force of law. United States v Smith, 13 USCMA 105, 32 CMR 105.

The pertinent Manual provisions, hereinbefore quoted, do limit the authorized maximum confinement imposable against officers to that listed in the Table of Maximum Punishments, but no similar provision governs other penalties, and the Manual expressly authorizes dismissal as a permissible sentence in the case of an officer. The formula outlined above is manifestly the one employed by the law officer in the case at bar, and his action conforms to the decision of this Court in United States v Goodwin, 5 USCMA 647, 18 CMR 271, where we were concerned with a similar problem. In that case we specifically adverted to paragraph 126d of the Manual, supra, as authorizing dismissal as a permissible punishment for officers convicted under the Uniform Code, and we expressly rejected the contention that where a punitive discharge could not be imposed against an enlisted offender, dismissal was legally inappropriate for a convicted officer. United States v Goodwin, supra, 5 USCMA at page 649.

. . .

Accordingly, we conclude the law officer did not err in his instructions on maximum sentence. Paragraph 126d, Manual for Courts-Martial, supra; United States v Goodwin, supra.

V

The final issue requires us to determine whether the law officer erred in not instructing the court-martial on multiplicity. . . .

. . .

While Judge Ferguson dissented in the first two mentioned cases, he agrees the above authorities are dispositive. Accordingly, we rule adversely to accused on the fifth issue.

VI

One additional problem remains, and that is the disposition we should order. Even though we have concluded the first specification of Charge III does not allege an offense, it is nonetheless apparent that the court-martial determined the accused had indeed committed the acts set forth in the invalid charge, for the separate conspiracy count included every item mentioned in the defective Article 133 specification. Moreover, had the averments of that Article 133 count included an overt act, the crime would have been multiplicious with the conspiracy offense with which accused were separately charged. Under those circumstances, it is evident that our ruling in favor of accused, in Part III herein, has no impact whatever on maximum sentence. And since we have determined that the law officer properly instructed the court-martial on imposable punishment, it is manifest that return of this case for reassessment of sentence would be fruitless and would constitute an empty ritual. Punishment has already been imposed based on the identical misconduct which remains after the invalid Article 133 offense is struck down, and based on the correct standard. See United States v Middleton, 12 USCMA 54, 58, 59, 30 CMR 54; United States v French, 10 USCMA 171, 180, 185, 27 CMR 245.

Accordingly, the accused's convictions under specification 1 of Charge III are set aside and ordered dismissed. In all other respects, the decision of the board of review is affirmed.

Chief Judge QUINN and Judge FERGUSON concur.

## UNITED STATES v. HOWE

United States Court of Military Appeals, 1967.
17 U.S.C.M.A. 165, 37 C.M.R. 429.

KILDAY, Judge:
Petitioner was arraigned before a general court-martial convened by the Commanding General, United States Army Air Defense
Center at Fort Bliss, Texas. He was charged with using contemptuous words against the President of the United States and conduct
unbecoming an officer and a gentleman, in violation of Articles 88
and 133, Uniform Code of Military Justice, 10 USC §§888 and 933,
respectively. He was also charged, originally, with public use of
language disloyal to the United States with design to promote disloyalty and disaffection among the troops and civilian populace, in
violation of Article 134, Uniform Code of Military Justice, 10 USC
§934. As to this last charge, the defense motion to dismiss was sustained by the law officer. He was convicted of the two charges, first
above-mentioned, and sentenced to dismissal, total forfeitures, and
confinement at hard labor for two years. The convening authority
reduced the period of confinement to one year and otherwise approved the sentence.* A board of review in the office of the Judge
Advocate General of the Army affirmed the findings and sentence.
In due time, petitioner filed with this Court, pursuant to
Article 67(b)(3), Uniform Code of Military Justice, 10 USC §867, a
petition for review. Upon consideration of that petition by this
Court, the same was denied. Thereupon, petitioner filed with this
Court his petition for reconsideration. This Court, by order, directed
that the petition for reconsideration be set for oral argument and that
briefs be filed by counsel for both parties. Briefs having been filed
and oral argument held, we proceed to the disposition of the petition
for reconsideration.
The specification under the charge of violation of Article 88,
supra, reads as follows:

"In that Second Lieutenant Henry H. Howe, Junior,
U.S. Army, Headquarters Company, 31st Engineer Battalion, Fort Bliss, Texas, did, in the vicinity of San
Jacinto Plaza, El Paso, Texas, on or about 6 November
1965, wrongfully and publicly use contemptuous words
against the President of the United States, Lyndon B.
Johnson, by carrying and displaying to the public a sign
reading as follows, to wit: 'LET'S HAVE MORE THAN
A CHOICE BETWEEN PETTY IGNORANT FACISTS IN

---

*Three months and two days after his trial he was released
from confinement under commandant's parole.

1968' and on the other side of the sign the words 'END
JOHNSON'S FACIST AGRESSION IN VIET NAM,' or words
to that effect."

The specification under the charge of violation of Article 133,
supra, reads as follows:

'In that Second Lieutenant Henry H. Howe, Junior,
U.S. Army, Headquarters Company, 31st Engineer Battalion, Fort Bliss, Texas, did in the vicinity of San
Jacinto Plaza, El Paso, Texas, on or about 6 November
1965, wrongfully take part in a public demonstration by
carrying and displaying to the public a sign reading as
follows, to wit: 'LET'S HAVE MORE THAN A CHOICE
BETWEEN PETTY IGNORANT FACISTS IN 1968' and on
the other side the words 'END JOHNSON'S FACIST
AGRESSION IN VIET NAM,' or words to that effect, his
acts constituting conduct unbecoming an officer and
gentleman in the United States Army."

Petitioner presents that the record reveals that a group of professors and students from a state college at El Paso, Texas, intending
to "demonstrate against American policy," requested permission from
the City Council of that city to hold a sidewalk demonstration in San
Jacinto Plaza, but that the council initially denied permission. Thereafter, "pressure" was brought on the City Council which persuaded
its members that there was a constitutional right to demonstrate.
The City Attorney then advised the council that under the Constitution
no permission was necessary for a group to hold a sidewalk demonstration. Petitioner also points out that one of the professors of the
above-mentioned group testified that the major purpose of the demonstration was to publicize "the other position in Vietnam," but after
the City Council denied permission to demonstrate, the rights guaranteed under the First and Fourteenth Amendments became a "second
point" of the demonstration.
    We note that the record of trial reveals that the proposal to
demonstrate had been a source of controversy for two weeks preceding the demonstration held on November 6, 1965. This controversy
had, during that period, consumed much space in the local press and
in broadcasts on local radio and television stations. At the time and
place set for the demonstration, a crowd of some 2,000 persons had
assembled and the picket line was met with pro-Vietnam sentiment,
including spectators with "Win in Vietnam" stickers pasted on their
foreheads, and American Legionnaires, distinctively attired, passing
out small United States flags. There was a counter-demonstration,
and "cat calls and comments" were aimed at the demonstrators by
spectators but otherwise the demonstration was peaceful.

The Assistant Chief of Police of El Paso testified that at the time of the demonstration he was a police captain in charge of the area of demonstration and had a force of thirty-three policemen stationed in the immediate vicinity of the park, with a reserve force one block away to preclude any violence which might occur or could occur. It also appears from the record that military policemen from the Provost Marshal's Office, Fort Bliss, Texas, were at the scene to aid the civilian police concerning any military personnel in uniform that might be involved in the demonstration by returning them to Fort Bliss.

The record further reveals that some twelve demonstrators walked in line about the park carrying signs reading, "let's get our boys out of Viet Nam," "get out of Viet Nam," "peace in Viet Nam," and "would Jesus carry a draft card." The demonstration was photographed and recorded on film by the El Paso Police Department and these photographs were admitted in evidence and the film projected for the court-martial. The demonstration was recorded on motion picture film by at least two of the local television stations and the same were broadcast by those stations.

The petitioner is a graduate of the University of Colorado where he majored in political science. While a student, he voluntarily participated in the Reserve Officers' Training Corps, and upon graduation he accepted a commission as a second lieutenant in the United States Army Reserve. He was ordered to active duty under that commission and had been on duty approximately twelve months at the time of this occurrence.

Petitioner was not a member of the group of professors and students which arranged for, and organized, the demonstration in San Jacinto Plaza. It appears as if he was not known to the members of that group. Prior to their assembly, he was observed at the site of the demonstration holding in his hand a rolled piece of cardboard. As the group began to march in its picket line, he joined the same at the rear thereof, unrolled the cardboard which he carried and held it before him as he walked, reversing the same from time to time so that each side was visible to the assembled crowd. On one side the placard contained the lettering: "LET'S HAVE MORE THAN A 'CHOICE' BETWEEN PETTY, IGNORANT, FACISTS in 1968"; and on the other side the lettering: "END JOHNSON'S FACIST AGRESSION IN VIETNAM."

One of the military policemen present testified he recognized three or four other servicemen at the scene. There is no means of knowing the number of other servicemen who may have been present, not in uniform, and not identified by the witness; nor the number of servicemen who may have seen the petitioner marching, on the films broadcast by the television stations.

In his initial petition for review, petitioner assigned the following as errors:

1. The charges against appellant violate the First Amendment to the Constitution.

2. Articles 88 and 133 are so vague and uncertain that they violate the Due Process clause of the Fifth Amendment.

3. The charge under Article 133 fails to state an offense.

4. The law officer erred to the substantial prejudice of the appellant in failing to instruct, sua sponte, that if the court-martial found the allegedly contemptuous words to have been uttered in the course of a political discussion, then it had to find that appellant intended them to be personally disrespectful.

5. Appellant was substantially prejudiced by the law officer's ruling that the maximum sentence for the charged offenses included confinement at hard labor for three years.

6. The law officer erred to the substantial prejudice of the appellant by instructing the court-martial, over defense objection, that in determining whether the words uttered by appellant were contemptuous of the President the court-martial "should apply the test of how the words were understood and what they were taken to mean by the persons who saw them, or some of them."

7. The appellant was prejudiced in his appeal before the board of review by Lieutenant Colonel Jacob Hagopian's participation in the oral argument and decision of the instant case.

. . .

The petitioner contends that this Article and the charge laid under it violate the Bill of Rights and the First Amendment thereof.

We note that this provision was not new to military law when it was adopted as a part of the Uniform Code of Military Justice. Actually, this provision, and its precursors, are older than the Bill of Rights, older than the Constitution, and older than the Republic itself.

. . .

The evil which Article 88 of the Uniform Code, supra, seeks to avoid is the impairment of discipline and the promotion of insubordination by an officer of the military service in using contemptuous words toward the Chief of State and the Commander-in-Chief of the Land and Naval Forces of the United States. Under the British Articles of War of 1765, the precursor to Article 88, Uniform Code of Military Justice, supra, was included with the offense of sedition under Section II thereof, entitled, "Mutiny." It is similarly separated in the American Articles of War 1776, being grouped with the offenses of sedition and mutiny. Winthrop's Military Law and Precedents,

2d ed, 1920 Reprint, at pages 932 and 961. We need not determine whether a state of war presently exists. We do judicially know that hundreds of thousands of members of our military forces are committed to combat in Vietnam, casualties among our forces are heavy, and thousands are being recruited, or drafted, into our armed forces. That in the present times and circumstances such conduct by an officer constitutes a clear and present danger to discipline within our armed services, under the precedents established by the Supreme Court, seems to require no argument.

The offense denounced by Article 88, supra, was an offense in the British forces at the beginning of our Revolutionary War and was readopted by the Continental Congress. It is significant that it was reenacted by the First Congress of which fifteen of the thirty-nine signers of the Constitution were members, including James Madison, the author of the Bill of Rights. United States v Culp, 14 USCMA 199, 211, 14 CMR 411. It is of even more significance that this provision was readopted by the Ninth Congress in 1806, after the Bill of Rights had been adopted and became a part of the Constitution. This action of Congress constituted a contemporary construction of the Constitution and is entitled to the greatest respect. United States v Culp, supra.

Speaking of a provision of this identical statute of 1806, the Supreme Court said in Ex parte Quirin, 317 US 1, 41, 87 L ed 3, 20, 63 S Ct 2 (1942):

> ". . . This enactment must be regarded as a contemporary construction of both Article 3, §2, and the Amendments as not foreclosing trial by military tribunals, without a jury, of offenses against the law of war committed by enemies not in or associated with our Armed Forces. It is a construction of the Constitution which has been followed since the founding of our government, and is now continued in the 82d Article of War. Such a construction is entitled to the greatest respect."

Since our decision in United States v Culp, supra, the Supreme Court has had occasion to again consider the question of contemporary construction of the Constitution. Growing out of the dispute occasioned by the order for the integration of the University of Mississippi, Governor Ross R. Barnett was cited for contempt and demanded trial by jury. In holding that he was not entitled to trial by jury, the Supreme Court said, in United States v Barnett, 376 US 681, 693, 12 L ed 2d 23, 32, 84 S Ct 984 (1964):

> ". . . Indeed, the short answer to this contention is the Judiciary Act of 1789 which provided that the courts of the United States shall have power to 'punish by fine or

imprisonment, at the discretion of said courts, all con-
tempts of authority in any cause or hearing before the
same.' It will be remembered that this legislation was
enacted by men familiar with the new Constitution. Madison urged passage of the act in the House and five of the
eight members of the Senate Committee which recommended adoption, were also delegates to the Constitutional
Convention of 1787. 1 Annals of Congress 18, 812-813.''

That Article 88, supra, does not violate the First Amendment
is clear. This conclusion is compelled and fortified by the recent
action of the Supreme Court in United States v Barnett, supra. The
reenactment by the First Congress on two occasions of the previously
existing Articles adopted by the Continental Congress and the action
of Congress in 1806 in reenacting the substantially identical provision, now contained in Article 88, must be regarded as contemporary
construction of the constitutional provisions. On no less than six
occasions since the enactment of 1806, the Congress has reenacted
the provision, with little or no change, as a construction of the Constitution which has been followed since the founding of our government.

. . .

What has been written historically of Article 88 of the Code,
supra, applies with equal force to Article 133 of the Uniform Code.
This codal provision reads:

> "Any commissioned officer, cadet, or midshipman
> who is convicted of conduct unbecoming an officer and a
> gentleman shall be punished as a court-martial may
> direct."

Article 47, Articles of War, enacted June 30, 1775*--identical to
Article 23 of the British Articles of War in force at the beginning of
the Revolutionary War--provided for the discharge from the service
of any commissioned officer convicted by a general court-martial
"of behaving in a scandalous, infamous manner, such as is unbecoming the character of an officer and a gentleman." Winthrop's Military
Law and Precedents, supra, at page 957. In this same text, it is to
be found as Article 21 of the Articles of War, enacted September 20,
1776, and as Article 20 of the Articles of War, enacted May 31, 1786.

---

*"Whatsoever commissioned officer shall be convicted before
a general court-martial, of behaving in a scandalous, infamous manner, such as is unbecoming the character of an officer and a gentleman, shall be discharged from the service." [Winthrop's Military
Law and Precedents, 2d ed, 1920 Reprint, at page 957.]

Winthrop, supra, at pages 969, 974. The scope of this provision was thereafter enlarged by the Articles of War, enacted April 10, 1806 (2 Stat 359), for Article 83 thereof omitted the original phrase "scandalous, infamous," providing simply, "Any commissioned officer convicted before a general court-martial of conduct unbecoming an officer and a gentleman, shall be dismissed the service." Winthrop, supra, at page 983. In the Articles of 1874 (Revised Statutes, section 1342), Article of War 61,* dismissal was made applicable for any conviction of an officer without regard to the trial forum, and, thereafter, of any "cadet"--by the Act of August 29, 1916, Article 95 (39 Stat 650).** The Act of June 4, 1920, Article 95 (41 Stat 787) brought no change. Other than including "Midshipmen" within the scope of the provision and removing the mandatory punishment of dismissal, this Article has since then remained the same. See Article 133 of the Uniform Code, supra, Act of May 5, 1950, 64 Stat 108, 142, and the Act of August 10, 1956, 70A Stat 36, 76.

Regardless, it is now argued that the charge founded upon this Article violates the First Amendment to the Constitution, fails to state an offense, and is so vague and uncertain that the due process clause of the Fifth Amendment is abridged.

That Article 133 affronts no constitutional concept has seemingly never been in doubt. In its present form, it is not a penal statute of sweeping and improper application. N.A.A.C.P. v Button, 371 US 415, 9 L ed 2d 405, 83 S Ct 328 (1963). Nor is it one "applied solely to terminate the reasonable, orderly, and limited exercise of the right to protest." Brown v Louisiana, 383 US 131, 142, 15 L ed 2d 637, 645, 86 S Ct 719 (1966). The right to free expression is not here curtailed. Indeed, in the military, it is specifically assured by AR 600-20, paragraph 46, January 31, 1967,* superseding, but

---

*"Any officer who is convicted of conduct unbecoming an officer and a gentleman shall be dismissed from the service." [Ibid., at page 991.]

**"Any officer or cadet who is convicted of conduct unbecoming an officer and a gentleman shall be dismissed from the service." [Act of August 29, 1916, Article 95 (39 Stat 650, 666).]

***"Participation in picket lines or any other public demonstrations, including those pertaining to civil rights, may imply Army sanction of the cause for which the demonstration is conducted. Such participation by members of the Army, not sanctioned by competent authority, is prohibited--

    a.  During the hours they are required to be present for duty.
    b.  When they are in uniform.
    c.  When they are on a military reservation.
    d.  When they are in a foreign country.
    e.  When their activities constitute a breach of law and order.
    f.  When violence is reasonably likely to result."

identical to, paragraph 46.1, then applicable. In truth, Article 133
concerns only the abuse of that right. De Jonge v Oregon, 299 US
353, 81 L ed 278, 57 S Ct 255 (1937). No one can quarrel with the
general proposition that "freedom of expression upon public questions
is secured by the First Amendment"; that this safeguard "was fashioned
to assure unfettered interchange of ideas for the bringing about of political and social changes desired by the people"; or "that public discussion is a political duty." New York Times Co. v Sullivan, 376 US 254,
269, 11 L ed 2d 686, 84 S Ct 710 (1964), with Annotation: Right to Free
Speech, 11 L ed 2d 1116. It must, on the other hand, be noted, the
"search for the outer limits of that right" (Curtis Publishing Co. v
Butts, -- US --, 18 L ed 2d 1094, 87 S Ct 1975, decided June 12, 1967)
has, in the main, been restricted to the civilian and not to the military
community and, even then, as we have said, the right is not to be exercised totally unrestricted. Dennis v United States, Schenck v United
States, Curtis Publishing Co. v Butts, all supra; see, also, Annotation:
Right of Free Speech, supra.

. . .

In short, we, too, find Article 133 of the Uniform Code, supra,
a constitutionally permissible exercise of statutory restraint.

By the same token, we find little merit to the defense argument
that the instant specification does not state an Article 133 offense,
in that the action or behavior proscribed must be limited to the accused's "official capacity." Suffice it to again say, an officer on
active duty is not a civilian and his off-duty activities do not fall outside the orbit of Article 133, AR 600-20, paragraph 46.1, notwithstanding insofar as an abuse to the right of free expression is
concerned.

. . .

Turning to the remaining question of constitutional import, we
do not consider Article 88 so vague and uncertain on its face that it
violates the due process clause of the Fifth Amendment. It has been
said that the constitutional requirement of definiteness is violated by
a criminal statute only if that statute fails to give a person of ordinary
intelligence fair notice that his contemplated conduct is denounced by
the statute. United States v Harriss, 347 US 612, 98 L ed 989, 996-
997, 74 S Ct 808 (1954). Moreover, the Supreme Court has held that
"if the general class of offenses to which the statute is directed is
plainly within its terms, the statute will not be struck down as vague,
even though marginal cases could be put where doubts might arise.
United States v Petrillo, 332 US 1, 7, 91 L ed 1877, 1882, 67 S Ct
1538. Cf. Jordan v DeGeorge, 341 US 223, 231, 95 L ed 886, 893, 71
S Ct 703. And if this general class of offenses can be made constitutionally definite by a reasonable construction of the statute, this
Court is under a duty to give the statute that construction." Id., at
page 618. In this regard, "the standard as defined is not a neat,
mathematical formulary. Like all verbalizations it is subject to

criticism on the score of indefiniteness." Dennis v United States, supra, at page 1156. So long as there are ascertainable standards of guilt, that is enough, for impossible standards of specificity are not demanded.

> ". . . The test is whether the language conveys a
> sufficient definite warning as to the proscribed conduct
> when measured by common understanding and practice
> (United States v Cardiff, 344 US 174, 73 S Ct 189, 97 L
> Ed 200; Cramp v Board of Public Instruction of Orange
> County, Fla., 368 US 278, 82 S Ct 275, 7 L Ed 2d 285,
> 292; Winters v New York, 333 US 507, 68 S Ct 665, 92
> L Ed 840; Champlin Refining Co. v Corporation Commis-
> sion, 286 US 210, 52 S Ct 559, 76 L Ed 1062, 86 ALR
> 403). . . ." [State v Hill, 189 Kan 403, 369 P2d 365,
> 371, 91 ALR2d 750, 760 (1962).]

Be that as it may, the Supreme Court has recently written:

> ". . . The objectionable quality of vagueness and
> overbreadth does not depend upon absence of fair notice
> to a criminally accused or upon unchanneled delegation
> of legislative powers, but upon the danger of tolerating,
> in the area of First Amendment freedoms, the existence
> of a penal statute susceptible of sweeping and improper
> application. Cf. Marcus v Search Warrant of Property,
> etc., 367 US 717, 733, 6 L ed 2d 1127, 1137, 81 S Ct
> 1708. These freedoms are delicate and vulnerable, as
> well as supremely precious in our society. The threat
> of sanctions may deter their exercise almost as potently
> as the actual application of sanctions. Cf. Smith v
> California, supra (361 US at 151-154); Speiser v Randall,
> 357 US 513, 526, 2 L ed 2d 1460, 1472, 78 S Ct 1332.
> Because First Amendment freedoms need breathing
> space to survive, government may regulate in the area
> only with narrow specificity. Cantwell v Connecticut,
> 310 US 296, 311, 84 L ed 1213, 1221, 60 S Ct 900, 128
> ALR 1352." [N.A.A.C.P. v Button, 371 US 415, 433,
> 9 L ed 2d 405, 418, 83 S Ct 328 (1963).]

Whatever the test, Article 88 meets the constitutional norm as to certainty. We need not dwell on its susceptibility of improper application for that possibility has had previous assessment. In the matter of "fair notice," we emphasize that Article 88 is designed to cover the use of "contemptuous" words toward holders of certain offices named therein. "Contemptuous" is used in the ordinary sense as is evidenced by the Manual for Courts-Martial, United States,

1951, paragraph 167. See Webster's Third New International Dictionary. The proscribed conduct having been made certain and the warnings sufficient, it follows that the language of the Article satisfies the test of definiteness, just as does Article 133, hereinbefore discussed. See United States v Fletcher, Smith v Whitney, and United States v Giordano, all supra. In sum, we answer issues 1, 2, and 3 adversely to the petitioner.

Counsel for the appellant also contend that the law officer erred to the prejudice of Lieutenant Howe in failing to instruct, sua sponte, that if the court-martial found the alleged contemptuous words to have been uttered in the course of a political discussion, it thereupon had to find he intended these words to be personally disrespectful.

It is argued that this record shows accused participating in a political discussion, and that, under the circumstances, personal contempt for the President was absent--this latter aspect being an ingredient of the offense.

Assuming the conduct in question amounts to a political discussion, as appellate defense counsel contend, the argument advanced nonetheless fails. A plain and unambiguous statute is to be applied and not interpreted. United States v Davis, 12 USCMA 576, 31 CMR 162. Neither the Manual nor the Code make "intent" an element of the offense. Admittedly, paragraph 167 of the Manual, supra, provides, in part:

> ". . . Adverse criticism of one of the officials or groups named in the article, in the course of a political discussion, even though emphatically expressed, if not personally contemptuous, may not be charged as a violation of the article." [Emphasis supplied.]

The above-quoted emphasized phrase, however, cannot be equated to the contemptuous language prohibited by this Article. Indeed, paragraph 167 further provides:

> ". . . However, giving broad circulation to a written publication containing contemptuous words of the kind made punishable by this article, or the utterance of such contemptuous words in the presence of military inferiors, would constitute an aggravation of the offense."

Neither the legislative history of the Uniform Code nor interpretation of comparable Articles of War lend themselves to any different interpretation. See United States v Poli, CM 235607, 22 BR 151, 161 (1943). Accordingly, the law officer did not err in failing to give a sua sponte instruction concerning intent.

The next issue to be considered is whether appellant was substantially prejudiced by the law officer's ruling that the maximum

sentence for the charged offenses included confinement at hard labor
for three years. The Table of Maximum Punishments, Manual for
Courts-Martial, United States, 1951, paragraph 127c, does not provide a stated punishment for either of the offenses here charged. It
should be noted that for punishment purposes they were treated as
multiplicious. In those instances where punishment is not stated, if
the offense is included within an offense listed in the Table of Maximum Punishments or is closely related to some other listed offense,
"the lesser punishment prescribed for either the included or closely
related offense will prevail as the maximum limit of punishment."
Paragraph 127c, supra. Since neither of the offenses here involved
is included within other offenses, it is the contention of the appellate
defense counsel that they are most closely akin to the offenses under
Article 89 of the Uniform Code, 10 USC §889, for it makes punishable
disrespect toward a superior officer. Six months is the maximum
authorized confinement for conviction under this Article. Such was
not the view taken by the law officer for he had instructed the court
on a three-year maximum for confinement, treating these offenses
as being similar to an Article 134 offense of uttering disloyal statements. To this, defense replies that even if the Article 134 offense
is possibly related, where an offense not listed in the Table of Maximum Punishments is similar to listed offenses, a preference for the
lesser of the two is manifest under paragraph 120c, Manual for
Courts-Martial, United States, 1951, and by our holding in United
States v Beach, 2 USCMA 172, 7 CMR 48.

For the charges and specifications in this case, it is our considered opinion that the offense of disloyal statements, in violation
of Article 134 and punishable by a maximum of confinement at hard
labor for three years, is most closely analagous to the instant
charges. . . .

Accordingly, as to the instant charges and specifications, we
find that the law officer gave the court-martial the correct maximum
punishment imposable.

Yet another issue is that the law officer erred to the substantial prejudice of the appellant by instructing the court, in spite of the
defense objection, that in determining whether the words used by
Lieutenant Howe were contemptuous, the court-martial "should apply
the test of how the words were understood and what they were taken
to mean by the persons who saw them."

The appellant takes the position that the test applicable in this
case is the same as that used in criminal prosecutions for obscenity.
Related to the case at bar, the proper measurement, counsel contend, should have been "whether to the average person, applying
contemporary community standards, on a national basis, the uttered
words taken as a whole are contemptuous of the specified public
official."

Be that as it may, on this record of trial we envision no prejudice befalling the accused because of the instructions actually given

in this area. The issue matters not, when as here, the language utilized by the appellant is obviously contemptuous per se. . . .

In the last error assigned, it is asserted the appellant was prejudiced at the board of review level when Lieutenant Colonel Hagopian refused to disqualify himself from participating as a board of review member in review of the case. This assignment is founded on an affidavit made by military appellate defense counsel. . . .

. . .

Appellate defense counsel, as we have heretofore pointed out, does not assert Lieutenant Colonel Hagopian was personally biased, only that there was the appearance of a predisposition of bias. It is error for one who is counsel on a case to participate thereafter as a judge, but, measured by the standards set out above, the instant affidavit does not, in our estimation, establish even a predisposition of possible harm. As we have noted, the specification in question is in fact legally sufficient. Lieutenant Colonel Hagopian was called upon to give no more than a legal evaluation of the specification. As a senior member of the Defense Appellate Division, and, therefore, acting as counsel, he set forth his views. His opinion did not change its legal sufficiency and his subsequent membership on the board of review, therefore, offers no possible prejudice to the appellant.

These are the considerations which prompted denial of the accused's petition in the first instance, and require us to deny the petition for reconsideration.

Chief Judge QUINN and Judge FERGUSON concur.

Article 134 of the Code is often referred to as the General Article or, less elegantly, as the "catch-all" Article. Judge Nott of the Court of Claims had the following comments about the contents of the article in the case of Swaim v. U.S., 28 Ct.Cl. 173 (1893):

> "What is conduct unbecoming an officer and a gentle-
> man, or what is conduct to the prejudice of good order
> and military discipline is beyond the bounds of exact
> formula, and must depend more or less upon the circum-
> stances and peculiarities of each case. To slap a woman
> in the face is no more violation of the law than to slap
> a man in the face. Yet under the code of military ethics,
> to slap a woman in the face might be regarded as a
> cowardly act and be classified as conduct unbecoming
> an officer and a gentleman. To commit an assault on
> any person is an offense at law; but under the other code,
> not to commit an assault, as where a ruffian was insulting

an unprotected girl, might be deemed conduct unbecoming
an officer and a gentleman.  The cases which involve conduct to the prejudice of good order and military discipline
are still further beyond the bounds of ordinary judicial
judgment, for they are not measurable by our inate sense
of right and wrong, of honor and dishonor, but must be
gauged by an actual knowledge and experience of military
life, its usages and duties.  All that a civil court can do
in these collateral cases is to look into the record and
see that the wide discretion which the Articles of War
give to a court-martial and the commanding officer who
approves the sentence has not been abused; that the sentence does not rest on suppositious or frivolous pretexts;
that the case presents facts which a body of experienced,
intelligent, impartial, military experts may reasonably
hold, in the exercise of sound discretion, to be prejudicial
to good order and military discipline.  When facts appear,
the civil court must concede that they constitute the offense embodied in the charge."

## UNITED STATES v. FRANTZ

United States Court of Military Appeals, 1953.
2 U.S.C.M.A. 161, 7 C.M.R. 37.

PAUL W. BROSMAN, Judge:
On his plea of guilty, the accused was convicted by special
court-martial (1-52-S-367) of four offenses, three of which are of
no consequence here.  A board of review set aside his conviction of
the offense, charged in Specification 2 of Charge II, on the ground
that its language did not allege a crime under the Uniform Code of
Military Justice, 50 USC §§551-736.  Thereupon, The Judge Advocate
General, United States Navy, certified the following question to this
Court:

"Whether, as a matter of law, specification 2 of
Charge II failed to allege an offense in violation of
Article 134 of the Uniform Code of Military Justice?"

The charge and specification in question alleged that the defendant violated Article 134 of the Uniform Code of Military Justice,
50 USC §728, "in that . . . [ he] did, at Long Beach, California, on
or about 28 February 1952, wrongfully have in his possession with

intent to deceive, an armed forces liberty pass . . . well knowing
the same to be false."

In brief, the board of review determined that the draftsman of
the specification intended to allege, via Article 134 of the Code, supra,
a violation of 18 USC §499, which renders criminal possession of a
military pass or permit "with intent to defraud." Thereafter its
members concluded that an "intent to deceive," as charged in the specification, was not equivalent to the "intent to defraud" proscribed by
18 USC §499, and, therefore, that the specification did not allege an
offense under Article 134 of the Code, supra.

Assuming arguendo--and only so--that an "intent to deceive"
is not in all essential respects tantamount to an "intent to defraud,"
we nevertheless believe that the board of review erred. First of all,
there is nothing to indicate that the draftsman of the specification in
question intended to lay the charge under 18 USC §499 through that
portion of Article 134, supra, rendering cognizable by court-martial
"crimes and offenses not capital, of which persons subject to this
code may be guilty." It will be recalled that Article 134 consists of
three distinct and separate parts. The first applies to "all disorders
and neglects to the prejudice of good order and discipline in the
armed forces"; the second extends to "all conduct of a nature to bring
discredit upon the armed forces"; and the third is that mentioned
above, "crimes and offenses not capital, of which persons subject to
this code may be guilty." United States v. Snyder, (No. 409), 4 CMR
15, decided June 5, 1952; United States v. Herndon (No. 570), 4 CMR
53, decided July 17, 1952; United States v. Long (No. 464), 6 CMR
60, decided December 3, 1952. Our conclusion from a reading of the
specification, together with the language of Article 134, supra, is
quite the reverse of that reached by the board of review. No reference was made in the charge to a statutory basis for the allegation
of a "crime or offense not capital"--although we need not now decide
whether such a reference is prerequisite to a sufficient allegation of
such an offense. The specification is palpably patterned on model
specification number 138, Manual for Courts-Martial, United States,
1951, Forms--Charges and Specifications, App. 6c, page 490. We
are quite certain that its draftsman was concerned primarily with the
accused's universally reprehended conduct, and that he gave no
thought to the third clause of Article 134, supra. United States v.
Herndon, supra. He was surely thinking principally in terms of the
first two clauses of that Article.

Viewing the charge in this light, there can be little doubt that
deceitful possession by an accused of a false liberty card was conduct "to the prejudice of good order and discipline"--for it constituted
a deliberate flaunting of the requirement that liberty cards be duly
and properly authenticated, and of the authority of the officer designated to issue such documents. It is unnecessary to decide whether
the act charged might at the same time have been "conduct of a nature
to bring discredit upon the armed forces."

That phase of accused's argument predicated on the facts is
readily answered by pointing out that he entered a plea of guilty to the
specification in question, and persisted therein in the face of full advice as to its consequences--thereby effectively removing purely
factual issues from the case. Also, departing somewhat from the
issue certified, accused argues that the Code's Article 134, supra, as
applied, is unconstitutional because of vagueness. The root of this
argument, of course, is his contention that the conduct charged here
is not so patently prejudicial to good order and military discipline
that the defendant could have known in advance that he was violating
the Article. We certainly believe--as noted above--that the conduct
involved was obviously of that prejudicial nature. To put the question
is to answer it in all reasonable minds.

The constitutionality of the Article, as applied, having been questioned by defense from the point of view of the certainty or definiteness of its proscriptions, we think it incumbent upon us to appraise it
on its face and generally as well. Surely, the third clause of the Article is not vague. However, we cannot ignore the conceivable presence
of uncertainty in the first two clauses. Assuming that civilian precedents in the field are applicable in full force to the military community, we do not perceive in the Article vagueness or uncertainty to
an unconstitutional degree. The provision, as it appears in the Uniform Code, is no novelty to service criminal law. Compare Champlin
Refining Company v. Corporation Commission, 286 US 210, 242-243,
76 L ed 1062, 1082, 52 S Ct 559; Connally v General Construction Co.,
269 US 385, 391-392, 70 L ed 322, 328, 46 S Ct 126. On the contrary,
it has been a part of our military law since 1775, and directly traces
its origin to British sources. Winthrop's Military Law and Precedents,
2d ed., 1920 Reprint, page 720. It must be judged, therefore, not in
vacuo, but in the context in which the years have placed it. Musser v.
Utah, 333 US 95, 97, 92 L ed 562, 565, 68 S Ct 397. That the clauses
under scrutiny have acquired the core of a settled and understandable
content of meaning is clear from the no less than forty-seven different offenses cognizable thereunder explicitly included in the Table of
Maximum Punishments of the Manual, supra, paragraph 127c, pages
224-227. Accordingly, we conclude that the Article establishes a
standard "well enough known to enable those within . . . [its] reach
to correctly apply them." Connally v. General Construction Co.,
supra, at 391; Hygrade Provision Co. v. Sherman, 266 US 497, 502,
69 L ed 402, 406, 45 S Ct 141; Omaechevarria v. Idaho, 246 US 343,
348, 62 L ed 763, 767, 38 S Ct 323; Nash v. United States, 229 US 373,
57 L ed 1232, 33 S Ct 780; International Harvester Co. v. Kentucky,
234 US 216, 223, 58 L ed 1284, 1288, 34 S Ct 853. A certain minimum
element of indistinction remains which, in legislation of this entirely
defensible character, can never be expunged completely, and must be
dealt with on a case-by-case basis. See Krichman v. United States,
256 US 363, 367-368, 65 L ed 992, 994, 41 S Ct 514. This can be accomplished readily and properly in accordance with respectable

analogues developed in courts of the civilian scheme. This latent and inescapable ambiguity cannot, in view of the recognized and measurable standard of the Article, be fatal, for "the law is full of instances where a man's fate depends on his estimating rightly . . . some matter of degree." Nash v. United States, supra, at 377.

It is evident that our conclusion in this branch of the case is buttressed by the presence of impressive civilian authority involving legislation operative principally, or even wholly, in the civilian scene. However, the briefest of terminal references must be made to the presence of special and highly relevant considerations growing out of the essential disciplinary demands of the military service. These are at once so patent and so compelling as to dispense with the necessity for their enumeration--much less their argumentative development.

The question certified is answered in the negative.

Chief Judge QUINN and Judge LATIMER concur.

Although it is not necessary to allege in the specification that the misconduct charged is "prejudicial to good order and discipline" (U.S. v. Sadinsky, 14 USCMA 563, 34 CMR 343 [1964]), the military judge must instruct the court-martial that it must find that the conduct was of such a nature (U.S. v. Williams, 8 USCMA 325, 24 CMR 135 [1957]).

## UNITED STATES v. NORRIS

United States Court of Military Appeals, 1953.
2 U.S.C.M.A. 236, 8 C.M.R. 36.

ROBERT E. QUINN, Chief Judge:

The accused, charged with larceny in violation of Article 121 of the Uniform Code of Military Justice, 50 U. S. C. §715, pleaded guilty to "taking without authority" in violation of Article 134, 50 U. S. C. §728. At the conclusion of the trial, the law officer advised the court that the accused could not be found guilty of any offense other than larceny or wrongful appropriation. The court found him guilty of wrongful appropriation and sentenced him to dishonorable discharge, total forfeiture of pay and confinement for one year. The convening authority approved, reducing the confinement to six months.

The board of review held that the law officer erred in not instructing the court on the legal effect of intoxication in relation to the specific intent required for both larceny and wrongful appropriation, and in withdrawing the offense of "wrongful taking" from the court's consideration. Because of these errors, the board affirmed only a finding of wrongful taking under Article 134, supra, and reduced the sentence to confinement for four months and forfeiture of $50.00 per month for a like period. The Judge Advocate General has certified the questions of whether there is any legal offense of wrongful taking under Article 134 and, if so, what is the maximum punishment for the offense.

. . .

Whatever may have been the state of the law prior to the Uniform Code, we are convinced that the general Article of the Code-- Article 134, supra--embraces no criminal conversion offense lesser than wrongful appropriation as defined by Article 121, supra. That Article includes larceny and wrongful appropriation--the distinction between the two lying in the required element, for the former, of an intent to deprive permanently and, for the latter, of an intent to deprive only temporarily. "Wrongful taking" is not mentioned as an offense anywhere in the Code or Manual. No sample specification governing such an offense is listed; it is not mentioned in the Table of Maximum Punishments; and it is not listed in the "Table of Commonly Included Offenses" as lesser included under larceny.

. . .

It is our view that, in accordance with the remarks of Professor Morgan, quoted earlier, Article 134 should generally be limited to military offenses and those crimes not specifically delineated by the punitive Articles. See Winthrop's Military Law and Precedents, 2d ed., 1920 Reprint, page 720. As the Manual itself notes, there is scarcely an irregular or improper act conceivable which may not be regarded as in some indirect or remote sense prejudicing military discipline under Article 134. Manual for Courts-Martial, United States, 1951, page 381. We cannot grant to the services unlimited authority to eliminate vital elements from common law crimes and offenses expressly defined by Congress and permit the remaining elements to be punished as an offense under Article 134.

We are persuaded, as apparently the drafters of the Manual were, that Congress has, in Article 121, covered the entire field of criminal conversion for military law. We are not disposed to add a third conversion offense to those specifically defined. It follows that there is no offense known as "wrongful taking" requiring no element of specific intent, embraced by Article 134 of the Code. The ruling of the law officer to that effect at the trial was correct. However, we concur with the board of review in holding that the law officer erred, considering the evidence presented, in not instructing the court on the legal effect of intoxication on the offenses charged.

There is no lesser offense not requiring specific intent which could be affirmed so as to purge the error. Accordingly, the decision of the board of review is reversed and a rehearing is ordered.

Judge LATIMER concurs.

BROSMAN, Judge (concurring):

It strikes me that, for reasons soundly based in function and policy, military law should recognize an offense in the nature of "wrongful taking," requiring only a general criminal intent. Although occasion for the proscription of such misconduct may obtain in the civilian community as well, inducements both more numerous and more compelling appear to me to be present in the military scene. The possible unfortunate future result in the case at bar, for example, affords an illustration of the sort of thing I have in mind.

Additionally, I had supposed that such a crime was known to military criminal law. However, I have been convinced by my brothers that no such offense exists under the Uniform Code of Military Justice and the Manual for Courts-Martial, United States, 1951, and I fully concur in their disposition of the instant case.

However, I am impelled to question what seems to me to be the clear implication of the majority opinion that Article 134, 50 U. S. C. §728, is and should be "generally limited to military offenses." I am inclined to doubt the correctness of this suggestion in both its present and imperative aspects. A glance at the Manual's Table of Maximum Punishments, under the heading of Article 134, demonstrates readily that many substantial non-military crimes are currently enumerated thereunder, and I see no overmastering reason why this should not be so. While it is perfectly true--as the Manual says--that "an irregular or improper act on the part of a member of the military service can scarcely be conceived which may not be regarded as in some indirect or remote sense prejudicing discipline," I would exercise care not to push this notion too far. I can easily conceive of wrongful takings which, principally as disorders, fall within the objectives of Article 134 with a much greater show of propriety than numerous offenses now included thereunder. My previous judicial conduct must indicate that I have every wish to protect fully the rights of accused persons. At the same time, I am anxious not to impede military commanders in the proper exercise of their responsibility to maintain discipline.

The Court has held that negligent homicide is an offense properly chargeable under Article 134 (United States v. Kirchner, 1 U.S.C.M.A. 477, 4 C.M.R. 69 [1952]; see also United States v. Greenfeather, 13 U.S.C.M.A. 151, 32 C.M.R. 151 [1962]). On the other hand, negligent indecent exposure is not an offense under Article 134 (United States v. Manos, 8 U.S.C.M.A. 734, 25 C.M.R. 238 [1958]). A specification alleging a violation of a capital offense may not be pleaded as a violation of Articles 133 or 134. See U.S. v. French, 10 U.S.C.M.A. 171, 27 C.M.R. 245 (1959).

Although a text in military law is usually restricted to a consideration of the laws related to the administration of military justice, there are many other laws that are administered by, or have a peculiar effect upon, members of the armed services. For example, the Department of Defense, as probably the largest independent contractor in the United States, administers a vast panoply of procurement laws, regulations, and directives. Another specialized field of law, termed "military affairs" by army judge advocates, encompasses the interpretation and application of regulations affecting day-to-day operations. Such problems as the legality of promotions and demotions, the determination of line of duty status, and the assessment of pecuniary liability for the loss or damage of military property are considered by these specialists. It is not feasible to attempt to discuss all these laws in a book of this type; however, certain specialized areas are briefly discussed in the following sections.

CONTROL OVER CONDUCT ON MILITARY INSTALLATIONS

CAFETERIA WORKERS v. McELROY*

Supreme Court of the United States, 1961.
367 U.S. 886, 81 S.Ct. 1743, 6 L.Ed.2d 1230.

*[ Footnotes have been omitted.  Ed.]

MR. JUSTICE STEWART delivered the opinion of the Court.
In 1956 the petitioner Rachel Brawner was a short-order cook
at a cafeteria operated by her employer, M & M Restaurants, Inc.,
on the premises of the Naval Gun Factory in the city of Washington.
She had worked there for more than six years, and from her employer's point of view her record was entirely satisfactory.
The Gun Factory was engaged in designing, producing, and in-
specting naval ordnance, including the development of weapons
systems of a highly classified nature.  Located on property owned by
the United States, the installation was under the command of Rear
Admiral D. M. Tyree, Superintendent.  Access to it was restricted,
and guards were posted at all points of entry.  Identification badges
were issued to persons authorized to enter the premises by the
Security Officer, a naval officer subordinate to the Superintendent.
In 1956 the Security Officer was Lieutenant Commander H. C.
Williams.  Rachel Brawner had been issued such a badge.
The cafeteria where she worked was operated by M & M under
a contract with the Board of Governors of the Gun Factory.  Section
5(b) of the contract provided:

". . . In no event shall the Concessionaire engage, or
continue to engage, for operations under this Agreement,
personnel who

459

. . .
> "(iii)  fail to meet the security requirements or
> other requirements under applicable regulations of the
> Activity, as determined by the Security Officer of the
> Activity."

On November 15, 1956, Mrs. Brawner was required to turn in
her identification badge because of Lieutenant Commander Williams'
determination that she had failed to meet the security requirements
of the installation.  The Security Officer's determination was subsequently approved by Admiral Tyree, who cited §5(b)(iii) of the contract as the basis for his action.  At the request of the petitioner
Union, which represented the employees at the cafeteria, M & M
sought to arrange a meeting with officials of the Gun Factory "for the
purpose of a hearing regarding the denial of admittance to the Naval
Gun Factory of Rachel Brawner."  This request was denied by Admiral Tyree on the ground that such a meeting would "serve no useful
purpose."

Since the day her identification badge was withdrawn Mrs.
Brawner has not been permitted to enter the Gun Factory.  M & M
offered to employ her in another restaurant which the company operated in the suburban Washington area, but she refused on the
ground that the location was inconvenient.

The petitioners brought this action in the District Court against
the Secretary of Defense, Admiral Tyree, and Lieutenant Commander
Williams, in their individual and official capacities, seeking, among
other things, to compel the return to Mrs. Brawner of her identification badge, so that she might be permitted to enter the Gun Factory
and resume her former employment.  The defendants filed a motion
for summary judgment, supported by various affidavits and exhibits.
The motion was granted and the complaint dismissed by the District
Court.  This judgment was affirmed by the Court of Appeals for the
District of Columbia, sitting en banc.  Four judges dissented.  We
granted certiorari because of an alleged conflict between the Court
of Appeals' decision and Greene v. McElroy, 360 U.S. 474.  364 U.S.
813.

As the case comes here, two basic questions are presented.
Was the commanding officer of the Gun Factory authorized to deny
Rachel Brawner access to the installation in the way he did?  If he
was so authorized, did his action in excluding her operate to deprive
her of any right secured to her by the Constitution?

## I

In Greene v. McElroy, supra, the Court was unwilling to find,
in the absence of explicit authorization, that an aeronautical engineer,
employed by a private contractor on private property, could be barred
from following his profession by governmental revocation of his
security clearance without according him the right to confront and

cross-examine hostile witnesses. The Court in that case found that neither the Congress nor the President had explicitly authorized the procedure which had been followed in denying Greene access to classified information. Accordingly we did not reach the constitutional issues which that case otherwise would have presented. We proceed on the premise that the explicit authorization found wanting in Greene must be shown in the present case, putting to one side the Government's argument that the differing circumstances here justify less rigorous standards for measuring delegation of authority.

It cannot be doubted that both the legislative and executive branches are wholly legitimate potential sources of such explicit authority. The control of access to a military base is clearly within the constitutional powers granted to both Congress and the President. Article I, §8, of the Constitution gives Congress the power to "provide and maintain a navy;" to "make rules for the government and regulation of the land and naval forces;" to "exercise exclusive legislation . . . over all places purchased by the consent of the legislature of the state in which the same shall be, for the erection of forts, magazines, arsenals, dock-yards, and other needful buildings;" and to "make all laws which shall be necessary and proper for carrying into execution the foregoing powers. . . ." Broad power in this same area is also vested in the President by Article II, §2, which makes him the Commander in Chief of the Armed Forces.

Congress has provided that the Secretary of the Navy "shall administer the Department of the Navy" and shall have "custody and charge of all . . . property of the Department." 10 U.S.C. §5031(a) and (c). In administering his Department, the Secretary has been given statutory power to "prescribe regulations, not inconsistent with law, for the government of his department, . . . and the custody, use, and preservation of the . . . property appertaining to it." 5 U. S. C. §22. The law explicitly requires that United States Navy Regulations shall be approved by the President, 10 U. S. C. §6011, and the pertinent regulations in effect when Rachel Brawner's identification badge was revoked had, in fact, been expressly approved by President Truman on August 9, 1948.

. . .

Article 0701 of the Regulations delineates the traditional responsibilities and duties of a commanding officer. It provides in part as follows:

"The responsibility of the commanding officer for his command is absolute, except when, and to the extent, relieved therefrom by competent authority, or as provided otherwise in these regulations. The authority of the commanding officer is commensurate with his responsibility, subject to the limitations prescribed by law and these regulations. . . ."

Article 0734 of the Regulations provides:

'In general, dealers or tradesmen or their agents shall
not be admitted within a command, except as authorized
by the commanding officer:
"1. To conduct public business.
"2. To transact specific private business with individuals at the request of the latter.
"3. To furnish services and supplies which are
necessary and are not otherwise, or are insufficiently,
available to the personnel of the command."

It would be difficult to conceive of a more specific conferral of
power upon a commanding officer, in the exercise of his traditional
command responsibility, to exclude from the area of his command a
person in Rachel Brawner's status. Even without the benefit of the
illuminating gloss of history, it could hardly be doubted that the phrase
"tradesmen or their agents" covered her status as an employee of
M & M with explicit precision. But the meaning of the regulation need
not be determined in vacuo. It is the verbalization of the unquestioned
authority which commanding officers of military installations have
exercised throughout our history.

This power has been expressly recognized many times. "The
power of a military commandant over a reservation is necessarily extensive and practically exclusive, forbidding entrance and controlling
residence as the public interest may demand." 26 Op. Atty. Gen. 91,
92. "[I]t is well settled that a post commander can, in his discretion,
exclude all persons other than those belonging to his post from post
and reservation grounds." JAGA 1904/16272, 6 May 1904. "It is well
settled that a Post Commander can, under the authority conferred on
him by statutes and regulations, in his discretion, exclude private
persons and property therefrom, or admit them under such restrictions as he may prescribe in the interest of good order and military
discipline (1918 Dig. Op. J. A. G. 267 and cases cited)." JAGA 1925/
680.44, 6 October 1925.

Under the explicit authority of Article 0734 of the Navy Regulations, and in the light of the historically unquestioned power of a commanding officer summarily to exclude civilians from the area of his
command, there can remain no serious doubt of Admiral Tyree's
authority to exclude Rachel Brawner from the Gun Factory upon the
Security Officer's determination that she failed to meet the "security
requirements . . . of the Activity." Her admittance to the installation in the first place was permissible, in the commanding officer's
discretion, only because she came within the exception to the general
rule of exclusion contained in the third paragraph of Article 0734 of
the Regulations. And the plain words of Article 0734 made absolute
the commanding officer's power to withdraw her permission to enter
the Gun Factory at any time.

## II

The question remains whether Admiral Tyree's action in summarily denying Rachel Brawner access to the site of her former employment violated the requirements of the Due Process Clause of the Fifth Amendment. This question cannot be answered by easy assertion that, because she had no constitutional right to be there in the first place, she was not deprived of liberty or property by the Superintendent's action. . . .

The Fifth Amendment does not require a trial-type hearing in every conceivable case of government impairment of private interest. "For, though 'due process of law' generally implies and includes actor, reus, judex, regular allegations, opportunity to answer, and a trial according to some settled course of judicial proceedings, . . . yet, this is not universally true." Murray's Lessee v. Hoboken Land and Improvement Co., 18 How. 272, 280. The very nature of due process negates any concept of inflexible procedures universally applicable to every imaginable situation. Communications Comm'n v. WJR, 337 U.S. 265, 275-276; Hannah v. Larche, 363 U.S. 420, 440, 442; Hagar v. Reclamation District No. 108, 111 U.S. 701, 708-709. "'[D]ue process," unlike some legal rules, is not a technical conception with a fixed content unrelated to time, place and circumstances." It is "compounded of history, reason, the past course of decisions. . . ." Joint Anti-Fascist Comm. v. McGrath, 341 U.S. 123, 162-163 (concurring opinion).

As these and other cases make clear, consideration of what procedures due process may require under any given set of circumstances must begin with a determination of the precise nature of the government function involved as well as of the private interest that has been affected by governmental action. Where it has been possible to characterize that private interest (perhaps in oversimplification) as a mere privilege subject to the Executive's plenary power, it has traditionally been held that notice and hearing are not constitutionally required. Oceanic Navigation Co. v. Stranahan, 214 U.S. 320, 340-343; Knauff v. Shaughnessy, 338 U.S. 537; Jay v. Boyd, 351 U.S. 345, 354-358; cf. Buttfield v. Stranahan, 192 U.S. 470, 497.

What, then, was the private interest affected by Admiral Tyree's action in the present case? It most assuredly was not the right to follow a chosen trade or profession. Cf. Dent v. West Virginia, 129 U.S. 114; Schware v. Board of Bar Examiners, 353 U.S. 232; Truax v. Raich, 239 U.S. 33. Rachel Brawner remained entirely free to obtain employment as a short-order cook or to get any other job, either with M & M or with any other employer. All that was denied her was the opportunity to work at one isolated and specific military installation.

Moreover, the governmental function operating here was not the power to regulate or license, as lawmaker, an entire trade or profession, or to control an entire branch of private business, but, rather, as proprietor, to manage the internal operation of an important federal military establishment. See People v. Crane, 214 N. Y. 154, 167-169, 108 N. E. 427, 431-432 (per Cardozo, J.); cf. Perkins v. Lukens Steel Co., 310 U.S. 113, 129. In that proprietary military capacity, the Federal Government, as has been pointed out, has traditionally exercised unfettered control.

Thus, the nature both of the private interest which has been impaired and the governmental power which has been exercised makes this case quite different from that of the lawyer in Schware, supra, the physician in Dent, supra, and the cook in Raich, supra. This case, like Perkins v. Lukens Steel Co., 310 U.S. 113, involves the Federal Government's dispatch of its own internal affairs. . . .

. . .

We may assume that Rachel Brawner could not constitutionally have been excluded from the Gun Factory if the announced grounds for her exclusion had been patently arbitrary or discriminatory--that she could not have been kept out because she was a Democrat or a Methodist. It does not follow, however, that she was entitled to notice and a hearing when the reason advanced for her exclusion was, as here, entirely rational and in accord with the contract with M & M.

Finally, it is to be noted that this is not a case where government action has operated to bestow a badge of disloyalty or infamy, with an attendant foreclosure from other employment opportunity. See Wieman v. Updegraff, 344 U.S. 183, 190-191; Joint Anti-Fascist Comm. v. McGrath, 341 U.S. 123, 140-141; cf. Bailey v. Richardson, 86 U.S. App. D. C. 248, 182 F. 2d 46, aff'd by an equally divided Court, 341 U.S. 918. All this record shows is that, in the opinion of the Security Officer of the Gun Factory, concurred in by the Superintendent, Rachel Brawner failed to meet the particular security requirements of that specific military installation. There is nothing to indicate that this determination would in any way impair Rachel Brawner's employment opportunities anywhere else. As pointed out by Judge Prettyman, speaking for the Court of Appeals, 'Nobody has said that Brawner is disloyal or is suspected of the slightest shadow of intentional wrongdoing. 'Security requirements' at such an installation, like such requirements under many other circumstances, cover many matters other than loyalty.' 109 U.S. App. D. C., at 49, 284 F. 2d, at 183. For all that appears, the Security Officer and the Superintendent may have simply thought that Rachel Brawner was garrulous, or careless with her identification badge.

For these reasons, we conclude that the Due Process Clause of the Fifth Amendment was not violated in this case.

Affirmed.

MR. JUSTICE BRENNAN, with whom THE CHIEF JUSTICE, MR. JUSTICE BLACK and MR. JUSTICE DOUGLAS join, dissenting.

I have grave doubts whether the removal of petitioner's identification badge for "security reasons" without notice of charges or opportunity to refute them was authorized by statute or executive order. See Greene v. McElroy, 360 U.S. 474 (1959). But under compulsion of the Court's determination that there was authority, I pass to a consideration of the more important constitutional issue, whether petitioner has been deprived of liberty or property without due process of law in violation of the Fifth Amendment.

I read the Court's opinion to acknowledge that petitioner's status as an employee at the Gun Factory was an interest of sufficient definiteness to be protected by the Federal Constitution from some kinds of governmental injury. Indeed, this acknowledgment seems compelled by our cases. Wieman v. Updegraff, 344 U.S. 183, (1952); United Public Workers v. Mitchell, 330 U.S. 75, 100 (1947) (dictum); Torcaso v. Watkins, ante, p. 488, decided today. In other words, if petitioner Brawner's badge had been lifted avowedly on grounds of her race, religion, or political opinions, the Court would concede that some constitutionally protected interest--whether "liberty" or "property" it is unnecessary to state--had been injured. But, as the Court says, there has been no such open discrimination here. The expressed ground of exclusion was the obscuring formulation that petitioner failed to meet the "security requirements" of the naval installation where she worked. I assume for present purposes that separation as a "security risk," if the charge is properly established, is not unconstitutional. But the Court goes beyond that. It holds that the mere assertion by government that exclusion is for a valid reason forecloses further inquiry. That is, unless the government official is foolish enough to admit what he is doing--and few will be so foolish after today's decision--he may employ "security requirements" as a blind behind which to dismiss at will for the most discriminatory of causes.

Such a result in effect nullifies the substantive right--not to be arbitrarily injured by Government--which the Court purports to recognize. What sort of right is it which enjoys absolutely no procedural protection? I do not mean to imply that petitioner could not have been excluded from the installation without the full procedural panoply of first having been subjected to a trial, with cross-examination and confrontation of accusers, and proof of guilt beyond a reasonable doubt. I need not go so far in this case. For under today's holding petitioner is entitled to no process at all. She is not told what she did wrong; she is not given a chance to defend herself. She may be the victim of the basest calumny, perhaps even the caprice of the government officials in whose power her status rested completely. In such a case, I cannot believe that she is not entitled to some procedures. "[T]he right to be heard before being condemned to suffer grievous loss of any kind, even though it may not involve the stigma and hardships of a criminal conviction, is a principle basic to our society." Joint Anti-Fascist Refugee Comm. v. McGrath, 341 U.S. 123, 168 (1951) (concurring opinion.) See also Homer v. Richmond, 110 U.S. App. D. C. 226, 292 F. 2d 719 (1961); Parker v.

Lester, 227 F. 2d 708 (C. A. 9th Cir. 1955). In sum, the Court holds that petitioner has a right not to have her identification badge taken away for an "arbitrary" reason, but no right to be told in detail what the reason is, or to defend her own innocence, in order to show, perhaps, that the true reason for deprivation was one forbidden by the Constitution. That is an internal contradiction to which I cannot subscribe.

One further circumstance makes this particularly a case where procedural requirements of fairness are essential. Petitioner was not simply excluded from the base summarily, without a notice and chance to defend herself. She was excluded as a "security risk," that designation most odious in our times. The Court consoles itself with the speculation that she may have been merely garrulous, or careless with her identification badge, and indeed she might, although she will never find out. But, in the common understanding of the public with whom petitioner must hereafter live and work, the term "security risk" carries a much more sinister meaning. See Beilan v. Board of Public Education, 357 U.S. 399, 421-423 (1958) (dissenting opinion). It is far more likely to be taken as an accusation of communism or disloyalty than imputation of some small personal fault. Perhaps the Government has reasons for lumping such a multitude of sins under a misleading term. But it ought not to affix a "badge of infamy," Wieman v. Updegraff, supra, at 191, to a person without some statement of charges, and some opportunity to speak in reply.

It may be, of course, that petitioner was justly excluded from the Gun Factory. But, in my view, it is fundamentally unfair, and therefore violative of the Due Process Clause of the Fifth Amendment, to deprive her of a valuable relationship so summarily.

[Section 1382 of Title 18 of the United States Code reads as follows]

Whoever, within the jurisdiction of the United States, goes upon any military, naval, or Coast Guard reservation, post, fort, arsenal, yard, station, or installation, for any purpose prohibited by law or lawful regulation; or

Whoever reenters or is found within any such reservation, post, fort, arsenal, yard, station, or installation, after having been removed therefrom or ordered not to reenter by any officer or person in command or charge thereof--

Shall be fined not more than $500 or imprisoned not more than six months, or both.

## WEISSMAN v. UNITED STATES

United States Court of Appeals, Tenth Circuit, 1967.
387 F.2d 271.

*[ Footnotes have been omitted.  Ed.]

BREITENSTEIN, Circuit Judge.

Appellants-defendants were charged in an information with a violation of 18 U.S.C. §1382 by the reentry to a military reservation after having been ordered not to do so.  The charge was a petty offense under 18 U.S.C. §1.  As permitted by 18 U.S.C. §3401(b), the defendants elected to be tried in the United States District Court and demanded and received a jury trial.  They were found guilty and appeal from the sentences imposed.

Fort Sill is a military reservation in Oklahoma.  In June, 1967, defendant Weissman attended a court-martial held there and participated in a demonstration which included "chanting, making noises, and the singing of certain phrases to the disruption of the court." The commandant received reports of these demonstrations and of the activities of both Weissman and Martin.  He ordered that they should not reenter Fort Sill.  On July 29, 1967, written notice of that order was served on the defendants personally.  On July 31 the military authorities, on the basis of statements of the defendants to the press and on the basis of surveillance of defendants suspected that the defendants might reenter the base to attend a court-martial.  Cars in which the defendants were riding were stopped at a traffic control point within the reservation because the cars did not have the required permit stickers.  The defendants were later identified and arrested.

Defendants say that they were free lance journalists and that the bar order violated the First Amendment guarantee of freedom of the press and the Sixth Amendment right to a public trial.  The claim that they were representatives of the press is based on affidavits submitted in support of a motion to dismiss.  At the time of their arrest they did not assert a right to enter the reservation because of any representation of the press.  We doubt that their belated self-serving declarations entitle them to be heard on the point.  In any event the argument is without merit.  If it be assumed that a defendant in a court-martial has the right to a public trial, there is grave doubt whether members of the press have standing to invoke that right. Even if they have, they may be ordered to conform to standards of conduct and may be excluded if necessary to maintain orderly proceedings.  Weissman participated in an unseemly demonstration at a previous court-martial and Martin solicited people to take part in such demonstrations.  The military authorities had the responsibility to forestall such conduct by excluding those responsible therefor. In our opinion no violation of either the First Amendment or Sixth

Amendment occurred by barring the defendants from entering the reservation.

The bar order is attacked on the ground that the government showed no valid reason for its promulgation. The argument is that Cafeteria & Restaurant Workers Union v. McElroy, 367 U.S. 886, 81 S.Ct. 1743, 6 L.Ed.2d 1230, requires that the reason for exclusion must be spelled out in detail. We do not read the Cafeteria Workers decision as requiring that detailed reasons are necessary to sustain a bar order. It holds that although the person challenging the order "could not have been kept out because she was a Democrat or a Methodist . . . ," she could be excluded on the showing that "the reason advanced for her exclusion was . . . entirely rational . . ." and the order was within the authority of the issuing officer.

We do not understand the argument of the defendants as attacking the authority of the commandant to make the order. In the Cafeteria Workers decision the Court recognized that a Post Commander in the exercise of his discretion could exclude from the Post private persons "in the interest of good order and military discipline." The question then is whether the order was rational.

General Brown, the commanding officer, ordered his staff to investigate the defendants' activities at Fort Sill. The staff intelligence officer prepared a report which went up the chain of command to the General. On the basis of the report the General made the bar order. He testified that he did so because he considered the conduct of the defendants "prejudicial to good order and discipline, and the accomplishment of my mission." In the facts presented the basis for the order appears more clearly than did the basis for the order in the Cafeteria Workers case. We believe that the order was reasonable. Even if we did not so believe, the order was within the discretionary power of the commandant and not reviewable by the courts.

While General Brown was on the witness stand, defense counsel made a demand under 18 U.S.C. §3500 for the production of written reports relevant to his testimony. The court refused to order such production. The argument is that under both §3500 and the decision in Jencks v. United States, 353 U.S. 657, 77 S.Ct. 1007, 1 L.Ed.2d 1103, the defense is entitled to the reports because of their bearing on the justification for the order. The answer is that the argument collides with the principle just recognized. As a matter of law there may be no challenge to the General's statement of the reason for the bar order. Because of this rule, it is unnecessary to consider whether the reports are statements subject to production under either §3500 or the Jencks decision. Absent the right to attack, the means or method of attack merit no consideration. In our opinion the trial court correctly denied access to the reports which were demanded.

Defendants argue that their arrests were illegal. Pursuant to orders the military policemen were stopping all cars at traffic control points to determine whether they bore the required permit

stickers. After the defendants were identified as passengers, they
were taken into custody. The cars were not searched and no statements were taken. Reliance on Henry v. United States, 361 U.S. 98,
80 S.Ct. 168, 4 L.Ed.2d 134, is misplaced. There a particular car
was stopped on a public street and searched without sufficient cause
to believe that the occupants were committing any crime. In the circumstances of that case the arrest occurred when the car was
stopped and, as the arrest was illegal, the search was illegal. An
arrest does not occur when a military policeman stops a car at a
traffic control point within a military reservation to ascertain if the
car is authorized to proceed.

A witness for the government testified that the point where the
cars were stopped was "exclusively owned by the United States and
within the exclusive jurisdiction of the United States." Under Army
Regulations a member of the army may make an arrest for "a misdemeanor amounting to a breach of the peace . . . committed in his
presence." The military police knew of the bar order. When they
saw the defendants on the reservation in violation of that order, a
misdemeanor was committed in their presence and they had full
power to arrest. The fact that the stopping of the cars and the identification of the defendants were not simultaneous does not change the
result. The offense occurred when the defendants entered the reservation. In our opinion the arrests were lawful and the testimony of
the military police in regard thereto was properly submitted to the
jury.

. . .

In Bridges v. Davis, 311 F.Supp. 935 (D. Hawaii, 1969), the
District Court upheld a commanding officer's right to exclude civilian
ministers from military reservations. The Court stated that it was
without authority to review the administrative order of exclusion even
though certain military prisoners would not be able to speak to the
clergymen whom they desired. In Küskilla v. Nichols, 433 F.2d 745
(CA, Seventh Cir, 1970), an exclusion order against a civilian employee working on Fort Sheridan was reversed on the grounds that
her rights to freedom of speech and association under the First
Amendment had been violated.

On May 27, 1969 a letter entitled "Guidance on Dissent" was issued by the Office of the Adjutant General, Department of the Army. Included therein was the following:

## On-Post Demonstrations by Civilians

A commander may legally bar individuals from entry on a military reservation for any purpose prohibited by law or lawful regulation, and it is a crime for any person who has been removed and barred from a post by order of the commander to re-enter. However, a specific request for a permit to conduct an on-post demonstration in an area to which the public has generally been granted access should not be denied on an arbitrary basis. Such a permit may be denied on a reasonable basis such as showing that the demonstration may result in a clear interference with or prevention of orderly accomplishment of the mission of the post, or present a clear danger to loyalty, discipline, and morale of the troops.

In United States v. Bradley, 418 F.2d 688 (4th Cir., 1969), the court reversed the conviction of three students from the University of North Carolina for distributing leaflets at Fort Bragg, North Carolina, allegedly in violation of a post regulation. The court held the regulation inapplicable to the particular conduct in question. In Committee to Free the Fort Dix 38 v. Collins, 429 F.2d 807 (3d Cir., 1970), the court refused to consider the denial by the commander of Fort Dix of an application to hold a demonstration on public highways on-post because the case had become moot.

In Overseas Media Corporation v. McNamara, 385 F.2d 308 (C.A.D.C., 1967), the Court of Appeals reversed the District Court's granting of summary judgment to the government on the grounds that the complaint tendered factual issues giving rise to a legally justiciable question. The complaint alleged that the corporation had been illegally denied the use of certain newsstand facilities of military post exchanges in the Far East.

CONTROL OF SERVICEMEN'S CONDUCT

The Department of the Army letter of May 27, 1969 (see p.
470, supra) also contained the following:

Possession and distribution of political materials.
In the case of publications distributed through official outlets
such as Post Exchanges and Post Libraries, a commander is authorized to delay distribution of a specific issue of a publication in
accordance with the provisions of para. 5-5 of AR 210-10. Concurrently with the delay, a commander must submit a report to the
Department of the Army, ATTN: CINFO. A commander may delay
distribution only if he determines that the specific publication presents a clear danger to the loyalty, discipline, or morale of his troops.
In the case of distribution of publications through other than
official outlets, a commander may require that prior approval be
obtained for any distribution on post. Distribution without prior approval may be prohibited. A commander's denial of authority to
distribute a publication on post is subject to the procedures of para.
5-5, AR 210-10, discussed above.
A commander may not prevent distribution of a publication
simply because he does not like its contents. All denials of permission for distribution must be in accordance with the provisions of
para. 5-5, AR 210-10. For example, a commander may prohibit distribution of publications which are obscene or otherwise unlawful
(e.g., counselling disloyalty, mutiny, or refusal of duty). A commander may also prohibit distribution if the manner of accomplishing the
distribution materially interferes with the accomplishment of a military mission (e.g., interference with training or troop formation).
In any event, a commander must have cogent reasons, with supporting evidence, for any denial of distribution privileges. The fact that
a publication is critical--even unfairly critical--of government policies or officials is not in itself, a grounds for denial.
Mere possession of a publication may not be prohibited; however, possession of an unauthorized publication coupled with an attempt
to distribute in violation of post regulations may constitute an offense.
Accordingly, cases involving the possession of several copies of an
unauthorized publication or other circumstances indicating an intent
to distribute should be investigated. . . .

Publication of 'Underground Newspapers.'

Army regulations provide that personal literary efforts may not be pursued during duty hours or accomplished by the use of Army property. However, the publication of 'underground newspapers' by soldiers off-post, on their own time, and with their own money and equipment is generally protected under the First Amendment's guarantees of freedom of speech and freedom of the press. Unless such a newspaper contains language, the utterance of which is punishable under Federal law (e.g., 10 U.S.C. Sec. 2387 or the Uniform Code of Military Justice), authors of an 'underground newspaper' may not be disciplined for mere publication. Distribution of such newspapers on post is governed by para. 5-5, AR 210-10. . . .

### DASH v. COMMANDING GENERAL, FORT JACKSON, SOUTH CAROLINA*

United States District Court, District South Carolina,
Columbia Division, 1969.
307 F.Supp. 849, aff'd 429 F.2d 427 (4th Cir. 1970).

*[Footnotes have been omitted. Ed.]

DONALD RUSSELL, District Judge.

This is an action for a declaratory judgment. The plaintiffs were at the time of the commencement of the action non-commissioned servicemen stationed at Fort Jackson, South Carolina. Their action is filed not only on their behalf but also on behalf of all enlisted personnel at such base and seeks a declaration of their constitutional rights of free speech under the Federal Constitution.

The record refers to a number of constitutional rights, which the plaintiffs claim the defendants, the Commander of the Post, and the Secretary of the Army, violated. For purposes of this proceeding, however, the plaintiffs, through their counsel, limit their claim of constitutional deprivation to two matters: (1) The regulation of the Post Commander, restricting the distribution of published materials on post; and (2) The refusal of the Post Commander to grant the plaintiffs' request to have a public, open meeting on base for the free discussion of the Vietnam war and other complaints connected therewith, as requested by a petition presented to such commander.

The circumstances that gave rise to this controversy are not disputed. They were established either by stipulation of facts or by evidence taken before me. On the basis of such record so established, both parties seek summary judgment, contending rightly that, basically, the issue is one of law, involving the constitutional rights of servicemen.

The plaintiffs--or, at least, some of them--prepared and distributed a petition requesting the Post Commander to allow them to

have an open, public meeting on base for the purpose of "freely dis-
cuss(ing) the legal and moral questions related to the war in Vietnam
and to the civil rights of American citizens both within and outside
the armed forces." The petition stated it to be their "intention to hold
a peaceful, legal meeting open to any enlisted man or officer at Fort
Jackson." They professed a desire "only to exercise the rights guaranteed to us as citizens and soldiers by the First Amendment to the
U.S. Constitution." Some twelve non-commissioned servicemen
signed such petition. It was presented at the office of the Post Commander, who, through an aide, refused to accept it, stating that the
Army did not engage in "collective bargaining". Some days before
this, an impromptu open discussion of the Vietnam war was held outside the quarters occupied by a number of the plaintiffs. In this discussion, a substantial number of servicemen took part. Considerable
acrimony developed; threats were exchanged; fighting began; officers
were disobeyed; and complete disciplinary control of the servicemen
was for a time lost.

The Post Commander prior to the commencement of this action,
issued a regulation limiting the right to distribute pamphlets on the
base. This regulation, the validity of which is challenged by the
plaintiffs, is as follows:

> "Distribution of publications such as books, periodi-
> cals, pamphlets, handbills, flyers, advertisements, and
> similar printed material at Fort Jackson may not be made
> except through regularly established and approved distribu-
> tion outlets unless prior approval is obtained from the in-
> stallation commander or his authorized representative.
> Approved outlets are the Post Exchange and its branches,
> the Post Library, and the official offices and designated
> agencies of the installation. Individuals desiring to dis-
> tribute unofficial publications of any kind within the
> reservation will submit copies to G1 for approval by the
> Commanding General prior to effecting dissemination."

So far as the record indicates, none of the plaintiffs had been denied
the right to distribute any pamphlet on base. In fact, there is no showing that the Post Commander had ever exercised his authority under
this regulation.

Since the commencement of this action, all of the plaintiffs
have either been released by the Army or been transferred to other
bases.

. . .

At the outset it should be noted that a serviceman's right of free
speech is not absolute. With his induction into military service, he
"necessarily accepts some abridgment of his right of free speech."
Thus, in a recent attempt to order and rationalize existing decisions

interpreting the First Amendment, a thoughtful commentator explicitly refrained from incorporating the military into the general scheme of such rights, remarking that, "To a certain extent, at least, the military sector or society must function outside the realm of democratic principles, including the principle of freedom of expression" and, "Certainly, members of the armed forces, at least when operating in that capacity, can be restricted in their right to open discussion." This is true because, as the Supreme Court as put it, "The military constitutes a specialized community governed by a separate discipline from that of the civilian." It has been aptly observed that, "An army is not a deliberative body." and, it may be added, it cannot function as a debating society. "Its law is that of obedience" and discipline, and its strength lies in "Vigor and efficiency on the part of the officer, and confidence among the soldiers. . . ." As a recent decision phrases it, "The need for discipline (in the Army), with the attendant impairment of certain rights, is an important factor" in the operation of an Army.

To say that a serviceman's right of free speech is limited is not an entirely anomalous principle. Even among civilians, the right of an individual to exercise First Amendment rights may be legally circumscribed by the character of his public employment or by the circumstances, place and time where the right is sought to be exercised. Accordingly, in Pickering v. Board of Education (1968) 391 U.S. 563, 568, 88 S.Ct. 1731, 20 L.Ed.2d 811, the Court said, "At the same time it cannot be gainsaid that the State has interests as an employer in regulating the speech of its employees that differ significantly from those it possesses in connection with regulation of the speech of the citizenry in general." See, also, United Public Workers of America (C.I.O.) v. Mitchell (1947) 330 U.S. 75, 67 S.Ct. 556, 91 L.Ed. 754. And, in Goldwasser v. Brown (D.C. Cir. 1969) 417 F.2d 1169, filed September 17, 1969, a civilian employee of the Air Force, discharged as a teacher because of comments made in the classroom to foreign officers on the Vietnam war, assailed his discharge as a violation of his First Amendment rights. In denial of such claimed violation, the Court said:

> "We would also be blinking reality if we did not recognize that a class of foreign military officers at an Air Force installation on invitational orders presents special problems affecting the national interest in harmonious international relations. We are certainly not equipped to second guess the agency judgment that the instructional goals of the Air Force program would be jeopardized by the teacher's volunteering his views on subjects of potential explosiveness in a multi-cultural group."

Moreover, "The rights of free speech and assembly, while fundamental in our democratic society, still do not mean that everyone with opinions or beliefs to express may address a group at any public place and at any time." In short, where First Amendment rights are involved, whether of civilian or serviceman, the issue always involves the balancing by the Courts of the competing private and public interests at stake in the particular circumstances.

It does not follow, however, that contrary to certain early judicial expressions, First Amendment rights are completely inapplicable to servicemen. Indeed, the Court of Military Appeals, applying as it understood the decision in Burns v. Wilson (1953) 346 U.S. 137, 73 S.Ct. 1045, 91 L.Ed. 1508, has held that "servicemen have all the protections of the Bill of Rights except such as are expressly or by necessary implication not applicable by reason of the peculiar circumstances of the military." But the Courts have been understandably loath to overturn military decisions where military personnel is concerned. After all, it is not the function of courts to "regulate the army" and "judges are not given the task of running the Army." Courts must be "scrupulous not to interfere with legitimate Army matters" and are required to give "a substantial degree of civilian deference to military tribunals. In reviewing military decisions," the Courts "must accommodate the demands of individual rights and the social order in a context which is far removed from those which" the Courts "encounter in the ordinary run of civilian litigation, whether state or federal. In doing so", the Courts "must interpret a legal tradition which is radically different from that which is common in civil courts." Chief Justice Warren in The Bill of Rights and the Military, 37 N.Y.Univ.L.Rev. 181, 186-7 (1962) has stated the proper judicial role in this connection thus:

> "So far as the relationship of the military to its own personnel is concerned, the basic attitude of the Court has been that the latter's jurisdiction is most limited. . . .
>
> "This 'hands off' attitude has strong historical support, of course. While I cannot here explore the matter completely, there is also no necessity to do so, since it is indisputable that the tradition of our country, from the time of the Revolution until now, has supported the military establishment's broad power to deal with its own personnel. The most obvious reason is that courts are ill-equipped to determine the impact upon discipline that any particular intrusion upon military authority might have."

There are few instances of a judicial application of these rules in a context similar to that posed by the plaintiffs. In United States

v. Bradley (4th Cir. 1969) 418 F.2d 688, filed November 28, 1969, which involved a distribution of hand bills on an army post but not by servicemen, the Court decided the case on other grounds and found it "unnecessary to decide constitutional questions raised". It is unlikely, however, that the Court would have found the rights of a serviceman on post identical with that of a civilian, even though on post. In Callison v. United States, supra, a draftee, in process of induction, sought to induce other inductees at the induction center to sign a petition opposing the draft and the war in Vietnam. Ordered to desist, he disobeyed, claiming the right to distribute his petition under the First Amendment. The Court held that "the order to refrain from soliciting signatures was not an impermissible intrusion upon appellant's First Amendment rights and was entitled to respect and obedience." 413 F.2d at p. 135. Professor Kester, in 81 Har.L.Rev. 1697, "Soldiers Who Insult the President: An Uneasy Look at Article 88 of the Uniform Code of Military Justice" (1968), was commenting critically on a case in which the offensive remark about his Commander in Chief made by a commissioned officer found violative of Article 88 was made off base "isolated from any military audience and was found by the Court of Military Appeals without constitutional protection" (page 1768, 81 Har.L.Rev.). He was particular to note, however, that, "A post commander's restriction on public statements after increased discipline problems caused by public dissent by his personnel might be constitutionally acceptable" (pp. 1764-5, 81 Har.L.Rev.). Actually, he suggested that Article 88 which forbids contemptuous words spoken of the President by a serviceman, "should be redrafted to exclude specifically all utterances but those published or made to public gatherings, or those made not in ordinary conversation but in an unsolicited effort to proselytize military personnel." (p. 1766, 81 Har.L.Rev.) Italics added. The author's criticism centered on the place where questioned statement was made, i.e., off post and to an almost wholly non-military audience. Goldwasser, to which reference has heretofore been made and in which no infringement of free speech rights was found, involved criticisms leveled at our involvement in Vietnam made within the classroom by a civilian employee of the Defense Department, serving as a language instructor for foreign military personnel being trained in this country.

Despite the absence of any specific decisional authority on our specific issues, it would appear plain from the foregoing general principles that, within certain limits, the military establishment should have authority to restrict both the distribution of printed materials and the holding of public discussion meetings on post. The right to restrict, however, must no doubt be kept within reasonable bounds; it is not, and cannot be, a completely limitless power. And, however hesitant they may be to "intrude", Courts will be available to determine whether there is a reasonable basis for such restrictions as may be placed on the serviceman's right of free speech by the military establishment.

The restriction placed on the distribution of printed material at Fort Jackson (T.C.Reg. 600-50), to which the plaintiffs direct their first challenge, may be, as plaintiffs argue, broad and indefinite; it does not incorporate within itself any plain standards by which a pamphlet's acceptability for distribution may be adjudged. The regulation must be read, however, in conjunction with the opinion of the Judge Advocate instructing authoritatively the Post Commander in the exercise of his powers under AR 210-10, paragraph 5-5e. By these instructions, the Post Commander is required to make specific findings in support of any restriction imposed by him under the Regulation. Specifically, he is advised against any denial based on "good taste" or "in the best interests of the command" and is instructed that he may delay distribution of a publication "only if he determines that the specific publication presents a clear danger to the loyalty, discipline, or morale of his troops." He is commanded that he "may not prevent distribution of a publication simply because he does not like its contents" and "The fact that a publication is critical--even unfairly critical--of Government policies or officials is not in itself, a ground for denial." The constitutionality of the regulation must be determined on the regulation as construed and defined in these instructions issued by the Judge Advocate, controlling the application by the Post Commander of the regulation. See the concurring opinion of Justices Black and Douglas in Gregory v. City of Chicago (1969) 394 U.S. 111, 113, 89 S.Ct. 946, 22 L.Ed.2d 134, and concurring opinion of Justice Harlan in Shuttlesworth v. City of Birmingham (1969) 394 U.S. 147, at p. 159, 89 S.Ct. 935, 22 L.Ed.2d 162. So limited and defined, the challenged Regulation would appear to be within the authority of the Post Commander. Whether the Post Commander, in the exercise of his authority under the Regulation as limited and defined by the commands of the Judge Advocate, acts arbitrarily or capriciously, without proper justification, in a particular instance is a question which will arise when the Post Commander has exercised his authority under the Regulation. So far as the record shows, he has never exercised the authority to restrict the distribution of any printed material. What is involved in this proceeding, so far as distribution of printed material is concerned, is the bare right of the Post Commander, in those cases where there is a reasonable basis for the conclusion that the distribution represents "a clear danger to the loyalty, discipline, or morale of his troops," to prohibit the distribution of such printed material. I find he has such power. As I have said, however, whether he has properly exercised such power in a particular situation is an issue that can only be resolved when that situation arises.

It is urged by the plaintiffs that, even if the challenged regulation be limited as the Judge Advocate has ruled, it still is too vague to meet constitutional requirements. In support of this contention, they rely on Shuttlesworth, supra. That case, however, involved a criminal ordinance and dealt with the rights of a civilian seeking to exercise his constitutional rights on the public streets. Here, on the

other hand, we are dealing with a military regulation governing conduct on a military training base. It seems settled that the Courts do
not require the same precision and specificity of standards in military regulations as in a criminal statute. Actually, language very
similar to that used in the Judge Advocate's instructions was sustained against constitutional attack in Cafeteria and Restaurant
Workers Union, Local 473, A.F.L.-C.I.O. v. McElroy (1961) 367 U.S.
886, 894-896, 81 S.Ct. 1743, 6 L.Ed.2d 1230. The regulation in that
case, which was upheld, phrased the Commander's authority in the
terms of "good order and military discipline". (p. 893, 81 S.Ct.
1743). In Weissman v. United States (10th Cir. 1967) 387 F.2d 271,
274, the action of the Post Commander was based on a finding that
the conduct was "prejudicial to good order and discipline"; it was
sustained against attack. As a matter of fact, the language used by
the Judge Advocate in marking out the limits of the regulation seems
as clear as the circumstances admit. Of course, the power under
such regulation may be abused. Should the Post Commander be unable to show any possible reasonable basis for his determination,
remedies are available for redress in the Courts. But there is, as I
have said, no contention that the power has been so abused; the
attack is on the power to restrict. That attack, in my opinion, must
fail.

Likewise, the Post Commander has the authority, in a proper
case, to deny servicemen under his command the right to hold on
post public meetings. So much, Professor Emerson, in his scholarly
and exhaustive discussion of the constitutional right of free speech
in 72 Yale L.Journal 936, quoted supra recognizes. Again, though,
this power must be exercised only where it is reasonably possible
that the meeting might represent "a clear danger to military loyalty,
discipline or morale of the military personnel" at the post. Moreover, Courts have both the responsibility and the duty to interfere
where such power is exercised, either arbitrarily or capriciously,
without a proper basis. Accordingly, the question becomes: Did the
Post Commander have a proper basis for denying the petition for an
open, public meeting and discussion on post?

It is the position of the defendants that the very nature of the
subjects to be discussed at the meeting, taken in conjunction with the
known views of the promoters of the meeting, warrants the conclusion
that the meeting would have created unrest, provoked disorder and
weakened discipline and morale among the military personnel at the
base.

While the plaintiffs assert the purpose of the meeting was to
discuss peaceably the justification of the Vietnam engagement and the
right of the Post Commander to abridge such right of discussion, their
own view of the issue to be discussed was plain: To them, the Vietnam war is an immoral war, engaged in wrongfully and carried on
inhumanely. It must be assumed that a meeting, promoted by the

plaintiffs, would seek to develop and expound that thesis.  Can it be disputed that such a meeting, held on post and directed particularly at servicemen being trained to participate in that very war, would likely be calculated to breed discontent and weaken loyalty among such servicemen?  Can training for participation in a war be carried on simultaneously with lectures on the immorality or injustice of such war?  In my opinion, the denial of the right for open, public meetings at advertised meetings on post for discussion of the propriety of the political decision to participate in the Vietnam war was justified "by reason of the peculiar circumstances of the military" and represented no infringement of the constitutional rights of the plaintiffs or others similarly situated.  Off base, as parts of the great mass of our nation's citizenry, they may well be entitled to First Amendment rights, they should no doubt be granted the right of all other citizens to exercise the freedom to dissent and to criticize.  This right was stated and upheld in the instructions of the Judge Advocate, already cited.  But to organize meetings on base, to seek to create of and within the military itself a cohesive force for the purpose of compelling political decisions--and political decisions directly related to the mission of the military itself--would undermine civilian government, especially civil control of the military, and would take from responsible civilian government the power of decision.  And this plainly was the purpose of the meeting sought by the plaintiffs.  They sought to generate, through their meeting, such discontent with the Vietnam war among servicemen that the political decision to involve this nation in such war might be influenced, if not reversed.  This they may have a constitutional right to do off base and as individual citizens, despite the fact that they were members of the armed services.  But this is quite different from their right to organize on base among military men meetings to promote discontent with their military responsibilites and tasks.

Moreover, the defendants offered proof that an impromptu open meeting, created by some of the plaintiffs and providing an opportunity for the discussion on base of the very subjects sought to be discussed at the public meeting solicited in the petition of the plaintiffs, had created disorder, fomented dissension, and given rise to serious breaches of discipline.  Such evidence clearly demonstrated the reasonableness of the Post Commander's action.

The plaintiffs, citing Tinker v. Des Moines Independent Community School Dist. (1969) 393 U.S. 503, 89 S.Ct. 733, 21 L.Ed.2d 731, and like cases, however, would liken their claim of a constitutional right to hold such meetings on post to the right of college or school students to have such meetings on school premises.  It should be noted at the outset that, in the Tinker Case, the Court was careful to point out that "the record does not demonstrate any facts which might reasonably have led school authorities to forecast substantial disruption of or material interference with school activities," as a result of permitting the plaintiff to wear an armband during school hours indicating his opposition to the war in Vietnam. (393 U.S. at p. 514, 89 S.Ct. at 740). In fact, the single question posted in the petition for certiorari in that case limited the claim of First Amendment right to acts "not disruptive of school discipline or decorum". Such is clearly not the case here. The events of the impromptu open meeting provide a reasonable basis for concluding that such a meeting as that proposed by the plaintiffs, held on post, would be "disruptive" of discipline and interfere with the military functions of the base. Moreover, there is a fundamental difference between both the role and the operations of a military training base and a school or college. At the military base, the serviceman's training is in discipline and obedience. The school or college, on the other hand, is, to quote the language of the Court in Keyishian v. Board of Regents (1967) 385 U.S. 589, 603, 87 S.Ct. 675, 17 L.Ed.2d 629, "peculiarly the 'market-place of ideas'." It is a place for free and unrestricted inquiry, for the discovery of truth through open discussion and the frank dissection of conflicting viewpoints. Commenting on the Tinker Case, the editors in 83 Har.L.Rev. 159, put it that schools are places for "open, vigorous, disputations, disturbing" discussions and speeches--certainly not an apt description of a military training base. Because of the obvious differences both in purposes and in necessary operations, it is thus clear that the rules applicable to conduct in a military base and in a school or college must be and are entirely different and that authorities sustaining First Amendment rights of students are inapplicable to the determination of the rights of servicemen on base.

It is, therefore, my opinion that the motion of the defendants for summary judgment should be granted, and

It is so ordered.

In Yahr v. Resor, 431 F.2d 690 (CA, 4th Cir. 1970), the refusal of a district court to grant a preliminary injunction against interfering with the distribution of a newspaper on base was affirmed. The newspaper was published by servicemen during their off-duty hours and had been distributed off the base.

## LOCKS v. LAIRD

United States District Court, Northern District California, 1969.
300 F.Supp. 915.

*[Some footnotes have been omitted.  Ed.]

ZIRPOLI, District Judge.
On or about October 10, 1968, the then Secretary of the Air
Force issued a general order which reads:

> "Recent developments have established a need for
> clarification of the circumstances in which Air Force
> members are not permitted to wear their uniform.  Ac-
> cordingly, pursuant to para 1-10d, AFM 35-10, 26 June
> 1968,* the Secretary of the Air Force has specified that
> Air Force members will not wear the uniform at any
> public meeting, demonstration, or interview if they have
> reason to know that a purpose of the meeting, demonstra-
> tion, or interview is the advocacy, expression or approval
> of opposition to the employment or use of the Armed
> Forces of the United States.  (Emphasis added)

-------------

*AFM 35-10, Paragraph 1-10 provides:

When Wear of the Uniform is Prohibited.  Air Force members will not wear the uniform:
    a. At any meeting or demonstration that is a func-
tion of, or sponsored by any organization, association,
movement, group, or combination of persons that:
    (1)  The Attorney General of the United States
has designated as totalitarian, Fascist, Communist, or
subversive.
    (2)  Advocates or approves the commission of acts
of force or violence to deny others their rights under the
Constitution of the United States.
    (3)  Seeks to alter the form of the United States
Government by unconstitutional means.
    b. During or in connection with the furtherance of
private employment or commercial interests when an
inference of official sponsorship for the activity or interest would be drawn.
    c. Under circumstances which would bring dis-
credit upon the Armed Forces.
    d. Under any other circumstances that Secretary
of the Air Force specifies and publishes.

Petitioner Locks, after court-martial proceedings, was convicted on two specifications of violation of Article 92 of the Uniform Code of Military Justice for failing to obey the above stated general order or regulation. This conviction is under military appellate review. Pending review of the record of trial, petitioner was ordered to be confined at the United States Air Force Retraining Center at Lowry Air Force Base, Colorado.

Since the issue raised by petitioner Locks in the instant case is the same issue that will be dealt with by the military appellate review, this court should not interfere with such military judicial process. "The military constitutes a specialized community governed by a separate discipline from that of the civilian. Orderly government requires that the judiciary be as scrupulous not to interfere with legitimate Army matters as the Army must be scrupulous not to intervene in judicial matters." Orloff v. Willoughby, 345 U.S. 83, 94, 73 S.Ct. 534, 97 L.Ed. 842 (1953). The very matter which brought petitioner Locks before the court-martial and for which he has a pending appeal is the very matter governed by the regulation here in question, hence we do not have "a situation in which defense of the State's [here the military's] criminal prosecution will not assure adequate vindication of constitutional rights." Dombrowski v. Pfister, 380 U.S. 479, 485, 85 S.Ct. 1116, 14 L.Ed.2d 22 (1965). Under such circumstances Dombrowski is not applicable. The controlling cases here are Gusik v. Schilder, 340 U.S. 128, 71 S.Ct. 149, 95 L.Ed. 146 (1950), and Noyd v. McNamara, 378 F.2d 538 (10th Cir. 1967) cert. denied, 389 U.S. 1022, 88 S.Ct. 593, 19 L.Ed.2d 667 (1967). These controlling cases dictate that this court is without jurisdiction as to petitioner Locks and as to him the complaint for injunction and declaratory relief and the petition for writ of habeas corpus are dismissed.

The remaining petitioners (plaintiffs) in this case--Bright, Williams and O'Connell--are members of the United States Air Force Reserve presently serving on extended active duty and currently stationed at Hamilton Air Force Base, California. They are not under physical restraint in any form and seek to enter this "controversy" on the allegation that they "desire and intend to participate in a similar demonstration [similar to the one petitioner Locks attended in uniform and for which he was convicted in court-martial proceedings] to be held off the Air Force Base on May 30, 1969, and that but for the regulation in question and the punishment being suffered by plaintiff Locks they would do so and wear their uniforms as an expression of their First Amendment freedoms."

These three petitioners contend that the regulation is "unconstitutional, vague, overbroad and discriminatory on its face." With this contention this court cannot and does not agree.

It was stipulated at the Court hearing on the order to show cause that the purpose of the demonstration of May 30, 1969, is the advocacy, expression or approval of opposition to the employment and use of the Armed Forces of the United States in Vietnam; that petitioners desire and intend to wear their Air Force uniforms at said demonstration; and that petitioners can reasonably expect that the regulation (general order) will be enforced against them if they wilfully violate the same. This stipulation adequately presents a "controversy" for the consideration of the court.

There is no constitutional right of a member of the Air Force to wear his uniform when and wherever he pleases. There can be no doubt that the Air Force may by proper orders regulate the use of the Air Force uniform by which individuals wearing that uniform are identified with the Air Force.

But, petitioners contend, conceding the above to be true, the regulation in question is not a "proper" regulation since, as they allege, enforcement thereof violates their assured freedom of speech.

The petitioners' claim rests on the fundamental proposition that the display of symbols can be "speech" which enjoys First Amendment protection. It has long been established that the display of unofficial symbols is protected by the First Amendment, Stromberg v. California, 283 U.S. 359, 51 S.Ct. 532, 75 L.Ed. 1117 (1931); Tinker v. Des Moines Independent Community School District, 393 U.S. 503, 89 S.Ct. 733, 21 L.Ed.2d 731 (decided February 24, 1969), and that freedom from coerced acceptance of official symbols in violation of religious scruples is also protected by the First Amendment, West Virginia State Board of Education v. Barnette, 319 U.S. 624, 63 S.Ct. 1178, 87 L.Ed. 1628 (1943).

The power and universality of symbolic forms of communication was recognized by the Supreme Court in West Virginia State Board of Education v. Barnette, supra at 632-633, 63 S.Ct. at 1182:

> Symbolism is a primitive but effective way of communicat-
> ing ideas. The use of an emblem or flag to symbolize some
> system, idea, institution, or personality, is a short cut
> from mind to mind. Causes and nations, political parties,
> lodges and ecclesiastical groups seek to knit the loyalty
> of their followings to a flag or banner, a color or design.
> The State announces rank, function, and authority through
> crowns and maces, uniforms and black robes; the church
> speaks through the Cross, the Crucifix, the altar and
> shrine, and clerical raiment. Symbols of State often con-
> vey political ideas just as religious symbols come to con-
> vey theological ones. Associated with many of these
> symbols are appropriate gestures of acceptance or respect:
> a salute, a bowed or bared head, a bended knee. A person
> gets from a symbol the meaning he puts into it, and what is
> one man's comfort and inspiration is another's jest and
> scorn.

The key that unlocks the present dispute is the understanding that there is no necessary relationship between the symbol and that which is symbolized. A common example of this fact is that a "v" formed with the forefinger and middle finger is today a symbol for peace, whereas twenty-five years ago it was a symbol for victory in war. The point is that a symbol takes on an assigned relationship to the thing symbolized based primarily on the context of its use.

A military uniform is a symbol, and the issue in this case is whether it may be used in a context expressly contrary to the purposes and values intended by the Secretary of the Air Force. This court holds that if the Secretary of the Air Force commands that the uniform not be worn at events of the nature in question, the First Amendment does not command otherwise. To permit members of the military to display at will the primary symbol of their military service would be to permit the destruction of the very symbolic effectiveness which the uniform is intended to enjoy.* This court does not find it violative of the First Amendment for the Secretary to limit the wearing of the uniform to contexts that will promote a sense, not just of membership in the Air Force, but of participation, allegiance, and achievement. The Air Force designs and furnishes the uniform according to its own criteria; the First Amendment does not forbid the Air Force from determining the uniform's use according to its own criteria.

This court is mindful that each petitioner took an oath in which he declared: "I do solemnly swear (or affirm) that I will support and defend the Constitution of the United States against all enemies, foreign and domestic; that I will bear true faith and allegiance to the same, and that I will obey the Orders of the President of the United States and the orders of the officers appointed over me, according to regulations and the Uniform Code of Military Justice. So help me God." (Emphasis added).

The general order (or regulation) here in question is an order of the President of the United States and the officers appointed over petitioners according to regulations.

------------

*The power with which a uniform can symbolize the values of patriotism and military prowess was exemplified in France prior to World War I. For almost a century the French army had sported blue coats, a red kepi, and red trousers. As developments in technology enable rifles to fire over greater distances, the need to escape visual detection increased. Efforts to change the uniform to a duller tone than red, however, were defeated by the assertion that "Le pantalon rouge c'est la France." Barbara W. Tuchman, The Guns of August 37-38 (1962). This court cannot say that the First Amendment deprives the military of authority to determine the circumstances in which such symbolic power is either generated or dissipated.

Petitioners overlook the fact that Armed Forces are mobilized for employment and use wherever the national interests require their employment and use; that such employment and use is the very purpose their presence in the Armed Forces is intended to serve; that while wearing the uniform of the Air Force they are subject to the commands of the President of the United States and the officers appointed over them; and that to effectively accomplish these objectives as members of the Armed Forces they can and should be subject to such restrictions as are reasonably necessary under the circumstances.

Here in considering the status of petitioners as members of the Air Force and the fact that they are subject to employment and use by the President pursuant to his constitutional authority, the time and circumstances which prompted the regulation may not be ignored.

Were we at peace and not engaged in a "war" in Southeast Asia, time and circumstances might cause us to seriously question the constitutionality of the regulation under review. But at a time of national emergency in which the nation is engaged in one of the costliest wars of our history in the number of lives lost, casualties otherwise sustained and resources expended, attendance in uniform at a demonstration clearly and directly aimed against the very purposes for which our Armed Forces are to be employed and used runs counter to the oath each petitioner took and constitutes such a flouting of elemental loyalty to the President and the officers appointed over petitioners that it cannot help but have some adverse and detrimental effect on the loyalty, discipline, morale and efficiency of the Armed Forces. To conclude that such activity or symbolic speech could not have such adverse effect is unreasonable. The extent of such adverse effect this court need not decide, once it determines, as it does, that some adverse effect could be reasonably expected to follow. The basic responsibility of determining what constitutes "for the good of the service" when it involves assigning significance to military symbols, is more a military decision than it is a judicial one and hence should be approached by the courts with caution.

"Military regulations must be considered in the light of military exigencies, 'must be geared to meet the imperative needs of mobilization and national vigilance . . .' and great and wide discretion exists in the executive department both in the formation and application of regulations and in their interpretation in such matters as what constitutes 'for the good of the service'." Noyd v. McNamara, supra at 540.

To ensure against arbitrary action of the state, a free society values robust, vigorous and essentially unlimited public speech and discussion by citizens and protects their right to do so by peaceful demonstrations. But when the purpose and very objective of the demonstration is opposition to the employment and use of the Air Force in Southeast Asia and when symbolic speech at such demonstration by wearing the uniform of the Air Force will tend to destroy

military values through the misuse of the most universal and powerful symbol of those values and thereby adversely affect its effort to
fulfill its primary purpose, the employment and use of its personnel
in Southeast Asia, a general order or regulation issued to avoid or
diminish the danger of such consequences to the Air Force is not only
reasonable but imperative.

What this court decides today applies to the Air Force's determination as to the use of its own symbols. Because of the unique
situation here involved, this court finds that the regulation, even
though restricting only opposition to the use of the United States Armed
Forces, is not violative of the First Amendment's ban on selective
suppression of expression, Cox v. Louisiana, 379 U.S. 559, 85 S.Ct.
476, 13 L.Ed.2d 487 (1965), and on coerced prescription of political
orthodoxy, West Virginia State Board of Education v. Barnette, supra
at 647, 63 S.Ct. 1178. As noted above, exclusion of the uniform from
the activity here proscribed is essential to the preservation of the
symbolic significance of the uniform. This court therefore finds that
the regulation is drawn with the requisite degree of precision and that
there is no violation of the doctrine of overbreadth, which the United
States Supreme Court has made applicable to cases of this type involving a conflict between the war power and the First Amendment,
United States v. Robel, 389 U.S. 258, 262-268, 88 S.Ct. 419, 19 L.Ed.2d
508 n. 20 (1967). The regulation does not circumscribe oral or
written speech. The regulation does not prohibit attendance or participation by members of the Air Force in meetings, demonstrations
or interviews of the type here in question. Finally, wearing the uniform is prohibited only if there is reason to know the nature of the
event in question.

The complaint and petitions are denied, the order to show cause
is discharged and the proceedings are in all respects dismissed as to
all parties in their capacities as plaintiffs and as petitioners.

Commanders have the authority to place civilian establishments
off-limits to military personnel if they find that visiting such establishments will have a significant adverse effect on their health, morale
or welfare. In the past, this authority has been used against houses
of prostitution and known drug outlets. The Department of the Army
has cautioned commanders not to use such powers to restrict soldiers
in the exercise of their Constitutional rights of free speech and association by barring attendance at coffee houses, unless the activities in the
coffee houses include counseling of soldiers to refuse to perform duty
or desert (see Department of the Army letter of May 27, 1969, supra).

Section 1381 of Title 18 of the United States Code reads as
follows:

"Whoever entices or procures, or attempts or en-
deavors to entice or procure any person in the Armed
Forces of the United States, or who has been recruited
for service therein, to desert therefrom, or aids any such
person in deserting or in attempting to desert from such
service; or

Whoever harbors, conceals, protects, or assists any
such person who may have deserted from such service,
knowing him to have deserted therefrom, or refuses to
give up and deliver such person on the demand of any
officer authorized to receive him--

Shall be fined not more than $2,000 or imprisoned
not more than three years, or both."

## RADERMAN v. KAINE

United States Court of Appeals, Second Circuit, 1969.
411 F.2d 1102.

MOORE, Circuit Judge:

Plaintiff-appellant, Harold Raderman instituted this action
against defendants-appellees, Major General J. W. Kaine, Commanding General, 77th United States Army Reserve Command and Captain
William Stanners, Commanding Officer, 146th General Support Company, whereby he sought permanently to enjoin them from enforcing
certain statutes and a directive issued as of July 1, 1968 which might
result in plaintiff being certified to his Selective Service Board for
immediate induction into the Armed Services. He also requested the
convocation of a three-judge court to rule upon alleged constitutional
issues. The defendants moved for an order dismissing the complaint
or alternatively for summary judgment in their favor. The district
court granted the motion for summary judgment, dismissing the
complaint and plaintiff appeals from that order.

### The Facts

The facts are to be found in the complaint and affidavits to
which correspondence between plaintiff and the Army, plaintiff's
employer and the Army and an inter-departmental memorandum are
annexed. The controversy is based upon the length of plaintiff's hair,
particularly during the period from July 15, 1968 to the present time.

Some six years ago plaintiff enlisted in the Army and, instead
of the two-year period of continuous service, elected to enlist in the
Reserves for six years, six months of which were to be active duty,

the balance by regular attendance at drills (two days a month) and by two weeks' annual summer camp training. He finished his active duty assignment on February 20, 1964, and was eventually assigned to the 146th General Support Company. Shortly thereafter plaintiff obtained employment with a theatrical agency and in 1965 became an agent for "rock and roll" bands. Because of this position plaintiff claims that he "has worn his hair longer than conventional length" (Compl. par. 8). Until July 1, 1968 an Army directive gave individuals "the right to retain long hair" if it contributed "to the individual's civilian livlihood." (Weekly Bulletin 42, October 20, 1967).

Subsequently this directive was superseded by the directive of July 1, 1968 which "prohibited reservists from wearing their hair as long as that then and still being worn by plaintiff." (Compl. par. 11). During his summer training period in July 1968 plaintiff was ordered to conform to the new directive and refused to comply. The penalty was a fine of some $20 but an additional and more serious consequence was the denial of credit for attendance at drills. Again on August 10, 1968 plaintiff was advised by defendant Stanners that unless he wore his hair at a conventional length he would not receive credit for attendance and that because of such defaults he would be inducted into military service for approximately fifteen months' active duty. Thereafter plaintiff wrote to Vice-President Humphrey and Congressman Ryan. These letters and others were unproductive of results favorable to plaintiff and on September 12, 1968 plaintiff was advised by a Major General of the Army that "Army regulations require that haircuts be well groomed, cut short or medium length, and trimmed at all times. Exceptions will not be made to this policy." A subsequent letter from plaintiff's employer to the Major General indicated that if plaintiff cut his hair his value to them "would be sharply curtailed."

At this time plaintiff had accumulated thirteen unexcused absences from drills. Some absences he disputes but if his absences, resulting from no credit because of his unkempt appearance, are counted, they exceed the allowable number.

The district court relied upon this court's recent decision in Smith v. Resor, 406 F.2d 141, in which the court said: "Further, the decision as to what constitutes the correct appearance of reservists is, absent extraordinary circumstances not present here, within the jurisdiction of the Army."

Plaintiff summons to his aid seven of the first ten amendments to the Constitution, probably on the theory that with seven pegs on the board his broadly hurled arguments might attach themselves to one. But such reliance points to the fallacy of plaintiff's position. If he asks: Does being in the Army curtail or suspend certain Constitutional rights?, the answer is unqualifiedly "yes". Of necessity, he is forced to surrender many important rights. He arises unwillingly at an unreasonable hour at the sound of a bugle unreasonably loud. From that moment on, his freedom of choice and will ceases to exist.

He acts at the command of some person--not a representative of his own choice--who gives commands to him which he does not like to obey. He is assigned to a squad and forced to associate with companions not of his selection and frequently the chores which he may be ordered to perform are of a most menial nature. Yet the armed services, their officers and their manner of discipline do serve an essential function in safeguarding the country. The need for discipline, with the attendant impairment of certain rights, is an important factor in fully discharging that duty.

In listing all his constitutional impairments plaintiff forgets that it is the Constitution which authorizes the creation of an Army. Plaintiff's and his fellow citizens' duly elected representatives enacted the draft legislation. He knew that he could fulfill his military obligations by enlisting in the Army for two or for six years. It is the same Army--only the period of service differs. Plaintiff concedes that, had he elected the two-year period, he would have had to conform to Army Regulations including the length of his hair. However, plaintiff chose the six-year enlistment undoubtedly because it offered certain inducements. Not the least of these inducements was probably the ability to carry on various civilian activities and to avoid the raucous sounds of daily bugles and the regimented day thereafter--or even possibly foreign service. But these civilian activities were permissive, they were not constitutional rights. Plaintiff was still in the Army and subject to Army discipline. He was not a free agent. Nor could he ignore his Army enlistment. For six years he, by his own choice, imposed restrictions upon his activities and his appearance. For various reasons, the Army decided (not subject to federal court review unless the courts take over the functions of the General Staff) that the equivalent of two years' intensive service was six months, followed by five and one-half years of bi-weekly drills and summer camp training.

Plaintiff now asks that an exception as to appearance be made in his case. The Army has advised him that such an exception cannot be made. Such a decision is within the exclusive jurisdiction of the Army.

How have the courts handled such requests for special treatment under allegedly special circumstances?

First it is necessary to set out the statutory and regulatory framework underlying the present action. Section 673a of Title 10 authorizes the President to order to active duty any member of the Ready Reserve who is "not participating satisfactorily" in his reserve duties. Members of reserve units are exempt from induction under 50 U.S.C. App. §456 only "so long as they continue to be such members and satisfactorily participate in scheduled drills and training periods as prescribed by the Secretary of Defense. . . ." No definition of "satisfactory participation" is contained in either statute. [Emphasis added]

Army Regulations No. 135-91, issued pursuant to the above authority, prescribes the "policies, procedures and responsibilities pertaining to satisfactory completion of the Ready Reserve service obligation." Members "are required to participate satisfactorily in paid drill units . . . for the full period of their Ready Reserve obligation." "Satisfactory participation" is defined in the Regulations as "Attendance at all scheduled unit training assemblies . . . unless excused by proper authority." A member is not satisfactorily participating "unless he is in the prescribed uniform, presents a neat and soldierly appearance, and performs his assigned duties in a satisfactory manner as determined by the unit commander," Army Regulations 135-91(5) (d) (2) [Emphasis added]. Failure to properly participate leads to loss of attendance credit and to an unexcused absence. The nature of the relief appellant seeks in this lawsuit is to have this Court become the arbiter of what constitutes "a neat and soldierly appearance," within the meaning of the Army regulations, inform the Army that his hair is the proper length for a reservist and then order the Army not to call him up for active duty.

This Court has repeatedly refused to grant relief in similar situations where men have been called to active duty because of unsatisfactory participation in training functions. Fox v. Brown, 402 F.2d 837 (2d Cir. 1968), cert. denied, 393 U.S. 1114, 89 S.Ct. 1007, 22 L.Ed.2d 120 (March 24, 1969); Winters v. United States, 281 F. Supp. 289 (E.D.N.Y., 1968), aff'd 390 F.2d 879 (2d Cir. 1968); United States v. Lonstein, 370 F.2d 318 (2d Cir. 1966). See also United States ex rel. Schonbrun v. Commanding Officer, 403 F.2d 371 (2d Cir. 1968). The rationale has been that determination of whether a reservist has fully discharged his duties was, absent extraordinary circumstances, for the Army and not for the Courts.

Smith v. Resor, supra, cited by plaintiff, is not to the contrary, although the facts are somewhat similar to the present case. There a reservist was called to active duty because of five "unsatisfactory" ratings for attendance at required meetings. See Army Regulations 135-91. He had received most of these ratings because his hair was too long. However, this Court in reversing the District Court's denial of relief remanded because the Army had failed to follow its own regulations. Weekly Bulletin 42, referred to above, was then in effect and Smith's employer had written the required letter indicating that longer hair was necessary to his employment but his commanding officer refused to allow him to wear his hair long. More importantly, this letter was not placed in his file, as is required, but was tucked in the commanding officer's desk, thereby rendering any in-service appeal fruitless. The Court, remanding for such an appeal, emphasized that what constituted proper or correct appearance was "within the jurisdiction of the Army," and declined to review the validity of the decision that Smith must cut his hair to get credit for attendance at drills. This is precisely the discretionary determination which plaintiff now asks this Court to review.

Discretionary power by its very nature is the power to choose among competing considerations. Although rarely is discretion absolute--even the broad discretion of governmental personnel officers in hiring and firing is limited where certain bases of action would violate the Constitution--this Court, because of the frequent need for expedition in call-up orders has expressed serious doubt how far this principle should apply to such matters. United States ex rel. Schonbrun, supra, 403 F.2d at 374. In Orloff v. Willoughby, 345 U.S. 83, 73 S.Ct. 534, 97 L.Ed. 842 (1953), the Supreme Court declined to review a military call-up order where an abuse of discretion may very well have been involved. The Court refused to review despite the claimed discriminatory character of the orders.

At the time of the present action, Raderman had not yet been formally ordered to report for active duty, and in anticipation of such order and to bar its issuance he brought this suit. He claims that his case is distinguishable from other cases cited above, since it is "an affirmative lawsuit before an induction order" has been received, rather than a habeas application after an induction order. [Emphasis added.] But the procedural posture of such an action is irrelevant to the merits. If it were otherwise, a reservist, who could reach the courthouse steps first, by commencing an action before a call-up order issued, presumably would have greater substantive rights than one who was not as agile.

Plaintiff claims that compliance with his commanding officer's order to trim his hair would have seriously impaired his ability to earn his living. Therefore, he alleges that the military's action has denied him "liberty" and "property" without due process of law, citing a quotation from Chief Justice Warren in Greene v. McElroy, 360 U.S. 474, 492, 79 S.Ct. 1400, 1411, 13 L.Ed.2d 1377 (1959), that "the alleged liberty is petitioner's freedom to practice his chosen profession" . . . "free from unreasonable governmental interference." The Greene case involved the question of whether an engineer, who for years had had security clearance and had worked on many defense projects, could be denied such clearance on the basis of confidential informant testimony without the opportunity to confront and cross-examine his accuser. The Court held that he could not be. The case is clearly distinguishable on its facts; it did not involve a reservist and Chief Justice Warren dictum must be viewed in the context of the factual situation of that case.

The problem with a reservist, such as Raderman, is that he is neither a civilian nor a full-time soldier. In effect he must live in two worlds, one military and one civilian and attempt to satisfy the requirements of both. As in this case, the demands of each may conflict and, while the result may appear harsh, he made the choice some time ago to join a reserve unit. Concomitant with that decision was the knowledge that he would be subject to Army rules and regulations concerning his appearance for six years. Certainly what constitutes a neat and soldierly appearance for a reservist within such regulations is within the discretion of the military. There is no claim here that plaintiff was treated any differently than any other reservist; in fact, he was advised by a Major General of the Army that "Exceptions will not be made to this policy." Throughout the ages the appearance of the military has changed radically. Pictures of Visigoths and our own Civil War soldiers illustrate these changes. But past practices afford no criteria for the present. At any rate, a court is in no position to make that kind of judgment. In the present case there is clearly no action by the military which goes far beyond any rational exercise of discretion. Relief must therefore be denied.

We have reviewed the other claims raised by the plaintiff and conclude that they are without merit.

The judgment below is affirmed.

For a very interesting and novel case in which a Federal District Court enjoined the army from transferring a soldier because of violation of his right to free speech, see Cortright v. Resor, No. 70 C 909 (D.C.E.D.N.Y., 1971). Compare Schlanger v. Seamans, 39 Law Week 4329 (U.S. Supreme Court, 1971).

## OFFENSES UNDER THE UCMJ AND THE FIRST AMENDMENT

Although the UCMJ and the administration of military justice are discussed in detail in Part Three, the following materials point up the specific problem of determining the possible proper restriction of the serviceman's rights under the First Amendment.

One of the earliest cases heard by the Court of Military Appeals concerning this problem was United States v. Voorhees, 4 USCMA 509, 16 CMR 83 (1954), a review of a conviction for publishing without obtaining prior army clearance. In 1966, the Court set aside the conviction of an accused for extortion and wrongful communication of a threat on the grounds of insufficiency of evidence; playing a part in that decision was a possible attempt by certain personnel to interfere with the accused's rights under Section 1034 of Title 10 of the

United States Code to communicate with a member of Congress (U.S. v. Schmidt, 16 USCMA 57, 37 CMR 213). The constitutionality of Article 88, UCMJ, which allows the court-martial of an officer who uses contemptuous words against the President or other specified persons, was upheld in United States v. Howe, supra, p. 435.

Section 2387 of Title 18 of the United States Code reads as follows:

> "Activities Affecting Armed Forces Generally
> (a)  Whoever, with intent to interfere with, impair, or influence the loyalty, morale, or discipline of the military or naval forces of the United States:
>
> > (1)  advises, counsels, urges, or in any manner causes or attempts to cause insubordination, disloyalty, mutiny, or refusal of duty by any member of the military or naval forces of the United States; or
> > (2)  distributes or attempts to distribute any written or printed matter which advises, counsels, or urges insubordination, disloyalty, mutiny, or refusal of duty by any member of the military or naval forces of the United States--
>
> Shall be fined not more than $10,000 or imprisoned not more than ten years, or both, and shall be ineligible for employment by the United States of any department or agency thereof, for the five years next following his conviction."

## UNITED STATES v. DANIELS

United States Court of Military Appeals, 1970.
19 U.S.C.M.A. 529, 42 C.M.R. 131.

QUINN, Chief Judge:
A general court-martial at Camp Pendleton, California, convicted the accused of eight specifications, laid under Article 134, Uniform Code of Military Justice, 10 USC §934, alleging that, with the intent to interfere with the loyalty, morale, and discipline of named members of the Marine Corps, he urged and attempted to cause insubordination, disloyalty, and refusal of duty on the part of said members contrary to 18 USC §2387. The findings of guilty were

affirmed by a board of review, but it modified the sentence by reducing the period of confinement from ten years to four years.

. . .

. . . [T]he accused challenges the sufficiency of the evidence to support the findings of guilty. His central contention is that the statements attributed to him were merely "expressions of grievances and private opinions" for which he cannot be prosecuted without violating his constitutional right to free speech and to the exercise of his religion. The right to believe in a particular faith or philosophy and the right to express one's opinions or to complain about real or imaginary wrongs are legitimate activities in the military community as much as they are in the civilian community. See United States v Schmidt, 16 USCMA 57, 36 CMR 213 (1966); United States v Wolfson, 36 CMR 722, 728 (1966). If the statements and the intent of the accused, as established by the evidence, constitute no more than commentary as to the tenets of his faith or declarations of private opinion as to the social and political state of the United States, he is guilty of no crime. However, if competent evidence reveals conduct not protected by the Constitution and condemned by statute, the findings are proper. Hartzel v United States, 322 US 680, 88 L Ed 1534, 64 S Ct 1233 (1944); United States v Howe, 17 USCMA 165, 37 CMR 429 (1967). We turn, therefore, to consideration of the requirements of the statute.

Title 18, United States Code, §2387, has its roots in the Espionage Act of 1917. The language of the current statute and its progenitor are substantially the same. Dunne v United States, 138 F2d 137 (CA 8th Cir) (1943), certiorari denied, 320 US 790, 88 L Ed 476, 64 S Ct 205 (1943). The judicial construction accorded the predecessor statute is, therefore, appropriate to the purposes and requirements of the current provision. United States v Cook, 384 US 257, 16 L Ed 2d 516, 86 S Ct 1412 (1966); United States v Rogan, 8 USCMA 739, 25 CMR 243 (1958).

In Hartzel, supra, the Supreme Court of the United States considered the predecessor statute. As in this case, the issue was whether the evidence was sufficient to sustain a conviction. The defendant had published three articles which, in material part, depicted World War II as a gross betrayal of the United States and advocated transformation of the war into an " 'internal war of race against race.' " Copies of the articles were disseminated among civilian and military organizations and persons. The Supreme Court held that inasmuch as the statute restricted the defendant's constitutional right to speak and write freely it was to be strictly construed. The Court determined that the statute required not only proof of prohibited acts, but two other "elements." One, which the Court described as the "subjective" element, was that at the time of commission of a prohibited act the defendant possessed the specific intent proscribed by the statute. The other element, which the Court characterized as an "objective" element, consisted of a requirement that there be "a clear and present danger that the activities in question will bring about the substantive evils" delineated in the statute. Id., 322 US, at pages 683, 686-687. With Hartzel's analysis of the elements of the offense as the frame of reference, we turn to the evidence against the accused.

The accused claimed membership in the Black Muslim sect. On frequent occasions he talked about the tenets of his faith to black members of his unit. He also talked about the involvement of the United States in the Vietnam war and the participation of black troopers of the Marine Corps in that war. Specification 1 of the charge alleges that starting in May 1967, at Cherry Point, North Carolina, and continuing into July 1967, at Camp Pendleton, California, with the intent to interfere with, impair, and influence the loyalty, morale, and discipline of Private First Class J. W. Jones, the accused urged and attempted to cause insubordination, disloyalty, and refusal of duty by Jones. Jones testified as a Government witness.

According to Jones, while stationed at Cherry Point, he spoke to the accused "quite frequently." Their conversations, which were largely "discussions" with other blacks in the unit, ranged over many subjects including the accused's religion and his attitude toward the Vietnam war. "[Q]uite often" the accused declared that blacks did not have a country; that the Vietnam war was a "white man's war" and blacks did not "belong over there." Some of the participants "sort of" made "fun" of the accused's religion, and "most of the time" Jones personally disagreed with the accused.

At different times, Jones and the accused were transferred to Camp Pendleton for further training in preparation for duty in Vietnam. At Camp Pendleton they again met "quite often," and again discussed the war in Vietnam. Riots occurred in several major cities in the country and the discussions included comments on the riots. The accused frequently reiterated his early declarations that Vietnam was a white man's war and blacks did not "belong" in it. Asked if the accused had ever "directly" told him not to go to Vietnam, Jones replied: "Yes, sir, he did. Not--In a way he did. He said I shouldn't go. He told me I shouldn't go to Vietnam."

On July 12, 1967, Captain H. J. Trautwein, Jr., the commanding officer of the unit, met with the accused, pursuant to the accused's request. The meeting lasted for more than three hours. The accused told Captain Trautwein that he could not "in conscience" go to Vietnam "because this was a white man's war" and he would only have to return to "fight the white man in the states." The accused requested a change in his military occupation specialty or release from active duty. Trautwein assured him he would "do all we could" to obtain either aspect of the requested relief. He asked that in the meantime the accused not "spread" his philosophy among company members because there were "people that didn't want to be there" and they were "particularly susceptible" persons. It may fairly be inferred from Jones' testimony, and the testimony of other witnesses, that Trautwein did not persuade the accused to silence. Jones continued to meet the accused sometimes two or three times a day and the accused continued to declare that blacks had no country and should not go to Vietnam because it was a white man's war.

On July 27, 1967, Jones and other members of the company were at the rifle range. On notification by the accused and a Corporal W. L. Harvey, Jr., the black troopers assembled at two meetings, one held immediately after the noon meal and the other after the evening meal. Several witnesses testified about the noon meeting. The substance of their testimony is to the effect that the accused addressed the assembled black troopers.* The accused told the assembled blacks that there was no need for them to go to Vietnam because Vietnam was a white man's war and he "didn't see . . . [any] sense in going overseas and fighting the white man's war." He told the assemblage that he would prepare a list of names of the "people that want to request mast," and that they would go to talk to the Captain. Jones did not attend the morning assembly, but he did attend the evening meeting. He testified that at that time the accused stated: "We were going to request mast the next day . . . and refuse to go and fight in Vietnam."

Jones and others put their names on a sheet of paper to request mast. The next morning when a call was issued for the persons who had requested mast, he joined the formation which was made up of persons who had attended the meetings the previous day. At the company office, Jones indicated he had requested the mast because he was going to refuse to go to Vietnam since it was a white man's war. However, when informed of the nature and consequences of a refusal to obey orders, he decided not to go through with his mast request. At trial, he maintained that he would not have requested mast on his own initiative, and had done so because of the meeting he had attended the previous day.

We consider first whether the evidence is sufficient to support the findings by the court-martial that the accused made the declarations attributed to him with the "intent to interfere with, impair, and influence the loyalty, morale, and discipline" of Jones as alleged in the specification. Appellate defense counsel argue that the accused lacked the requisite intent because for the most part his declarations were made in barracks "bull sessions" and represented "expressions of . . . personal beliefs . . . and . . . grievances" lacking any "element of urging others to do anything." The form and the place of a declaration may indeed indicate the intent with which the declaration is made, but they are not determinative. The intention of a speaker may be determined from surrounding circumstances as well

---

*Some white Marines stood at the edge of the group of blacks.

as from the language in which his declarations are framed. Hartzel v United States, supra, 322 US, at page 691; see United States v Noriega, 7 USCMA 322 (1956). The fact that a declaration is phrased in the form of personal belief does not necessarily negate the existence of an intention to impair or influence the listener's loyalty, morale, or discipline. United States v Dembowski, 252 Fed 894 (ED Mich) (1918). Nor is an intent to impair loyalty and discipline negated by the fact that the effort is made in a place commonly used for innocuous gossip and social conversation. Schoborg v United States, 264 Fed 1 (CA 6th Cir) (1920), certiorari denied, 253 US 494, 64 L Ed 1029, 40 S Ct 586 (1920); United States v Dembowski, supra.

The accused's declarations can reasonably be construed differently from the construction accorded them by his counsel. They propounded a racial doctrine that contemplated not merely separation and lack of cooperation between the races, but violent confrontation. The declarations were addressed directly and specifically to members of the accused's race who were members of the Marine Corps. The listeners were engaged in training that would qualify them for transfer to, and participation in, the war in Vietnam. That war was constantly called a white man's war, and a war in which blacks should not fight. Blacks were enjoined to remain in this country to fight whites for black causes. To that end, the accused proposed to his listeners that they join in a mass mast as a means of effecting their discharge from the Marine Corps.

Appellate defense counsel and the amicus curiae contend that the accused's exhortation to join in a mass request for a mast was a call for lawful action. A request for mast is unquestionably lawful, but the court-martial could reasonably conclude that the accused's call was not a call for the exercise of a lawful right for a lawful purpose. There is no evidence the accused knew or honestly believed that Jones, or his other listeners, had independent reasons to request mast. There is an abundance of evidence to support a conclusion that the accused urged Jones to join the mass request for mast because blacks were obligated not to serve in the Vietnam war because it was a white man's war.

The Court members were entitled to weigh all the circumstances, and the reasonable inferences to be drawn from them. They could reasonably conclude that the accused's exhortations to Jones and his call for action in the form of a mass mast was a subtle and skillful way of leading the black troopers in the company into insubordination and disloyalty. Considering the totality of the accused's declarations and the circumstances in which they were uttered, we are satisfied that the court members could find beyond a reasonable doubt that the accused's declarations were intended to interfere with or impair the loyalty, morale, and discipline of Jones.

Turning to whether the accused's activities presented a clear and present danger which could bring about insubordination and disloyalty, the evidence demonstrates that propagation of the accused's theses occurred at a time when Jones and other blacks in the company were undergoing training to prepare them for duty in Vietnam. The accused had been informed that many persons in the company "didn't want to be there" and they were a particularly "susceptible" group. He also knew that the blacks in the company were "aware" of race riots in some of the large cities and were sensitive to the tensions between blacks and whites. Knowing these things, he spread the doctrine that the Vietnam war was a white man's war and blacks could not and should not fight there but remain at home to "fight." The joinder of the Vietnam war with racial violence in the cities was not mere rhetoric or political hyperbole, but a call for refusal of duty. The call was accompanied by the presentation of an alleged means of practical achievement of the objective without penalty. The means proposed by the accused did not contemplate reliance upon the ordinary and the usual reasons for separation from the service or excuse from duty but depended upon the implied force of the number of blacks who availed themselves of it. The aggregate of the accused's activity was not a trivial hazard but a clear and present danger to impairment of the loyalty and obedience of Jones and other blacks in the company. We conclude, therefore, that the evidence satisfies the objective requirement of 18 USC §2387, as propounded by the Supreme Court of the United States in Hartzel v United States, supra, and amply supports the findings of guilty of specification 1 of the charge.

The remaining seven specifications involve other statements and other persons exhorted by the accused not to go to Vietnam. There are some differences in the content of the declarations. Specification 5, for example, alleges that the accused called Private First Class J. C. Griffin an "'Uncle Tom' for wanting to go over to Vietnam and fight." The amicus curiae contend that the expression is no more than a pithy epithet which "cannot be deemed" sufficient to incite others to illegal actions. Evidence, however, indicates that the term "Uncle Tom" was understood as insult or derision. In appropriate circumstances, insult, derision, or coarse epithet can be as effective a cause of insubordination, disloyalty, and refusal of duty as direct incitement. Schaefer v United States, 251 US 466, 478, 64 L Ed 360, 40 S Ct 259 (1920); Seebach v United States, 262 Fed 885 (CA 8th Cir) (1919). Other statements are attacked as too trivial to incite to disloyalty or insubordination. Specification 4, for instance, alleges, in part, that the accused urged Private R. L. Burwell to "disobey the order of his platoon sergeant to get a hair cut." This allegation is viewed as "too ludicrous to be worthy of the consideration of this court." By itself, the allegation may indeed be insignificant, but other averments and proof indicate the accused exhorted Burwell to get out of the Marine Corps because it was a "white man's outfit"; that he should "refuse to go to Vietnam" because there was "no need" for him to fight the white man's war; that Burwell should request mast to refuse to fight in Vietnam; and if all the black troopers "stick together" and request mast, they "could probably get out" of the Marine Corps because "the Captain didn't want us to start a riot in the service." From all the evidence, the court-martial could reason that urging Burwell to disobey the order to get a hair cut was an integral part of accused's intention and effort to influence Burwell to disobedience and disloyalty.

As in the case of Jones, the accused's declarations to other blacks ultimately failed in their intended purpose. The failure did not immunize the accused from prosecution. Schenck v United States, 249 US 47, 63 L Ed 470, 39 S Ct 247 (1919); Dennis v United States, 341 US 494, 509, 95 L Ed 1137, 71 S Ct 857 (1951). On consideration of the record, we are satisfied that the evidence is legally sufficient to support a conclusion that the accused's conduct was intended to impair the loyalty, morale, and discipline of the persons mentioned in the specifications and that there was a clear and present danger that disloyalty and insubordination would result from his activities.

Determination of the legal sufficiency of the evidence from our viewpoint does not necessarily mean the triers of the facts found the same facts and drew the same inferences. The only way we can be certain they reached the same ultimate conclusions is to consider the instructions tney were given as to the facts they were required to find to return findings of guilty.

Prompted by questioning by the Court on argument of the appeal, appellate defense counsel have filed a supplemental brief challenging the sufficiency of the instructions. Relying upon Yates v United States, 354 US 298, 1 L Ed 2d 1356, 77 S Ct 1064 (1957), appellate defense counsel contend that whether the accused's declaration had the natural and probable tendency to generate the kind of action prohibited by 18 USC §2387, is a question of fact for the court members. Yates dealt with 18 USC §2385. The two sections deal with the same general subject, but whether the rationale of Yates applies to conduct violative of section 2387 need not detain us.

Hartzel v United States, supra, 322 US, at pages 686-687, specifically held that one of the "elements" of section 2387's predecessor statute was whether the alleged activities presented a "clear and present danger" that they would "bring about the substantive evils" prohibited by the statute. It determined that this "objective" element and the "subjective" element of the accused's intent to cause insubordination must both be "proved by the Government beyond a reasonable doubt." The district judge's instructions at the trial covered both elements of the offense as follows:

> ". . . Now, the two things must concur, and it must appear that the publication was calculated to have that effect, and that the defendant intended it to have that effect.

"Now, you are to determine whether the publications were calculated to have that effect from the publication itself, it is for you to determine whether these
publications, the language used in these publications,
was calculated to have that effect, and then you will have
the question of intent. I might say in this connection, I
might, in describing the limitations on free speech, I
might use the language that was used by Justice Oliver
Wendall Holmes: He said: 'The question in each case
is whether the words used are used under such circumstances or of such a nature as to create clear and present
danger that they will bring about the effect that Congress
has a right to prevent.'

"That is the rule that you must apply in determining whether these publications were calculated to have
that effect, as to whether the words used in these publications are such, or were used under such circumstances
or were of such a nature as to create a clear and present
danger that they would interfere with enlistment or recruiting or . . . would cause insubordination in the army,
because then they are prohibited by the statute that I have
read to you.

"Then there is a question of intent. It is charged
in the indictment they were intended to produce those results. In determining whether they were used with that
intent, you will take into consideration all of the circumstances in the case, and you must take into consideration
the words used, and whether from the words used themselves you could find that there was such intent, and you
are at liberty to infer that, to take into consideration the
language used, the intention and the probable result of
such language used, you are at liberty to infer that from
all of the facts and circumstances that you have heard
testified to here in the evidence, the circumstances under
which they were issued." [Transcript of Record filed
with the Supreme Court of the United States, No. 531,
October Term 1943.]

On the appeal before the Supreme Court of the United States,
the Government conceded that the trial judge had properly submitted
to the jury the question of the tendency of the defendant's activities
to cause insubordination or disloyalty. In its brief, at page 18, it
said:

"Clear and present danger. The jury found that
the petitioner's acts during time of war constituted a
clear and present danger of causing disloyalty, refusal

of duty, or insubordination in the armed forces. As Mr.
Justice Brandeis observed in Schaefer v United States,
251 US 466, 483, 'because it is a question of degree the
field in which the jury may exercise its judgment is,
necessarily, a wide one', though the duty rests on the
courts to withdraw the case from the jury if 'men,
judging in calmness, could not reasonably say that (the
words) created a clear and present danger that they
would bring about the evil which Congress sought and had
a right to prevent'. We submit that the trial court properly left the issue to the jury."

Pierce v United States, 252 US 239, 244, 64 L Ed 542, 40 S Ct
205 (1920), which involved a conspiracy to cause insubordination and
disloyalty and a substantive count of attempting to cause insubordination and disloyalty under the predecessor statute is to the same effect.
Rejecting a contention that a demurrer to the indictment should have
been sustained, the Supreme Court said: "Whether the statements
. . . had a natural tendency to produce the forbidden consequences,
as alleged, was a question to be determined not upon demurrer, but
by the jury at the trial." (Emphasis supplied.) We conclude, therefore, that the instructions in a prosecution of this kind must advise
the court members, as triers of the facts, that they must find beyond
a reasonable doubt that the language and the circumstances of the accused's declarations presented a clear and present danger that those
declarations would cause insubordination, disloyalty, or refusal of
duty. With this requirement in mind, we turn to the instructions in
this case.
During an out-of-court hearing on proposed instructions, trial
counsel raised the question of the likelihood of the accused's conduct
to create insubordination and disloyalty. He noted his belief that the
circumstances under which the accused's statements were made could
be considered in determining the "apparent present danger." He also
called attention to evidence that the accused's listeners were persons
"about to complete their training to go to Staging Battalion," which
would be their last duty station in the United States before going to
Vietnam. However, the law officer rejected trial counsel's remarks
with the comment that this evidence went to "the gravity of the offense rather than to the element of the offense." As a result, the
instructions make no mention of the tendency of the accused's activities to produce the prohibited results as an element of the offense.
Thus, the court members were entirely uninformed on a matter essential to determination of the accused's guilt or innocence. This serious
instructional deficiency requires reversal of the findings of guilty of
a violation of section 2387. United States v Rhoden, 1 USCMA 193, 2
CMR 99 (1952); United States v Soukup, 2 USCMA 141, 7 CMR 17
(1953).

An out-of-court hearing at the close of the defense case provides the subject matter for the accused's final assignment of error. The last defense witness was Private First Class J. L. Honesty. In his testimony, Honesty had referred to a pretrial statement he had made in connection with the mass mast, and he indicated his "attitude" changed later when he went on leave and talked to members of his family. He denied that he had previously said he did not want to fight the white man's war in Vietnam. When Honesty concluded his testimony, the law officer excused the court members and held the out-of-court hearing. He noted that, while Honesty had been testifying, he had read Honesty's pretrial statement, which was included in the Article 32 Investigation Report that counsel had given him at the beginning of trial and which had been referred to during the trial. The law officer stated that he was "highly disturbed" by what he had read and that he would "not be a party to anything even remotely" connected with certain remarks in the statement. He indicated he would "direct [the trial] counsel to pursue" the matter. However, after some colloquy, in which defense counsel argued that Honesty's statement reflected his own "feelings and opinion" and "never implicated" the accused, the law officer acknowledged that he was not "an advocate in the case" and that "perhaps . . . [he had been] a little carried away . . . [by] the situation." He reiterated that he was "profoundly shocked" at parts of Honesty's statement, but he terminated the out-of-court hearing. Later, at another out-of-court hearing after the luncheon recess, the question of a mistrial was raised. Defense counsel indicated he had no "desire to make" any such motion.

Inasmuch as the accused affirmatively disclaimed any desire to inquire into effect of the incident on the law officer's qualification to function impartially during the remainder of the trial, it may now be too late to press the incident as ground for reversal. United States v Law, 10 USCMA 573, 28 CMR 139 (1959); United States v Weaver, 9 USCMA 13, 25 CMR 275 (1958). Apart from waiver of the right to object to the law officer's remarks, no reasonable risk of prejudice to the accused from the incident appears in the record. The law officer's concern was with Honesty's veracity, not with the accused's guilt or innocence. Nothing in the incident reflects adversely upon the impartiality and fairness he demonstrated throughout the trial. His remarks were not known to the court members, and Honesty was never examined in open court on the contents of his statement. Appellate defense counsel insist that disregard of the incident will result in a miscarriage of justice. See United States v Russell, 15 USCMA 76, 35 CMR 48 (1964). We have scrutinized the record but find no indications of bias or prejudice on the part of the law officer which even hint at an "appearance of evil." Certainly, the law officer was impetuous and injudicious in his comments on Honesty's personal beliefs, but his loss of composure was temporary and unknown to the court members. The incident may be regrettable, but it does not amount to reversible error. United States v Lindsay, 12 USCMA 235, 30 CMR 235 (1961).

We turn now to the nature of the relief to be accorded the accused because of the instructional error noted earlier. In the companion case of United States v Harvey, 19 USCMA 539, 42 CMR 141, decided this date, we dealt with the same issue. We determined that some of the findings of guilty were not affected by the error and could properly be affirmed as a lesser included offense.

In Harvey, we assumed but did not decide that the statements set out in the specifications were disloyal to the United States. Some of the statements in this case are like those in Harvey; others, such as the statement to Private Burwell to disobey an order to get a haircut, are not. As in Harvey, however, we need not determine whether the statements are disloyal to the United States as a political entity. The findings of guilty of section 2387 treat the statements as conduct the effect of which could impair the obedience or loyalty of particular persons; they do not explicitly indicate that the statements as such disavow allegiance to the United States. Depending upon the circumstances, reasonable persons might reach different conclusions as to the nature of the statements; thus, the question is essentially one of fact for fact finders, rather than one of law for this Court. However, as in the Harvey case, "the court-martial's findings indicate, as a minimum, that the accused solicited a member of the Marine Corps to commit a military offense." Considering the time that has elapsed since the accused's trial, we deem it appropriate to affirm those findings rather than continue the proceedings by ordering a rehearing on the charges on which the accused was arraigned.

The decision of the board of review is reversed. The record of trial is returned to the Judge Advocate General of the Navy for submission to the United States Navy Court of Military Review for reassessment of the sentence upon the basis of the approved findings of guilty.

Judge DARDEN concurs.

Judge FERGUSON concurs in the result.

See also U.S. v. Harvey, 19 USCMA 539, 42 CMR 141 (1970); and U.S. v. Gray, 20 USCMA 63, 42 CMR 255 (1970).

The concept of sovereign immunity--that is, that a government
is not liable for harm done to a person unless it has so consented--
is a venerable fundamental principle of common law. The idea that
an aggrieved party may be denied redress because the defendant is
the government or one of its employees, however, has seemed unjust
to many persons. Accordingly, the doctrine of immunity has been
progressively eroded, first by acts of Congress granting private
relief and later by the enactment of many statutes allowing a suit in
the courts by an injured party against the government or by allowing
a claim through administrative action. The most comprehensive of
this type of statute is the Federal Tort Claims Act (28 U.S.C. 1346),
which was interpreted in the following cases.

## BROOKS v. UNITED STATES*

Supreme Court of the United States, 1949.
337 U.S. 49, 69 S.Ct. 918, 93 L.Ed. 1200.

*[ Footnotes have been omitted. Ed.]

MR. JUSTICE MURPHY delivered the opinion of the Court.

This is a suit against the United States under the Federal Tort
Claims Act, 60 Stat. 842, 28 U. S. C. (1946 ed.) §931, now 28 U. S. C.
§2674. The question is whether members of the United States armed

forces can recover under that Act for injuries not incident to their service. The District Court for the Western District of North Carolina entered judgment against the Government, rendering an unreported opinion, but the Court of Appeals for the Fourth Circuit reversed, in a divided decision. 169 F. 2d 840. We brought the case here on certiorari because of its importance as an interpretation of the Act. 335 U.S. 901.

The facts are these. Welker Brooks, Arthur Brooks, and their father, James Brooks, were riding in their automobile along a public highway in North Carolina on a dark, rainy night in February, 1945. Arthur was driving. He came to a full stop before entering an intersection, and proceeded across the nearer lane of the intersecting road. Seconds later the car was struck from the left by a United States Army truck, driven by a civilian employee of the Army. Arthur Brooks was killed; Welker and his father were badly injured.

Welker and the administrator of Arthur's estate brought actions against the United States in the District Court. The District Judge tried the causes without a jury and found negligence on the part of the truck driver. The Government moved to dismiss on the ground that Welker and his deceased brother were in the armed forces of the United States at the time of the accident, and were therefore barred from recovery. The Court denied the motion, entered a $25,425 judgment for the decedent's estate, and a $4,000 judgment for Welker. On appeal, however, the Government's argument persuaded the Court of Appeals to reverse the judgment, Judge Parker dissenting.

We agree with Judge Parker. The statute's terms are clear. They provide for District Court jurisdiction over any claim founded on negligence brought against the United States. We are not persuaded that "any claim" means "any claim but that of servicemen." The statute does contain twelve exceptions. §421. None exclude petitioners' claims. One is for claims arising in a foreign country. A second excludes claims arising out of combatant activities of the military or naval forces, or the Coast Guard, during time of war. These and other exceptions are too lengthy, specific, and close to the present problem to take away petitioners' judgments. Without resorting to an automatic maxim of construction, such exceptions make it clear to us that Congress knew what it was about when it used the term "any claim." It would be absurd to believe that Congress did not have the servicemen in mind in 1946, when this statute was passed. The overseas and combatant activities exceptions make this plain.

More than the language and framework of the act support this view. There were eighteen tort claims bills introduced in Congress between 1925 and 1935. All but two contained exceptions denying recovery to members of the armed forces. When the present Tort Claims Act was first introduced, the exception concerning servicemen had been dropped. What remained from previous bills was an exclusion of all claims for which compensation was provided by the

World War Veterans' Act of 1924--43 Stat. 607, 38 U. S. C. §421,
compensation for injury or death occurring in the first World War.
H.R. 181, 79th Cong., 1st Sess. When H.R. 181 was incorporated into
the Legislative Reorganization Act, the last vestige of the exclusion
for members of the armed forces disappeared. See also Note, 1
Syracuse L. Rev. 87, 93-94.

The Government envisages dire consequences should we reverse
the judgment. A battle commander's poor judgment, an army surgeon's
slip of hand, a defective jeep which causes injury, all would ground
tort actions against the United States. But we are dealing with an
accident which had nothing to do with the Brooks' army careers, injuries not caused by their service except in the sense that all human
events depend upon what has already transpired. Were the accident
incident to the Brooks' service, a wholly different case would be presented. We express no opinion as to it, but we may note that only in
its context do Dobson v. United States, 27 F. 2d 807, Bradey v.
United States, 151 F. 2d 742, and Jefferson v. United States, 77 F.
Supp. 706, have any relevance. See the similar distinction in 31
U. S. C. §223b. Interpretation of the same words may vary, of course,
with the consequences, for those consequences may provide insight
for determination of congressional purpose. Lawson v. Suwannee
Fruit & Steamship Co., 336 U.S. 198. The Government's fears may
have point in reflecting congressional purpose to leave injuries incident to service where they were, despite literal language and other
considerations to the contrary. The result may be so outlandish that
even the factors we have mentioned would not permit recovery. But
that is not the case before us.

Provisions in other statutes for disability payments to servicemen, and gratuity payments to their survivors, 38 U. S. C. §701,
indicate no purpose to forbid tort actions under the Tort Claims Act.
Unlike the usual workman's compensation statute, e. g., 33 U. S. C.
§905, there is nothing in the Tort Claims Act or the veterans' laws
which provides for exclusiveness of remedy. United States v.
Standard Oil Co., 332 U.S. 301, indicates that, so far as third party
liability is concerned. Nor did Congress provide for an election of
remedies, as in the Federal Employees' Compensation Act, 5 U. S. C.
§757. Thus Dahn v. Davis, 258 U.S. 421, and cases following that
decision, are not in point. Compare Parr v. United States, 172 F. 2d
462. We will not call either remedy in the present case exclusive,
nor pronounce a doctrine of election of remedies, when Congress has
not done so. Compare 31 U. S. C. §224b, specifically repealed by the
Tort Claims Act, §424(a). In the very Act we are construing, Congress provided for exclusiveness of the remedy in three instances,
§§403(d), 410(b), and 423, and omitted any provision which would
govern this case.

But this does not mean that the amount payable under servicemen's benefit laws should not be deducted, or taken into consideration,

when the serviceman obtains judgment under the Tort Claims Act.
Without the benefit of argument in this Court, or discussion of the
matter in the Court of Appeals, we now see no indication that Congress
meant the United States to pay twice for the same injury. Certain elements of tort damages may be the equivalent of elements taken into
account in providing disability payments. It would seem incongruous,
at first glance, if the United States should have to pay in tort for hospital expenses it had already paid, for example. And whatever the
legal theory behind a wrongful death action, the same considerations
might apply to the Government's gratuity death payment to Arthur
Brooks' survivors, although national service life insurance might be
considered a separate transaction, unrelated to an action in tort or
other benefits.

But the statutory scheme and the Veterans' Administration
regulations may dictate a contrary result. The point was not argued
in the case as it came to us from the Court of Appeals. The court
below does not appear to have passed upon it; it was unnecessary,
in the view they took of the case. We do not know from this record
whether the Government objected to this portion of the District Court
judgment--nor can we tell from this record whether the Court of
Appeals should consider a general objection to the judgment sufficient
to allow it to consider this problem. Finally, we are not sure how
much deducting the District Judge did. It is obvious that we are in
no position to pass upon the question of deducting other benefits in
the case's present posture.

We conclude that the language, framework and legislative history of the Tort Claims Act require a holding that petitioners' actions
were well founded. But we remand to the Court of Appeals for its
consideration of the problem of reducing damages pro tanto, should
it decide that such consideration is proper in view of the District
Court judgment and the parties' allegations of error.

Reversed and remanded.

MR. JUSTICE FRANKFURTER and MR. JUSTICE DOUGLAS
dissent, substantially for the reasons set forth by Judge Dobie, below,
169 F. 2d 840.

FERES v. UNITED STATES*

Supreme Court of the United States, 1950.
340 U.S. 135, 71 S.Ct. 153, 95 L.Ed. 152.

*[Footnotes have been omitted. Ed.]

MR. JUSTICE JACKSON delivered the opinion of the Court.
A common issue arising under the Tort Claims Act, as to which
Courts of Appeals are in conflict, makes it appropriate to consider
three cases in one opinion.

The Feres case: The District Court dismissed an action by the executrix of Feres against the United States to recover for death caused by negligence. Decedent perished by fire in the barracks at Pine Camp, New York, while on active duty in service of the United States. Negligence was alleged in quartering him in barracks known or which should have been known to be unsafe because of a defective heating plant, and in failing to maintain an adequate fire watch. The Court of Appeals, Second Circuit, affirmed.

The Jefferson case: Plaintiff, while in the Army, was required to undergo an abdominal operation. About eight months later, in the course of another operation after plaintiff was discharged, a towel 30 inches long by 18 inches wide, marked "Medical Department U.S. Army," was discovered and removed from his stomach. The complaint alleged that it was negligently left there by the army surgeon. The District Court, being doubtful of the law, refused without prejudice the Government's pretrial motion to dismiss the complaint. After trial, finding negligence as a fact, Judge Chesnut carefully reexamined the issue of law and concluded that the Act does not charge the United States with liability in this type of case. The Court of Appeals, Fourth Circuit, affirmed.

The Griggs case: The District Court dismissed the complaint of Griggs' executrix, which alleged that while on active duty he met death because of negligent and unskillful medical treatment by army surgeons. The Court of Appeals, Tenth Circuit, reversed and, one judge dissenting, held that the complaint stated a cause of action under the Act.

The common fact underlying the three cases is that each claimant, while on active duty and not on furlough, sustained injury due to negligence of others in the armed forces. The only issue of law raised is whether the Tort Claims Act extends its remedy to one sustaining "incident to the service" what under other circumstances would be an actionable wrong. This is the "wholly different case" reserved from our decision in Brooks v. United States, 337 U.S. 49, 52.

There are few guiding materials for our task of statutory construction. No committee reports or floor debates disclose what effect the statute was designed to have on the problem before us, or that it even was in mind. Under these circumstances, no conclusion can be above challenge, but if we misinterpret the Act, at least Congress possesses a ready remedy.

We do not overlook considerations persuasive of liability in these cases. The Act does confer district court jurisdiction generally over claims for money damages against the United States founded on negligence. 28 U. S. C. §1346(b). It does contemplate that the Government will sometimes respond for negligence of military personnel, for it defines "employee of the Government" to include "members of the military or naval forces of the United States," and provides that

" 'acting within the scope of his office or employment', in the case of a member of the military or naval forces of the United States, means acting in line of duty." 28 U. S. C. §2671. Its exceptions might also imply inclusion of claims such as we have here. 28 U. S. C. §2680(j) excepts "any claim arising out of the <u>combatant</u> activities of the military or naval forces, or the Coast Guard, <u>during time of war</u>" (emphasis supplied), from which it is said we should infer allowance of claims arising from non-combat activities in peace. Section 2680(k) excludes "any claim arising in a foreign country." Significance also has been attributed in these cases, as in the <u>Brooks</u> case, <u>supra</u>, p. 51, to the fact that eighteen tort claim bills <u>were</u> introduced in Congress between 1925 and 1935 and all but two expressly denied recovery to members of the armed forces; but the bill enacted as the present Tort Claims Act from its introduction made no exception. We also are reminded that the <u>Brooks</u> case, in spite of its reservation of service-connected injuries, interprets the Act to cover claims not incidental to service, and it is argued that much of its reasoning is as apt to impose liability in favor of a man on duty as in favor of one on leave. These considerations, it is said, should persuade us to cast upon Congress, as author of the confusion, the task of qualifying and clarifying its language if the liability here asserted should prove so depleting of the public treasury as the Government fears.

This Act, however, should be construed to fit, so far as will comport with its words, into the entire statutory system of remedies against the Government to make a workable, consistent and equitable whole. The Tort Claims Act was not an isolated and spontaneous flash of congressional generosity. It marks the culmination of a long effort to mitigate unjust consequences of sovereign immunity from suit. While the political theory that the King could do no wrong was repudiated in America, a legal doctrine derived from it that the Crown is immune from any suit to which it has not consented was invoked on behalf of the Republic and applied by our courts as vigorously as it had been on behalf of the Crown. As the Federal Government expanded its activities, its agents caused a multiplying number of remediless wrongs--wrongs which would have been actionable if inflicted by an individual or a corporation but remediless solely because their perpetrator was an officer or employee of the Government. Relief was often sought and sometimes granted through private bills in Congress, the number of which steadily increased as Government activity increased. The volume of these private bills, the inadequacy of congressional machinery for determination of facts, the importunities to which claimants subjected members of Congress, and the capricious results, led to a strong demand that claims for tort wrongs be submitted to adjudication. Congress already had waived immunity and made the Government answerable for breaches of its contracts and certain other types of claims. At last, in connection with the Reorganization Act, it waived immunity and transferred the burden of examining tort claims to the courts. The primary purpose of the Act was to extend a remedy to those who had been without; if it incidentally benefited those already well provided for, it appears to have been unintentional. Congress was suffering from no plague of private bills on the behalf of military and naval personnel, because a comprehensive system of relief had been authorized for them and their dependents by statute.

Looking to the detail of the Act, it is true that it provides, broadly, that the District Court "shall have exclusive jurisdiction of civil actions on claims against the United States, for money damages. . . ." This confers jurisdiction to render judgment upon all such claims. But it does not say that all claims must be allowed. Jurisdiction is necessary to deny a claim on its merits as matter of law as much as to adjudge that liability exists. We interpret this language to mean all it says, but no more. Jurisdiction of the defendant now exists where the defendant was immune from suit before; it remains for courts, in exercise of their jurisdiction, to determine whether any claim is recognizable in law.

For this purpose, the Act goes on to prescribe the test of allowable claims, which is, "The United States shall be liable . . . in the same manner and to the same extent as a private individual under like circumstances . . . ," with certain exceptions not material here. 28 U. S. C. §2674. It will be seen that this is not the creation of new causes of action but acceptance of liability under circumstances that would bring private liability into existence. This, we think, embodies the same idea that its English equivalent enacted in 1947 (Crown Proceedings Act 1947; 10 and 11 Geo. VI, c. 44, p. 863) expressed, "Where any person has a claim against the Crown after the commencement of this Act, and, if this Act had not been passed, the claim might have been enforced, subject to the grant . . ." of consent to be sued, the claim may now be enforced without specific consent. One obvious shortcoming in these claims is that plaintiffs can point to no liability of a "private individual" even remotely analogous to that which they are asserting against the United States. We know of no American law which ever has permitted a soldier to recover for negligence, against either his superior officers or the Government he is serving. Nor is there any liability "under like circumstances," for no private individual has power to conscript or mobilize a private army with such authorities over persons as the Government vests in echelons of command. The nearest parallel, even if we were to treat "private individual" as including a state, would be the relationship between the states and their militia. But if we indulge plaintiffs the benefit of this comparison, claimants cite us no state, and we know of none, which has permitted members of its militia to maintain tort actions for injuries suffered in the service, and in at least one state the contrary has been held to be the case. It is true that if we consider relevant only a part of the circumstances

and ignore the status of both the wronged and the wrongdoer in these
cases we find analogous private liability. In the usual civilian doctor
and patient relationship, there is of course a liability for malpractice.
And a landlord would undoubtedly be held liable if an injury occurred
to a tenant as the result of a negligently maintained heating plant.
But the liability assumed by the Government here is that created by
"all the circumstances," not that which a few of the circumstances
might create. We find no parallel liability before, and we think no
new one has been created by, this Act. Its effect is to waive immunity
from recognized causes of action and was not to visit the Government
with novel and unprecedented liabilities.

It is not without significance as to whether the Act should be
construed to apply to service-connected injuries that it makes
". . . the law of the place where the act or omission occurred" govern any consequent liability. 28 U. S. C. §1346(b). This provision
recognizes and assimilates into federal law the rules of substantive
law of the several states, among which divergencies are notorious.
This perhaps is fair enough when the claimant is not on duty or is
free to choose his own habitat and thereby limit the jurisdiction in
which it will be possible for federal activities to cause him injury.
That his tort claims should be governed by the law of the location
where he has elected to be is just as fair when the defendant is the
Government as when the defendant is a private individual. But a
soldier on active duty has no such choice and must serve any place
or, under modern conditions, any number of places in quick succes-
sion in the forty-eight states, the Canal Zone, or Alaska, or Hawaii,
or any other territory of the United States. That the geography of an
injury should select the law to be applied to his tort claims makes
no sense. We cannot ignore the fact that most states have abolished
the common-law action for damages between employer and employee
and superseded it with workmen's compensation statutes which provide, in most instances, the sole basis of liability. Absent this, or
where such statutes are inapplicable, states have differing provisions
as to limitations of liability and different doctrines as to assumption
of risk, fellow-servant rules and contributory or comparative negligence. It would hardly be a rational plan of providing for those disabled in service by others in service to leave them dependent upon
geographic considerations over which they have no control and to laws
which fluctuate in existence and value.

The relationship between the Government and members of its
armed forces is "distinctively federal in character," as this Court
recognized in United States v. Standard Oil Co., 332 U.S. 301, wherein
the Government unsuccessfully sought to recover for losses incurred
by virtue of injuries to a soldier. The considerations which lead to
that decision apply with even greater force to this case:

". . . To whatever extent state law may apply to
govern the relations between soldiers or others in the

armed forces and persons outside them or nonfederal
governmental agencies, the scope, nature, legal incidents
and consequences of the relation between persons in
service and the Government are fundamentally derived
from federal sources and governed by federal authority.
See Tarble's Case, 13 Wall. 397; Kurtz v. Moffitt, 115
U.S. 487. . . ." Pp. 305-306.

No federal law recognizes a recovery such as claimants seek. The
Military Personnel Claims Act, 31 U. S. C. §223b (now superseded by
28 U. S. C. §2672), permitted recovery in some circumstances, but it
specifically excluded claims of military personnel "incident to their
service."
    This Court, in deciding claims for wrongs incident to service
under the Tort Claims Act, cannot escape attributing some bearing
upon it to enactments by Congress which provide systems of simple,
certain, and uniform compensation for injuries or death of those in
armed services. We might say that the claimant may (a) enjoy both
types of recovery, or (b) elect which to pursue, thereby waiving the
other, or (c) pursue both, crediting the larger liability with the proceeds of the smaller, or (d) that the compensation and pension remedy
excludes the tort remedy. There is as much statutory authority for
one as for another of these conclusions. If Congress had contemplated
that this Tort Act would be held to apply in cases of this kind, it is
difficult to see why it should have omitted any provision to adjust these
two types of remedy to each other. The absence of any such adjustment is persuasive that there was no awareness that the Act might be
interpreted to permit recovery for injuries incident to military service.
    A soldier is at peculiar disadvantage in litigation. Lack of time
and money, the difficulty if not impossibility of procuring witnesses,
are only a few of the factors working to his disadvantage. And the few
cases charging superior officers or the Government with neglect or
mis-conduct which have been brought since the Tort Claims Act, of
which the present are typical, have either been suits by widows or
surviving dependents, or have been brought after the individual was
discharged. The compensation system, which normally requires no
litigation, is not negligible or niggardly, as these cases demonstrate.
The recoveries compare extremely favorably with those provided by
most workmen's compensation statutes. In the Jefferson case, the
District Court considered actual and prospective payments by the
Veterans' Administration as diminution of the verdict. Plaintiff received $3,645.50 to the date of the court's computation and on esti-
mated life expectancy under existing legislation would prospectively
receive $31,947 in addition. In the Griggs case, the widow, in the
two-year period after her husband's death, received payments in excess of $2,100. In addition, she received $2,695, representing the six
months' death gratuity under the Act of December 17, 1919, as
amended, 41 Stat. 367, 57 Stat. 599, 10 U. S. C. §903. It is estimated

that her total future pension payments will aggregate $18,000. Thus the widow will receive an amount in excess of $22,000 from Government gratuities, whereas she sought and could seek under state law only $15,000, the maximum permitted by Illinois for death.

It is contended that all these considerations were before the Court in the Brooks case and that allowance of recovery to Brooks requires a similar holding of liability here. The actual holding in the Brooks case can support liability here only by ignoring the vital distinction there stated. The injury to Brooks did not arise out of or in the course of military duty. Brooks was on furlough, driving along the highway, under compulsion of no orders or duty and on no military mission. A government owned and operated vehicle collided with him. Brooks' father, riding in the same car, recovered for his injuries and the Government did not further contest the judgment but contended that there could be no liability to the sons, solely because they were in the Army. This Court rejected the contention, primarily because Brooks' relationship while on leave was not analogous to that of a soldier injured while performing duties under orders.

We conclude that the Government is not liable under the Federal Tort Claims Act for injuries to servicemen where the injuries arise out of or are in the course of activity incident to service. Without exception, the relationship of military personnel to the Government has been governed exclusively by federal law. We do not think that Congress, in drafting this Act, created a new cause of action dependent on local law for service-connected injuries or death due to negligence. We cannot impute to Congress such a radical departure from established law in the absence of express congressional command. Accordingly, the judgments in the Feres and Jefferson cases are affirmed and that in the Griggs case is reversed.

Nos. 9 and 29, affirmed.

No. 31, reversed.

MR. JUSTICE DOUGLAS concurs in the result.

---

The "incident to service" test set forth in the Feres case has engendered a great deal of litigation in the lower Federal Courts, but the Supreme Court has not decided any other cases concerning this issue. It has been held that incident to service includes more than actual performance of duty by plaintiff at time of injury; for example, the widow and children of a serviceman who was riding in a car from a South Dakota military base to Seattle to receive training with respect to a new type of airplane and who was killed as the result of the negligence of another serviceman driving on service business were denied recovery because the decedent was traveling under military orders (Callaway v. Gerber, 289 F.2d 171 [9th Cir. 1961], certiorari denied 368 U.S. 874 [1961]). On the other hand, when the serviceman has been riding in a car while on leave or pass, recovery has been allowed. See, inter alia, Knecht v. U.S., 242 F.2d 929 (3rd Cir. 1957). To the apparent temporal requirement that recovery is barred if the serviceman is injured during activities incident to service, some Courts have distinguished situations on a purely geographic basis; hence, recovery was denied when a U.S. aircraft crashed into an officer's post quarters killing him while he slept but was allowed when a similar incident occurred off post. Compare Orken v. U.S., 239 F.2d 850 (6th Cir. 1958) with Sapp v. U.S., 153 F.Supp. 496 (W.D. La. 1957).

One of the reasons cited in Feres and other cases for withholding the right of recovery is the substantial scheme of other benefits available to the serviceman or his dependents through administrative action. For example, the Military Personnel and Civilian Employees Claims Act of 1964 provided for the settlement of claims of military personnel for damage to or loss of personal property incident to service. This Act affords no compensation for personal injury or death. The Military Claims Act (10 U.S.C. 2733) does allow such recovery for injuries incident to a "noncombat activity," but severe administrative restrictions are placed on such recovery. There are other claims statutes that allow limited recovery in certain situations. See, e.g. 10 U.S.C. 2734 and 10 U.S.C. 2737. The settlement of claims under these statutes is often decentralized throughout the armed services to certain judge advocates and legal officers.

The foregoing pertains to claims against the United States. Judge advocates and legal officers are also engaged in the investigation and preparation of claims in favor of the United States. For example, Sections 2651 and 2652 of Title 42 of the United States Code provide as follows:

§2651. Recovery by United States--Conditions; exceptions; persons liable; amount of recovery; subrogation; assignment

(a)  In any case in which the United States is authorized or required by law to furnish hospital, medical, surgical, or dental care and treatment (including prostheses and medical appliances) to a person who is injured or suffers a disease, after the effective date of this Act, under circumstances creating a tort liability upon some third person (other than or in addition to the United States and except employers of seamen treated under the provisions of section 249 of this title) to pay damages therefor, the United States shall have a right to recover from said third person the reasonable value of the care and treatment so furnished or to be furnished and shall, as to this right be subrogated to any right or claim that the injured or diseased person, his guardian, personal representative, estate, dependents, or survivors has against such third person to the extent of the reasonable value of the care and treatment so furnished or to be furnished. The head of the department or agency of the United States furnishing such care or treatment may also require the injured or diseased person, his guardian, personal representative, estate, dependents, or survivors, as appropriate, to assign his claim or cause of action against the third person to the extent of that right or claim.

Enforcement procedure; intervention; joinder of parties;<br>State or Federal court proceedings

(b) The United States may, to enforce such right, (1) intervene or join in any action or proceeding brought by the injured or diseased person, his guardian, personal representative, estate, dependents, or survivors, against the third person who is liable for the injury or disease; or (2) if such action or proceeding is not commenced within six months after the first day in which care and treatment is furnished by the United States in connection with the injury or disease involved, institute and prosecute legal proceedings against the third person who is liable for the injury or disease, in a State or Federal court, either alone (in its own name or in the name of the injured person, his guardian, personal representative, estate, dependents, or survivors) or in conjunction with the injured or diseased person, his guardian, personal representative, estate, dependents, or survivors.

Veterans' exception

(c) The provisions of this section shall not apply with respect to hospital, medical, surgical, or dental care and treatment (including prostheses and medical appliances) furnished by the Veterans' Administration to an eligible veteran for a service-connected disability under the provisions of chapter 17 of Title 38. Pub.L. 87-693, §1, Sept. 25, 1962, 76 Stat. 593.

§2652.   Regulations--Determination and establishment of reasonable value of care and treatment

(a) The President may prescribe regulations to carry out this chapter, including regulations with respect to the determination and establishment of the reasonable value of the hospital, medical, surgical, or dental care and treatment (including prostheses and medical applicances) furnished or to be furnished.

### Settlement, release and waiver of claims

(b)  To the extent prescribed by regulations under subsection (a) of this section, the head of the department or agency of the United States concerned may (1) compromise, or settle and execute a release of, any claim which the United States has by virtue of the right established by section 2651 of this title; or (2) waive any such claim, in whole or in part, for the convenience of the Government, or if he determines that collection would result in undue hardship upon the person who suffered the injury or disease resulting in care or treatment described in section 2651 of this title.

### Damages recoverable for personal injury unaffected

(c)  No action taken by the United States in connection with the rights afforded under this legislation shall operate to deny to the injured person the recovery for that portion of his damage not covered hereunder.  Pub.L. 87-693, §2, Sept. 25, 1962, 76 Stat. 593.

Judge advocates and legal officers at various command levels have been delegated authority to initiate and settle claims under the above statute.  If the claim is to be asserted through litigation, such action must be taken by the Department of Justice.

## PURPOSE

Section 510 of the Appendix to Title 50 of the United States Code reads as follows:

§510.   Purpose; suspension of enforcement of civil liabilities

In order to provide for, strengthen, and expedite the national defense under the emergent conditions which are threatening the peace and security of the United States and to enable the United States the more successfully to fulfill the requirements of the national defense, provision is made to suspend enforcement of civil liabilities, in certain cases, of persons in the military service of the United States in order to enable such persons to devote their entire energy to the defense needs of the Nation, and to this end the following proceedings and transactions which may prejudice the civil rights of persons in such service during the period herein specified over which this Act [sections 501-548 and 560-590 of this Appendix] remains in force. Oct. 17, 1940, c. 888, §100, 54 Stat. 1179.

### BOWSMAN v. PETERSON

United States District Court, Nebraska, 1942.
45 F. Supp. 742.

DELEHANT, District Judge.
In an action to recover judgment for personal injuries and property damage allegedly resulting from an automobile collision, the defendant, upon written motion, supported by affidavits, seeks a stay of proceedings under the provisions of the Soldiers and Sailors Civil Relief Act of 1940, 50 U.S.C.A. Appendix §521 et seq., for the

519

period of his military service in the United States Army into which he has been inducted since the institution of the suit, and for three months thereafter.

Counsel for the parties have submitted the issue to the court by oral argument. Without neglecting the possibility that recourse to the indulgence of the act may be available, and actually had, in many instances where the legitimate protection of the person in the country's service is more apparent than real, the court is convinced that the stay must be allowed; and the motion is, therefore, being sustained.

It has been said that, ordinarily, "to be a sufficient ground for a continuance, it must appear that the absence of a party is unavoidable and not voluntary, that the party's presence is necessary, that the application is made in good faith, and that the party will be able to attend at some reasonable future time." 17 C.J.S., Continuances, §27, p. 210 (see also 9 R.C.L. 551, Title Continuances Sec. 8).

In this instance, the inevitability of absence must be affirmed upon the premise of the national emergency, irrespective of the basis of the defendant's induction into the military service. The necessity of the presence of a party at the trial of a civil action for damages against him is admittedly not absolute, but it is at least reasonable. Within due limitations, he ought to be allowed to testify personally before the jury rather than through the notoriously indifferent medium of deposition. He should be allowed to scrutinize the jury list, to confront the jury as it is empanelled to observe the responses of its members on the voir dire examination, to make suggestions and have them and his preferences and his possible relation to the jurymen considered, in the very important step of peremptory challenges. He should, if reasonably possible, have the opportunity to be personally before the court and the jury during the entire progress of his trial, manifesting his interest in its event and allowing those charged with the burden of decision to observe him, either for his advantage or to his possible detriment. The good faith of the present application is not seriously in question. As to the defendant's probable attendance upon trial "at some reasonable future time", the court, in the current circumstances, will abstain from clairvoyance; but will give the applicant the full benefit of any uncertainty upon the point.

So, even in the absence of a controlling statute, the court would be disposed to grant some indefinite and discretionarily terminable continuance upon the defendant's request. Both upon considerations of general judicial discretion and on the basis of precedent such indulgence may be supported.

But here the statute seems to be imperatively controlling both as to the necessity for the stay, 50 U.S.C.A. Appendix §521, and for practical purposes, as to its duration, 50 U.S.C.A. Appendix §524.

. . .

The Soldiers and Sailors Civil Relief Act of 1940 (in like manner with all similar previous acts in our history) was prompted by

at least two considerations, first, the maintenance in the armed forces
of a reasonable measure of that unbothered serenity and security in
respect of personal responsibilities which effectively promotes military efficiency and the national defense; and secondly, the assurance
that in the field of individual justice no advantage in judicial proceedings by or against a soldier or sailor will result from his absorption
in his country's defense.

The soldier or sailor in seasons of war has neither time nor
mental aptitude for litigation.  Without unnecessary discussion, it may
simply be stated that while the Act recognizes that in some instances
"the ability of . . . the defendant to conduct his defense is not materially affected by reason of his military service", such instances will
be relatively rare.  And the court is not made aware of any circumstances upon which it may be concluded that this is one of them.

There is nothing novel either in the legislation which the defendant now invokes, or in the policy of judicial and social indulgence
towards the absent soldier.  Only presumption would impel a judge,
in a memorandum of this character, to assemble from legal and general literature the abundant examples of the latter grace.  And as to
the former, it will be sufficient merely to mention the numerous
statutes enacted during the Civil War upon the point (vide: 13 C.J.
143, Title, Continuances Sec. 42(2), Note 68 and cases cited; 17 C.J.S.,
Continuances, §30) and the more recent Soldiers and Sailors Civil
Relief Act of 1918, 50 U.S.C.A. Appendix §101, et seq., especially
Secs. 112 and 115.

It may be granted that a continuance will probably operate at
least temporarily and perhaps permanently to the disadvantage of
the plaintiff.  That result is unfortunate.  But it is a reasonable exaction by society from one of its members for its own preservation;
a proper imposition by the state upon an individual citizen in the
course of its discharge of its constitutional obligation to "provide for
the common Defence".

## HUNT v. JACOBSON

Supreme Court, New York, 1942.
178 Misc. 201, 33 N.Y.S. 2d 661.

EDER, Justice.

Ex parte application.  Judgment of foreclosure and sale is
sought in an action brought to foreclose a mortgage on real property.
It appears that none of the defendants are in the military service of
the United States except the defendant Harold P. Janpole, who was
personally served in this action but has entered no appearance herein that at the time said service was effected he was in the military
service of the United States, at Camp Dix, in New Jersey.

This court is requested to incorporate in the judgment, in the
exercise of discretion, a finding that in its opinion the ability of said

defendant Janpole to comply with the terms of the mortgage under foreclosure herein is not materially affected by reason of the fact that he is or may be in such military service as defined in the Act of Congress known as the Soldiers' and Sailors' Civil Relief Act of 1940, 50 U.S.C.A. Appendix, §501 et seq., Act of October 17, 1940, c. 888, 54 Stat. 1178.

. . .

No application for a stay under the provisions of the Act has been made by the said defendant, the court is advised that said defendant Janpole is a member of the Bar of this state; it may therefore be presumed he is cognizant of his rights under said Act.

. . .

Statutes enacted for the benefit of persons engaged in military service are a recognized institution in this country, and, being remedial, are to be construed liberally (Greening v. Sheffield, Minor, Ala., 276), possessing as they do, attributes of privilege and exemption (Land Title & Trust Co. v. Rambo, 174 Pa. 566, 34 A. 207), and it has been held that even in the absence of such a statute public policy demands the recognition of such exemption. Land Title & Trust Co. v. Rambo, supra.

While such exemption, as respects civil actions, is by the Act under consideration made applicable to persons in the military service of the United States, such protection has also been enacted for persons engaged in the military service of a state. Cases, supra; Andrews v. Gardiner, 185 App. Div. 477, 173 N.Y.S. 1; People ex rel. Gaston v. Campbell, 40 N.Y. 133.

Section 100 of Article I of the Act, 50 U.S.C.A. Appendix §510, entitled "Purpose of Act; suspension of enforcement of civil liabilities," declares: "In order to provide for, strengthen, and expedite the national defense under the emergent conditions which are threatening the peace and security of the United States and to enable the United States the more successfully to fulfill the requirements of the national defense, provision is hereby made to suspend enforcement of civil liabilities, in certain cases, of persons in the military service of the United States in order to enable such persons to devote their entire energy to the defense needs of the Nation, and to this end the following provisions are made for the temporary suspension of legal proceedings and transactions which may prejudice the civil rights of persons in such service during the period herein specified over which this Act remains in force." [Emphasis Editor's.]

The purpose of such enactments is to relieve a person so engaged in military service from the mental distress occasioned by the handicap of his being in the military service, resulting in his inability to function with the freedom of action which he possessed prior to his induction into the military establishment, causing inability to meet financial and other obligations and commitments, the mental distress resulting from inability to adequately protect legal rights and interests or to make proper defense to suit brought against him, it being recognized that such distress has the tendency to impair his efficiency as a member of the militia, and, as well, the tendency to impair his efficiency as a member of the militia, and, as well, the tendency to impair the efficiency of the organization with which he may be associated:--the design was "to prevent interference with military duties." Andrews v. Gardiner, supra [185 App.Div. 477, 173 N.Y.S. 2].

To meet this situation, and to overcome this condition, if possible, such statutes are enacted whereby he is given a degree of mental repose through the intervention of the court for his protection to the end that this rights and remedies shall not be imperiled or jeopardized in consequence of such military service. This does not mean to imply that the statute is to be made applicable to every situation, without limitation, merely because such person is in the military service; it is not to be employed as a vehicle of oppression or abuse; its invocation is not to be permitted for any needless or unwarranted purpose; it is to be administered as an instrument to accomplish substantial justice. This is plainly indicated by the very language of section 532,--"unless in the opinion of the court the ability of the defendant to comply with the terms of the obligation is not materially affected by reason of his military service" and empowering the court to make such disposition of the case "as may be equitable to conserve the interests of all parties." (Emphasis mine.) In other words, as illustrated by Andrews v. Gardiner, 185 App.Div. 477, 173 N.Y.S. 1, 2, which involved an exemption provision of the Military Law of this state, "The statute should be construed to accomplish the purpose for which it was enacted. . . ."

The criterion, then, is the combination of two factors, i. e. (1) whether the defendant's inability to comply results by reason of such military service, and (2) that such military service has materially affected the ability to comply.

This determination can only be properly arrived at by an examination of the facts.

In the instant case it appears that the said defendant is only a nominal party to the action having merely a one-sixth interest in a mortgage, which, if still unpaid, is nevertheless subordinate to the mortgage being foreclosed herein; it is set forth that no personal judgment is sought or will be sought against the said defendant; it also appears that the mortgage under foreclosure herein is dated May 14, 1906, and was duly recorded on May 15, 1906; that said defendant has no equity of redemption or other claim or interest arising out of this mortgage.

In this state of the record I am of the opinion that the plaintiff is entitled to the finding sought and it is so adjudged. Judgment of foreclosure and sale signed.

## PERSONS PROTECTED

Section 511 of the Act reads in part:

(1) The term "persons in military service" and the term "persons in the military service of the United States", as used in this Act [sections 501-548 and 560-590 of this Appendix], shall include the following persons and no others: All members of the Army of the United States, the United States Navy, the Marine Corps, the Coast Guard, and all officers of the Public Health Service detailed by proper authority for duty either with the Army or the Navy. The term "military service", as used in this Act [said sections], shall signify Federal service on active duty with any branch of service heretofore referred to or mentioned as well as training or education under the supervision of the United States preliminary to induction into the military service. The terms "active service" or "active duty" shall include the period during which a person in military service is absent from duty on account of sickness, wounds, leave, or other lawful cause.

### MANTZ v. MANTZ

Court of Common Pleas of Ohio, Summit County, 1946.
69 N.E.2d 637.

EMMONS, Judge.
This cause came on to be heard upon the petition of the plaintiff and the evidence, and the Court finds that Henry Mantz, the defendant, is confined in Camp Bowie, Texas, under a general court martial for a period of five years and sentenced to be dishonorably discharged at the termination of his sentence and to forfeit all pay and allowances due or to become due.

The Court finds that a copy of the petition, together with summons and motion for temporary alimony and support, was sent to this defendant by registered mail; that an affidavit for publication had been made, and that service by publication had been completed.

The Court finds that plaintiff and defendant were married in 1938; that the plaintiff has been a resident of the State of Ohio and Summit County for more than a year immediately last past from the filing of her petition in divorce; that the plaintiff and defendant have four children as issue of said marriage: Carol, aged six; Karl, aged two; Alyce and Henry, twins, aged six months. That the defendant is guilty of gross neglect of duty as charged in the petition, and that the plaintiff is entitled to a divorce as prayed for.

An interesting question arises in this case as to whether the defendant, being a prisoner under general court martial, still has the protection under the Soldiers' and Sailors' Civil Relief Act of 1940, 50 U.S.C.A. Appendix, §501 et seq.

. . .

It is true that the defendant was drafted into the Army of the United States, but the question is whether he is still considered to be in active service or duty. He is not absent from duty because of sickness, wounds or leave, so his absence can only be excused under the head of other lawful causes. He was lawfully committed under general court martial, but the cause of this incarceration was an illegal one under army rules and regulations. The benefits of the Soldiers' and Sailors' Relief Act are extended to those who are in active service or duty and do not inure to benefit or protect those who through their voluntary aggressions and conduct remove themselves from the role of soldiers and sailors in active service or duty.

It would be asinine to imagine that the law was passed to grant a cloak of immunity from civil laws of the state by way of the Soldiers' and Sailors' Relief Act to one who stands in the position of a felon, having been convicted by general court martial.

It does not matter in this instance whether a dishonorable discharge is to come in the future or not; his pay as a soldier has stopped; those dependent upon him for support no longer get the government allotment; the government certainly does not regard him as a soldier on active duty or service, and this Court takes the same attitude. Wilson v. Wilson, 14 Ohio Supp. 92.

It is within the province of the Court to protect the wife and children and to see that a sufficient amount is awarded them to provide for the reasonable necessaries of life while the defendant is in military service, and service by publication is sufficient to decree the relief sought.

I do not mean to infer that commitment for any violation of the army's rules and regulations would divest the soldier of his rights under the Soldiers' and Sailors' Relief Act, but the gravity of the offense charged and the sentence of the court martial are factors which must be considered in determining this question.

Considering the facts in this case, the Court therefore finds that the defendant is not entitled to the immunities and benefits under the Soldiers' and Sailors' Relief Act, that he is not actively on duty or in service in the army, and therefore, since he cannot be served in the State of Ohio with summons, service by publication is properly made.

. . .

## BORREGO v. del PALACIO

Court of Civil Appeals of Texas, 1969.
445 S.W.2d 620.

WARD, Justice.

## OPINION

In County Court at Law No. One, El Paso County, Texas, Edward del Palacio filed suit against Joe Borrego, Leo Escandon, and Oscar Madrid to recover certain musical instruments and rental for their use. We will refer to the parties as they appeared in the trial court. Citations were duly issued and served on the defendants. Pursuant to notice to show cause, the court, on January 19, 1968, issued a temporary injunction restraining and enjoining the defendants from disposing of or damaging the instruments in question. This order recites that the defendants appeared by and through their attorney and the same appears to have been approved by their attorney of record. No answer in any form was ever filed by the defendants to the suit on file. On August 7, 1968, default judgment was entered by the court without a jury, in favor of the plaintiff. . . .

. . .

The defendants, by two of their points, complain of the failure of the plaintiff to comply with the Soldiers' and Sailors' Civil Relief Act in any of its requirements. 50 U.S.C.A. Appendix §520. A default judgment, taken without the affidavit or other requirements of section 520, is not rendered void, but merely voidable at the instance of the service man upon proper showing of prejudice and injury. The act is for the exclusive benefit of the service man. He alone can take advantage of it, and then only upon showing that his interest has been deleteriously affected. These principles seem to be well settled by adjudicated cases upon the subject. Mims Bros. v. N. A. James, Inc., Tex. Civ. App., 174 S.W.2d 276 (refused 141 Tex. 554, 175 S.W.2d 74). A default judgment against these defendants could not be opened because the plaintiff failed to file an affidavit showing the defendants were not in the military service, unless the record shows that the defendants were, as a matter of fact, in the military service. The record in this case does not so reflect, nor is there even any claim made by the defendants to this effect. These points are overruled.

. . .

The judgment of the trial court is affirmed.

## NASSAU SAV. & LOAN ASS'N v. ORMOND

Supreme Court, Queens County, 1942.
179 Misc. 447, 39 N.Y.S.2d 92.

DALY, Justice.

Application pursuant to the Soldiers' and Sailors' Civil Relief Act of 1940, as amended October 6, 1942, Public Law 732, 77th Congress, 50 U.S.C.A. Appendix §501 et seq., 530, for an order to stay the plaintiff from proceeding with the instant action to foreclose a mortgage.

The moving defendant, Johanna V. Ormond, and her brother, the defendant John J. Carey, are the co-owners of the one family house covered by a bond and mortgage executed by them on June 25, 1931, and upon which there is an unpaid balance of $2,633.67. Since October 1, 1942, there has been a default in the payment of $35 per month, required to be paid under said mortgage on account of principal and interest. In addition the defendants have failed to pay real estate taxes commencing with the October, 1940, payment, as well as an assessment levied against the property; the total tax arrears and assessment amount to $495.60.

According to the motion papers the son of the moving defendant contributed to the household prior to his induction into the armed forces of the United States, the sum of $20 each week, and her husband is receiving the sum of $60 per month from the New York Telephone Company, which retired him in November, 1941, because of illness. The co-owner, John Carey, is said to contribute nothing to the upkeep of the house and has in fact been a drain on the family resources. Under these circumstances it is contended that all proceedings should be stayed unconditionally without requiring any payments whatsoever to be made.

The plaintiff has offered to accept interest at the rate of 4% plus a reasonable amount on account of the arrears of taxes, plus the payment of current taxes. This has been refused. Upon the instant application the plaintiff contends that if a stay be granted "there should be some arrangement made in the order for the payment of interest and taxes".

Section 306 of the 1942 Amendment, 50 U.S.C.A. Appendix, §536, provides that "Dependents of a person in military service shall be entitled to the benefits accorded to persons in military service under the provisions of this article upon application to a court therefor, unless in the opinion of the court the ability of such dependents to comply with the terms of the obligation, contract, lease, or bailment has not been materially impaired by reason of the military service of the person upon whom the applicants are dependent". Thus, "Article III . . . Rent, Installment Contracts, Mortgages, Liens, Assignments, Leases" of the Act of 1940 has been extended to dependents of persons in military service. Subdivision (2) of Section 302 of said Article, 50 U.S.C.A. Appendix, §532, provides:

"In any proceeding commenced in any court during the period of military service to enforce such obligation arising out of nonpayment of any sum thereunder due or out of any other breach of the terms thereof occurring prior to or during the period of such service the court may, after hearing, in its discretion, on its own motion, and shall, . . . on application to it by such person in military service or some person on his behalf, unless in the opinion of the court the ability of the defendant to comply with the terms of the obligation is not materially affected by reason of his military service--

"(a)   stay the proceedings as provided in this Act; or

"(b)   make such other disposition of the case as may be equitable to conserve the interests of all parties."

This provision, it has been held, "is not to be employed as a
vehicle of oppression or abuse; its invocation is not to be permitted
for any needless or unwarranted purpose; it is to be administered as
an instrument to accomplish substantial justice." Hunt v. Jacobson,
178 Misc. 201, 33 N.Y.S.2d 661, 664. It is clear that complete immunity was not intended; the language of the statute itself authorizes
the court to stay the proceedings or make such other disposition "as
may be equitable to conserve the interests of all parties". (Italics
mine.)

If the movant's son, prior to his induction, contributed to the
support of the household, as contended in the moving papers, a large
part of such contribution may be continued under the Servicemen's
Dependents Allowance Act of 1942, 37 U.S.C.A. §201 et seq. Under
said Act, in addition to the serviceman's contribution of $22 per month,
the Government will contribute $15 per month to one parent, if one
only, and an additional $5 for each brother or sister, the whole not to
total more than $50, or $25 to two parents and an additional $5 for each
additional brother or sister, the whole not to total more than $50.

It seems clear under the circumstances that the stay should not
be unconditional.  The allotment by the son and the allowance by the
government, plus the pension received by the movant's husband, are
sufficient to justify the payment of current taxes on the property in
order to maintain the status quo at least to some extent.  Accordingly
the application will be granted on condition that the defendants pay to
the plaintiff the sum of $15 per month commencing February 1, 1943.
This sum will be applied to the payment of current taxes and if any
balance remains, such balance will be paid on account of the tax arrears.

Settle order on notice.


## SPECIFIC RIGHTS


Section 521 of the act provides for proceedings, in which a member of the military service is a plaintiff or defendant, to be stayed on
his application unless in the opinion of the Court the ability to prosecute or defend is not materially affected by his service.  Section 523
of the act provides for a stay upon his application or on the Court's
own motion of any judgment entered against him and any attachment
or garnishment of property.

## McCOY v. McSORLEY

Court of Appeals of Georgia, 1969.
119 Ga. App. 603, 168 S.E.2d 202.

BELL, Presiding Judge.

1. Under the Soldier's and Sailors' Civil Relief Act, the trial courts have a discretion in granting or denying stays in judicial proceedings where persons in the military service of the United States are involved. Of course, the Act should be liberally construed in favor of the serviceman. The discretion denying a stay may be exercised where the court concludes from all the circumstances of the case that the civil rights of the serviceman will not be prejudiced. 50 U.S.C.A. App. §§510, 521. The Supreme Court of Georgia has recognized the existence of the discretion to deny stays. Gates v. Gates, 197 Ga. 11, 28 S.E.2d 108; Lankford v. Milhollin, 197 Ga. 227, 28 S.E.2d 752. And so has the Supreme Court of the United States. Boone v. Lightner, 319 U.S. 561, 63 S.Ct. 1223, 87 L.Ed. 1587. The discretion is not an absolute one, but virtually no discretion is absolute. In all cases the exercise of discretion will be reversed only where it is abused. Historically this has been the policy of the Georgia Appellate Courts. Williamson v. Lunsford, 119 Ga.App. 240 (4), 166 S.E.2d 622. Here, the serviceman was the driver of the vehicle in which the plaintiff's daughter was riding at the time of the collision in which she was killed. The serviceman was sued as a party along with his father under the family purpose car doctrine. At the hearing on the motion for a stay under the Soldiers' and Sailors' Civil Relief Act, the deposition of the serviceman consisting of 94 pages of direct and cross examination was in evidence. Also at the hearing the plaintiff stated in a binding and enforceable fashion (see Division 2) that the absent serviceman defendant will not be asked to pay any portion of any judgment which is not payable by his liability insurer. This means simply that if the serviceman has liability insurance, the plaintiff is legally committed not to seek additional sums personally from him beyond that protection. It also means that if the serviceman has no liability insurance, the plaintiff is legally committed not to seek any sum at all from him. Based on all these circumstances, the trial judge concluded that the serviceman's ability to defend himself would not be materially impaired and denied the stay. We cannot say he abused his discretion. It is perfectly proper for a trial judge to consider matters such as these noted here and on these facts to form his opinion and to exercise his discretion by denying a stay. See the numerous decisions annotated in 50 U.S.C.A. App. §521, Notes 11 and 54. Also see the very excellent discussion in Koons v. Nelson, 113 Colo. 574, 160 P.2d 367 [7] [8] [9] [10].

2. Attorneys are expected to exercise exemplary fiducial conduct on behalf of their clients and toward the courts. Code §9-601. The strong presumption arises from an attorney's appearance in court on behalf of a litigant that he is authorized to appear and to act for that party. Edwards v. Wall, 153 Ga. 776, 113 S.E. 190. Clients are bound by statements of their attorneys made in open court. Travelers Ins. Co. v. Miller, 104 Ga.App. 554, 122 S.E.2d 268. The scope of an attorney's authority to act for his client is determined by the contract of his employment. In absence of express restrictions on the attorney's authority in the contract of employment, the authority is plenary. Dean v. Jackson, 219 Ga. 552, 134 S.E.2d 601. Acts of an attorney on behalf of a party cannot be questioned unless wholly unauthorized and then only if the aggrieved party is not guilty of unreasonable delay in acting to correct the improper acts after notice or knowledge of them. Jackson v. Jackson, 199 Ga. 716, 35 S.E.2d 258.

It follows that the solemn pronouncement in open court by plaintiff's counsel, as recited in the order of the trial judge, that no collection would be sought of any judgment against the absent serviceman beyond the limits of liability insurance afforded the serviceman, is binding and enforceable.

The judgment denying the stay is affirmed.

EBERHARDT and DEEN, JJ., concur.

## MOULDER v. STEELE

Court of Appeals of Georgia, 1968.
162 S.E.2d 785.

HALL, Judge.

The plaintiff sued the owner and the driver of an automobile, the son of the owner, alleging that her property was damaged by a collision of the automobile caused by the negligence of the driver. Only the owner was served with process. The trial court denied the plaintiff's motion for summary judgment against the defendant. Thereafter in February 1968 the defendant filed an application for stay under the Soldiers and Sailors Civil Relief Act (50 U.S.C.A. App. §521) alleging that the driver of the vehicle was enlisted in the United States Air Force in February 1967 for four years and was actively engaged and stationed in New Mexico, was expected to be able to return to Atlanta on leave during late December 1968, and was the only witness to the accident except his wife, a passenger in the automobile, who also resided in New Mexico. The court granted the application ordering that the action be stayed until the driver "is able to attend trial or is no longer in military service." On this appeal the plaintiff enumerates as error the order staying the action and the antecedent order denying her motion for summary judgment.

. . .

2. The Soldiers and Sailors Civil Relief Act, supra, provides for stay of proceedings to which persons in military service are parties, it does not authorize a stay because witnesses are in the service. . . .

The trial court erred in granting defendant's application for a stay under the Soldiers and Sailors Civil Relief Act.

. . .

Judgment reversed for the reason stated in Division 2.
BELL, P. J., and QUILLIAN, J., concur.

See Halstead v. Halstead, 165 P.2d 513 (D.C. of Appeal, First District, 1946).

Prior to the entry of a default judgment based on lack of appearance by the defendants, section 520 of the act requires the filing of an affidavit by the plaintiff stating whether the defendant is in the military service. Failure to comply does not affect the validity of a judgment taken by default against a person who was not then in the military service, but if the defendant was in the military service he has a right to apply to reopen the judgment for ninety days after termination of his service. The defendant on application must show that he has a meritorious defense that he was prejudiced from asserting at the time judgment was entered. See In re Cool's Estate, 19 N.J. Misc. 236, 18 A2d 714 (Orphans' Ct. of N.J., Warren County, 1941); Blankenship v. Blankenship, 236 Ala. 297, 82 So.2d 335 (Sup. Ct of Ala., 1955) discussed in 33 N.Y.U. L. Rev. 975 (Nov 1958); and Davidson v. General Finance Corp., 295 F.Supp. 878 (D.C.N.D.Ga., 1968).

Section 525 of the Act reads as follows:

§525.   Statutes of limitations as affected by period of service

The period of military service shall not be included in computing any period now or hereafter to be limited by any law, regulation, or order for the bringing of any action or proceeding in any court, board, bureau, commission, department, or other agency of government by or against any person in military service or by or against his heirs, executors, administrators, or assigns, whether such cause

of action or the right or privilege to institute such action or proceeding shall have accrued prior to or during the period of such service,
nor shall any part of such period which occurs after the date of enactment of the Soldiers' and Sailors' Civil Relief Act Amendments of
1942 [Oct. 6, 1942] be included in computing any period now or hereafter provided by any law for the redemption of real property sold
or forfeited to enforce any obligation, tax or assessment. Oct. 17,
1940, c. 888, §205, 54 Stat. 1181; Oct. 6, 1942, c. 581, §5, 56 Stat.
770.

CALDERON v. CITY OF NEW YORK

Supreme Court, New York County, 1945.
184 Misc. 1057, 55 N.Y.S.2d 674.

KOCH, Justice.
This is an application by defendant to set aside the verdict of
a jury awarding damages of $122,000 in favor of plaintiff against de-
fendant. Sufficient evidence was presented to raise a question of fact
on the issue of negligence. This motion presents two points which
will be here discussed.
Defendant contends that the service of a notice of claim, as required by §394a--1.0, subd. c of the New York City Administrative
Code, L. 1937, Ex.Sess., ch. 929, was not timely and therefore plaintiff's action is barred. Plaintiff was in the military service of the
United States at the time of the occurrence and for the entire six
months during which the notice should have been served. Despite
this conceded fact, defendant nevertheless contends that, 50 U.S.C.A.
Appendix §525 as amended (section 205 Soldiers' and Sailors' Civil
Relief Act) does not relieve plaintiff of the necessity of serving the
proper notice within the statutory period, since a statute requiring
a plaintiff to serve a "notice of claim" is not strictly a statute of
limitation. In the opinion of this Court, it is entirely immaterial
what label or legal designation be applied to the notice of claim,--
whether it be called a statute of limitation, a condition precedent,
or even a "circumstance necessary to the creation of such right".
The nomenclature is unimportant and defendant's contention is untenable.

. . .
The motion to set aside the verdict and for a new trial is accordingly granted.

## DAMERON v. BRODHEAD*

Supreme Court of the United States, 1953.
345 U.S. 322, 73 S.Ct. 721, 97 L.Ed. 1051.

*[ Footnotes have been omitted. Ed.]

MR. JUSTICE REED delivered the opinion of the Court.

The facts here are simple and undisputed. Petitioner is a commissioned officer of the United States Air Force. He was assigned to duty at Lowry Field, near Denver, Colorado, in 1948 and, throughout that year, resided in a privately rented apartment in that city. Respondent, acting Manager of Revenue and ex-officio Treasurer and Assessor of the City and County of Denver, assessed a tax of $23.51 on his personal property, mostly household goods in the apartment, which he valued at $460, by virtue of 4A Colorado Statutes Annotated (1935 ed.), c. 142. Petitioner paid the tax under protest, and sued to recover. His complaint pleaded as a fact that he, "during the whole of the calendar year 1948, and for many years prior thereto, was, and at the present time is, a citizen and a resident of the State of Louisiana, domiciled in the Town of Port Allen, in the Parish of West Baton Rouge, in the State of Louisiana, and remains a domiciliary of that town, parish, and state, and a citizen and resident of said state, in which during all of the period of time pertinent hereto the plaintiff was and is a qualified voter." He claimed that §514 of the Soldiers' and Sailors' Civil Relief Act, 54 Stat. 1186, as amended, 56 Stat. 777, 58 Stat. 722, 50 U. S. C. App. §§501, 574, therefore forbade imposition of the Colorado tax. Respondent moved to dismiss, argument was had and the trial court entered judgment for petitioner. The Colorado Supreme Court, on appeal, reversed. Cass v. Dameron, 125 Colo. 477, 244 P. 2d 1082. It held that the purpose of the statute was to prevent multiple taxation of military personnel, but that since Louisiana had not taxed petitioner's personal property, Colorado was free to do so. Our grant of certiorari rested on 28 U. S. C. §1257 (3). 344 U.S. 891.

Section 514 of the Act was added, in large part, in 1942. It then provided essentially that:

> "For the purposes of taxation in respect of any person, or of his property, income, or gross income, by any State, Territory, possession, or political subdivision of any of the foregoing, or by the District of Columbia, such person shall not be deemed to have lost a residence or domicile in any State, Territory, possession, or political subdivision of any of the foregoing, or in the District of Columbia, solely by reason of being absent therefrom in compliance with military or naval orders, or to have

> acquired a residence or domicile in, or to have become
> resident in or a resident of, any other State, Territory,
> possession, or political subdivision of any of the fore-
> going, or the District of Columbia, while, and solely by
> reason of being, so absent."

The 1944 Amendment thereto, which is crucial here, first concerned
personal property taxes. It stated:

> "personal property shall not be deemed to be located or
> present in or to have a situs for taxation in such State,
> Territory, possession, or political subdivision, or dis-
> trict."

It also interpolated "personal" in the second line of §514 (1). 58 Stat.
722.

Respondent's argument that the statute in this form cannot
affect Colorado's attempt to tax petitioner is two-fold--either it does
not apply or is unconstitutional.

The constitutionality of federal legislation exempting servicemen from the substantial burdens of seriate taxation by the states in
which they may be required to be present by virtue of their service,
cannot be doubted. Generally similar relief has often been accorded
other types of federal operations or functions. And we have upheld
the validity of such enactments, even when they reach beyond the
activities of federal agencies and corporations to private parties who
have seen fit to contract to carry on functions of the Federal Government. Carson v. Roane-Anderson Co., 342 U.S. 232, and cases cited;
cf. James v. Dravo Contracting Co., 302 U.S. 134, 160-161.

Nor do we see any distinction between those cases and this.
Surely, respondent may not rely on the fact that petitioner here is not
a business contractor. He is not the less engaged in a function of the
Federal Government merely because his relationship is not entirely
economic. We have, in fact, generally recognized the especial burdens
of required service with the armed forces in discussing the compen-
sating benefits Congress provides. Le Maistre v. Leffers, 333 U.S.
1; Boone v. Lightner, 319 U.S. 561. Cf. Board of Commissioners v.
Seber, 318 U.S. 705. Petitioner's duties are directly related to an
activity which the Constitution delegated to the National Government,
that "to declare War," U.S. Const., Art. I, §8, cl. 11, and "to raise
and support Armies." Ibid., cl. 12. Since this is so, congressional
power such as this statute must be upheld. Pittman v. Home Owners'
Corp., 308 U.S. 21, 32-33; Federal Land Bank v. Bismarck Co., 314
U.S. 95, 102-104. Carson v. Roane-Anderson Co., supra, at 234.
What has been said in no way affects the reserved powers of the states
to tax. For this statute merely states that the taxable domicile of
servicemen shall not be changed by military assignments. This we
think is within the federal power.

We turn, then, to the interpretation of the statute within the factual confines of this particular case. Respondent's theory here also has no merit. It is based on the statements of the legislative history that, for instance, the provision was "designed to prevent multiple State taxation." H.R. Rep. No. 2198, 77th Cong., 2d Sess., p. 6. The short answer to the argument that it therefore only applies where multiple taxation is a real possibility is that the plain words of the statute do not say so. In fact, they are much broader: "personal property shall not be deemed to be located or present in or to have a situs for taxation" in the state of temporary presence in any case. There is no suggestion that the state of original residence must have imposed a property tax. Since the language of the section does not establish a condition to its application, we would not be justified in doing so. For we are shown nothing that indicates that a straight-forward application of the language as written would violate or affect the clear purpose of the enactment. See United States v. Public Utilities Comm'n, ante, p. 295, decided today, and cases cited. In fact, though the evils of potential multiple taxation may have given rise to this provision, Congress appears to have chosen the broader technique of the statute carefully, freeing servicemen from both income and property taxes imposed by any state by virtue of their presence there as a result of military orders. It saved the sole right of taxation to the state of original residence whether or not that state exercised the right. Congress, manifestly, thought that compulsory presence in a state should not alter the benefits and burdens of our system of dual federalism during service with the armed forces.

For similar reasons, we reject the argument that the word "deemed" as used implies a rebuttable presumption so as to permit taxation by the state of temporary presence in some cases. Such a construction would nullify the statute. For in every case, the absence of the property from the state of the serviceman's temporary presence would be a fiction, rebuttable by further evidence.

Reversed.

[Dissenting opinion of Justice Douglas, with whom Justice Black concurred, omitted.]

## CALIFORNIA v. BUZARD

Supreme Court of the United States, 1966.
382 U.S. 386, 86 S.Ct. 478, 15 L.Ed.2d 436.

MR. JUSTICE BRENNAN delivered the opinion of the Court.

Section 514 of the Soldier's and Sailors' Civil Relief Act of 1940, 56 Stat. 777, as amended, provides a non-resident serviceman present in a State in compliance with military orders with a broad immunity from that State's personal property and income taxation. Section 514 (2) (b) of the Act further provides that

"the term 'taxation' shall include but not be limited to
licenses, fees, or excises imposed in respect to motor
vehicles or the use thereof: Provided, That the license,
fee, or excise required by the State . . . of which the
person is a resident or in which he is domiciled has been
paid."*

The respondent here, Captain Lyman E. Buzard, was a resident
and domiciliary of the State of Washington stationed at Castle Air
Air Force Base in California. He had purchased an Oldsmobile while
on temporary duty in Alabama, and had obtained Alabama license
plates for it by registering it there. On his return, California
refused to allow him to drive the car on California highways with the
Alabama plates, and, since he had not registered or obtained license
tags in his home State, demanded that he register and obtain license
plates in California. When he sought to do so, it was insisted that he
pay both the registration fee of $8 imposed by California's Vehicle

---

*50 U. S. C. App. §574 (2) (b). Section 514, 50 U. S. C. App.
§574, reads in relevant part as follows:
"(1) For the purposes of taxation in respect of any person, or
of his personal property, income, or gross income, by any State, . . .
such person shall not be deemed to have lost a residence or domicile
in any State, . . . solely by reason of being absent therefrom in
compliance with military or naval orders, or to have acquired a
residence or domicile in, or to have become resident in or a resident
of, any other State, . . . while, and solely by reason of being, so
absent. For the purposes of taxation in respect of the personal
property, income, or gross income of any such person by any State,
. . . of which such person is not a resident or in which he is not
domiciled, . . . personal property shall not be deemed to be located
or present in or to have a situs for taxation in such State, Territory,
possession, or political subdivision, or district. . . .
"(2) When used in this section, (a) the term 'personal property'
shall include tangible and intangible property (including motor vehicles), and (b) the term 'taxation' shall include but not be limited to
licenses, fees, or excises imposed in respect to motor vehicles or
the use thereof: Provided, That the license, fee, or excise required
by the State . . . of which the person is a resident or in which he is
domiciled has been paid." (50 U. S. C. App. §574.)
The unitalicized text was enacted in 1942, 56 Stat. 777. Concern whether nonresident servicemen were sufficiently protected from
personal property taxation by host States led to a clarifying amendment in 1944, 58 Stat. 722. That amendment gave §514 its two subsections. The italicized words in subsection (1) are the relevant
additions to the original section. Subsection (2) was entirely new.

Code* and the considerably larger "license fee" imposed by its Revenue and Taxation Code.** The license fee is calculated at "two (2) percent of the market value of the vehicle," §10752, and is "imposed . . . in lieu of all taxes according to value levied for State or local purposes on vehicles . . . subject to registration under the Vehicle Code. . . ." § 10758. Captain Buzard refused to pay the 2% fee,*** and was prosecuted and convicted for violating Vehicle Code §4000, which provides that "[N]o person shall drive . . . any motor vehicle . . . upon a highway unless it is registered and the appropriate fees have been paid under this code." The conviction, affirmed by the District Court of Appeal, 38 Cal. Rptr. 63, was reversed by the Supreme Court of California, 61 Cal. 2d 833, 395 P. 2d 593. We granted certiorari, 380 U.S. 931, to consider whether §514 barred California from exacting the 2% tax as a condition of registering and licensing Captain Buzard's car. We conclude that it did, and affirm.

The California Supreme Court's reversal of Captain Buzard's conviction depended on its reading of the words "required by" in the proviso of §514 (2) (b). In the context of the entire statute and its prior construction, it gave those words the effect of barring the host State from imposing a motor vehicle "license, fee, or excise" unless (1) there was such a tax owing to and assessed by the home State and (2) that tax had not been paid by the serviceman. The mandatory registration statute of Washington, as of most States, imposes the duty to register only as to cars driven on its highways, and Captain Buzard had not driven his car in Washington during the registration year. The court reasoned that there was thus no "license, fee, or excise" owing to and assessed by his home State. Since there was on this view no tax "required by" Washington, the court concluded that California could not impose its tax, even though Captain Buzard had not paid any Washington tax.

If this reading of the phrase "required by" in the proviso were correct, no host State could impose any tax on the licensing or registration of a serviceman's motor vehicle unless he had not paid taxes

---

*The relevant provisions of the Vehicle Code, enacted in 1935, and recodified in 1959, are §§4000, 4750 and 9250.

**The relevant provisions of the Revenue and Taxation Code, enacted in 1939, are §§10751, 10752 and 10758.

***Captain Buzard did not have sufficient cash to pay the $8 registration fee and the approximately $100 demanded in payment of the 2% tax and penalties. He testified without contradiction that at that time he "didn't refuse to pay" the tax. "He [the registration officer] said, 'Do you want to pay it now?' and I said, 'I don't have the money in cash with me, will you accept a check?' and he said, 'No.'" It was thereafter that Captain Buzard asserted his contention that the tax could not legally be assessed.

actually owing to and assessed by his home State. If the serviceman were under no obligation to his home State, and payment of taxes was a prerequisite of registration or licensing under the host State statutes, the host State authorities might consider themselves precluded from registering and licensing his car. The California court did not confront this consequence of its construction, because it regarded the relevant provisions of California statutes as allowing registration and licensing whether or not taxes were paid; hence, the possibility of unregistered cars using the California highways was thought not to be at issue.* The court's construction, however, pertained to the federal, not the state, statute; if correct, it would similarly restrict the imposition of other host States' registration and licensing tax provisions, whether or not they are as flexible as California's. We must therefore consider the California court's construction in the light of the possibility that in at least some host States, it would permit servicemen to escape registration requirements altogether.

Thus seen, the California court's construction must be rejected. Although little appears in the legislative history to explain the proviso (H.R. Rep. No. 1514, 78th Cong., 2d Sess.; S. Rep. No. 959, 78th Cong., 2d Sess. There were no debates.), Congress was clearly concerned that servicemen stationed away from their home State should not drive unregistered or unlicensed motor vehicles. Every State required in 1944, and requires now, that motor vehicles using its

---

*"Defendant does not contend that California may not, as an exercise of its police power, require him to register his automobile. In fact, his attempt to register the vehicle independently of the payment of fees and penalties was frustrated by the department. Defendant's position is simply that the Soldiers' and Sailors' Civil Relief Act of 1940 . . . prohibits the collection of such fees as an incident to a proper exercise of the police power or otherwise. As a consequence of the narrow question thus raised by the defendant, contentions which look to the purpose of registration in furtherance of proper law enforcement and administration fail to address themselves to the issue." 61 Cal. 2d, at 835, 395 P. 2d, at 594.

The statutory scheme severs the 2% tax provision of the Revenue and Taxation Code from the flat registration fee of $8 requirement in the Vehicle Code. Vehicle Code §4000, under which respondent was prosecuted, refers only to payments of "the appropriate fees . . . under this code" and Vehicle Code §4750 refers only to "the required fee." (Emphasis supplied.) The severability clause of the Revenue and Taxation Code, §26, provides that if application of any provision of that Code to "any person or circumstance, is held invalid . . . the application of the provision to other persons or circumstances, is not affected."

highways be registered and bear license plates.  Such requirements
are designed to facilitate the identification of vehicle owners and the
investigation of accidents, thefts, traffic violations and other violations of law.  Commonly, if not universally, the statutes imposing
the requirements of registration or licensing also prescribe fees
which must be paid to authorize state officials to issue the necessary
documents and plates.  To assure that servicemen comply with the
registration and licensing laws of some State, whether of their home
State or the host State, we construe the phrase "license, fee, or excise required by the State . . ." as equivalent to "license, fee, or
excise of the State. . . ."  Thus read, the phrase merely indicates
Congress' recognition that, in one form or another, all States have
laws governing the registration and licensing of motor vehicles, and
that such laws impose certain taxes as conditions thereof.  The
serviceman who has not registered his car and obtained license plates
under the laws "of" his home State, whatever the reason, may be required by the host State to register and license the car under its laws.

The proviso is to be read, at the least, as assuring that §514
would not have the effect of permitting servicemen to escape the obligation of registering and licensing their motor vehicles.  It has been
argued that §514 (2)(b) also represents a congressional judgment that
servicemen should contribute to the costs of highway maintenance,
whether at home or where they are stationed, by paying whatever
taxes the State of registration may levy for that purpose.  We conclude, however, that no such purpose is revealed in the section or its
legislative history and that its intent is limited to the purpose of
assuring registration.  Since at least the 2% tax here involved has
been held not essential to that purpose as a matter of state law, we
affirm the California Supreme Court's judgment.

It is plain at the outset that California may collect the 2% tax
only if it is a "license, fee, or excise" on a motor vehicle or its use.
The very purpose of §514 in broadly freeing the nonresident serviceman from the obligation to pay property and income taxes was to relieve him of the burden of supporting the governments of the States
where he was present solely in compliance with military orders.
The statute operates whether or not the home State imposes or
assesses such taxes against him.  As we said in Dameron v. Brodhead, 345 U.S. 322, 326, ". . . though the evils of potential multiple
taxation may have given rise to this provision, Congress appears to
have chosen the broader technique of the statute carefully, freeing
servicemen from both income and property taxes imposed by any
state by virtue of their presence there as a result of military orders.
It saved the sole right of taxation to the state of original residence
whether or not that state exercised the right." Motor vehicles were
included as personal property covered by the statute.  Even if Congress meant to do more by the proviso of §514 (2) (b) than insure that
the car would be registered and licensed in one of the two States, it

would be inconsistent with the broad purposes of §514 to read sub-section (2)(b) as allowing the host State to impose taxes other than "licenses, fees, or excises" when the "license, fee, or excise" of the home State is not paid (Contra, Whiting v. City of Portsmouth, 202 Va. 609, 118 S. E. 2d 505; Snapp v. Neal, 250 Miss. 597, 164 So. 2d 752, reversed today, post, p. 397).

. . .

Whatever may be the case under the registration and licensing statutes of other States, California authorities have made it clear that the California 2% tax is not imposed as a tax essential to the registration and licensing of the serviceman's motor vehicle.* Not only did the California Supreme Court regard the statutes as permit-ting registration without payment of the tax, but the District Court of of Appeal, in another case growing out of this controversy, expressly held that "[t]he registration statute has an entirely different purpose from the license fee statutes, and it is clearly severable from them." Buzard v. Justice Court, 198 Cal. App. 2d 814, 817, 18 Cal. Rptr. 348, 349-350 (see note, p. 538). The California Supreme Court also held, in effect, that invalidity of the "license fee" as applied was a valid defense to prosecution under Vehicle Code §4000. In these cir-cumstances, and since the record is reasonably to be read as show-ing that Captain Buzard would have registered his Oldsmobile but for the demand for payment of the 2% tax, the California Supreme Court's reversal of his conviction is

Affirmed.

## SNAPP v. NEAL

Supreme Court of the United States, 1966.
382 U.S. 397, 86 S.Ct. 485, 15 L.Ed.2d 445.

MR. JUSTICE BRENNAN delivered the opinion of the Court.

This is a companion case to California v. Buzard, ante, p. 386, decided today. The State of Mississippi levied an ad valorem tax against a house trailer of the petitioner, Sergeant Jesse E. Snapp. Sergeant Snapp was stationed under military orders at Crystal Springs Air Force Base, Mississippi. He bought the trailer in Mis-sissippi and moved it on Mississippi highways to a private trailer park near the Air Force Base where he placed it on movable con-crete blocks and used it as a home. He did not register or license the trailer, or pay any taxes on it in his home State of South Carolina.

---

*It is not clear from the California courts' opinions whether they regard the $8 registration fee as a fee essential to the registra-tion and licensing of the motor vehicle. Therefore that question re-mains open for determination in the state courts.

He challenged the Mississippi tax as a tax on his personal property prohibited by the Soldiers' and Sailors' Civil Relief Act of 1940, 54 Stat. 1178, as amended in 1944, §514, 50 U. S. C. App. §574.* The Mississippi Supreme Court sustained the levy on the ground that, as applied to motor vehicles, §514 (2) (b) conditions the nonresident serviceman's immunity from its ad valorem tax on the serviceman's prior payment of the fees imposed by his home State. The court reasoned that since §514 (2) (b) "stipulat[es] expressly that the taxation should not be limited to privilege and excise taxes, it necessarily follows that the prohibited tax must include the only other general branch of taxation, that is, ad valorem. It is emphasized that the federal statute is meant to include ad valorem taxes as being one of the taxes for which the serviceman is immune, provided he complies with the laws of his home state concerning registration of the motor vehicle. If he fails to so comply, as was done in this case at bar, he is no longer entitled to protection of the Act of Congress." 250 Miss. 597, at 614-615, 164 So. 2d 752, at 760. We granted certiorari, 380 U.S. 931. We reverse on the authority of our holding today in Buzard that the failure to pay the motor vehicle "license, fee, or excise" of the home State entitles the host State only to exact motor vehicle taxes qualifying as "licenses, fees, or excises"; the ad valorem tax, as the Mississippi Supreme Court acknowledged, is not such an exaction. We thus have no occasion to decide whether the Mississippi Supreme Court was correct in holding that the house trailer was a "motor vehicle" within the meaning of §514 (2) (b).

Reversed.

## SULLIVAN v. UNITED STATES*

Supreme Court of the United States, 1969.
395 U.S. 169, 89 S.Ct. 1648, 23 L.Ed.2d 182.

*[Footnotes have been omitted. Ed.]

MR. JUSTICE STEWART delivered the opinion of the Court.
The issue raised by this appeal is whether §514 of the Soldiers' and Sailors' Civil Relief Act prohibits Connecticut from imposing its sales and use taxes on servicemen stationed there who are residents or domiciliaries of other States. The United States instituted this action in federal court against the appropriate Connecticut officials on behalf of the aggrieved servicemen. The District Court entered a declaratory judgment that the federal statute prevents collection of the sales and use taxes from such servicemen, and the Court of Appeals affirmed. We noted probable jurisdiction of this appeal.

---

*The relevant text of the statute is in California v. Buzard, ante, p. 388, n. 1.

The sales and use taxes imposed by the Connecticut Education, Welfare and Public Health Tax Act are typical of those enacted by the vast majority of States. A tax of 3-1/2% is levied on the gross receipts from sales of tangible personal property at retail within the State. Although the retailer is liable for payment of the tax, he is required to pass it on to purchasers by adding it to the original sales price of all items sold. The use tax is imposed at the same rate on "the storage, use or other consumption" in the State of tangible personal property purchased from any retailer. The use tax provisions-- designed to reach the use or consumption in the State of property purchased outside it--exempt all transactions which are subject to the sales tax. And while the consumer is liable directly to the State for the use tax, he can discharge his liability by paying it to the retailer if the retailer is "engaged in business" within the State and therefore required to collect the use tax. The use tax is also imposed upon purchasers of motor vehicles, boats, or airplanes from non- retailers. The amount of any tax under the Act is reduced by what- ever sales or use tax has already been collected "by any other state or political subdivision thereof." Finally, the Act commands that all proceeds of the sales and use taxes "shall be allocated to and expended for public health, welfare and education purposes only."

By stipulation and affidavits in the District Court, the parties offered some examples of the imposition of these taxes on naval per- sonnel stationed in Connecticut but domiciled elsewhere. Lieutenant Schuman, a Nebraska domiciliary, and Commander Carroll, a Michi- gan domiciliary, bought used motorboats from nonretailers in Connecticut and were assessed a use tax. Schuman paid the tax under protest, and Carroll has refused to pay, each claiming that he is exempt under the Soldiers' and Sailors' Civil Relief Act. Lieu- tenant Commander Shaffer and Commander Foster, who are domi- ciled in Pennsylvania and Texas respectively, each purchased a new car; the Connecticut retailer collected and paid the sales tax. Foster registered his car in Texas, which also exacted a sales or use tax. Finally, Commander Roloff, whose home State is Wisconsin, pur- chased a used car in Florida and paid that State a 2% sales tax. When he registered the car in Connecticut, he was assessed and paid the use tax, with credit for the Florida sales tax.

As enacted in 1942, §514 of the Soldiers' and Sailors' Civil Relief Act provided that for purposes of any state "taxation in re- spect of any person, or of his [personal] property, income, or gross income," he shall not be deemed to have lost his residence or domi- cile in his home State or acquired a residence in any other State "solely by reason of being absent [from home] in compliance with military or naval orders." Clarifying language was added in 1944 to provide that for purposes of taxation in respect of personal prop- erty, the "personal property shall not be deemed to be located or present in or to have a situs for taxation in such State." Also in 1944

Congress enacted a special subsection for automobiles: servicemen
are exempt from "licenses, fees, or excises imposed in respect of
motor vehicles or the use thereof" if they have paid such levies in
their home States. Finally, in 1962, Congress added the provision
that §514 applies to property in any tax jurisdiction other than the
serviceman's home State, "regardless of where the owner may be
serving" in compliance with military orders.

We think it clear from the face of §514 that state taxation of
sales to servicemen is not proscribed. A tax on the privilege of
selling or buying property has long been recognized as distinct from
a tax on the property itself. And while §514 refers to taxes "in respect of" rather than "on" personal property, we think it an overly
strained construction to say that taxation of the sales transaction is
the same as taxation "in respect of" the personal property transacted.
Nor does it matter to the imposition of the sales tax that the property
"shall not be deemed to be located or present in or to have a situs
for taxation" in Connecticut. The incidence of the sales tax is not
the property itself or its presence within the State. Rather it is the
transfer of title for consideration, a legal act which can be accomplished without the property ever entering the State. Had Congress
intended to include sales taxes within the coverage of §514, it surely
would not have employed language so poorly suited to that purpose
as "taxation in respect of the personal property."

It is contended on behalf of the servicemen that, even if §514
does not encompass sales taxes, at least it prohibits taxation of the
use of personal property. Not only are use taxes said to fall literally
within the meaning of the phrase "taxation in respect of the personal
property," but §514 specifically refers in two places to property "or
the use thereof." Moreover, it is argued, the sole jurisdictional
basis of the use tax is the location of the personal property in Connecticut; yet imposition of a tax with such incidence on a serviceman
contravenes the command of §514 that his personal property "shall
not be deemed to be located or present in or to have a situs for
taxation in such State." While we agree that use taxes are not so
clearly excluded by the language of §514 as are sales taxes, neither
do we believe that they are clearly included. And consideration of
the purpose and legislative history of §514 along with its language
and other factors has led us to the conclusion that Congress did not
intend to free servicemen stationed away from home from the sales
or use taxes of the host State.

The legislative history of the 1942 enactment and the 1944 and
1962 amendments of §514 reveals that Congress intended the Act to
cover only annually recurring taxes on property--the familiar ad
valorem personal property tax. . . .

. . .

Section 514 does not relieve servicemen stationed away from
home from all taxes of the host State. It was enacted with the much

narrower design "to prevent multiple State taxation of the property." And the substantial risk of double taxation under multi-state ad valorem property taxes does not exist with respect to sales and use taxes. Like Connecticut, nearly every State which levies such taxes provides a credit for sales or use taxes paid on the transaction to another State. Of course it is true, as we held in Dameron v. Brodhead, 345 U.S. 322, that §514 prevents imposition of ad valorem property taxes even though the serviceman's home State does not tax the property. But the predominant legislative purpose nonetheless remains highly relevant in determining the scope of the exemption, and the absence of any significant risk of double taxation under state sales and use taxes generally is therefore strong evidence of congressional intent not to include them in §514.

. . .

We think that, in light of the clear indications of congressional intent discussed above, the most sensible inference to be drawn from this language is that the only taxes on the use of property from which servicemen are exempted are the special registration taxes imposed annually by all States on the use of motor vehicles. Indeed, this interpretation is supported by the structure of §514 itself. There is no reference to "use" of property in those portions of subsection (1) which set out the basic exemption and in which Congress would naturally have been expected to mention use taxes had it meant to include them. Moreover, subsection (2)(b) does not say that for purposes of §514 "taxation" includes "licenses, fees, or excises" on the use of all personal property except those in respect of motor vehicles for which such fees have not been paid at home. Rather it says that "taxation" includes such levies only on motor vehicles when they have been paid at home. Thus, as we held in California v. Buzard, 382 U.S. 386, subsection (2)(b) does not encompass ordinary revenue-raising excise or use taxes, but is limited to "those taxes which are essential to the functioning of the host State's licensing and registration laws in their application to the motor vehicles of nonresident servicemen." Id., at 395. The Court held in Buzard that §514 exempted servicemen from the California tax on automobiles, not because it was an excise tax on use covered by subsection (2)(b), but rather because it was not such a tax. The so-called "license fee" there in question was an annual tax in the amount of 2% of the assessed market value of the car--a levy which was indistinguishable from the annually recurring ad valorem taxes that §514 was designed to cover.

It is thus evident that in subsection (2)(b) Congress was dealing solely with a unique form of state "tax"--the motor vehicle registration fee. Because such fees are not always clearly classifiable as property taxes, servicemen would not be exempted from many of them by subsection (1) of §514. Since annually recurring license fees raise much the same risk of double taxation to transitory military personnel as do property taxes, Congress evidently decided in 1944 to extend the exemption of §514 to include motor vehicle registration fees as well as property taxes. From 1944 to 1962 the only reference in §514 to "use" of property was found in subsection (2)(b). And, in view of the narrow purpose of that subsection and the absence for 20 years of any other reference to "use" in §514, we cannot believe the repetition of that word in the 1962 amendment--described by Congress as a mere clarification of the existing law--can be deemed to have added all use taxes to the coverage of the statute. The 1962 amendment merely reflected the prior reference to the "use" of motor vehicles in subsection (2)(b).

Finally, we find unpersuasive the appellees' contention that, since the Connecticut use tax can be applied only with respect to personal property used within the State, its imposition on servicemen away from home cannot be squared with the declaration of §514 that "personal property shall not be deemed to be located or present in or to have a situs for taxation in such State." That clause is modified by the opening words of the sentence--"[f]or the purposes of taxation in respect of the personal property." Section 514, therefore, does not in terms relieve servicemen from every state tax which is somehow dependent on the presence of personal property within the State. Rather, it provides only that a State cannot justify imposing the taxes to which §514 was initially intended to apply--annually recurring ad valorem property taxes--on the ground of the property's presence within the State.

This construction is confirmed by the explanation which Congress itself gave for the addition in 1944 of the language on which the appellees rely:

> "The purpose of the proposed legislation is to
> clarify the intent of section 514 of the Soldiers' and
> Sailors' Civil Relief Act. . . . When that provision of
> law was added to the act to relieve persons in service
> from liability of double taxation by being moved from
> one State to another under orders, it was intended that
> it should apply to personal-property taxes as well as to
> income taxes. As presently constituted, it primarily
> affects taxes in respect to income and other taxes based
> on residence or domicile, but it does not prevent the
> State of 'temporary residence' from taxing tangible per-
> sonal property actually located in such State so long as
> the tax does not depend on residence or domicile. A few
> States have taken the position that tangible personal
> property of military personnel who are only temporarily
> within their jurisdiction does not acquire a situs for
> taxation, but it has been held that section 514 of the act
> as now written does not affect the right of a State to

> assess personal-property taxes on property within its
> jurisdiction."

The 1944 amendment, therefore, had only the limited purpose "to
clarify" Congress' original intent to cover "personal-property taxes
on property," not to expand the exemption in a manner which would
include sales or use taxes.

For these reasons we hold that §514 of the Soldiers' and
Sailors' Civil Relief Act does not exempt servicemen from the sales
and use taxes imposed by Connecticut. Accordingly, the judgment is
Reversed.

The principal case is discussed in 74 Dickinson L.Rev. 536
(Spring 1970).

The preceding paragraphs and cases will give the reader a general idea of some of the interests of servicemen that are protected
and some rights available to them. Additional sections of the act not
specifically noted above extend the benefits of the act to persons
ordered for induction or military service (§516) and preclude application of the act to written agreements entered after commencement
of service (§517). There are specific sections concerning eviction
(§530), installment contracts (§531), mortgages (§532), leases (§534),
life insurance policies (§535), public lands (§561), homestead entries
and settlement claims (§562), mining claims (§565), irrigation rights
(§568), and income taxes (§573). Obviously the solution of a specific
problem will require research of the applicable sections and decided
cases.

Although the original act was to terminate on May 15, 1945,
Congress has extended all provisions to remain in full force and effect
until repealed or otherwise terminated by a subsequent act (50 U.S.C.
App. 464).

Department of the Army Pamphlet 27-166, March, 1962, contains selected cases and materials concerning the act up to that date.
The act is also discussed in 55 ABAJ 1053 (November, 1969).

## ABOUT THE EDITOR

WILLIS E. SCHUG is Assistant Dean at the School of Law, Columbia University, New York. A Colonel, U.S. Army (Ret.), Dean Schug served in the Army as counsel in more than seventy-five general courts-martial, supervised lawyers and other personnel in the administration of military justice, and was Assistant Professor of Law at the United States Military Academy. He received an LL.B. from Columbia; an M.S. in Public Administration from Ohio State University; and a B.S. from the United States Military Academy.